AMERICAN
WILLS PROVED IN LONDON
1611–1775

AMERICAN
WILLS PROVED IN LONDON
1611–1775

Compiled by
Peter Wilson Coldham

Genealogical Publishing Co., Inc.

INTRODUCTION

The landed property, goods and money remaining in his native land which belonged to any Englishman dying abroad were rigorously protected by law and convention which required that a regularly appointed executor or administrator be recognized before any part of that person's assets could be touched. The Prerogative Court of Canterbury (P.C.C.) — so named because it conducted its business under the jurisdiction of the Archbishop of Canterbury, the highest ecclesiastical personage in England (and not, as is sometimes conjectured, because of any association with the county of Kent!) — acted as the foremost probate court in the land from its seat in Doctors' Commons in London. In theory, and for the most part in practice also, the P.C.C. was the only probate court entitled to issue grants of probate and administration relating to English (and Welsh) subjects dying abroad who had assets in England, although the probate courts of the Bishop of London until well into the seventeenth century occasionally exercised the same prerogative, probably because of the polite fiction that an Englishman dying abroad came under that Bishop's jurisdiction. The wills abstracted in this volume represent, therefore, the widest spectrum of contemporary society, from dynastic families with vast landed estates in the American colonies to illiterate soldiers and sailors, both British and colonial, who died in the preservation or extension of the borders of Empire, leaving their wages to their wives, sweethearts or mothers. On the other side of the Atlantic, English testators, some recently retired to enjoy a comfortable old age on the profits of a career in the colonies, and others who had never left their native shore but who had despatched relatives to the New World, frequently remembered their American kinsfolk, friends and business acquaintances in their wills.

The superb collection of wills in the P.C.C., register copies of which survive in an unbroken series from 1600 (but with many wills also registered from well before that date) to 1858, was quickly recognized as a unique and authoritative genealogical resource once a serious academic approach had been adopted in the mid-nineteenth century towards investigation of the origins of the first American settlers. Foremost in this field was Henry FitzGilbert Waters who, between 1883 and 1889, transcribed several hundred P.C.C. wills relating to the Pilgrim Fathers and their families for the *New England Historical and Genealogical Register*, and in 1901 brought out his monumental work *Genealogical Gleanings in England* [1] in which his researches were consolidated. He noted, but did not publish, details of those wills relating exclusively to Virginia. This work was left to Lothrop Withington who inherited Waters' unpublished notes about Virginia and, with the addition of researches of his own, published a series of "Virginia Gleanings" in the *Virginia Magazine of History and Biography* between 1903 and 1916. The series was continued by two other collaborators until 1929 when it was concluded. The complete collection of notes and will transcripts has been published as *Virginia Gleanings in England.*[2] A more modest, but still valuable, contribution in this field was made by George Sherwood with the publication of some additional will abstracts relating to American colonists under the title of *American Colonists in English Records.*[3]

The genesis of this present volume lies in the series of P.C.C. administration and probate acts abstracted for serialization in the *National Genealogical Society Quarterly* between 1973 and 1980 and subsequently published in a consolidated form as *American Wills & Administrations in the Prerogative Court of Canterbury, 1610-1857.*[4] That volume, the first to attempt a comprehensive listing of P.C.C. wills and administrations with an American association, was intended primarily as a finding aid to the hundreds of individual documents of interest to the historian and genealogist working in this field, and will continue to fulfill that purpose. It was not, however, possible, working to such a strictly defined objective, to provide the complete information such as names of close relations, legatees, witnesses, ownership of property, business interests, precise documentary references, and much else besides, that is essential to an adequate identification and interpretation of probate sources. The decision to present this further volume containing summaries of those wills not included in Waters, Withington or Sherwood was taken, therefore, because of the demonstrable need to provide the present-day researcher with an accessible compendium to American wills proved in London to complement and stand comparison with the three already mentioned.

Many of the wills now appearing for the first time as printed abstracts were proved first in one or other of the American colonial courts, and their re-appearance in the P.C.C., sometimes after an interval of years, may be taken as a sure indication that the testator had lands or assets in England requiring the grant of letters of administration. It is worth remarking here that certain probate records survive in the P.C.C. which perished during the vicissitudes of conflict in the U.S.A., or suffered considerable neglect or damage there. Something must also be said, however, about some less auspicious aspects. The concentration accorded in the last 150 years to P.C.C. records of the sixteenth and seventeenth centuries has meant that the calendars and indexes for those periods are in every respect superior to those of a later date. While finding aids for the years up to 1700 may, therefore, be accepted as reasonably comprehensive, thereafter the sheer volume of business conducted by the P.C.C., combined with inadequate means of reference, make it inevitable that a small number of American wills are likely still to lurk undiscovered within the registers.

A further important qualification has to be made. The will so laboriously copied out in its every last detail into the P.C.C. register, now the first recourse available to the searcher, would be at best a third-generation copy: the lawyer's or testator's first draft would usually be written out again in a "fair" hand and then copied once more for registration in the P.C.C. Of the many so-called original wills preserved in the Public Record Office (P.R.O.), a substantial proportion are clearly copies. When a will had to be obtained from a colonial probate court, the likelihood is that the register copy in the P.R.O. will be five or six generations away from the original version. The likelihood of clerical error must clearly have increased in direct proportion to the number of times a transcript was made. Those who regularly handle documents dating from before the nineteenth century will know just how impenetrable certain styles of writing, and particularly florid or idiosyncratic signatures, can be. While the P.C.C. clerks clearly did their best to obtain an exact transliteration — and all their work was rigorously checked — it would be surprising if certain names of people and places unfamiliar to the clerks were not written down as a "best guess." The registers are notable for their almost total innocence of any editorial question marks! (It appears, nevertheless, that the delightful name of Fishlake Chubb which appears on a will of 1754 is authentic.)

In presenting these abstracts, the overall aim has been to reduce the content of each will to the essential genealogical and geographical facts, stripping out both the traditional religious formulae which prefaced most and the ponderous legal phraseology, especially those windy conditional inheritance clauses so beloved of learned clerks, hopefully without distorting the broad intentions of the testator. For each abstract every effort has been made to provide both the date of the will and of the grant of probate or administration, and the names of the principal legatees, executors and witnesses. Where essential information additional to that contained in the will and its endorsements has been culled from an Act Book, it has been included between square brackets. In every case a precise reference to the original source, either in the P.R.O. or the London Guildhall, has been provided, occasionally with a reference to a printed source from which supplementary information may be gleaned.

Every cliché used about the drawing up of a will — the "voice beyond the grave" — makes its appearance in these pages. We find relations literally struck out, others cut off with the proverbial shilling, and a few denied all benefit unless they complied with certain imposed conditions. Many testators, given the opportunity of committing their deepest emotions to paper without fear of argument or opposition, took full advantage. Quakers could subtly proclaim their beliefs by insisting on their own dating system and pointedly omitting any reference to saints after whom many English places, and almost all churches, were named; those of a Catholic persuasion could leave money so that prayers might be offered for the repose of their souls; while those of an agnostic disposition simply failed to take up the first page of their wills with the customary pious reference to the hope of resurrection. At a more personal level, we find a number of sons condemned for their undutiful ways, burial rituals for their extravagance, and wives for their unfaithfulness. Few husbands, however, went as far as John Dunton of London who in 1733 bequeathed to his second wife a ring inscribed "Forgive your enemies."

The contemplation of "inescapable dissolution," an emollient phrase often used in wills as a circumlocution for death, seemed also to bring out the most deep-seated fears and ambitions. At one extreme there were those like Francis Nicholson, Governor of South Carolina, who appeared preoccupied to ensure that his travels and appointments were chiselled in stone for the benefit of posterity, or John Custis of Williamsburg who left detailed instructions for the erection of a marble memorial inscribed with his coat of arms and a description of the interment rituals which were to be conducted on his own estate. At the other extreme were those who obviously harboured a morbid anxiety for the future welfare of their mortal remains. Peter Moulson in 1674 left firm orders for his grave to be dug so deep that his bones would not be thrown about at some distant time, but even he was less obsessive than Henry Jerningham of Maryland who went into gruesome detail about the disposal of his remains. They were, after medically supervised treatment, to be packed into a black box and taken by his family across the Appalachians to be finally buried wherever they settled.

In this short preface I have attempted to avoid repetition of the more detailed description of the work of the P.C.C. and of the various categories of probate grants which was included in the introduction to *American Wills & Administrations in the Prerogative Court of Canterbury, 1610-1857*. Those with a particular interest in these matters should refer to that work.

Peter Wilson Coldham　　　　　　　　　　　　　　　　Pentecost 1992
　　　　　　　　　　　　　　　　　　　　　　　Purley, Surrey, England
　　　　　　　　　　　　　　　　　　　　　　　　　　　　　　AMDG

---

1. 2 vols. Boston: New England Historic Genealogical Society, 1901.

2. Baltimore: Genealogical Publishing Co., Inc., 1980.

3. 2 vols. London, 1932-1933.

4. Baltimore: Genealogical Publishing Co., Inc., 1989.

The following abbreviations have been used throughout this volume:

Admon.	=	Administration
Adr.	=	Administrator
Adx.	=	Administratrix
AWW	=	Administration with will annexed
Beds.	=	Bedfordshire
Berks.	=	Berkshire
Bucks.	=	Buckinghamshire
Cambs.	=	Cambridgeshire
Chesh.	=	Cheshire
Co.	=	County
Ct.	=	Connecticut
Cumb.	=	Cumberland
Derbys.	=	Derbyshire
E. Fla.	=	East Florida
Exec.	=	Executor
Exex.	=	Executrix
Ga.	=	Georgia
Glos.	=	Gloucestershire
Hants.	=	Hampshire
Heref.	=	Herefordshire
Herts.	=	Hertfordshire
Hunts.	=	Huntingdonshire
I.O.W.	=	Isle of Wight
Lancs.	=	Lancashire
Leics.	=	Leicestershire
Lincs.	=	Lincolnshire
LMC	=	*Lord Mayor's Court of London Depositions Relating to Americans 1641-1736*
Mass.	=	Massachusetts
Md.	=	Maryland
Mddx.	=	Middlesex
Mon.	=	Monmouthshire
N.A.	=	North America
N.C.	=	North Carolina

N.C.	=	North Carolina
N.E.	=	New England
NGSQ	=	*National Genealogical Society Quarterly*
N.H.	=	New Hampshire
N'hants.	=	Northamptonshire
N.J.	=	New Jersey
N'land.	=	Northumberland
N.Y.	=	New York
N.Y.C.	=	New York City
Norf.	=	Norfolk
Notts.	=	Nottinghamshire
O'seer	=	Overseer
OW	=	Original will
Oxon.	=	Oxfordshire
Penna.	=	Pennsylvania
Pr.	=	Proved
PRO	=	Public Record Office, London
R.I.	=	Rhode Island
Salop.	=	Shropshire
S.C.	=	South Carolina
Som.	=	Somerset
Staffs.	=	Staffordshire
Suff.	=	Suffolk
Sy.	=	Surrey
Va.	=	Virginia
Warw.	=	Warwickshire
W. Fla.	=	West Florida
Wilts.	=	Wiltshire
Worcs.	=	Worcestershire
Yorks.	=	Yorkshire

AMERICAN
WILLS PROVED IN LONDON
1611–1775

1611

Arthur Pett of Stepney, Mddx., master of the *Unity* of London but now sick aboard the *Blessing* of Plymouth at James Town, Va., dated 30 Aug 1609. Bequests to: my mother, now wife of Richard Nottingham; my brother William Pett; my brother William Welche; my wife Florence Pett and my daughter Elizabeth Pett. Execs: my said wife and Thomas Johnson of Ratcliffe, mariner, master of the *Lyon* of London, now at James Town. O'seer my father-in-law Richard Nottingham. Wits: Thomas Johnson, Robert Addames, William Milward. Pr. 19 Mar 1611 in Commissary Court of London by Florence Pett. (Guildhall 9172/25).

1613

John Gerarde, citizen and barber surgeon of London, dated 11 Dec 1612. Bequests to: my son-in-law Richard Houlden; my daughter Elizabeth his wife; my niece Agnes Houlden. My adventure of £25 in Va. to my nieces Margaret and Katherine Houlden. Exex. my wife Agnes Gerarde. Wits: William Johnes and Freeman Fox. Pr. 20 Mar 1613 in Archdeaconry Court of London by Agnes Gerarde.

1617

Alexander Whitaker of Blackfriars, London, now crossing the seas to Va., dated 16 Feb 1611. Bequests to: my brothers Samuel, William and Jabez Whitaker; my sisters Frances Whitaker, Susanna Lothrop, and Mary Clarke wife of Raynes Clarke; my cousin William Gouge. I leave to my brother Samuel my Bill of Adventure to Va. and the profits thereof if I die without issue. Christopher Levitt, linen draper of the City of York, my cousin Anthony Culverwell and Mr. Crashawe owe me money. Sir Henry Griffith of Burton Agnes, Yorks., owes me for a chest of viols. Exec. to be my said brother Samuel and overseer my cousin William Gouche of Blackfriars, clerk. Wits: Richard Culverwell and Caleb Gouge. Pr. 4 Aug 1617 in Commissary Court of London by Samuel Whitaker and, on his death, admon. granted in PCC 3 Sep 1617 to the sister Susan Lothrop. (Guildhall: 9171/23/75 & PRO: PCC PROB 11/130/95).

1619

John Mynterne dated at Manigo, Va., 15 Mar 1618. To my wife (Alice) while she remains a widow £30 but if she marries this sum to go to my cousin Elizabeth Wills, daughter of John Wills. To my said wife a three-quarters share of the *Consent*. To John Staining a book called *The Seaman's Calendar*. Other bequests to: my brothers Samuel, William, Nathaniel and Byngey Mynterne; my brother-in-law Thomas Gee; John Wynter; my boy George Lang; John Davies of Foye (Heref.); Owen Pomerye; George Cheltnam. Wits: John Wynter, Owen Pomerye; William Clement. AWW granted 6 Jan 1619 to the relict, Alice Mynterne, no exec. having been named. (PROB 11/133/7).

1624

Henry Jacob [of St. Andrew Hubbard, London], dated 5 Oct 1620. I give my goods to my wife Sarah Jacob and, if she dies before my children come into Va., they are to have equal parts when they are 21. None of the said children are to have anything unless they go to Va. before the end of May 1621 and Nathaniel Page, who now dwells with me, shall account with my said children. Wits: James Page and George (x) Crouch. Pr. 5 May 1624 by the relict. (PROB 11/143/38).

George Keynell [of St. Katherine by the Tower, London], undated. The will takes the form of a memorandum of goods sent by the testator (in 1622) to Va. by the *James*, Mr. Tobias Felgate, under the charge of his mate William Barker. Out of the sale of these goods, 3s.4d. is to be paid to John Harrison of the ship's company and of the residue half is to go to my wife (Frances) and half to my child born on her body. AWW 8 Nov 1624 to the relict Frances Keynell, no exec. having been named. (PROB 11/144/105).

1625

George Ruggles, sailor of the ship *Due Return* bound for Va. Nuncupative will given at the beginning of Mar 1625. Bequests to: Henry Furton; Peter Masters, surgeon of the *Due Return*. Wits:

Simon Kitchin, master of the ship, and Edward Pepper. AWW 3 May 1625 in Commissary Court of London to Henry Furton. (Guildhall: 9171/24/422).

1630

Robert Manstidge of Taunton, Somerset, [who died overseas], son of Thomas Manstidge of Taunton, deceased, dated 6 Jan 1625. My friend and o'seer Tobias Felgate, is to dispose of my goods aboard this ship, the *James* of London, by sale in Va. and collect all my debts there, and to deliver the proceeds to my friend Symon Whetcombe of London, Turkey merchant, for the credit of my uncle and exec. Richard Longe of Taunton. My estate is to be divided between my sister Jone Manstidge and my brothers William, Isaac and Emanuel Manstidge. Wits: John Sparkes, Robert Dennes, Richard Brewster and William Greene. Pr. 9 Feb 1630 by Richard Longe. (PROB 11/157/14).

Andrew Parkes of London, haberdasher [who died overseas], dated 2 Jly 1628. All my goods to my brother John Parkes now in the Island of Va. if he is living when the ship *Hopewell* of London wherein I am embarked arrives there. Other bequests to: my aunt Sewzan Parkes of London, widow; my aunt and exex. Elizabeth Warden of Christ's Hospital, London, widow. O'seer my friend Thomas Ward, citizen and cordwainer of London. Wits: Richard Merydale, Sir Anthony Mosley, John Clarke, Joseph Bryan, apprentice of Ric. Merydale. Pr. 13 Feb 1630 by Elizabeth Warden. (PROB 11/157/19).

Richard Price [of St. Margaret, Westminster, Mddx.], citizen and vintner of London, dated 28 Jly 1630. To be buried at St. Margaret, Westminster. My lands in Hayes and Ruislip, Mddx., and Denham, Bucks., the Angel with Hope in the parish of St. Clement Danes, and tenements in King Street, Westminster, to my son Richard Price when he is 21 with due allowance to my wife Margaret who is to be my exex. Other principal bequests to: my daughters Margaret, Ann and Olive; my cousin Richard Dale, a son of my sister Joan Dale, widow; my brother John Price and his wife, my sister Mathewe; my cousin Margaret Burgen, now wife of Henry Towers. To my cousin Thomas Burgen the lands and tenements I ought to have for my adventures in Va. and the money I have lent to the Society of St. Martin's Hundred there, or if he dies to my cousin Richard Dale.

O'seers: Thomas Carpenter, sheeregrinder, and Nicholas Butcher, citizen and salter of London. Wits: Robert Wood, Richard Hilton & others. Pr. 5 Nov 1630 by Margaret Price. (PROB 11/158/94).

Francis Dickinson [of Northam, Devon, mariner], bound for Va., undated. Bequests to: the poor of Northam and Barnstaple; Elizabeth Moore, my wife before God; Stephen Jefferie; Mr. Laskam; Henry Petteres; Rebeckah Petteres; Anne Buyes; Orvis Buyes; Petternell Buyes. Residue of estate which is in the hands of Richard Draper, to Laurence Draper and Philip Draper. Wits: Richard Draper, Johane Draper, Elizabeth More and William Limbre. AWW 24 Sep 1630 to Richard Draper, father and guardian during their minority of Laurence and Philip Dickinson. (PROB 11/158/77).

1635

Anne Garrard of Up Lambourne, Berks., widow, dated 19 Jun 1634. Bequests to: my grandchild and exex. Jane Busher, daughter of Abraham Busher, my daughter's former husband; my grandchild Anne Busher, now wife of Thomas Hinton, gent, who has lately gone to Va.; my grandchildren Philip, Edward, John and Charles Kistell, sons of Philip Kistell. O'seers: Tobias Greenbury, minister of Lambourne, and John Maslyne of Up Lambourne. Wits: John Harris and Thomas Deane. Pr. 13 Feb 1635 by Jane Busher. (PROB 11/167/9).

George Parkhurst of Ipswich, Suffolk, gent, now bound for Va. by the *Primrose* of London, dated 22 Jly 1634. My whole estate to my exex. Anne Wonham, gent(lewoman) with the profits now in the hands of Mr. John Cotton dwelling in Cannon Street, London. Wits: Thomas Draper, Richard Thoroton, Johan Browne, Humphrey Bruan and John Owsebie. Pr. 9 Feb 1635 by Anne Wonham. (PROB 11/167/14).

Richard Hill, son of William Hill of Cookham, Berks., husbandman deceased, now bound on a voyage to N.E. [who died overseas, bachelor]. Bequests to: my brother George Hill and my sisters Mary, Alice and Elizabeth Hill; my cousin and exec. Nicholas Greene of Cookham, tailor. My cottage and three acres in Cookham which are held on lease by Nicholas Greene is to be used as payment of my legacies. Wits: Thomas Pennant, scrivener, his apprentice Andrew Griffith and Thomas Greene. Pr. — Sep 1635 by Nicholas Greene. (PROB 11/169/96).

1636

Richard Rogers Esq., Controller of H.M. Mint within the Tower of London [and of St. Michael Crooked Lane, London]. To be buried in the church of St. Michael near the grave of Sir William Walworth in the chancel. Principal bequests to: my wife Joane; my son Edward Rogers who is to have all my lands and tenements in Va. during his lifetime, after which they are to pass to my grandson Richard Rogers; Lidia Rogers, wife of my said son Edward; my daughter Anne, wife of Jasper Draper; my kinsmen Abraham Rogers and John Rogers; my grandchildren Richard Rogers, Edward Rogers and Lidia Rogers; my son-in-law William Hewson; the poor of Little Ness, Salop., where I was born. Wits: Robert Hanson, scrivener, Bartholomew Hill, William Salisburie, John Smith and William Stevens. Pr. 8 Sep 1636 by Edward Rogers and Jasper Draper. (PROB 11/172/97).

1637

George Pewsey of Limehouse, Mddx., [master of the *Marmaduke* and trader to Va.], dated 19 Sep 1634 aboard the *Assurance* at sea. Bequests to: my wife and exex. Rebecca Pewsey; my son (unnamed); my mother Ursula Pewsey; my sisters Martha and Annis Pewsey; my daughter Joane Phillips. O'seers: Mr. Isaac Bromell (who is to be master of my ship) and Mr. Robert Freeman, merchant. Pr. by Rebecca Pewsey 16 Jan 1637. (PROB 11/173/6). See NGSQ 68/116.

1641

Winifred Greene of London [of Kingsbury, Mddx.], widow, dated 1 Feb 1641. Bequests to: the children of my brothers John Finch and Francis Finch; the children of my sister Joane Coomes by her husband Thomas Coomes and by her late husband Morris Price deceased; Mary Finch, daughter of my said brother John; my sister Ann Fegon, widow; my sister Grace Finch, wife of the said Francis Finch; the rector of St. Michael Bassishaw, London; my son John Green (who went to Va.), if he be alive. Wits: Richard Rochdale, scrivener, and Henry Firebrace his servant. Pr. 5 Oct 1641 by the brother, John Finch. (PROB 11/187/121 & 128). See NGSQ 69/117.

1643

Thomas Newton, citizen and clothworker of London, dated 24 Jly 1640. To be buried in the new churchyard by Moorfields, London. The lease of my house in Gutter Lane to my wife and exex. Sara Newton during her lifetime and then to my son Jonathan Newton. My two shares of lands in Martins Hundred, Va., turned over to me by Hugh Evans, citizen and clothworker of London in 1622, to my said son. Wits: Edward Osborne, John Horne, scrivener, and Roger Wilford his servant. Pr. Archdeaconry Court of London 13 Jan 1643 by Sara Newton.

Joseph Tilden, citizen and girdler of London [of St. John Walbrook, London], dated 1 Feb 1643. Bequests to: my brother Freegift Tilden; my niece Sarah Smith; my sister Lidia Tilden, late wife of my brother Nathaniel Tilden; my brother's two daughters who are married in N.E.; the poor of St. John the Baptist, London; my nephew and exec. Joseph Tilden, son of my brother Nathaniel Tilden; my brother and o'seer George Thatcher to have the rents of my lands in Sussex. My brother Hopestill Tilden is to act as my administrator in trust until Joseph Tilden can take executorship. Wits: Henry Randall, Francis Nelmes and Val. Crome. AWW 18 Mar 1643 to the brother Hopestill Tilden during the absence overseas of the nephew Joseph Tilden. (PROB 11/191/28).

1644

Robert Speed of Va., planter, now in the City of London but intending to depart again for Va., dated 14 Oct 1643. Bequests to: Capt. Nathaniel Oldis; Hanna Wilkinson; Mary Wilkinson; William Wilkinson, son of Thomas Wilkinson of Ellington [?Cambs.]; Clare Tompson, wife of George Tompson; my cousins William, Elizabeth and Sara Speed, children of my kinsman William Speed, citizen and fishmonger of London; my godchildren John Austion, son of Richard Austion, Jane Watkins, daughter of Richard Watkins, Temperance Waterman, Susanna Bassnett, daughter of William Bassnett; my cousin Walter Oxley; Mary Browne, daughter of Nicholas Browne; William Baulke; my servant John Thomas. Half the money owed to me by Anthony West, surgeon, to be given to Ann, wife of William Wilkinson, and the other half to Elizabeth, wife of Thomas Oldis. A decent pulpit, the ten commandments and the King's Arms to be bought for the church in Kynothan (*sic*) in

Elizabeth Co., Va. O'seers Capt. Leonard Yeo and William Wilkinson. Sole exec. my cousin the said William Speed who is to have my plantation and lands in Va. Pr. 16 Sep 1644 in the Archdeaconry Court of London. (NGSQ 69/195).

Katherine Morley of Great Stanmore, Mddx., widow, dated 3 Jly 1645. A Portugal piece to my daughter Mrs. Ann Gate. To my youngest son James Morley my tenement at Lucas End and nine acres of land in the manor of Cheshunt, long since surrendered by my son-in-law Thomas Gate Esq. of the Inner Temple, London. To my poor eldest son John Morley, now living in N.E., a quarter of the profits from my estate during his lifetime, a bible and £10. To my grandchildren Judith and Katherine Gate I leave cloth, etc. £5 to my grandson (blank) Morley, resident at Norremberg (?Nuremberg), son of my late son Thomas Morley. To the servants in the house of my brother-in-law Mr. Thomas Burnell whatever seems fitting to my son James Morley who is to be my exec. Wits: Thomas Burnell, Hester Burnell and Mary Thomas. Pr. 6 Aug 1645 in Commissary Court of London by the named exec. Guildhall: Reg. 1644-46 f.58)

1646

John Sheppard of Towcester, Northants., mercer, dated 16 Jly 1633. To my eldest son William Sheppard now in N.E. all the goods I sent him in May and Jun 1643 by the *Concord* and my brother William Sheppard of Cambridge, N.E., and Mr. Collins of the same town to be my o'seers there. To my said son William my house in Northbarr Street, Banbury. To my son John, when he is 21, my house in the High Street, Towcester which I purchased of Thomas and John Winfield. To my son Samuel, when he is 21, the house in Towcester I purchased of John Hayles. To my youngest son Daniel four acres I purchased of my father-in-law William Kingston, two acres purchased of Michael West and two acres purchased of Anne Jennings. Bequest to my brother George Waples. Wits: William Pitchford, Andrew Paine and Peter Deakin. Pr. 6 Jun 1646 by the relict Frances Sheppard. (PROB 11/196/88).

1647

Mary Sadler of Mayfield, Sussex, widow, dated 16 Jan 1646. Bequests to: my daughter and exex. Elizabeth James; my son John Sadler; my daughter Mary Sadler and her children which I suppose to live in N.E.; my daughter Ann Allin and her daughter Mary; my grandchildren Mary Russell, Thomas Russell, Mary James and Elizabeth James. Wits: John Ricken and Mathew Hudley. Pr. 13 Nov 1647 by Elizabeth James. (PROB 11/202/231).

1649

William Thomas of Llantwit Major, Glamorgan, dated 15 Jan 1647. Land and goods of £500 due to me in the West Indies and America to the child my wife may be carrying or, if not, to my wife during her lifetime and then to my brother Samuel Thomas. Other principal bequests to: my wife (unnamed) and her children by her first husband; my brother Alexander Thomas and his sons. Wits: John Lloyd, William Tobee and Jane Sander. Pr. 6 Jun 1649 by the brother Alexander Thomas. (PROB 11/209/153).

1651

William Taylor, citizen and haberdasher of London [of Hackney, Mddx.], dated 29 Mar 1650. To be buried in the parish church of Hackney. To my brother Robert Taylor at the Somers Islands 40 shillings and to his son Samuel Taylor of N.E. £8. My leases of tenements near Paul's Chain, London, lately purchased of Stephen Goodyeare and held of St. Bartholomew's Hospital, to the use of my wife Margaret. My house called the Three Nuns in Paternoster Row, London, to my son Daniel Taylor. The lease of my houses at Charing Cross to my daughter Rebecca Taylor. Other principal bequests to: my son and exec. Samuel Taylor; my son and heir Daniel Taylor and Rebecca his wife; my second son Edmond Taylor; my two daughters Margaret Webb, wife of William Webb, and Hannah Claxton, wife of Robert Claxton, mercer; my daughter-in-law Rebecca Howard; my sister Elizabeth Owen in Buckingham; my sister Martha Vocher, widow. Wits: Thomas Conn, notary, and Daniel Bunting his servant. Pr. 19 Jly 1651 by the son Samuel Taylor. (PROB 11/217/155). Further grant on 12 Dec 1674 to Thomas Lawes.

1652

Richard Wood of Whaddon in the City of Gloucester, gent., dated 7 Sep 1650. My house and five acres called the Bourne in Brookthorpe and five acres at Harescombe to my daughter Margaret Dewxell, widow. Other bequests to: my son and heir Richard Wood and his wife Julian; my son William Wood and his wife Edith; my kinsmen Robert Wood, John Roberts and Richard Dewxell; the children of my sister Millicent Addis, wife of William Addis; the daughter of my cousin William Barnes, which daughter is in N.E.; Mary Wood, my now wife, to be exe. O'seers: my brothers-in-law Thomas Atkins and Robert Beard. Wits: Thomas Jennins, Thomas Atkins, John Symons and Richard Taylor. Pr. 17 Feb 1652 by Mary Wood. (PROB 11/220/50). See NGSQ 61/115.

1653

Thomas Mills of Exeter, Devon, vintner, dated 18 Mar 1653. An annuity to my wife Honor Mills to be paid by Alan Penny of Exeter, merchant. Bequest to my sister Mary Reddock's child. Residue of estate to my only child William Mills whom I suppose to be in Va. and who is to be my exec. if he returns, otherwise my exex. is to be my said wife. Wits: Robert Buckland, Samuel Alford and Jonathan Carter. Pr. 26 Sep 1653 by Honor Mills. (PROB 11/228/178).

1654

Thomas Bludder of Clewer, Berks., gent., dated 25 Jly 1653. To my brother Marmaduke Bludder, if there be such a man living, 40 shillings. Other bequests to: my wife Emma; my sister Dionisia Beard; our parson Joel Barnard; my cousin Charles Aldworth; my brother May's two children, George and Susan May; my goddaughter Mrs. Alice Miller of Clewer and her daughter Emma Miller. As for my kindred in Va., I do not know whether any of them be living not having heard from any of them these five years, and the rest of my kindred have been strangers unto me a long time. No witnesses shown. Pr. 16 Mar 1654 by Emma Bludder. (PROB 11/240/396).

1657

Richard Quiney [of St. Stephen Walbrook], citizen and grocer of London, dated 16 Aug 1655. To be buried at Stratford on Avon, Warw., where my father and ancestors are. I have no wife. Bequests to: my children Richard, Adrian, Thomas and William Quiney, Ann wife of Thomas Booth, and Ellen wife of Edward Pilkington; my brother Thomas Quiney; my brothers-in-law Master John Sadler and William Smith; my cousins Richard Bayley, Master William Wheate, Dr. John Willby, Master George Nash, Richard Chaundler, William Watts, William Smith, John Smith and Robert Smith. All my lands in Va. I bequeath to my son Richard during his lifetime and he is to be my exec. if he is resident in England at my death. Pr. 3 Jan 1657 by the son Richard Quiney. (PROB 11/261/6).

William Boys of Cranbrook, Kent, clothier, dated 14 Aug 1656. My wife Joane is to be my exex. and to have seven-eighths of my lands in Cranbrook during her lifetime. If it should happen that the other part which now belongs to John Stow, son of Thomas Stow in N.E., should be sold, my wife is to consult with my sons John, Thomas, William and Joseph Boys (all under 21) to whom my lands are to descend. Bequests to my daughters Sibylla Boys and Mary Boys when they are eighteen. If my wife marries again she is to give security to my brother Edmund Colvill of Maidstone for payment of my children's legacies. No witnesses shown. Pr. 24 Feb 1657 by the relict. (PROB 11/262/72).

Thomas Letchworth, younger son of Thomas Letchworth, citizen and fishmonger of London, intending to voyage to Va., [and who died overseas] dated 8 Jan 1654. Whole estate to my said father who is to be sole exec. Wits: William Pettey, John Phillips, Richard Ames, John Rawlins, scrivener. Pr. 13 Mar 1657 by the said father. (PROB 11/263/104).

Thomas Alderne of London, merchant, dated 21 Apr 1756. I am to be buried in Hackney church near my late mother and the cost of my funeral is not to exceed £200. To my wife Dorothy an annuity of £200 out of my manors of Monnington Stradle, Old Hill and Hunderton in the parishes of Vowchurch, Madley and Clehonger, Heref., and houses in the City of Hereford. To my son Owen Alderne my part of a sawmill and lands belonging to the New England Co. and purchased by me and Col. Beale from Richard Leather and John B-----. Other principal bequests to: my sons Thomas and Owen Alderne; my daughter Dorothy; my brothers Edward Alderne, doctor of laws, and Daniel Alderne; the children of my brother Charles; my father-in-law Col. Owen Rowe and my mother-in-law Rowe; my brothers Samuel and Joseph Rowe and my sister Hannah Rowe; my brothers Elias, Tobias, Samuel, Edmond and Rowland Crispe; my brother George Brett; my kinsman Francis Griffith; my nephew and nieces John, Frances and Eleanor Greene, children of my sister Greene; my kinsman Jonathan Dryden; my kinsman and servant Edmond Alderne; Mary, Francis, Constance, Robert and Henry Dryden, children of my cousin Martha Dryden; my sister Clarke; my brother Doctour. Execs: my wife, my said father-in-law, my friend Thomas Loddington and my nephew John Greene. Wits: William Stringer, Thomas Weaver and George Carlton, servant to Jo. Mayne, scrivener. Pr. 20 Jun 1657 by the relict. (PROB 11/265/218).

William Moult, residing with James Jones of Nasswadax Creek, Accomack, Northampton Co., Va., who died in Accawacke, Va. This will takes the form of a letter dated 18 Sep 1653 from William Moult to his brother Francis Moult at Ashby Folvill, Leics. I have received your letter with a joyful heart and can expect the token with my sister Luice for which I give her thanks. I understand my tobacco is sold at Plymouth but at a very low rate: I had as much in London for one hogshead as I have there for two. I received the 20 shillings of George Maivill, the carrier. I may be in England this month but when I come to Va. I shall not fail to write to you. If I do any other you must write to James Jones ordering him to sell my goods and return them in tobacco—he is an honest man and you may trust him. If I should die single you should have it all. Help our dear mother and our good sisters and brothers. I dare not venture to take my sister Dorithie over with me. I have been dangerously ill but am well recovered. AWW 20 Jun 1657 to the brother, Francis Moult; no exec. having been named. (PROB 11/265/249).

Simon Lloyd [of Va.], mariner, dated 25 Dec 1655. To my brothers Edward and William Lloyd one shilling each. To my sisters 12 pence each. The residue of my estate to my execs. Mr. Robert Conway, citizen and joiner of London, and my cousins Margaret Conway and Evan Lloyd. The said Margaret Conway is not to marry without the consent of her uncle, the said Robert Conway. Wits: Thomas Lloyd, John Parrey and William (x) Davies. Pr. 30 Jly 1657 by Robert Conway. (PROB 11/266/280).

John Tuttie [of St. Bartholomew by the Exchange], citizen and fruiterer of London, son of William Tuttie of London, gent., deceased, dated 3 Sep 1657. Bequests to: my sister Hannah Knight of N.E. for her children; my brother William Tuttie of Totteridge, (Herts.); my sister Hester Blissett; my sister Elizabeth Tew and her son Nicholas Tew; my brother Samuel Tuttie and his four children; my brother Micklethweight; my uncle John Ling. My wife Rachel Tuttie is to be sole exex. Wits: Thomas Dunne and Robert Corney. Pr. 3 Oct 1657 by the relict. (PROB 11/268/372).

Robert Cochet of Mickleover, Derbys., gent., dated 5 Sep 1657. Lands in Staffs. and Derbys. to: my wife and exex. Anne Cochet; my daughters Anna and Sarah Cochet; my sons Nathaniel and Thomas Cochet. £5 to my sister Dorothy Joyce, wife of John Joyce of N.E., and £5 to their children. O'seers: my brother-in-law Joseph Swetnam and friend Samuel Berisford, ministers in Derby. Wits: James Wright, William Nepton and Stephen Wall. Pr. 30 Apr 1657 by the relict. (PROB 11/274/128).

1658

John Lyon, formerly of N.E. but now of the *Elizabeth* frigate in State service. For the care shown to me by my landlady Alice Linsey I leave my whole estate to her. Wits: William Sheare, Thomas Ralstone, Francis Hodgson and George Wyatt, scrivener. Admon. granted 30 Oct 1658 to principal legatee Alice Linsey. (PROB 11/282/559).

1659

Simon Sharp of Scatham (?Scothorne), Lincs., now aboard the frigate *Grantham* in America in State service, dated 20 Sep 1657. Bequests to: my friend and exec. Charles Brandon, steward of this ship; my friend Henry Whitehart. Pr. 31 Mar 1659 by Charles Brandon. (PROB 11/289/157).

Kempo Sybada [of Stepney, Mddx.] of London, mariner, dated 19 Mar 1659. £15 from my estate in England and Holland and one-eighth of my lands and plantations in Africa (*sic*), i.e. in N.E. and Jamaica, to my daughter Anne Sybada when she comes of age. The residue to my wife and exex. Mary Sybada. O'seers: Capt. John Wentworth of Bermuda, at present in London, and John Penny of London, mariner, commander of the *America*. Wits: Richard Napper, Ann Napper, William James, Redmond Rolle and James Witter. Pr. 18 Apr 1659 by the relict. (PROB 11/289/189).

John Ellis [of Va.], dated 25 Oct 1658. My Irish servant (unnamed) is to reckon his time as 10 years since coming to me and then to be free. Thomas Clarke is to serve one year from Mar next and then to be free. My servant Tayler is to serve the four years on his indenture. Bequests of cattle to Alexander Mitcheler, Mary Hudson and Elizabeth Jordan. An annuity to my mother Anne Milton out of the proceeds of my estate which are to be sent home for England. Residue to my brother Henry Ellis which, after his decease, is to be divided amongst his children. Execs: Living Denwood, Richard Bayley, Stephen Horsy and William Jordan. Wits: John Parmoore, William Coulborne and John Dixon. Pr. 22 Jun 1659 by William Jordan with the consent of the brother Henry Ellis. (PROB 11/293/370).

William Colcutt, seaman of the *Planter* in Va. Nuncupative will in the form of a memorandum dated 29 Mar 1659. Understanding his wife to be dead, the deceased left bequests to: his sister Anne West; John Nossiter; Thomas Prenderges, mate of the said ship; Ward Reddish; John Frost and David Man. The residue was to go to Patience Dandy, his wife's kinswoman, whom he had brought up from a child. Wits: Thomas Prenderges and David Man. AWW 5 Aug 1659 to Anne West, aunt and guardian of Patience Dandy. (PROB 11/294/446).

Margaret Blunt [of St. Thomas, Southwark, Surrey], widow. £10 to my sister Mary Welch in Martin's Hundred, Va., and £20 more if she outlives my cousin Sybilla Levitt. Other bequests to: my brother Captain Audry; my brother Edward Barber and his wife; my cousin John Levitt; Bridget Filby; Elizabeth Bull. Residue to the said Sybilla Levitt who is to be exex. O'seers: my brethren John Fogwell, said Edward Barber and Richard Levitt. Wits: Thomas Gibson and Alwine Burton. Pr. 23 Sep 1659 by Sybilla Levitt. (PROB 11/295/459).

1660

Francis Wheeler of London, merchant, now bound for Va., dated 6 Oct 1656. Bequests to: my friend Mr. John White, his wife and children; the children of my sister Marie Smith; the children of my sister Lettice Toms; the children of my sister Jane Man; the children of my sister Elizabeth Price; my brother-in-law Ralph Tustian; the poor of Bushley, Worcs., where I was born. My son Francis Wheeler, if he be of age when I die, to have my goods and ships in England and overseas. Wits: Henry Traverse, scrivener, John Budd, John Newland, his servant. Pr. 14 Mar 1660 by the son Francis. (PROB 11/297/19).

Thomas Mapson of Bethnal Green, Mddx., whitebaker, dated 23 Oct 1656. £25 to my niece Susanna, daughter of my eldest son Thomas who is supposed to have been lost at sea in a voyage to N.E. £25 to my other niece Elizabeth, daughter of the said Thomas, when she is 21 or on marriage. I have given £5 to my daughter-in-law Elizabeth Mapson, wife of my said son Thomas. To George Mapson, son of my uncle George Mapson, journeyman shoemaker living in London, 3s.6d., and to his other children 1s. each. To the children of Lodowicke Peele, ship carpenter, who married my uncle, 3s.6d. each. To my wife Joane Mapson £500. To my only son James Mapson, silk weaver, £200. Wits: Robert Gell, William Weardale, Robert Forster and Thomas Smith. Pr. 17 Jly 1660 by the relict. (PROB 11/299/137).

John Curtyce of Burghfield, Berks., gent., dated 20 Sep 1660. To my uncle Richard Curtyce my lease in Radley, Berks. Bequest to my sister Elizabeth Curtyce on marriage provided she gives £5 to my sister Jane Collyer, wife of Thomas Collyer, in N.E., and 5s. to all her children. Other bequests to: John Curtyce, son of John Curtyce of Tilehurst, (Berks.); my son-in-law John Richards; my two children John and Mary Curtyce. Execs: my kinsmen John Curtyce of Tilehurst and John Curtice of Radley, John Cole of London, merchant, and James Maynard of Reading, woollen draper. Wits: Thomas Petter, Roger Avenill, Richard Brewen and Elizabeth Bucknell. Pr. 31 Oct 1660 by named execs. (PROB 11/300/178).

1662

Francis Carpender of London, draper, now living in Hereford, dated 15 Mar 1660 with codicil of 9 Feb 1661. To my cousin Simon Carpender in Va. £5 and the debt of £20 I sent him as an adventure. I have debts owing to several men arising out of the bankruptcy of William Halse of Kingston, Heref. Other principal bequests to: my wife Helen Carpender who is to have my house in Kings Pyon, (Heref.), during her lifetime; my mother Phillip Carpender; my sister Phillip Carpender; my brother Mr. William Carpender of Chilston (dead at the time of the codicil) and his wife; my brother Thomas Carpender of London, his wife and his children William and Mary; my sister-in-law Alice Carpender, relict of my brother Richard Carpender deceased; my cousin Thomas Carpender and his wife; my cousin William Carpender of Oxford who is to have the lease of the Blackboy in Cheapside, London; my cousin Walter Carpender of Gloucester; my cousin Francis Carpender; my cousin Ann Simonds; my cousin Phillip Carpender; my cousin Mary Carpender; my cousins John and Elizabeth Berrington of Winsley and my cousin John Berrington near Norwich; my cousin Thomas Berrington; my cousin John Barneby of Kings Pyon, Heref.; my wife's sisters Elizabeth Moore and Mary Bradshaw; the poor of Hope under Dinmore, Heref., where I was born. O'seers: my cousin Thomas Carpender, Thomas Berrington and John Barneby. Wits: John Rawlins, John Philpotts, Abraham Seward, Susanna Meredith and John Parker. Pr. 9 May 1662 by the relict. (PROB 11/308/63).

Robert Peere of Clerkenwell, Mddx., butcher, dated 22 Jun 1655. Bequests to: my son Thomas Peere; my daughter Dorothy, wife of John Carter, butcher; my granddaughter Joane Carter, daughter of the said Dorothy, when she comes of age; my daughter Elizabeth, now wife of Robert Rayment of Va., planter, and to their children when they come of age. Residue to my wife Joane Peere who is to be sole exec. O'seers to be my son Thomas Peere and Jeremy Dance of Clerkenwell, blacksmith. Pr. 21 Oct 1662 in Archdeaconry Court of London. (Guildhall OW 9052/13).

1663

Robert Clark of Rotherhithe, Sy., mariner, now resident at Boston, N.E., dated 16 Sep 1662. My estate is to be divided between my wife (Mary) and my (minor) children John, William, Robert, Mary, Elizabeth, and the child born to my wife since I came from her. O'seer for my estate in N.E. to be Jonathan Wilson, carpenter. Wits: Thomas Savage Sr., Nicholas Page, William Pearse and William Smith. Note of 23 Sep 1662 signed by Edward Rawson, Recorder of Boston, that the estate of the deceased and of the owners of the ship *Relief* in N.E. was to be inventoried and sold under authority given to Captain (Thomas) Savage, Mr. Stoddard, Mr. Houchin, said Jonathan Wilson and Mr. Nicholas Page. AWW 1 Mar 1663 to Walter Rogers, guardian of the minor son John Clark. Revoked and granted 3 Aug 1663 to Mary Clark, widow, mother and guardian of the said John Clark. (PROB 11/310/33).

Humphrey Ley [who died overseas, bachelor]. The will takes the form of a letter written on 20 Sep 1658 on board the *Phoenix*, Mr. Robert Church, then bound for James River in Va. "and up the bay to Md. and so for Holland" to "my deare harte and loveinge sister," Judith Ley. I send love to my aunt and my sister Mary and her children. I am now in the Downs in good health and, had our merchant been aboard, we would have sailed sooner. My brother James Eirde is in good health and desires to be remembered to his wife and children and to my aunt. I was with him at Chatham when his ship was paid off. William Granger is one of our company and asks to

be remembered to his mother. That which I gave you a hint of is
in the hand of Elizabeth Fosse, the fifty (pounds?), if I never see
you again. I give that and all the materials I have in the world to
you, my sister. AWW 9 Mar 1663 to the said sister Judith Skinn
alias Leigh. (PROB 11/310/38).

John Hatton of London, salter, [who died in Va.], dated 14 Dec 1654.
To my brother Thomas Hatton the lands bequeathed to me by the
will of my late father John Hatton. Other bequests to: my brothers
Henry and Samuel Hatton; my sister Susan Hatton. Execs: my brother
Thomas Hatton and Mr. Robert Llewellin of London, salter. Wits:
Richard Colchester and Hercules Commander, scrivener. Pr. 22 Jly
1663 by Thomas Hatton, the other exec. having died. (PROB 11/311/93).

Hannah Wallin alias Poulter of St. Andrew Undershaft, London,
spinster, dated 15 Mar 1662. To be buried at St. Mary at Hill where
my brother John Wallin alias Poulter is buried. £10 to Thomas
Poulter now in Va. or overseas, brother of Mary Poulter who is
daughter of my cousin John Poulter of Hitchin, Herts. Other
principal bequests to: Mr. Joseph Alstone of London, Norwich
merchant, Mary his wife and their children Joseph, Edward, Isaac
and Clare Alstone; Mr. Edward Alstone; John Baldridge; my
kinsman Thomas Hunt and his children Thomas and Hannah Hunt;
the son and daughter of my cousin Isaac Poulter of Hitchin,
deceased, whose names I know not; the poor of Hitchin where I
was born. Execs: Joseph Alstone Sr. and Mary his wife. Wits:
Thomas Goodwin, scrivener, and Timothy Howford. Pr. 7 Aug 1663
by Joseph Alston. (PROB 11/312/112).

Thomas Walker of St. Michael Bassishaw, citizen and salter of London,
dated 20 Apr 1661. To my son Thomas Walker in Boston, N.E.,
£200. Other bequests to: my wife and exex. Hannah Walker; my
son Thomas Walker now at Boston, N.E.; my daughter Hannah
Straing; my brother William Walker; my sister Mrs. Hannah Fening,
widow, and her daughters Mrs. Mary Horrocks and Mrs. Hannah
Lowdham. O'seers: my said brother William Walker and my son
Paul Stoninge. No wits. shown. Pr. 2 Dec 1663 in Archdeaconry
Court of London by Hannah Walker. (Guildhall OW 9052/14).

1664

Arthur Blackmore of St. Gregory, citizen and painter stainer of London,
dated 7 Dec 1663. Bequests to: my son Humphrey Blackmore; my
son Arthur Blackmore (under 21); my daughters Frances, Mary and
Sarah Blackmore; my brother-in-law Mr. John Knight and his wife;

Mr. Anthony Reed; my wife and exex. Rebecca (*sic*) Blackmore. O'seers: said John Knight and Mr. Patrick Barrett. Wits: Thomas Laundis, Anthony Ryder, notary public, and John Hartry. Pr. 31 Mar 1664 by the relict Elizabeth (*sic*) Blackmore. (PROB 11/313/28).

N.B. This appears to be the Arthur Blackmore who married Susan Burnett in Holland and by her had a daughter Susan who married first Humphrey Robinson of London, merchant, and second Capt. William Corker of Va., surgeon, by whom she had issue. See NGSQ 67/215.

Ralph Story of Wapping, Mddx., mariner [who died in Va.], dated 14 Aug 1663. Bequests to: my wife and executrix Avis Story; my wife's mother Barbara Greene; my cousin Rowland Story, son of my brother Rowland Story deceased; my cousin Katherine Story, daughter of my brother Robert Story deceased. Wits: John Watley, scrivener, John Price and George Holloway. Pr. 1 Jun 1664 by the relict. (PROB 11/314/73).

1665

Richard Lee of Stratford Langton, Essex, who died in Va. The Probate Act Book records grant of probate in Jan 1665 to Thomas Griffith and John Lockey with similar powers reserved to John and Richard Lee but the will is to be found neither in the Register for that year nor amongst the collections of original wills.

John Clarke of Great Yarmouth, Norfolk, mariner, [master of the ship *Unity*, who died in Va.], dated 30 Nov 1657. Bequests to: my kinsman and exec. William Clarke the elder of Yarmouth, mariner; my sisters Joane and Mary Clarke. Wits: John Woodroffe and James Barnes. Pr. 26 May 1665 by William Clarke. (PROB 11/316/47).

N.B. Depositions were taken in Plymouth, England, in Sep and Oct 1666 to establish the validity of a codicil written in Amsterdam on 2 Aug 1664 by which the testator, who died in Va. on 4 Mar 1665, devised his estate in Va. to his partner William Browne. See NGSQ 66/219.

Hester Oakings of St. Botolph Aldgate, London, widow, dated 17 Oct 1664. £6 to Samuel Loveday of Creechurch, London, to be distributed to the poor but this bequest to be made void if my son Joseph Oakings returns from Va. My friend Richard Norwood of this parish to be exec. in trust for my said son who is to have the residue of my estate if her returns; if not the residue is to go to my kinsmen Harman Echballs and Joan Hall. O'seers: William Lambly and Randall Roper. Wits: John Packwood, Randall Roper

and William Lambly. Pr. 26 Jly 1665 in Archdeaconry Court of
London by the named exec. (Guildhall OW 9052/15).

George Elliot, now resident at the Hermitage, Dockhead, Whitechapel,
Mddx., mariner, but bound on a voyage to Va. in the *Accamacke*
under Capt. Smith, dated 27 Oct 1664. Bequests to: my brother
William Elliott; my sister Katherine Butler; my sister Margaret, wife
of Thomas Wiggett of Portland, Dorset, yeoman, and her daughter
Susannah Wiggett; my exex. Elizabeth, wife of John Corbin of
Whitechapel, mariner, who is to have my house and lands in Portland.
Wits: John Browne, Elizabeth Bayley and Anthony Errington,
scrivener. Pr. 19 Jly 1665 by Elizabeth Corbin. (PROB 11/317/72).

Arthur Pine, citizen and cordwainer of London, dated 1 Sep 1665. £10
to my daughter Hannah Johnson of Accamack, Va. Other bequests
to: my daughter Elizabeth Chandler and her husband Jacob
Chandler; my son-in-law Edward Christmas and his daughter Susan-
na Christmas; my kinswoman Elizabeth Jetter; my friends Mr. John
Poynter and Mr. Thomas Nelson the elder of St. Mary Abchurch.
Residue to my said daughter Susanna Christmas who is to be my
exex. Wits: ---?--- Rowse, William Medley and John Hiller. Pr. 6
Sep 1665 in Archdeaconry Court of London by the named exex.
(Guildhall OW 9052/15).

James Loughman of St. Botolph Aldgate, citizen and saddler of London,
dated 8 Jly 1665. Bequests to: My son William Loughman of Md.
in Va.; my youngest son Daniel Loughman in Md.; my brother John
Loughman, citizen and haberdasher of London; my wife Jane Loughman who is to be exex. O'seers to be John Pleadwell, citizen and
blacksmith of London, and William Sherly, citizen and hatbandmaker
of London. Wits: William Hewitt, Robert Soley and Henry Waller,
scrivener. AWW 2 Nov 1665 to the relict. Pr. 2 Nov 1665 in
Archdeaconry Court of London (Guildhall OW 9052/15).

1666

Thomas Read of Colchester, Essex, carpenter, dated 13 Jly 1665. My
house in All Saints parish, Colchester, to my son Thomas Read now
living in N.E. but, if he should not return, it is to be sold to purchase
lands in America for him, his wife and children. £320 to my son-
in-law Samuel Bacon and my daughter Mary, his wife, now living
in N.E., to be laid out similarly. My lands in Langham, Essex, of
which John Warner and his wife have the right of redemption, to
be settled upon my son Isaac Read and his wife. Other bequests to:

my daughter Rachel Hocker and her husband Joseph Hocker; my brother George Read and his son Thomas Read. Execs: my son Isaac Read and John Clarke. Wits: Thomas Lucas and John Waterhouse. Pr. 3 Mar 1666 by the execs. named. (PROB 11/320/51).

Arthur Cobb of London, gent., now bound for Syranum in America, dated 29 May 1663. Bequests to: my brothers Sir Thomas Cobb and Francis Cobb; my brother and exec. James Cobb, citizen and merchant tailor of London; my sister Winifred, wife of Steward Walker Esq.; my sister Alice Croker, widow; my sisters Susan and Margaret Cobb. Wits: Marmaduke Fleming and Charles Bird, both living in Holborn. Pr. 10 Apr 1666 by James Cobb. (PROB 11/320/56).

William Coltman of Greenbank, Stepney, Mddx., mariner, [who died in Va.]. My whole estate to my mother and exex. Alice Coltman of Greenbank. Wits: Mary Ward, Elizabeth Cadd and Robert Rose, scrivener. Pr. 1 Nov 1666 by Alice Coltman. (PROB 11/322/159).

1667

James Drumont of Stepney, Mddx., mariner [who died in Va., bachelor]. My friend Christian Mustard of Stepney, widow, to be my attorney and exex. and to have all that is due to me from my service at sea, including H.M. service. Wits: Robert Gray and James Wallace, scrivener. Pr. 7 Feb 1667 by the exec. named. (PROB 11/323/19).

William Allright the elder of Arborfield, Berks., yeoman, dated 18 Mar 1667. To my eldest daughter Margaret Avery in N.E. 20 shillings. To my wife Jone the £60 owed me by Thomas Moore of Whitley, Berks. Other bequests to: my sons William and Thomas Allright; my wife's sister Alice Wright; my cousin James Brant; my son-in-law Edward Ellis and his children Mary and Margaret Ellis, my grandchildren. O'seers: my brother James Allright and my friend Samuel Norris. Exec. my son William. Wits: John Mileham, Mathew Mileham and William Biddle. Pr. 21 May 1667 by the named exec. (PROB 11/323/56).

Samuel Crosse, citizen and embroiderer of London, [of St. Saviour, Southwark, Sy.], dated 20 May 1667. My estate to be divided between my son Samuel Crosse, my wife and exex. Mary Crosse and my sister Anne Glossopp. Rings for mourning to my father-in-law William Fluellin, my brother-in-law Philip Coltby and my brother-in-law Thomas Aspely and his wife. To my cousin Richard Crosse of Spondon, Derbys., 12 pence. Wits: John Byorr, George

Bennett and Thomas Hudson, scrivener. Pr. 27 Jun 1667 by the relict. (PROB 11/324/77).

N.B. The testator was a creditor of John Checkley of St. Saviour's, cooper, who emigrated to Boston, N.E. See LMC pp. 42-43.

John Achley of London, merchant, bound on a voyage to Tangier and Va. and back to London [by the *Hope* but who died in Va., bachelor], memorandum dated 6 Feb 1666. During my absence at sea I make my friend Dr. John Dolman of Ratcliffe, Stepney, Mddx., physician, my attorney and sole exec. so that he may demand all my goods and tobacco. Will dated 15 Aug 1666. To my father Mr. Anderson Achley Sr. all my clothes and bedding in Va. Other bequests to: Mr. Robert Mathewes at the Flower de Luce in Friday Street, (London), a creditor of Mr. Richard Read of Stepney, merchant; Captain Richard Longman and Mr. William Martin to whom I am factor; Mrs. Barbary Newman; my brother and sisters (unnamed). Wits: Patrick Napier, Samuel Bowker(?) and Richard Longman. Pr. 16 Nov 1666 and 6 Aug 1667 by Dr. John Dolman. (PROB 11/324/101). See NGSQ 67/61.

Abraham Oker now belonging to the flyboat *Salisbury*, Capt. Smith of Limehouse, bound for Va., [who died at sea on the *Bendish*, bachelor], dated 11 Mar 1666. My whole estate to my friend, creditor and exec. James Farthing of Redriffe, Sy., gent. AWW 3 Aug 1667 to the principal creditrix, Elianor Hitchcock, the named exec. renouncing. (PROB 11/324/109).

William Corderoy, merchant of Va., [bachelor], dated 16 Sep 1667. The charges are to be paid on my 13 hogsheads of tobacco in the *Charles* of London, commander Samuel Cooper, including a Bill of Exchange passed by John Smith upon James Nuttmaker, and the balance of my account with James Jenkins. I appoint as my sole exec. in England my brother Jasper Corderoy and he is to have my entire estate there and to pay what I owe to my father and mother. Ten shillings each to my brother Francis Corderoy and sister Anne Corderoy. Wits: Nathaniel Hitchinson, Christopher Derne, Mary Cobley, Anna Iremonger and Joseph Pike, scrivener. Pr. 10 Oct 1667 by the named exec. (PROB 11/325/130).

1668

James White, late of Barbados, merchant, [who died in Boston, N.E.], dated 10 Sep 1666. Principal bequests to: my wife Katherine White; the parish of Hornchurch, Essex, where I was born; Josiah, James (student at Oxford), John, William, Anne and Dorothy, children of my brother William White, late of London, in order that they may purchase their said father's farm of Fethes in Essex. Execs. in trust: Col. Henry Hawley, Edward Pye, James Beake Esq., William Bate Esq., my brother William White and Mr. Jeremy Edgington, merchant. Wits: John Gobble, Francis Punchard and Richard Gregory. Note that on 28 Mar 1667 before Governor Richard Bellingham, Edward Rawson and others, John Gobble aged 43, Francis Punchard aged 38, and Richard Gregory aged 24, made depositions as to the testator's will. Pr. 11 Feb 1668 by William White with similar powers reserved to the other execs. (PROB 11/326/26).

1669

John Thurmur living in Calvert Co., [Md.], dated 4 Apr 1668 and sworn before Charles Calvert [in Md.] 10 Apr. All my goods to my daughter Anne Elwes and my son Thomas Elwes. A silver tobacco dish to my friend Captain Sampson Waring; a silver beer bowl to his wife; to their son Basil Waring two heifers which I refused for myself when I sold my cattle to William Worgan. Wits: Richard (x) Gibbs and Francis Buckston. AWW 10 Feb 1669 to the principal legatee Thomas Elwes, no exec. having been named. (PROB 11/329/24).

George Morgan [who died at sea or in Va., bachelor], undated. Bequests to: Bridget Morgan; my cousin Margaret Lingom living near Shrewsbury, (Salop.); my cousin Anne Owens of London. Exec. Richard Knewstubb. Pr. 15 Apr 1669 by the named exec. (PROB11 /329/42).

1670

Samuel Filmer, formerly of East Sutton, Kent, [and formerly of Va. but who died in Westminster, Mddx.], dated 17 Jly 1662. Bequests to: my mother Lady Anne Filmer; my brothers Sir Edward Filmer and Robert Filmer Esq.; my sister Lady Anne Godscall, widow; my friends and cousins Frances Stephens, wife of Mr. Samuel Stephens of Va., Archibald Pinkard of Lynton, Kent, gent., Mr. Warham Horsmonden and Susan his wife, and Mr. Anthony Horsmonden; my cousin and exex. Mary Horsmonden, eldest daughter of said Warham Horsmonden, and Susan Horsmonden of Ham, Lenham,

Kent, between whom and myself there is an agreement of marriage. Wits: Anne Godscall, Ursula Horsmonden, Susannah Chapman and Warham Horsmonden. AWW 28 May 1670 to Warham Horsmonden, father of Mary Filmer alias Horsmonden, during her absence in Va. Revoked and granted to the said Mary Filmer 12 Apr 1671. (PROB 11/332/58).

Daniel Flower of London, citizen and merchant tailor of London, now bound on a voyage to sea [to Va.], dated 20 Aug 1663. I appoint as my execs. Richard Ellis and Walter Myles, citizens of London, to whom I am indebted. Wits: Timothy Gardner, Edward Pert and John Fisher, scrivener. Pr. 18 Jun 1670 by Richard Ellis. (PROB 11/333/75). Grant of admon. of 12 May 1670 to Alexander Martyn revoked.

John Ottway of Horsham, Sussex, labourer, dated 29 Mar 1639. To the first born of my brother Thomas my nine acres of land in Point in the parish of Cobham, (Sy.); to my second brother William 12 pence; to John Horrall my house called Hachford. Wits: John (x) Rise (?), John Hunt and Thomas (x) Hunt. Memorandum of same date that the testator was then bound to the new plantation called N.E. AWW 1 Mar 1670 to the principal legatee Elizabeth, wife of Thomas Ernall, no exec. having been named. (PROB 11/332/39).

Lewis Phillips of Huntingdon, gent., dated 24 Aug 1668. To be buried in the parish church of Brampton, Hunts., under the stone where Alice, wife of my deceased brother John Phillips, was buried in 1640. To my cousin John Throckmorton in Va. £5. Other principal bequests to: my sister Alice Throckmorton; my brother Gabriel Throckmorton in Ireland; Lewis Phillips, son of my nephew John Phillips, eldest son of my eldest brother John Phillips who was slain in the service of Charles I; Margaret, widow of my said brother John; my nephew Thomas Phillips; my cousin Albion Throckmorton; my sister Hutchenson; my sister Dunn, formerly wife of my brother Henry Phillips, and her daughter Hester Phillips; my niece Ann Brownsmith; Judith, late wife of my nephew Charles Phillips. Wits: John Negus, William Jeay, Benjamin Sheppeard and Samuel Butler. Pr. 3 Mar 1669 by John Halley. (PROB 11/332/39).

Raphael Throckmorton [of St. Gregory, London], dated 10 Sep 1669. £10 to my wife's brother William Walthall now living in Va. which my father Holland of Islington, Mddx., is to send him; £10 to my wife's sister Mrs. Elizabeth Clayton, now wife of John Clayton Esq.; £10 to my cousin Mary Throckmorton, second daughter of Sarah Throckmorton deceased. Other bequests to: the poor of Warrington, Bucks., where I was born; my cousin Edward Throckmorton; my cousin Mrs. Frances Throckmorton of Warrington; my cousin Martha Holland, second daughter of Solomon Bolton in the parish of St. Martin in the Fields; my sister Mary Castle of Olney, Bucks., widow, and her daughter Elizabeth Castle; my sister King. Execs: Edward Bringhurst, attorney who lived in my house in Aldermanbury, (London), and my cousin Edward Throckmorton. Wits: John Geneway and Thomas Tilsted. Pr. 3 May 1670 by Edward Throckmorton. (PROB 11/332/66).

Richard Preston of Patuxent, Md., dated 2 Dec 1699. To my son James Preston, if he is alive and returns from England to Md., the use of my plantation in Patuxent during his lifetime until such time as my grandchild Samuel Preston comes of age. In the meantime my daughter-in-law Margaret Preston is to be provided for if she decides to give him maintenance. My said son James, on the same conditions, is to have my patent for 200 acres called the Neglect and the island upon the Eastern Shore called Barren Island. My land in Great Choptank called Herne lately purchased of Walter Smith as per patent for 600 acres to my two daughters Rebeckah and Sarah Preston during their lifetimes, then to my son James, but if all should die, then to my kinsmen James and John Dassay. My 500 acres at the head of Little Choptank River is to be divided between my kinsmen Raphe Dassay and John Dassay. I have a covenant with William Tick, a Dutchman living in Little Choptank, relating to the delivery of cattle by us in partnership and, when this covenant expires, the said Raphe Dassay is to have all my cattle remaining. My friend and o'seer Edward Norman is to be paid his full wages and at the end of his service 585 lbs of tobacco. Thomas Brockson is to be paid his full wages and given 1,200 lbs of tobacco and a cow. William Purnell is to be given a cow, etc. and to be made free on 20 Oct next. The said John Dassay is to have goods to the value of £20 from my house or from the goods being sent from England this year. I leave £20 to George Harris to be paid in goods if he comes from England this year and half of the debts due to me in tobacco according to the promise I made him when he went with my son James to England. To my grandchildren William and James Berry 5,000 lbs of tobacco and to my grandchild Rebeckah Berry some plate which is to come from England. To my kinsman James Dassay 4,000 lbs of tobacco. To my said son James half the money I have sent for by James Coneway. To Thomas Preston upon the Clifts I give the tobacco he owes me. To Isaac Hunt I give goods to the value of £5. To William Harper I give what is due to him by my Bill. The residue of my estate to my said three children. Execs: my friends William Berry, Peter Sharpe, John Taylor of Kent and John Meeres upon the Clifts. Wits: Enoch Coombes, George Denline, Thomas Peale and William Jones. AWW 20 Aug 1670 to the son James Preston during the absence of the named execs. (PROB 11/333/101).

1671

Samuel Mew, citizen and salter of London [of St. Mildred Poultry], dated 6 May 1671. To be buried in the church of St. Mildred Poultry near my late wife Jane Mew. To my sister Sarah Cowper, wife of [blank] Cowper of N.E. £20. To my brother Ellis Mew of N.E. £20. Other principal bequests to: my sister Hester, wife of Christopher Blake; Hester Williams, wife of [blank] Williams, painter, daughter of the said Hester; Mary and Ruth Blake, daughters of the said Hester; my brother James Mew; my brother Peter Mew, if living when I die; my (minor) grandchildren Samuel, Henry, Hester and Thomas Withers, children of my late daughter Elizabeth, wife of Thomas Withers; my daughter-in-law Rachel Cason, now wife of John Cason, in Ireland; my son-in-law Joseph Ling; my daughter Mary Dod, wife of John Dod; my friends Sir Thomas Boyde, Mrs. Anne Fithes, David Cunningham and Richard Bogan of London, merchants; William Hills of London, druggist; Zachary Bartram, apothecary, etc. The residue to my friends and execs. Edward Bilton Sr. and Thomas Lamb of London, oilman. O'seers: John Worth and Francis Packe, gent. Wits: John Allen, Thomas Ligon, Peter Knowles and George Townrow, notary. Pr. 17 May 1671 by the execs. named. (PROB 11/336/65).

Hugh Stanley [of Md.], dated 30 Jly 1667. My wife Dorothy Stanley is to have my personal estate, my 200 acres at the eastern end of the Eastern Shore, and a quarter of 13,050 acres in Rappahannock, and is to be my exex. My brother John Stanley is to have 200 lbs of tobacco and to occupy my other lands during his lifetime, after which they are to descend to his two sons John and Edward Stanley. I leave cattle etc. to Salina Frances A. Jacob, the child I now keep. My will is to be recorded by the Commissioners of Calvert Co., Md. Wits: John Owen, Margaret (x) Weekes and Roger Blackhurst. AWW 8 Dec 1671 to Elizabeth Stanley, mother of the testator's minor nephews, John and Edward Stanley, in Md. (PROB 11/337/149).

1672

Roger Price, citizen and leatherseller of London, now bound to Va. by the *Salisbury*. The Vintners' Company owe me £25 out of which I make these bequests. To my brothers Richard and William Price £6 each. To my cousins Elizabeth and Jane Price, daughters of my brother Richard, £5 each. To my cousin Sampson White, son of my uncle Sampson White, late of Edmonton, Mddx., deceased, 40 shill-

ings. To my aunt Jone Piggot 20 shillings. My said brothers are to
be execs. Wits: George Allder, scrivener, Henry Sergent his servant.
Pr. 2 May 1672 by Richard Price. (PROB 11/339/64).

John Edmonds of Collingbourne Abbots, Wilts., cutler [who died in Va.,
bachelor], dated 2 Dec 1667. To my mother Elizabeth Collins during
her lifetime £20 and then to my sisters Eddey and Joane Edmonds or,
if they die, to my brother Thomas Collins and my sister Marie Collins.
To my cousin Marie Jones 50 shillings. My father Richard Collins is
to have my household goods. My uncle George Blanchard is to be my
exec. Wits: Thomas Jones, William Adman and William ----ll. Pr. 6
Jly 1672 by the named exec. (PROB 11/339/86).

Anthony Salwey of Ann Arundell Co., Md., gent., dated 23 Oct 1668.
If I should die in England where I now am, I am to be buried in
the church of Severn Stoke, Worcs., near my father and mother. To
my sister Dorothy, wife of Richard Stephens, £30 within a year of
her husband's decease if it can be raised on the return of tobacco
from my plantation. To my kinsman John Sollers 50 acres, cattle,
etc. To my sisters Dorothy, Helen and Joane 20 shillings each. To
my wife's goddaughter ----linda Mylls a mare. To my kinsman
Richard Harris one hogshead of tobacco. To my cousins Hanbury
Harris and Robert Harris 10 shillings each. To my brother Richard
Salwey of the city of Worcester, draper, my lands and plantation in
America and he is to be my exec. Wits: George Mill and Richard
Harris. Pr. 23 Aug 1672 by the named exec. (PROB 11/339/103).

Thomas Middleton Esq. of London, dated 5 Dec 1672. My legacies are
to be paid out of my estate in England, Barbados, N.E. and Antigua.
The children or execs. of Capt. Henry Colleton, deceased, are to
give to my execs. a release in respect of my dealings with him.
Principal bequests to: my wife Elizabeth; my sister Rebecca Wilkins;
my son and exec. Benjamin Middleton who is to have all my
plantations overseas; the children of my daughter Elizabeth Freere
by Capt. Toby Freere; Ursula, now wife of William Gold, and
Arabella, now wife of Samuel Pett, daughters of the said Henry
Colleton. O'seers: Mr. John Buckworth, Major Nehemiah Bourne
and Mr. Nicholas Dawes. Wits: Simon Nicholls, Nicholas Dawes,
John Nicholls, Roger Shiller and John West, scrivener. Pr. — Dec
1672 by the named exec. (PROB 11/340/152).

1673

William Parker [of Stepney, Mddx.], dated 3 Jan 1672. All my goods
in England, profits from my shares in ships, the produce of the

goods now in the *Richard and Martha* and £500 due to me from
the Hamborough Company are to be divided between my wife and
exex. Grace Parker and my daughter Elizabeth Parker. To my said
daughter a negro woman, cattle and mares in Md. My household
goods in Md. are to be divided between my wife, my son William
Parker, and my said daughter. My said wife is to have one negro
woman and one English servant. Bonds of £400 from the Hamborough Company to be shared between my daughters Thomasine
Kent, Sarah Edmondson and Dorothy Whittle. The tobacco due to
me in Md. and all my lands there to my son William Parker. Wits:
Edward Lloyd and Jane Harris. Pr. 24 Jly 1673 by the named exex.
(PROB 11/342/93).

Samuel Jones of Gloucester, N.E., mariner, [of the ship *Warspight* in
the King's service, who died in St. Thomas, Southwark, Sy.], dated
20 Mar 1673. I appoint as my attorney, exex. and sole legatee my
sister Susanna, wife of Richard Smith of Southwark, Sy., smith.
Wits: Susanna Morgan, Richard (x) Abbott, Thomas Lewis and J.
Simkins, scrivener. Pr. 1 Oct 1673 by the exex. named. (PROB
11/343/126).

1674

Mary Neeve, spinster, daughter of John Neeve, citizen and brewer of
London, [who died in Va.], dated 17 Oct 1661. To Samuel and
Mary Stanley, children of Michael Stanley of Cheapside, London,
hosier, 20 shillings each. To my sister Hannah Neeve £6. To my
said father 12 pence. To my sister and exex. Sarah, wife of Stephen
Lewis, citizen and stationer of London, £12. Wits: John Rowland,
Martha Sayer and John Man, scrivener. Pr. 13 Jan 1674 by the
named exex. (PROB 11/344/9).

Peter Moulson of [St. Bartholomew the Less], London, gent., dated 29
May 1674. To be buried at St. Bartholomew the Less behind the
south door and my grave to be made deep so that my bones may
not be thrown about. To my brother Foulke Moulson, now as I
conceive in Va., £200 if he comes to England but £100 if he does
not. If he dies before me, £100 is to be divided between my three
kinsmen Ann Roades, widow, Mrs. Margaret Pemmell, and Mary,
wife of Mr. Daniel Cary, and the other £100 to my friend and
exex. Mrs. Margaret Blague. £100 and my lease from Peter Dutton
Esq. of a house occupied by Ann Roades to my nephew Peter
Moulson of Waverton, Chesh. Other principal bequests to: the parish
of Waverton where I was born; St. Bartholomew's Hospital, Lon-

don; Gaines Moulson, brother of the said Peter Moulson; Margaret Harding, wife of Mr. Edward Harding, and their three sons. Wits: Thomas Cooke, John Haslipp and William Cawthorne. Pr. 30 Jun 1674 by the exex. named. (PROB 11/345/74).

Thomas Bache of Over Penn, Staffs., dated 21 Jan 1674. £100 to Thomas, Elizabeth, Mary and William Bache, children of my son Thomas Bache deceased, when they reach the age of 30. To my son William Bache 10 shillings. To my grandchild Gravenor Dyson 40 shillings. The residue to my daughter Mary Dyson. Wits: Elizabeth Dovey, Ann Muchalt and John Daulton. AWW granted 2 Jly 1674 to the daughter Mary Dyson. (PROB 11/345/83).

N.B. Peter Bache, a nephew of the testator, was stated to have emigrated to Va. in 1676 and to have had several children there. See NGSQ 62/273.

1675

Henry Knight of St. Martin in the Fields, Mddx., mariner [who died in Md.], dated 25 Nov 1672. Bequests to: my cousin Ann Meakin; my uncle and exec. Robert Day of St. Martin in the Fields, coachman. Wits: Robert Tendring, Sarah Tendring, Nicholas (x) Blackman and Thomas Gilbert, scrivener. Pr. 12 Jan 1675 by the named exec. (PROB 11/347/6).

Henry Grey [of St. Botolph Aldgate, London, who died in Va.], dated 8 Aug 1674. All my estate in Va. to my wife Elizabeth. To George Bennet two years of his time. My friend John Mann to be o'seer. Wits: Mordecai Cooke, William Holyday, George Bennet and Elizabeth Ironmonger. AWW 5 Jun 1675 to the principal creditor Richard Bankes, the relict Elizabeth Kerby *alias* Grey renouncing. (PROB 11/348/64).

Nicholas Tovey of St. George's parish, Somerset, (*sic*, perhaps Bristol?), mariner, [who died in Md.], dated 9 Jan 1675. My wife and exex. Anne Tovey is to have all my goods and my house in the Marsh in Bristol during her lifetime and thereafter it is to go to my brother Robert Whiting. To my brother George Irish a ring. My friend Samuel Gibbon is to dispose of all my unsold goods in Md. and to ship the proceeds to my wife. Written at Mr. Henry Ward's house, Elsie River, Cecil Co., Md. Wits: Henry Ward, John Gilbert and John Moll. Admon. granted at St. Mary's Probate Office, Md., 23 Feb 1675 to John Ward. Pr. London 30 Jun 1675 by the relict. (PROB 11/348/71).

Ambrose Fielding [who died in Va.], dated 26 Jun 1673. My estate is
to be divided between my three children Richard, Edward and Ann
Fielding. My brother Edward Fielding and my said son Richard are
to be execs. If I die here in Va. in the absence of my execs., I
appoint my friends Thomas Brereton and Thomas Hobson to be
o'seers. To my wife Ann Fielding 10 shillings. Wits: Henry Roach
and Samuel Hartnell. Pr. 1 Jly 1675 by the brother Edward Fielding.
(PROB 11/348/74).

Isaac Brookesbancke surgeon of the *Anne*, Capt. Benjamin Cooper,
[who died at sea bound for Md.], dated 29 Aug 1674. I appoint
my brother William Brookesbancke sole exec. and he is to pay my
mother Frances Walker £5. To my sisters Sarah Brookesbancke and
Mary Walker 20 shillings each. To my brother Cornelius Walker
20 shillings. To my brother Thomas Walker five shillings. To Ann
Mills 20 shillings. Wit: John Hunt. Pr. 4 Aug 1675 by the named
exec. (PROB 11/348/81).

Ann Dafforne of Shoreditch, Mddx., widow, dated 14 Oct 1675. To
my son John Dafforne now resident in N.E. 12 pence for all that
he may claim from my estate. Bequest to my younger son and
exec. Benjamin Dafforne. Wits: Mary Holwell, F. Johanna, I. (x)
Jacob and Samuel Shawser. Pr. 27 Nov 1675 in Archdeaconry Court
of London by named exec. (Guildhall OW 9052/19).

1676

David Anthony of Stepney, Mddx., mariner [who died in Va., bachelor],
dated 4 Jly 1675. My whole estate to my friend, creditor and sole
exec. James Dicks of Wapping, gent. Wits: John Hamblin and John
Marten, notary public. AWW granted 8 Jly 1676 to Margaret, wife
of James Dicks, during his absence overseas. (PROB 11/351/86).

Margaret Stone of St. Peter le Poor, London, widow, nuncupative will
dated 2 Nov 1676. My whole estate to my daughter Sarah Stone
during whose minority I appoint as my exec. in trust my brother-
in-law Joseph Godwin. Wits: Richard Heyward and Mary Heyward.
Pr. 21 Nov 1676 by the named exec. (PROB 11/352/146).

N.B. William Stone, tailor of Norton Folgate, London, husband of the
testatrix, went to Va. in about 1670. See LMC p. 68.

1677

Robert Tavernor of London, merchant, now intending for Md. [who died in Va.], dated 18 Oct 1675. Money for mourning rings to my brother Jeremy Tavernor and John Fowlkes of the Barbican, London, upholster. My exex. Bridget Fowlkes of the Barbican, spinster, is to have my goods in England and Md. Wits: John Webster, Mary Fowlkes and Thomas Ayton, scrivener. Pr. 31 Jan 1677 by exex. named after sentence for the validity of the will. (PROB 11/353/9).

Anne Grave of St. Botolph Aldgate, London, widow, "ancient and crasey of body," dated 10 Feb 1675. To George Grave Sr. of Hartford, Connecticut, and John Grave of Guildford, Newhaven, N.E., an annuity of £6 out of my tenements in Great Maplestead and Sible Hedingham, Essex. My house in Great Minories Street, London, in the occupation of Andrew Furzland, surgeon, and a house in Sible Hedingham known as Hunwicks to my grandson Jonathan Hardey. Other principal bequests to: my grandson Joseph Hardey; my cousins Charles and John Ellis; my kinsman Thomas Williams resident in Barbados and Anne Butler his sister; Godfrey Watkinson of Chesterfield, Derbys.; my cousin Francis Smith, grocer; my cousin Bennet, late wife of James Bennet deceased. Wits: Daniel Dyke, Lawrence Wise, Thomas Hicks, Timothy Lane, Prudence Wickes and Thomas Sondel, servant to John Wickham, scrivener. Pr. 20 Mar 1677 by William Kiffin. (PROB 353/31).

Leonard Southcot, quartermaster of the *Loyal Rebecca* now in York River, Va., dated 18 Dec 1676. My friend Thomas Short to have my entire wages and estate and to be my exec. Wits: James Tubb, William Watkins and John Mickilman. Pr. 21 Jun 1677 by the named exec. (PROB 11/354/68).

John Prise of London, [of Shadwell, Mddx.], mariner, now bound to Va. by the *Recovery* of London. My entire estate to my wife Joanna Prise who is to be my exex. Wits: Edward Thompson and Anthony Gester. Pr. 26 Sep 1677 by the named exex. (PROB 11/354/93).

Robert Huggins of Bristol, mariner, now bound overseas [who died in Carolina, bachelor], dated 11 Aug 1673. My friend William Peasley of Ratcliffe, Stepney, Mddx., to be my attorney and exec. Wits: Manley Man, William Dray, Joseph Hall and John Jenkin, scrivener. Pr. 22 Nov 1677 by the exec. named. (PROB 11/355/117).

Robert Terrell of London, merchant, dated 26 Oct 1677. To my cousin William Terrell, son of my brother William Terrell, £10 and £5 to his sister. To my cousin John Alpen £5. To my friend Robert Vaulx, merchant, £10, and he is to be o'seer. To my brother Richmond

Terrell 10 shillings. To my friend Mrs. Elizabeth Wickins the elder
£10. These legacies are to become chargeable only after my
accounts with Mr. Johnson and others in Va. are settled, and my
lands in Hants. are to be sold. To my sister Mary Mew a silver
cup. Exec. to be my cousin Robert Alpen, citizen and cook of
London. Wits: Anthony Horsmonden, Richard Wicking, John Wicking and Elizabeth Wicking. Pr. 23 Nov 1677 by exec. named.
(PROB 11/355/120).

N.B. The testator, son of Robert Terrell (or Tyrell) of Reading, Berks.,
was brother of Richmond, Charles and William Terrell who all
settled in New Kent Co., Va. See NGSQ 72, pp. 288-289.

1678

Thomas Todd of Baltimore Co., Md., dated 26 Feb 1676. To my wife
Ann Todd £400 which is in the hands of Alderman Richard Booth
in London and £176 in the hands of Robert Gossedy, and she is
to have the piece of land in England of which Gossedy is possessed.
To my four daughters Ann, Johanna, Francis and Avarilla the profits
from 87 hogsheads of tobacco now shipped for England, a mare
each, etc. If there is need for additional money, my share of the
ship *Augustine* is to be sold. To my brother Christopher Todd £20
to be paid to him in England and the 700 acres called Todd in
Cosica Creek, Chester River. My son Thomas Todd is to be exec.
Wits: Ebenezer Milam and Simon (x) Whithall. Pr. 30 Mar 1678
by the exec. named. (PROB 11/356/29).

James Turpin of the Liberty of the Tower, London, tobacconist, now
bound on a voyage to sea, [widower who died in Va.], dated 27
Nov 1675. My whole estate to my brother-in-law John Smith of St.
Botolph Aldgate, London, who is to be my exec. Wits: Joseph Cooke,
scrivener, and Daniel Shilling his servant. (PROB 11/356/54).

Jehosaphat Smith, citizen and ironmonger of London [who died in
Boston, N.E.], dated 23 Jly 1677. My estate to be divided between
my wife Margaret Smith and my brother and exec. Jacob Smith.
Wits: Thomas Smyth, Mary Smyth and Nicholas Wilkins. Pr. 29
Jly 1678 by the exec. named. (PROB 11/357/79).

Robert Wynne of Jordans parish, Charles City, Va., gent., dated 1 Jly
1675. To be buried in Jordans Church near my son Robert Wynne.
Regarding my estate in England I leave to my eldest son Thomas
Wynne (a minor) my farm in Whitstable, Kent, known as Linchett
Banks with remainder to my son Joshua Wynne and my daughter

Woodleif. My said son Thomas is also to have two houses in St. Mildred's parish, Canterbury and my said son Joshua a house and oatmeal mill in Dover Lane outside St. George's, (Canterbury), called the Lily Pot. To my said daughter a tenement in the parish of Hernehill, (Kent). Regarding my estate in Va. I leave to my son Thomas the cattle of his own mark; to my son Joshua my plantation called George's; and to my daughter a servant of four years to serve the next shipping out or else 2,000 lbs of tobacco to buy a servant. To my grandchild George Woodleif a filly. All my other estate in Va. I leave to my wife Mary who is to be sole adx. My friends Thomas Grendon, merchant, and my son-in-law Capt. Francis Poythres are to be o'seers. Wits: Thomas Brome and John (x) Burge of Charles City. Pr. in Charles City 3 Aug 1675. AWW London 15 Aug 1678 to Thomas Crane, attorney for the relict Mary Wynne in Va. (PROB 11/357/79).

John Baker of Poplar, Stepney, Mddx., mariner, [who died in N.E.], dated 2 Nov 1675. My wife Sarah Baker is to be my attorney and exex. Wits: Nathaniel Atkinson and Parnall (x) Westoll. Pr. 22 Oct 1678 by the exex. named. (PROB 11/358/17).

1679

Joseph Stocker of Wiveliscombe, Som., mercer, dated 5 Mar 1679. My farm and lands called Chubworthy in the parish of Raddington, Som., to my wife and exex. Mary Stocker during her lifetime and thereafter to my (minor) son Ephraim Stocker with remainder to my (minor) son Obadiah Stocker and my daughter Mary Stocker. To my said son Obadiah the tenement which I purchased in the Manor of Wiveliscombe and is in the possession of my father Amos Stocker. My brother William Stocker is to have my watch and my sister Joan 40 shillings. Wits: Anthony Stocker, William Lanterow and Ethelred (x) Lanterow. Pr. 28 May 1679 by the relict. Further grant 16 Feb 1681 to Amos Stocker and others as guardians of the minor children. (PROB 11/359/63).

N.B. The son Ephraim Stocker took passage from Bristol to Va. in about 1688 but the ship in which he embarked was never heard of again. See NGSQ 67, p. 212.

Mary Whitehead of Binfield, Berks., widow, dated 28 Feb 1679. To be buried in Binfield churchyard beside my husband. My wedding ring to my son Richard Whitehead living in Va. £5 to my grandson Francis Reynolds in order to bind him as an apprentice. My clothing to my daughter Mary Herbert. My daughter Philadelphia Whitehead is to be sole exex. Wits: Elizabeth Angell, William Angell and Richard Dewell. Pr. 2 May 1679 by the exex. named. (PROB 11/359/65).

Joseph Austin, late of N.E. but now of Shadwell, Mddx., mariner, dated 28 Sep 1678. My friend Mary Yems, wife of Nathaniel Yems of Shadwell, mariner, is to be my attorney and exex. Wits: David Gwynn, James Lakin, scrivener, and Nicholas Man his servant. Pr. 1 Sep 1679 by the exex. named. (PROB 11/360/113).

1680

Richard Smith of Stepney, Mddx., mariner [of the *Duke of York* who died in Va.], dated 17 Feb 1679. My friend Elizabeth Davis, wife of Mathew Davis of Stepney, mariner, to be my attorney and exex. Wits: John (x) Jeffryes and James Smith, scrivener. Pr. 9 Jun 1680 by the exex. named. (PROB 11/363/86).

George Moone of Fremington, Devon, mariner, [who died in Va.], undated. Bequests to: my brother Hugh Moone; my sisters Katherine Barnacot, Dorothy Coster and Christian Briant. Residue to my wife Alice who is to be sole exex. Wits: John Hellyer and John (x) Ash. Pr. 12 Nov 1680 by the exex. named. (PROB 11/364/151).

N.B. Depositions were taken in 1678 to establish the validity of the will which was written in James Town, Va. See NGSQ 69, pp. 199-200.

Hugh Nevett [of Va., bachelor], dated 27 Jly 1673. To my kinsman John Nevett, son of Richard Nevett, all my 1,100 acres upon the Blackwater in the North River held by patent bought of George Curtis and all the cattle and servants belonging thereto, with remainder to my kinswomen, the daughters (unnamed) of my brother William Nevett. To my kinswomen, the daughters (unnamed) of my brother Richard Nevett 40 shillings each. Maintenance is to be provided for the daughter of my brother Arthur Nevett whom I have sent for to come to my plantation in Va. To Major Thomas Walker and his wife £5 each. O'seer to be my kinsman Edward Cotton. Execs: Mr. George Seaton and Mr. John Throckmorton. On 5 Oct 1680 William Nevett appeared in order to declare that he had received a true copy of the will with notice that the named execs. had died. Thomas Walsh declared that he was employed in Va. by the heir John Nevett at whose request he had disposed of the estate. When he was in Va. in Feb 1679 he spoke to the exec. Throckmorton but Seaton was then dead. AWW 5 Oct 1680 to the nephew John Nevett. (PROB 11/364/132).

William Toms of Topsham, Devon, mariner [who died in Va., bachelor], dated 19 Aug 1675. My friend Richard Evans of Redriffe, Sy., waterman, to be my attorney and exec. Wits: William Phillips and Richard Ordway. AWW 14 Jly 1680 to Elizabeth Evans, wife of the named exec., during his absence overseas. (PROB 11/367/113).

Edmund Goddard, citizen and cooper of London, now bound on a voyage to Va. [who died in Va., bachelor], dated 3 Sep 1662. My house and lands in Thorndon, Suff., to my sister Hannah Goddard, widow, who is to be exex. £5 to my sister Mary Goddard. Wits: William Bower, scrivener, Thomas Woodward and Edward Allen his servant. Pr. 5 Dec 1680 by the named exex. Hannah Sheffield alias Goddard. (PROB 11/368/181).

1682

Henry Meese, citizen and draper of London, [of St. Katherine Cree-church], merchant, dated 12 Jan 1681. By articles of 16 Apr 1675 between me, Frances Pert of Mountnessing, Essex, widow and exex. of Henry Pert Esq. of Mountnessing, I contracted to marry my now wife, the eldest daughter of the said Henry Pert, and to settle estate on her to the value of £200. I therefore leave to my wife my entire estate save for the following legacy. To my four (minor) children Henry, John, Anne and Frances Meese all my plantations and lands in Va. My said wife to be exex. Wits: Benjamin Mosse, scrivener, Thomas Birchall and Thomas Johnson. Pr. 5 Apr 1682 by the exex. named. (PROB 11/369/47).

Thomas Teere of St. Botolph, Aldgate, London, citizen and blacksmith of London, dated 28 Nov 1681. To my son Thomas Teere, now resident in N.E., one shilling and no more. The residue to my wife and exex. Elizabeth Teere. Wits: Robert Bayley, John Tym and Daniel Shyling. Pr. 31 May 1682 in Archdeaconry Court of London by the relict. (Guildhall OW 9052/23).

Ralph Kinsey of St. Botolph Aldersgate, London, yeoman, dated 23 Jun 1682. To my wife Anne Kinsey my house in Allostock in the parish of Great Budworth, Chesh., during her lifetime and then to my son John Kinsey. To my said wife and my children John, Anne and Mary Kinsey the value of lands in Pennsylvania I purchased of William Penn and Thomas Holmes which are now to be sold. To John Tisoe 20 shillings to be distributed to the poor. Execs: my brothers William Kinsey and Robert Browne, both of Westminster, tailors. Wits: Thomas Higgs, John Tysoe, Peter Bowen and Edward

Lambert, servant to John Bland, scrivener. Pr. 29 Jun 1682 by the execs. named. (PROB 11/370/72).

John Johnson of Lubeck, [Germany], at present living in Wapping, Mddx., mariner, suddenly bound to sea in the *Concord*, Capt. Thomas Hurlock, [and who died in Va., bachelor], dated 26 Oct 1680. My friends Robert Cheny of Wapping, mariner, and Joane his wife to be my attorneys and execs. Wits: James Lyddall, John Marlar, scrivener, and William King. Pr. 27 Jly 1682 by Joane Cheny. (PROB 11/370/85).

1683

Robert Nelson of Shadwell, Mddx., mariner, now bound to sea [who died in Carolina, bachelor], dated 23 Jun 1681. My friends Thomas Wellin of Shadwell, ballastman, and Dorcas his wife to be my attorneys and execs. Wits: John Standbridge and Richard Man, scrivener near New Crane, Wapping. Pr. 8 Jan 1683 by Dorcas Wellin. (PROB 11/372/7).

Thomas De Lavall of N.Y.C., dated 10 Jun 1682. To my son-in-law William Darvall all my lands within the bounds of Harlem upon the Island of N.Y., an island called Great Barnes Island near Harlem and my mill at the Ecopus? To my son John De Lavall my houses and lands at the Ecopus? except the mill. To my daughter Margaret Coddrington £50. To my sister Anne Cornewell an annuity of £5 during her life and thereafter to her daughter Anne. My son John is to allow my brother-in-law Edward Dyer maintenance. Exec. my son John. *Codicil.* To my son John De Lavall my part of Yonkers Mill on Hudson River. To my son-in-law Thomas Coddrington my lands and houses at Gravesend on Long Island. My son-in-law William Darvall is to pay what is due to Mr. Samuel Simcock of London, merchant. To my granddaughter Frances Darvall my land lying by the Smith's Fly in N.Y. known as the Cherry Garden. Wits: Edward Dyer and John Tuder. Copy taken from the Office of Records, N.Y. AWW 7 Feb 1683 to Thomas Landon, attorney for the son John De Lavall now overseas. (PROB 11/372/17).

John Avery of Dorchester Co., Md., shipwright, dated 25 Apr 1677. All my real and personal estate to my wife Anne Avery during her lifetime and then to my grandson John Granger. Wits: George Powry, Thomas Pattison, Mary Meredith and Mary Lane. Admon. granted at St. Mary's, Md., in Jly 1680. AWW 11 Aug 1683 to

Cuthbert Haslewood, brother of John Haslewood now overseas, husband of the relict Anne Haslewood alias Avery deceased. (PROB 11/373/92).

1684

Thomas Jarvis, late of Va. but now of London [St. Olave, Old Jewry], merchant, dated 6 Apr 1684. My estate in Va. is to be sold and the proceeds sent to George Richards of London, merchant. My brother Christopher Jarvis, in consideration of his duty to my aged mother during her lifetime, is to be sent clothing and linen in a sealskin trunk and I forgive him all the rents he owes me for the farm at Holton, Suff., where he lives provided he pays my goddaughter Mary Worlick £20. Residue to my wife Elizabeth Jarvis and my (minor) son Thomas Jarvis. Execs: my said wife, my brother Edmond Foster and the said George Richards. Wits: Richard Tyms, John Pool and Michael Bignall, scrivener. Pr. 18 Apr 1684 by the execs. named. (PROB 11/375/43).

Nicholas Prynn of Stepney, Mddx., mariner [who died in Va.], dated 11 Aug 1682. To my daughters Judith Edgcomb and Abigall Burford 12 pence each. Residue to my wife Dorothy Prynn who is to be my exex. Wits: Robert Robinson, Anna Soloman and Samuel Wills, scrivener. Pr. 5 May 1684 by the relict. (PROB 11/376/61).

James Swift of [St. Mary Abchurch], London, [who died in Hackney, Mddx.], dated 17 Apr 1684. Whole estate to my wife and exex. Sarah for the maintenance of my four children James, Sarah, Elizabeth and Judith Swift. Wits: Thomas White and Judith Jones. Pr. 12 Jun 1684 by the relict. (PROB 11/376/81).

N.B. The testator traded frequently to N.E. See LMC pp. 38-39.

Benjamin Acrod of Hackney, Mddx., gent., [who died in Pennsylvania], dated 12 Jan 1683. Of my personal estate consisting of £200 owing to me by my sister Susanna Kirke I leave £10 to my brother John Acrod and £100 between my sisters Susanna, Lydia Dismarett, Priscilla White and Phebe Acrod. I leave to my son John Acrod the £200 owed me by Edmond Thomas which I am taking with me to Pennsylvania. The 5,000 acres which I shall purchase there I leave to my nephew Richard White. Execs: my son John Acrod and the said Richard White. Wits: Thomas White and Hannah Garnett. Pr. 10 Dec 1684 by the relict after sentence for validity of the will. (PROB 11/378/158).

1685

William Gibson of [St. Edmund the King], London, haberdasher, dated 31 Jly 1683. My 500 acres in Pennsylvania and £200 to my (minor) son John Gibson. Household goods and £300 to my wife and exex. Elizabeth Gibson. £200 to my (minor) daughter Patience Gibson. £100 to my brother John Gibson with remainder to the children of my two sisters Elizabeth Steers and Anne Lucas. Wits: Harbert Springett, Thomas Cox and Sell. Craske. AWW 9 Jan 1685 to Jane Barnes, guardian of the children, John, William, and Patience Gibson, during their minority; the relict renouncing. (PROB 11/379/5).

Davey Wyett of St. Gregory Stoke, Som., husbandman [who died in Carolina, bachelor], dated 2 Sep 1682. All my goods which may be left in Ireland or carried with me to Carolina are to go to my brother John Wyett of Uplyme, Devon, serge weaver, and he is to be my exec. Wits: Toby Welles, Martin Dunsford and Katherine (x) Browne. Pr. 4 May 1685 by the named exec. (PROB 11/380/65).

George Derickson of Shadwell, Mddx., [who died on the ship *Unicorne* in Va., bachelor], dated 18 Oct 1683. My friend Thomas Anderson of Shadwell, shipwright, to be my attorney and exec. Wits: Rachel Howlett, Peter Peterson and George Jewell, scrivener. AWW 7 Jun 1685 to Anne Anderson, wife and attorney of Thomas Anderson, now overseas. (PROB 11/380/70).

John Wise [who died in Va.], dated 27 Jly 1684. My clothing, books and instruments aboard the *Golden Fleece*, Capt. James Coote, to my brother William Wise. All my wages for service on the said ship to my mother Anne Miller living in Deal, (Kent), who is to be my exex. Wits: Edward Horspitt, Richard Beard, William Wise and Richard Richardson. Pr. 29 Jun 1685 by named exex. (PROB 11/380/79).

Nicholas Painter of Anne Arundell Co., Md., gent, now residing in London, dated 8 Sep 1684. To my cousin Henry Bray of London, glazier, my 4,000 acres in Dorchester Co., Md., held by three patents granted by Lord Baltimore. To my brother Roger Painter of Andover, Hants., husbandman, my 700 acres on Wye River, Talbot Co., Md. To my sister Katherine Painter of Andover, spinster, my 700 acres in Anne Arundell Co. To Mrs. Barbara Trinder of Abchurch Lane, London, spinster, my 1,050 acres in Cecil Co., Md. To Katherine Keate, daughter of John Keate of Andover, my 400 acres in Tuckahoe, Talbot Co. To William Hawkins of London, scrivener, a half part of 1,000 acres on Chester River, Talbot Co., half of 1,700 acres in Dorchester Co. and half of 900 acres in Cecil Co. To John Hawkins of London, distiller, £5. I give their freedom to my negroes Tom and Sarah. Residue to my exec. Henry Bray. Wits: William Evans, Joseph Huckebutt and John Jenkins. Pr. 8 Oct 1685 by the named exec. (PROB 11/381/123).

Thomas Pope of St. Philip and Jacob, Bristol, merchant, now bound on a voyage to sea. To my wife Joanna my house and land called Nobles Corner in Barton Regis, Glos., and my plantation at Pope's Creek in Westmoreland, Va., during her lifetime and then to my sons Charles and Nathaniel Pope. My wife is to have a one-third part of the Clifts Plantation on Potomack River, Westmoreland, Va., belonging to my sons Richard and John Pope. I appoint my friends and kinsmen Mr. William Hardridge, Mr. Lawrence Washington and Mr. John Washington of Va. to help my sons Thomas, Richard, John, Charles and Nathaniel Pope in the management of their plantations until they come of age and to consign the profits thereof to my wife in England. The residue of my estate to my wife and three daughters, Mary, Elizabeth and Margaret Pope. My execs. in trust for England are to be Richard Gotley and Charles Jones the younger of Bristol, merchants. Wits: John Churchman, William Meredith, William Brayne and John Selwood. Pr. 20 Oct 1685 by Richard Gotley. (PROB 11/381/124).

George Read of Whitechapel, Mddx., mariner, shortly to go on a voyage in H.M. ship *Swallow*, Capt. Crevatt, [and who died on the ship *Culpepper* in Va.], dated 27 Nov 1682. Whole estate to my wife Margaret Read who is to be my attorney and exex. Wits: Alexander Arnett, William Athy and Thomas Craven, scrivener. Pr. 14 Oct 1685 by the relict. (PROB 11/384/125).

William Sterry of Bristol, mariner, now in Boston, N.E., dated 30 Aug 1684. My whole estate to my wife Charity Sterry. My friend Mr. Adam Winthrop to be exec. Wits: William Colman and Thomas Kemble. AWW 26 Oct 1685 to the principal creditor in Boston Giles Merricke, the relict renouncing. (PROB 11/384/125).

Thomas Weare of Charfield, Glos., yeoman, dated 20 Dec 1684. To my sister Hannah Summers 40 shillings, to her sons John and Peter Summers 40 shillings each, and to her daughters Elizabeth, Mary, Sarah and Jane Summers 40 shillings each. To my brother Daniel Weare half of my household goods and to his daughter Mary 40 shillings. I make my eldest brother Peter Weare of York in N.E. my sole exec. and leave him the lease on the estate where I dwell and all the residue of my goods with remainder to his eldest son. O'seer: my friend Joseph Poole of Charfield. Wits: Ewan Christian, Richard (x) Cussens and Elizabeth (x) Haile. Pr. 3 Oct 1685 by the named exec. (PROB 11/384/128).

Samuel Shute of [St. Peter] Cornhill, London, Esq., dated 8 Apr 1684. To my wife the lease of my house at Theobalds, my household goods and £1,500. To my daughter, wife of Mr. Thomas Andrews £1000. To my nephew Benjamin Shute, son of my deceased brother Benjamin, £500 when he is 21. To my nephew Joseph Shute £2,200 when he is 21. I have made settlement of my lands in Montgomeryshire and Salop. by deed. The residue of my estate to my son Joseph Shute, my daughter Andrews, and my daughter Elizabeth. My wife Anne is to be my exex. Wits: Robert Gilpin, John Strickson and John Greene. Pr. 15 Dec 1685 by the relict. (PROB 11/381/156).

N.B. The testator had trading partners in N.Y. See LMC pp. 20 & 58.

1686

Richard Watson of St. Margaret, Westminster, Mddx., gent., dated 18 Apr 1685. To my brother-in-law Theodore Wilkins of New Ross, Ireland, £20 and to his children Elizabeth, Katherine and Michael Wilkins £20 each. To my late wife's son, Robert Boodle of Rappahannock River, Va., £100 a year from which he shall pay Mr. John Ward of St. Andrew, Holborn, London, tailor, what he owes him for the clothes he took when he went to Barbados. To my late wife's daughter, Cicely Brandreth of St. Margaret, Westminster, now wife of William Brandreth, tailor, £100. Other bequests to: Thomas Jones of Westminster, apothecary; Mrs. Elizabeth Plumpton of Westminster, widow, and her daughters Mrs. Elizabeth Arnold and Mrs. Sarah Juxon, and her niece Alice Willey. The moiety of my mansion house called Blendon Hall in Bexley, Kent, lately in the occupation of Sir Edward Brett and by him bequeathed to me, to be divided between Elizabeth, Katherine and Michael Wilkins and Brune Clench of St. Martin in the Fields, Mddx., gent., who is to be my exec. Wits: Roger Worrall, Thomas Gilbert, scrivener, and Abraham Gilbert. Pr. 6 Jan 1686 by the named exec. (PROB 11/382/9). New grants made in 1733 and 1808.

William Hawkins of Kingston-on-Thames, Sy., barber-surgeon, bound to N.E. by the *Society* of Boston, Mr. Christopher Clarke, dated 27 Feb 1666. To my sisters and exexs. Rachel Sudell and Frances Blaunch, wife of Robert Blaunch, a property in Kingston bequeathed to me by my father John Hawkins. Bequests to: Simon Smith of Kingston, gent.; Edward Baldin of London, cooper; and John Hawkins, son of my brother John Hawkins. Wits: Thomas Wallis, John Alsop, scrivener of Fenchurch Street, London, and Thomas

Watkin his servant. Pr. 27 Jly 1686 by Rachel Wade alias Sudell, wife of Christopher Wade, with powers reserved to the other sister. (PROB 11/384/96). Grant revoked in Nov 1700 on presentation of a later will of 1 Aug 1685 in which the testator describes himself as of Boston, N.E., and of which the testator's wife Dorothy was made exex.

N.B. Depositions were taken in Boston in Jly 1700 from Thomas Clarke, pewterer; Eleazar Moody, scrivener; Isaac Addington Esq., former clerk of Boston Co. Court; James Meers, haberdasher; Humphrey Parsons, merchant; and Samuel Checkley, surgeon, former apprentice to the testator. These establish that two sons and two daughters of the testator were then still living (in Boston). See NGSQ 65, p.219.

William Balfoure of London, surgeon, now bound overseas, [who died in Va.], dated 2 Apr 1685. Alexander Blair of the Middle Temple is to be my attorney and exec. and deliver the residue of my estate to the first Scottish surgeon that shall come home of a broken voyage. Wits: Thomas Wallis and Anthony Goodwin. Pr. 1 Sep 1686 by the named exec. (PROB 11/384/113).

Oliver Smith of Ratcliffe, Stepney, Mddx., mariner, now bound to Va. in the *John*, commander Thomas Groves, [and died in Va. on the *Susanna*], dated 26 Nov 1680. My wife Mary Smith is to be my attorney and exex. Wits: Per Milners and Thomas Quiller, scrivener. Pr. 4 Oct 1686 by the relict. (PROB 11/385/139).

John Royse of London, merchant, now bound on a voyage to N.Y. [but who died in Gravesend, Kent], dated 18 Jun 1683. To my father Mr. Daniel Royse and my friend Mr. James Wancklen 40 shillings each for a mourning ring. To my wife £200. The residue of my estate to my brother Daniel Royse, the children of my sister Winne and the children of my sister Wiche. My said father and James Wancklen to be my execs. Wits: Tobiah Winne, scrivener, Daniel Chandler and George Copping his servant. Pr. 9 Dec 1686 by the father. (PROB 11/385/154).

Mary Langhorne alias Ingoldsby [of Holborn, Mddx., but who died in Staughton, Hunts.], dated 24 Nov 1686. I leave to my son and exec. Sir William Langhorne £100 and a new suit I brought to Charlton. To my son Thomas Langhorne £300. To my daughter Katherine James £20. To my daughter Dorcas Pordage £30. To my grandson John Conyers Esq. £10 and to his three sons 40 shillings each. To my brother Clement Oxenbridge and his wife £4 and to their daughter Katherine 40 shillings. I owe the children of my brother John Oxenbridge £40 which was borrowed by Capt. Ingoldsby: those children are now all dead but for one in Jamaica and one in N.E. who, if they are still alive, should be repaid if they come to England. Wits: Christopher Jeakins, Edward Rolt and Ann Keer. Pr. 16 Dec 1686 by the named exec. (PROB 11/385/167).

1687

Thomas Mather of London, mariner, now bound to N.Y.C. and W.I. by the *Thomas & Anne*, Mr. Andrew Elton, [but who died at sea, bachelor]. I leave my estate, including my wages due for my service on board this ship, to my sister Martha Coppocke who is to be my exex. Wits: John (x) Carpenter, Nicholas Thornton, William (x) Bew and W. Curson. Pr. 7 Mar 1687 by the exex. named. (PROB 11/386/39).

William Strachey of St. Austin, London, merchant, dated 27 Oct 1686. To be buried in the church of Camberwell, Sy. To my wife Martha Strachey £120 and the rents due at my decease from my estate in Essex. To my daughter Arabella Waters, wife of John Waters, now in Va., planter, £10 a year. To my granddaughter Elizabeth Cox, daughter of Arabella Waters, the rents and profits of my houses and estates to a total of £200 and possession of the same after the deaths of the said John and Arabella Waters. My friend George Richards of London, merchant, to be my exec. Wits: Mary Wither, John How, scrivener, and Samuel Pollett. Pr. -- Mar 1687 by the named exec. (PROB 11/386/42).

Daniel Axtell [of Stoke Newington, Mddx., who died in Carolina], dated 3 Aug 1678. £500 each when they come of age or marry to my children: Sibilla, Daniel, Mary, Holland, Rebeckah, Elizabeth and Anne. When my estate is gathered in from abroad my wife and exex. Rebeckah is to have £2,000 but, if there is not sufficient to pay my other legacies, her portion is to be reduced accordingly. O'seers: Henry Danvers Esq. and Mr. William Pennington. Wits: Anne Cooper, Mary Catchpoule and Sarah Hill. AWW 2 Jly 1687 to Walter Needham, doctor of medicine, attorney for the relict now in Carolina. (PROB 11/388/90).

Richard Bacon of Stepney, Mddx., seaman of the *Thomas & Richard*, merchantman of London, Capt. Thomas Winn, now bound for Va., dated 18 Aug 1686. William Chalke of St. Andrew, Holborn, London, farrier, to be my attorney and exec. Wits: Henry Tomlinson and Cyprian Southake, scrivener. Pr. 12 Dec 1687 by the named exec. (PROB 11/389/146).

1688

John Pargiter of St. Martin in the Fields, Mddx., dated 10 Feb 1688. £10 each to Robert, Edward, Samuel, William Pargiter, sons of my deceased brother William Pargiter, and £10 to the children of his daughter Knight. £20 to Frances Meade, wife of Mr. Francis Meade of Battersea, (Sy.). £20 to my kinsman Mr. Thomas Pargiter, son of my brother Thomas Pargiter. £5 to George Pargiter, son of my said brother. £10 to my cousin Sarah Lovell at York River, Va. £12 to Elizabeth Pargiter, widow of my cousin Robert Pargiter deceased. Twenty shillings for mourning to my cousin Austin of Hampton, (Mddx.), and his wife. £5 to my cousin Benjamin Billingsby, bookseller. Twenty shillings for mourning to my cousin Callendrine and his wife Mary. To my grandchildren John and Mary Fleetwood, children of Sir Gerald Fleetwood, £2,000 when they come of age. To my son John Pargiter all my lands in Nordley Wood, Astley and Astley Abbotts in Salop., my estate in Pamber and Bramley, Hants., and tenements in London and Mddx. To my son Samuel Pargiter houses in Fleet Street and elsewhere in London. My said two sons to be execs. O'seers Sir William Cowper. Wits: Richard Adams, W. Meritt, John Feram, Richard Netter and William Grimes. Pr. 24 Feb 1688 by the execs. named. (PROB 11/390/21).

John Wyron of Reading, Berks., tinplate worker, dated 29 Apr 1688. My two houses in Bread Street, Reading, to my wife Elizabeth during her lifetime with remainder to my daughter Sarah, wife of John Neale of Reading, clothworker, and my daughter Mary, wife of John Moore of New Windsor, Berks., tinplate worker. My meadow in Longworth, Berks., and £100 to my said daughter Mary. To my daughter Grace, wife of William Rackstraw, now in Penna. or possibly returning from there, £100. Exec. to be my friend Thomas Smith. Wits: Richard Blissett, Richard (x) Willmutt and Richard (x) Irons. Pr. 10 May 1688 by named exec. (PROB 11/391/71).

Simon Keech [of Stepney, Mddx., bachelor, who died in Va.]. Joakim Pagett and Katherine Farbour depose that Simon Keech, master of the ketch *Truelove* of London now in Chickonessex, declared that his entire estate should go to his poor sisters. The depositions were proved as a nuncupative will on 13 Feb 1688 in Accomack Co., Va. AWW in London 2 Aug 1688 to Ellis Kelly of St. Michael Cornhill, London, merchant, attorney for the sisters Mary and Joanna Keech, Elizabeth Woodnett, widow, and Sarah Tilly, widow. (PROB 11/392/108).

Joseph Morton of Carolina, landgrave, dated 14 Apr 1685. To my son Joseph Morton books including those recording Assembly

proceedings and £1,000 sterling. To my daughter Deborah Blake
£400 sterling. To my son John Morton £1,000 sterling, lands in
Berrow, Som., and all other lands in England and Carolina. £5
to Mr. Nehemiah Cox of London £100 to be distributed by Mr.
William Collins and Mr. Nehemiah Cox to poor ministers in
England. To my sister Rebeccah the use of £50 and cattle and
hogs, and she and her husband are to have the use of a negro
man and woman. The residue of my estate to my wife Elinor
who is to be my exex. Wits: Edward Bowell, John Bletchley and
John Ansted. Recorded in Carolina 25 May 1685. On 7 Nov 1685
John Bletchley of Weston near Bath, Som., carpenter, deposed
that he was a servant to the testator for four years and was a
witness to his will with Mr. Edward Bowell, the testator's brother-
in-law, John Ansted, another servant now deceased, and Mrs.
Elizabeth Gower. The said Elizabeth Gower, widow living near
Thavies Inn in Holborn, milliner aged 34, also deposed that she
knew the testator for many years and lived in his house in
Carolina for 1½ years. AWW 20 Nov 1688 to the sons Joseph
and John Morton, the relict having died; revoked and granted on
19 Mar 1706 to Anne Wills alias Morton, wife of Thomas Wills,
who was the relict of the testator's son John Morton deceased.
(PROB 11/393/153).

1689

Alexander Parker of George Yard, [St. Edmund Lombard Street],
London, haberdasher of small wares, dated 6 Mar 1689 with codicil
of same date. My daughter Anne Parker is to have my goods and
wares. My real estate in England and Penna. is to be sold for the
benefit of my execs. and the profits divided between my other
children Mary, Ellen, Elizabeth, Alexander and John Parker. My
youngest son John Parker had no legacy from his grandfather
William Goodson deceased and should therefore receive maintenance. O'seers: my friends William Crouch, William Ingram,
Daniel Wharley and Henry Goldney. Execs: my daughter-in-law
Prudence Wager and my daughter Mary Parker. Wits: Thomas
Howkins, Charles Fox, Edmund Cox and Robert Bicknell. Pr. 25
Apr 1689 by execs. named. (PROB 11/395/53).

Henry Whearley of Barbados now bound on a voyage to England,
dated 22nd of the third month called May 1685. £70 to my brother
Abraham Whearley, now in Penna., to whom I forgive the £30 he
owes me, and he is to have a further £100 if he has need. My

estate known as Chelmsford in Hunsdon, Herts., I leave to the use of my brother and exec. Daniel Whearley of London. Other bequests to: my wife Sarah Whearley; my sister Anne Phillips, wife of George Phillips of London. Exec. in trust for England to be my friend William Walker of London, ironmonger. Execs. in trust for Barbados to be my friends William Bicknall, merchant, and Capt. William Dymmock. Wits: Thomas Bread, John Summers, Valentin Tregenow and Richard Vaux. Pr. 26 Apr 1689 by Daniel Whearley. (PROB 11/395/55).

Charles Stepkin Esq. of London [who died in Va.], dated 1 Mar 1688. To my children Charles Stepkin and Theodosia Stepkin all my lands in Milk Yard, Wapping, Stepney, Mddx., and my plantation in Ware parish, Gloucester Co., Va., with remainder to my cousins John Lane, minister, and Mary Lane. To my wife Elizabeth Stepkin one shilling. To Mr. William Bower 20 shillings for a ring. If my two children die without issue I leave £100 each to Sarah Richards, daughter of Mr. George Richards, and Joseph Low. Wits: Roger Denniston, George Williams and Thomas Smith. AWW 5 Jly 1689 to the relict Elizabeth Stepkin, guardian of Charles and Theodosia Stepkin during their minority. (PROB 11/396/104).

Robert Clarke, now of St. Giles Cripplegate, London, but late of Md., planter, dated 14 Dec 1689. My plantation in Md. and all my goods aboard the *Exeter Merchant*, Mr. John Coyle, to my mother Jane Clarke and my brother John Clarke who are to be my execs. Wits: Edward Gray, Richard Clarke, Mary Roberts and Charles Medgate. Pr. 20 Dec 1689 by John Clarke. (PROB 11/397/172).

1690

Richard Wharton of Boston, N.E., merchant, bound to sea on a long voyage, dated 10 Jly 1687 with codicil of 9 Sep 1687. To my wife half of my plate, household goods and rents and one-third of my personal estate during her lifetime. To my son William Wharton my moiety of the island called Recompense Island and my lands in the province of Maine. To my daughter Sarah Wharton household goods, a farm near Haverell Line which was granted to her grandfather Higginson, and £250 when she comes of age or is married. To my second daughter Bethia Wharton household goods belonging to her deceased mother and 1,000 acres at Dunstable, N.E., with the consent of her grandfather or

uncle Higginson. To my daughters Ann, Martha and Dorothy
Wharton my three shares of land in the Narragansett Country and
£300 each when they are of age. The portions for my eldest
daughters Sarah and Bethia are to be put into the hands of their
uncle Capt. John Higginson. To Mary Read 40 shillings and two
acres by the waterside in Stoake Hall Farm at Narragansett for
a house to be erected for her when a town shall be settled. Execs
in trust for America: Waite Winthrop Esq., Capt. John Higginson,
Mr. Isaac Addington and Mr. John Eyres, merchant. Execs in
trust for England: Mr. Samuel Read and Mr. Nathaniel Whitfield
of London, merchants. Pr. 15 Apr 1690 by Samuel Read and
Nathaniel Whitfield. (PROB 11/399/64).

Joshua Holland of Shadwell, Mddx., mariner, dated 17 May 1690. To
my son John Holland now in America my four messuages at King
David Fort, Shadwell, with remainder to my sons Thanks Holland
and Francis Jackson who are to have £200 each and to be my
execs. £150 to my daughter Elizabeth now in Penna. To my
granddaughter Mary Slany £50 to be held by my son Francis
Jackson while she is a minor. My servant Sarah Wilkinson is to
have the lease of my lower tenement at King David Fort paying
the rents to my son John Holland. Wits: Nicholas (x) Mansfell,
Ann Pritchard and Thomas Quilter. Pr. 26 May 1690 by Thanks
Holland. (PROB 11/399/73).

Patrick Carroll of Aldgate, London, now bound to sea, [who died in
May 1690 on the ship *St. Thomas* in Va., bachelor], dated 2 Dec
1689. My whole estate to my friend Margaret Souldsby of Aldgate,
spinster, and she is to be my exex. Wits: James Frankling, Ann (x)
Black and William Daintrey, servant to John Marlar, scrivener. Pr.
27 Nov 1690 in the Archdeaconry Court of London by the named
exex. (Guildhall OW 9052/28).

Thomas Barnes [of H.M. ship *Rose*, who died near N.E.], dated 8 Apr
1687. To my son Merrick £5. Residue to my wife and exex.
Elizabeth Barnes. Wits: Richard (x) Miller, Robert (x) Lawrance,
George (x) Blake and John Cross. AWW 1 Nov 1690 to Susan
Harvison, daughter of the relict Elizabeth Barnes *alias* Harvison,
who died before administering. (PROB 11/402/176).

Elizabeth Matthews of St. Mary Woolnoth, London, widow [who died
in N.E.], dated 2 Jun 1686. To my mother Susanna Lonsdale of
St. Michael, Cornhill, London, widow, all my estate and goods here
or overseas with remainder to my brother John Lonsdale, and they
are to be my execs. Wits: John Pimms, Benjamin Gladman, Edward
Watkins and John Wickhams, scrivener. Pr. 17 Nov 1690 by
Susanna Lonsdale. (PROB 11/402/187).

1691

John Enton [of St. Paul, Covent Garden, Mddx., who died in Va.], dated 7 Apr 1689. I appoint John Smith of Christ Church Hospital, writing master, as my attorney in case I should not return to England. He is to collect my wages for service in H.M. ship *Deptford* and transmit any residue to my father, brother and sisters (unnamed). AWW 27 Jan 1691 to John Smith. (PROB 11/403/5).

Francis Macaire, native of Pont en Royan, merchant of Lyons, at present in Carolina, dated 2 Nov 1687. Will in French with English translation. I have taken to bed in the house of Mr. Alexander Pepin in Charles Town. To my servant Michael Anthony I give his freedom and one-third of his passage from London. I give his freedom to my servant Francis Bonnet. Other bequests arising out of the testator's partnership with Mr. Boyd and De Giguilliat. Pr. 6 Apr 1691 by Cephas Tutet. (PROB 11/403/44).

John Mayo Esq. of Bayford, Herts., dated 15 Mar 1675. My son Israel Mayo Esq. of Bayford has been charged with the payment of all my legacies and is to be my exec. My son-in-law Benjamin Albyn owes me £2,000 by his bond which is now to be delivered to my daughter Elizabeth Albyn who is to receive £1,000 and her children the other £1,000. The bond from my son-in-law Richard Fleetwood is to be delivered to my daughter Anne Fleetwood and £600 paid to her son Samuel Fleetwood. £100 to my daughter Mary Sclater. My son Israel Mayo is to erect a free school at Kingswood, Wilts., where I was born. To my grandchildren George, Alice, Ann, Margaret, Phebe, Rebecca and Sarah Mayo, children of my said son Israel, £200 each. Wits: George Nevill, John Cooke, Mary Underhill and John Mayo. Pr. 6 May 1691 by the named exec. (PROB 11/404/83).

N.B. The daughter Mary Sclater (or Slater) was wife of Col. Henry Slater, Governor of N.Y. Province—see her will proved in 1705.

Elias Provoast of N.Y., carpenter, [who died in Va.]. I appoint my friend John Castle of Deptford, Kent, carpenter, as my attorney and exec. to collect my wages due for my service on H.M. hired ship *Samuel & Henry* and to give my father Johannes Provoast of N.Y. six crowns to be disposed among my brothers. Wits: Theodoret Lambkin, Nathaniel Scarlett and John Ward. Pr. 12 Jun 1691 by the named exec. (PROB 11/405/103).

Hugh Arrowsmith of N.Y., mariner of the ship *Edgar*, [who died at sea], dated 25 Jan 1691. I leave my clothing to Thomas Bishop and my wages to him, Thomas Anger and John Tongue who have appointed Elizabeth Anger as their adx. Wits: Edward Moore, T. Legg and William Fitzhugh. AWW 11 Sep 1691 to Elizabeth, wife of Thomas Anger, and attorney for Thomas Bishop and John Tongue during their absence abroad. (PROB 11/405/131).

William Coward of Boston, N.E., mariner [who died in the King's service on the ship *Neptune*], dated 3 Apr 1690 aboard the said ship in Piscataqua. My whole estate to my wife Christian Coward. Wits: Benjamin Bullivant, Joseph Love and James Atkins, scrivener. AWW 10 Oct 1691 to the relict. (PROB 11/406/157).

Lawrence Deladicq, citizen and joiner of London, now bound to sea in the *Bever* of London for N.Y., [and who died overseas], dated 6 Oct 1690. I appoint my brother-in-law Paul Ray of Stepney, Mddx., weaver, as my attorney and exec. Wits: William Davie, Peter Jesses and Christopher Howard, scrivener. Pr. 12 Oct 1691 by the named exec. (PROB 11/406/160).

Thomas Wyborne, late of N.E., surgeon, [who died at sea], dated 19 Nov 1690. I appoint Nathaniel Wickham of Whitechapel, Mddx., surgeon, as my attorney and exec. Wits: John Warwell, Sarah Hissey, John Mainstone and John Dennis, scrivener. Pr. 2 Oct 1691 by the exec. named. (PROB 11/406/183).

John Wayte of Worcester, glover, dated 13 Aug 1691. I have empowered Millicent Hoskins to sell my lands in Penna. and the money so raised is to go to my son Benjamin Wayte when he comes of age. To my daughter Elizabeth £5 when she is of age or marries. To my servant Francis Willis ten shillings. The residue to my wife and exex. Elizabeth Wayte. Wits: John Lacy, Stephen Cosens and Thomas Taylor. Pr. 14 Nov 1691 by the relict. (PROB 11/407/200).

1692

John Follet, [mariner of H.M. ship *Deptford* who died in Va.]. The testator's will was dictated at the end of Jly 1689 in the said ship off Cape Henry, Va., in the presence of George Molins, surgeon, Richard Thomas, Richard Sharpey and John Peirson. The testator gave his goods aboard the ship to his messmate Richard Mills and made him his exec. On 26 Aug 1689 the ship overturned in Potomack River and the will was lost. Pr. 22 Jan 1692 by Richard Mills. (PROB 11/408/8).

John Stolpys of Wapping, Mddx., mariner [who died in Va.], dated 20 Nov 1690. I appoint Albert Albertson of Wapping, victualler, and

Anne his wife as my attorneys and execs. to collect my wages for sea service. Pr. 18 Apr 1692 by Albert Albertson. (PROB 11/409/73).

Elizabeth Whitbourne of St. Botolph, Aldgate, London, widow, dated 17 Nov 1690. To my granddaughter Elizabeth, wife of William Erby of Va., planter, a silk gown, etc. Other bequests to: Joyce Gomm, widow; Thomas and William Sheppard, sons of Thomas Sheppard, weaver, deceased. The residue, including my lease from the Merchant Taylors' Company, to my exec. John Strong, citizen and woodmonger of London, and after his decease to the said Elizabeth Erby. O'seers to be Mr. John Hawkins, distiller, and Mr. Richard Bolton, pumpmaker. Wits: John Answorth, Robert (x) Burdon and Andrew Haynes, scrivener in the Minories. Pr. 18 Aug 1692 in Archdeaconry Court of London by the named exec. (Guildhall OW 9052/29).

Walter Upington of Bristol, mariner, [who died in Md.], dated 4 Dec 1691. To be buried at the discretion of James Wathen and Robert Sullivant. My son Robert Upington is to be apprenticed to my kinsman John Upington and to receive £100. To my daughter Sarah £100. My wife is to receive the interest on the £200 so bequeathed. Execs: Mr. George Tice and Mr. Roger Bagg. Wits: James Wathen, Robert Sullivant and Joseph Hayman. Pr. 6 Sep 1692 by the execs. named. (PROB 11/411/177).

John Gibson of H.M. ship *Assurance*, [who died at James River, Va.], dated 4 Dec 1691. I appoint Edward Kerby, citizen and merchant tailor of London, as my attorney and exec. Pr. 11 Oct 1692 by the named exec. (PROB 11/411/185).

Stephen Sargent [of H.M. ship *Swan*, bachelor]. On 4 Oct 1692 John David, mariner aged 45, and William Blair, mariner aged 26, late of the *Swan*, deposed that they had known Sargent for two years. In Nov 1691 Sargent made a will leaving his estate to Joseph Nash, purser of the ship, whom he named as his exec. The witnesses were Samuel Snelling, John Davis, the said William Blair and a scivener. In Jun 1692 the will and the exec. were lost in an earthquake at Jamaica. AWW 10 Oct 1692 to Frances Nash, relict of Joseph Nash. (PROB 11/411/191).

John Seaman, citizen and cooper of London [of St. Dunstan in East, who died in Md.], dated 31 Aug 1696. My whole estate to my wife Elizabeth who is to be my exex. Wits: William Hiccocks, Richard Bell, scrivener, and William Parsons his servant. Pr. 7 Oct 1692 by the relict. (PROB 11/411/192).

Joseph Topping of Islington, Mddx., merchant, dated 4 Sep 1692. My brother and sister Samuel and Hannah Topping to be my execs. and to have all my houses and lands in Va. and my tobaccos in the hands of Mr. Micajah Perry and Mr. Thomas Lane of London, merchants. To each of the children of my sister Tithick £10. To all my relations by my mother and father 20 shillings each. Wits: John Mountford, Cuthbart Harrison, John Mountford and Francis Robinson. Pr. 14 Oct 1692 by the named execs. (PROB 11/411/192).

John Archbell of Shadwell, Mddx., mariner [who died on the ship *Ephraim* in Va.], dated 23 Oct 1691. I appoint Alexander Thompson of Shadwell and Hannah his wife as my attorneys and execs. Wits: John (x) Wheatly, Mary (x) Meade and John Poultney, scrivener. Pr. 13 Nov 1692 by Hannah Thompson. (PROB 11/412/195).

William Weedon of London [of St. Botolph Bishopsgate], gent., dated 30 Sep 1686. To my nephew William Weedon of Pocomoke River, Md., and now of London, my copyhold of tenements in Hayes, (Mddx.), now in the tenure of William Melham, yeoman, and tenements in Rickmansworth, Herts., late in the occupation of Mary Weedon, widow, and now of Thomas Weedon; and a leasehold on the west side of London Bridge known as Nonsuch in the tenure of Edward Mitton and Thomas Wood. To my niece Ann Weedon, late of Pocomoke and now of London, spinster, a freehold tenement in Mark Lane in the parish of St. Olave, Hart Street, London, late in the occupation of Thomas Brasbridge and now of Thomas Hamond. My last brother, James Weedon, died indebted to William Clarke of Hertford and this debt is to be paid. Execs: my friend William Burton, citizen and merchant tailor of London, during the minority of my said nephew and niece. Wits: Charles Burdett, William Simpson, Abraham Hemingway, scrivener in Threadneedle Street, and John Nye his servant. Pr. 2 Nov 1692 by the nephew William Weedon, the niece Ann Weedon having died. (PROB 11/412/215).

Caleb Phillips of H.M. ship *Expedition*, [of N.E.], sailmaker, dated 22 Jly 1692. I appoint my wife Elizabeth Phillips of N.E. as my attorney and exex. Wits: Edward Dover, Ezekiah Vass, John Yeomans and William Holloway. AWW 24 Jan 1693 to James Harris of Bermondsey, Sy., mariner, during the absence overseas of the named exex. (PROB 11/413/13).

1693

Samuel Jones of London, mariner, now bound to Va. in the *Jacob*, commander Thomas Adley, [and who died on the ship *York*, bachelor], dated 30 Oct 1690. I appoint my brother John Jones, citizen and pewterer of London, as my attorney and exec. Wits: Henry Turner and Thomas Simkins, scrivener. Pr. 30 May 1693 by the named exec. (PROB 11/414/82).

Samuel Topping of Stepney, Mddx., weaver, dated 10 Dec 1692. To my sister Hannah Topping my share of the houses and lands in Va. given to me and my said sister by the will of my late brother Joseph Topping. To my sister Elizabeth Tizack five shillings. To my mother Anne Topping 20 shillings. My said sister Hannah to be exex. Wits: Edward Manton, Richard Moore and John Knowles, servant to William Badham, scrivener. Pr. 4 May 1693 by the exex. named. (PROB 11/414/88).

John Harris of Goatacre, Hillmarton, Wilts., clothier, dated 1 Apr 1693. To my son Samuel Harris my leasehold in Hillmarton which my wife Jane is to occupy during her lifetime. To my son John Harris £500 when his apprenticeship expires and he is to have my lands in Penna. To the Charlcutt (Quaker) Meeting £10. The residue of my estate to my daughters Sarah, Jane, Hannah and Mary Harris. My wife and son Samuel to be my execs. O'seers: my friends Jonathan Scott of Bremhill, (Wilts.), clothier, and Roger Cook of Calne, (Wilts.), yeoman. Wits: John Phillips, Stephen Dangerfield and John Ranger. Pr. 9 Jun 1693 by the execs. named. (PROB 11/415/96).

John Noore of Wapping, Mddx., mariner, now bound for Va., dated 2 Dec 1691. To my daughter Sarah, now wife of John Colson of Wapping, mathematician, one shilling. Bequest to daughter Anne. My house in Broad Street, Wapping, to my youngest daughters Rachel and Naomi. The residue of my estate to my wife Anne who is to be my exex. O'seers: my friends Richard Diamond, citizen and loriner of London, and Thomas Cooper, citizen and merchant tailor of London. Pr. 21 Jly 1693 by the relict. (PROB 11/415/114).

Peter Johnson of Shadwell, Mddx., mariner [of the ship *Anne*, who died in Va., bachelor], dated 13 Nov 1691. I appoint Gabriel Whithorne of Shadwell my attorney and exec. Wits: Ralph Steere, Joseph Grimes and Samuel Willis, servant to John Cosin, scrivener. Pr. 8 Aug 1693 by the exec. named. (PROB 11/415/125).

John Nicholson of Cecil Co., Md., [who died on the ship *Anne*], dated 13 Nov 1691. I leave all my real and personal estate to my wife Catherine Nicholson and appoint her exex. Wits: Gerrardus Messell, Benjamin Ham----- and Elias King. Pr. 11 Aug 1693 by the relict. (PROB 11/415/128).

Francis Petty second mate of the ship *Hope*, commander Samuel Kelly, bound for N.E. and W.I., dated 12 Oct 1692. My wife Sarah Petty is to be my exex. and to collect the wages of £3.7s.6d. per month which are due to me. Wits: Isaac Marwood, Thomas Osborne and Richard Carter. Pr. 30 Sep 1693 by the relict. (PROB 11/416/145).

John Coles of Exeter, Devon, cheesemonger, intending to take a voyage to sea [and who died in Penna.]. I have given a letter of attorney to my friend James Kerle of Catcott, Som., shargemaker (*sic*), so that he may gather in what is due to me to provide maintenance for my wife Joane Coles. She is to have the serge which is in the house of George Wiggington of Exeter, tailor, as well as my house and goods in England. If I die at sea and the goods I carry arrive safely in Penna., they are to be taken care of by my friends John Parsons and William Tyler who now live there. I have purchased 1,000 acres in Penna. which I devise to the said Parsons and Tyler. I leave to my two sisters Elizabeth Woodland and Ruth Gudridge two-thirds of my goods (in Penna.) and to my wife the other third. Wits: Robert Skinner, John Sparke, George Wiggington and William Wilson. Pr. 17 Oct 1693 by James Kerle. (PROB 11/416/513).

William Campbell of Wapping, Mddx., mariner of H.M. ship *Expedition* [who died on the ship *Anne* in Va.], dated 6 Dec 1691. I appoint David Watson of Wapping as my attorney and exec. Wits: Alexander Burn, William Potter and Joseph Clutterbuck. Pr. 24 Nov 1693 by the exec. named. (PROB 11/417/180).

Hendrick Harrison now bound to sea [mariner of the ship *Barnardiston*, who died in Va.], dated 28 Oct 1689. My whole estate to my friend and exex. Ann Hollyday, widow. Wits: Robert Montgomerie, Elizabeth Halleday and Nathaniel Milton. Pr. 2 Mar 1694 by Ann Thomson *alias* Hollyday. (PROB 11/419/56).

1694

John Booth of Stepney, Mddx., mariner, [who died on the ship *Industry* in Va.], dated 26 Jan 1691. My wife Sarah Booth to be my attorney, exex. and sole legatee. Wits: Joseph Dawson and Edward (x) Mills. Pr. 7 Apr 1694 by the relict. (PROB 11/419/71).

Sir Peter Colleton of St. James, Westminster, Mddx., dated 12 Jan 1694. To my son John Colleton when he comes of age all my lands in England, Barbados and Carolina and my one-eighth part of the Province of Carolina with remainder to my brother James Colleton. My brother-in-law Col. John Leslie of Barbados, my daughter Katherine Colleton and Mr. William Thornburgh of London to be my execs. in trust for my said son and to have guardianship of him. £1,000 to my said daughter Katherine. £1,500 to my younger daughter Anne Colleton when she comes of age or is married. To my natural son Charles Colleton £30 a year out of my tenements in the City of Exeter. £1,000 to Elizabeth Johnson, heretofore my wife, daughter of William and Elizabeth Johnson. £100 to Barbara Thacker. O'seers: Anthony Weldon Esq. of the Middle Temple, London, and John Hothersall Esq. of Gueddy Hall, Romford, Essex. Wits: Anthony Weldon, Nathaniel Tull, Benjamin Durzy and Thomas Hellasar. Pr. 4 Apr 1694 by the daughter Katherine, with similar powers reserved to William Thornburgh; Col. John Leslie having died overseas. (PROB 11/419/72).

Abraham Cully of Stafford Co., Va., gent. [bachelor], dated 31 May 1692. All my personal estate in Va. which is in the house of Mr. Samuel Hayward to be delivered to James Hearse, now of Stafford Co., who is to be my sole exec. My personal estate in the Chamber of London to my brother John Cully, gent., in London. Wits: John Wheatcraft and Robert Richards. On 25 Apr 1694 Nicholas Hayward of St. Bartholomew by the Exchange, London, notary public, deposed that James Hearse, the deponent's brother, was Deputy Clerk of the Court of Stafford Co. under Mr. Samuel Hayward who had copied the will for transmission to London. AWW 26 Apr 1694 to the brother John Cully. (PROB 11/419/72).

Mary Janson of Newland in the parish of Exhall, Coventry, (Warw.), widow of Bryan Janson Esq., late of Ashby St. Ledgers, Northants., dated 8 Jun 1689. To my son William Janson my tenement in Ashby with remainder to my sons John and George Janson. £50 to my daughter Anne, now wife of William Marsh. £100 to my daughter Barbara Janson. My said sons [all minors] to be my execs. O'seer to be my friend Thomas Pryor of Daventry, Northants., gent. Wits: Thomas Grascombe, John Yardley, John Bayley and Nathaniel Apletree. Pr. 22 May 1694 by William Janson with similar powers reserved to George Janson; the other exec., John Janson, having died. (PROB 11/420/102).

N.B. The son George Janson married Mary Edwards in 1689 without her father's consent before failing in his trade as an apothecary and fled to Va. in 1693 to escape his creditors. See NGSQ 67/290.

Thomas Austin of Wapping, Mddx., mariner [of H.M. ship *Richmond*, who died in N.Y.], dated 13 Mar 1689. My friend Thomas Frampton of Wapping, tobacconist, is to be my attorney, legatee and exec. Wits: Joan Wills, Richard Pinnard, servant to Samuel Wills, scrivener. Pr. 6 Jun 1694 by the named exec. (PROB 11/420/114).

John Osgood of London, merchant, [of Leytonstone, Essex], dated 17 May 1694. My two-hundredth part of West Jersey in America to be divided equally between my three sons Salem, John and Obadiah

Osgood. The rents of my tenements in Lombard Street, London, held
on lease from the Haberdashers' Company, to go to my wife Mary
Osgood, late daughter of William Welce of London, merchant,
deceased, during her lifetime. She is also to receive a third of the
rents of my lands in Langley, Bucks., which fall to me after the
decease of my mother Hannah Webb. Thereafter my son Salem is
to have all my lands in Langley, my warehouse in White Hart Court,
Gracechurch Street, London, and my tenements in Long Acre which
I have on lease from the Earl of Clarendon. My son John Osgood
is to have my tenements in Plow Court, Lombard Street, and £2,000
when he is 21. My son Obadiah Osgood is to have my tenements
in Spitalfields and £1,000 when he is 21. £4,500 to my daughter
Rebecca, wife of Francis Platt. £5 to my sister Marriott. £50 to the
children of my sister Sarah Bonifield, to be paid into the hands of
their father Abraham Bonifield. £5 each to my partners Hester Davis,
Isaac Davis and Henry Gouldney. £50 to the children of my sister
Hester Billingsly by her late husband Richard Billingsly. £20 to the
poor of the parish of (St.) Lawrence, Reading, Berks. £20 to the
poor of Castle Green, Bristol. Execs: my son Salem Osgood and my
friends Theodore Ecclestone and John Hall. Wits: Daniel Coxe,
Richard Day and Thomas East, clerk to Mr. Day. Pr. 15 Jun 1694
by the named execs. (PROB 11/421/136).

Samuel Thomson of Shadwell, Mddx., mariner [who died in Va.], dated
3 Dec 1691. My friends Thomas Anderson and Anne his wife are
to be my attorneys, legatees and execs. Wits: Denis Benseks, Richard
Gibbs and Samuel Willis, servant to John Cosin, scrivener. Pr. 6 Jun
1694 by Thomas Anderson. (PROB 11/421/143).

Thomas Arnall of Goodmans Fields, Whitechapel, Mddx., mariner, now
bound on a voyage [who died at sea on a voyage to Va.], dated 18
Nov 1691. To my now wife Katherine during her lifetime my lease of
a house held from Bridewell Hospital and thereafter to my son Goldsmith
Arnall with remainder to my sons Thomas and James Arnall. Execs:
my wife and son Goldsmith. Wits: William Wood, Richard Bowles and
Ladd. Hayles. Pr. 26 Jly 1694 by the relict, the son Goldsmith Arnall
having died. (PROB 11/421/148). See NGSQ 70/41.

Joseph Newton, outward bound for Va. as cook in the *Baltimore*,
Captain Mitchell, [who died on the ship *Dreadnaught*], dated 7 Feb
1693. I appoint Richard Martin of Wapping as my attorney, legatee
and exec. Wits: Garrett English and Samuel Wills, notary public.
Pr. 20 Oct 1694 by the named exec. (PROB 11/421/174).

William Davis of N.Y., mariner, now of the *Aldborough* ketch, Captain
Vincent, dated 10 May 1694. My wife Ellen Davis to be my attorney,
legatee and exex. Wits: Mary Enosin, Mary Griffin and Elizabeth
(x) Skilton. Pr. 25 Aug 1694 by the relict. (PROB 11/422/191).

Samuel Crabb of Boston, N.E., who died in Stepney, Mddx., bachelor, dated 25 Sep 1691. Nuncupative will leaving entire estate to William March, master of the *Thomas and Richard*. Wits: Thomas Turner and Elizabeth (x) Turner. AWW 4 Sep 1694 to William March. (PROB 11/422/212).

1695

William Pawlett Esq. of Bicton, Hants., [who died in Md.], dated 23 Apr 1693. I appoint my wife Martha as my attorney, legatee and exex. Wits: A. Fitzharry, Alles Lloyd and Florence McCartey. Pr. 6 Mar 1695 by the relict. (PROB 11/424/37). See NGSQ 68/118 alleging the existence of a will made by the testator in Md. in 1694.

Thomas Broome of H.M. ship *Dunkirk* bound from the Leeward Islands to Boston, N.E., dated 22 May 1693. I appoint Capt. James Ward as my attorney, legatee and exec. Wits: Samuel Lancaster, Charles Dicus and Henry Ward. AWW 5 Jun 1695 to John Aldred, attorney for Francis (*sic*) Ward now in distant parts. (PROB 11/426/88).

John Colvill of Cranbrook, Kent, clothier, dated 13 Aug 1691. Forty shillings to my sister Jane, late wife of John Oare the elder of Cranbrook, yeoman, deceased. Twenty shillings each to John Colvill, now in N.E., and to Stephen, Thomas and Elizabeth Colvill, children of my late brother Stephen Colvill. Twenty shillings each to Thomas Colvill, son of my late brother Edward Colvill. To poor Quakers of Cranbrook 20 shillings. To my daughter Elizabeth Colvill six pieces of old gold and £500 in goods when she is 21. To my wife Susanna during her lifetime my lands and tenements in Benenden, High Halden, Bethersden and Staplehurst, Kent, and thereafter to my son John. On my marriage to Susanna I gave to John Grinsted of Staplehurst, clothier, an annuity of £16 from my rents in Benenden, and I now ratify this. My said wife to be my exec. Wits: Richard Crampton, John Botting and John Allen. Pr. 15 Jly 1695 by the relict. (PROB 11/426/112).

William Carpenter of St. George, Southwark, Sy., mariner of H.M. ship *Essex*, [who died in N.Y. on H.M. ship *Richmond*], dated 15 Jly 1689. My wife Elizabeth Carpenter to be my attorney, legatee and exex. Wits: John Prusen, master, Peter Goff and John Chadborne, boatswain. Pr. 1 Jly 1695 by the relict. (PROB 11/426/113).

Samuel Hill of London, intending to take a voyage to Va. [and who died there, bachelor], dated 21 Oct 1693. My whole estate to my father Edward Hill Esq. of Adwell (?Ashwell), Northants., and he is to be my exec. Wits: Thomas Whincopp, Ann Lucy and Henry Mounsell. Pr. 2 Aug 1695 by the father. (PROB 11/427/131).

Robert Smithett [of Bermondsey, Sy.], mariner of H.M. ship *Lumley Castle* [who died in Boston, N.E.], dated 19 Jan 1693. My wife Proteza Smithett of Bermondsey is to be my attorney, legatee and exex. Wits: George Misher, T. Meads and Thomas Campion. Pr. 4 Oct 1695 by the relict. (PROB 11/427/161).

Joseph Fary of London, merchant, now bound to Va. by the *Ruth* [and who died on the ship *James* in Va.], dated 2 Feb 1693. To my brothers Francis and Robert Fary 20 shillings each. The residue of my estate to my mother Mary Fary of London, widow, during her lifetime, and then to my sister Mary, wife of James Wagstaffe, and my brother Charles Fary. My said mother to be my exex. Wits: William Braxton, scrivener, Benjamin Edmonds and John Marriott his servant. Pr. 7 Nov 1695 by the mother. (PROB 11/428/187).

Isaac Reed of Boston, N.E., mariner of H.M. ship *Tyger*'s prize, dated 11 Oct 1695. Mark Pooyd of Deptford, Kent, mariner, to be my attorney, legatee and exec. Wits: Thomas Loving and Thomas Weekes, churchwardens of Deptford, and Jerome Collins. Pr. 21 Nov 1695 by the named exec. (PROB 11/428/189).

William Marsh of Charles Town, N.E., but now residing in Stepney, Mddx., mariner, [who died on the ship *Mary* in Stepney], dated 29 Oct 1695. My friend Mr. Richard Robison of Shadwell, Mddx., shipwright, to be my legatee and exec. "I can hold my pen no longer." Wits: Ann Pearce and James Willoughby. Pr. 13 Dec 1695 by the named exec.; admon. of Aug 1695 to the principal creditor John Casey now revoked. (PROB 11/429/220).

Francis Atkinson, mariner of H.M. ship *Deptford* [who died in Va.], dated 8 Sep 1694. James Bowerman, mariner of this ship, to be my attorney, legatee and exec. Wits: P. Bridges, John Aldred and John Swan, master. Pr. 30 Dec 1695 by the named exec. (PROB 11/429/226).

Thomas Cornwell of London, merchant, [who died in Md., bachelor], dated 27 Mar 1694. I have received several cargoes from my brother Anthony Cornwell of London, merchant, and disposed of them for tobacco which is now to be shipped to my said brother in London. Regarding my estate in Md., my clothing is to go to my landlord John Turner and a kettle and other effects to Margaret his wife for her care of me in my sickness. Bequests of clothing to my late servant Richard Homes, William Dawkins and James Dawkins. To Captain Thomas Wharton my bed and furniture aboard his ship. My watch to Capt. Richard Smith. Execs: Thomas Wharton and

John Turner. Wits: C. Butler, Walsingham Cooke and John Newton. AWW 24 Dec 1695 to the brother Anthony Cornwell, the named exec. John Turner renouncing. (PROB 11/429/231).

1696

Andrew Percivall Esq. of Westminster, Mddx., dated 20 Feb 1696. All my estate in England to my wife Essex Percivall and my cousin Samuel Percivall, the produce of which is to be used to purchase lands for the use of my said wife and my son Andrew Percivall when he is of age. My estate in Carolina to the same to be sold in order to raise £3,000 for my daughter Mary when she is 21 or married, with remainder to my son James Percivall and my other children. My wife to be exex. Wits: Anthony Bromwich, Thomas Lake and Peter Marsh. Pr. 27 Mar 1696 by relict. (PROB 11/430/37). New grant made in Jun 1730.

Daniel Johnson of Lynn, N.E., trumpeter [of H.M. ship *Advice*, who died in St. Thomas's Hospital, Southwark, Sy.], dated 22 Jun 1695. Patrick Hayes of Bermondsey, Sy., victualler, is to be my attorney and exec. I leave my whole estate to my children (unnamed). Wits: John Kingked, Luke Prichard and John Allen, notary public. Pr. 6 Apr 1696 by the named exec. (PROB 11/431/50).

Edward Lloyd of Whitechapel, Mddx., merchant, and late of Md., planter, dated 7 Mar 1696. To my grandson Edward Lloyd my plantation in Wye River, Md., now in the occupation of my daughter-in-law Henrietta Maria Lloyd, a dividend of rough land in Langfords Bay in Chester River, and land on the north side known as Deirby. To my grandson James Lloyd 500 acres in Tuckahoe Creek near the head of Choptank River which I formerly had of my son Philemon Lloyd in exchange for my land upon the island in Wye River. To my wife Grace all my negroes. To my sister Mary Hughes 50 shillings. To my daughter-in-law Elizabeth Buckerfield £3. My said wife is to be my exex. O'seers: my friends Mr. Anthony Stratton and Mr. John Ewens. Wits: Thomas Lunn, John Outridge and Daniel Outridge. Pr. 14 Jly 1696 by the relict. (PROB 11/432/121).

Samuel Huckstep of Stratton Major parish, King and Queen Co., Va., [and of Ewhurst, Sussex], dated 9 Aug 1693. My whole estate to my wife Jane Huckstep who is to be my exex. Wits: William Todd, Edward Bates and Ignatius Turner. Published 18 Jly 1694. Wits:

William Scorey, William Smith and John Edwards. Pr. 3 Jan 1696
by the relict. (PROB 11/433/139).

William Nall, late of Boston, N.E., but now of London, mariner of
H.M. ship *Greenwich*, [bachelor], dated 23 Jan 1696. One shilling
each to my father-in-law Mr. Clements, my uncle John Nall and
my cousin Mathew Nall. The residue of my estate to my friend
Henry Causton, citizen, bricklayer and tiler of London, who is to
be my exec. Wits: Christopher Clayton, Thomas Causton and
William Causton. Pr. 22 Jan 1696 by the named exec. (PROB
11/433/143).

William Roydon, citizen and grocer of London, intending a voyage to
America [who died in Philadelphia], dated 20 May 1692. £40 and
all my lands and tenements in West N.J., Penna. and England to
my brother Robert Roydon of Witham, Essex, maltster. £20 each
to my nieces Elizabeth, Ann and Margaret Wright, daughters of my
late sister Elizabeth Wright of (Great) Totham, Essex. £10 to Emme,
wife of Richard Crews of St. George, Southwark, Sy., carman. £10
to John Tizack of London, merchant, who is to be my exec. £5
each to my friends and trustees Andrew Robinson and William
Cooper of West N.J. for their care of my estate. Wits: Joseph (x)
Stevens, Ruth Maynwaring and Henry Holland. Pr. 3 Jan 1696 by
the named exec. (PROB 11/433/147).

Joseph Swett of Boston, N.E., cooper [of H.M. ship *Defiant*], dated 20
Aug 1689. John Gill of Wapping, Mddx., waterman, is to be my
attorney, legatee and exec. Wit: Samuel Wills Jr. at Wapping New
Stairs. Pr. 24 Jan 1696 by the named exec. (PROB 11/433/148).

Benjamin Whitmore of Middletown, N.E., dated 25 Jun 1696 on board
H.M. ship *Royal Katherine* at sea. My whole estate to Charles Hill
of New London, Ct., who is to be my exec. Wits: Moses Tiller,
Ebenezer Daness and Charles Crowley. AWW 30 Sep 1696 to Isabel
Edwards, wife of Hugh Edwards, attorney for the named exec.
(PROB 11/434/195).

John Geary of Tring [and Dunsley], Herts., yeoman, dated 28 Mar
1696. My lands and tenements in Tring and Wiggington, Herts., to
my cousin Henry Geary, younger son of my cousin Henry Geary
of Wiggington, and he is to pay 40 shillings a year from my lands
in Tring to the poor Quakers there. All my freeholds in Chesham,
(Bucks.), to my cousin Joseph Geary, son of the said Henry Geary,
and he is to pay my sister (unnamed), widow of my brother Henry
Geary £16. My lands at Whelpley Hill near Chesham in trust to
my friend John Foster of the Bank to pay an annuity of £6 to my
cousin Mary Davy during her lifetime, and thereafter an annuity of
£10 to her son William Davy who is to have my 500 acres in

Penna. The residue of my estate to my cousin Henry Geary the younger who is to be my exec. Wits: Ralph Dagnall, William Lake and Daniel Baston. Pr. 9 Dec 1696 by the named exec. (PROB 11/435/249).

Job Tookey of H.M. ship *Newport*, mariner [and bachelor], dated 26 Nov 1695. Robert Fitzhugh of Boston, N.E., mariner, to be my attorney and exec. Wits: Michael Sanders, Christopher Cockrell and John Champlyn. AWW 11 Dec 1696 to Henry Fitzhugh, brother and attorney of the exec. Robert Fitzhugh of Boston, N.E. (PROB 11/435/262).

Simon Wotton of Calvert Co., Md., surgeon, bound for Jamaica, dated 13 Jan 1696. To my wife Susanna Wotton £50 or 2,000 lbs of tobacco per annum according to an order of court of 2 Feb and 20 Jan 1691/2. £30 to William Fisher, son of my brother John Fisher, when he is 21. £10 to my exec. in trust Thomas Wharton on behalf of my daughter Anne Wotton who is to have all my real and personal estate when she reaches the age of 18. Wits: John Hyde, William Clapcott and T. Suckle. Pr. 29 Dec 1696 by Thomas Wharton. (PROB 11/435/263).

1697

Seth Southell Esq. of Albemarle Co., Carolina, dated 25 Jan 1690. To my friend Mr. Francis Heartley I give for five years the plantation where he now dwells and during the lifetime of himself and his wife two-thirds of my Seignory bounding on Flatly Creek and Pascobank River which thereafter is to descend to my wife Anna Southell and her heirs. To my father-in-law Edward Forster my plantation at Custopinum for ever with cattle and one negro man. £5 to William Duckenfield Esq. To Edward Waad Esq. during his lifetime all my plantation where Mr. Thomas Evens now dwells on Little River and thereafter to his wife. To my wife Anna Blunt (*sic*) all my lands on Solomon Creek, Kendrick Creek, Little River, Flatly Creek and Pascobank River, Carolina, and she is to be my exex. Wits: William Wilkinson, Henderson Walker, John Lewis, William Woolward and Sarah Woolward. AWW 8 Feb 1697 to the principal creditor William Bowtell, the relict having died. (PROB 11/436/39).

Benjamin Willdy of London, Norwich factor, [late of Carolina], dated 17 Dec 1694. £50 to my sister Martha, wife of Edward Wood, with remainder to my mother Martha Dagget. £50 to my sister Mary, wife of Thomas Manwaring, with remainder to her children Mary

and Martha Manwaring. £10 to my brother Robert Cranstone. £10
to my sister Elizabeth, wife of Joseph Willdy. My said mother to
be my exex. Wits: Edward Wood, Sarah Brereton and Isaac Miller.
AWW 15 Feb 1697 to the sister Martha Wood, the mother Martha
Dogget having died. (PROB 11/436/42).

Winifred Mallett [*alias* Wolseley], of Charles Co., Md., [widow], dated
20 Apr 1685. To my nieces Helen Spratt and Anne Knipe all my
money in the hands of Sir John Worley after deduction of what is
due to James Amos and Margery his wife. To my niece Brookes
all my goods in her possession and thereafter to her daughter Anne.
Clothing to the negro Cis, Mary Davis and Mary Wathan. To Mrs.
Anne Pye whatever she may choose in Mr. (Edward) Pye's house.
To Mr. Edward Pye a bay nag left to me by Mr. Dagget. Residue
to my niece Mary Brookes who is to be my exex. Wits: Elizabeth
Dent, Anne Pye, Margaret (x) Harrison, Sara (x) Godson and
Cornelius (x) Buttwell. AWW 3 Mar 1697 to the principal creditor,
James Amos, the niece Mary Brookes having died and the surviving
legatee, Helen Spratt, wife of the Bishop of Rochester, renouncing.
(PROB 11/437/59).

Richard Foote [of St. Dunstan in the East], London, merchant, dated
19 Mar 1695. To my son Richard Foote 3,000 acres in Va. To
each of my sons George, Francis and Henry Foote 1,000 acres in
Va. £200 to my grandson Topham Foote to be employed in trade
by his father Samuel Foote, and 1,500 acres in Va. Other bequests
to my wife Hester Foote, my son Samuel Foote, and my daughter
Elizabeth Holmes. My said wife and my son Samuel Foote to be
execs. Wits: James Stone, Richard Stacey and Randolph Stacey. Pr.
23 Apr 1697 by the relict, the son Samuel Foote having died.
(PROB 11/437/73).

John Mundell of Newcastle Co., Penna., merchant, at present in Boston,
N.E., dated 5 Dec 1694. To my friend Mr. Thomas Hill of Boston,
merchant, £30. The residue of my real and personal estate to my
brother William Mundell of Deriston, Timvale parish, Nethsdale
Co., Scotland, who is to be my exec. with the said Thomas Hill.
Wits: Robert Maxwell, John Mulligan and John Edgar. On 27 Apr
1697 Robert Maxwell of Boston, merchant, deposed that this will
had been proved in Boston and that Thomas Hill, who had been
the testator's partner for three years, died in Dec 1696. The brother
William Mundell deposed that, while he was in Dundee, he had
received a letter dated 26 Jly 1696 from Mr. William Arbuckle,
Hill's correspondent in Scotland, containing a copy of the above
will. Pr. 27 Apr 1697 by William Mundell. (PROB 11/437/78).

Thomas Griffin of Shadwell, Mddx., mariner [of the ship *Hope*, who
died in Va., widower], dated 24 Sep 1695. Solomon Amos of

Stepney, Mddx., is to be my attorney, legatee and exec. Wits: William Wharton, William Reasley and Henry Reade, notary public. Pr. 28 Jly 1697 by the exec. named. (PROB 11/439/140).

Gabriel Predix of Stepney, Mddx., mariner [who died in Va.], dated 5 Jly 1697. My wife Susanna Predix to be my attorney, legatee and exex. Wits: Mary Larwens, Jane Wright and Henry Reade, scrivener. AWW 5 Jly 1697 to the principal creditor, Peter Senth, the relict renouncing. (PROB 11/439/146).

Lewis Perdrian [of Carolina], dated in Barbados 23 May 1694. [Will dictated in French from his deathbed]. Mr. Henry Le Noble living at Carolina shall put into the hands of my sister Mrs. Judith Perdrian in London all the effects in his hands. Wits: Peter Fleurian, Nicholas Richard, Samuel Durousseau and James Chaband. Letter dated Barbados 12 Aug 1694 to Mr. Simon Duport of London, merchant: I give you the sad news of the death of poor Mr. Lewis Perdrian, who formerly lived at Carolina at Mr. Le Serurier's house. He died on 24 May last of a high fever the day after he arrived from N.Y. He said he had left an inventory of his goods and his will in the house of Mr. Henry Le Noble in Carolina. Simon Duport of London deposed on 10 Jly 1697 that he had received the above letter and will. AWW 12 Jly 1697 to Judith Fanueil *alias* Perdrian, wife of Paul Fanueil. (PROB 11/439/146).

John Sinckler of Shadwell, Mddx., mariner [of the *Owners Adventure* who died in Va., widower], dated 30 Jan 1692. Anne Hill, wife of Thomas Hill of Shadwell, distiller, to be my attorney, legatee and exex. Wits: Mary Carpenter and George Carpenter Sr. of Ratcliffe. Pr. 1 Jly 1697 by the exex. named. (PROB 11/439/149).

Joel Horwood [elsewhere Harwood] of Boston, N.E., mariner [of H.M. ship *Sheerness*], dated 22 Jun 1697. Henry Horwood of Boston to be my attorney, legatee and exec. Wits: John Housden, Robert Bonner and Richard Rooles. Pr. 12 Aug 1697 by the brother Henry Horwood. (PROB 11/439/161).

William Robinson [of Md.], dated 29 Nov 1696. All my clothes aboard ship and on shore to William Colvert of England, upholsterer, who is to be my exec. and pay all my debts in England and Md. To Mary King of Md., spinster, £6 which is in the hands of Capt. Thomas Ely of the *Society* of London. To Caleb Phipherd one guinea in the hands of Capt. Ely. The residue to my father William Robinson in Yorks., England. Wits: Robert Jones, Andrew Steuert and Charles Kilburne. On 5 Dec 1696 the witnesses depose that this will was signed by the testator. Pr. 14 Aug 1697 by the named exec. (PROB 11/439/167).

James Gault of Stepney, Mddx., mariner [who died on H.M. ship *Dove*'s prize in Va.], dated 1 Jun 1695. My wife Alice Gault is to be my attorney, legatee and exex. Wits: Robert Jenkins and Thomas Pomeroy, notary public of Shadwell. Pr. 1 Sep 1697 by the relict. (PROB 11/440/184).

William White of Stepney, Mddx., mariner [of H.M. ship *St. Albans*' prize, who was drowned in Va.], dated 9 Aug 1692. My friend Edward Daniel of Stepney to be my attorney, legatee and exec. Wits: Christopher King, captain, Bartholomew Candler, master, John Penn, boatswain, and J. Ward, clerk. Pr. 7 Sep 1697 by the exec. named. (PROB 11/440/194).

William Barton, mariner of H.M. ship *Play*'s prize, dated 26 Jun 1697. While sick in his hammock, the deceased desired the surgeon's mate of the said ship, Charles Reed, to bring him a blank letter of attorney and will form but, there being none on board, he declared his will in the presence of Reed, the quartermaster Robert Finch and the gunner's servant William Wood. He left his wages to his messmates Mathew Butts and Robert Walker and the residue of his estate to his children (unnamed) in Penna. AWW 26 Jun 1697 to John Bunce, attorney for Matthew Butts and Robert Walker now at sea or abroad. (PROB 11/440/196).

Gawen Lawry, late Governor of East Jersey, dated Elizabeth Town, N.J., 12th of the month called Aug 1687. To my brother Arthur Lawry and his wife (unnamed) £20 with remainder of £10 to their children and £10 to the children of my sister Christian. £10 to my sister Agnes. £20 to George and John Watt. Of the debts due to me from John Swinton of Swinton deceased and John Swinton his son, £20 is to be paid to Robert Barkley and £20 to Henry Stout, Richard Thomas or Thomas Burr of Hertford. The residue of my estate is to be divided between my grandchildren, i.e. the children of my son James Lawry deceased, of my daughter Mary Haige and of my daughter Rebecca Foster. My execs. are to send to my wife, if she is then living, the portion due to my grandchildren in America or otherwise to some friends in York or East Jersey. My friends George and John Watt are to be my execs. O'seers: Frances Camfield and Robert Barkley. Wits: William Haig, Miles Forster and Charles Seddon. AWW 7 Oct 1697 to the grandson by a daughter, Obediah Haige; the exec. John Watt renouncing. (PROB 11/440/205)

John Primus of Shadwell, Mddx., mariner of H.M. ship *St. Alban*'s prize, [who died in Va., bachelor], dated 10 Apr 1693. Prudence Poulson, wife of Captain Edward Poulson of Shadwell, is to be my attorney, legatee and exex. Wits: John Ore, John Paine and Bernard Hunt, Captain's clerk. Pr. 8 Oct 1697 by the exex. named. (PROB 11/440/207).

Richard Baker of Stonedeane, Chalfont [St.] Giles, Bucks., yeoman, dated 6th of 12th month called Feb 1695. To my wife Mary all my stock and implements, furniture, etc. To my daughter Elizabeth Blatt half my houses in Aylesbury and Walton Fields which I hold by descent, and to my daughter Ann Chester the other half. To my grandchildren Rebecca Blatt and Joseph Chester a golden guinea each. To my two younger daughters Rebecca and Winifred Baker my ground in Lime Street, London, which is let to Philip Stower, a lease and meadow in Aylesbury which I bought from my uncle Alexander Stevens, and all my land in Penna. and West N.J. £10 to James Smith and Thomas Olliffe of Aylesbury towards the building of a new Meeting House there. £5 to Rebecca Webb to be paid into the hands of her aunt Mary Baker. Execs: my daughters Rebecca and Winifred. O'seers: My uncle Thomas Ellwood and my son John Chester. Wits: Robert Meade, George Millus and William Tuckwell. Pr. 18 Nov 1697 by Rebecca Baker. (PROB 11/441/221).

Ambrose Cleare of Stratton Major parish, New Kent Co., Va., dated 28 May 1686. To my son-in-law John Hayes, when he comes of age, a rug, blankets and a horse called Prince. To my wife Anne Cleare my horses Toby and Button, my negro man and the boy Will. To my daughter Mary my Scotch boy. To John Drummond 12 shillings. The residue to my said wife and daughter. My wife is to be my exex. Wits: John Gough, William Leigh and Thomas Nelson. AWW 10 Nov 1697 to Richard Parke, merchant, attorney for the relict Anne, now wife of Thomas Tea, in Va. (PROB 11/441/226).

John Nevill, Vice-Admiral [of St. Margaret, Westminster, Mddx., who died in Va.], now bound on a voyage to the Streights, dated 2 Nov 1696. My whole estate to my wife Mary and daughters Mary and Elizabeth Nevill who are to give £50 each to my sisters Elizabeth Nevill and Martha Carpender. Wits: John Sabbartony, Stephen Thexer and Hannah Finch. Pr. 2 Nov 1697 by the relict. (PROB 11/441/247).

William Penn of the City of London, mariner, now in Patuxent River, Md., dated 20 Sep 1696. To my three sisters (unnamed) £50 each. The residue to my wife (Elizabeth) who is to be my exex. Wits: Robert Marsham, John Wight and Thomas Greenfield. Pr. 18 Nov 1697 by the relict. (PROB 11/441/249).

Lovet Goring Esq. of the Inner Temple, Common Cryer and Serjeant at Arms of the City of London, dated 30 Aug 1695. To my brother Henry Goring all my lands in Uttoxeter, (Staffs.], during his lifetime and then to my nephew Lovet Saunders. My said nephew is to have my lands in Lichfield, Staffs., and to be my exec. when he comes of age. To my cousin John Goring Esq. my lands in

Callowhill in the parish of Kingstone, Staffs., and he is to pay my niece Elizabeth Saunders an annuity of £20. My execs. in trust to be the said John Goring and my cousin William Wolley the elder. Wits: Samuel Doody, Francis Birchfield and Joseph Stringer. Pr. 29 Dec 1697 by William Wolley, the other exec. John Goring having died. Revoked on 5 Aug 1701 and admon. to Lovet Saunders. On 10 Apr 1710 admon. to Susan Lambe, wife of Joshua Lambe of Roxbury, N.E., who was the exec. of Lovet Saunders now deceased, for the benefit of the latter's mother Elizabeth Saunders in N.E. (PROB 11/442/283).

1698

Thomas Yale of London, merchant, [who died in Grone, Denbighshire], dated 29 Sep 1697. My trustees at Fort George, Rev. George Lewis and Captain Charles Metcalfe, are to have the care of my estate in India. £5 to Mr. John Pine, vicar of Wrexham. My estate in Denbighshire to my mother Mrs. Ursula Yale and my brother Mr. Elihu Yale with remainder to the heirs male of my uncle Thomas Yale in N.E. O'seers: Dr. John Evans of London and Mr. Robert Harbine of London. Wits: Robert Lloyd, Mary Rock, Elizabeth Cole and Thomas Bradshaw. AWW 10 Jan 1698 to John Evans and Robert Harbin, no exec. having been named. (PROB 11/443/26).

Robert Fargusion of Kenton, N'land, mariner of the ship *Falkland*, [who died in N.E.], dated at Tarpaulin Creek, Elizabeth Island, N.E., 21 Jan 1697. George Wallis of Benwick (?Benwell), N'land, and now of the said ship, is to be exec. in trust on behalf of my father Thomas Fargusion of Kenton and to pay two guineas to my friend Margaret Springet of Poplar, Mddx. Wits: Andrew Seton, First Lieut., James Couch, Master, and Stephen Fox, Captain's clerk. Pr. 11 Feb 1698 by George Wallis. (PROB 11/443/35).

John Fly, late of Piscataway, N.E., but of H.M. ship *Catherine*, formerly the *Chester*, [widower], dated 22 Jun 1696. Nuncupative will dictated at Torbay, Devon, whereby the testator bequeathed half his wages to William Taverner and half to his children (unnamed). Wits: Robert Wilson and Peter Carey. AWW 1 Mar 1698 to William Taverner. (PROB 11/444/71).

James Trent, resident of Sweden but now in the City of London [Captain of the ship *Charles* in the King's service, who died in Penna.], dated 26 Nov 1695. My whole estate to my mother Isabella Stuart of Inverness, Scotland. Exec: Mr. Thomas Coats of London, merchant. Wits: John Ruck, William Brookhouse and William Scordy, notary. Pr. Apr 1698 by the named exec.; revoked in Nov 1699 and granted to the brother William Trent. (PROB 11/445/109).

John Bennett of St. Gabriel, Fenchurch Street, London, merchant, dated 12 Apr 1698. I have disposed of my tenements, lands and personal estate in Md. by a deed of 29 May 1695 which I have left in Md. with Thomas Homewood. To John Pettit, his wife, son and daughter 20 shillings each. Other bequests to: Joshua Walklyn and his wife; David Dennis and his wife; my cousin Ann Daking, her three sons and two daughters; Mrs. Doncastle. £50 each to: my cousin Mary Herbert; Elizabeth Daking when she is 18 or married; and Samuel Daking, her brother. My silver tobacco box etc. to the said David Dennis. Of the residue I bequeath half to my mother Margery Jones, who is to be my exex., and half to my cousin Hester Ginnott. Wits: William Bates, George Hammond and Mary (x) Bates. Pr. 14 May 1698 by the named exex. (PROB 11/445/114).

Michael Dickenson [of Altrincham, Chesh.], dated 20 Aug 1695. To my nephew James Talier, now or lately in Va., all my lands in Manchester, (Lancs.), with remainder to William, Hugh, Michael and Jonathan Colley, sons of his sister Alice Colley. To my niece Elizabeth Colley £500 when she comes of age or is married. The land in Sale, Chesh., which I purchased of Mrs. Anne Moseley to my nephews Hugh, Michael and Jonathan Colley. The tenement at Moss Side bequeathed to me by the will of Sir Edward Moseley I leave to my nephew Michael Colley and his sister Elizabeth Colley. To my godson Michael Charleton £10 and to his sister Anne Bartlett in Twittenham (?Twickenham, Mddx.), £20. To my cousin Richard Kay £20 to be secured for his two sons. To Mr. Gamaliel Chester and his sister Mrs. Ann Chester £5 each. To Mary Moss of Stratford, widow, 40 shillings. To my cousin William Colley £10. Execs: my nephews Hugh and Michael Colley. No witnesses shown. Pr. 17 May 1698 by Michael Colley. (PROB 11/445/120).

Charles Lidgett Esq., late of Boston, N.E., but now of [St. Bride's] London, dated 9 Apr 1698. To my wife Mary Lidgett all my lands and tenements in N.E. and the £3,000 which I promised to her father William Hester of Southwark, Sy., soapmaker, deceased, should be hers. She is to be my exex. and guardian of my children Peter, Charles and Ann Lidgett. My money and effects from N.E. are to be delivered to my brother-in-law John Hester of Southwark, soap boiler, who is to be my exec. in trust until my said wife arrives from N.E.: in the meantime I recommend her to the kindness of Mr. Francis Foxcroft of Boston. Wits: Thomas Richards, John Joursey and William Wharton. AWW 16 May 1698 to John Hester; further grant Mar 1701 to the relict. (PROB 11/445/126).

Rigault Bew of Ware, Gloucester Co., Va., planter, [who died in St. Giles Cripplegate, London, bachelor], dated 30 Dec 1696. To poor housekeepers of Ware parish £20. To Francis Ironmonger, son and heir of Samuel Ironmonger deceased, when he is 21, the house where I live with my plantation and dividend of land of 600 acres, with remainder to the heirs of my sister Elizabeth Ironmonger or the heirs of my sister Thurston, or of my sister Sarah Dawson. To my godson Drumon and goddaughter Johanna Carew a cow and calf. To my godsons John Thurston and Rigault Dawson a negro when they are 21. To my godson Wortham a negro when he is 21. To Elizabeth Thurston £25 when she is married. £25 each to my goddaughters Sarah and Elizabeth Ironmonger to be paid in two women negroes over the age of 16 and under 22. A gold ring to Mr. Samuel Vaudry. A gold ring of 20 shillings to my sisters and brothers Capt. Robert Thurston and Mary his wife, and Elizabeth Ironmonger and her husband (if married). The residue to my sisters Mary, Sarah and Elizabeth. My execs. in Va. and England to be Capt. Robert Thurston, Samuel Dawson and Elizabeth Ironmonger. Wits: William Grymes, Thomas (x) Blessingham and Mary (x) Whistler. Pr. 29 Jly 1698 by Samuel Dawson; limited admon. Sep 1697 to Micajah Perry of London, merchant, as attorney for the sisters, now revoked. (PROB 11/446/157).

David Edwards of Boston, N.E., mariner, dated 21 Sep 1696. (Will copied from Boston Registry). To my eldest son Sweet Edwards £100 when he is 21 and to my daughter Susanna £50 when she is 21. To my wife Mary Edwards the residue of my estate and my house and lands in Boston during her lifetime with remainder to my three children Sweet, Susanna and David Edwards. My wife to be my exex. Wits: John Phillips, Edward Procter and Joseph Prout. AWW 27 Jly 1698 to Edward Hull, attorney for Mary Edwards in Boston. (PROB 11/446/161).

Thomas Baker, formerly of Aaron, Isle of Purbeck, Dorset, mariner, but now of London, master of the *Elizabeth* of London, now in Plymouth bound for Newfoundland [who died in Va.], dated 16 May 1693. My attorneys to be my brother-in-law John Bennett of London, mariner, and his wife Mary Bennett, my sister, who look after my children Thomas and Mary Baker. My lands called Crannie in Dorset to my son Thomas with remainder to my daughter Mary and they are to be my execs. To my sisters Ann and Margaret Baker £5 each. To my sisters Joane Baker and Edeth Farrell, widow, 20 shillings each. Wits: Henry Bradshaw, Rose Bradshaw and Samuel Eastlake, notary public. Pr. 19 Aug 1698 by the sister Mary Bennett *alias* Baker. (PROB 11/447/182).

Adam Kennedy of St. Michael, Crooked Lane, London, merchant, now intended for N.Y. [who died in Antigua], dated 14 Sep 1697. Mourning rings to: Mr. William Gordon of London, merchant; Andrew Martine of London, merchant; George Martine of Sy., chapman; Alexander MacConell of Sy., chapman; William Walker, servant of William Gordon. £6 each to the said Andrew Martine and to my sisters Mary, Margaret, Anne and Jane Kennedy, all in Galloway Co., Scotland. The residue to my brother Robert Kennedy who is to be my exec. with the said William Gordon. Wits: John Brigge, Richard Harrison Jr. and William Walker. Pr. 18 Aug 1698 by William Gordon. (PROB 11/447/188).

John Eades of Stepney, Mddx., surgeon's mate, now going to sea, [who died in N.E.], dated 17 Jly 1694. My father-in-law George Hallam of Shadwell, Mddx., tailor, and his wife, my own mother, Winifred Hallam, to be my attorneys and legatees. Wits: Mary Eades, Susanna Willis and John Johnson, notary public. Pr. 17 Sep 1698 by George Hallam. (PROB 11/447/199).

Thomas Plowden of Lasham, Hants., gent., dated 16 May 1698. Ten shillings to each of my children and grandchildren. To my son Francis Plowden my lands in the Province of New Albion in North Va. and America which were granted to my father Sir Edward Plowden of Wansted, Hants., by patent of Charles I. This patent is now in the hands of my son-in-law Andrew Wall of Ludshott(?), Hants., who has wrongfully detained it for many years. The residue to my wife Thomazine Plowden who is to be my exex. Wits: Christopher Cowper, John Page, William Pryor and Armiger Bayly. Pr. 10 Sep 1698 by the relict. (PROB 11/447/204).

Thomas Hobbs [of St. Clement Danes, Mddx.], dated 13 Oct 1697. To my wife Catherina Hobbs the farm rents I purchased of the Earl of Danby on 26 Jly 1688, the rent charges out of the Manor of Aston Botterell and my other lands in Salop. conveyed to me by Edward Norton on 9 Sep 1681, my houses in Lincolns Inn Fields, Mddx., and in Rookley, Hants., with remainder to my son Thomas Hobbs when he is 21 and my nephew Abraham Weekes. Other bequests to: my nephews Francis, Thomas and Hobbs Weekes; my sisters-in-law Elizabeth and Susanna Stanyan. Execs: Sir John Sommers, Sir John Hawles, John Lilly and my said wife. Wits: R. Adney, P. Perschouse and Samuel Newton. Pr. 20 Oct 1697 by Sir John Hawles (Solicitor-General), John Lilly and Catherina Hobbs. (PROB 11/447/215).

N.B. The testator's sister Elizabeth was wife of Francis Weekes of Mddx. Co., Va., the father of the testator's nephews. See NGSQ 62/38.

Owen Jones [of N.Y.], of H.M. ship *Richmond*, dated 6 Jun 1697. Copy of will taken from the Registry of N.Y. Province. I leave my whole estate to my wife Elizabeth Jones who is to be my exex. AWW 27 Oct 1698 to George Farewell, attorney for the relict in N.Y. (PROB 11/447/217).

Thomas Jones, mariner of H.M. ship *Pembroke*, dated at Point Comfort, Va., 16 Aug 1697. Thomas Stinte and Jonathan (x) Spence depose on 15 Sep 1698 that the testator was carried ashore with many others to Hog Island, Va., where he died on 20 Aug 1697 after declaring his wish that his whole estate should go to his messmate Dyer Wade. Pr. 7 Oct 1698 by Dyer Wade; admon. of Nov 1697 to Elizabeth, wife of Richard Jones, now revoked. (PROB 11/447/217).

George Robotham of Talbot Co., Md., dated 28 Feb 1698. All my real and personal estate in Md. and England to my nieces Mary Erp and Ann Cook, daughters of my sister Ann Wilson of Findern, Derbys., and to my niece Ann Cotton, daughter of my sister Mary Keeling of Staffs., England. To William Wrench Jr. my plantation called Wrench's Farm and my land called the Vineyard of 700 acres. To Margaret Pemberton, wife of John Pemberton, 100 acres called Epsom in Talbot Co. To Walter Quinton a tract called Robotham's Range in Dorset Co. I leave 2,000 lbs of tobacco towards enlarging the Meeting House between Tuckahoe and King's Creek in Talbot Co. I leave 2,000 lbs of tobacco each to John Harrington, Roger Baddy, Francis Holmes, John Lane and Edward Sarsafitt. My execs. in trust John Pemberton, Mr. Edward Lloyd and Thomas Smithson are to sell the residue of my estate and remit the proceeds to Capt. Anthony Stratton in England. Wits: William Wrench Sr., Roger (x) Baddy, Mary Thomas and Robert Noble. AWW 8 Nov 1698 to Mary, wife of John Erp, Anne, wife of John Cooke, and Anne, wife of William Cotton. (PROB 11/448/237).

Sarah Eckley of Philadelphia, widow and exex. of John Eckley of Philadelphia, dated 17th day of sixth month 1692. To my three children William Burge, Mary Burge and Sarah Eckley, when they are of age, all the tenements and lands left to me by my late husband's will. £10 to the Meeting House in Philadelphia. Five guineas to my late husband's son John Eckley. My daughter Sarah is to be placed with my friend Hannah Delavall to be educated. Execs for Penna.: my friends Thomas Lloyd, Samuel Carpenter and John Delavall of Philadelphia. Execs for England: James Lewis, Peregrine Musgrave and Richard Stafford Jr., all of South Wales. Wits: John Goodsonne, Alexander Beardsly, James Fox, Abraham Hardiman and David Lloyd. Pr. 7 Dec 1698 by James Lewis, Peregrine Musgrave and Richard Stafford. (PROB 11/448/248).

1699

John Eckley, late of Kimbolton, Heref., but now of Haverfordwest, (Pembrokeshire), merchant [of Philadelphia], dated 17 Jly 1686. £5 to my brother John Daston of Docklow, Heref., yeoman, who is to be the guardian of my son John Eckley. To my said son John the £50 which I lent to George Phillips of Lawton, Kingsland parish, Heref., deceased, and all my goods at the Lee provided he confirms the lease made to John Powles of Bodenham, Heref. To my mother-in-law Mary Pritchard of Almeley, (Heref.), if she be living, £ (blank). £5 to my brother-in-law Sampson Lloyd of the Lee. £10 provincial currency to the poor of Philadelphia. To my now wife Sarah Eckley the house where I now dwell, a house on the west side of Bridge Street in Haverfordwest, my plantation adjoining Radnor Township in Penna., and my lands in Rudbaxton, Pembrokeshire. The residue of my estate to my said wife who is to be exex. Wits: Roger Pritchard, John Hardyman and Thomas Evans. AWW 1 Feb 1699 to James Lewis, Peregrine Musgrave and Richard Stafford, execs. of the relict Sarah Eckley deceased. (PROB 11/449/22).

John Langley of St. Saviour, Southwark, Sy., physician, dated 9 Feb 1698. £50 each to my sons William and Richard and £100 each to my daughters Elizabeth and Thomazine. To my daughter Margaret Day now in Md. £40. To my wife Thomazine my copyhold estate in Lambeth, Sy. To my friend Richard Drew, citizen and merchant tailor of London, £5. To my friends James Moor and his wife 20 shillings each for a ring. The residue to my wife who is to be my exex. Wits: Samuel Hilliard, Thomas Legg and John Martin. Pr. 15 Feb 1699 by the relict. (PROB 11/449/26).

Josiah Dixon of Aldgate, Mddx., mariner, now bound to sea [of the ship *Preservation*, who died in Va.], dated 3 Jan 1698. Richard Yates of Aldgate, mariner, and Sarah Yates his wife to be my attorneys, legatees and execs. Wits: Jane Efford, Mary Ungle and Richard Efford, notary public of Hermitage Bridge. Pr. 10 Mar 1699 by Sarah Yates. (PROB 11/449/39).

John Morton of London, merchant, [of Carolina], dated 7 Aug 1694. To my wife Ann £20. To my daughter Ann £100 when she comes of age. To my friend Robert Cuthbert Jr. of London, goldsmith, £10. To my sister Deborah Blake a negro man named Dick and a negro woman named Dina. To my aunt Rebeccah Bowell a negro man named Lewis, a negro woman named Flora, 30 cows and my plantation in Carolina called Pittinwan(?) during her life with remainder to my brother Joseph Morton. My said brother is to have the residue of my estate in Carolina. My friend Robert Cuthbert is to be guardian of my said daughter and to be sole exec. Wits: John Byard, John Arnold and John Stuckey Sr. Pr. 28 Apr 1699 by the named exec. Further grant 19 Mar 1706 to the relict Ann Wills *alias* Morton, now wife of Thomas Wills, the exec. Robert Cuthbert having died and his mother and exex. Eleanor Cuthbert renouncing. (PROB 11/450/61).

Robert Throckmorton of Little Paxton, Hunts., dated 1 Mar 1699. To my wife Mary during her lifetime a close called Westwood in Ellington, Hunts., with 166 acres and a windmill. Thereafter my son Robert Throckmorton is to have all my estate in Ellington on condition he pays £600 to my daughter Susanna and £500 each to my daughters Alice and Mary. My eldest son Bromsall Throckmorton is to have my Manor of Little Paxton and a house called Bricke in Paxton. To my brother Albion Throckmorton my plantation in Gloucester Co., York River, Va. To my brother Gabriel Throckmorton my plantation in New Kent Co., near Rappahannock River, Va. My father-in-law Thomas Bromsall Esq. and my uncle Edward Mason to be my execs. Wits: Mary Keene, Mary Mason, Mary (x) Jones and Richard Lee. Pr. 3 May 1699 by the named execs. (PROB 11/450/83).

Charles Hall citizen and fishmonger of London, bound on a voyage to Va. [who died in Va., bachelor], dated 28 Feb 1698. The goods which I have shipped with me on the account of Peter Martell of London, merchant, are to be credited to him and he is to be my exec. Wit: William Fashion, scrivener. William Clarke of St. Bride's, London, gent., deposes on 10 Jun 1699 that he well knew the testator, late of Md., and had often received letters from him. The will is in his writing. Pr. 12 Jun 1699 by Peter Martell. (PROB 11/451/94).

John West citizen and girdler of St. Sepulchre, London, dated 20 May 1698. To be buried in the Quaker ground in Bunhill Fields, Mddx. To my son Benjamin West £500 and to his wife Sarah £50. Bequests to: my grandchildren Thomas and John Harris, sons of Simon Harris and my daughter Mary his wife, both deceased; my grandchildren Mary, Richard and Anne West, children of my son Richard West and Anne his wife; my son-in-law Daniel Streete and my daughter Hannah his wife, and their son Benjamin Streete. To my grandchildren John and Mary East, children of my son-in-law Benjamin East deceased and my daughter Hannah his wife, now residing in Penna., £50 when they are 21. All my tenements in Penna. are to descend to my said grandchildren John East, Mary East and Benjamin Streete. An annuity of £10 is to be paid out of the rents of the Bull in Snow Hill, London, to my daughter Hannah Streete of Penna. £5 to my wife Mary West. Fifty shillings each to Anne

Marsh and Mary Selwood, her daughters by a former husband. To my son Richard West my copyhold tenement in Wandsworth, Sy., a tenement in Banbury, Oxon., and my lease from the Sadlers' Company of a messuage in Snow Hill. £4 to my friends John Edge of Hatton Garden and Peter Briggins of Bartholomew Close for the poor of Peele Meeting in St. John Street, Mddx. I forgive the debts owed to me by my brother Thomas West and my nephew Robert Axton of Princes Risborough, Bucks. Exec: my son Richard West. Wits: George Newland, scrivener, Bartholomew Browne and Samuel Robinson. Schedule of properties and leases annexed. Pr. 1 Jly 1699 by the named exec. (PROB 11/451/124).

Thomas Hunt of Chalfont St. Giles, Bucks., yeoman, intending to pass over the seas [and who died in Carolina, bachelor], dated 7 Dec 1689. £30 each to my sisters Ruth and Mary Hunt with remainder to my uncle John Grimsdalle Sr. of Chalfont, yeoman, and my cousin John Grimsdalle Jr. who are to be my execs. To my brother Andrew Hunt my tenement called Morehows at Hedgerley Green, Bucks. Wits: Thomas Grimsdalle, Ralph Evered and Henry Redding. AWW 14 Aug 1699 to the brother Andrew Hunt, the named execs. renouncing. (PROB 11/452/133).

Jacob Tompson of Bristol, mariner of the ship *Sarah* of Bristol, will dictated in Va. at the end of Sep or beginning of Oct 1698. The testator wished his entire estate to go to his wife. Wits: Edward Foye and Walter Cecill. AWW 18 Aug 1699 to the relict Susanna Tompson. (PROB 11/452/139).

Peter Noyes of Sudbury, N.E., now bound to sea, dated 10 Jan 1698. I leave to the town of Sudbury all my houses, lands and mills known as New Mill with uplands meadows in the hands of John Sheers and Richard Graves for the use of the poor for ever. £10 each to John and Peter Haines. £20 to my cousin Mary Noyes. The residue of my estate to my four sisters Mary Mountjoy, Dorothy Noyes, Sarah Noyes and Esther Noyes who are to be my exexs. Wits: James Sherman, Joseph Noyes and John Parmeter. AWW 10 Sep 1699 to William and John Crouch, attorneys for the named cxcxs. Dorothy, wife of Samuel Parris, Sarah, wife of Thomas Frinck, and Ester Noyes, all in N.E. (PROB 11/452/149).

Jacob Gradwell [who died on the ship *Preston* on Cooper River, S.C.]. This will takes the form of a promissory note dated Charles Town, S.C., 3 Apr 1699, whereby Gradwell undertook to repay Edward Hoole a sum of £11.10s. when the ship arrived in Barbados or, in case of his death, to recoup himself from Gradwell's goods on board with any residue being remitted to Mr. Thomas Gradwell of Preston, Lancs. On 24 Oct 1699 John Crowther of Whitechapel, Mddx., commander of the *Preston*, deposed that the testator was supercargo of the ship and the promissory note is in his hand. Thomas Molyneux Esq. of St. Martin Outwich, London, deposes similarly. AWW 25 Oct 1699 to Edward Hoole. (PROB 11/452/156).

Richard Tull of London, gent., now bound for Barbados, [of Md., bachelor], dated 27 Jan 1682. My closes of six acres near Stratford at Bow, Mddx., and Temple Mills, Essex, two acres called Bullivants on Mill River near Lee River, two acres between Mill River and the Lee in Hackney, Mddx., and West Ham, Essex, and the goods I intend to carry with me to Barbados, in trust to my friends and execs. Henry Medlicott, citizen and haberdasher of London, and John Ewer, citizen and skinner of London, to be used to support my sister Dorothy during the coverture between her and her husband Thomas Peck, citizen and dyer of London, with remainder to her daughter Jane Peck, the children of my uncle Henry Hanslapp and Elizabeth his wife, and my father-in-law James Best of London, gent. Wits: William Northey, Samuel Knowles and Henry Wills. AWW 13 Oct 1699 to the principal creditor Daniel Biddle, the named execs. and Jane Peck renouncing; grant of Jly 1692 revoked. (PROB 11/452/163).

1700

John Braine of Wapping, Mddx., merchant, dated 12 May 1699. To my wife Margaret Braine during her lifetime my lands and farm in Hornsey, Mddx., with remainder to the persons named in the will of my late father-in-law Thomas Farley. My tenements in London to my said wife during her lifetime and thereafter to my children Thomas Braine, Margaret wife of Robert Barclay, Farley Braine and Mary Braine. My said children are to be paid the legacies given them by their said father Thomas Farley. To my son Thomas Braine my one-eighth share of the ship *Susan* of which he is master and my lands in East N.J.. £10 to Joseph Caydle and William Saunders for the poor of the Quaker Meeting at Ratcliffe, Mddx. £50 each to my grandchildren John Braine, son of my son Thomas, and Margaret Barclay, daughter of my daughter Margaret. A golden guinea each to my brother James Braine and my friend Roger Newham who are to be execs. with my said wife. Wits: Benjamin Braine, Mary Cudlip and Thomas Butler. Codicil of 4 November 1699 revising the bequest to the testator's daughter Margaret, now married to Abraham Coleman. Wits: William Ruddock and Thomas Butler. Pr. 3 Jan 1700 by the execs. named. (PROB 11/454/3).

James Fidler of Stepney, Mddx., mariner, [who died on the ship *Dispatch* in Penna.], dated 16 Apr 1691. My wife Deborah Fidler to be my attorney, legatee and exex. Wits: John Manning, Henry Faulcon and Paul Symson. AWW to the principal creditor Thomas Coutts, the relict renouncing. (PROB 11/454/6).

John Johns, citizen and clothworker [of St. Botolph Bishopsgate], London, [who died in Carolina], dated 22 Aug 1698. My whole estate to my wife Frances Johns and daughter Mary Johns who are to be my exexs. Wits: Lan. Kerby and George Briant, clerk to Thomas Carr. Pr. 17 Jan 1700 by the relict. (PROB 11/454/9).

Nicholas Spencer of Nominy, Westmorland Co, Va., dated 25 Apr 1688. I am now the only surviving son of my late father Nicholas Spencer Esq., and heir to my late brother William Spencer Esq., and I leave to my son William Spencer, now in England, all my lands and tenements (in England) in Cople, Beds., Barford, Blunham and St. Neots, Hunts., and Codham Hall in Essex. To my wife Frances during her life my lands and tenements in the neck of land called Kingcopsco which I bought of Mr. Richard Wright, Mr. James Hardige and Richard Awburne, and which were formerly William Newberry's, with remainder to my son Mottrom Spencer. To my son Nicholas Spencer all my lands at the head of Nominy I bought of Mr. Foster, Mr. Hawkins and Mr. Manley. To my son John Spencer I give the title of land near Pope's Creek and lands I bought of Mr. William Horton, Capt. John Lord, Jacob Reny and Mr. John Froadsham (the last lying near Col. William Peirce's land and dwelling seat). To my son Francis Spencer my moiety of 5,000 acres which will fall to me and Capt. Lawrence Washington as joint tenants. To my son Mottrom Spencer £500 sterling out of my lands in England when he is 21. My son William Spencer to be exec. for England and my wife and sons Nicholas and John Spencer for Va. My friends Col. Isaac Allerton and Capt. Lawrence Washington to be o'seers. My debts are to be paid in money and not in commodities according to that unequal and dishonourable law of Va. Wits: George Luke, Thomas Hobson Jr. and Nathaniel Webster. AWW 15 Jan 1700 to John Rust of All Saints, Lombard Street, London, silkman, the sons Nicholas and John Spencer not appearing and William Spencer renouncing. (PROB 11/454/14).

Allen Stevenson of the City of Chester, merchant, about to make a voyage to America, dated 8 Mar 1699. £110 to the children (unnamed) of my brother John Stevenson of Nelson, Scotland. £110 to my brother James Stevenson of Nelson. £25 to my cousins Alexander Stevenson and James Gibb of Paisley, Scotland. £100 to my friend Andrew Symme who is about to go with me to America to assist me in gathering in my debts. £20 to the poor of Nelson.

Residue to Robert Sparke of Chester, linen draper, who is to be
my exec. Pr. 3 Jan 1700 by the named exec. (PROB 11/454/15).

Robert Codenham, late of Shadwell, Mddx., but now of N.Y. [who
died in N.Y.], mariner. All my estate to my wife (unnamed) at
Shacksby's Walk in Shadwell for herself and the education of (my?)
children. Exec: my friend Richard Jones of N.Y., merchant. Wits:
George Heathcott, Thomas Clarke, Edward Buckmaster and George
Brewerton. On 4 December 1688 admon. in N.Y. to Richard Jones
and an inventory made dated 28 Jan 1689. AWW 26 Feb 1700 to
John Chapman, guardian of the children, Jane, Robert and William
Codenham, the named exec. having died. (PROB 11/454/21).

William Nickolls of Kent Co. annexed to Penna., dated 13 Jan 1697.
To my granddaughters Dinah Mohan and Mary Nickolls, when they
are 14, a heifer each. To my son William Nickolls the males of
the said heifers. My said son is to buy a colt for my grandson
Jeremiah Nickolls when he is 18. All my lands in England, including
those at Bridgwater, Somerset, to my said son who is to sell them
and give £10 current to my grandson William Nickolls, son of
Robert Nickolls, when he is 18. My son William to be my exec.
Wits: Gartree Lober Sr., Mary (x) Nickolls Sr., Margaret (x) Lober
and Richard Busby. On 6 Mar 1698 Mary Nickolls and Richard
Busby depose in Kent Co., Penna., that they witnessed the above
will. Pr. 21 Mar 1700 by William Nicholls. (PROB 11/454/37).

Noel Mew [of Newport, R.I., and Providence Plantation, N.E.], now
intended for Old England, dated 3 Aug 1691. All my real and
personal estate to my wife Mary during her widowhood but, if she
marries, £110 out of my estate in England. My farm called Rocke
Farm, a mulatto boy called George and £50 to my son Richard
Mew who is to allow £5 a year to his sisters for their upbringing
while they are under age. To my daughter Mary Mew £100 and
an Indian girl called Jenny. To my daughter Patience Mew £100
and a negro woman named Bess. My lands in West Jersey are to
be sold and the profit divided between my said three children. My
wife to be my exex. O'seers: William Allen, Benjamin Newberry
and Peter Sandford. Wits: Richard Jones, Joseph Blydenburg,
Thomas Roberts and William Cload. True copy of will certified on
22 Dec 1692 by John Easton, Governor, John Greene, Deputy,
Walter Clarke, Benjamin Newberry, William Allen and Christopher
Almy. AWW granted 4 Apr 1700 to Thomas Zachary, attorney for
the relict Mary Mew in Newport, R.I. (PROB 11/455/59).

Samuel Shrimpton Esq. of Boston, Mass., dated 5 Jun 1697. My brick
tenement called the Exchange Tavern in Boston, my brick warehouse
near the Town Dock with land at the north end of Boston to my
son Samuel Shrimpton. To my kinswomen Abigail and Elizabeth

Bourne of London £300 each besides the legacies left to them by their grandfather Shrimpton deceased. The residue to my wife Elizabeth who is to be my exex. Wits: Ursula Cooles and Eliezer Moody, scrivener. True copy certified by Isaac Addington, Registrar. AWW granted 3 Jun 1700 to Elizabeth Roberts, widow, mother and attorney of [blank] Shrimpton, widow, mother and attorney of the relict Elizabeth Shrimpton in Boston. (PROB 11/456/89).

Richard Shaw, now resident in Wapping, Mddx., mariner, bound on a voyage to Guinea and Va. [who died in Va.], dated 21 Nov 1698. To my friend Moses Lacy all my goods and wages and he is to be my exec. Wits: John (x) Browne, Jane (x) Rownson and William Alderson. Pr. 4 June 1700 by the named exec. (PROB 11/456/90).

Launce Speermaine of Stepney, Mddx., mariner of H.M. ship *Royal William* [who died in Va.], dated 6 May 1697. David Speermaine and Elizabeth his wife are to be my attorneys, legatees and execs. Wits: Benjamin Hoskins, Matthew Teate, John Coattam and Daniel Call. Pr. 24 Jun 1700 by Elizabeth Speermaine. (PROB 11/456/90).

John Alexander of St. Olave, Southwark, Surrey, bound for Carolina by the *Edward Francis*, Mr. Thomas Man, and son and heir apparent to my father Robert Alexander of Manchester, Lancs., dated 12 Sep 1698. One shilling each to my brothers Robert and Charles Alexander and my sisters (unnamed). The estate which is to descend to me from my father, including 70 acres in Middlewich, Cheshire, to my wife Jane Alexander with remainder to Ann Nicholls of St. Olave, Southwark, who is to give £30 each to Thomas Manning of St. Olave's and Joseph Manning of St. Thomas's, Surrey, sons of Thomas Manning of Weldon, Northants. My said wife to be my exex. Wits: John Yorke, George Guilliames, Elizabeth Fanster and John Stichfield, scrivener. Pr. 27 Jly 1700 by the relict. (PROB 11/456/94).

Thomas Cleaver of Stepney, Mddx., mariner, [who died in Va., bachelor], dated 5 Apr 1693. My sister Mary Cleaver is to be my attorney, legatee and exex. Wits: Mary Cole and William Hippertree, servant to Samuel Ling, notary public in Wapping Wall. Pr. 24 Jly 1700 by the named exex. (PROB 11/456/96).

Mary Izard, wife of Ralph Izard of Berkeley Co., S.C., gent. To my said husband the 3,000 acres where we now dwell and my right and title in the plantation known as Boshee of 1,800 acres on Ashley River. My said husband is to be my exec. Wits: Jean Le Palle, Daniel Donevan and William Skamadine. Pr. 26 Jly 1700 by the husband. (PROB 11/456/101).

Frederick Clarke [of Carolina who died in Barbados, bachelor], dated 13 Nov 1697. My books and instruments now in this island

(Barbados) to Capt. John Bramble. The residue of my real and personal estate to my sisters Mary Stephen who lives in Carolina and Hester Vikarage. Execs: my brother Robert Stephen in Carolina and Mr. James Chaband. AWW 20 Aug 1700 to John Trott, attorney for Robert Stephen in Carolina. (PROB 11/456/111).

Patrick Lacy of H.M. ship *Restoration* [of H.M. ship *Essex* prize, who died in Va., bachelor], dated 9 Jly 1700. My uncle Thomas Connaway of Stepney, Mddx., gent., is to be my attorney, legatee and exec. Wits: Thomas Fowlis, Captain, Thomas Lawrence, Lieut., and Edward Eaton, Captain's clerk. Pr. 5 Aug 1700 by the named exec. (PROB 11/456/116).

John Ormandey [who died overseas, bachelor], will dated Md. 8 Feb 1700. To my youngest sister (unnamed) the cargo that was sent to Va. by the *Dolphin* pink. To Jane Helme that part of the cargo in the Streights. To Arthur Helme my tools and clothes aboard the *Anne and Mary*. £10 to John Dawson Jr. Wits: James Mackclanan, Arthur Helme, Jane (x) Maclaning and Sarah (x) Ratford. AWW 31 Aug 1700 to Arthur Helme. (PROB 11/456/117).

Lawrence Washington of Washington parish, Westmoreland Co., Va., gent., dated 11 Mar 1698. If I die in this county I am to be buried beside my father and mother and near my brothers and sisters and children. A mourning ring to my friends Mr. William Thomson, clerk, and Mr. Samuel Cross. To the children of my sister Anne Writt a manservant each or 3,000 lbs of tobacco when they are 20. To my sister Lewis a mourning ring. To my cousin John Washington Sr. of Stafford Co. my clothes. A manservant or 3,000 lbs of tobacco to my godson Lawrence Washington, eldest son of my cousin John Washington. My tract of 275 acres adjoining Meridah Edwards and Daniel White to my godson Lawrence Butler and Lewis Nicholls. A pulpit cloth and cushion to each of the upper and lower churches of Washington parish. My personal estate is to be divided between my wife Mildred, my son John Washington, my son Augustin Washington and my daughter Mildred Washington. To my son John Washington the seat of land where I now live, a tract from the mouth of the Mathodack to a place called the Round Hills with the addition I have made of William Webb and William Rush, my watermill and the 200 acres I bought of my brother Francis Wright near Stocks Quarter. To my son Augustin the dividend of 400 acres of land I bought of Mr. Robert Lessons' children in England between my brother's and Mr. Baldridge's land where Mr. David Lessons formerly lived, the land that was Mr. Richard Hill's and, after the decease of Mr. Lewis Markham and his wife, the tract of 700 acres where Mr. Lewis Markham now lives. To my daughter Mildred Washington all my 2,500 acres in Stafford Co. on Hunting Creek where Mrs.

Elizabeth Minton and Mr. William (*sic*) now live. Execs: my cousin John Washington of Stafford, my friend Mr. Samuel Thompson and my said wife. Wits: Robert Readman, George Waden, Thomas Howes and John Rosier. Pr. 10 Dec 1700 by Mildred Gale alias Washington, wife of John Gale. (PROB 11/458/186).

1701

Arthur Spicer of Sittenburne, Va., dated 18 Sep 1699. My whole estate in Va. and England to my son John Spicer subject to the following legacies. My said son to be sent to England to be educated, preferably at Charterhouse, and to be subject to guardians Jeffrey Jeffreys and Col. Robert of Lancaster Co. If my said son dies during his minority my estate is to descend to Lydia Spicer, daughter of my brother John Spicer, and £200 to be paid to her younger sister Elizabeth Spicer. Frances Robinson, daughter of Capt. Samuel Bloomfield to be paid what is due to her "in such like sort as came to my wife and after to my hands." My execs. in trust to be William Colston, Capt. John Bataille, (---?---) and John Lloyd. Wits: John B. Burkett and Mary Hardige. Pr. 18 Dec 1700 in Richmond Co., Va. This will was included as part of a lawsuit Spicer v. Ellis, Purvis and Bataille of 1701 in PRO: C5/261/75 but appears not to have been formally proved in the Prerogative Court of Canterbury. In the suit Alice Spicer, mother of the testator, claimed to have taken out letters of administration to his estate. See NGSQ 67/212-213.

Elizabeth Birch, widow of Mathew Birch deceased [of Penna.], dated 26 Nov 1700. All my real and personal estate, my right in a farm called Eggerton in Ashton, Kent, three farms in the Weald of Kent, and in houses at Coptree near Maidstone, Kent, to my three daughters Elizabeth, Alice and Ellinor Birch. My daughter Alice to be my exex. Wits: Francis Zouch and James Claypoole. Pr. 29 Jan 1701 by the exex. named. (PROB 11/459/2).

Thomas Bland of London, merchant, dated 25 Jan 1700. £200 to my cousin Lawrence Pendrill to be invested for my sister Sarah Day. An annuity of £10 to Mary Kermish. £20 each to my brother's two daughters, Sarah and Margaret Bland. A gold ring to every person named on the back of this will. To my cousin Sarah Pendrill, wife of Mr. Lawrence Pendrill, all my lands and plantations in Anne Arundell Co., Md., and they are to be my execs. Wits: Anthony Wells, Edward Grove, George Clifton and Anthony Wells Jr. Pr. 13 Jan 1701 by the named execs. (PROB 11/459/2).

Richard Hoskins of Penna., merchant, now resident in [St. Stephen Coleman Street], London, dated 4 May 1700. My lands and tenements in Penna. to my son Aurelius Hoskins. To my four daughters Martha, Mercy, Mary and Anne Hoskins, household furniture, my late wife's and daughters' clothing, etc. All my plantations in Barbados to Phillip Collins, planter, and John Groves, merchant, on trust to sell the same and remit the proceeds to my friends Edward Shippen and Samuel Carpenter who are to be my execs. in Penna. £15 in Barbados money is to be sent to my physician Dr. Thomas Loure. All my goods and personal estate in London to my friend Theodor Eccleston who is to be my exec. for London and to ship the proceeds thereof to Penna. £30 to my friend David Lloyd for his pains in educating my son. Wits: John Ellis, Charles Owen and John Brooker. Pr. 20 Mar 1701 by the solemn declaration of Theodore Eccleston. (PROB 11/459/38).

Michael Martyn of London, [of Boston, N.E.], mariner, now bound on a voyage to N.E., dated 1 Feb 1698. My estate in England, N.E. and alsewhere to my wife and exex. Sarah during her lifetime and thereafter to my son Richard Martyn with remainder to my sister Jane Rudkin. A guinea for a ring to my friend Thomas Webb of London, merchant. Wits: Thomas Taylor, G. Wharton and Thomas Lawrence, notary. Pr. 1 Mar 1701 by the relict. (PROB 11/459/39).

Ralph Try, cooper of the merchantman *Fairfax*, commander Samuel Thornbury, bound to Guinea [who died in York Town, Va.], dated 20 Sep 1697. My wife Frances Try is to be my attorney, legatee and exex. Wits: Samuel Thornbury, Nathaniel Bloxham, Joseph Green, mate, living at Deptford, Alexander Winn, boatswain, living at Greenwich, and George Soffrith, gunner, living by the Valiant Seaman at East Smithfield. Pr. 7 May 1701 by the relict. (PROB 11/460/73).

Richard Chambers, citizen and skinner of London, now going to sea [of Md.], dated 10 Dec 1697. Of the £100 I left in the hands of my mother and exex. Mary Chambers I bequeath half to my brother Thomas Chambers and the other half to my brother Nicholas Chambers, now an apprentice in London. My said mother is to dispose of the goods which I have taken to sea for the benefit of my brothers and sisters. Ten shillings each for mourning to: my brother Mr. Benjamin Pyke and my sister Mary his wife; my brother Thomas Chambers and his wife Elizabeth; my brother Nicholas Chambers; and my uncle Mr. John Elliston of West Malling, (Kent). Wits: Mary Elliston, Elizabeth Elliston and Peter Elliston. Pr. 16 July 1701 by the mother. (PROB 11/461/93).

John Swan of Wapping, Mddx., mariner, [who died at sea near N.E.], dated 13 Dec 1695. Richard and Margaret Heading of Wapping are to be my attorneys, legatees and execs. Wits: Margaret (x) Silver and Thomas Faldo, notary public. Pr. Aug 1701. (PROB 11/461/118).

Peter Charles [of Va.], mariner of H.M. ship *Shoreham*, dated 28 Nov 1700. My friend Hendrick Cloyson is to have all my goods on board the said ship and to be my exec. Wits: James Pack, David Herd and Henry Heath. Pr. 16 Oct 1701 by the exec. named. (PROB 11/461/135).

John Fernald of N.E., shipwright, now in London and bound to sea in the *Portsmouth* galley of London, dated 26 Feb 1701. I leave my whole estate to my friends George Rowe of Shadwell, Mddx., cordwainer, and Phebe his wife who are to be my execs. Wits: Nathaniel Sawarey, Mebello Smith and Francis Emerton, servant to Theo. Pomeroy, notary public in Upper Shadwell. Pr. 21 Oct 1701 by George Rowe. (PROB 11/462/138).

John Broadhurst the younger of London [of Va.], factor, dated 13 Sep 1699. My estate in Hudsfield near Macclesfield, Cheshire, to my wife and exex. Elizabeth Broadhurst during the minority of my children Elizabeth, Ann, Thomas and John Broadhurst. My cousin Roger Bolton is to be o'seer. Wits: R(oger) Bolton, Arthur Foresight and Cor. Nedham. Pr. 4 Dec 1701 by the relict. (PROB 11/462/164).

1702

Elizabeth Roberts of London, widow, dated 26 Feb 1701. £200 in trust to my son Nicholas Roberts and my daughter Elizabeth Shrimpton, widow, in N.E., for the purchase of lands in England for the use of my grandson Samuel Shrimpton and Elizabeth his wife (one of the daughters of my late daughter Sarah Richardson deceased) with remainder to their heirs. My son-in-law Robert Breedon, my daughter Mary his wife, and John Wildman of London, scrivener, are to receive the grant of £28 per month which is remitted to me by the Excise during the lives of my granddaughters Mary and Anna Richardson, and the £391 in the Chamber of London and to pay the profits to my granddaughter Sarah Wells, daughter of John Wells. My son-in-law John Richardson of Bristol, deceased, appointed me exex of his will dated 1 Sep 1692 and I make bequests to my grandchildren Stephen, Samuel, John, Mary and Anne Richardson. My daughter Mary Breedon, my grandson John Richardson and my friend Mr. William Burgis of Bristol, grocer, are to be my execs. O'seers: the said William Burgis and John Chard of Bristol, mercer. Wits:

James Albin, John Grace and John Wildman. Codicil of 11 Jly 1701 witnessed by Nathaniel Wade, John Grace and John Wildman. Pr. 13 Jan 1702 by Mary Breedon. (PROB 11/463/11). Further grant made in Mar 1702. See NGSQ 63/200 re the marriage in 1670 of Samuel Shrimpton of Boston and N.Y. to Elizabeth, daughter of Nicholas Roberts, citizen and ironmonger of London, who died intestate in Aug 1676 leaving children Sarah (Richardson), Mary (Breedon), and Nicholas Roberts.

Peter Guillum, [master of the brigantine *Jane and Margaret* who died in Va., bachelor]. This will takes the form of a letter from the testator to his brother John Greenwood of Southampton, sailsman, dated Cowes 22 Feb 1700. My desire to you and my father is that from what you have in your hands £50 should go to my sister Mary, £30 to my brother Thomas, and £20 to the child of my sister Frances. The residue should go to my father and mother. On 22 Feb 1702 John Greenwood deposed that the above letter was written from on board the said ship then bound to Va. and is in the testator's handwriting. On the following day John Drinkwater of St. Saviour, Southwark, Surrey, citizen and joiner of London, deposed that he also knew the testator and his handwriting. AWW 23 Feb 1702 to the father John Guillum. (PROB 11/463/21).

Perez Savage of Salem, N.E., dated Mackeness, Barbary, 23 May 1694. To Robert Carvel a French livre. To Henry (*sic*) in the Indees a ducat of gold. To John Borch and Elias Fortune a silver ducat each. I forgive Elyas Ayacat and Mr. Joanas the debts they owe me. The residue of my estate in the hands of Mr. Richard Hill, merchant in Cadiz or London, N.E., I leave to Thomas Thatcher, son of Thomas Thatcher, in Boston, N.E. Wits: John Thomas and Robert Carnes. On 8 Feb 1702 John Thomas of the Scilly Isles deposed that in 1680 he was master of the *Amity* ketch bound for Newfoundland and from there to Lisbon when he was captured by a pirate ship of Barbary and taken to Mackeness to work as a slave until Jly 1701. In 1692 Perez Savage of Boston, his young cousin Thomas Thatcher and other seamen who had been taken at sea were also brought to Mackeness as slaves. On 20 May 1694 Savage died of a bloody flux, having handed his will to the deponent in the presence of Robert Carver, another slave. Robert Carver of Salem, N.E., deposed that in Nov 1691 he joined the *Society* of Salem, of which the testator was captain, for a voyage from London to Bilbao and Cadiz. On 9 Apr 1692 they were captured by pirates and Savage, his nephew Thatcher, a youth, and the ship's company were taken to the City of Mackeness in Barbary as slaves. AWW 21 May 1702 to the nephew Thomas Thatcher. (PROB 11/464/56).

Abraham Bonnifield of Reading, Berks., distiller, dated 16th day of the 5th month called Jly 1701. To be buried near my late wife. To my daughters Sarah and Mary Bonnifield £500 each when they are 21 or married. £100 each to my grandchildren Sarah and Lucy Bonnifield, daughters of my son Joseph Bonnifield. To my cousins William and Elizabeth Roost three guineas each. To my cousins John Clayton and Margaret Lane 40 shillings each. Bequests to the poor of Quaker Meetings in Reading, Sun Lane and London Street. My 1,000 acres in Penna. is to be divided between my children Abraham, Sarah and Mary Bonnifield. My said son Abraham is to be my exec. O'seers: my friends Leonard Key and Andrew Hall of Reading. Wits: Thomas King, Christopher Stephens and Henry Freeman. Pr. 15 Apr 1702 by the affirmation of the named exec. (PROB 11/464/58).

William Hawkins of Boston, N.E., surgeon, dated 1 Aug 1685. The whole of my estate in N.E. and England to my wife and exex. Dorothy Hawkins for the use of my children (unnamed). Wits: Thomas Clarke and Eliezer Moody. Pr. 2 Apr 1702 (after sentence for the validity of this will and against validity of will dated 27 Feb 1667). (PROB 11/464/62).

John Hudson of Boston, N.E., [and of the ship *Paget*], dated 20 Aug 1700. My whole estate to William Jenkinson and Jane his wife who are to be my execs. Wits: Thomas Parsons, Thomas Bird and James Newton, clerk to John Dennis, notary public. Pr. 3 Jly 1702 by Jane Jenkinson. (PROB 11/465/116).

Patrick Townsend (alias Dudgeon) of Whitechapel, Mddx., [of Boston, N.E., who died in the West Indies], weaver. My brother William Townsend and my sister Hannah Greene, wife of James Greene, are to be my legatees and execs. Wits: Mary Milton, William Milton and Owen Callaham. Pr. 14 Jly 1702 by William Townsend. (PROB 11/465/123).

Francis Halley of [All Hallows Staining], London, gent. [who died in Va.], dated 28 Jun 1698. My two messuages in Mincing Lane, Fenchurch Street, London, to my son Francis Halley with remainder to my sister Mary Ward, wife of John Ward, and Nicholas Wright of St. Giles Cripplegate, London. £5 to my brother Thomas Waller. A guinea for a mourning ring to: my cousin Edmond Halley, Mary his wife, and their daughters Margaret and Katherine; my father and mother Richard and Eleanor Pyke; my brothers Thomas and William Pyke and Edward Day; my sisters Jone Day and Susan Pyke. Residue to my said son Francis. Execs: my cousin Edmond Halley and my father Richard Pyke. Wits: David Griel, Thomas

Carr, William Dean and Lancelot Kerby, clerk to Mr. Carr. Pr. 28 Sep 1702 by the execs. named. (PROB 11/466/149).

Lewis Davis of H.M. ship *Tyger*, mariner, [who died on H.M. ship *Advice* in N.E.], dated 14 Dec 1695. My wife Hannah Davis of Aldgate, London, to be my attorney, legatee and exex. Wits: Richard Cooke, Lieut., David Holland, Stephen Barnerd, master, and Richard Blake. Pr. 22 Dec 1702 by the relict. (PROB 11/467/193).

Richard Godson of Ratcliffe, Stepney, Mddx., [who died on H.M. ship *Advice* in N.Y.], dated 18 Sep 1696. My wife Agnis Godson to be my attorney, legatee and exex. Wits: Henry Willoughby, Paul Phillips and Thomas Quilter, notary public. AWW 2 Dec 1702 to the principal creditor Henry Willoughby, the relict renouncing. (PROB 11/467/196).

John Scott of Mattox, Westmoreland Co., Va., merchant, now bound to sea, dated 28 May 1700. £100 to my two sisters and their children whom I believe to be in Ireland and whose names are Jane and Rebecca Scott. £30 to Gustavos Scott, son of my brother James, to be paid from the money his father and mother owe me. £20 to my brother Gustavos Scott of Bristol who is to be my exec. If the *Potomack Galley* on which I have shipped most of my tobacco should not arrive safely, only one half of these legacies are to be paid. To my son John the plantation where I now dwell which I bought of Capt. Thomas Mountjoy with remainder to my daughter Jane. To my said daughter my tract of 500 acres on the north-east branch of the Potomack River in Md. called in the patent Strabane. My plantation at the head of Pope's Creek which I bought of Abraham Field to my wife Sarah. My son John is to be sent to England to his uncle Gustavos to be kept at school until he is of age. A new tobacco house is to be built at Pope's Creek. A ring for mourning to my godson John Hoare and Mr. David Wilson. My part of the £100 due to my wife's former husband Mr. George Crosse from Mr. Gould in the parish of Ceviton (?Chevington) in England I give to George Crosse, son of the said George Crosse. My execs. in trust are to be my wife Sarah and my kinsman Mr. William Graham and my said brother Gustavos Scott. Wits: Nathaniel Pope, Charles Tankersly, James Mason, David Wilson and Thomas Wickens. Copy of letter dated Cork, (Ireland), 29 (-----) 1702 from Gustavus Scott [to his wife]: My dear, I am safe arrived here and shall be clear to sail when there is a convoy. I have received a letter from my cousin William Graham in Va. and a copy of my brother's will, of which I am whole exec., which I have sent you and brother Galbraith with a letter of attorney. I hear the *Little John* is come for Bristol . . . Copy of letter (from Gustavus Scott to William Galbraith): Loving brother, Enclosed is a letter from Mr. Graham, a power of attorney from me and a copy of my brother's to Capt. Francklen for Gustavus Scott. William Galbraith of Bristol, merchant, deposes on 14 Dec 1702 that on 20 Aug 1702 Gustavus Scott of Bristol, mariner, sailed from Bristol for Cork and Montserrat; and on 17 Oct 1702 the deponent received from him a letter enclosing a copy of John Scott's will which he delivered to Mrs. Elizabeth Scott. AWW 19 Dec 1702 to Elizabeth Scott, wife and attorney of the named exec. Gustavus Scott. (PROB 11/467/206).

1703

William Giles of St. Giles in the Fields, Mddx., at present in the City of N.Y., merchant, dated 9 Sep 1702. To my father and mother and my brothers Thomas, George, John and Joseph Giles all my personal estate subject to the following bequests. £20 to my nephew John Giles, son of my brother George Giles. £5 to my sister Anne Underhill. £5 for my soul to be prayed for. Execs: Peter Rogers, gent., Charles Rhodes, surgeon, my brother George Giles, staymaker, and John Burroughes of N.Y. City, merchant. Wits: William Bisill, Christina (---?---) and Richard Harris. Pr. 26 Jan 1703 by George Giles, Peter Rogers and Charles Rhodes. (PROB 11/468/6).

Ouzeel Van Swieten, inhabitant of N.Y. at present in London, [bachelor], dated 23 Jan 1694. All my real and personal estate to my friend Mr. Valentine Cruger of London, merchant, who is to be my exec. Wits: Edward King, Edward Holmes, Benjamin Ashe and Robert Sinclair. AWW 2 Jan 1703 to Jacob Myna Cruger, relict and adx. of the named exec. (PROB 11/468/14). New grant in Jly 1705 to the sister Beatrice Ouzeel.

Micajah Lowe formerly of Charles City Co., Va., but now of Carshalton, Surrey, merchant, dated 20 Jan 1703. A gold ring to my uncle Mr. Micajah Perry and my mother-in-law Mrs. Elizabeth Hamlin. A ring for mourning to my sisters Susanna Lowe, Johanna Jarrett and Johanna Lowe, and to my friends Capt. Christopher Morgan and Capt. James Morgan. The residue of my estate to my wife Sarah who is to be my exec. with my uncle Micajah Perry. Wits: Sarah Barnes, Joseph Cooper, Robert Dalley and Thomas Dewbery. Pr. 17 Mar 1703 by Micajah Perry. (PROB 11/469/53).

James Rae of Stirling, Scotland, merchant, at present in London [who died in Md.], dated 28 Nov 1699. My debts to Thomas Gilchrist and Walter Blare of Glasgow are to be paid and the residue of my estate to go to my friend and exec. Mr. John Glissel of London, merchant. Wits: William Scorry, John Ruck, his clerk, and William Brookhouse. Pr. 12 Mar 1703 by the exec. named. (PROB 11/469/57).

Vincent Lambert [of Md., who died as a prisoner in France], dated 2 Feb 1703. Three guineas to my friend Capt. John Haselwood who is to receive my body for burial. Residue to my two sisters Anne Robinson and Margaret Lambert. My father Mr. Edward Lambert is to be my exec. Wits: Samuel Oliver, John Tayler, William Wallis and John Blenkern. Pr. 30 Jly 1703 by the father. (PROB 11/470/114).

Thomas Opie of Bristol, mariner, [who died in Va.], dated 16 Nov 1702. To be buried with my grandfather Mr. David Lindsay and a tombstone to be sent to Va. to be put over his and my grave. To my brother John Opie my second best bed etc. To my brother Lindsay Opie my best bed etc. To my sisters Helen, Susannah and Sarah the residue of my household goods and my one-eighth part of the *Adventure* and her cargo. If my brother John has my father's signet ring I bequeath mine to my brother Lindsay. All that was left to me by my father to my brothers and sisters except the plantation which will fall to my brother John. Mourning rings to: my uncle Edward Opie, Francis Thruppe, and Mrs. Anne Keen, widow, and Mrs. Sarah Keen, both of Cherry Point, Potomack, Va. £3 to my old servant Mary Edwards. To my brother Lindsay the proceeds of my watch which I sent to Jamaica by Mr. William Williamson. My sister Susannah to be my exex. and she is to pay my debts to George Bartlett and any others incurred since I was last in Va. Wits: Francis Thrupp, William Burwood and Edward Evans. Pr. Jly 1703 by the named exex. Susannah Cole. (PROB 11/470/116).

William Reed of H.M. ship *Southampton*, Capt. James Moody, dated on board the said ship at James River, Va., 22 Nov 1702. My whole estate to my friend David Cluny of the said ship who is to be my exec. Wits: William Hodshon, William Robeson, Jonas Reif and Thomas Else. Pr. 21 Jly 1703 by the named exec. (PROB 11/470/118).

Willoughby Hill of St. Andrew Holborn, London, marine [of the ship *India King*, who died in Va.], dated 21 Aug 1697. My wife Joan Hill is to be my attorney, legatee and exex. Wits: Thomas Cooke and Thomas Heath Jr. Pr. 21 May 1703 by the relict. (PROB 11/471/131).

Mottrom Spencer of Nomini, Westmoreland Co., Va., and late of the Essex Regiment, who died in St. Giles in Fields, Mddx., dated 24 Oct 1691. From the estate left to me by the will of my father I give £500 sterling to my wife out of the estate of my brother

William Spencer Esq. of Cople, Beds., and £300 which I require my mother Mrs. Frances Spencer to pay her. Mourning rings to: my sister Mrs. Lettice Barnard; my brother William Spencer; and my aunt Anne Armiger. My said wife is to be my exex. Wits: Richard Kitchiner, Lettice Barnard and William Saveige. AWW 15 May 1703 to the brother Capt. William Spencer, the named exex. renouncing. (PROB 11/471/135).

David Walters of Charlestown, N.E., mariner, now of H.M. ship *Britannia* but aboard the hospital ship *Smyrna Factor*, dated 15 June 1703. Thomas Pike of Boston, N.E., also now aboard the *Smyrna Factor*, is to be my only legatee and exec. Wits: Thomas Jones, James Mackmillan and John Whittingham. Pr. 30 Oct 1703 by the named exec. (PROB 11/472/176).

John Anthony of R.I., mariner, dated 16 June 1701. My whole estate to my son John Anthony. Richard and Elinor Potts to be my execs. Wits: Jo. Wood, Mary Pinkny and John Dennis, notary public. Pr. 10 Dec 1703 by affirmation of the relict. (PROB 11/473/205).

James Frisby of Cecil Co., Md., dated 10 Sep 1702. To my sons Thomas and William Frisby the five patents where I now live called Burtie's Journey, Frisby's Addition, Frisby's Wild Chase, Baltimore Field and Frisby's Points. To my son James Frisby my plantation called the White Marsh contained in three patents and one deed of sale from Samuel Wheller to myself and called Hardgrove's Choice, Frisby's Prime Choice, Frisby's Farm and Frisby's Forest. To my son Peregrine Frisby my tract beside the land belonging to Mr. John Atkey called Frisby's Meadows. To my son William Frisby my land called Cocks and all the plantation of 200 acres on which William Saunders lived on the south side of Sassafras River. To my son James Frisby a tract of 300 acres called Broad Oak on the south side of Sassafras River behind the land of Thomas Bostick. To my daughter Sarah Robinson £10 sterling and her mother's clothes and, if she comes to the country to inhabit, her mother's riding horse. The residue of my estate in America and Europe to my said sons. My son William is to be put to school in England and my son Peregrine to be bound apprentice. My son-in-law Thomas Robinson is to have my sloop. My sons Thomas, James and Peregrine are to be my execs. Wits: Clement Bankston, James Bowers, Ann Hewet, John Keye and Elizabeth Keye. On 8 Dec 1703 James Frisby of Whitechapel, Mddx., merchant, deposed that he was a son of the testator who died in Oct 1702 and that the above is a true copy of his will. Peregrine Browne of St. Catherine Creechurch, London, merchant, deposed on the same day that, having married the testator's sister and having arranged the education of the testator's sons Thomas, James and Peregrine, he can attest to the signature on the will. Pr. 3 Dec 1703 by the son James Frisby. (PROB 11/473/215). Double probate granted to the sons Thomas and Peregrine Frisby in Dec 1706.

Edward Hughes of West Chester City, (N.Y.?), mariner, now bound to sea, dated 23 Sep 1702. My estate to my sister Catherine Hughes of West Chester City and my friend William Clayton of Stepney, Mddx., grazier. My friend Elizabeth Clayton of Stepney to be my exex. Wits: William Owles, Margaret Ward and John Cudlipp. Pr. Dec 1703 by Elizabeth Clayton, widow. (PROB 11/473/220).

Edward Randolph Esq. [of Acquamat, Va.], Surveyor of Customs of all H.M. plantations and colonies in America, being about to make my seventeenth sea voyage to America, dated 15 June 1702. To my youngest daughter Sarah Randolph the salary due to me not already given to my daughters Williams or Deborah Randolph and all my plate in London in the hands of my friend Mr. Edward Jones of the Savoy. All the money received for my use from Gilbert Nelson, late Chief Justice of Bermuda and from George Plater Esq. of Patuxent, Md., which he may receive from Samuel Willson, is also to go to my daughter Sarah but, if she marries without the consent of Mrs. Mary Fog and Nathaniel Bladen Esq. of Lincolns Inn, her portion will go to my daughter Elizabeth Pim and her son Mr. Charles Pim. Wits: Humphrey Walcot, gent., Mrs. Catherine Bladen and Nathaniel Bladen. AWW 7 Dec 1703 to Sarah, wife of John Howard, guardian of the daughter Sarah Randolph. (PROB 11/473/234).

1704

Matthew Ham of N.E., mariner, now in St. Olave's, Southwark, Surrey, dated 10 Mar 1698. My friend Alice Pomery of St. Olave's, widow, is to be my attorney, legatee and exex. Wits: Mary Parry, Philip Jones and John Parry, notary public by St. Saviour's, Dockhead, Southwark. Pr. 3 Jan 1704 by the exex. named. (PROB 11/474/13).

Abraham Kenyan of Warfield, Berks., clerk, dated 15 Apr 1693. All my estate in Va. to my eldest son John Kenyan. My estate in Bollington and Millington to my second and third sons Jabez and Joseph Kenyan who are to be my execs. and pay their sister Jacinta £100. The freehold lease I bought of William Sturt to my son Joseph. Wits: John Newall, Martha Newall and Ann (x) Byrom. Pr. 28 Jan 1704 by the son Jabez Kenyan. (PROB 11/474/15).

Edward Rymes of St. Botolph Bishopsgate, London, mariner of H.M. ship *Royal Sovereign*, Capt. Sanders, [of Captain Wemm's Company, who died in N.Y.], dated 3 May 1691. My wife Elizabeth Rymes is to be my attorney, legatee and exex. Wits: Humphrey Sanders and Richard Scale. Pr. 14 Feb 1704 by the relict. (PROB 11/475/48).

Hugh Jones, Minister of Christ Church, Calvert Co., Md., dated 3 Jan 1702. All my books to Christ Church library. To Colonel John Bigger of Calvert Co. my riding horse. To Mr. Thomas Cockshutt, minister of All Saints parish, my gown and sash. The perquisites due to me in Christ Church parish are to go to the use of the glebe land given by Capt. Richard Ladd and are to be disposed of at the discretion of Capt. Richard Smith of Calvert Co. The residue of my estate to my eldest brother Mr. Richard Jones, late minister of Landasteroh (*sic*) in Anglesey with remainder to my younger brother Mr. John Jones and my eldest brother's children. My execs. Mr. Thomas Cockshutt and Col. John Bigger are to convey any surplus to Capt. John Hyde of London, merchant. Wits: Robert Skinner, John Mackoll, John Holdsworth and John Fisher. AWW 15 June 1704 to Barbara Jones, the relict of the brother Richard Jones deceased. (PROB 11/477/132).

Alexander Cornwall of St. Botolph Aldgate, London, mariner, now bound to sea [of the ship *Maryland Factor*, who died in Md.], dated 13 Jly 1703. My whole estate to my brother Walter Cornwall. My friend William Findlason of St. Botolph Aldgate, merchant, is to be my exec. Wits: Philip Stevens and T. Paley, notary public at Hermitage Bridge. Pr. 8 Aug 1704 by the exec. named. (PROB 11/477/160).

Robert Hornbe of St. Botolph Aldgate, London, now bound overseas by the ship *Benjamin*, Capt. Edward Smith, [and who died in Va.], dated 27 Jan 1702. My whole estate to my wife Elizabeth Hornbe who is to be my exex. Wits: Samuel Morgan, Margaret (x) Lacy and John Rutton of Gravesend, Kent. Pr. 25 Aug 1704 by the relict. (PROB 11/477/164).

Thomas Ogden of the Precinct of St. Katherine, Mddx., now bound to sea, [master of the ship *Thomas and Elizabeth*, who died in Va.], dated 11 Apr 1700. My whole estate to my wife Alice who is to be my exex. Wits: Joseph Fletcher and John Nunn. Pr. 7 Aug 1704 by the relict. (PROB 11/477/168).

James Bowker of St. Peter's parish, New Kent Co., Va. To my brother Edward Bowker of London £30 sterling. £10 for the purchase of plate for the new brick church in this parish. £40 sterling to my friend John Lyddall. A ring for mourning to my friend Capt. Joseph

Foster, my sister and Madame Barbarah Lyddall. The residue of my estate, including my tobacco, is to be divided between the children of my brother Ralph Bowker. The said Ralph Bowker is to have my books and to be my exec. My horse is to be sold and the proceeds remitted to my brother Edward Bowker. Wits: (--?--) Brebant, Elizabeth Portlock and Thomas (x) Soso. On 17 Mar 1703 Nathaniel Burwell of Va., merchant, and Nicholas Humfrey of Mile End, Stepney, Mddx., mariner, deposed that they know George Clough, Clerk of New Kent Co., who has certified the copy of the above will. AWW 17 Nov 1704 to Micajah Perry, attorney for the brother Ralph Bowker. (PROB 11/479/224).

Roger Newman of Baltimore, Md., dated 10 May 1704. To my friend Charles Greenbury, who is to be my exec., my negro man called Tom, a negro woman called Young Genny and her two negro children and a bay horse. My said exec. is to have the disposal of the plantation of 700 acres where I now dwell on the Bay Side near the north side of Petaphs River and to pay £500 to my sister Susannah Coatsworth who is also to have the residue of my estate. A silver cup and cover to Mrs. Rachel Greenbury. £20 sterling each to my friends Henage Robison and Edward Hancox. £10 for mourning to my brother Dr. Caleb Coatsworth. Elizabeth Samson is to have the girl Betty. £10 to James Read. Wits: Samuel Young, William (x) Hawkins, Charles Greenbury and Edward Hunt. Certificate of Thomas Brooke and William Dent Esqs., Judges of the Probate Court of Md., that the above is a true copy. AWW 30 Dec 1704 to the sister Susannah, wife of Caleb Coatsworth. (PROB 11/479/258).

1705

Robert Cherry of St. Thomas the Apostle, citizen and draper of London, dated 27 Dec 1704. To my friends and o'seers Mr. Lionel Sharpe and Mr. John Theed, both of London, I leave £10 for the poor. The residue of my estate to be divided between my son John Cherry and his children now overseas, and my daughter Mary, wife of Samuel England of Penna., and their children. My daughter Mary England and my friend Richard Beckett of Little Moorfields, London, to be my execs. Wits: Martha Hatten, John Wildman and Samuel Round, his servant. Pr. 10 Jan 1705 by the affirmation of Richard Beckett. (PROB 11/480/4).

Mary Slater, widow of Col. Henry Slater, formerly Governor of N.Y. Province, dated 14 Sep 1704. All my real and personal estate to

Mrs. Mary Leaver of N.Y.C. who is to be my exex. Wits: Margaret (x) Magregory, Mary Harris and Richard Harris. AWW 13 Mar 1705 to Charles Lodovick, attorney for the exex. in N.Y.C. (PROB 11/481/63).

N.B. The testatrix was daughter of John Mayo (see his will proved in 1691) and died in N.Y. at the end of 1704. See NGSQ 64/48.

Samuel Smith, citizen and haberdasher of London, dated 24 Mar 1690. Twelve pence each to: my brother Daniel Smith at Charlestown in N.E.; my brother Daniel (*sic*) Smith of Leicester; my nephews Thomas, Daniel and Samuel Smith; my niece Elizabeth Dungey, wife of [blank] Dungey, late of St. Botolph Bishopsgate, London. Residue to my wife and exex. Dorothy Smith. Wits: Jon. Clarke, George Ford and Richard Smith. Pr. 17 Nov 1705. (PROB 11/485/230).

John Weaver of Bristol, [who died in Md., gent.], dated Charles Co., Md., 17 June 1705. Nuncupative will declared in the presence of Capt. Elisha James, Col. Philip Hoskins and Dr. William Lock by which the testator left his whole estate to Mrs. Mary Weaver of Bristol, spinster, and named John Pilsworth of Bristol, surgeon, his exec. Certificate made on 25 June 1705 by Richard Broughton, Deputy Commissary for Charles Co., that the above will was declared before witnesses. Memorandum that the testator died on 17 June 1705 in Md. in Va. while on a journey. AWW 1 Nov 1705 to the sister Mary Weaver, the named exec. renouncing. (PROB 11/485/232).

Robert Read of St. Olave, Southwark, Surrey, mariner of the ship *Baltimore* bound for Va., dated 15 Jan 1703. My whole estate to my wife Elizabeth Read who is to be my exex. Wits: Samuel Acres and Edward Knowles, notary public in Bermondsey Street, Southwark. Pr. 17 Dec 1705 by the relict. (PROB 11/485/252).

1706

John Ash of Danho, Colleton Co., S.C., gent., dated 9 Apr 1703. My wife Mary, daughter of Samuel Batt, late rector of (East) Coulston, Wilts., to be my exex. and to have my whole estate subject to the following legacies. To my son John by Martha Jess the product of a £100 tally payable to me from the Exchequer and two-fifths of another tally for 14% on £400 during his lifetime. To my son William that which is due on survivorship of the said £100 tally during his lifetime. The said tallies are in the hands of Sir William Simpson. To my said son William the advowson of Cotleigh vicarage in Devon which I bought from Mr. Mayne. Execs. in trust for the disposal of my estate are to be Landgrave Joseph Morton and Lady Elizabeth Blake. Wits: Edmund Bellinger, James Byres and James Kinloch. AWW 31 Jan 1706 to William Methuen, attorney for the relict in S.C. (PROB 11/486/1).

Thomas Flint of N.E., now on board H.M. ship *Severn* at the Isle of Bombay in the East Indies, [bachelor], dated 19 Jly 1704. My whole estate to my friend William King of Boldre, Hampshire, also aboard this ship, who is to be my exec. Wits: Charles Lott, Joseph Hutchinson and Richard Cornelius. AWW 23 Feb 1706 to Elizabeth King, widow and adx. of the named exec. (PROB 11/486/37).

Christopher Morgan [of Bromley by Bow, Mddx., bachelor]. This will takes the form of a statement of account by Micajah Perry, Thomas Lane and Richard Perry, Va. merchants, of disbursements made on behalf of the deceased to his relatives and friends. Payments were made to: his brother John Whitemill; his brother James; his brother Robert and his children; his sister Jone; Edmund Forest Sr. and his children; Edmund Forest Jr. who received one-sixteenth part of the ship *Richard & Sarah*; James Morgan Jr. who received one-eighth of the ship *Gloucester*; Sarah Morgan who received one-sixteenth part of the ship *Hartwell*; his brother John's children; his cousin Gabriel Knight; Lydia, daughter of his brother John; Gabriel, son of his brother Robert; Henry Jones of Ratcliffe, smith, who had assets in Va.; and the poor of Stepney and Bromley by Bow, (Mddx.), Frome, (Somerset), the churches of Lombard Street, Creechurch, Aldermanbury and St. Dunstan in the East, (London). AWW 22 Feb 1706 to the brother John Morgan. (PROB 11/487/45).

Thomas Starke of London, merchant, [who died in West Ham, Essex], dated 22 Mar 1704. One-third of my estate to my wife Sarah but, if this is less than £2,000, all my estate in Suffolk to her during her lifetime with remainder to my son John Starke. To my said son my five plantations in Va. and one-fifth of my personal estate but all in excess of £1,500 to my daughter Martha Starke who is also to have the gold which was my aunt Dennis's. One-fifth of my personal estate to my said daughter but not more than £1,000. One-fifth of my personal estate to each of my daughters Frances and Elizabeth Starke but not more than £1,000. Francis Lee and William Downer to have £10 each for mourning. My wife and my son to be execs. Wits: Anne Stephens, W. Ford, John Hodgkin and Jeffery Bass. Pr. 4 Mar 1706 by the execs. named. (PROB 11/487/72). See NGSQ 70/39-45.

Salem Osgood of London, merchant, dated 10 June 1703. To my wife Anna £100 for uses which I have confided to her and she is to be my exex. To my brother Obadiah Osgood £50. To my aunt Hester

Stapleton £10. To my cousin Mary, wife of William Cole of Reading, (Berks.), £5. To my cousin Elizabeth Slack £10. To my friend Oliver Marton of the Middle Temple, London, gent., 20 guineas. To William Zankey of Areley, Worcs., £10. To John Bowater of London £10. To Henry Gouldney, citizen and goldsmith of London, £5. To John, Hannah and Mary Mills, children of Elizabeth Mills, relict of John Mills deceased, £20 each when they come of age. My house and warehouse in White Hart Court, Gracechurch Street, London, houses at Long Acre, Mddx., and houses and lands at Langley Green, Bucks., to my wife during her lifetime with remainder to my daughters Rebeccah and Anne Osgood and my brother Obadiah Osgood. By indentures of 29/30 Nov 1698 between my father John Osgood's execs., Francis Platt of London, gent., and Rebeccah his wife (daughter of the said John Osgood), and myself, estates in Scaldwell, Northants., were conveyed to the said Platt and his wife: Rebeccah Platt is lately dead without issue and, on the death of her husband, this estate to which I have the right of inheritance I devise to my daughters Rebecca and Anne Osgood. My said daughters are also to have my one-twohundredth part of West Jersey devised to me and my brothers by my said late father. Wits: Oliver Marton, Elizabeth Slack, Christian Hanson and Thomas Meanes. Pr. 9 Apr 1706 by the solemn declaration of the relict. (PROB 11/488/95).

Nathaniel Young of Shadwell, Mddx., mariner, now bound on a voyage in the *Eagle* galley of London [and who died in Carolina], dated 16 Dec 1704. My whole estate to my friends Joseph Dearing of Shadwell, mariner, and Mary his wife and they are to be my execs. Wits: Thomas Jacobs and Thomas Pomeroy, notary public. Pr. 8 Apr 1706 by Mary Dearing, widow. (PROB 11/488/101).

William Freshwater of Clerkenwll, Mddx., citizen and haberdasher of London, dated Va. 9 Mar 1704. My whole estate including my tenement on the east side of Old Artillery Ground and goods in my house in St. John Street, Clerkenwell, to my sister Elizabeth Freshwater who is to be my exex. Wits: Henry Thornton, William Long and Alexander Rives. AWW 3 May 1706 to relict Elizabeth Freshwater. Revoked on her death Apr 1714 and granted to the sister Elizabeth, wife of Richard Freshwater. (PROB 11/488/106).

Thomas Stratfold of Bierton, Bucks., now going to sea [late of Va.], dated 26 Mar 1701. To my friend Henry Ilmore, whom I appoint as my exec., all my houses and lands subject to the following bequests. My aunt Plasance Knight to receive 10 shillings a quarter during her lifetime. £20 to my cousin William Knight. Forty shillings to Jane Attes, wife of John Attes, or if she be dead, to my aunt Elizabeth Durant. Wits: Griffin Crane, James Tompson,

John Hughes and John Tompson, notary public at the end of Blewgate Fields, Shadwell, Mddx. Pr. 7 May 1706 by the exec. named. (PROB 11/488/114)

Nathaniel Hunton of East Ham, Essex, gent., dated 3 Aug 1705. To my nephew Samuel Hunton, whom I appoint as my exec., my farm known as Master John's in Mountnessing and Shenfield, Essex, now in the occupation of William Lambert, and my farm in Chelmondiston near Ipswich, Suff., called Chelmondiston Hall, subject to the following bequests. £20, my copyhold estate in Whitechapel, Mddx., held of the Manor of Stepney, and my four acres in London Fields near Hangman's Acre to my sister Lucretia Swallow, with remainder to her daughter Sarah Swallow, my nephew Nathaniel Hunton, and Hunton March, son of John March. Ten shillings to my sister Mary, wife of Thomas Ford. £100 to my sister Elizabeth March of N.E. and £100 to each of her children. Wits: Thomas Leaver, William Marden and Thomas Gouge, all of East Ham. Pr. 21 Aug 1706 by the named exec. (PROB 11/489/179).

Jasper Ellixon of Ratcliffe Highway, Stepney, Mddx., mariner [of the merchant ship *Preservation* who died in Va.], dated 11 Jan 1698. My wife Margery Ellixon is to be my attorney, legatee and exex. Wits: John Strayne, Thomas Gibbon and John Johnson, notary public near the Gun in Upper Shadwell. Pr. 17 Dec 1706 by Mary Ellixon alias Alexon, widow. (PROB 11/490/224).

John Connop of Ratcliffe, Stepney, Mddx., mariner [of the merchant ship *Olive Tree*] now bound to sea, [who died in Va.], dated 6 Sep 1704. My whole estate to my friend Edmond Castle of Ratcliffe, gunsmith, who is to be my exec. Wits: John Bond and Thomas Quilter, notary public. Pr. 16 Dec 1706 by the named exec. (PROB 11/491/252).

William Dover of St. Olave, Southwark, Surrey, shipwright [of the merchant ship *Old Neptune*, who died in Va., bachelor], dated 20 Dec 1702. My whole estate to my father Thomas Dover of St. Olave's, scrivener, and my sister Anne Dover. My said father to be my exec. Wits: Sarah Wortley, Hannah Warr and John Warr. AWW 9 Dec 1706 to the sister Anne Dover, the father having died. (PROB 11/491/253).

Thomas Skinner of London, shoemaker, [who died in Md.], dated 14 Nov 1695. To my sisters Mary Pointer and Elizabeth Skinner an annuity of 40 shillings each payable from my lands in Blofield, Norfolk. To my kinsman John Pointer £5 when he reaches the age of ten. The residue to by brother John Skinner who is to be my exec. Wits: Elinor Berry, Elizabeth (x) Warner and William Lane, scrivener. Pr. 12 Dec 1706 by the exec. named. (PROB 11/491/265).

1707

Dame Mary Sargeant alias Phipps, relict of Sir William Phipps of Boston, N.E., deceased, dated 19 Feb 1704 (and copied from the Mass. Registry). By indenture of 24 Sep 1701 I reserved to myself all right and title in my estate before my marriage to Peter Sargeant Esq. I leave £10 to my said husband. To my mother-in-law Mrs. Mary Howard, widow, an annuity of £10, and I forgive her son Philip White all his debts to me. My adopted son Spencer Phipps *alias* Bennett is to be my heir and to inherit all my real estate when he is 21. My house at the north end of Boston in the tenure of Samuel Avis to Mary Armstrong. Other principal bequests to: my sister Mrs. Rebecca Bennett; Rev. Increase Mather; my friend Mr. John White; Margaret, wife of Matthew Armstrong, and her daughter Mary Armstrong; Dorcas, wife of Thomas Salter. My friends John Foster and Andrew Belcher Esq. are to be my execs. in trust during the minority of my said son. Wits: Robert Earle, Samuel Aves and Frances White. AWW 29 Jan 1707 to John Metcalfe, attorney for Spencer Phipps alias Bennett in N.Y. (PROB 11/492/16).

Benjamin Wright [of the merchant ship *Levite*, who died in Va.], dated 12 Aug 1706. My whole estate to my friend Robert Jones. Wits: Thomas Howard, George Sweetland and Cornelius Shipton. AWW 13 Jan 1707 to John Hunt, attorney for Robert Jones now at sea. (PROB 11/492/23).

William Aylward, late of Va., merchant, now in London, [but who died in France, bachelor], dated 6 Nov 1701. My whole estate in England and Va. to my friend Robert Cary living in Watling Street, London, who is to be my exec. Wits: Edward Garrett, Elizabeth (x) Lane and William Scorey, notary public. Pr. 20 Feb 1707 by the named exec. (PROB 11/492/24).

Thomas Colles of Deptford, Kent, shipwright [who died on the ship *Nicholson* in Va.], dated 8 Jan 1706. My whole estate to my wife Mary Colles who is to be my exex. Wits: Samuel Sherwin, Henry Rider and Jerome Collins, scrivener near Queen's Yard Gate, Deptford. Pr. 5 Feb 1707 by the relict. (PROB 11/492/27).

William Bowyer, late of Jamaica but now of N.Y.C., merchant, [who died in N.Y.], dated 15 Jan 1706. £20 each for mourning to Mr. David Jamison and his wife. Twenty shillings each for a mourning ring to: Mrs. Mary Johnson; William Turner; Richard Mill of Jamaica; Mr. Thomas Mitchell; Mr. Archibald Cunningham; Mr. Benjamin Dogett. My negro boy Richmond is to be sent to the said Richard Mill. The residue of my estate to my brothers and sisters (unnamed).

David Jamison of N.Y., Mr. William Turner of London and Richard
Mill of Jamaica are to be my execs. Wits: David Law, Nathaniel
Maiston and Richard Willett. Pr. 30 May 1707 by William Turner.
(PROB 11/494/99).

Samuel Elson of Black Point, N.E., mariner of H.M. ship *Greyhound*,
dated 20 Aug 1706. My whole estate to my friend Robert Harding
of Peterhead, Aberdeenshire, Scotland, mariner of this ship, and he
is to be my exec. Wits: William Herriott, Captain, Richard Tippett,
master, Thomas Betts, boatswain, and Philip Wiseman. Pr. 11 Sep
1707 by the named exec. (PROB 11/496/204).

John Hastings of London, mariner, late of Prestonpans, Scotland,
outward bound on a voyage [master of the ship *James*, who died
in Va.], dated 15 Jly 1701. My whole estate to my sister Jeanet
Hastings of Prestonpans. My friend William Brock of London,
mariner, to be my exec. Wits: J. Campbell, Patrick Bapty and
Samuel Wills, notary public in Wapping. AWW 27 Sep 1707 to
William Finlason, attorney for the only sister Janette Hastings in
Prestonpans, the named exec. renouncing. (PROB 11/496/206).

Randolph Nickols of Charlestown, Massachusetts, mariner, dated 6 Aug
1701. My whole estate to my wife and exex. Sarah Nickols. Wits:
George Thorold, John Gyles and Edward Turfrey. Pr. 5 Dec 1707.
(PROB 11/497/266).

1708

John Guest of the Inner Temple, London, gent., [of Philadelphia,
widower], dated 28 Aug 1697. To my brother Thomas Guest one
shilling. The residue of my estate to my cousin Capt. John Geast,
citizen and haberdasher of London, who is to be my exec. and to
act as trustee in my place of the estate of Mr. Anthony Death.
Wits: Daniel Geast, Roger Harris and Susannah Merrick. Pr. 22
Apr 1708 by the exec. named. (PROB 11/500/86).

Andrew Johnson of Woodford, Essex, mariner [of the merchant ship
Sussex, who died in Va., bachelor], dated 14 Aug 1705. My whole
estate to my sister Martha Splitt of Woodford, spinster, who is to
be my exex. Wits: Ann (x) Warwick, Robert Bramble of Milton
next Gravesend, Kent, and Thomas Rutton, attorney at Gravesend.
Pr. 28 Apr 1708 by Martha Tilbury alias Splitt, wife of Thomas
Tilbury. (PROB 11/501/95).

Edmund Payne [of Stepney, Mddx., who died in Md.], dated 3 Jly
1688. My whole estate to my wife Katherine Payne and she, my

cousin Katherine Mappell, and her brother Payne Mappell are to be my execs. Pr. 1 Jly 1708 by the relict. (PROB 11/502/167).

Samuel Jobson the elder of Bermondsey, Sy., woolstapler, dated 29 Jly 1706. To my wife Mary Jobson £400 and my tenement in Bermondsey with remainder thereof to my children. £450 to my son Samuel Jobson. £150 to my daughter Hannah Maling, wife of Thomas Maling, £10 to my grandson Samuel Maling, and £5 each to my grandchildren Abigail, Thomas, Elizabeth and Hannah Maling. To my son Michael Jobson of Philadelphia I give his bond to me of £100, which bond is now in the hands of my daughter Hannah Maling. I also give to my said son all my lands and houses in Penna. and leave £40 to his recently born son Samuel. £400 each to my daughters Sarah Jobson, Mary Jobson and Katherine Jobson when they come of age or are married. I forgive my brother John Jobson his debt to me of £125 and leave £5 to his daughter Mary. £10 to Walter Miers and Joseph Grove in trust for the poor of the Monthly Meeting at Horsleydown, Southwark, Surrey, and to John Powell, Steward of the Friends' Meeting at the Workhouse to be used for the poor there. Execs: Joseph Grove, Silvanus Grove, my son-in-law Thomas Mayling (*sic*), and my son Samuel Jobson. Wits: William Fukes, Charles Walton and George Chalkley Jr. Pr. 9 Nov 1708 by the affirmation of Thomas Mayleigh (*sic*) and Samuel Jobson. (PROB 11/505/262).

John Lowe of Hingham near Boston, N.E., mariner of H.M. ship *Triton*, [bachelor], dated 9 Jly 1707. My whole estate to my friend William Mason of Howton (Houghton), Durham, mariner, who is to be my exec. Wits: Henry Meyer, Charles Blakey and Isaac Bartholomew. AWW 12 Nov 1708 to Adam Bird, attorney for William Mason, father and administrator of the named exec. William Mason deceased. (PROB 11/505/264).

Peter Hance of Ratcliffe, Stepney, Mddx., mariner [of the merchant ship *Providence*, who died in Va.], dated 11 Jan 1698. My wife Sarah Hance and my friend Robert Townsend of Ratcliffe, cordwainer, to be my attorneys, legatees and execs. Wits: Thomas Ellis and Thomas Porter Jr., his clerk, at Upper Shadwell. Pr. 11 Dec 1708 by the relict. (PROB 11/505/286).

1709

Abraham Ballew, mariner [of the merchant ship *Robert*, who died in Va.], dated 28 Jan 1704. My whole estate to my wife Mary Ballew who is to be my exex. Wits: Peter Girard, Mary Cruickshank and

Charles Power, scrivener near the Navy Office, London. Pr. 17 Jan 1709 by the relict. (PROB 11/506/7).

Jacob Manning of Salem, N.E., mariner of H.M. ship *Rumney*, dated 28 Dec 1708. My whole estate to my cousin Warwick Palfray of Salem, mariner, who is to be my exec. Wits: John Quick and Christopher Gardiner. Pr. 5 Jan 1709 by the named exec. (PROB 11/506/14).

Philip Blackalar, late of N.E., mariner of H.M. ship *Ruby*, dated 26 Aug 1708. My whole estate to my wife Mary Blackalar of N.E. and Margaret Allsell, wife of Joseph Allsell of Wapping, Mddx., mariner, and she is to be my exex. Wits: Abraham Sharp and John Allen, notary public at Hermitage Bridge. Pr. 3 Feb 1709 by the named exex. (PROB 11/506/24).

James Griffiths, Landgrave of Port Royal, Carolina, [who died in the Palace of St. James, Westminster, Mddx.], dated 6 Jan 1709. All my patents in Carolina amounting to 48,000 acres to my father John Griffiths of Carmarthenshire who is to be my exec. One shilling each to my uncles and aunts on my father's and mother's side, to their sons and daughters and their children. Wits: Jane Harriman, Margery (x) Carpenter and Anthony Thomas. Pr. 3 Feb 1709 by the father. (PROB 11/506/33).

Flower Walker [of Md.], now in London but not settled here, being on a voyage from Brompton to Northallerton, (Yorks.), where I was born, and desiring to take ship for Md., dated 10 June 1700. To my eldest brother William Walker 20 shillings and one shilling to each of his children. To my brother Christopher Walker 20 shillings. To my sister Elizabeth Richardson 20 shillings and one shilling to each of her children. To my brothers Richard and Thomas Walker £10 each and 5 shillings to each of their children. To my brother-in-law George Dunn £10 and 5 shillings to each of his children. £8 each to my father Richard Walker and mother Isabell Walker. On the deaths of my uncle Peter Richardson and his son-in-law George Richardson an estate in Manby, (Lincs.), reverts to me which I now leave to my execs. who are to pay £50 to my niece Ann Walker. Execs: my brothers Thomas and Richard Walker and brother-in-law George Dunn. Wits: Henry Russell, William (x) Hollingsworth and Zachary Hollings (*sic*). Pr. 12 Feb 1709 by the brother Richard Walker. (PROB 11/506/43).

Benjamin Dogett of Kingston, Jamaica, but formerly of London, merchant. Will in the form of a letter written from Kingston to his brother John Dogett in London on 8 Jly 1703. The letter refers to: my sister de Bary; my brother Otgher who gave an account of his mother's death in S.C.; my (said) brother John Dogett who left his wife and children in S.C. and is alleged to be in the Fleet Prison in London. The mother of the three brothers Benjamin, John and Otgher Dogett is stated to have left a will appointing the said Otgher her sole exec. Pr. by John Dogett Mar 1709 after testimony on 14 Nov 1706 from Anthony Grindall Esq. of St. Bride's, London, and John Seymour of St. Botolph without Aldgate, distiller, that they had known Benjamin Dogett for ten years and recognized his handwriting. (PROB 11/507/53).

James Fowler of Mile End, Stepney, Mddx., late inhabitant of Nansemond Co., James River, Va., gent., dated 27 Apr 1709. My stock in trade in Va. to be disposed of by my exec. and the proceeds to be remitted to England. My wife Elizabeth Fowler is to consign goods delivered to my account to my friend Mr. John Goodwin, merchant in London. Mr. Robert Betty who, with my wife, manages my concerns in Va., is to be retained at the salary agreed with Capt. Richard Lovett, late of Norfolk Co., Va., deceased. During her lifetime my said wife is to have my manor house and plantation in the upper parish of Nansemond Co. where she lives, and thereafter they are to go to my brother Daniel Fowler's eldest son named Roarry Fowler. My lands known as Earle's Plantation to the said Roarry Fowler. My plantation at Summerton called Oadham's Plantation, now in the tenure of Mr. Crawford, to my goddaughter Margaret Sullivan, daughter of Mr. Daniel Sullivan, with remainder to her brother Daniel Sullivan. A riding horse etc. to Robert Betty. A negro boy called Cudger to my friend Richard Parker. To Hester Mackey 12,000 lbs of tobacco, cattle, etc. when she comes of age or is married. To my servant boy John Tavor(?), when he is free, two suits of clothes and mathematical instruments. A mourning ring to Mr. Joseph Meredith. All my negroes, household goods, cattle and stock to my wife and, if the said Roarry Fowler should come to Va., she is to fit up a handsome lodging room for him. My said wife and friend Mr. John Goodwin are to be my execs. Wits: Adam (x) Watson, Richard Waplington and Philip Traheron. Pr. 13 May 1709 by John Goodwin. (PROB 11/508/115).

John Baker of Fairlight, Sussex, yeoman, proposing to take a journey to East N.J., [who died in East Jersey], dated 23 Mar 1687. My lands in East N.J. to my wife with remainder to my two brothers John Fuller and Joseph Wakeham, and they are to be my execs. To Mr. William Dockwra, merchant in London, £5 for his help in managing my estate. Wits: Susanna Cater and Elizabeth (x) Swaine in Little St. Helen's, London. Pr. 30 June 1709 by Joseph Wakeham. (PROB 11/509/135).

Hercules Coutts of the City of London, merchant, [who died in Newcastle, Penna.], dated 2 Sep 1697. To my brother and exec.

James Coutts of London, merchant, all my real and personal estate but, if I marry and have issue, my wife is to have my estate for the benefit of any children. Wits: Alexander Straton and George Brewster. Pr. 26 Aug 1709 by the named exec. (PROB 11/510/190).

George Fullerton of Charles Town, S.C., merchant, dated 8 Oct 1708. To William Rhett Jr., son of William Rhett of Charles Town, merchant, £200 current. To Sarah and Catherine Rhett, daughters of the same, £200 current each. To William Rhett Sr. and Sarah his wife £200 current and £100 sterling now in the hands of Mr. Robert South of London, merchant. To the said Sarah Rhett my negro boy called Snowhill. To the poor of St. Philip's, Charles Town, £20 current. The residue to my brother Mr. William Fullerton living in Ayrshire, Scotland. My friends Mr. William Rhett and Sarah his wife to be my execs. Wits: Bentley Cooke, Mary Pearce and Sarah Cocke. Pr. 8 Sep 1709 by William Rhett. (PROB 11/510/211).

George Fane, Captain of H.M. ship *Lowestaff*, now in the harbour of N.Y., dated 31 Mar 1709. All my real and personal estate to my brother Charles Fane Esq. of Barcledon near Reading, Berks., who is to be my exec. in England. Gyles Shelley of N.Y., merchant, and Capt. Gordon, commander of H.M. ship *Maidstone* to be my execs. in N.Y. Wits: Adr. Philiptes (*sic*), T. Braine and Thomas George. Pr. 24 Oct 1709 by the brother Charles Fane. (PROB 11/510/219).

John Towsey [of Boston, N.E., bachelor], dated 10 Mar 1699. To Mrs. Abigail Henchman, widow, dwelling in Boston, £300 current. The residue to my brother Thomas Towsey who is to be my exec. Wits: Abraham Adams, Abigail Adams and John Soames. AWW 19 Sep 1709 to Benjamin Smith, attorney for the brother Thomas Towsey in Boston. (PROB 11/511/229).

1710

Samuel Kenyon, formerly of Manchester, Lancashire, but late of Boston, N.E., mariner. Copy of will probated in Boston to the relict, Elizabeth Kenyon, at PROB 20/2952. (Jan. 1710).

John Crow of Shadwell, Mddx., mariner [of the merchant ship *Providence*, who died in Va.], dated 6 Jly 1707. My whole estate to my friend Thomas Jackson of Shadwell and Mary his wife who are to be my execs. Wits: Henry Hewis, Edward Ivory and John Forrest. Pr. 9 Jan 1710 by Thomas Jackson. (PROB 11/513/10).

Jeffery Cockshudd of Great Harwood, Lancs., mariner, [who died in Va., bachelor], dated 15 Apr 1691. To brother Edmund Cockshudd £10, brother Thomas Cockshudd £20, and brother John Cockshudd £30. Execs: brothers Thomas and John. Wits: Elizabeth Shaw and Thomas Webb, scrivener. Pr. 14 Jan 1710 by Thomas Cockshudd. (PROB 11/513/10).

Thomas Ward of N.E., mariner of the merchant ship *Industry*, [who died in Lisbon, bachelor], dated 13 May 1710. My friend John Kast to be my legatee and exec. and collect my wages from William Jordan, master of said ship. Wits: David Sheppard, John Burton and John Hamilton. AWW 16 Jan 1710 to Joan Keast (*sic*), wife and attorney of the exec. in Va. on the ship on the merchant ship *Elizabeth and Martha*. (PROB 11/513/30).

Livellet Jones of Fairfield, N.E., mariner of H.M. ships *Suffolk* [and *Lancaster*, who died in hospital in N.Y.], dated 18 May 1709. My friend William Collins of Aldgate, London, to be my legatee and exec. and to collect my wages from Capt. William Cleaveland of the *Suffolk*. Wits: James Emerson, Jonathan Trotter and Richard Jones. Admon. 29 Mar 1710 to Mary, wife of William Collins now at sea. (PROB 11/514/70).

Patrick Spence of Copley, Westmoreland Co., Va., but now of Allington, Dorset, gent., dated 25 Marh 1710. To be buried at the discretion of Daniel Gundry of Allington, merchant. Bequests to: my cousin Patrick Spence, son of my late uncle Patrick Spence, who is to have my forest land near the Courthouse in Westmoreland Co. and two slaves called Aggedy and Bess; my sister Mary Spence who is to have my land near Potomack River; my cousins Rose and Dorcas Neele, daughters of my late sister Dorcas Neele, when they are 16 or married; my cousin Robert Mason, son of my late sister Elizabeth Mason, when he is 16; my cousin Thomas Spence, son of my late uncle Patrick Spence; Captain George Eskridge of Va. who is to have all my law books. My slave Mulatto Tom to be freed. Residue of estate in England and Va. to my sister Mary Spence. Execs. Daniel Gundry and George Eskridge. Wits: John Symes, Deborah Gundry and John Symes Jr. Pr. 4 May 1710. (PROB 11/515/116).

Joseph alias Jotham Grover of the merchant ship *Providence*, [bachelor], dated 4 May 1710. Nuncupative will directing all his wages to be put in the hands of William Lanchester for the benefit of his grandmother in Boston, N.E. Wits: Robert Godber and William Clark. AWW 27 May 1710 to William Lanchester for benefit of the testator's grandmother Grover in Boston. (PROB 11/516/138).

Robert Beadle, late of Salem, N.E., now of London, mariner, dated 23 Mar 1708. My whole estate to Joanna Mann of Bermondsey, Surrey, widow, who is to be my exex. Wits: Samuel Allen and John Allen, notary public at Redriffe Wall. Prob. Sep 1710 to named exex. (PROB 11/517/197).

Edward Tynte Esq., Governor of Carolina, dated 19 Jly 1709. My whole estate to Mrs. Frances Kilner of Brownlow Street, St. Giles in the Fields, Mddx., spinster, who is to be my exex. Wits: William Morgan and Abel Ketelby. Prob. 6 Oct 1710 by named exex. (PROB 11/517/220).

Isaac Robson of Stepney, Mddx., mariner [of merchant ship *Britannia*, who died in Va.], dated 17 Feb 1704. My whole estate to my wife Mary Robson who is to be my exex. Wits: Vincent Hurley and John Thomas, notary public inb Wapping. Prob. 27 Sep 1710 by relict. (PROB 11/518/232).

Philip Oyles, one of the sons of Philip Oyles, citizen and clothworker of London, being minded to go overseas, [of Md., bachelor], dated 15 Mar 1707. All my freeholds in Flaunden, Herts., devised to me by my said father in his will of 20 Aug 1697, after the death of his wife Sarah Oyles, to my brother Thomas Oyles of Limehouse, Mddx., grocer, who is to pay £20 to my sister Mary Oyles. £6 to my master Thomas Dry, citizen and skinner of London, and his wife Mary Dry. £5 each to my cousins Jennie and Mary, daughters of the said Thomas Dry. £3 to the poor Quakers of Ratcliffe. Residue to my said brother Thomas who is to be exec. Wits: Charles Humphreys, Samuel Clarke and Thomas Silater. Pr. 10 Nov 1710 by solemn declaration of named exec. (PROB 11/518/251).

William Paine of Stepney, Mddx., mariner [of the ship *Charles*, who died in Va.], dated 5 Apr 1703. My whole estate to my wife Susanna Paine who is to be my exex. Wits: William Gully and John Renells, clerk to John Dennis, notary public. Pr. 13 Nov 1710 by relict. (PROB 11/518/251).

1711

Henry Thorpe, late of Liverpool, Lancs., but now residing in Knowsley, Lancs., dated 19 Jun 1710. To be buried in the Quaker ground in Hartshaw near my late wife. All my lands and houses in Penna., of which the deeds are in the custody of Samuel Carpenter of Philadelphia, to my brothers Thomas and John Thorpe and my sister Elizabeth Smalman. Household goods to Elizabeth, wife of my brother Thomas, and their daughter Elizabeth. To Richard and Samuel Smalman, son of my said sister, my pocket watch etc. £10 and clothes to my brother William Thorpe of Yorkshire. Other principal bequests to: Cicely, wife of James Kemp, gardener; Benjamin Boult of Liverpool, shoemaker; John Smallwood of London, merchant, and Thomas his son; Mary Collins of Liverpool; my cousin Lettice Kenrick of Liverpool; James Laithwait, Hannah his wife, and their daughters Martha and Hannah; my kinsman Richard Kelsall of Liverpool, draper. Execs: my brother Thomas Thorpe and my sister Elizabeth Smalman. O'seer: Richard Kelsall. Wits: John Nayler, Arthur Parr and Richard Gardner. Pr. 18 Jan 1711 by solemn declaration of Thomas Thorpe. (PROB 11/519/15). Revoked 28 Jly 1733 on death of Thomas Thorpe and admon. to William Henderson, husband and adr. of Elizabeth Henderson alias Smalman deceased, the only surviving legatee Elizabeth Savage alias Thorpe, wife of Henry Savage, renouncing.

Thomas Leeth of Stepney, Mddx., mariner [of the merchant ship *Anne and Mary*, who died in Va.], dated 24 Oct 1693. My sister Jane Usher, wife of John Usher of Stepney, mariner, to be my attorney, legatee and exex. Wits: Elizabeth Welborn, Grace Emerson, Nathaniel Hake and John Dennis, notary public. Pr. 11 May 1711 by Jane Holmes alias Usher, now wife of John Holmes. (PROB 11/521/109).

John Paston of Old Stratford, Warw., gent., [who died in America], dated 10 Jan 1702. My lands in Dorsington and Bragington, Glos., and in Old Stratford, Welcombe and Bishopston, Warw., to my brother Samuel Paston of Bath, Som., apothecary. £50 to my mother Elizabeth Paston who is to be my exex. £50 each to my sisters Elizabeth and Mary Paston. A golden guinea each to my uncle Mr. William Rawlins and my aunt Mrs. Jane Rawlins. Wits: Thomas Woolmer, John Hunt Jr. and John Woolmer. Pr. 5 Jun 1711 by the mother. (PROB 11/521/136).

Nathaniel Sale of London, merchant, [who died in Charles Town, Carolina], dated 18 Mar 1709. £10 for mourning to my friend and former partner Mr. Crispin Newcombe of Exeter, merchant. My watch to my nephew William Johnson of Lincoln. My sister Mrs. Mary Johnson, widow of Mr. George Johnson of the Close, Lincoln, is to be exex. Residue to my said sister and her children Jane, William and Mary Johnson, with remainder to my brother Henry Sale of London, peruke maker, my brother John Sale of London, joiner, and my sister Anne Clarke near Laworth, Lincs. Wits: Joseph Hawkins and Susanna Hawkins. Pr. 5 Jun 1711 by named exex. (PROB 11/521/138).

Eusebius King of Bristol, Prince George Co., Va., dated 9 Feb 1709. £20 to John Spaine in whose house I live. £30 to Daniel Sturdivant.

£10 to James Thweats the elder. £20 to Capt. John Bayley of
Barbados, merchant, or if he is dead to his widow, formerly the
wife of Thomas Burnham. £150 to my friend William Randolph
the elder of Henrico Co. who is to be my exec. To Chichester
Sturdivant my 100 acres adjoining Henry Reed. The residue to my
brother William King and Richard Oakley of Wisbech, Cambs. Wits:
John Epes and William Swaine. Pr. 9 Feb 1709 in Prince George
Co. AWW granted London 17 Sep 1711 to Isham Randolph,
attorney for William Randolph in Henrico Co. Further grant in Jan
1713 to Richard Oakley. (PROB 11/523/188).

Thomas Bourne citizen and grocer of London, [tobacconist who died
in Md.], dated 4 August 1703. To be buried in the Quaker ground
in London. My whole estate including houses in White Bear Court
which were mortgaged to Jacob Camfield deceased, to my wife
Mary Bourne who is to be my exex. and maintain and apprentice
my son Jesse Jacob Bourne. If my wife dies before me, my sons
Benjamin and Jesse Jacob Bourne are to be my execs. Wits: William
Leman and William Thomas. Undated codicil. I leave to my wife
my estate in Calvert Co., Md., known as Eltonhead Manor, and she
is to confirm the agreement of 8th day of 2nd month 1704 between
me and my daughter Elizabeth Bourne and release my son Samuel
Bourne from all his debts to me. Wits: Richard Johns, Arthur Young
and William Pollard. AWW granted 2 Oct 1711 by his solemn
affirmation to Benjamin Bourne, attorney for Richard Johns in Md.,
exec. of the relict Mary Bourne now deceased. (PROB 11/523/199).

William Webb of Bristol, mariner, at present residing in Md., dated
Md. 20 Oct 1710. £20 to my daughter Anne, wife of John Hodges
of Bristol. The residue to my said daughter, my son William Webb
and my daughter Elizabeth Webb. My wife Sarah Webb is to be
exex. Wits: William Loch, Francis Holland and James Heath. Pr.
in Md. 24 Nov 1710. Pr. London 30 Oct 1711 by the relict. (PROB
11/523/224).

1712

Benjamin Browne of Salem, Massachusetts, merchant, dated 8 Nov
1708. £200 current to Harvard College, Cambridge, Mass., and £200
current for bringing up poor scholars. £50 current to Salem church,
half to be used for furnishing the Lord's Table and half to purchase
a baptismal bowl. £60 current towards making the grammar school
in Salem a free school. £70 current to the town of Salem for
building an almshouse. £10 to my friend Mr. Nicholas Noyes. £8

to my housekeeper Hannah Elsey. £1,000 current to my nephew Mr. John Winthrop of Boston. £1,000 current to my niece Mrs. Ann Winthrop. £2,000 current to my niece Mrs. Sarah Woodward who dwells in England. £1,000 to my niece Mrs. Mary Lynd, wife of Mr. Benjamin Lynd. £50 to Samuel Browne, son of my nephew Maj. Samuel Browne. £20 to Sarah Browne, daughter of my nephew Capt. John Browne. £50, linen and clothing to my late wife's two sisters. To my brother William Browne Esq. my Indian boy named Peter. £10 to my sister Mrs. Rebecca Browne. My ten acres in North Field, Salem, to Benjamin Lynd, son of my niece Mrs. Mary Lynd, during his life. My dwelling house and new warehouse, the most western on my wharf, to Benjamin Browne, son of my nephew Capt. John Browne. The residue of my estate in Britain, Barbados and N.E. to my said nephews who are to be my execs. Wits: Walter Price, Benjamin Wolcot, T. Barton, Thomas Barnard and Stephen Sewall. AWW granted 10 Jan 1712 to John Ive, attorney for the execs. in N.E. (PROB 11/525/3).

Andrew Cook of St. Giles in the Fields, Middlesex, gent., dated 21 Dec 1711. My two houses in Plumtree Street, St. Giles, known as the Cherry Tree and my land called Cooke Point at the mouth of Great Choptank River, Dorchester Co., Md., to my children Ebenezer Cook and Anne Cook who are to be my execs. Wits: Edward Ebbitt, Katherine (x) Richardson and Francis Simkins. Pr. 2 Jan 1712 by named execs. (PROB 11/525/4).

John Bluck of Shadwell, Middx., mariner, [who died in N.E. on the ship *Samuel*], dated 23 Feb 1711. One shilling each to all who have lawful title to be my relations. Residue to my wife Amy Bluck who is to be my exex. Pr. 7 Feb 1712 by Amy Bluck, mother of the named exex. now deceased. (PROB 11/525/20).

John Fountain of Abingdon, Berkshire, gent., dated 24 Feb 1711. Principal bequests, to be paid after the death of his wife Margaret, to: my cousin Alice Woolhead, daughter of my sister Martha Woolhead deceased; my cousin Thomas Partridge of Leighton Buzzard, Bucks, butcher, and his daughters Mary, Martha and Katherine; my cousin John Ireland of Woburn, Beds., labourer, and his children Anne, Susannah, Henry and Hannah; my cousin Susannah Lake, daughter of my sister Woolhead and wife of Robert Lake of Potsgrove, (Beds.), and their daughters Martha and Susannah; my cousin Elizabeth Partridge, daughter of Robert Partridge, formerly a brewer in Goswell Street; John Carpenter, son of John Carpenter, late of Burford, Oxon., brewer, by his first wife; my cousin Katherine Cheyney, daughter of the said John Carpenter; Mary, wife of John Eustace and one of the daughters of my cousin Mary Phillips, widow; the two children of my cousin Robert Leath;

my cousin Benjamin Kenner of the City of Oxford, tailor, and his
daughter Mary Kenner; Kenner Cooke, son of Martha Cooke. My
six messuages in Abingdon to my said wife with remainder to my
cousin Robert Fountain, now aged about 40, son of my brother
Roger Fountain, wine cooper, who died at Lynn Haven in Va. My
wife Margaret to be sole exex. Wits: Joseph Spinage, Thomas Knapp
and William Holmes. Pr. 16 Feb 1712 by relict. (PROB 11/525/28).

James Thomas [of Philadelphia who died in St. Margaret Lothbury,
London, bachelor], dated 22nd of 4th month 1706. £30 to my
brother Micah Thomas and his children. £20 to my brother Gabriel
Thomas. £20 to my sister Mary Snead and her children. £40 to my
sister Rachell Wharton. An annuity of £20 to my uncle James
Thomas. £50 each to my nieces Elizabeth, Mary and Rachell
Williams. £20 each to my cousins, children of Thomas Wharton
and my sister Rachell his wife. £20 to Edward Shippen Sr. and his
grandchildren Edward and Elizabeth Shippen. £30 to Samuel Preston
and his daughters Margaret and Hannah. Residue to the poor of
Philadelphia. The said Edward Shippen and Samuel Preston of
Philadelphia, merchants, to be my execs. Wits: Philip Russell,
Walton Huling, Jonathan Bayly and Morris Edwards, Sussex Co.
in Delaware Bay. Published 7 Nov 1710. AWW granted 11 Feb
1712 to John Askew, attorney for the named execs. in Philadelphia.
(PROB 11/525/38).

Thomas Cox, citizen and vintner of London, dated 20 May 1709. £80
to be paid to my son Thomas Cox for the benefit of the two
daughters of my late daughter-in-law Mary Test, late wife of Daniel
Test. Forty nobles to my daughter-in-law Mary Frankling and 20
nobles to her six children Thomas, Jacob, Mary, Sarah, Anne and
Elizabeth Frankling. Forty nobles to my daughter-in-law Sarah
Plumstead and 20 nobles to her daughter Mary Plumstead. Other
bequests to: my cousin Richard Cooper near Upton, Glos.; my
cousin Anne Weekes in Trinity Lane; Mary Edwards of Tiddington
near Tewkesbury, Glos.; the poor of Whitechapel, Mddx.; my cousin
Hannah Print, daughter of Thomas Clark of Cheltenham, Glos.;
Mary Plumstead, wife of Clement Plumstead of Pescod Street. To
my wife Anne Cox alias Hinde the interest of £400 by bond from
the Vintners' Company and the rents from two tenements I lately
built in the Quaker burial ground near Coverlid Fields. £100 to my
son Thomas Cox and Grace his wife. To my said son in trust for
his six children Grace, Thomas, John, Anne, Russell and Mary Cox,
800 of my 920 acres in Philadelphia Co., Penna. The other 120
acres and £30 to my cousin Mary Chandler now dwelling in Penna.
To my son John Cox £100 and 400 acres on a branch of Cooper's
Creek, Gloucester Co., West New Jersey. To my son-in-law Lassells

Metcalfe and Christian his wife, my daughter, £100 and my shares in the Penna. Land Co. and the first Old Penna. Co., and in trust for their children £100 which I disbursed to assist William Penn in his composition with Philip Forde. Execs: my wife Anne and my brother-in-law John Antrim of Martin's le Grand, London. O'seers: Jacob Frankling, Samuel Waldenfield and John Field. Wits: John Craig next door to the George in Greek Street, John Saunders at the George, and Matthew Hopkinson, scrivener in Greek Street. Codicil of 13 Dec 1711. Pr. 14 Mar 1712 by affirmation of the relict. (PROB 11/526/46).

Edmund Littlepage [formerly of York River, Va., but late of St. Mary Abchurch, London, who died in Enfield, Middlesex, bachelor], dated 6 May 1712. £500 to my nephew Richard Littlepage on York River, Va. £600 to my niece Elizabeth Walker and £600 to her two children. £200 to my niece Elizabeth Elliott in Thame, Oxon. £100 each to Richard, Edmund, Robert, Hannah, Anne and Elizabeth Page, children of my niece Hannah Page of Lambeth, (Sy.), deceased, and £16 to Richard Page, father of the said children. £50 each to my sister-in-law Mrs. Mary Trull in Horseshoe Alley, Moorfields, and her eldest daughter Mary. £50 to Mrs. Smith at the Feathers, a toyshop in Fore Street. £100 to Mr. Owen, minister at Pewterers' Hall in Lime Street, and £400 for deserving non-conformist ministers. £500 to the Corporation children in Bishopsgate. £30 to the poor of Mary Abchurch. Residue to my nephew Joseph Littlepage who is to be my exec. O'seers: Mr. William Prince and Mr. Thomas Hodgson. No witnesses shown. On 8 Aug 1712 Thomas Mercer, book-keeper to the Bank of England, and John Howse of St. Mary Abchurch, citizen and goldsmith of London, deposed that they knew the testator who died on 30 Jly last. The deponents were present with John Brumwich, Benjamin Joseph Jr., Joseph Littlepage and Mr. Cooke, attorney, when the will was drawn up. Pr. 8 Aug 1712 by exec. named. (PROB 11/528/157).

Henry Fielding of King and Queen County, Va., gent., dated 26 Oct 1704. My plantation which I bought of John Durratt and £30 to John Adamson who is to have his freedom after he has gathered in my tobaccos and bills of exchange. £20 each to John and Mary Howell. £2 each for mourning to Mme. Mary Lane, Col. Gawin Corbin and Mme. Jane Corbin. £20 to my cousin Francis Thompson in England. £10 to Jane Corbin, daughter of Mme. Jane Corbin. £10 to Mrs. Frigatt for her care of me. £10 for mourning to Mr. John Story. Residue to my daughter Frances Fielding but, if she dies before she comes of age or marries, my estates in England and Va. are to go to my mother Mme. Frances Fielding and John and Mary Howell. If any negro ships of the Royal Africa Co. arrive from the West Indies consigned to me, Col. Gawin Corbin is to have the sales and management thereof. Mourning rings to Mme. Mary Lane and Capt. Edward Lewis. £5 to Mr. Isaac Hill. Execs: my said mother, Arthur Bayly Esq. and Mr. Francis Thompson in England; Col. Gawin Corbin and Mr. John Story in Va. Wits: John Spicer, James (x) Dinglass and William (x) Collins. Pr. 27 Nov 1712 by Francis Thompson. (PROB 11/529/208).

Henry Sway of N.Y., mariner of H.M. ship *Star Bomb*, dated Port Royal, Jamaica, 5 Dec 1711. My friend Morgan Williams, bombadier of the said ship, is to be my sole legatee and exec. Wits: Charles Trewbody, John Kirkdell and Henry Antrobus. Pr. Nov 1712 by the named exec. (PROB 11/529/220).

1713

David Bell of St. Giles in the Fields, Mddx., surgeon, [who died in Albany Fort, America], dated 25 Apr 1702. My whole estate to my wife Elizabeth Bell who is to be my exex. Wits: Timothy Davison and Robert Johnson, notary public. Pr. 26 Jan 1713 by relict. (PROB 11/531/2).

John Fox of Camberwell, Sy., mariner of H.M. ship *Rochester*, [who died in Boston, N.E.], dated 27 Oct 1708. My friend Anne Perry of St. George the Martyr, Southwark, Sy., spinster, is to be my legatee and exec. Wits: Emanuel Hillington and Roger Beavans, scrivener near St. Margaret's Hill, Southwark. Pr. 12 Jan 1713 by named exex. (PROB 11/531/7).

Sem Cox of St. Mary's, Richmond, Va., dated 18 Oct 1710. To be buried beside my late daughter at Robert Peck's plantation. My tobacco is to be shipped to Mr. John Collyer, merchant in Bristol. My water grist mill called Head's Mill to Joseph Downing, son of George Downing by Anne his wife and she is to receive the rents thereof during her son's minority. A good pair of stones is to be funished for the said mill. My Indian man called Will is to be freed and to have clothes and 1,000 lbs of tobacco. My negro woman Rose and her two children to the said Joseph Downing. An orphan child Elizabeth Colins is to have 1,000 lbs of tobacco and is to be cared for by the said Anne Downing. Jim Richardson, son of James Richardson, is to stay with my exec. or return to his father. The land which was given to me by deed by William Bury is to go to his daughter Margaret Bury, and she is to have three ewes and a lamb. I confirm that I have sold 220 acres and another 136 acres which I lately bought of Robert Taliaferro and Margaret his wife in St. Mary's Richmond to Thomas White. To George, son of the said George Downing, 2,000 lbs of tobacco. To my friend Edward Tuberville 1,000 lbs of tobacco. Benjamin Deverill and George Downing are to be my execs. Wits: Thomas Evans, George Alsup and Edward Tuberville. On 12 Oct 1711 Marmaduke Beckwith of Richmond Co. deposes that he well knew the testator and that the will is a true copy. Pr. same day by named Benjamin Deverill. (PROB 11/523/204).

Thomas Markin of London, [of Stepney, Mddx.], mariner, now bound to sea, [master of the *Sarah & Hannah* who died in Md.], dated 13 Nov 1711. £2,000 to my wife Sarah Markin in accordance with the bond I made before our marriage. £200 in trust to Benjamin Bradley and James Bradley of London, merchants, for the benefit of my mother Sarah Sevencraft, widow, with remainder to the children of my sister Ann Alderton. My said wife is to be exex. but, if she dies before me, I leave £1,000 to each of her children by her first husband John Harrison, mariner. To each child of my brother Nicholas Markin of London, mariner, £ [blank]. Wits: Thomas Willing, Thomas Markey, William Young and Samuel Prigg, attorney in Bristol. On 7 Nov 1712 Sarah Markin, widow, deposed that she married the testator in Dec 1710 and knows that he made no other will save one which he burned shortly after their marriage. On 22 Nov 1711 her husband sailed from Bristol in his ship bound for Md. where he died. Pr. 17 Feb 1713 by relict. (PROB 11/531/42).

N.B. Depositions were taken in Bristol in 1712 to establish the circumstances in which this will was drawn up - See NGSQ 66/220.

Robert Paston Esq., Captain of H.M. ship *Feversham*, dated 12 Sep 1711. My whole estate to Ann Hyde, now at N.Y., spinster. Execs: my friends Adolph Phillips and George Clarke, both of N.Y. Wits: Catharina Brett, Robert Fog and Robert Milward. AWW, after sentence for validity, granted 13 Feb 1713 to Benjamin Edmonds, attorney for execs. in N.Y.; admon. of Jly 1712 to Thomas Sandford revoked. (PROB 11/531/44).

Thomas Harwood Esq. of Streatley, Berks, dated 22 Apr 1704. My son Richard Harwood to have all my plantations in Md. By his will of 24 Aug 1700 my late son John Harwood left half his estate to his son Swanley Harwood. Other bequests to: my grandchildren Mary, Thomas and Anne Burley; my son Thomas Harwood; my daughter Sarah Abery; my grandsons Thomas, John and Harwood Abery; my grandchildren Elizabeth, Mary, Anne and Martha Wyld; my daughter Elizabeth Brent. Wits: John Hosea, Alexander Hoggon and John Booker. Pr. 14 Mar 1713 by the son Rev. Thomas Harwood. (PROB 11/532/61).

Thomas Nowell of [St. Dunstan in the West], London, gent., dated 24 Jan 1713. My estate to my exec. in trust Alexander Nesbett Esq. for the benefit of my daughter Mrs. Martha Marshall. Wits: Elenor Ryder, Rebeccah Pagett and Eli Brooke. AWW granted 18 Mar 1713 to legatee Martha Marshall, wife of John Marshall in N.E., the named exec. renouncing. (PROB 11/532/65).

Richard Wharton, eldest son of William Wharton late of Waitby near Wharton, Westmorland, gent., and now resident in Williamsburg, Va., dated 26 Jly 1712. My whole estate to my brothers Thomas and John Wharton of London, gents., who may sell the same, with the exception of slaves, only with the approval of Henry Holdcroft in trust for the benefit of my child or children. My son William Wharton is to inherit the said lands but none shall go to my daughter. My wife Ruth is to employ an honest attorney to demand her dower from lands in Westmorland which are under any old mortgage to the Lowthers or others. All my negroes and other servants are to be sold forthwith to meet my debts. My cattle and other goods in Va. are to be sold by my friend Henry Holdcroft and his neighbour Mr. Richard Richardson and I make them my execs. for Va. My said wife is to be exex. for England. I leave £5 to my goddaughter Mary, daughter of Henry Holdcroft. The poor widow Skelton alias Broadbent and her daughter are to live in my stone house or turret and to have apples for their use, pasturage for a cow and a yearly allowance of corn. Wits: Dionysia Hadley, Christopher Philipson, William Smith, Samuel Boy and John Sarjanton. AWW granted 1 Apr 1713 to the brothers Thomas and John Wharton, the relict renouncing. (PROB 11/532/93).

John Ryley, mariner [of H.M. ships *Winchelsea* and *Chester*, who died in Boston, N.E.], dated 31 Mar 1712. My house in Greenwich, (Kent), to my brother-in-law Bryan Northen, and I forgive the rents due by the tenant thereof, John Ingham. To my brother William Ryley my two houses in Crane Street, Greenwich. Wages due to me for my sea service and any money in the hands of my uncle Nathaniel Ryley to my brother Croucher. My brothers Hugh Dyer and Bryan Northen to be execs. Wits. John Scrivener, John Shaw and William Fervis. Pr. 16 Jun 1713 by Bryan Northen, the other exec. having died. (PROB 11/534/144).

John Buy the elder of Reading, Berks., mealman, dated 4 Jly 1707. £200 to my wife Mary. To my son John Buy my tenement and malthouse in London Street, Reading, which I purchased of William Castell, with remainder to my son William Buy. My lands in Penna. to my said two sons, the £25 paid by William Lamboll for my use to the Free Society of Traders in Penna., and the money owed to me by my brother Robert Buy. Residue to my wife and she and my sons to be execs. Wits: James Quarrington, William Douglas Sr., Mary Coad and William Douglas Jr. Pr. 18 Aug 1713 by affirmation of the sons. (PROB 11/535/184).

William Bessill of Southampton, mariner [of St. Margaret, Westminster, Mddx., who died in Va.], dated 9 Jan 1707. My whole estate to my wife Mary who is to be my exex. and one shilling each to any relations who may have a claim on me. Wits: William Winter, Stephen Sibley Sr. and Mary Winter. Pr. 17 Sep 1713 by relict. (PROB 11/535/201).

Arthur Jackson of Bristol, surgeon, [who died at Quarry Creek, Potomack River, Stafford County, Va., bachelor], dated 18 Jun 1702 aboard the *John* near Lundy Island. My estate to be divided between my father Arthur Jackson Sr., my sister Elizabeth Jackson, my sister Rachel Jackson and my brother Thomas Jackson. Copy letter from John Waugh [of Stafford Co., Va.] to James Kelson of Bristol: I will do all possible to get what is due to you on the death of your brother and have taken out letters of administration in your name. Your brother's negro is not yet sold and there was another negro sent to your brother by Mr. Elton for sale. A Bill of Exchange was drawn by Mr. Benoni Thomas when he was bedridden with gout on Mr. John Gooding, merchant in London. I am obliged to employ an attorney at Williamsburg. Deposition sworn Bristol 7 Nov 1713 by Elizabeth Kelson alias Jackson, wife of James Kelson, whip-maker, and Rachel End alias Jackson, wife of Joseph End of Bristol, carpenter. They are sisters of the testator who died in Va. on 9 May 1713 leaving them, his brother Thomas Jackson and his father (since deceased) as his only relatives. On 13 Jly 1713 the deponents received the above letter which enclosed a copy of the testator's will endorsed by Henry Parry, Deputy Clerk of Stafford Co. It was brought over by the *Hartford*, Capt. Scandrith. AWW granted 18 Nov 1713 to the said sisters; admon. of Jly 1712 to the father now revoked. (PROB 11/537/258).

William Glencross of N.Y., about to depart thither from London, dated 11 Feb 1709. Broughton Wright to be my sole legatee and exec. Wits: Joseph Ward and John Dennis, notary public. Pr. 9 Dec 1713 by exec. named. (PROB 11/537/271).

1714

Humphrey Todd of Wapping, Mddx., mariner [of H.M. ship *Deptford*, who died on H.M. ship *Adventure* in Boston, N.E.], dated 11 Feb 1709. My friends John Slater of Wapping, carver, and Elianor his wife to be sole legatees and execs. Wits: Gilbert Heath, Owen Byrne and William Lanman, notary public. Pr. 4 Feb 1714 by John Slater. (PROB 11/538/40).

Joseph John Jackman of Surrey Co., Va., gent. [who died in Deal, Kent], dated 27 Apr 1714. £5 to my mother Catherine Jackman. To my godson Josiah John Halliman my 100 acres on the south side of Notoway River in Isle of Wight Co. known as Joseph's Mount, my large bible, cattle, etc. £10 to my brother William Jackman. £5 to each child of my sister Mary Harris. £20 to my brother-in-law Richard Slade and Catherine his wife and £20 each to their children Thomas and Mary Slade. £5 each to my friends Maj. Nathaniel Harrison of Surrey Co., William Robertson of Williamsburg, York Co., gent., Ethelred Tayler of Surrey Co., gent., and Nathaniel Ridley of Isle of Wight Co., gent. £5 to the poor of Lower Wallop, Hampshire. Twenty shillings each for mourning to my sister-in-law Catherine Allen and my cousins John and Arthur Allen. A ring of 20 shillings to Capt. Isham Robertson. My plantation of 300 acres in Lawnes Creek in Surrey Co. where I lately dwelt, the 590 acres adjoining which I bought of Mr. William Butler, a water mill I purchased of Capt. Robert Kea at the head of Lawnes Creek, and my other lands of 1,000 acres on the south side of Notoway River to my friends Nathaniel Harrison, William Robertson, Ethelred Tayler and Nathaniel Ridley in trust to be sold and the produce thereof with my tobaccos to be remitted to Micajah and Richard Perry of London, merchants, for the use of my wife Mary Jackman who is to be my exex. Wits: Isham Randolph, Jeremiah Lirland, Graves Parke, Robert Jordan Jr. and Godfrey Pole. Pr. 22 May 1714 by the relict. (PROB 11/540/98).

John Rowland of Shadwell, Mddx., mariner, [of N.E., who died on passage from France to London], dated 15 Sep 1709. My whole estate to Joseph Dearing of Shadwell, mariner, and Mary his wife who are to be execs. Wits: Mary Sally and Marina Hodgson, servant to Mr. Pomeroy. AWW 19 Jly 1714 to Francis Cane, attorney and husband of the mother Abigail Cane in N.E., Joseph Dearing renouncing and Mary Dearing having died. (PROB 11/541/145).

Richard Chandler of Portobacco Creek, Charles Co., Md., dated 12 Apr 1712. My entire estate including plantations to my only brother Mr. William Chandler. All debts to be paid including one to my exec. Mr. Ralph Pigott, son of Nathaniel Pigott Esq. of the Middle Temple, London. Wits: Jonas Buckley, Francis Lynch and John Howard. Pr. 7 Oct 1714. (PROB 11/542/189).

John Dunkan of Stepney, Mddx. [of the merchant ship *Society*, who died in Va.], dated 13 Dec 1712. My whole estate to my friend

Elizabeth Browne who is to be my exex. Wits: Thomas Calderwood, James Findley and Margaret Findley. Pr. 8 Nov 1714 by Elizabeth, wife of David Browne. (PROB 11/543/217).

1715

William Jeffreys of St. James, Westminster, mariner [of the merchant ship *Mary and Francis*, who died in Va., bachelor], dated 7 Sep 1711. My whole estate to my uncle John Jeffreys of St. James, haberdasher, who is to be my exec. Pr. 9 Jan 1715 by exec. named. (PROB 11/544/10).

Moses Wickham of Southampton, master of H.M. ship *Sorlings*, now in N.Y., dated 13 Apr 1713. My whole estate, including what is due to me as prize money from the taking of the *Dolphin*, to my wife Eleanor Wickham who is to provide for my children. £3 for mourning to Thomas Orr, gent., purser of the said ship, who is to be my exec. in trust. Wits: Nathan Simpson, Thomas Braines, Robert Robinson, Thomas Graham and Robert Neeres. Pr. 22 Jan 1715 by exec. named. (PROB 11/544/17).

John Aderne of Bickton, Cheshire, gent., bound for Carolina by the *Carolina Merchant*, commander Thomas Foster, [who died in Carolina], dated 28 Feb 1699. £10 to my brother Ralph Aderne. £5 each to my sisters Mary Aderne and Margaret Hall, wife of James Hall. A golden guinea to my brother-in-law Robert Meeke of Slaithwaite, Yorks., clerk. A golden guinea to Mr. Ralph Aderne, second son of Sir John Aderne of Arderne, Chesh. The goods in my house at Clayton Bridge, Manchester, Lancs., to my sister Margaret Hall. Residue to my cousin Edward Warren of London, merchant, who is to be my exec. Wits: John Robins, Charles Boddam and Thomas Furnivall. Pr. 28 Apr 1715 by exec. named. (PROB 11/545/63).

Thomas Waple of London, distiller, [of Md., bachelor], dated 4 Apr 1713. £5 to the charity school of Shoreditch, Mddx. The residue to my brothers Osmund and Henry Waple and my sisters Susannah Forward and Sarah Waple. My brother Henry Waple and brother-in-law Jonathan Forward to be execs. Wits: John Scrimshire and James Cruley. Pr. 8 Apr 1715 by execs. named. (PROB 11/545/79).

Daniel Hamson of Stepney, Mddx., mariner [of H.M. ship *Mermaid*, who died on the merchant ship *Hamilton*, bachelor], dated 26 Sep 1712. My friend John Newby to be my sole legatee and exec. Wits: Richard Yerbury, Philip Townsend and William Hoyden. AWW 27

Jun 1715 to Thomas Newby, attorney for John Newby in N.E. (PROB 11/546/114).

Peter Clifford of Whitechapel, Middx., gunsmith, [who died in Annapolis in the West Indies], dated 20 Sep 1719. My whole estate to my wife Mary Clifford who is to be my exex. Wits: Mary Halford, Edward Bellas and Jonathan Cranwell, scrivener. Pr. 7 Jly 1715 by relict. (PROB 11/547/131).

John Fulham [of Carolina], sergeant in Capt. Henly's Company of Col. Holt's Regiment of Marines on board H. M. ship *Royal Oak*, dated 19 Jan 1703. My wife Ursula Fulham to be my sole legatee and exex. Wits: John Suffield, notary public, and Anthony Seager. Pr. 1 Sep 1715 by relict. (PROB 11/548/173).

Edward Jukes of Charles Town, S.C., dated 4 Oct 1710. My wife Dorothy Jukes to be my sole legatee and exex. Wits: Charles Craven, Gideon Johnston, Nicholas Trott and James Baron. Pr. 14 Nov 1715 by relict. (PROB 11/549/221).

1716

John Burnett of Stanstead Abbots, Herts, [of N.E., who died abroad or at sea], dated 19 Jly 1704. All my real and personal estate in Stanstead to my brother Samuel Burnett including my 5 acres called the Moores on condition that he pays my mother Deborah Lowd an annuity of £3 with remainder to my aunt Mrs. Sarah Aunger of Ware, Herts. Thomas Aunger of Ware to be my exec. Wits: Edward Burnett, Isaac Ducasse and Elizabeth Norris. Pr. 11 Jan 1716 by the named exec. (PROB 11/550/1).

Edward Scott of H.M. ship *Nightingale*, dated Annapolis, Md., 4 Sep 1714. My father James Scott to be my sole legatee and exec. Wits: William Ball, Robert Boddell and Godfrey Withers. AWW 27 Mar 1716 to the brother William Scott, the father being dead and the mother Bridget Scott renouncing. (PROB 11/551/58).

Samuel Stacy of H.M. ship *Nightingale* now at Annapolis, Md., [who died in N.E.], dated 18 Aug 1715. £16 sterling to my aunt Elizabeth Ross in Annapolis to be paid out of my wages. Residue to my father John Stacy of St. Clement Danes, Mddx., and after his decease to my brother and exec. John Stacy who is to share my estate between himself, Benjamin, Jeremiah, Hannah, Mary and Katherine Stacy. Wits: Richard Shaw, David (x) Millew and Eli Bilton. Pr. 9 Mar 1716 by named exec. (PROB 11/551/59).

Samuel Barlow of Deptford, Kent, mariner of H.M. ship *Montague* [of H.M. ship *Shoreham* who died in Va.], dated 1 Mar 1694. My wife Elizabeth Barlow to be my attorney, legatee and exex. Wits: Henry Dabdin, John Wadham and Thomas Benson, churchwardens of Deptford, and Jerome Collins. Pr. 4 Jun 1716 by the relict. (PROB 11/552/111).

Thomas Davenport of London, merchant, [of N.Y.], dated 22 Feb 1699. All my household goods to my sister Alice, wife of Mr. Matthew Measures. Residue to my brothers Richard and William Davenport and my sisters Elizabeth, wife of John Cartwright, Annis, wife of Thomas Hunt, and the said Alice Measures. William Horsepool of London, merchant, to be my exec. Wits: P. Belin, Thomas Martin and John Stelfax. Pr. 8 Aug 1716 by named exec. (PROB 11/553/161).

James Dumotier, merchant living in London, dated 27 Mar 1713. (Translated from French). £20 to the French church in Threadneedle Street, London. To my son Peter Dumotier the £40 I promised when he gave me his general release of 31 May 1708. £10 to my nephew Gardon or his wife who live in Carolina. £10 each to my cousin Bretevil, wife of Mr. Baille, and to Mr. Le Bessin and his wife. £5 to my godson, the son of Mr. Chois, buttonmaker. The residue to my wife Judith Dumotier, John Raynold and Theodore Marnasse who are to be execs. in trust for my said son, for James Dumotier, grandson of my deceased brother John Dumotier, and for the children of my niece, the wife of the said Mr. Theodore Marnasse. Wits: James Douxsaint and James de Brissac. Pr. 10 Feb 1715 by the relict. (PROB 11/544/23). Revoked and granted Nov 1722 to James Dumotier of St. Paul Covent Garden, Middlesex.

Samuel Creake of Limehouse, Middx., [master of the ship *Britannia*, who died in Md.], dated 23 Jan 1710. To my mother Mary Creake £50 and half my freeholds in Whaplode, Lincs., during her life with remainder to my wife Mary Creake who is to be my exex. My said mother and wife to have my customary holding in the Manor of Gedney and Welby, Lincs., which I have surrendered to the uses of my will. Wits: Nathaniel Goodwin, Humphrey Brent, scrivener, and Henry Wills Jr., his servant. Pr. 1 Oct 1716 by affirmation of the relict. (PROB 11/554/187).

Humphrey Taylor [of Penna.], now of Stepney, Mddx., shipwright, [who died in N.Y., widower], dated 29 Nov 1710. To my wife Mary Taylor £20 a year from the rents of my tenements wherever they are. The residue of the rents to my mother Elizabeth Taylor. To the eldest daughter of my cousin Joan Lyden £5 a year until £100 is paid, and she is to pay my wife £20 a year with remainder to my sister Mary Ragg. The residue to my wife who is to be exex. Wits: Samuel Samson, Sarah Symonds and Richard Symonds, notary public at Marine Square, Ratcliffe. Pr. 16 Oct 1716 by the mother Elizabeth Taylor, widow, the wife having died. (PROB 11/554/198).

John Sadler, late of [St. Stephen Walbrook], London, and now of Hunsdon, Herts., dated 2 Jan 1799. To my exec. Sir Charles Ingleby my moiety of a plantation of 6,400 acres called Martins Brandon near James River, Va., and a moiety of another nearby called Martins Hope of 1,900 acres, in trust to pay my the rents thereof to my daughter Elizabeth Sadler. I forgive Thomas Jackson, my tenant in Va., what he owes me. Other bequests to Mr. Charles Spencer and Mr. Charles Stafford. Wits: John Jenkinson, John Bennett and Francis Demayne. Pr. 16 Nov 1716 by named exec. (PROB 11/555/215).

1717

Richard Haman of St. Olave, Southwark, Surrey, mariner [who died on the merchant ship *New York* in N.Y.], dated 20 Feb 1715. My wife Anne Haman to be my sole legatee and exex. Wits: W. Holloway, notary public, and N. Campbell, his servant. Pr. 1 Feb 1717 by relict. (PROB 11/556/32).

William Bevis of Topsham, Devon, mariner, [master of the merchant ship *Hope*, who died in Va.], dated 7 Oct 1715. To my son William Bevis my house in Monmouth Street in the occupation of John Mead and Robert Yonge. To my son Benedict Bevis my house in Topsham. Residue to my wife Margaret who is to be exec. in trust with Mr. John Weston of Topsham, baker, for the benefit of my said children. Wits: George Godard, Elizabeth Furse and John Harris. Pr. 26 Mar 1717 by relict. (PROB 11/557/54).

Robert Hilton of Dukes's Place, Mddx., merchant, [formerly of N.E., but late of London], dated 15 Feb 1717. My whole estate to my friends Samuel Lilly and Alexander Holmes of Duke's Place, merchants. Wits: John Trobell, notary public, Lawrence Bath and Abigail (x) Manchester. Pr. 13 Mar 1717 by Samuel Lilly. (PROB 11/557/61).

Thomas Keech surgeon of the merchant ship *Goodwill*, Capt. John Crawley, [who died in Md.], dated 2 Mar 1716. To my friend George Fisher, citizen and surgeon of London, £14.12s.6d. and he is to be my exec. Residue to my wife Elizabeth Keech. Wits: Katherine Charriot, John Bayly and S. Wilcocke, notary public. Pr. 29 Nov 1717 by exec. named. (PROB 11/561/215).

Gresham Otway of St. James, Westminster, Mddx., [of the environs of Boston, N.E.], spinster, dated 1 Nov 1710. I am indebted by bond for £110 to my uncle Edward Benskin of St. Martin the in the Fields, Mddx., gent., and I bequeath all my estate to him and to his wife Frances Benskin whom I make my execs. Any residue of my estate is to be distributed as they think proper to my sisters. Wits: Richard Duke, Ann Duke, Mary Hill and Joseph Hunt, scrivener near St. James's House. Pr. 28 Nov 1718 by Edward Benskin, the other exec. having died. (PROB 11/561/217).

John Marshall of Shadwell, Mddx., mariner [of the merchant ship *Resolution*, who died in Md.]. My wife Sarah Marshall to be my sole legatee and exex. Wits: Ellinor Cosin, John Cosin and Robert Pickering. Pr. 3 Dec 1717 by relict. (PROB 11/561/236).

1718

William Topping, surgeon of the merchant ship *Boughton*, Capt. Thomas, [who died on the merchant ship *New York Postilion* in N.Y.], dated 14 Aug 1707. My wife Ann Topping to be my sole legatee and exex. Wits: John Sheen, John Davis and John Bright. Pr. 21 Jan 1718 by relict. (PROB 11/562/19).

Joseph Dunn of St. Olave, Southwark, Surrey, [who died in Md.], dated 25 Dec 1714. My wife Elizabeth Dunn to be my sole legatee and exex. Wits: Ralph Studd, Alexander Hume and Robert Hume. Pr. 10 Apr 1718 by relict. (PROB 11/563/76).

Thomas Howson [of Md.], son of Mary Howson, the daughter of Mr. Street, and my lawful mother, who is to be my exex. and to have whatever is in the hands of my uncle and Mr. Raye. I cut off my sister Mary Hanson with a shilling. "So ends my last will because I shall not be here after Christmas. I write now that it may come into force in January 1701(/2)." Wits: Thomas Goodman, Obadiah King and Thomas Frances. Pr. 10 Jun 1718 by the mother. (PROB 11/564/119).

James Traiell of Shadwell, Mddx., mariner, [who died on H.M. ship *Shoreham* in Va.]. My wife Margery Traiell to be my sole legatee and exex. Wits: Mary (x) Burch, Elabathes Gotes and James Thompson, notary public. Pr. Jun 1718 by the relict. (PROB 11/564/134).

John Chrystie, surgeon [of the merchant ship *Rumsey*, who died at York River, Va., bachelor], dated 25 Jly 1716. My friend Elizabeth Cheshire of Wapping, Mddx., spinster, to be my sole legatee and exex. Wits: Richard Cheshire Jr., Sarah (x) Alexander and Jon. Thomas, notary public in Wapping. Pr. 28 Nov 1784 by Elizabeth Grimes alias Cheshire, wife of William Grimes. (PROB 11/566/211).

William Jones of Rotherhithe, Surrey, shipwright, bound overseas by the *Tunstone* Indiaman, Capt. Adams, [and who died in Va.], dated 22 Jan 1717. My friend Thomas May to be my sole legatee and exec. Wits: Sampson Barrett, Sarah Crump and Isaac Crump, scrivener in Rotherhithe. Pr. 18 Dec 1718 by named exec. (PROB 11/566/241).

1719

John Page of Gloucester County, Va., now designing a voyage to England [who died in Bethnal Green, Mddx., merchant], dated 20 Apr 1709. To my daughter Elizabeth Page all her mother's clothes etc. and five guineas when she is 12 on 4 Nov 1714 and all that is due to her from the estate of Capt. Francis Page and Mrs. Elizabeth Page, her mother, deceased, which will make £3,000 when she is 21. To my daughter Mary Page £3,000 when she is 21 on 26 Jan 1728 or is married. To my daughter-in-law Martha Page all her mother's rings and jewels etc. To my son-in-law Mann Page on his arrival in Va. a saddle horse, a large bible, and a picture of his father and mother, the late Matthew Page and Mrs. Mary Page, himself and his two sisters Alice and Martha. By deed of 20 Sep 1705 before my marriage to my late wife, mother of the said Mann Page, I agreed to confer on her £2,000 in negroes, cattle and stock and 13s.4d. for every 100 lbs of tobacco on Mann Page's plantation in New Kent Co. The said Mann Page shall now have all my negroes, except the carpenters George and Jenny and the house wenches Doll and Poll, cattle and stock for his plantation in Gloucester Co. £20 to my godson Bouth Napier, son of Robert Napier, when he is 21. To my godson Matthew Walker, son of Mr. Joseph Walker of York Co., when he is 21, £30 for the purchase of two negro children. The residue to my son John Page when he is 18 on 22 Dec 1717 and then to be my exec. My execs. in trust are to be Edmond Berkley of Gloucester Co., the said Mr. Joseph Walker, Mr. Robert Anderson Jr. of New Kent Co. and Mr. Richard Wilsheir of Gloucester Co. Wits: Guy Smith, John Pratt and Hugh Hughes. On 2 January 1719 Micajah Perry and Richard Perry of St. Catherine Creechurch, London, merchants, and John Page of York Co., Va., gent., depose that the testator died at Bethnal Green in 1710 and that this will is in his hand. Pr. 2 Jan 1719 by the son John Page. (PROB 11/567/14).

William Wright Esq. of St. Ann, Westminster, shortly to go beyond the seas [who died in Annapolis Royal], dated 21 Jun 1715. My wife Sarah Wright to be my sole legatee and exex. Wits: John Parris, John Blacksley and Edward Yonge. Pr. 25 Feb 1719 by relict. (PROB 11/567/38).

Peter Hemard of Spitalfields, Mddx., weaver, [who died in Va.], dated 14 Sep 1713. On the marriage of my daughter Anne to John Jacob Cailleau I gave them what I could in the circumstances and I now give them and their children one shilling each. The residue to my wife and exex. Elizabeth with remainder to my said daughter and the deacons of the French Church in Threadneedle Street, London, for the poor and appoint Messrs. Claude Baudouin and Peter Geneves execs. in trust. By his will of 16 Oct 1712 Daniel Brulon of Jamaica, merchant deceased, appointed me guardian of his sons Daniel and Isaac Brulon and I now commit the guardianship to my wife. Wits: Isaac Delpeech, notary public, and Daniel Olivier. Pr. 17 Mar 1719 by relict. (PROB 11/567/47).

James Barbot of St. Margaret, Westminster, Mddx., merchant, bound on a voyage to sea [who died in Md.], dated 20 Mar 1703. One-third of my estate to my wife Mary Barbot and two-thirds to my children. I entrust to the care of my brother John Barbot the education of any child my wife may bear. My said wife and brother to be my execs. Wits: James Barbot Sr. and Susan Assally. Pr. 27 Apr 1719 by the relict, the brother John Barbot having died. (PROB 11/568/60).

Mary Buy of Reading, Berkshire, widow (of John Buy whose will was proved in 1713), dated 22 Aug 1717. £10 to my son-in-law John Buy who is to be my exec. My household goods to my daughters Mary Dell and Mary Foster. I leave to my son-in-law Thomas Dell the house and plantation of 375 acres in Ridley, Chester Co., Penna., which he mortgaged to William Passmore, now of Hurst, Wilts., but late of Philadelphia, clothier, and which he assigned to me. Bequest to my kinswoman Dorothy Walker of High Wycombe, Bucks., widow. My friends William Lamboll of Reading, mealman, and Peter Briggins of Bartholomew Close, London, to be overseers. Wits: Timothy Wesley, Margaret Cane and William Douglas. Pr. 11 Jun 1719 by the affirmation of John Buy. (PROB 11/569/100).

Lady Catherine Fairfax, Baroness Dowager of Cameron, Scotland, dated 21 Apr 1719. To be buried in Broomfield church, (Kent) near my mother Lady Margaret Culpepper. My lands and plantation in Va. to my execs. in trust William Cage Esq. of Milgate in Bersted, Kent, and Edward Filmer Esq. of East Sutton, Kent, to the use of my eldest son Thomas Lord Fairfax with remainder to my sons Henry Culpepper Fairfax and Robert Fairfax. I made a bond with

George Sayer Esq. deceased to pay £800 to my daughter Catherine but she has died intestate and I invest her estate in my execs. in trust. Other bequests to my daughters Margaret and Frances. Wits: D. Fuller, John Mason and E. Finch. Pr. 3 Jun 1719 by William Cage. (PROB 11/569/105).

Michael Arlington [of Stepney, Mddx., mariner of H.M. ship *Lyme* [who died in Va.]. My friends Nathan Movelty and Sarah his wife to be my legatees and execs. Wits: John (x) Stargicall and Richard Symonds, notary public. Pr. 18 Aug 1719 by Nathan Movelty. (PROB 11/569/140).

Michael Cole of Ratcliffe, Mddx., mariner, setting out to sea, dated 31 Jan 1717. My lands in Poplar, Mddx., and houses in Harry's Court near Brooke Street, Ratcliffe, in trust to my friends Mr. Samuel Vaus, Mr. George Manwaring, Mr. William Ricketts and Mr. Jonathan Shakespeare of London, merchants, for the use of my son Philip Cole during his life with remainder to my children Michael Cole, Thomas Cole, Rachel Cole, Mary wife of Richard Davister and Elizabeth wife of Paul Lillywhite. To my sons Michael and Thomas Cole £1,800 in bonds in the hands of Col. William Rhett of S.C. Accounts annexed show that the testator owned seven-sixteenths of the ship *Elizabeth*. Pr. 3 Aug 1719 by Samuel Vaus and Jonathan Shakespeare. (PROB 11/569/142).

George Walker of St. Giles Cripplegate, London, cook of H.M. hospital ship *Pembroke* [who died on H.M. ship *Pearl* in Va.], dated 29 Mar 1709. One shilling to my wife Margaret Walker. Residue to my friends George Chapman of St. Margaret, Westminster, chandler, and Hannah his wife who are to be execs. Wits: Thomas Marlow, George Baker and Stephen Bellas, clerk to Mr. Huett, attorney near the Navy Office. Pr. 13 Aug 1719 by George Chapman. (PROB 11/570/154).

William Marriott Esq. of Grays Inn, Mddx., dated 2 Aug 1717. To Mr. Gerard Vander Neden of Trinity College, Cambridge, £1,500 for the benefit of my late wife's relations. To my half-brother Mr. George Marriott all my lands in Towcester and Heathencote Fields, Northants., with remainder to his eldest son. £300 to my cousin William Cooper in trust for my cousin Jane Rayner. Other bequests to: my cousin Dorothy Plumpton, widow; my friend Henry Boult; my cousin Benjamin Sharp. The residue to be divided between my said brother George Marriott, the three sons left by my sister (Dorothy) Waters at her death in Va., and my exec. William Cooper. Wits: Thomas Bullock, Jane Bullock, his wife, and Jane Bullock, his daughter. Pr. 9 Sep 1719 by named exec. (PROB 11/570/167). See NGSQ 62/199.

John Hawkins of Queen Anne Co. Md., dated 23 Apr 1717. To my
eldest son John Hawkins £200 and he is to discharge his mortgage
to Richard Bennet Esq. To my daughter Elizabeth Marsh £100, an
annuity of £50, 10,000 lbs of tobacco and a negro boy called David.
I forgive the sums which were owed me by Mr. Thomas Marsh,
her deceased husband. £60 to my granddaughter Sarah Marsh with
remainder to her sisters. To my grandson John Hawkins, eldest son
of my son John, my lands called Barrons Neck at Double Creek
and £60. To my other grandson Ernault Hawkins the remainder of
the tract called Tully's Delight and a plantation at Beaver Marsh
on Tukahoe Branch when he is of age. To Michael Turbut, son of
my nephew William Turbut, and Maryann Turbut, daughter of my
nephew Foster Turbut, the remainder of my tract called Jaspers on
Red Lion Branch. To my nephew Samuel Turbut the money I paid
for him to Mr. Charles Carroll. To John Tuckey a cow and calf.
To my old servant John Creamer 500 lbs of tobacco. I forgive Jane
Clothier, widow of Robert Clothier, all her husband's debts. My
old negro woman called Naomi to be set free. £15 to St. Paul's
parish to buy church plate on which my name is to be engraved.
My tombstone is to be ordered and inscribed to the directions of
Mr. Christopher Wilkinson. A mourning ring to my brother Col.
William Coursey, my sister Sarah Covinton and Elizabeth Coursey.
If my son Ernault dies before my now wife Elizabeth Hawkins, she
shall have the lands conveyed to me by Charles Vanderford on
Coursey Creek. Residue to my son Ernault Hawkins who is to be
my exec. Wits: Arthur Emory, Nathaniel Tucker and Ann Emory.
Pr. 20 Nov 1719 by the named exec. (PROB 11/571/209).

1720

Benjamin Deverall of Va. [and formerly of Bristol], dated 22 Oct 1716.
A guinea each to my brother Jeremiah Deverall and his two children
John and Susannah. To my cousin William Morgan £5 for his
education, all my clothes in Va., and my white horse called Prince.
£20 to Mary Taylor, wife of Humphrey Taylor. Residue to my wife
Rachel and my daughter (Rachel) with remainder to the children
of my brother John Deverall and my sister Hannah Morgan. Execs.
for England to be my wife and my brother Jeremiah Deverall; and
for Va. my friend William Bronaugh and Samuel Matthews. Wits:
Benjamin Strother, William Morgan and John (x) Davis. Pr. 1 Feb
1720 by execs. named and pretended wills of 21 Jan 1714 or May
1717 declared invalid. (PROB 11/572/27). Copy of will at PROB

20/2896 with deposition by the nephew William Morgan of Bristol. New grant made 5 Aug 1730 to Rachel Russell alias Deverall, wife of John Russell and daughter of the testator.

William Nicholson of Anne Arundell Co., Md., merchant, dated 25 Sep 1719. To my son William Nicholson my 1,000 acres in Baltimore Co. called Poplar Neck and two lots in London Town which I purchased of Thomas Holland and Mehittable Parepoint. To my son Joseph Nicholson three tracts called Batchelor's Delight of 298 acres, Clark's Directions of 702 acres (both in Anne Arundell Co.) and Lockwood's Adventure of 400 acres in Baltimore Co. with a lot in London Town taken up by Capt. Richard Jones deceased. To my son Benjamin Nicholson a lot in London Town next to Mr. Turner Wooten's lot originally taken up by Capt. Edward Burgess. To my sons Benjamin, Samuel and Edward Nicholson my part of a tract called Nicholson's Manor in Baltimore Co. of 4,200 acres. My friends and execs. in trust for Md. are to sell my tracts called Covell's Troubles, Rockey Point, part of Covell's Cove, Turkey Island, part of Mitchell's Chance, part of Puddington's Harbour, Elk Thicket, Williams' Addition and Poplar Neck in Anne Arundell Co. and remit the proceeds to Mr. William Hunt, merchant in London, for the benefit of my said sons. My sisters Mrs. Elinor Foster, Mrs. Anne Nicholson and Mrs. Elizabeth Nicholson to have the care of my children until they come of age and to be my execs. in England with Mr. William Hunt. My execs. in Md. to be Mr. James Mouat, Mr. Stephen Warman, John Beale and James Nicholson. Wits: John Arnold, William Sim and Margaret (x) Kinnorston. Pr. 5 Feb 1720 by William Hunt. (PROB 11/572/37).

Robert Hall of [Marlborough], Prince George Co., Md., gent., dated 4 Dec 1719. My wife Elizabeth to have one-third of my estate. £30 to Benjamin Allen. A horse to Josiah Wilson. My man Richard Chubbard is to be made free and have my clothes. Residue to Mr. James Haddock and Welden Jefferson who are to be my execs. Wits: Ann Head, Mary Head and Bigger Head. AWW 18 May 1720 to Thomas Sprigg, attorney for execs. in Md. (PROB 11/574/109).

John Livingston of New London, Connecticut, now in London, [who died in St. James, Westminster, Mddx.], dated 17 Feb 1720. Decent and complete mourning to my brother-in-law Col. Samuel Vetch, my sister Margaret Vetch his wife, and my kinsman Mr. James Douglass of London, merchant. Residue to my wife Elizabeth with remainder to my brothers and sisters. Said James Douglass to be my exec. Wits: John Pawlett, John Borland, Bartholomew Jackson and Philip Davis. Pr. 12 May 1720 by named exec. (PROB 11/574/112).

John Smart of Rotherhithe, Sy., surgeon, [who died in Md.], dated 24 May 1712. My whole estate to my wife Ann who is to be sole exex. Wits: W. Holloway, notary public in Shad Thames, ----- Capell, his servant, and Hester (x) Cockwell. Pr. 21 Jun 1720 by the relict. (PROB 11/574/144).

George Marshall of Shadwell, Mddx., [of the merchant ship *Bayly*, who died in Va., bachelor], dated 11 Apr 1719. My whole estate to my friends Edward Coggin of Shadwell, mariner, and Ann his wife who are to be my execs. Wits: Daniel Curtis, Rebecker Powell and Timothy Thompson, notary public at Cock Hill, Shadwell. Pr. 18 Jun 1720 by Ann Coggins. (PROB 11/575/140).

Elizabeth Fawkner of Epsom, Sy., widow, dated 4 Jun 1720. £500 to the children and grandchildren of my uncles Edward Bulkley, Peter Bulkley and Gersham Bulkley, late of N.E. Other bequests to: the building of a dissenting church in Epsom; my nephew Thomas Bulkley, factor at Fort St. George, East Indies; my cousin Edward Bulkley, his wife Sarah and their daughter Elizabeth Bulkley; my three nieces Sarah, Jane and Susannah Fawkner, sisters of my nephew Everard Fawkner; my cousin Mary Rotheram; my brother-in-law William Brudenall; my cousin Ann Barrow, daughter of my cousin Thomas Barrow. My execs. to be Stanley West, gent., and Rev. William Harris, both of London. Wits: John Wildman and John Nurden. Pr. 1 Jly 1720 by execs. named. (PROB 11/575/153).

John Arderne of N.C., dated 22 Oct 1707. My whole estate in America and England including my plantation called Salmon Creek with slaves and stock, my gold ring engraved with a death's head now in the hands of my relation Sir John Crew of Uskinton, Chesh., my part of a house at Clayton Bridge in the parish of Manchester, Lancs., where my brother Ralph lives, and two guineas bequeathed to me by my relation Lady Crew, to my kinsman William Duckinfield Esq. of N.C. who is to be my exec. "Were I worth 10,000 millions . . . I would leave him every farthing." Wits: Charles Barber, John Taylor, Henry Sisle, Thomas Arnold and George Blaney. Pr. 3 Sep 1720 by named exec. (PROB 11/575/188).

1721

Samuel Harris, late of Charles Town, N.E., mariner of the merchant ship *Martha and Hannah*, Mr. Francis Norris, nuncupative will of 20 Nov 1720. His brother Amos Harris, mariner of the said ship to be exec. in trust for the benefit of the tetator's wife and children.

Wits: John Parkman and William Bedson. Pr. 4 Jan 1721 by the named exec. (PROB 11/578/7).

Mary Hawkins of Tothill Fields, St. Margaret, Westminster, Mddx., widow, business calling me to go beyond the seas [and who died in Boston, N.E.], dated 30 May 1715. To my son John Hawkins my annuity of £8 payable by the Merchant Taylors' Co. provided he pays £60 to his sister Mary Hawkins and does not marry Ann Undee, the young woman with whom he keeps company. The said annuity is mortgaged for £20 to Mr. John Keck in King Street, Westminster. Remainder to my daughter Mary Clarke who is now with me.One guinea each to my children's uncle and aunt Hopley. My brother Randolph Hopley and my cousin Randolph Hopley to be execs. Wits: John Rowland, John Merzeau and John Egelsham. Pr. 17 Feb 1721 by Randolph Hopley Jr. (PROB 11/578/28).

Mary Gledhill [of the Isle of Wight, Va., widow], only surviving exex. of my deceased husband James Day and sole exex. of my deceased husband John Johnson, dated 30 Nov 1712. My sons James Day and Nathaniel Ridley are to be my execs. and are to honour the unpaid legacies of my said husbands and administer monies in the hands of Micajah Perry & Co. of London and of John Lear and Elizabeth his wife who is exex. of Mrs. Isabella Harveild who was exex. of Capt. Luke Harveild of Nansemond Co. and an exex. of my husband Day. Wits: Francis Wrenn, Thomas (x) Wrenn and John Ogburne. AWW 23 Jun 1721 to Micajah Perry, attorney for execs. in Va. (PROB 11/580/109).

Richard Martin of Bristol, merchant, now going on a journey, [who died in Va.], dated 30 Sep 1719. £100 to my sister Elizabeth, wife of Samuel Groves of Dursley, Glos., and £100 to her daughter Sarah Groves when she is 21 or married, with remainder to the children of my brother John Martin. £100 to be placed at interest for my sister Ann Martin of Dursley. Other bequests to my nieces Ann and Mary Martin, daughters of my late brother John Martin, and my brother George Martin. Nathaniel Wraxall, Lyonell Lyde and Andrew Pope, all of Bristol, merchants, to be my execs. Wits: Peter Mugleworth, Jacob Marler Jr. and John Safford. Pr. 1 Jun 1721 by named execs. (PROB 11/580/114).

Francis Brinley Esq. of Boston, N.E., dated 19 Oct 1719. £20 to my wife Hannah Brinley. To my daughter-in-law Mrs. Katherine Lyde £20 and an annuity of £60 payable from the rents of my tenements at the south end of Boston Neck in Kingston and Narragansett Co. also called King's Province. I have already given £800 to my granddaughter Elizabeth Hutchinson as part of her portion and she is now to have £20 which is to be delivered to her husband Mr.

William Hutchinson, and £2,200 more so that her husband may settle a good jointure on her. She is also to have my 170 acres in Kingston not already disposed of which I purchased of Capt. Josiah Arnold of James Town, and £200 in obligations entered into by two persons in England which are now in the hands of Thomas Brandon of the Inner Temple. To Eliakim Hutchinson, eldest son of my said granddaughter, all the estate I purchased of John Richmond of Taunton, now called Norton. £10 to Edward Lyde Esq. of Boston. £5 to Mrs. Mary Cole, daughter of Mr. John Cole of Kingston deceased. Forty shillings each to Mr. Mahos of Roxbury and my kinswoman Mary Vial of Barrington. My books to Alice Wait, wife of Samuel Wait of Kingston, and Mr. Samuel Warkeman of Newport. My map of the world to Timothy Clark Esq. of Boston. All my household goods to my grandchildren Francis Brinley and Elizabeth Hutchinson. £20 to Deborah, wife of my grandson Francis Brinley. All my lands in Hoxton, Mddx., and Stanwell and my messuage at the northern end of Quonouaquatt Island alias James Town. Execs. to be my grandsons Francis Brinley and Mr. William Hutchinson. Wits: Samuel Lynde, Thomas Newton and George Cradock. Pr. 1 Jly 1721 by grandson Francis Brinley. (PROB 11/580/123).

Richard Mahier, late of N.E. but now of London, mariner, [who died in Rotherhithe, Sy.], dated 4 Mar 1721. My exec. John Lloyd of London, merchant, is to consign to James Bowdoin, merchant in Boston, the proceeds of my three-eights of the cargo I brought to London and of the *Friendship* of which I was master, for the benefit of my wife Mary Mahier, daughter of Capt. Thomas Savage of Cherrystone on the eastern shore of Accomack Co., Va. My said wife is also to have the money in the hands of my friend Mary Pyke, widow, dwelling near the Salutation in Boston, a promissory note in the hands of Mr. John Marshall, a bond of £114 from Capt. Abinezer Wentworth of Boston, one of £100 from Abigail Jervis of Boston, widow, and one of £125 from Mary Huss of Boston, widow. To my nephew Richard Mahier a bond of £50 on Solomon Townsend of Boston, blacksmith. To my nephew John Mahier, son of my brother John Mahier of the island of Jersey, 600 crowns. To my sister Katherine Renoff, late Mahier, 400 crowns. £5 to my friend Sarah Bass of Boston, widow. A ring for mourning to my friend Anthony Todder, merchant. To the poor of the eleven parishes of Jersey 100 livres for the poor. Residue to my nephew Richard Mahier of Boston, mariner. John Lloyd to be exec. for England and Jersey and James Bowdoin and Anthony Todder of Boston, merchants, for N.E. Wits: Mathew Cooter, Henry Bewes and John Crump, scrivener in Rotherhithe. Pr. 4 Jly 1721 by John Lloyd. (PROB 11/580/135).

John Ash of Westfield, Colleton Co., S.C., dated 30 Mar 1711. Twenty square feet to be laid out for a burial place. My mulatto slave Jemmy to be freed. Bequests to: my brother William Ash if he is living at the time of my death; my sister Isabella Ash; the church of St. Paul's; Joseph Briant, Stephen Ford, Mr. Thomas Waring and Mr. Ralph Izard. Residue to my wife Ann, daughter of Thomas Bolton, who is to be my exex. Wits: John Hayes, John Wilkinson and Mary Hayes. AWW 16 Aug 1721 to William Livingston, husband and administrator of the relict Ann Livingston alias Ash, late of Westfield, S.C., who died in Wilts., England, before administering. (PROB 11/581/142).

William Andrews of Cote, Bishops Canning, Wilts., [who died in Va., bachelor], dated 16 May 1712. £50 to Elizabeth Andrews of Cote. £10 to my uncle Nicholas Nash and £20 to his daughter, now wife of Edward Browne. £5 to my aunt Nash. £5 to my brother John Andrews. Residue to Hester, Mary and William Nash, children of my said uncle. The said Nicholas Nash and Elizabeth Nash to be my execs. Wits: Francis Gilbert, Thomas Shipp and Prescott Pennyston. Pr. 7 Dec 1721 by Nicholas Nash. (PROB 11/582/215). Further grant in Aug 1726 to Hester Browne alias Nash.

Thomas Oswin, mariner of the *Essex*, Capt. Thomas Dansey, [who died in York River, Va.], dated 5 Jan 1721. My whole estate to my father Christopher Oswin of St. Saviour, Southwark, Sy., butcher, who is to be my exec. Wits: Mary Bright and John Bright, scrivener in Red Lion Street, Southwark. Pr. 16 Dec 1721 by the father. (PROB 11/582/227).

1722

George Pattison of Shadwell, Mddx., mariner [of the *Betty*, who died in Va., bachelor], dated 28 Feb 1719. My whole estate to my mother Jane Pattison of Shadwell, widow, who is to be my exex. Wits: Thomas Jones and John Helsing, attorney near Wapping Wall. Pr. Jan 1722 by the mother. (PROB 11/583/13).

William Romman of Woodborough, [Wilts., who died in Philadelphia, bachelor], undated. £20 to my brother Roger Oram. Richard Smith, son of Edmund Smith, to be apprenticed. One guinea to Henry Briant. A ring for mourning to Mary, daughter of William Chandler of Woodborough, and to Elizabeth Strotton. A bible each to William, son of Henry Robbonce and to Samuel, son of Samuel More. One guinea to my mother. A pair of gloves to Simon Rudle.

My brother Richard Romman to be my exec. Wits: Richard Paul and John Stagg. Pr. 1 Mar 1722 by exec. named. (PROB 11/584/61).

Thomas Winfield, citizen and currier of London, [of Va.], dated 4 Jan 1720. To my uncle Bezell Wright £5. A guineas for a ring each to John Orton and his wife and John Sturgis. To my sister Hannah Page three-quarters of my estate free of the control of her husband William Page. The other quarter to my brother Edward Winfield. The said John Orton to be my exec. Pr. 5 Mar 1722 by the named exec. (PROB 11/584/65).

Charles Lucas of Shadwell, Mddx., mariner [of the *Hopewell*, who died in Md.], dated 5 Nov 1718. My one-eighth share of the *Hopewell* to my sister Elizabeth, wife of Edward Poulter. A ring of twenty shillings to my brothers Robert Lucas, William Lucas and the said Edward Poulter, and my sisters Elizabeth Poulter and Elizabeth Lucas. £10 to John Poulter, son of the said Edward Poulter. Exec. to be the said Edward Poulter. Wits: Thomas Campion, Aaron ---datt and John Kelsing near Wapping Wall. Pr. 20 Jun 1722 by named exec. (PROB 11/585/122).

John May of Coldash, Thatcham, Berks., bucket maker, dated 5th of the month called July 1720. My lands in Penna. to my son William May. My leasehold dwelling and residue of my estate to my wife Mary May who is to be my exex. Wits: Thomas Titcom, Jane Wells and Joseph (x) Beneat. Pr. 18 Jun 1722 by affirmation of the named exex. (PROB 11/585/122).

William Richards, [of St. Martin in the Fields, Mddx.], carpenter of the transport ship *George* hired into H.M. service [who died on the merchant ship *Easter* in Carolina], dated 13 May 1709. My whole estate to my wife Elizabeth Richards who is to be my exex. Wits: Margaret Bissell, Thomas Ellery and William Mitchell, clerk to Mr. Bissell. Pr. 30 Jun 1722 by relict. (PROB 11/585/126).

John Hampton of Somerset Co., Md., minister of the gospel, dated 28 Oct 1719. A silver tankard and spoons to my cousin James Rownd. A silver cup and spoon to my cousin Edward Rownd, son of William Rownd deceased. My gold buttons to my brother-in-law Mr. Robert King. A bible to my sister-in-law Ellenor Ballard, wife of Capt. Charles Ballard. A negro called Pompey to my son-in-law Robert Jenkins Henry and a negro called John Mingo to my son-in-law John Henry. Residue of my estate and one-third of my money in Europe to my wife Mary Hampton who is to be my exex. Two-thirds of my money in Europe to my brother Robert Hampton, merchant in Londonderry, (Ireland), and my two sisters Margery and Frances Hampton. The said Robert Hampton is to be my exec. in Britain. Wits:

John Clement, John Chonan and Robert Truman, scrivener. Pr. 8 August 1722 by Robert Hampton. (PROB 11/586/158).

George Whitehorne of Whitechapel, Mddx., mariner, [of Boston, N.E.], dated 23 Feb 1714. All my copyhold estate in reversion in Ealing, Mddx., to my friends James Warren of Shoreditch, Mddx., thread-man, and Benjamin Thorp, citizen and weaver of London, in trust for my wife Katherine Whitehorne who is to bring up my minor children. Wits: Richard Hoo(?), Mary Knowles and John Knowles, scrivener. Pr. 16 Aug 1722 by Benjamin Thorp, James Warren having died. (PROB 11/586/166).

William Waters of Northampton Co., Va., dated 3 Jly 1720. To my son William Waters my plantation on the north side of Hunger's Creek, my gold seal ring, my servant John Robins, my sloop the *Isabel*, a one-eighth part of my sloop *Dolphin*, and all my negroes except the boy called Amsbury who is to go to my grandson Thomas, son of Zerubabel Preeson and Margaret his wife. To my granddaughter Isabel Preeson £25 for the purchase of a female negro. To my said daughter Margaret Preeson my white woman servant and her daughter Mary for the time they have to serve. £10 to Robert Baynton. My son William Waters to be my exec. Wits: Robert Baynton and James Locker, clerk of Northampton Co. Pr. 22 Oct 1722 by the exec. named. (PROB 11/587/205).

Robert Stevens Esq. of St. James, Goose Creek, S.C., dated 8 Sep 1720. I wish to be buried beside my daughter Mariane Stevens. To my wife Mary during her lifetime all my lands in Berks. or elsewhere in England, including the lands I purchased of the heirs of the late William Holloway of Berkcome (*sic*), Berks., plumber. My kinsman Mr. John Vicaridge, who now resides with me, is to maintain his aunt, my said wife, on my plantation, and she is to have my negro girl. To my kinsman Mr. Joseph Alexander of Bury St. Edmunds, Suff., clerk, £100 sterling. The remainder of my estate to the said John Vicaridge who is to be my exec. Wits: John Moore, John Green and John Bayly. Pr. 7 Nov 1722 by the named exec. (PROB 11/588/222).

Richard Waters of Somerset Co., Md., planter, dated 21 Apr 1720. To my son William Waters my tract of 620 acres called Waters' River on which my dwelling house stands. To my cousin John Waters my 70 acres of marsh which was in the occupation of myself, my brother John Waters deceased and Charles Hall deceased. To my sons William, Richard and Littleton Waters the remaining marsh on Manokin called Flat Lands. To my brother William Waters my sloop *Elizabeth*. To my wife Elizabeth Waters my negroes Scipio, Aleck, Hager and Major, and after her demise the said Scipio is to be freed and to have two cows and calves. If any of my children marry without the consent of the West River Quaker Meeting, they are to be deprived of their inheritance. My sons Richard and Littleton are to be left in the care of Richard Hill and Thomas Chalkley of Philadelphia. To my daughter Ester a negro called Rose and to my daughter Sarah a negro called Peg. £250 out of the estate in England left to me by my uncle William Marriott of Towcester, now in the hands of William Cooper, to my sons Richard and Littleton. I appoint the said Cooper and John Hyde Sr., merchant in London, to dispose of my said uncle's estate. My wife and son William to be my execs. Wits: John (x) Brown, William Pearson, Edward (x) Harper and Thomas (x) Fairclo. AWW 13 Nov 1722 to Jonathan Scarth, attorney for the execs. in Md. (PROB 11/588/227).

Henry Wigington, late of S.C. but now of York Buildings, Villiers Street, [St. Martin in the Fields, Mddx.], dated 27 May 1722. I desire to be buried in the chancel of the church of Kingston on Thames, Sy., where most of our family lie. Bequests to: Mr. Robert Hume of S.C., attorney at law, and his wife and daughter Sophia Hume; my mother Mrs. Ann Wigington; my brother and sister Lowfield; my brother and sister Lason; my aunt Henrietta Thomas; my cousins Edward and Henrietta Harradin; John Penny Esq. of Clements Inn. Execs. in England Mr. Robert Hume of Tooley Street, Southwark, apothecary, and Mr. James Dunnidge of Birchin Lane, London, notary public. Execs. in Carolina Robert and Sophia Hume. Pr. 17 Dec 1722 by Robert Hume. (PROB 11//588/248).

1723

Stephen North, late of Boston, N.E., but now of London [who died in St. Botolph Aldgate, London], son of Stephen North of Boston, vintner, deceased, dated 13 Jan 1722. My whole estate to my uncle and exec. Francis North of St. Botolph Aldgate, apothecary, and my aunt Martha Keating of London, widow. Wits: Edward Willis, Eliner Page, servant to Mr. Francis North, and Ar. Avis, attorney near Aldgate. Pr. 5 Jan 1723 by exec. named. (PROB 11/589/14).

John Bressey of St. Clement Danes, Mddx., gent., [who died in Md., bachelor], dated 30 Jun 1717. Five shillings to my brother Charles Bressey. Residue to my friend Mrs. Ellinor Lloyd of St. Clement Danes, spinster, who is to be my exex. Wits: Catherine Thistelweat and Alice Hicks. Pr. 26 Apr 1723 by exex. named. (PROB 11/590/68).

Benjamin Shemans of Stepney, Mddx., mariner, shortly bound on a voyage to sea, [who died on H.M.S. *Dolphin* in Carolina], dated 31 Oct 1722. My whole estate to Mrs. Mary Jordan of Stepney, widow, who is to be exex. Wits: Joseph Bradley and Richard Burbydge. Pr. 2 Aug 1723 by exex. named. (PROB 11/592/174).

Jonas Yesline, mariner of H.M. ship *Seaford*, [bachelor], dated N.Y. 14 Dec 1719. My whole estate to my kinswoman Mary Scot of Highgate, Mddx., widow, who is to be my exex. Wits: James Collins and J. Cudlipp, clerk. AWW 22 Oct 1723 to Margaret, wife of John Cudlipp on H.M. ship *Blandford* in S.C., attorney for the exex. (PROB 11/593/221).

Samuel Buttall of Topsham, Exeter, Devon, sugar baker, dated 24 Jan 1719. Bequests to: my wife and exex. Mary Buttall, including 1000 acres in Carolina on Edistow River near New London and a sum left to her by her mother Mrs. Woods; my sons Benjamin, John, Humphrey and Charles Buttall; my said son Charles to have a lease of property in Wrexham, Denbigh, left to me by the will of my uncle George Buttall deceased; my daughters Mary Hodges, wife of Mr. Nathaniel Hodges; Sarah Wiggington, wife of Mr. Thomas Wiggington; Elizabeth Wells, wife of Mr. Abraham Wells; my cousin Mr. Joshua Buttall; my cousin Mr. Thomas Green; my niece Dorcas Jackson, wife of Mr. Abraham Jackson of Moreton, Devon. Wits: Daniel Coleman, Thomas Sampson and John Conant. Pr. 12 Nov 1723 by relict. (PROB 11/594/228). See also will of Mary Buttall pr. Feb 1731.

Andrew Hart of Wapping, Mddx., mariner, [who died on the *Amity* in Va.], dated 8 Feb 1717. My whole estate to my friend Robert Wilson who is to be my exec. Wits: John Lucas, Joseph Gambling amnd Samuel Sharman, notary public near Union Stairs, Wapping. Pr. 18 Nov 1723 by John (*sic*) Wilson. (PROB 11/594/235).

John Jones of Philadelphia, dated Philadelphia 17 Jan 1723. All my estate in England, Wales and Penna. to my wife and exex. Jean Jones but, if my friends and trustees Mr. John Lloyd of Ragat (?Raglan) and Robert Price of Cefn Weg see fit, it shall be sold to pay my debts. Wits: John Cadwallader, Edward Roberts and Peter Evans. Pr. 11 Dec 1723 by the relict. (PROB 11/594/260).

1724

Philip Lenthall of London, mariner, [of Philadelphia], dated 20 Jan 1714. My tenements in Hornchurch, Essex, and other real estate to my brother John Lenthall of St. Dunstan in the West, London, stationer, who is to be my exec. £40 to my sister Frances Lenthall, spinster. I revoke my will of 19 Jan 1714 which devised my estate to Sarah Wheeler, spinster. Wits: E. Fazakerly, James Smith and Jacob Turner. Pr. 15 Jan 1724 by exec. named. (PROB 11/595/11).

Gilbert Peterson of London, mariner, now bound overseas, [who died on the *Prince Royal* in Va., bachelor], dated 14 Aug 1721. My whole estate to my friend James Carrack who is to be my exec. Wits: John Maxwell and John Crump, scrivener in Rotherhithe. Pr. 10 Jan 1724 by exec. named. (PROB 11/595/16).

John Edge of St. Andrew, Holborn, Mddx., gent., considering the danger of the seas [who died in Boston, N.E.], dated 8 Jun 1717. My whole estate to my sisters Martha Comby and Johanna Edge who are to be my exexs. Wits: John Darby and Darby Stapleton of Doctors' Commons. Pr. 17 Feb 1724 by Martha Darby alias Comby. (PROB 11/595/30).

Thomas Thorpe of Stepney, Mddx., mariner, [who died in Va.], one of the sons of John Thorpe, citizen and apothecary of London deceased, dated 9 Mar 1722. To my wife and exex. Jane Thorpe my half of a woodland in the parishes of Ruckinge and Orlestone, Kent. £10 to my mother-in-law Mrs. Mary Thorpe of Poplar, Mddx., widow. Wits: Thomas Harris, John Smith and Gilbert Hawker. Pr. 13 Feb 1724 by relict. (PROB 11/596/47).

Edward Warner, citizen and distiller of London, dated 31 Aug 1722. My plantations in Md. to my wife Mary who is to be my exex. My personal estate to be divided between my wife and my children Edward, Richard and Samuel Warner and Mary, wife of Richard Wright. Certificates by William Rolfe of St. Edmund the King, London, haberdasher and Quaker, and Richard Wright of St. Gabriel, Fenchurch Street, London, as to the testator's handwriting. Pr. 20 Mar 1724 by the son Edward Warner of St. Botolph Aldgate, London, the relict renouncing. (PROB 11/596/73).

Thomas Porter of the island of Curacao, dated 16 Jly 1722. My friend John Fread of N.Y., mariner, to be my attorney, legatee and exec. Wits: Thomas Ince and Ichabod Loutitt. On 23 Jly 1724 Capt. Thomas Smith of St. Olave, Southwark, Sy., deposed that he witnessed a letter of attorney sent by John Fred of N.Y. dated 5 Nov 1723 appointing Mr. George Streatfield and Mr. David Clarkson of London, merchants. AWW 23 Jly 1724 to George Streatfield, attorney for John Fred in N.Y. (PROB 11/598/175).

David Rice, sergeant of Hon. John Doncell's Co. and Lieut-Gov. of H.M. Garrison of Annapolis, dated 6 Jan 1722. To my sisters Katherine and Jane Rice one shilling each. Residue to my wife

Anne Rice who is to be exex. Wits: John Clark, William Barkley and Robert Arundell. Pr. 14 Sep 1724 by relict. (PROB 11/599/213).

Christopher Arthur of Sypruss Barony, S.C., [who died in Stepney, Mddx.], heir and devisee of my uncle Dominick Arthur of the same, deceased, dated 24 Oct 1724. To my friend Mr. Thomas Akins 500 acres from my estate which is now in his tenure, my servant boy Quintus and a negro boy called Cuffy. To my mother Mrs. Christian Arthur an annuity of £20 sterling. To my goddaughter Miss Ann Harlston £200 current when she is 18 or married and my negro girl called Mary. £5 sterling each to Mr. Samuel Wragg and Mrs. Mary Young. Half of the residue of my real and personal estate to my kinsman Patrick Roche of Limerick, (Ireland), merchant, son of my uncle Francis Roche deceased, and Anstace Roche alias Arthur his wife; and half to my kinsman Bartholomew Arthur, son of my uncle Patrick Arthur of Limerick, deceased, and Katherine Arthur his wife. Capt. John Harlston, John Asby and Thomas Akins, gents., and Patrick Roche to be execs. Wits: William Burr, Philip Cooke and Thomas Ing. Pr. 21 Dec 1724 by Patrick Roche. (PROB 11/600/260).

Francis Rolle of Md., dated 17 November 1724. To my wife Dorothy Rolle [daughter of Richard Feddeman of Talbot Co.] her dowry of my estate. The residue to my four sons Robert Rolle, Francis Rolle, Feddeman Rolle and Henry Rolle. My exec. to be Arnault Hawkins of Md. Wits: John Dunkin, George Coats and William Curtis. Pr. 7 Dec 1724 by exec. named. (PROB 11/600/282).

John Turner of Bagendon, Glos., yeoman, [but late of Whitechapel, Mddx., who died in Md., bachelor], dated 12 Oct 1717. One shilling each to my brothers Samuel and Henry Turner. Residue to my cousin and exec. Rachel Eycott, daughter of my cousin Thomas Eycott of Bagendon, innholder. Wits: Anthony Carpenter, John (x) Rodway and Henry Timbrell. AWW 4 Dec 1724 to Thomas Eycott, father and guardian of the named exec. (PROB 11/600/283).

Christopher Vernon of Md., planter, [who died in St. Dunstan in the West, London], dated 8 Dec 1724. £100 each to my nephew William Vernon and niece Anne Moore, children of my deceased brother John Vernon, and £100 to Jane their mother which is to be paid to Mr. Thomas Hare for her use free from the control of her now husband John Ashford. £100 to my kinsman Robert Atkins, his wife and children. £52 to Mr. Peter De Frene for his daughter-in-law Maria Haveningham as soon as she comes of age. Residue to my aunt Anne Vernon who is to be my exex. Wits: Bartholomew Cooper, William Cooper and William Gill. Pr. 14 Dec 1724 by exex. named. (PROB 11/600/285).

John Smile of H.M. ship *Greyhound*, Capt. Solguard, now going overseas, [who died in N.Y.], dated 16 Aug 1722. £40 to my brother James Smile of Muenross (?Melrose), Tweedale, Scotland, weaver. £30 each to my sisters Janet and Mary. My friends Mr. William Hogg of Edinburgh, merchant, and Alexander Bibb of St. Martin in the Fields, Mddx., victualler, to be my execs. Wits: Robert Bird and Thomas Cartwright. Pr. 11 Dec 1724 by Alexander Bibb. (PROB 11/601/20).

1725

Thomas Cockburn [of Penna.], mariner of the *Newberry*, Capt. Henry Coombe, latitude 17° north and longtitude 58.40° west, dated 5 Sep 1724. My brother John Cockburn to be my exec. and to pay £10 to my sister Martha Cockburn. Wits: Isa. Cardel and Henry Coombe. Pr. 4 Jan 1725 by exec. named. (PROB 11/601/4).

John Davis of Deptford, Kent, mariner [of H.M. ship *Sea Horse*, who died in Boston, N.E.], dated 10 Feb 1719. My whole estate to my mother Elizabeth Davis of Swansea, Glamorgan, widow. Evan Jones of Deptford, shipwright, and Mary his wife to be my execs. Wits: Edward Brickdell and Thomas Wellings, notary public in King Street, Deptford. Pr. Feb 1725 by Evan Jones. (PROB 11/601/34).

Jacob Furness of Bermondsey, Sy., mariner, dated 3 Sep 1723. One shilling to all my near relations. To my wife Elizabeth Furness my freeholds in N.Y. purchased by my late father John Furness and all my other estate, and she is to be my exex. Wits: Richard Heathfield, Henry Gamble and Thomas Watts, scrivener in Long Lane, Southwark. Pr. 11 Feb 1725 by relict. (PROB 11/601/34).

David Maybank of Christ Church, Berkeley Co., S.C., carpenter, dated 27 Apr 1713. To my eldest daughter Ann £25, a negro boy Will, six cows or calves and an annuity of £5. To my daughter Elizabeth Hyde a negro girl Statira and £10. To my daughter Susanna a negro girl Bess and £100 when she is 18. To my son Joseph £100 when he is 18 and my plantation of 500 acres at Owendan, being half of the 1,000 acres I purchased with my brother Wigfall. To my wife Susanna the plantation where I now live, the negro men Mathias and Surry, a negro woman Moll and a negro boy Bookey which I purchased of my son Hyde. My house and land in Charles Town purchased of Joseph Croskeys where John Jackson dwells is to be sold for the benefit of my children. Residue to my wife who is to be exec. with my brother Joseph Wigfall and Benjamin Quelch.

Wits: John Hutchinson, Thomas Herbert and Benjamin Quelch Jr.
AWW 27 Feb 1725 to Samuel Wragg, attorney for Susanna Bond
alias Maybank, wife of James Bond, and for Thomas Barton in
S.C. (PROB 11/601/46).

Susanna Maybank of Christ Church, Berkeley Co., S.C., widow, dated
14 Jun 1716. To my son Joseph Maybank my house and land in
Broad Street, Charles Town, in satisfaction for what was left him
by his father, and a negro Mathias. He is to pay the interest due
from me to Ann Maybank. To my daughter Elizabeth Wigfall Hyde,
widow, a negro called Bookey. To my son William Hyde the first
son born of my negro woman Moll. To my daughter Susanna
Maybank the house and plantation where I now dwell, a negro man
called Surry and negro woman called Moll. To my daughter Anne
Maybank a bed, etc. £5 to Mrs. Anne Barton. One guinea to be
sent to my cousin William Mason, son of my uncle William Mason
in England. To my daughters Elizabeth and Susanna the produce
of what was left to me by my brother Wigfall on his plantation.
My friends Col. George Logan and Mr. Thomas Barton are to be
guardians of my son Joseph. My said daughter Susanna is to be
my exex. Wits: Thomas Fairchild, Ann Davoll and Ann Barton.
AWW 27 Feb 1725 to Samuel Wragg, attorney for Susanna Bond
alias Maybank, wife of James Bond, and for Thomas Barton in
S.C. (PROB 11/601/45).

Christopher Billop, a prisoner in the Fleet Prison, London, gent., dated
25 Apr 1724. My plantation in Bentley and Manor of Bentley, my
mansion house and other estate in Staten Island, N.Y. Province, to
my daughter Mary, now wife of Rev. William Skinner, with
remainder to Christopher, Thomas, Brook, Robert, Samuel and
William Farmar, sons of my son-in-law Thomas Farmar, on condition that whichever of the brothers shall inherit shall take the
surname of Billop. Jasper Farmar, eldest son of the said Thomas
Farmar, is to have only £20. My plantation near Rareton River
known as Innion's Land in N.Y. Province to my daughter Anne,
wife of the said Thomas Farmar. Of the £5,200 due to me from
the estate of Sir Alexander Rigby deceased I give £200 to Mr.
James Fittar of London, merchant, and £500 to my nephew Thomas
Billop of Deptford, Kent. To my niece Hannah Booth £50. Execs.
to be James Fittar and my nephew Thomas Billop. Wits: Thomas
Frank, William Abell, William Abbott, John Baker and Edward
Games. Pr. 24 Apr 1725 by execs. named. (PROB 11/602/80).

Martha Lee of Goodman's Fields, Whitechapel, Mddx., widow, dated
26 Apr 1725. To my son George Lee my tenements in Gracechurch
Street, London, and in Cople parish, Westmoreland Co., Va. My
tenements in Suffolk to my two daughters Martha and Lettice Lee,

subject to the payment of £100 to Daniel Watts when he is 21 pursuant to the will of my former husband Thomas Moore deceased. In case of my children's death, my estate in London is to descend to the children of my late brother John Silk and of my brother Abraham Silk, and my estate in Suffolk to my brother Tobias Silk. £10 each to my friend Mr. Oliver Marton of the Temple, my brother Tobias Silk and William Wareham, citizen and barber surgeon of London. £5 each to Ruth Hill, widow, and Naomi Hill her daughter. Residue to the said Tobias Silk and William Wareham who are to be my execs. and guardians of my three children. Wits: John Mathew, Oliver Marton and Edward Marton. Pr. 5 May 1725 by execs. named. (PROB 11/603/114). See NGSQ 63/131.

James Brown of Wapping, Mddx., [and late of Rotherhithe, Sy., who died on the *Champion* in Md.], dated 12 Apr 1715. My whole estate to my wife Abigall Brown of Wapping who is to be my exex. Wits: Daniel Males, Katherine (x) Smith and John Shallder, notary public at Wapping. Pr. 28 Sep 1725 by the relict. (PROB 11/605/193).

James Parnell of Lincolns Inn, Mddx., gent., [of Penna.], dated 17 Dec 1724. £10 to my sister Bridget Stevenson. A guinea for a ring to my brother John Penn. To my brother and exec. Ambrose Stevenson all monies due to me or in the right of my late wife Elizabeth Parnell, all my tenements at Fillongley, Warw., and coppice woods bequeathed by the will of William Brierly to his sister Mary Clancay. Wits: Thomas Stevenson, Thomas Grey and Mary Polly. Pr. 1 Oct 1725 by exec. named. (PROB 11/605/216).

Benjamin Motteux of London, jeweller, [of S.C., bachelor], dated 1 Jan 1724. My whole estate to my brother John Anthony Motteux of London, merchant, who is to be my exec. Wits: Moses Motteux and Samuel Smith. Pr. 14 Dec 1725 by exec. named. (PROB 11/606/256).

1726

Nathaniel Glover, late of Dorchester, N.E., but now of Bermondsey, Sy., tanner, dated 9 Mar 1726. My whole estate to my friend Jane Davis of Bermondsey, widow, who is to be my exex. Wits: Sarah Beamore and John Kidder, notary public. Pr. 21 Mar 1726 by exex. named. (PROB 11/608/48).

Barbara Danson of Holborn, Mddx., spinster, dated 8 Apr 1726. To Margaret Mollison and Daniel Dolly my plantation of 3,000 acres on the neck of land on the north-east side of Pascotank River, N.C., my four Baronies of 48,000 acres, and £43 in the hands of my execs. Daniel Oliver and William Welstead living in Boston, N.E. Wits: William Leader, Thomas Solley and Thomas Anderson. Pr. 23 Apr 1726 by affirmation of Daniel Dolley. (PROB 11/608/68).

Augustine Long, citizen and wheelwright of London, dated 8 Feb 1726. To my daughter Elizabeth Ireson one shilling. To my granddaughter Elizabeth Rise, now living in Va., for herself and her children £100. Residue to my wife Alice Long who is to be my exex. Wits: Theophilus Joyner, Samuel Lee and Stephen Mills, scrivener in Smithfield. Pr. 14 Apr 1726 by relict. (PROB 11/608/75).

Richard Tookerman of S.C., gent., now bound on a voyage to West Indies, dated 11 Dec 1723. All my debts to be paid including that to Nathaniel Barnardiston of London, merchant, who is to be my exec. with Thomas Matthew of London, gent. All my estate including that which came to me on my marriage to my wife Katherine Tookerman and my children. Wits: Benjamin Heath, John Lawsone and John Heaton. Pr. 22 Apr 1726 by execs. named. (PROB 11/608/84).

Samuel Cox Esq. of Barbados [who died in Md.], dated 10 Apr 1724. My whole estate to my wife Elizabeth Cox who is to be my exex. My sons-in-law Hon. Thomas Beckles, George Graeme Esq. and Henry Peers Esq. of Barbados to be execs. in trust for the children of my three daughters Maud Beckles, Elizabeth Graeme and Sarah Peers. Wits: Mary Sharpe and Joseph Walker. Pr. Barbados 5 Feb 1725. AWW London 25 Jun 1726 to Henry Palmer, attorney for the relict in Barbados. (PROB 11/609/118).

William Lanman of London, gent., [of Boston, N.E.], dated 11 Jly 1724. Forty shillings to my mother Johan Lanman of Pilton, Devon. Twenty shillings each to my brothers John and Samuel Lanman of Pilton, butchers, and ten shillings each to their wives and children. To my friends Thomas Morrison and Hugh Donogan a half-guinea each. To Jane, wife of Charles Hopkins of Chancery Lane, London, mariner, a half-guinea. To my said brother John Lanman £40 in satisfaction of our agreement of Aug or Sep 1721 for the maintenance of Chrisogon Lanman. Residue to my son William Lanman of London, gent., who is to be exec. Wits: Nathan Bayley Jr., John Harrison and Francis Brooke. Pr. 8 Sep 1726 by exec. named. (PROB 11/611/186).

Hugh Drysdale, late of Col. Charles Churchill's Regiment of Dragoons, [Lieut-Gov. of Va. who died in Va.], dated 23 Feb 1722. My whole estate to my wife Hester Drysdale who is to be my exex. Wits: John Moyle, James Powell and Terence Collins. Pr. 12 Dec 1726 by relict. (PROB 11/612/255).

1727

Henry Clarke of Shadwell, Mddx., mariner, now bound to sea [who died in Penna.], dated 27 Jly 1719. My whole estate to my wife Elizabeth Clarke who is to be my exex. Wits: Elizabeth Power, William Marriner and John Kinge, attorney in Ratcliffe. Pr. 9 Mar 1727 by the relict. (PROB 11/614/58).

Elisha Bennett of Rumney Marsh, N.E., dated 9 Apr 1726. My whole estate at Rumney Marsh and Boston to my wife Dorothy Bennett with remainder to my children John Bennett, Elis Bennett and Sarah Viall. £100 each to my grandson John Bennett in N.Y. and my grandson Samuel Viall. My wooden house at Boston is to be sold to pay the cost of my wife's burial and my brick house there is to be brought in with the rest of my estate. Wits: Joshua Billett, Samuel Breeden and Robert (x) Wait. AWW 30 May 1727 to Henry Palmer, attorney for the relict in Rumney Marsh. (PROB 11/615/108). Granted 16 Feb 1734 to the son John Bennett on the death of the relict.

Robert Hughes of Wapping, Mddx., mariner, [who died on H.M. ship *Tartar* in Va.], dated 12 Feb 1708. My whole estate to my wife Mary Hughes who is to be my exex. Wits: Thomas Withinson, John Knight and John Bull. Pr. 30 May 1727 by the relict. (PROB 11/615/117).

Tobias Bowles of London, merchant, dated 19 Feb 1725. To be buried in St. George's church, London, near my late wife. To my son-in-law Henry Alexander Primrose my leasehold house the Greyhound in Deal, (Kent), in trust for the use of my daughter Mary Underdowne, now wife of Capt. John Underdowne, during her lifetime, with remainder to her son John Underdowne; and the leasehold of the Royal Exchange in Deal for the use of my said grandson with remainder to my son James Bowles. To Richard Burbridge of London, merchant, my leasehold of the Royal Oak in Deal and the dwelling house where my daughter Margaret Primrose now lives in trust for her. Thomazine Bowles, daughter of my late brother Phineas Bowles, to be released from her servitude in Va. to Mr. Willis in York River. To my said son James Bowles my interest in a tenement in Dunster's Court, Mincing Lane, London, where I now dwell, if he shall leave Md., where he now lives, and returns to carry on trade to Md. Bequest to my daughter Jane Bowles. The said Henry Alexander Primrose and grandson John Underdowne to be my execs. Wits: Gabriel Neve, Robert Phillimore and Richard Brouncker. Codicil of 17 Feb 1727 witnessed by Daniel Lamport, Gabriel Neve and Thomas Pruning. Codicil of 13 Jun 1727 witnessed by Johanna Moutravers, Mary Bean and Elizabeth (x) Kerby. Pr. 3 Jly 1727 by execs. named. (PROB 11/616/156). Double probate to James Bowles Aug 1727. See NGSQ 62/36.

Nicholas Kidgell of Charles Town, S.C., [late of Stepney, Mddx.], mariner, dated 5 Aug 1726: copied from S.C. Register Book E, pp. 94-95. My whole estate to my wife Sarah Kidgell living in Chivers Court, Nightingale Lane, Limehouse, Mddx. Mr. Benjamin Godin of Charles Town, merchant, to be my exec. in trust for her. Wits: Henry Hargrave, Daniel Gibson and Jeremiah Milner. AWW 22 Jly 1727 to the relict. (PROB 11/616/167).

William Burley [of N.Y.], midshipman of H.M. ship *Torbay* now at sea, dated 12 May 1727. £50 to my mother Elizabeth Burley of St. Andrew, Holborn, London, widow. Residue to my wife Susanna Burley of N.Y. Three trunks of linen at the house of my grandfather William Blakeway in Garland Court near Stepney church and the wages due for my service in H.M. ships *Tartar*, *Kent* and *Torbay* are to be reckoned in my estate. Peter Seignoret of Greenwich, Kent, and Mark Anthony Ravaud of Hammersmith, Mddx., Esq., to be execs. Wits: William Allip, Thomas Dove and Edward Rant, clerk of the *Torbay*. Pr. Aug 1727 by execs. named. (PROB 11/616/179).

Edward Plesto of Kent Co., Md., carpenter. Ten shillings each to Col. Thomas Smith and Martha his wife, Edward Wornel and Sarah his wife, Daniel Farrell and Agnis his wife, Thomas Piner, John Tilden, John Woodel and Martha his wife. To the said John Woodel all my carpenter's and cooper's tools. To John Wilson's wife a heifer and calf. To Thomas Lee in Britain £10. To Dorothy, daughter of my brother John Plesto in Britain, £10. To my sister Catherine Eales in Britain the lands and plantation I bought of Col. Richard Tilghman known as Tilghman's Farm. Col. Thomas Smith and William Thomas to be my execs. Wits: John (x) Wilson, Joseph (x) Cox and Edward Scott. AWW 2 Aug 1727 to Mary Boardman, wife of Charles Boardman, niece and next of kin of Catherine Eales alias Yates who was sister of the testator. (PROB 11/616/190).

Samuel Beesley of Bristol, merchant, designed on a voyage overseas [who died in Va.], dated 13 Jun 1726. £10 to my brother William Beesley of Worcester who is to be my exec. Residue to my mother Martha Beesley and my sister Martha Beesley. Wits: Robert Yeascombe and George Hall. Pr. 3 Sep 1727 by affirmation of exec. named. (PROB 11/617/201).

William Alexander of St. Gregory by St. Paul's, London, gent., [who died in Philadelphia], dated 17 Oct 1707. My manor called Ruddock's and my lands in Roydon, Much Farindon and Nasing, Essex, to my wife and exex. Mary Alexander with remainder to my sons William and Charles Alexander. Wits: Bathiah Tyllott, Robert Boz(?) and Philip Tyllott Jr. Pr. 6 Oct 1727 by relict. (PROB 11/617/222).

Henry Maynard of Dublin, Ireland, merchant, [who died in Va.], dated 21 Dec 1719. My whole estate to my wife and exex. Henrietta who is to give £600 each to my children. Wits: Christopher Downes, George More and Thomas Cooke, notary public. Pr. 13 Oct 1727 by the relict. (PROB 11/617/238).

Isaac Lee of Rappahannock River, Va., mariner, but now of Stepney, Mddx., dated 18 Nov 1726. One of my best negroes to my mother Sarah Lee of America, widow. My next best negro to my brother Richard Lee of America. All my lands and houses in America to my brothers John and Hancock Lee with remainder to my sisters Anne Eustace and Elizabeth Lee. Col. Robert Carter and my said brother Richard Lee to be my execs. in America and William Dawkings of London exec. in Britain. Wits: Thomas Freestan, James Lang, Thomas Dove, Sarah Kent, Mary (x) Goodwin and John Newby, attorney at law. AWW Nov 1727 to exec. named. (PROB 11/618/267).

William Phillips of Boston, N.E., merchant, dated 13 Oct 1726. To my friend and exec. John Lovelock, son of William and Jone Lovelock of Chippenham, Wilts., my estate in the occupation of Job Bull and Henry Cox known as Pickers Lea; the house where I live known as the Blew; my three ships *Robert*, *Success* and *Nassau*; a quarter part of the ships *Charming Peggy*, *Bombay* and *William & Mary*, and half of the *New England Chacer* now bound for Lisbon under Mr. John Groves. To my cousins John, Mary and Sarah Phillips one shilling each. To my friend John Hurd Esq. of Boston £500. To my cousins Elizabeth Wilks, Jane Morrice, Mary Morrice and Hannah Farmer £50 each. Wits: John Turner, Henry Dutton and Roger Thompson. Pr. 22 Dec 1727 by exec. named. (PROB 11/618/305).

James Willing of Bristol, soap boiler, dated 25 Nov 1727. £100 each to: my brother Richard Willing of Bristol, merchant; my brother Thomas Willing of Philadelphia, merchant; Mary, Jane and Anne, daughters of Stephen Burcombe of Stinchcombe, Glos., clothier, when they are of age. Two shillings to my brother-in-law George Willing. Residue to my said brother Richard who is to be my exec. Wits: Richard Price, John Bedford, William Naish and G. Tyndall. Pr. 5 Dec 1727 by exec. named. (PROB 11/618/311).

1728

Francis Nicholson Esq., Governor of S.C., now residing in St. George, Hanover Square, Mddx., dated 4 Mar 1728. A white marble tombstone to be erected over my grave inscribed to say that I was born at Downham Park near Richmond, Yorks., on 12 Nov 1655, to give my age at death, and to express my travels and the offices I have held in Europe, Africa, Asia and America. All my papers and manuscripts concerning America are to go to the Society for Propagating the Gospel in Foreign Parts. To my friend and exec. Kingsmill Eyre Esq. my lands in Va., N.E. and Penna. which are to be sold and the produce used to pay the passage of persons coming from N.E. to receive ordination and return as missionaries. Other principal bequests to: Landgrave Abel Ketelby; the children of my sister Phipps; Sir Thomas Frankland; Mr. Frederick Frankland; Robert Ketelby Esq. and his wife and their son Abel Ketelby; Alderman Micajah Perry and his wife; the widow of the late Mr. Richard Perry; Mr. Samuel Wragg and his wife and children. Wits: Eliza Dreury, Francis Bonifant, John Wright and Moody Gilbert. Pr. 5 Mar 1728 by exec. named. (PROB 11/621/91).

John De Lanne of Charles Town, S.C., surgeon, now living in Stepney, Mddx., dated 16 Sep 1727. My whole estate to my cousins and execs. Robert Aubert of Old Artillery, watchmaker, and Anne de Lannay of Stepney, spinster, in trust for my wife Mary De Lanne. £200 each to Peter De Lanne, Mary De Lanne and Susanna De Lanne. Mr. Isaac Chardon of Carolina has been empowered to transmit to my execs. the produce of my effects in Carolina. Wits: James Miffant and George Schutz, clerk to Mr. Isaac Delpech, notary public in Threadneedle Street. Pr. 24 May 1728 by execs. named. (PROB 11/622/145).

George Atchison, late of Charles Town, S.C., but now of Islington, Mddx., merchant. My real estate to my youngest brother John Atchison of S.C. who is to pay annuities to my mother Jane Paterson alias Atchison and my eldest brother David Atchison. Other bequests to: my sisters Jennett and Grizell Atchison; my cousin John Atchison; Mr. James Pain of Charles Town, merchant; Mary Atchison, daughter of my said brother David. Residue of personal estate to my brother John Atchison. Execs: my cousin David Atchison and the said James Pain. Wits: William Glencross, Cane Glencross and Robert Crosby. Pr. 12 Sep 1728 by David Atchison and 27 Oct 1729 by James Pain. (PROB 11/624/256).

Henry James of Bristol, merchant tailor, dated 20 Apr 1724. £5 to my son John James. One guinea to my son Joseph James, for whom I have already provided, a piece of gold to his wife Frances, and £10 to my grandson Joseph James. £5 to my daughter Elizabeth for whom I have also provided since her marriage. £5 to my friend Mary Pratt. My lands and plantations in Penna. to my only unmarried daughter Hannah James who is to be my exex. Wits: Walter Kipping, John Cray and George Hardwicke. Pr. 1 Oct 1728 by exex. named. (PROB 11/625/294).

John Harman of Bermondsey, Sy., mariner, [who died on the merchant ship *Forward* in Va.], dated 12 Feb 1711. My whole estate to my wife Mary Harman who is to be my exex. Wits: Sarah (x) Allen, John Allen and John Kidder, notary public. Pr. Dec 1728 by the relict. PROB 11/626/354).

1729

Jonathan Bull of Boston, N.E., mariner, dated 2 Aug 1727. To be buried at the discretion of my friend Samuel Storke of London, merchant. One-third of my estate to my wife Elizabeth Bull and two-thirds to my children Elizabeth, John and Samuel Bull when they come of age or are married. My said wife and my brother Mr. Samuel Greenleafe to be execs. Wits: Mary Hyatt of Ratcliffe, widow, Mudd Fuller of Broad Street, Ratcliffe, scrivener, and J. Hacket, his servant. Pr. 7 Jan 1729 by the relict. (PROB 11/627/2).

Albert Muller [of Bristol who died in S.C., bachelor], dated 21 Jun 1724. £50 to the poor of the Danish Lutheran Church in Well Close Square, London. £10 to my sister Inger, widow of Christen Hesselberg, now resident in Norway. £10 each to Elizabeth Couch and Barbara Evans. £5 to Ann Evans. Residue to Lyder Muller, son of my brother Jochim Muller, now reported to be residing in Amsterdam. Wits: Barbara Evans and John Cable. AWW 21 Jan 1729 to the nephew Lyder Muller. (PROB 11/627/17). 9 Jan 1738 granted to Walter Lougher, adr. of Lyder Muller deceased.

George Smith of Va. [who died in St. George the Martyr, Mddx.], dated 7 Oct 1728. My estate in Va. and West Indies, lately descended to me by the death of my father Christopher Smith, to my aunt Sarah Tayler, wife of Richard Tayler of St. George the Martyr, and they are to be my execs. Wits: John Bincliffe, Isaac Sugden and Robert Jones. Pr. 28 Jan 1729 by execs. named. (PROB 11/627/25).

William Stuart, now resident in Boston, N.E., mariner, bound to sea, dated 14 Oct 1724. My estate in Boston to my friend Thomas Steel Esq. of Boston who is to be my exec. My estate in Britain to my brother Joseph Stuart and my sister Deborah. Wits: Benjamin Eliot, Benjamin Bridge and Samuel Tyley. Pr. Boston 18 Mar 1717. AWW granted London 3 Feb 1729 to John Dod, attorney for the exec. in Boston. (PROB 11/628/56).

Charles Faldo of Yateley, Hants., gent., [who died in Carolina], dated 1 Mar 1725. My estate to my wife Mary Faldo. My brother-in-law William Palmer of St. Bride's, London, turner, to be exec. in trust for the benefit of my children. Wits: Thomas Lucas, Edward Bremer and George Elly. Pr. 1 Apr 1729 by exec. named, the wife having died in the testator's lifetime. (PROB 11/629/104).

Robert Willison, late of S.C. but now of St. Saviour, Southwark, Sy., merchant, dated 2 Feb 1729. £120 and an annuity of £10 to my wife Elizabeth Willison. £100 each to my uncle George Oldner and to Mr. Zaccheus Routh who are to be execs. in trust for such purposes as my aunt Alice Oldner shall appoint. Wits: Thomas Davis, Samuel Carberley and Francis Priest. Pr. 16 May 1729 by affirmation of George Oldner and 14 Apr 1732 by Zaccheus Routh. (PROB 11/630/154).

James Bowles of St. Mary's Co., Md., merchant, dated 13 Jun 1727, (copied from Md. records). To my daughter Elenor Bowles my plantation called Half Pond and land in Scotch Creek where Robert Phillip, Daniel Curr, John Gibbons and Henry Tucker dwell. To my daughter Mary Bowles the land where Hector McLain lived adjoining John Read's, and land called Hog Neck along the branch called Break Neck Hill to the main road to our church, and land to the south side from where Owen Read lived to the headline between John Hall and William Wilkinson. To my daughter Jane Bowles the residue of my lands in St. Mary's Co. where my dwelling house stands and all my land called Masson's and over St. Thomas's Creek where Dr. Magill lives. My wife Rebecca Bowles may choose one-quarter of the above lands on which to dwell during her lifetime and is to be my exex. I forgive the debt owed me by my uncle George Bowles. £50 to my poor relations in England. Wits: William Brogden, John Mitchell, Josias Jeffery, D. Makill and Edmund Plowden. Pr. 23 Jun 1729 by the relict. (PROB 11/630/159).

Evan Evans, vicar of Sutterton, Lincs., [who died in Md.], dated 2 Nov 1716. To my wife Alice my mortgage of part of William Robinson's estate in Denbighshire during her lifetime with reversion to my son-in-law Thomas Lloyd and his heirs by my daughter Mary. If I die before my return from America, I request the Bishops of London and Lincoln to influence the King to present the living of Sutterton to my son-in-law. My estate in America, including what may be due to me from Philadelphia or the Society for Services of Churches Abroad, and what may be due from my living at

Sutterton to Mr. John Brace of London, clothworker, who is to be my exec. Wits: Robert Cock, John Rogers and George Ho (*sic*). Pr. 8 Aug 1729 by the named exec. (PROB 11/631/223).

Pinchback Hamerton of London [of Va., bachelor], son and heir of Edmond Hamerton, tobacconist and planter, who died in Va., now bound on a voyage thither to see after the estate he has left me, dated 6 Jan 1721. My sister Hannah Cloke, wife of Richard Cloke, shoemaker of the Minories, London, to be my legatee and exex. Wits: Thomas Hollis, Thomas Howell and Joseph Nurse, servant to Thomas Hollis. Pr. 29 Dec 1729 by exex. named. (PROB 11/634/339).

James Tenant [of Princess Ann Co., Va.], clerk, dated 23 Dec 1726. To my wife Elizabeth Tenant my five negroes Caesar, Tom, Jack, --ndy and Sarah and her two mulatto children Davis and Lewis. To my daughter Elizabeth Tenant my five negroes Alifa and her two children, Betty, Sarah, Abednego and Pegg, with remainder to her brothers James and Samuel Tenant. To my eldest son James when he is of age £200 in the hands of Capt. John Hide, merchant in London. To my son Samuel when he comes of age £100, also held by Capt. John Hide. All my tobacco in this Co. and in Norfolk Co. to my said sons. My execs. to be my said wife, Capt. Charles Sayer and Maj. Anthony Walke. Wits: Francis Laud and Thomas Thorowgood. Pr. Va. 1 Mar 1727. AWW granted London 20 Dec 1729 to Thomas Sandford, attorney for the relict Elizabeth, now wife of Lewis Conner, in Va. (PROB 11/634/355).

Roger Whitley, Ensign of Gen. Francis Nicholson's Independent Company at Fort King George, S.C., dated 7 Oct 1726. To be buried at the discretion of my commanding officer Lieut. James Watt. To my creditor Mr. Alexander Nisbett all my wages in the hands of Kingsmill Eyres and my effects at Barton's, Charles Town. Wits: Philip Delegat, Thomas Hamilton and Christopher Clarke. AWW 10 Dec 1729 to William Livingston, attorney for Alexander Nisbett in Edinburgh, Scotland. (PROB 11/634/357).

1730

Thomas Simson Esq., born in Port Royal, Jamaica, and now of St. Martin the Fields, Mddx., [of N.Y. and Philadelphia, who died in Jamaica], dated 7 Jly 1725. Neither my wife nor her relations are to be invited to my funeral. £200 each to my brothers and sister now in Jamaica John, William, James and Love Simson and Mary Simson. £500 held by Mr. Nathaniel Barnardiston of Budge Row,

London, merchant, to Tablay James, natural son of the late Capt.
Edward James of Jamaica, merchant. Thirty guineas each to: Mr.
George Oxenden of Hungerford Market, St. Martin in the Fields,
victualler, and Sarah his wife; and William Burley Esq. of Hungerford Market, Margaret his wife and William their son. £30 each to
Andrew Flinge of Cross Lane near Spur Alley in the same parish,
waterman, and Mary his wife. £50 each to Mr. Peter Valette and
my mother Ann, now his wife, in Jamaica. £50 to Mr. John Cavalier
of Kingston, Jamaica. Many other bequests. My friends Mr. Nathaniel St. Andre, Mr. William Parrott, Mr. Joseph Macham and Mr.
Thomas Steele to be execs. in Britain; Mr. Peter Valette and Ann
his wife, and Mr. John Cavalier to be execs. in Jamaica. Wits:
Matthew Hudson, John Jackson and Richard Titt. Pr. 19 Feb 1730
by Nathaniel St. Andre; admon. of Mar 1729 to the relict Ann
Simson revoked. (PROB 11/636/50).

Francis Stocking [of Hilborough, Norfolk], dated 27 Jan 1730. To my
kinsman and exec. John Stocking of Hilborough, blacksmith, my
plantation in Philadelphia which was left to me by the will of my
son Thomas Stocking. Twenty shillings to William Alcock, son of
William Alcock. Wits: Mary Carpenter, Rebecka Andrews and John
Carpenter. Pr. 7 Feb 1730 by the nephew John Stocking. (PROB
11/636/51).

Thomas Kerr of Stepney, Mddx., mariner of H.M. ship *Chatham*, [of
Portsmouth, Hampshire, who died in N.Y.], dated 28 Feb 1716. My
whole estate to my wife Jane Kerr who is to be my exex. Wits:
Margaret Britcher and Francis Warner. Pr. 13 Apr 1730 by the
relict. (PROB 11/636/89).

William Crockett of H.M. ship *Alborough*, now in S.C., [who died in
Providence Island, S.C. bachelor], dated 15 Sep 1729. My friend
Thomas Vinter of London to be my exec. and legatee. Wits: J.
Daniell, J. Culforth and John Kingland. Pr. 13 Jun 1730 by exec.
named. (PROB 11/638/153).

William Burnett, Governor of N.Y. and N.J., dated 6 Dec 1727. To
be buried at the chapel of the Fort in N.Y., if I die there, near my
wife Mary and one of my children. My estate in Holland and
England is to be sold by my brother-in-law David Mitchell and my
sister, his wife Mary, and the proceeds from my father's *History*
are to be added and be used to satisfy my debt to the estate of
my brother Gilbert Burnett. My personal estate in America is to be
sold for the use of my children William, Mary and Thomas which
I had by my late wife Mary Vanhorn. Abraham Vanhorn and Mary
his wife are to be my execs. and take care of my minor son Gilbert
Burnett. Wits: Is. Bovin, John Haskett and Stephen Deblois. Pr. 9
Jly 1730 by execs. named. (PROB 11/638/183).

Alexander Denny of Charles Town, S.C., mariner, [who died in Stepney, Mddx.], dated 10 May 1728. My whole estate to my wife Lucy Denny during her lifetime with remainder to the children of my late brother James Denny of Crawford's Dock near Glasgow, Scotland, the children of my wife's late brother Thomas Botley of Sarum, Wilts, shoemaker, and the children of my wife's sister whose maiden name was Elizabeth Botley. Mr. John Brome, master of H.M. ship *Scarborough* to be exec. Wits: Christopher Ruby, Thomas Atkinson and William Smith, Register at Charles Town. AWW 4 Aug 1730 to the relict, the named exec. renouncing. (PROB 11/639/234).

Robert Traweek of Butomocke, Va., mariner of H.M. ship *Plymouth*, widower, dated 10 May 1729. My whole estate to my son George Traweek who is to be exec. Wits: Thomas Bignall, Jonathan Bennett and J. Tyler, clerk. AWW 17 Aug 1730 to Thomas Bignall, guardian of the son George Traweek. (PROB 11/639/267).

Theophilus Rogers of Northampton, dated 30 Jan 1730. To be buried where my sister Bridget lies. All my manors and lands in trust to my friends and execs. Jonathan Warner Jr. and William Bevor of the Exchequer, and my brother Robert Rogers. My household goods and an annuity of £100 to my mother Elizabeth Rogers. An annuity of £40 to my sister Elizabeth Goodfellow and £200 each to her three children when they come of age. An advowson to such son of Mr. Wilmer of Sywell, (Northants.), as shall be educated as a priest. An annuity of £20 to my sister Woodburn. An annuity of £20 to my sister Anne Rogers and £500 to buy lands. To the four children of my late unhappy brother John Rogers £1,000 when they come of age. To my brother William Christopher Rogers £200 and to each of his children £100. £50 each of to Dorothea, Penelope and Sarah Poreton, daughters of my late master Poreton. £500 for the education of William and Bennet Wilmer, younger sons of William Wilmer. Two silver servers to Mrs. Penelope Merriott, wife of George Merriott. £20 for mourning to Mrs. Rebecca Rokeby of Stratford, Essex, and £500 to her daughter Elizabeth Rokeby. Other bequests to: the poor of Moreton Pinkney, (Northants.); the children of my brother Wills; my nephews John and Richard Rogers, sons of the late John Rogers; my nephews Theophilus and Timothy Goodfellow. Wits: Jane Rushworth, William Orme and John Harper. Deposition made 11 Sep 1730 by Timothy Rogers of Northampton, gent., brother of the testator, that he discovered the will in a drawer in the house of his mother. The deceased left only three sisters, Elizabeth, Christian and Ann. Pr. 11 Sep 1730 by Robert Rogers and William Beevor. (PROB 11/640/89). See NGSQ 62/205 which indicates that Richard Rogers, son of "the late unhappy John

Rogers" who was a ship's captain in the Guinea trade, emigrated to Va. in 1754 but no trace of him or his descendants was discovered there in 1774.

Edward Henry Calvert Esq. of Annapolis, Md., dated Md. 24 Apr 1730. My whole estate to my wife Margaret Calvert who is to be my exex. Wits: Benedict Leonard Calvert (Governor of Md.), Charles Calvert and Samuel Stringer. Pr. Md. 15 May 1730. Pr. London 20 Nov 1730 by the relict. (PROB 11/640/300).

Richard Cary of Bristol, merchant, bound on a voyage to sea [who died in Va., bachelor], dated 26 Feb 1712. Half my estate to my father John Cary Esq. of Bristol during his lifetime with remainder to my brother and exec. Warren Cary who is to have the other half of my estate. Wits: George Payne and Thomas Cary. AWW 24 Nov 1730 to Jane Cary, spinster, niece by a brother, the named exec. having died. (PROB 11/640/301).

Joseph Myatt, commander-in-chief at Albany Fort, America, for the Hudson's Bay Co., [widower], dated 6 Mar 1728. £20 to my friend Mr. Thomas Bird, Secretary to the Co. £10 to Margaret Hall, daughter of my master John Hall of Congleton, Cheshire. £2 to the poor of Congleton. The residue to my three brothers William, Philip and Jonathan Myatt in Congleton. The said John Bird and Mr. Richard Staunton of London, gent., to be my execs. Wits: Richard White and John Bricker. Depositions made 7 Nov 1730 by George Spurrell and Christopher Middleton of Stepney, Mddx., mariners, that the testator died in June last and the will is in his hand. Pr. same day by named execs. (PROB 11/641/310).

William Donkester of Broadstairs, St. Peter in Thanet, Kent, mariner [of the merchant ship Henrietta, who died in Boston, N.E., bachelor], dated 18 Apr 1729. £10 each to my cousin Elizabeth Huson of Margate, (Kent), and my aunt Ann Pearce of Upton. The residue to my aunt Judy Cooke who is to be my exex. No witnesses shown. Depositions made 9 Dec 1730 by Anthony Curling of St. Peter in Thanet and Jeremiah Jones of Stepney, Mddx., mariners, that the will was signed by the testator and left by him with his aunt Judy Cooke at Broadstairs. Pr. same day by the named exex. (PROB 11/641/329).

Elizabeth Levett of Prince George Co., Md., widow, dated 22 Sep 1725. To my son Robert Levett when he is 18 my interest in an estate in Beverley, Yorks., which may be due to me as the relict of Robert Levett deceased. To my son John Levett £150 and furniture when he is 18. To my daughter Elizabeth Duskin a negro called Tom. £5 to Col. James Haddock. To my brother Daniel Mariartee and my sister Margaret Sprigg a ring of 20 shillings. The residue to my two daughters Margaret and Ruth Clark. The said Col. Haddock and Margaret Clark to be my execs. Wits: Josiah Wilson, Margaret (x) Dick and Lingan Wilson. (Copied from Md. Will Book No. 1, folio 416). Pr. Md. 4 Jan 1729 by George Buchanan and Margaret his wife and James Haddock. Pr. London 5 Dec 1730 by James Haddock and Margaret Clark alias Buchanan, wife of George Buchanan. (PROB 11/641/335).

1731

Mary Buttall of Exeter, Devon, widow, dated 23 Mar 1730. Bequests to: my grandchildren Joseph, Jory, Nathaniel, Mary, Valentine and Frances Hodges, children of my daughter Dame Mary Hodges, widow; my grandchildren George, Samuel, Benjamin, Humphrey, Mary, Sarah and Elizabeth Wiggington, children of my daughter Sarah Wiggington; my grandchildren Mary and John Wells and their brother, whose name I have forgotten, children of my daughter Mary Wells; my grandchildren Mary, Sarah, Samuel and their brother whose name I have forgotten, children of my son Humphrey Buttall; my granddaughter Mary, daughter of my son Charles Buttall; my sons-in-law Thomas Wiggington and Abraham Wells; my estate near New London, Edistow River, Carolina, to go to Dame Mary Hodges in trust for my son Charles Buttall; my sons Benjamin and Humphrey Buttall. Execs. to be my said sons and daughters. Wits: Joan Badcock, John Grant and John Stoodly. Pr. 10 Feb 1731 by Mary Hodges. (PROB 11/642/26).

John Hackett [of Penna., bachelor], dated 27 Mar 1721. In case I die this voyage I make this as my will. £5 each to my sister Mary Bolter and my brothers Thomas Bolter and Thomas Hackett. The residue to my father John Hackett of Worcester. Wits: Lydia Pocock and Elizabeth Allibon. AWW 25 Feb 1731 by affirmation to the brother Thomas Hackett, the father having died. (PROB 11/642/37).

Daniel Webber of Stepney, Mddx., now intending a voyage to N.E., mariner, dated 19 Feb 1724. My whole estate to my wife Susanna Webber who is to be my exex. Wits: Anne (x) Allen and John Coverly in Whitechapel. Pr. 26 Apr 1731 by the relict. (PROB 11/644/108).

John Pratt, formerly of Va., merchant, at present residing in Manor Street, Chelsea, Mddx., dated 12 Feb 1731. My friends Joseph Windham of London, linen draper, William Hunt of London, merchant, Philip Perry of London, merchant, and Roger Tublay

of Chelsea are to be my execs. The £1,000 which was devised
by my nephew, the late William Pratt of Gloucester Co., Va.,
merchant, to his daughter Elizabeth Pratt is to be paid and she
is to have £500 from my own estate when she comes of age,
with remainder to her brother Keith William Pratt and my nephew
James Pratt who now live with me. The said William Keith Pratt
is never to be bound to the Va. trade. £30 to my brother William
Pratt and his wife Cresswell who live at Peterhead, Aberdeenshire,
Scotland. The residue to my said nephew James Pratt. Wits: John
Oldfield, Henry Anderson and Thomas Arslett. Pr. 22 Jly 1731
by Joseph Windham, Roger Tublay and Philip Perry. (PROB
11/645/193).

Graves Packe of London, mariner, now bound on a voyage overseas,
[of Va., master of the merchant ship *Gooch*], dated 16 Dec 1728.
To my wife Elizabeth Packe £100 and a negro woman Patt with
her children, and she is to relinquish her right of dower to my
exec. Mr. Edward Randolph. Rings for mourning to my friends Col.
David Bray, Maj. John Holloway and Mr. John Randolph. £50 each
to my godson Graves Packe, son of my son Richard Packe, and
my godson Beverly Randolph. To my friend Edward Randolph of
London, merchant, my 350 acres in James City Co. on Skitles Creek
bequeathed to me by Mr. Samuel Pond of Skitles Creek, merchant,
by his will of Jly 1717, 250 acres near the mouth of Skitles Creek
lately purchased of Mr. Holden in London, a tract of 275 acres in
Hanover Co. (formerly New Kent Co.) on Maddade Creek, now in
the tenure of John Holden, and four lots at Queen Mary's Port near
Williamsburg with the houses thereon. My execs. to be Mr. Edward
Randolph of London and John Randolph of Williamsburg. Wits:
Jacobus Lone, notary public, Arthur Lane Bowman, his clerk, and
Thomas Green. Pr. 14 Aug 1731 by Edward Randolph. (PROB
11/646/215).

Philip Boldry of Wapping, Mddx., mariner [of the merchant ship *Patsey*,
who died in Va., bachelor], dated 1 Feb 1731. My friend William
Greene of Wapping, victualler, to be my legatee and exec. Wits:
Richard Corddaux and John Lordor. Pr. 15 Sep 1731 by named
exec. (PROB 11/646/222).

Henry Lowe Sr. of St. Mary's Co., Md., gent., dated 25 Oct 1717.
To my son Henry Lowe the tract of 1,300 acres where he now
lives and a tract called Green Oak. To my son Bennet Lowe the
tract where he now lives and all my lands in Baltimore Co.
between Mr. Darnall and myself. To my son Thomas Lowe my
old plantation in the Freshes. To my son Nicholas Lowe the
plantation where I now dwell. To my three daughters Ann,
Elizabeth and Henrietta Maria Lowe my tract called Golden

Grove. To my daughter Dorothy my New Design in Freshes. To my daughter Mary a tract called Wood's Quarters. To my daughter Susanna Maria, wife of Mr. Charles Digges, £100. The residue of my estate in England and Md. to my children excepting Susanna Maria Digges. My sons Henry and Bennet to be execs. Wits: Samuel Grastis, Richard Brooks and Michael Jennifer. (Copied from Md. Wills Book No. 6, folio 453). Pr. Md. 6 Nov 1717. Further undated will. To my sister Susanna Digges the resurveyed tracts called Bennett's Lowe in Kent Co. and Green Oak, and land in Cecil Co. called Sprie's Hill, on condition that her husband relinquishes to my sister Mary Neale any title he claims to a plantation in Prince Co. where his dwelling stands. To my sister Elizabeth Darnall my plantation known as part of Delabrook Manor in St. Mary's Co. and three tracts near St. Mary's Court House, formerly occupied by Maria Farthing. To my said sister Mary Neale my 1,500 acres in Charles Co. called Barbados which I exchanged with Mr. John Digges. To my sister Dorothy Lowe the tract called Golden Grove in Dorchester Co. To Mrs. Mary Young of St. Mary's Co. four working slaves and a tract called Workenton during her lifetime with remainder to my sister Elizabeth Darnall. The negro families are not to be parted at the division of my estates. The residue to my said sisters. Mr. Charles Digges and Mr. Henry Darnall are to be my execs. Depositions taken 23 May 1729 from Christian Geist of Annapolis, gent. aged 30, Robert Elliot of St. Mary's Co., gent., Philip Key of the same, aged 32, and Edward Cole of the same, gent., that the above will is in the testator's hand. Pr. 8 Sep 1731 by the daughters, Elizabeth, wife of Henry Darnall, and Dorothy, wife of Francis Hall; the sons, Henry Lowe and Bennet Lowe, having died in Antigua. (PROB 11/646/233).

Charles, Earl of Orrery, dated 6 Nov 1728. To William Bird Esq. of Va. a gold watch. Other principal bequests to: my only son John, Lord Boyle; my exec. Henry, Earl of Uxbridge; Viscount Windsor; Col. William Cecil; Dr. Robert Friend, master of Westminster School; Mrs. Swordfeger; the poor of Burnham, Bucks. Wits: William Marrow, J. Delval and L. Poly. Pr. 15 Sep 1731 by named exec. (PROB 11/646/236).

William Bamber of Bermondsey, Surrey, shipwright of the *Five Sisters*, Capt. Gideon Holmes, now going on a voyage, [of the merchant ship *Bugill* who died in N.Y., bachelor], dated 1 Apr 1729. My whole estate to Anne Scott, daughter of my exec. Thomas Scott of Bermondsey, victualler. Wits: Thomas Swan, John Barwick and Samuel Clark, scrivener in Jacob Street near Rotherhithe Wall. Pr. 20 Dec 1731 by exec. named. (PROB 11/648/298).

1732

Thomas New of Bristol, now residing in Philadelphia, commander of the brigantine *Faro*, dated 30 May 1728 in the port of Philadelphia. My whole estate to my wife Elizabeth and the child she carries, if born alive. My friend William Attwood of Philadelphia, merchant, to be my exec. for Penna. and N.J.; and my said wife for England. Wits: John White, John Smith, Charles Brockden and Joseph Breintall. Pr. 11 Jan 1732 by the relict Elizabeth, now wife of Joseph Reynolds. (PROB 11/649/20).

John Smith of Hartford, Connecticut, merchant, now in Cork, Ireland, dated 18 Nov 1731. My house and warehouse in Hartford and £100 to my wife Ann Smith. The residue of my estate to be sold for the benefit of my three (minor) children George, Mary and William Smith. My said wife and David Williams, master of my ship *William*, to be execs. My said ship and my sloop *Mary*, both in Cork harbour, to be sent to Mr. James Calwell at Bristol, merchant, for disposal. Wits: Elizabeth Bartlett, Samuel Bartlett and Robert Wallis, notary public. Pr. Jan 1732 by David Williams. (PROB 11/649/23).

William Richardson Jr. of Md., mariner, [who died in Rotherhithe, Surrey], dated 17 Sep 1731. To be buried in the Friends' burial ground. My estate to be divided between William and Richard Richardson, sons of my brother Joseph Richardson. My friend Thomas Plumsted, merchant in London, to be exec. Wits: Richard Petty, Thomas Barton and David Maude. Pr. 3 Mar 1732 by affirmation of named exec. (PROB 11/650/81).

Charles Dunster of Perth Amboy, Mddx. Co., [N.J., bachelor], dated 25 Apr 1706. £200 to my sister Margaret, wife of Daniel Roy. £100 each to: John MacCallow of Chiswick, Mddx., gent.; Isaac Ashby of London, merchant; Thomas Nicholas of London, merchant. £50 each to: my niece Mary, wife of Andrew Donalson; John Weymss of St. Martin's in the Fields, Mddx., surgeon; William Sinclair of the same, wigmaker; Margaret Wallice of the same; Nicholas Mandell of the same, gent.; Gilbert Elliot of the same, gent.; John Boughton of the New Inn, Mddx., gent; my friend George Robison of the White Horse, Lombard Street, London; Mrs. Janet Sutton, wife of Thomas Sutton; Mr. James Stevens, usher at Edinburgh; Evander Markwer of Edinburgh, vintner. To my nephew Duncan Wright, gent., now in France, one shilling. To my friend James Alexander, Attorney-General of the Jerseys, one-quarter of all the lands I have taken up in the Jerseys, and one-quarter of my share of the estate in America of the late Joseph Ormston of

London, but reserving to my heirs the tract of 1,650 acres commonly called (blank) formerly belonging to Lord Niell Campbell. One hundred acres to Michael Kearney. My relations and friends in Perthshire, Scotland, are to be given an account of my estate by my execs. James Alexander, Mr. Michael Kearney of Perth Amboy and Mr. John Boughton, attorney at law. Wits: Thomas McIntosh, Alexander MacDowall and Marcela Fagan. Codicils of 16 and 17 Feb 1727. A tract of 1,650 acres on the north branch of Rareton River above the upper end of Reed's Island to my kinsman Daniel Donalson who is to fulfil my agreement with John Fraser relating to the same. Marcela Fagan is to receive one shilling only. Wits: Robert King, John Watson and Alexander MacDowall. Pr. 6 Apr 1732 by John MacCulloch and John Boughton. (PROB 11/651/103).

Thomas Mason of Cecil Co, Md., merchant, [who died in Philadelphia, bachelor], only son and heir at law of John Mason, late of Philadelphia, tailor, dated Philadelphia 4 Nov 1731. My exec. John Copson of Cecil Co., merchant, is to pay £15 current to William Carter Esq. of Philadelphia. To my sister Mary, when she is 21, the balance of the £150 legacy she was bequeathed by Amy Lee of Eton or Windsor, (Berks.). Wits: Owen Owen, John Jones and Francis Sherrard. Pr. Philadelphia 13 Mar 1732. Deposition made 5 Jun 1732 by Andrew Duchee as husband of Mary Duchee alias Mason of Philadelphia, sister of the testator, that John Copson had renounced admon. AWW 6 Jun 1732 to Andrew Duchee. (PROB 11/652/171).

William Hammond of Ratcliffe, Mddx., gent., dated 9 Jly 1732. My farm in Thundersley, Essex, to my uncle William Clopton of Va. during his lifetime with remainder to his children. Other bequests to: my friends and execs. Samuel Skinner Esq. and Josiah Cole, apothecary, of Ratcliffe; Mary Hammond Waters; Christian Waters. Wits: Thomas Taylor, Hannah (x) Norman and Mudd Fuller, scrivener. Pr. 17 Jly 1732 by the named execs. (PROB 11/652/188). See NGSQ 60/260.

Hickford Leman of London, gent. [of Piscatua, Md., bachelor], dated 14 Aug 1703. To my brother Daniel Cooper my half of a lead mine in Derbyshire with remainder to his son John Cooper. The residue of my estate to my said brother who is to be exec. Wits: Joseph Quilter, John Hill and John Overman of Aldgate without. Pr. 30 Aug 1732 by named exec. (PROB 11/653/211).

Samuel Ranolds of Stepney, Mddx., mariner [of H.M. ship *Fox*, who died in S.C., bachelor], dated 10 Aug 1730. My friend Richard Miller of Stepney, waterman, to be my legatee and exec. Wits: Richard Jones and Timothy Thompson, notary public at Cock Hill, Shadwell. Pr. 7 Aug 1732 by the named exec. (PROB 11/653/215).

Gerard Collingwood of Wapping, Mddx., mariner [of the merchant ship *Three Brothers*, who died in Va., bachelor], dated 24 Sep 1728. My friends John Slater and Elinor his wife to be my legatees and execs. Wits: Thomas Grimes and John Worthy. Pr. 20 Oct 1732 by Eleanor Slater, widow. (PROB 11/654/244).

Elias Solomon, late of N.E. and now of Rotherhithe, Surrey, mariner, dated 14 Sep 1725. My whole estate to Sarah Pike of Rotherhithe, widow, and Sarah Pike her daughter who are to be my exexs. Wits: John Teale and John Allen, notary public on Redriffe Wall. Pr. 28 Aug 1732 by Sarah Pike Sr. (PROB 11/653/217).

James Greive, mariner, outward bound to Va. in the *Sarah*, dated 28 Jan 1729. My whole estate to my friend Catherine Scott of Stepney, Mddx., who is to be my exex. Wits: John Parsons and John Newby, attorney at law. Pr. Dec 1732 by Catherine Scott, widow. (PROB 11/655/284).

1733

Peter Jeffreys, mariner of H.M. ship *Kinsale* [of the merchant ship *Prosperous Ann* who died in Md., bachelor], dated 20 May 1731. My whole estate to my brother Robert Jeffreys of London who is to be my exec. Wits: John Brome, James Reddall and James Rickman. Pr. 22 Jan 1733 by the named exec. (PROB 11/656/15).

James Smith, [late Secretary of N.J. who died at Burlington, N.J.], dated 17 Mar 1721. All my estate in N.J. to Sir Thomas Mackworth of Normanton, Rutland, who is to be my exec. Wits: Ann Luffingham Sr., Ann Luffingham Jr. and John Minskipp. Pr. 22 Apr 1736 by exec. named. (PROB 11/657/63).

John Dunton, citizen and stationer of London, late of St. Giles Cripplegate, [formerly of N.E. but late of Stepney, Mddx.], dated 22 Apr 1733. £300 to my adopted child Mrs. Isabella Edwards, widow, late of Dean Street, Holborn, for the devotion she has shown me since our first acquaintance in Ireland. Other principal bequests (in an exceedingly long will) to: Mr. William Lutwich and Mrs. Susannah Lutwich and her mother Mrs. Elizabeth Collings, widow; my cousins William and Nathaniel Reading; my brother-in-law Mr. John Sudbury, watchmaker, and his wife Hesther, "once a destitute sister"; my old landlord Mr. Richard Wilkins of Boston, N.E., and his daughter Comford Wilkins; Mr. Zechariah Marriott in New Street, London, wire drawer, who is to inherit the portion left to me by my brother Luke Denton before he went to the East Indies; my cousins James, Ann and Mary Townsend of Brainsford (?Braintree, Essex); My sister Elizabeth Guise of Hertford; Mary Richard-

son, sister of my first wife Elizabeth (Annesley); my sister Anne
Annesley; my sister Sarah Fromantle; my cousin Richard Woolhouse; Mrs. Brick, widow, living at Boston, N.E. To my second
wife Sarah Dunton a ring inscribed either "Set your affection on
things above" or "Forgive your enemies and die in malice with no
man." I am to be buried beside my first wife Elizabeth who died
on 28 May 1697. Richard Nowland to be my exec. Wits: John
Reef, Adam Rossor and Robert Owen Jr. Pr. 24 Mar 1733 by exec.
named. (PROB 11/657/82). New grant Jun 1744.

Edward Brailsford of S.C., dated 24 Mar 1730. To be buried near my
late wife in the churchyard of St. Andrew. To my son Edward
Brailsford £5 current. My 12,070 acres called Coeshah Island to be
sold. Residue to my sons John Joseph Morton and Samuel Brailsford.
Arthur Middleton Esq. and Mrs. (Sarah) Middleton to be execs. Wits:
Andrew Leslie, Burrl. M. Hyrne and Henry Hyrne. AWW to Samuel
Wragg, attorney for named execs. in S.C. (PROB 11/658/110). 25
May 1762 granted to Samuel Brailsford, attorney for surviving exec.
Sarah Middleton, widow.

William Fleet of Alderbury, (Wilts.), [formerly of Martin Worthy,
Hampshire, but late of Choptank, Talbot Co., Md., who died at sea
on the ship *Peach Blossom*, bachelor], dated 6 Apr 1727. £10 each
to my brothers Mathew, Henry, Giles, John and Richard Fleet and
my sisters Mary and Elizabeth Fleet. A mourning ring to Mr.
Richard Widmore and Mrs. Elizabeth Widmore of Longparish,
(Hants.), and Mr. and Mrs. Thomas King of the Sack, Winchester.
My brother Mathew and sisters Mary and Elizabeth to be execs.
On 14 Mar 1733 Henry Fleet of Rosemary Lane, Whitechapel,
Mddx., salesman, and Richard Fleet of Alderbury, Wilts, hus-
bandman, deposed that the above will was in the hand of the
testator. Pr. 11 Apr 1733 by the surviving exec. Mary Tanner alias
Fleet, wife of Robert Tanner. (PROB 11/658/115).

Daniel Webb Esq. of Monkton Farley, Wilts., dated 13 Feb 1732. All
my lands and tenements at South Wraxall, Bathford and Bradford,
Wilts. and Somerset, in trust to John Talbot Esq. of Lacock, (blank)
Northey Esq. of Compton, James Powell of Rodbourne Court and
Thomas Dycke of Limpley Stoke, gent., for the benefit of my
grandson John Webb Seymour until he is aged 24, with remainder
to my grandsons William, Francis and Edward Seymour. Other
bequests to: my nephews Michael Smith Webb, Daniel Webb and
Isaac Webb, sons of my late brother Isaac Webb of N.E., watchmaker; my sister-in-law Susannah Hunt, sister of my late wife. My
son-in-law Edward Seymour Esq. to be exec. Wits: John Harris, John
Perry and Richard Lovemore. Pr. 8 Jun 1733 by exec. named. (PROB
11/660/189).

James Grape of New Windsor, Berks., gent., dated 22 Apr 1733. To be buried with my late wife. All my real estate in Wokingham, Berks., to my son Richard Grape who is to pay an annuity of £24 each to my daughters Esther and Arabella. £200 to my son Samuel Grape in S.C. £20 to my granddaughter Mary Grape when she comes of age. O'seers: my friends Hon. John Sale, Mr. William Waterson and Mr. Elliot Salter. My said son Richard to be exec. Wits: Thomas Hobbs, Nathaniel Richardson and W. Sumner. Pr. 18 Jly 1733 by exec. named. (PROB 11/660/198).

Samuel Cornock of London, mariner, now bound to Philadelphia, [master of the ship *Molly*, who died in S.C., bachelor], dated 31 Aug 1730. £10 to my brother Daniel Cornock. Residue to Thomas Plumsted of Gracechurch Street, London, ironmonger, who is to be exec. Wits: S. Martyn in Birchin Lane, Anthony Welden, his clerk, and John Ditcher. Pr. Aug 1733 by affirmation of named exec. (PROB 11/660/218).

Benedict Leonard Calvert Esq. of [Epsom], Surrey, [bachelor], at present of Md., dated 22 Apr 1732. One-third of my estate to the King William Free School in Annapolis for the encouragement and education of youth in the province. £50 each to my sisters Charlotte Brerewood and Jane Hyde. An annuity of £40 to Mrs. Theodosia Lawrence. £10 to my servant Robert Young. £10 to the poor of Annapolis. My negro boy called Osmyn to my goddaughter Elizabeth Calvert, daughter of Charles Calvert Esq., Commissary-General of Md. Mourning rings to my sister Lady Baltimore and my brother Charles, Lord Baltimore. £10,000 to my brother Hon. Cecilius Calvert, if he has need, with remainder to the children of my brother-in-law John Hyde Esq. of Kingston Lisle, Berks. My said brother to be exec. for Europe and Edmund Jennings Esq. of Annapolis for Md. Wits: George Plater, (-----) Ross and Thomas Doughty. Pr. 17 Aug 1733 by named exec. (PROB 11/660/219).

Alexander Trench of Granville Co., S.C., merchant, dated 1 Jan 1730. To be interred in Charles Town where my wife Hester Trench is buried. My debts to be paid out of money raised by the sale of effects in my house in Whitehall and my lodging in Charles Town. My cattle on Trench Island and stock in the hands of John and Mathew Nelson in my Barony of Raplioe to be sold and surplus to be remitted to my brother Councillor Frederick Trench in Dublin for the use of my son Frederick Trench until he is 18. My pew in the church at Port Royal to be used by strangers and transient persons. Execs: Mr. John Wright, merchant, and Benjamin Whitaker Esq., both of Charles Town. Wits: John Wallis, John Lining and Peter Shipard. Pr. 4 Dec 1733 by the surviving exec. Benjamin Whitacre. (PROB 11/662/321).

1734

Charles Blake [of Md.], dated 24 Aug 1723, (copy from Md. records). If I die in Md. I am to be buried by my wife. To my son John Blake my two tracts called Rissendale and Courseys on Wye River with remainder to my son Philemon Blake. To my said son John the residue of my lands on Wye River and the wading place on condition that he quitclaims Peter Harwood for the title of land I sold him on account of the will of my late uncle Sayers. To my said son Philemon my lands called White Banks, Coursey Neck and Long Neglect on Chester River. From the estate in England left to me by the will of my father £500 and an annuity of £50 to my daughter Dorothy Carroll. A mourning suit to my daughter Henny. Codicil of 3 Sep 1725: Charles Carroll of Annapolis, surgeon, has sued me in the Chancery Court for a sum of £500 which he claims I owe him on account of his marriage to my daughter Dorothy, but I made no such promise. My said sons to be execs. Wits: Richard Tilghman, Otho Coursey, Richard Tilghman Jr., Philemon Lloyd, R. Bennett and John Stevens. Pr. 14 Jan 1734 by Philemon Blake Esq. (PROB 11/663/1).

Abraham Downe, late of Md. but now of Broadoakes, Wimbish, Essex, dated 27 Apr 1729. A mourning ring to my brother Joseph Downe if he be alive at my death. Residue to my wife Elizabeth Downe who is to be sole exex. Wits: M. and W. Clagett. Pr. 3 Apr 1734 by relict. (PROB 11/664/81).

Edward Young of St. Botolph Aldgate, Mddx., mariner [of the merchant ship *Daniel and Anna*, who died in Md., bachelor], dated 1 Jan 1734. My whole estate to my mother Mary Young, widow. My friends William Speven and Lydia his wife to be execs. Wits: John Fallows and Sa. Wilcocke, attorney and notary, Butcher Row, East Smithfield. Pr. 4 Jly 1734 by William Speven. (PROB 11/666/173).

Henry Russell, mariner of H.M. ship *Alborough*, [who died in S.C., bachelor], dated 20 Jun 1730. Forty shillings each to John, Elizabeth, Richard and Mary Muncreef. Residue to my brother William Russell of Liams (*sic*) near London, ship carpenter. William Randal of Charles Town, S.C., blacksmith, to be exec. Wits: Thomas Allin, Thomas Carter and William Smith. AWW 30 Aug 1734 to John Pick, attorney for named exec. in S.C. (PROB 11/666/187).

Stephen Clay, mariner [of the merchant ship *Anne*, who died in Va., bachelor], son of Robert Clay of Lambeth, Surrey, distiller, dated 19 May 1730. To my uncle William Norwood of Margate, Kent, vintner, £100 out of the legacy of £1,000 given to me by the will

of my late aunt Elizabeth Clay, widow, and payable after the death
of her sister Mrs. Mordit of Fetter Lane, London. Residue to my
brother William Clay and my sisters Elizabeth and Sarah Clay when
they come of age. My said uncle to be exec. Wits: Jon. Rooff and
Daniel Butler. Pr. 22 Oct 1734 by exec. named. (PROB 11/667/212).

William Nicholas of H.M. ship *Winchelsea*, [who died in Va., bachelor],
dated 4 Jun 1734. Thomas Page of the said ship to be sole legatee
and exec. Wits: James Graham, Thomas Heddell and Joseph Hind.
Pr. 24 Oct 1734 by exec. named. (PROB 11/667/223).

Nicholas Reeks, mariner of the *William and Sarah*, Mr. William Stanton,
[who died in Md.], dated 21 Jan 1734. Samuel Spurrier of St. John,
Southwark, Surrey, victualler, to be sole legatee and exec. Wit:
Abraham Harman, clerk to William Holloway, notary public in Shad
Thames. Pr. 17 Oct 1734 by named exec. (PROB 11/667/225).

1735

Thomas Barton Esq. of Berkeley County, S.C., dated 29 Jan 1732. To
my son Thomas Barton 150 acres where he now dwells if he pays
the mortgage in the hands of Capt. John Vandrose; and to my sons
William Barton and John Barton 150 acres each. To my daughter
Ann a negro wench and cattle. My estate in England which came
to me on the death of my brother John Barton to be divided equally
between my said four children. Wits: Jonathan Stock, John Baker
and John Young. AWW 17 Jan 1735 to Samuel Wragg, attorney
for the sons William and John Barton in S.C. (PROB 11/669/3).

Edward Peters of Bristol, mariner, now bound on a voyage overseas,
dated 23 Oct 1724. To my mother Elizabeth Peters of Bristol,
widow, £50 and the house in Old Market Street where she dwells
and a cellar and warehouse near Leonards Lane, Bristol, with
remainder to my brother Warren Peters. My tenements in Back
Lane and Ann Street, Bristol, and a tract in Penna. of 500 acres
to the said Warren Peters with remainder to my cousin James Peters,
gent, son of my late uncle John Peters, pewterer, who is to pay
£50 each to my sister Sarah Peters and my cousin Susan Tilly,
widow. My said mother and brother to be execs. Wits: Henry
Woolnough, Stephen Stringer and Richard Daniell. Pr. 25 Feb 1735
by surviving exec. Elizabeth Peters. (PROB 11/669/35).

Ayliffe Williams, late of N.C. but now residing in Westminster, Mddx.,
dated 22 Nov 1734. Money in the hands of my attorneys Christopher
and Edmund Gale Esqs. of N.C., including a receipt by David

O'Sheal of Nansemond, Va., to be remitted to England. My land and buildings on New River to be sold. My debt to Mr. Henry Nean of Compton Street, Westminster, to be paid. £10 to Mr. James Webb of Broad Street, (London). Residue to my mother Mrs. Esther Williams of Old Gravel Lane, Wapping, (Mddx.), during her lifetime and then to my brother John Williams and my sister Esther Taylor whom I ask to assist the children of our unhappy brother Daniel. Execs. the said Henry Nean and James Webb. Wits: Oliver Farmer and William Coumbe. Pr. 2 May 1735 by named execs. (PROB 11/671/113).

Edward Walbank [of Philadelphia], dated 16 Apr 1733. My debts in America and elsewhere are to be paid and the residue is to go to my wife Agnes Walbank who is to be my exex. Wits: Clement Plumsted and Arent Hassert. Pr. 18 Jun 1735 by the relict. (PROB 11/671/136).

Lewis Bradley, mariner of H.M. sloop *Happy*, Capt. James Lloyd, [who died in S.C.], dated 4 Jly 1734. My whole estate to my friends Mr. John Owen, tailor in Charles Town, and Mr. William Mallard, clerk of the said ship, and they are to be execs. Wits: James Whaley, Roger Goff and Michael Cliff. AWW 27 Aug 1735 to John Bryan and and Paul Debell, attorneys for execs. in S.C. (PROB 11/672/165).

Robert Johnson Esq., Governor of S.C., dated 25 Dec 1734. Principal bequests to: my eldest son Robert Johnson; my sons Nathaniel and Thomas; my daughters Margaret and Mary; my brother-in-law Col. Thomas Broughton Esq.; my nephews Nathaniel and Andrew Broughton; my brother-in-law Archibald Hutcheson Esq.; my kinsman Gabriel Manigault; my kinsmand John Schutz Esq.; my kinsman John Cooke Esq.; my sister-in-law Phebe Bonner. Execs. for S.C.: Thomas, Nathaniel and Andrew Broughton. Execs. for England: Archibald Hutcheson, John Schutz, John Cooke and Phebe Bonner. Wits: G. Anson, James Lloyd, John Fenwick and Andrew Rutlidge. AWW 9 Aug 1735 to the son Robert Johnson Esq., the named execs. renouncing. (PROB 11/672/172).

George Armstrong, second mate of the *Concord*, Capt. Samuel Rush, outward bound to Md. [and who died there], dated 6 Mar 1735. A clock and ring given me by my late grandmother Lock and the residue of my estate to ny uncle Robert Pitt Esq. of Bethnal Green, Mddx., who is to be my exec. Wits: John Scott, Mathew Jackson and Betty England. Pr. 5 Dec 1735 by named exec. (PROB 11/674/242).

Robert Barker of London, merchant, [late Collector of Customs in Burlington, West N.J.], dated 4 Apr 1730. My whole estate in trust to Nathaniel Hurdd Esq. of Stidd, Derbyshire, and James Worthington of Love Lane, Aldermanbury, London, gent., for the benefit of my mother Mary Barker of London during her lifetime, with remainder to my sister Mary, wife of Francis Hurdd of London, merchant. Wits: Thomas Lithered and John Elford Jr., notary public. AWW 20 Dec 1735 to the sister Mary Hurdd, the named execs. renouncing. (PROB 11/674/242).

1736

John Baker of Bristol, merchant, dated 9 Oct 1734. £500 to satisfy my bond with John Bound Sr. and Philip Freeke Esq., both since deceased, on the marriage of my daughter Isabella with John Bound, son of the said John. £500 to my son John Baker and Thomas Pearce in pursuance of an agreement made by me with James Pearce, mariner, and Ann his wife, my daughter Ann Baker, and my said son John Baker and Thomas Pearce. My late father Henry Baker by his will left a glass house at Strawberry Hill to be divided between his grandchildren and all were paid except (blank) Baker, son of my brother Ebenezer Baker, who married and settled in S.C. Other bequests to: my daughter Sarah Wayne; my sons Stephen and Francis Baker; my grandchildren Sarah Bound, Ann Bound, James Smith, James Bound and James Pearce. O'seers John Elbridge Esq., James Pearce, John Wayne and John Platt. Exec. my son Stephen Baker. Wits: Philip Watkins, John Peacock and James Harris. Pr. 23 Jan 1736 by exec. named. (PROB 11/675/2).

Ann Gibson, widow of Daniel Gibson of S.C., surgeon. My whole estate including my plantation near Charleston, S.C., to my friend Rev. Lawrence Neill who is to be sole exec. Wits: Philip Cadet, Thomas Cooke and Ralph Kent, scrivener. Proved 2 Jan 1736 by named exec. (PROB 11/675/8).

Zachariah Richardson, [formerly of Bermondsey, Surrey, but late of Philadelphia], dated 21 Dec 1735. To be buried in Friends' burial ground. I appropriate all the costs due to me in the Chancery suit I have obtained against Andrew Hamilton of Philadelphia (See NGSQ 61/3). My whole estate to my wife (Rebecca Richardson) who is to give £5 each to my four sisters. My friend John Warner is to be exec. Wits: Samuel Binks, Nathaniel Reed, John Warriner and Elizabeth Clark. Pr. 23 Feb 1736 by affirmation of the relict and Thomas Binks, execs. of will of John Warner deceased. (PROB 11/675/41).

Richard Way, [of N.E.], mariner of H.M. ship *Namur*, dated 1 Jun 1735. My whole estate to my friend and exec. John Nightingirl of the said ship, mariner, for the benefit of my wife Hannah Way of N.E. Wits: Peter Sporle, Joseph Atkins and Bartholomew Pitts, clerk. Pr. 29 May 1736 by the named exec. (PROB 11/676/73).

Duncan Mackenzie of St. Martin in the Fields, Mddx., gunsmith, about to undertake a long voyage [of N.Y., bachelor], dated 26 Apr 1728. £10 to my brother Alexander Mackenzie. The residue to my son Glenn Mackenzie and daughter Elizabeth Mackenzie when they are 21 or married, with remainder to my said brother, who is to be exec., and my sister Anne Mackenzie. Wits: Amelia Sedwell and Robert Crosby. Pr. 1 Apr 1736 by named exec. (PROB 11/676/85).

William Timson of Bruton parish, York Co., Va., dated 25 Apr 1726. To my brother John Timson all my land at the mouth of Queen Creek, York River, and at Mannikin Town. £10 to my cousin Laindon. One guinea each to: my cousin Frances Jones; my cousins Elizabeth and Mary Barber; my cousins Mary, John, Elizabeth, Juxon and Samuel Timson, children of my uncle Samuel Timson; all the children of Thomas Crips. £50 to my cousin and godson William Timson when he is 21. £30 to the poor of Bruton and for the purchase of plate for the church. An annuity of £20 sterling to my mother which is to be paid by my said brother, but if he dies my mother (Anna Maria Timson) is to have £500 out of the estate left to me by my aunt Milener. £25 to John Robinson. My said brother to be exec. Wits: William Barber, Lain Jones and Philip Burt. AWW 2 Jun 1736 to Neil Buchanan, exec. of John Timson deceased, the mother not appearing. (PROB 11/677/140).

Thomas Thomson [of Scotland] bound for Md., dated 10 Apr 1711. My whole estate to my brother James Thomson of Tilieallen(?), Perthshire, Scotland, who is to be exec. Wits: Alexander Nevill, Charles Warmingham and Robert Teppets, scrivener against Beauford Street, Strand. Pr. Jun 1736 by the named exec. (PROB 11/677/141).

John Walter Esq. of Tooting, Surrey, dated 30 Dec 1734. To my eldest son and exec. Abel Walter my manors and lands in Britain and Barbados; to my son Henry Walter half of my lands in Granvill Co., S.C., purchased from Capt. Douglas, and 1000 acres of Crown land in the Barony of Days Creek in Granvill Co. To my son William Walter the other half of my lands in S.C. To my sons James, Alleyne and Meynell Walter 2,000 acres in the said Barony. To my daughters Lucy and Mary Walter £2,000 each when they are 18. 1,000 acres in the said Barony to my son Richard Walter. To my grandson John Walter, son of my son Abel Walter, all my lands in Goose Creek, S.C., known as Red Bank. To my daughter Elizabeth Dottin £500 in trust. To my daughter Lucy Walter £500 when she is 21. Wits: Thomas Bund, E. Alleyne and Benjamin Maynard. Codicil dated 18 Mar 1736: my son Henry Walter to have £1,250 if he shall settle in S.C. within four years. Pr. 5 Jun 1736 by named exec. (PROB 11/677/142).

Christopher Gildemaster of London, merchant, knowing the danger of
voyages [who died in East N.J., bachelor], dated 13 Aug 1731. My
2,000 acres near St. Lawrence's Brook in East N.J. which I bought
of Peter Sonman Esq. to my two brothers John Frederick Gildemaster of Bremen and Daniel Gildemaster of Rotterdam, merchants, and they are to be execs. Wits: Peter Stapleton, Thomas
Cocke and Nathaniel Patten, notary public. Pr. 9 Jly 1736 by execs.
named. (PROB 11/678/153).

Joseph Wilkinson of Calvert Co., Md., merchant, dated 25 Apr 1734.
A mourning suit and ring to my brother-in-law Mr. John Skinner.
One-third of my personal estate and tobacco in England and
elsewhere, slaves and cattle, etc. to my wife, (or two-thirds if she
is with child); one third to my daughter Elizabeth; and one-third
to my son Joseph. My said wife to be exex. and my brother-in-law
guardian of my children. Wits: Posthumus Thornton, Roger Boyce
and Alexander Lawson. AWW 22 Jly 1736 to William Torver,
attorney for the relict in S.C. (PROB 11/678/168).

David Mallortie of London, mariner, now bound on a voyage to the
coasts of Africa and thence to Carolina and other parts of America
by the *Susannah* of which I am commander, [of Port Royal, S.C.,
bachelor], dated 2 Jly 1735. A mourning ring to my first mate Mr.
Benjamin Wych who is to be captain of my ship. Residue to my
father James Mallortie of London, merchant, who is to be exec.
Wits: P. Villepontoux and Benjamin Bonnet, notary public. Pr. 6
Oct 1736 by exec. named. (PROB 11/679/224).

John Watts of Workington, Cumberland, mariner, at present bound on
a voyage overseas [who died in Md.], dated 4 Apr 1728. One
quarter of my estate to my brother and exec. Richard Watts of
Workington; one half to Richard Watts and Joseph Millner of
Workington who are to pay the interest thereon to my sister
Dorothy, wife of John Lawrence, and my sister Isabell, wife of
John Carr, Excise Officer at Whitby; and one quarter to the children
of my late sister Ann Burkitt of Workington. Wits: Jacobus Lone,
notary public, Arthur Lone Bowman, his clerk, and Henry Erswell.
Pr. 1 Oct 1736 by exec. named. (PROB 11/679/230).

1737

Samuel Curry of St. Martin in the Fields, Mddx., peruke maker,
[who died in Boston, N.E.]. My whole estate to my sister Ester,
wife of Henry Herbert of St. Martin in the Fields, goldsmith. Mr.

John Le Sage to be exec. Wits: Ezekias Lever and John S---eer.
AWW 7 Jan 1737 to Ester Herbert, the named exec. renouncing.
(PROB 11/681/2).

John Baker of Bristol but now of Charles Town, S.C., merchant, dated
14 Nov 1735. To my nephew James Bound, now resident in Charles
Town, £500 sterling when he is 21 and an annuity of £30. £100
sterling each to my nieces Sarah and Anne Bound and Henrietta
Pearce when they are 21 or married. £100 to the charity school for
girls in Temple parish, Bristol. £30 to Mr. Obediah Arrowsmith of
Ledbury, Heref. £40 to Benjamin Weale of London, brazier. £25 to
Joseph Lewis of Bristol, tobacconist. To my brother Francis Baker
a snuff box given to me by my late father. A memorial stone to be
placed on my late wife's grave in S.C. Residue to my sons Francis
and Stephen Baker. Execs. in trust for Carolina are to be Mr. Paul
Innys, Mr. Thomas Lamboll and Mr. Richard Hill; and for Great
Britain Mr. Paul Fisher of Bristol, merchant, and Mr. James Pearce
of London, merchant. Wits: Thomas Jenys, Thomas Ovens and G.
Tyndale. Pr. 5 Feb 1737 by Stephen Baker. (PROB 11/681/18).

Walter Newberry of Gracechurch Street, London, merchant, dated 22nd
of 12th month called February 1734. £100 Carolina money to my
sister Sarah Parson of Charles Town, S.C. £100 N.E. money to be
paid by John Wheelwright of Boston to: my brother-in-law John
Cranston of Newport, R.I., to be divided between the children of
my sister Anne Mary Cranston deceased; my sister Elizabeth Bordon
of Newport, R.I., widow, to be divided between her children; my
sister Martha, wife of Nathan Allen of Allen Town, N.J., to be
divided between her children; my sister Mary, wife of Jeremiah
Williams of Hempstead Harbour, Long Island, to be divided between
her children. £30 N.E. money to my kinsman Joseph Jacob of
Newport, R.I. to be divided between the children of my sister Sarah
Parson. £20 N.Y. money to my brother-in-law Thomas Rodman of
Flushing, Long Island. All my houses and lands in the hands of
the said Rodman and £500 N.E. money to my daughter Margaret
Newberry when she is 21 or married. £10 to Martha Gipson. My
(late) wife's clothes to my sisters Patience Reed and Anne Hyam.
If both my sisters die, the proceeds of my estate are to be shipped
in goods to my kinsmen Thomas Richardson and Joseph Jacob of
R.I. While Joseph Symmonds lives, the portion due to my daughter
Anne is to remain in the hands of my friend Thomas Plumsted who
is to be exec. with Margaret Wyeth. Wits: Thomas Mildred, John
Mason and William Shephard. Pr. 4 Mar 1737 by affirmation of
execs. named. (PROB 11/682/64).

Robert Sibbet of St. Luke, Mddx., mariner, [who died in Md.,
bachelor], dated 17 Jly 1735. My friend Catherine Stringfellow of

Shoreditch, Mddx., spinster to be my legatee and exex. Wits: Arthur Parker and John Palmer, scrivener in the Temple. Pr. 24 Mar 1737 by exex. named. (PROB 11/682/69).

Joshua Gabourel of London, master of the *Maxwell*, now bound for Barbados, [of Cape Fear, N.C., bachelor], dated 23 Sep 1726. £100 each to my brother Amos Gabourel of Jersey, mariner, and my sisters Rachael and Jane Gabourel of Jersey, spinsters. Residue to my brother Thomas Gabourel of Jersey, yeoman, who is to be exec. Wits: John Vaughan, Jacobus Lone, notary public, and Arthur Lone Bowman. Pr. Apr 1737 by the brother Amos Gabourel, the brother Thomas Gabourel having died. (PROB 11/683/120).

Bryan Taylor of St. Stephen, Coleman Street, London, merchant, [who died in Md., bachelor], dated 16 Jan 1731. All my freeholds in Langtoft, Lockington, Aike, Scarborough, and elsewhere in Yorkshire to my mother Mary Taylor of London while she remains a widow, otherwise to my brother Everard Taylor who now resides overseas on condition that he returns to reside in Britain, otherwise to my brothers Freeman and Francis Taylor, with remainder to my friend Mr. Philip Smith, son of Mr. Philip Smith of St. Stephen, Coleman Street. Exec: Mr. Philip Smith Sr. Wits: John Chamberlain, Mary Tate and Richard Middleton, attorney of Common Pleas. AWW 13 May 1737 to the brother Freeman Taylor, the named exec. having died and the mother renouncing. (PROB 11/683/120).

James Slone of London, merchant, now in possession of £1,500 in merchandise to dispose of in Madeira and the West Indies, [of Boston, N.E.], dated 4 Mar 1735. My whole estate to my friends Mr. John Hayes of Ratcliffe Cross, Mddx., peruke maker, and James Adams of Bishopsgate Street, London, stationer, who are to be execs. Wits: Kentish Kiggell and William Adams. Pr. 3 Aug 1737 by execs. named. (PROB 11/690/182).

Thomas Fitch Esq. of Boston, Mass., merchant, dated 19 Jly 1735. £30 to my sister Sarah Warren. £100 each to my nieces Priscilla and Mary Hunt. £200 to my nephew Jabez Hunt. £80 to my niece Sarah Watts. To the poor of Boston the interest on £300. To the college at Cambridge, Mass., £300. To my daughter-in-law Martha Fitch £10. To my wife Abiel Fitch £6,000 and one-third of my real estate during her lifetime. £10 to Rev. Dr. Sewall, £20 to Rev. Mr. Thomas Prince, and £5 each to the ministers of Boston who preach in public on Thursdays. Half the residue of my estate to Martha Allen and half to my grandson Andrew Oliver *alias* Thomas Fitch Oliver when he is 21, with remainder to my son-in-law Andrew Oliver. £600 to my sister Sarah Warren. Execs: my said wife and sons-in-law Mr. James Allen and Mr. Andrew Oliver. Wits: Jonathan Loring, Samuel Tisley and Stephen Higginson. Pr. Boston 30 Jun 1736. AWW 5

Sep 1737 to Thomas Gainsborough, attorney for execs. in Boston. (PROB 11/685/205).

Herbert Haynes of Abingdon parish, Gloucester Co., Va., [who died in St. Peter Cornhill, London], dated 20 Jan 1737. To be buried at the discretion of my friend and attorney Mr. Job Wilkes who is to receive my rents in London. Residue to my wife Sarah Haynes and my father Thomas Haynes who are to be execs. Wits: Thomas Shickles, Thomas Thompson and George Fox. AWW 15 Dec 1737 to Job Wilkes, attorney for execs. in Va. (PROB 11/686/275).

1738

William Allcock of Mollington, Oxon., mason, dated 29 Sep 1733. My lands in Mollington to my brother John Farmer and my sister Joan his wife with remainder to my friend Francis Abbitts of Mollington. An annuity of £6 left to my sister Anne Elkington by the will of her late husband Richard Elkington is to be paid. My tenement in the occupation of William Nicolls to my nephew John Farmer. All my other lands in Mollington and Farnborough, Warw., in trust to my friends John Gorstelowe of Mollington, gent., and Robert Sparrow of Wardington, Oxon., gent., to be sold for the benefit of my said nephew. £10 each to the children and grandchildren of my late brother George Elkington of N.J. £50 each to my nieces Elizabeth and Mary Rymer, daughters of Hugh Rymer and Elizabeth his wife of Liverpool, Lancs. £30 each to my niece Mary Farmer, daughter of my brother John Farmer and his wife Joan. £200 to the poor of Farnborough and Mollington. The said Francis Abbitts to be exec. Wits: Richard Woodward, Anthony Harris and John Burrowes. Codicil of 25 Apr 1735. Bequest to the children and grandchildren of my deceased brother in N.J. increased to £50. £10 to my kinsman Joseph Ball of Banbury, (Oxon.), and £5 each to William Osborne, son of William Osborne, carpenter, and William Hunt of Cropredy, Oxon., weaver. Wits: Philip Coleman, William Coleman and Alice Smith. Pr. 27 Jan 1738 by named exec. (PROB 11/687/2).

Francis Brown of Philadelphia, merchant, [late of Madeira, who died in Philadelphia, bachelor], dated 29 Jly 1728 (copy from Philadelphia records). My friend and relation Robert Kirwan is to take into his hands all my books and papers relating to Madeira in order to collect my debts, and is to be exec. Wits: John Richason and Edward Pleadwell. AWW 13 Mar 1738 to creditor Robert French; the named exec. having died and the father Andrew Brown, the brother Andrew

Brown, and the sister Mary Brown, having been cited but not having appeared. (PROB 11/688/57).

Michael Howard of Talbot Co., Md., gent., dated 1 Feb 1735. To my father and mother £10 to be remitted to London by my brothers Adam or Francis Howard to Mr. Samuel Hyde. £1,500 to be invested by Messrs. Samuel and Herbert Hyde of London, merchants, for the benefit of my nephew Michael William Howard, son of my late brother Matthew Howard of Dublin, who is now with me. My said nephew is to be educated at Westminster School and King's College, Cambridge, until he is 21. The excess from this investment is to be paid to my sister-in-law Sarah Howard, relict of my said brother, for the use of his daughter Elizabeth Howard, with remainder to the two eldest sons of my brother Mr. Adam Howard in Westmeath, Ireland. My nephew Michael William Howard is to have the use of my law library. Other bequests to my sister Rose Wilson and my brother Rochfort Howard. Execs. in Britain: Samuel and Herbert Hyde, Adam, Francis and Michael William Howard. Execs. in Md.: Daniel Dalany Esq. of Annapolis and Mr. Walter Carmichael of Queen Anne Co., merchant. Wits: Edward Fottrell, James Lloyd, James Farrell and William Ruddle. Pr. 23 Mar 1738 by the brother Francis Howard. (PROB 11/688/66). Revoked Aug 1757 on the death of Francis Howard and admon. granted to Christopher Plunkett, son of Ann Plunkett, widow.

Adam Greves of Charles Town, S.C., [of H.M. ship *Rose*, bachelor], dated 27 Jun 1737 (copy from Md. records). My whole estate to my friend Edward Stephens who is to be exec. Wits: Benjamin Marriott, William Hume and Archibald Ferguson. AWW 13 Apr 1738 to Edward Jasper, attorney for exec. in S.C. (PROB 11/688/91).

Thomas Owen of Granville Co., S.C., planter, dated 29 May 1735. All my debts incurred since 29 Sep 1734 are to be paid. To my wife Frances Owen all my plantation called Owen's Lodge, negroes, stock, etc., and land on Cussahatchey Creek in Granville Co., with remainder to my daughter Elizabeth Owen. Residue to my said wife. Execs: Joseph Wragg and William Yeomans, both of Charles Town, merchants, and my brother Jeremiah Owen. Wits: Richard Woodward, Joseph Edward Flower, Jennit Cobley and Ambrose Reeve. Pr. 14 Jly 1738 by the brother Jeremiah Owen. (PROB 11/690/182).

Samuel Stringer of Epsom, Surrey, doctor of physick, undated. All my manuscripts and papers relating to medicine to my son (unnamed) now in Md. A guinea for a ring to Mr. William Tomlin. Residue to my wife Louisa Stringer who is to be exex. Pr. 26 Jly 1738 by relict. (PROB 11/690/185).

John Tute, now of London, mariner, bound on a voyage to Va. by the *Hope* of which I am commander, [of James River, Va.], dated 9 Apr 1736. To my executors in trust John Comer of St. Katherine by the Tower, London, sailmaker, and Thomas Parr of Crutched Friars, London, notary public, £200 to provide an anuity for my sister Elizabeth, now wife David Heard, with remainder to the said Thomas Parr. £10 to my goddaughter Sarah Staples. Residue to my wife Elizabeth Tute. Wits: Michael Coulter, Joseph Johnson and Mary Fast. Pr. 7 Jly 1738 by Thomas Parr. (PROB 11/690/186).

Richard Munday of Stepney, Mddx., mariner, [master of the merchant ship *Europa*, who died in Va., bachelor], dated 3 Aug 1737. £25 to my father. A small parcel marked R.M. to my sister Elizabeth Munday. Residue to Samuel Bonham of Stepney, merchant, who is to be exec. No witnesses shown. Depositions 10 Jly 1738 by Joseph Stephens of Rotherhithe, Surrey, mariner, and George Wilson of Shadwell, Mddx., mariner, that the testator died off the coast of Va. and that he wrote the above will in their presence. Pr. 2 Aug 1738 by exec. named. (PROB 11/691/200).

Andrew Faneuil of Boston, Mass., merchant, dated 12 Sep 1734. (Copy from Mass. records). My house in Boston to the minister of the French church in Boston with remainder to my heirs excluding Benjamin Faneuil of Boston. £100 to the poor of the said church and £100 to the other poor of Boston. A suit of mourning to Dr. Benjamin Colman. £100 to my brother John Faneuil of Rochell. £50 each to my brother-in-law Peter Cossart of Cork, Ireland, and his sister Susannah Cossart of Amsterdam. Five shillings to Benjamin Faneuil of Boston, son of my late brother Benjamin Faneuil. Eight thousand ozs. of silver are to be laid out for the benefit of my niece Mary, wife of Mr. Gillam Phillips, and 500 ozs. in pieces of eight for her son Andrew Phillips when he is of age. £2,000 each to the daughters of my said late brother, Anne Faneuil and Marian Faneuil, when they are 21 or married. £1,000 to my sister Susannah Faneuil, widow of Abraham de la Croix of Rochell. To my servant maid Hendrine Boyltins a suit of mourning and 500 ozs. in pieces of eight, and to her son Henry Johnson 150 ozs. in pieces of eight. Residue to my nephew Peter Faneuil, son of my late brother Benjamin, who is to be my exec. Wits: John Read, William Price and Charles Morris. Pr. 4 Sep 1738 by named exec. (PROB 11/691/212).

Jonathan Cay, Rector of Christ Church parish, Calvert Co., Md., dated 24 Jun 1714 (copy from Md. records). To my brother John Cay all my books except those chosen by my wife. To my wife and exex. Dorothy Cay any 20 books she may choose and the residue of my estate. Wits: Phillis Clodius, Frederick Clodius and Owen Ellis. Pr. 19 Oct 1738 by relict. (PROB 11/692/229).

James Thomson of St. Botolph, Aldgate, London, mariner [of H.M. ship *Rose*, who died in Carolina, bachelor], dated 19 Nov 1733. My whole estate to my sister Agnes, wife of James Spenston. My friend William Livingston of St. Botolph, Aldgate, victualler, to be exec. Wits: Alexander Benston and Samuel Wilcocke Jr., East Smithfield. Pr. 18 Dec 1738 by exec. named. (PROB 11/693/297).

George Uriell of London, mariner, [of Md., master of the ship *William*], dated 5 Mar 1731. All my estate in Cockermouth, Cumb., to my mother Rebeccah Uriell, with remainder to my sister and exex. Rebecca Iredell and her children. One guinea to my sister Ruth Martin. Wits: Benjamin Richardson of Shadwell, Mddx., William Olbie of Wapping, Mddx., pilot, and Robert Cragg of Whitehaven, Cumb. Pr. 8 Dec 1738 by Rebecca Iredell, widow. (PROB 11/693/298).

1739

Neel Philips or Phips of St. Anne, (Limehouse), Mddx., [of the merchant ship *Brunswick*, who died in Boston, N.E.], dated 5 Dec 1737. My whole estate to my friends William Thompson of Limehouse, victualler, and Johanna his wife, who are to be execs. Wits: Robert Smith, Benjamin Thompson, George Watts and Jonathan Greenwood, servant to Mr. Joseph Lester, notary public. Pr. 1 Feb 1739 by William Thompson. (PROB 11/694/40).

John Elbridge Esq. of Bristol, dated 20 Feb 1739. £10,000 to my niece Frances Mudge, daughter of my late brother (unnamed). £10,000 to my niece Rebecca, now wife of Henry Woolnough, gent., and only daughter of my eldest brother Aldworth Elbridge deceased. £500 each to my friends Samuel Creswick, D.D., and his wife. To the said Samuel Creswick, Peter Davies, gent., and Earle Benson Esq., all of Bristol, £3,000 in trust for the maintenance of a charity school lately erected by me on St. Michael's Hill, Bristol. To my friend Mr. Henry Bodman £2,000 and £5,000 in trust to dispose of as I have instructed. £5,000 to the infirmary of St. James, Bristol. £20 each to Mr. Charles Jones, Mr. Nathaniel Stevens, Mr. John Jocham and Mr. Whittington Rooke. £25 each to Henry Fane Esq., Jeremiah Burroughs Esq. and Pearce Griffith Sr. Esq. £8,000 to all the daughters of my late sister Smith and their children now living in N.E. My messuage at Westbury on Trym, Glos., to my nephew Thomas Elbridge. My messuage at the Royal Fort, Bristol, to my niece Rebecca Woolnough. My messuage in King Street, Bristol, to Henry Rodman. Execs. in trust: John Scrope Esq. of London,

John Cosens Esq. of Redland, Glos., and Samuel Creswick. Wits: Francis Pitts, One. Tyndall and Robert Sandford. Codicil of same date with bequests to servants. Pr. 27 Mar 1739 by named execs. (PROB 11/695/53).

N.B. The testator and his sisters Rebecca Sanders and Elizabeth Russell were born in Pemaquid, N.E. See NGSQ 60/185.

John England of Alder Mill, Tamworth, Staffs., gent., [of Md.], dated 6 Apr 1730. To my son Allen England the goods I left in my house at Alder Mill when I first went to America. All my working tools and implements and the real estate demised to me by James Burslem of Packington, Leics., and Francis Stratford Esq. of Merevale, Warw., to my sons Allen and Joseph England. To my sons John, Allen and Joseph England my one-tenth part of a furnace and forge, negroes, iron ships, utensils, etc. near a place called North East in Principio, Md. One guinea each to Thomas Robinson of Tamworth and Samuel Lythall of Polesworth, (Warw.). All my other personal estate in Penna. and Md. to my said sons John, Allen and Joseph England who are to be execs. Wits: Othniel Storrs, Robert Parker and John Lofthouse. Pr. 28 Mar 1739 by affirmation of named execs. (PROB 11/695/53).

Daniel Rivet, living in Stepney, Mddx., weaver, intending very soon to go beyond seas, [of Ga.], dated 8 Sep 1733 (translated from French). I have done all I could for my three sons Daniel, Lewis and Enoch Rivet and I give to each of them one shilling. Residue to my wife and exex. Barbe Rivet with remainder to my two daughters Susanna Louisa and Rose Elizabeth Rivet. Wit: Isaac Delplech, notary public. Pr. 19 May 1739 by relict. (PROB 11/696/114).

Jeremy Dummer, late agent of Massachusetts and Connecticut, now resident at Plaistow, Essex, dated 7 Jun 1738. All the N.E. gentlemen in London are to be invited to my funeral and given a ring with my name inscribed on it. £100 each to Mrs. Kent in the house where I live and to Mrs. Mary Stephenson of the same house. £100 to my kinswoman Mrs. Lloyd of N.E. (formerly Pemberton and Campbell).£50 to Dudley Woodbridge of Barbados. A £50 N.E. bill to Mrs. (Elizabeth) Burr of N.E. in acknowledgment of the civility I received from her husband (Samuel Burr), a schoolmaster at the college in Charles Town, (Mass.). Ten guineas each to Col. and Capt. Mandell, Swedes in London. My library to Stephen Whatley of Grays Inn, gent. £20 N.E. money to my brother Dummer of Newbury, (Mass.), for the poor Indian squaws that come begging at his door. To my sister Dummer a picture of her husband. The bulk of my estate should go according to an Act of Assembly in N.E. Execs: Francis Wills Esq. and Mr. Samuel Storke. Wits:

Benjamin Rutland and Ann Silver. Depositions 30 May 1739 by
Francis Hatton of Grays Inn, gent., and James Howgill of the Middle
Temple, London, gent., that the testator died in May 1739 and that
the above will was signed by him. Pr. 1 Jun 1739 by execs. named.
(PROB 11/696/126). See NGSQ 64/219.

Alexander Collier of St. Katherine's Precinct, London, mariner [of
H.M. ship *Wolf*, who died in Va., bachelor], dated 1 Jun 1734. My
whole estate to my friend William Culling of St. Katherine's who
is to be exec. Wits: William Scott and Charles Freeman. Pr. 12
Nov 1739 by exec. named. (PROB 11/699/229).

Isaac Amyand of Charles Town, S.C., gent., now in London, dated 26
Aug 1738. Bequests to: my friend Thomas Corbett of Charles Town;
my friend Childermas Croft Esq. of Charles Town. Gabriel Manin-
goult Esq. of Charles Town to be executor in trust for my estate
in Carolina which is to be sold and the proceeds to be held by my
uncle and executor Claudius Amyand Esq., H.M. Serjeant Surgeon
of St. Martin in the Fields, Mddx., in trust for my mother Justina
Amyand of Aberystwyth, Wales. After her death one half is to be
paid to my cousin Claudius Amyand, son of my said uncle, and
half to the other children of my said uncle. My estate in England
is to be applied to the same uses. Wits: Elizabeth Rimes, John
Walker and Francis Bowry, clerk to Mr. Byron of Nassau Street,
St. Ann's. Pr. 20 Dec 1739 by Claudius Amyand. (PROB
11/699/250).

Amos Garrett of Annapolis, Md., merchant, son of James and Sarah
Garrett, late of St. Olave Street, Southwark, Surrey, dated 4 Sep
1714. If I die in America I am to be buried with a marble tombstone
near the new house at the plantation where Robert Hewett lives as
overseer. £600 to my brother-in-law Henry Woodard and £60 to
the children of my sister Mary Woodard when they are 17 or
married. £1,000 to my mother Sarah Garrett. Other bequests in an
exceedingly long will to: my cousins Henry Facer, daughter (*sic*)
of Seth Garrett, and James Garrett, son of the same; my kinsman
Thomas Facer; my kinsman James Facer, son of Thomas and Martha
Facer, late of Rugby, (Warw.); my niece Elizabeth Woodard,
daughter of my brother-in-law Henry Woodard; my nephew William
Woodard, son of the same. Execs: my mother Sarah Garrett and
my sisters Elizabeth Ginn and Mary Woodard. 22 Dec 1739 admon.
with will to William Woodward (*sic*), son of the exec. of the
residuary legatee Mary Woodward deceased; Sarah Garrett, mother
of the testator, having died in his lifetime. (PROB 11/699/258).
Admons. of Jly 1728 to the sisters, Elizabeth Ginn and Mary
Woodard, widows, and of Jan 1735 to Elizabeth Ginn on the death
of Mary Woodard, now revoked.

John Jago, a negro, cook of H.M. ship *Mediterranean*, Capt. Harris, [who died on the merchant ship *Humphrey* in Va., bachelor], dated 30 Oct 1731. My whole estate to John Coldham Jr., son of John Coldham of Bermondsey, Surrey, victualler. Wits: Jeremiah Wheatley and Joseph Harries. Pr. Dec 1739 by John Coldham, father and guardian of John Coldham; no executor having been named. (PROB 11/699/262).

1740

Charles Crommelin of N.Y. province but now in London, dated 27 May 1735. My losses in trade have drawn me from home to seek succour among my relations in Europe which I have obtained partly from France by securing a right to three-quarters of debts due to the estate of the late James Smith of St. Thomas's Island, America, now in the hands of Mr. Jerome Joseph Le Jeune of Martinique. The said estate having been partly seized by the Danish Government and partly by embezzlement, and an application having been made to the Danish Court, I am preparing to embark for Martinique and St. Thomas to effect recovery. My debts, including those to Mr. Samuel Baker and Mr. Francis Gourdon, merchants of London, and Mr. Jenvrem(?) of London, are to be paid and any residue remaining is to remitted to my eldest son Daniel, at present resident in Rotterdam, and used for the benefit of my children. The said Samuel Baker is to be exec. for England and my son Daniel, John and Joseph Read, merchants, for N.Y. Wits: Anthony Frost and James Fleming. Pr. 22 Apr 1740 by the son Daniel Crommelin. (PROB 11/701/103).

Thomas Sharp of Bristol, mariner, now bound on a voyage to sea, [of Philadelphia, bachelor], dated 25 Feb 1723. My whole estate to my friend John Thomas of Bristol, baker, who is to be my exec. Wits: Samuel Tyler, William Blackmore and William Scammell. Pr. 29 Apr 1740 by exec. named. (PROB 11/702/125).

William Goddard of St. Margaret Moses, London, mariner, [who died in S.C.], dated 26 Nov 1733. My whole estate to my aunt Mary Darby of St. Margaret Moses, spinster, who is to be my exex. Wits: Jonathan Wells and Charles Hatt. Pr. 2 May 1740 by named exex. (PROB 11/702/140).

John Thompson of Bermondsey, Surrey, distiller, dated 6 Apr 1740. To be buried in Bermondsey in the same vault as my son Robert Thompson. I have already advanced £500 to my son John Thompson and the same sum to my daughter Jane on her marriage to Thomas

Ford, surgeon, and settled on her my messuage in Rotherhithe. Mourning rings to Mr. Langdon of Bermondsey, gent., and his wife, and Capt. Daniel Russell of Bermondsey and his wife. £10 to my cousin Alexander Thompson of R.I., distiller. £5 for mourning to my cousin Catherine Garth, daughter of my sister Jane Dix. My one-sixteenth share of the ship *Goodwin*, Mr. Robert Arbuthnot, to the two daughters of my late uncle Robert Thompson of Montrose, Scotland. My wife Jane Thompson to have the rents of my tenements in Bermondsey and Rotherhithe during her lifetime and to pay two shillings a week to my sister Jane Dix, widow. To my children John Thompson, Jane Ford and Andrew Thompson (a minor) my shares in coal and lead mines. My said wife to be exex. Wits: Patrick Shea, Abraham Harman and Daniel Stowy. Pr. 2 May 1740 by relict. (PROB 11/702/157).

John Crokatt of Charles Town, S.C., merchant, at present in Lisbon, dated 21 Nov 1738. £50 each to my brother-in-law John Jolly of Edinburgh, merchant, and my brother James Crokatt of Charles Town. £100 to my brother-in-law William Woodrop. £200 to Margaret Strachan who has lived with James Crokatt. Residue to my father Charles Crokatt of Edinburgh who is to be exec. with Alexander Robertson. Witness: Edward Burn. Pr. 28 Jun 1740 by the father. (PROB 11/703/166).

Robert Jesson of Philadelphia, merchant [and widower], dated 3 Apr 1732. My whole estate to Rebecca, wife of Solomon Goade of Philadelphia, mariner, and she is to be my exex., with remainder to my sister Ann Jesson. Wits: Nicholas Reddish, Alexander Paxton and Thomas Hopkinson. Pr. 18 Jun 1740 by named exex. (PROB 11/703/173).

John Brathwaite Esq. of S.C., dated 1 April 1740. Bequests to: my mother Mrs. Silvester Brathwaite of Dover, (Kent), widow; my nephew Thomas Brathwaite; the daughter of Mrs. Hannah Ives; my wife Silvia; my eldest son (unnamed). Half the interest on my estate is to be used for the education and maintenance of my children. My estate in England is in the hands of Edward Jasper Esq. of Tower Hill, (London), and estate in Carolina in the hands of Chief Justice Benjamin Whitaker and Mr. George Austin, merchant. Execs: my said wife, Mrs. Margaret Pultney, wife of Daniel Pultney Esq., Mrs. Elizabeth Tichburn, sister of the said Mrs. Pultney, and Thomas Revell Esq., Member of Parliament. Wits: Peter Colleton and J. Colleton. Pr. Charles Town, S.C., 29 Apr 1740 and in London 27 Aug 1740 by Silvia Brathwaite and Elizabeth Tichborne, spinster. (PROB 11/704/219).

Arthur Middleton of St. James, Goose Creek, Berkeley Co., S.C., dated 7 Jun 1734. To my wife Sarah one-third of my estate in

Great Britain, Barbados and S.C., including all the negroes I settled on her before our marriage, and the land and tenements in Charles Town which I bought of Mr. Andrew Allen. Half of my lot No. 100 in Charles Town to my son William and the other half to my son Henry. To my son Henry Middleton the tract of 1,630 acres where I now live which I bought of the late Mr. Benjamin Gibbs, 100 acres I bought of the Lords Proprietors, 131 acres on the west side of Goose Creek which I bought of Ralph Izard Esq., 70 acres of swamp and 1,300 acres at the head of Cooper River. A tract of 60 acres to my son William Middleton. To my son Thomas Middleton a tract of 1,500 acres on Wassamscue Swamp, 500 acres I bought of Mr. Thomas Clifford, a town lot in Dorchester, 750 acres called Beechon which I bought of Mrs. Margaret Beeching, and 50 acres I bought of the late Benjamin Schenckingh. Residue to my minor sons Henry and Thomas Middleton. My said wife to be exex. Wits: Timothy Millechamp, Jane Millechamp and Thomas Corbett. Adminon. with will to William Middleton Esq., attorney for Sarah Middleton in S.C. (PROB 11/704/230).

Stephen Nicolls of Salem, N.E., mariner of H.M. ship *Lyon*, [bachelor], dated 8 Feb 1740. All my goods to my friend John Gobell in Love Lane, Cock Hill, Stepney, [Mddx.]. Note: signed by the testator with a mark because of rheumatism in his right hand. Wits: Abel Raymond, William Stevens and John Ridgen. AWW 22 Aug 1740 to Hannah Gobell, wife and attorney of John Gobell now on board H.M. ship *Lichfield*. (PROB 11/704/231).

John Barnes of Christ Church, Surrey, dyer, [who died in Ga., widower], dated 15 Jun 1733. The reversion of a lease in Princes Street, Brick Lane, Spitalfields, due to me on the death of Mary Wells, devisee under the will of Thomas Rich, citizen and dyer of London, to John Whorlton of Christ Church, silk dyer, for the use of my friend and exec. William Graves of St. Giles Cripplegate, London. Wits: Henry Cary and Samuel Downes. Pr. 21 Oct 1740 by named exec. (PROB 11/704/231).

Kezla Caswall of Queen Street, London, and now of Camberwell, Surrey, widow, [formerly of Boston, N.E.], dated 17 Jly 1735. To my sister Lydia, widow of John Houlton of Clapham, Surrey, her family picture. Other bequests to: my son John Caswall of Boston, N.E., merchant; William Cave of Essex Street, Strand, Mddx., tallow chandler; Thomas Lane of Clements Inn, London; my daughter Susannah, wife of John Warner of Camberwell. My said son, William Cave and Thomas Lane to be execs. Wits: Anne Downes and Benjamin Sparrow. Pr. 5 Dec 1740 by John Caswall. (PROB 11/706/316).

1741

Adam Cromartie of Wapping, Mddx., mariner [of H.M. ship *Colchester* who died in Va.], dated 20 Nov 1736. My whole estate to my wife Marjery Cromartie. Execs: John Crafts of Wapping, shopman, and Elizabeth his wife. Wits: James Donald and William Moor, attorney at law at the Hermitage. Pr. 13 Jan 1741 by Elizabeth Crafts. (PROB 11/707/5).

Robert Thomlinson of Boston, N.E., merchant [and bachelor], dated 11 Apr 1739. My whole estate to my brother Richard Thomlinson and my sisters Isabel Robinson and Catherine Robinson. Wits: Robert York and M. Robinson. AWW 29 Jan 1741 to the brother Richard Thomlinson. (PROB 11/707/22).

Benjamin Plummer Esq. of Portsmouth, New Hampshire, dated 7 May 1740. My negro boy Juba, gold watch and a ring to my friend Mrs. Mary Macphederis. My saddle horse to Theodore Atkinson Esq. and a gold ring to his wife. A mourning suit to Mr. John Loggin. My clothing is to be sold in Boston. £10 to my mother. Residue to my brothers. Execs: my brother Mr. Thomas Plummer of London, merchant, and Theodore Atkinson of Portsmouth, New Hampshire. Wits: Arthur Browne, James Jeffrey and Joshua Peirce. Pr. 12 Mar 1741 by Thomas Plummer. (PROB 11/708/73).

Edward Fraunces Esq. of Bere, Jamaica, but now of London. A gold ring each to Henry Smallwood Esq., John Bordon Esq., Barney Phelp Esq. and Moses Kerrett Esq. An annuity of 20 shillings Jamaica money each to my negro servant maids called Madge and Maria. Residue to my brother James Fraunces of Cheapside, London, apothecary, with remainder to my cousins Elizabeth Jacquelin, now wife of Richard Ambler Esq. of York Town, Va., Mary Jacquelin, now wife of John Smith of Gloucester Co., Va., merchant, and Martha Jacquelin of York Town. Execs: my said brother, Barney Phelp and Moses Kerrett. Wits: John Hyde, John Harwood and John Hawkesworth. Pr. 3 Apr 1741 by James Fraunces. (PROB 11/708/89).

Benjamin Edmonds [the younger] of Boston, Mass., mariner, now bound on a voyage to sea, dated 2 May 1735. My whole estate to my wife Rebecca Edmonds who is to be my exex. Wits. Ezekiel Goldthwait, Joseph Marion and William Story. AWW 3 Jun 1741 to Albert Dennie, attorney for the relict Rebecca, now wife of Moses Penniman in Braintree, N.E. (PROB 11/710/150).

Adam Sewell of Shadwell, Mddx., mariner [of H.M. ship *Phoenix* who died in Carolina, bachelor], dated 1 Dec 1737. My whole estate to my friends George Powers of Shadwell, victualler, and Mary his wife who are to be execs. Wits: John Brunifield and John Tayer. Pr. 1 Jly 1741 by George Powers. (PROB 11/710/188).

Archibald Cummings of Philadelphia, clerk, dated 23 Mar 1741. All my plate and household goods, my two negroes Cato and Hannah, and £600 curent to my wife (Jane Elizabeth) with remainder to my nephew George Craige. To my said nephew my two houses in Arch Street, Philadelphia, and the £50 I have already given to him for his voyage to St. Kitts. £100 to my wife's niece, Margaret Valner. £10 to Margaret Hooper. Out of the £100 held by the Chamberlain of London, for which Thomas Moore has the bond, I give £25 to my said nephew, £25 to his sister and £20 to my brother, Rev. George Cummings. To Dr. John Kearsley £20 current. Residue in Penna. to the poor of Christ Church, Philadelphia. Dr. Thomas Moore of Aldersgate, London, to be exec. for Great Britain and my said wife and John Kearsley execs. for Penna. Wits: Samuel Holt, Alexander Annaud and Peter Evans. Pr. 1 Aug 1741 by Rev. Thomas Moore. (PROB 11/711/197).

Jacob Wickeat, mariner of H.M. ship *Hampton Court*, [bachelor], born of Indian parents in N.E., dated at Cartagena 22 Mar 1741. All my wages due for my service on this ship, Capt. Digby Dent, to my friend Richard Jeffery, mariner. Wits: Arthur Seymour, John Miller and John Torkinge. AWW 30 Sep 1741 to Alexander Godwin, attorney for Richard Jeffery, now at sea. (PROB 11/712/248).

Anna Barnard of Hendon, Mddx., widow, dated 2 Sep 1739. Clothing to my sister Rachael Marriott of St. John's Lane, Clerkenwell, Mddx., spinster. A nightgown etc. to my sister, the wife of Job Goodson of Penna. A gown etc. to Ann, wife of Henry Hitchcock of Hendon, Mddx., wheeler. A bed etc. to Mary Tinsley. Residue to my nephew William Dolley of St. Andrew, Holborn, Mddx., ironmonger, who is to be exec. Wits: Watt Crook and John House. Pr. 20 Nov 1741 by named exec. (PROB 11/713/295).

Andrew Newell of Charles Town, Mass., but now in Rotherhithe, Surrey, mariner. To my eldest son Joseph my interest in the new wharf at Nantucket when he is of age. Residue of my estate to my wife Eunice Newell for use in bringing up my children Joseph, Andrew, Eunice and Mary Newell. My said wife exex. for Mass. and my friends Henton Brown and John Owen, merchants in London, execs. for Great Britain. Wits: Margaret Comean, Mary (x) Romein and Martha Tapley. Pr. 4 Dec 1741 by affirmation of Henton Brown. (PROB 11/714/356).

1742

Richard Lawrence, mariner of H.M. ship *Squirrel*, Capt. Peter Warren, now residing at Boston, N.E., and bound on a voyage to sea [who died overseas], dated 17 Aug 1739. My whole estate to my wife Mary Lawrence who is to be my exex. Wits: Edmond Cottle, (blank) Lindsey, George Wallis and Joseph Marion. AWW 22 Jan 1742 to Peter Warren Esq., attorney for the relict in Boston. (PROB 11/715/21).

John Prichard of All Hallows, Barking, London, mariner, [of Bell Town, Md.], dated 10 Feb 1733. £5 to my wicked wife Katherine Prichard. £5 each to my kinsman Anthony Donne and his son John Donne. Residue to my mother Luce Prichard with remainder to my sister Ruth Prichard. Anthony Donne Sr. of Red Lion St., Holborn, Mddx. to be exec. Wits: John Jenkins, Robert Donn and Robert Baynham. Codicil of 11 Feb 1737. Having purchased one-sixteenth of the Patuxent iron works in Md., I leave to my exec. Anthony Donne all money due from Mrs. Christian and Arthur Vaughan and all the money due to me in Barbados which is in the hands of Messrs. Sherge and Forte, merchants. A quarter of my profits from the said works to Edward Mathews, son of Franklyn Mathews, with remainder to my sister Ruth Prichard; and half of profits to the daughters of my aunt Ruth Pugh. Wits: Ch. De Lafontaine, George Napier and Mary Donn. Pr. 28 Jan 1742 by named exec. (PROB 11/715/28).

John Pattison of Rochester, Kent, mariner, [of S.C., who died on H.M. ship *Windsor*], dated 15 Jly 1732. My whole estate to my daughter Isabella Pattison of Rochester who is to be my exex. Wits: John Stath, Henry Joyce and Abraham Jenkinson. Pr. 8 Feb 1742 by the daughter Isabella, now wife of George West. (PROB 11/716/61).

Alexander Spotswood Esq. of Orange Co., Va., now going upon an expedition, [late Maj-Gen. and Col. of the American Regiment who died at Annapolis, Md.], dated 19 Apr 1740. My lands, negroes and slaves in Va. to my eldest son John with remainder to my son Robert. During the minority of my sons, my execs. may lease any lands except a tract of 15,000 acres called Mine Tract in Spotsylvania Co. which I have set apart as an ironworks. At least 80 slaves with 20 of their children should be employed in the said works. £3,000 sterling to my son Robert when he is 21. £2,000 sterling each to my daughters Anna Catharina and Dorothea when they come of age. To my cousin Elliott Benger and Dorothea his wife during their lifetime my 200 acres at Mattaponney Creek excepting the tenement of Peter Johnson. £20 to my godson Alexander Greme, son of my cousin John Greme of William and Mary College. To the said college all my books and maps. The residue of my estate to my wife Butler and my four children. Execs: my said wife, Elliott Benger and Robert Rose of Essex Co., clerk. Wits: R. Francis, Benjamin Waller, Sterling Clark and E. Dorsey. AWW 23 Feb 1742 to Robert Cary, attorney for the execs. in Va. (PROB 11/716/68).

George Abell of Clarges Street, St. George, Westminster, gent., [of Charles Town, S.C., widower], dated 19 Aug 1737. £5 for mourning to Frances, wife of Matthew Denton of Gosmore, Herts. A guinea ring to each of my sisters. All the residue of my lands and personal estate to my brother Thomas Abell Esq. of Coleshill, Warw., who is to be my exec. Wits: Elizabeth Greenshaw, Deighton Carter and Robert Smith. Pr. 12 Mar 1742 by named exec. (PROB 11/716/75).

George Forbes of St. Mary's Co., Md., dated 10 Oct 1739. If I die here I am to be buried in the same grave in Broadneck as my son George. To my granddaughter Mary Gordon a tract of 400 acres in Cecil Co. near Elk River called Simms' Forest which I bought of Anthony Simms, with remainder to James Forbes, son of my late nephew John Forbes, and to George Gordon. To my brother Thomas Forbes in Scotland £100 sterling which is in the hands of Mr. William Hunt, merchant in London. To Robert, Margaret, Anne and Margery Forbes £200 which is in the hands of Mr. William Black, merchant in London. To Mary McWilliams, widow, the use of the negro boy Oronoko and negro girl Phillis, 40 barrels of wheat, corn, etc. My son-in-law George Gordon and Kenelm Jones of St. Mary's Co., gent, to be my execs. and guardians of my granddaughter. Wits: John Urquhart, William McWilliams and Thomas Truman Greenfield. Codicil of same date. Whatever is due to me from my sister-in-law Dryden Forbes is to be given to her son James Forbes. AWW 16 Jun 1742 to William Black, attorney for execs. in Md. (PROB 11/718/183).

Joseph Renton of Northumberland, surgeon [of the merchant ship *Rose*, who died in Va., bachelor], dated 16 Feb 1739. My whole estate to my friend Cuthbert Birkley of Shadwell, Mddx., victualler, who is to be my exec. Wits: Joseph Fish and Humphrey Owen. Pr. 20 Jly 1742 by named exec. (PROB 11/719/230).

Charles Watkins of S.C., planter, [a bachelor who died at sea on the merchant ship *Dolphin*, Mr. John Fraser, dated 25 Aug 1742. All my effects are to be delivered to Mr. William Parker, bookseller in St. Paul's Churchyard, London, to be forwarded to my brothers and sisters John, William and Mary Watkins and Honour Trumper. £5 sterling each to John Williams in S.C. and to Thomas Joans for his attendance on me on board this ship. Wits: John Fraser, Thomas (x) Joans and Walter Duhigg. AWW 19 Oct 1742 to the brother, William Watkins. (PROB 11/721/313).

William Harding of Rotherhithe, Surrey, [who died in Va., bachelor], dated 13 Nov 1739. My clothes to my brother Philip Harding and residue of estate to my exex. Mrs. Adrianna Oakley of Rotherhithe. Wits: William Paulding and William Wright. Pr. Nov 1742 by Adriana Dunn *alias* Oakley, wife of Samuel Dunn. (PROB 11/721/329).

N.B. A cause was promoted in 1743 by Samuel and Adriana Dunn against Elizabeth Perry, widow, claiming that the defendant owed money to the estate. The testator was employed by Mr. John Hanbury, merchant of London, and went to Va. to take command of the *Dunkirk* but died there In September or October 1742. See NGSQ 64/288.

Andrew Hamilton Esq. of Philadelphia, dated 31 Jly 1741. Since the marriage of my daughter Margaret to William Allen of Philadelphia, merchant, I have given her 500 acres near the borders of Bucks Co., a lot in Philadelphia adjacent to that given me by George Willox (*sic*), another lot at Wicocoa on the River Delaware, 19 acres of pasture and 10 acres of swamp. To my grandson John Allen all my bank and water lots, late the estate of Joshua Tittery, a messuage in the possession of Stephen Benezet of Philadelphia, merchant, etc. Other bequests to: my sons James and Andrew Hamilton, my grandson Andrew Allen, and George Gale of Somerset Co., Md., who married the daughter of Bridget Lotherbury. Execs: William Allen and my sons James and Andrew Hamilton. Wits: Abraham Taylor, William Till, Septimus Robinson and Tench Francis. AWW 8 Dec 1742 to Ferdinando John Paris, attorney for execs. in Penna. (PROB 11/722/355). See NGSQ 60/181-182 and 61/4-10 for lawsuits relating to the testator.

Edward Hext of Charles Town, S.C., gent, dated 6 Oct 1739. £1,000 to St. Philip's church in Charles Town for the relief of the poor. £1,500 to be invested for my niece Sarah Rutlidge and her children, with remainder to the children of my kinsman John Hext of S.C. The messuage where I live on Charles Town Bay to the said John Hext, with remainder to (blank) Hext, son of my brother Thomas Hext. Other bequests to: my brothers Thomas, Francis, Alexander and David Hext; Hugh and Amias Hext, sons of my brother Amias Hext; my kinsman Philip Hext of Frome, Somerset, father of Thomas Hext whom I brought with me to S.C.; my sister Martha Bee and her children William Bower, Mary Bryan and Tabitha Peter. Execs: my brothers David and Thomas Hext, my kinsman John Bee Jr., Jonathan Bryan, Philip Prioleau and John McCall, all of S.C. Pr. 30 Dec 1742 by David Hext and John McCall. (PROB 11/722/357).

1743

Thomas Bedingfield of Dorking, Surrey, gent., dated 17 Nov 1739. I am far advanced in years and writing is become troublesome. I confirm that by my marriage articles £600 is to be placed at interest for my wife's benefit. My freehold on Cornhill, Newmarket, Suffolk, to my sister Ann Johnson, relict of Ezekiel Johnson, with remainder to my niece Ann, wife of James Le Counte of the Strand, Mddx., gent. £5 to my nephew Bedingfield Johnson and my niece Elizabeth Cornelius, widow, daughter of my sister Ann Johnson. My nephew Thomas Bedingfield Hands is at so great a distance from me as perhaps Md. in the West Indies and, since his presence here may be needed to negotiate affairs concerning my will, my niece Ann Le Counte may determine these matters as if he were here. Execs: my said niece and my nephew Bedingfield Johnson. Wits: Thomas Collins Sr. and William Collins. Pr. 25 Feb 1743 by Ann Le Counte. (PROB 11/723/33).

Richard Neilson [of Brigadier Guise's Regiment of Foot], now bound on an expedition to the West Indies as a volunteer, [who died in Carolina, bachelor], undated. Half my personal estate to my eldest brother William Neilson of Edinburgh and half between my brothers John and Samuel Neilson. £20 is to be used to put my bastard daughter Mary Neilson to Mr. Crossmith, dancing master in Beaufort Buildings, or to Mr. Morgan near the Bear Tavern, Strand, Mddx., haberdasher. Mr. William Chancellor to be exec. Wits: Mr. Henry Halsey, linen draper in Portsmouth, and Henry Halsey, his nephew. Pr. 22 Feb 1743 by named exec. (PROB 11/724/49).

John Remnant of Kingston on Thames, Surrey, lighterman and waterman, now of H.M. ship *Pearl*, [who died in Va., bachelor], dated 19 Jun 1741. My whole estate to my friend John Mackey who is to be my exec. Wits: Henry Bowler and William Beale. Pr. 16 Feb 1743 by named exec. (PROB 11/724/53).

Mary Walley of Bruton near Williamsburg, York Co., Va., but now of St. Margaret, Westminster, Mddx., [widow], dated 16 Feb 1742. I am to be buried in Bellfound, Mddx. Co., under a black marble stone. Ten acres in Bruton parish with Mattey's schoolhouse, a dwelling lately erected for a schoolmaster adjoining Mr. Pope's land, and £50 to the parish church of Bruton, £100 to my husband's nephew James Allen, with remainder to his brothers and sisters on his mother's side. £200 to Mr. James Franceys who is to be my exec. or, if he dies, my kinsman Abraham Jordan. £20 to James Matthew Delony with remainder to his mother Ann Delony. £5 to Mary Jauncey, wife of John Jauncey, notary public. Residue to

Bruton parish. Wits: John Galley, Hannah Stretch and John Jauncey. Pr. 1 Feb 1743 by James Franceys. (PROB 11/724/60).

John Rush of N.Y., hatter, whither I shall return as soon as I have health, dated 13 May 1743. To my wife in N.Y. my clothes and stock in trade in London excepting hat boxes which are to be sold and the proceeds sent to her with £10 in copper half pence. £20 to Edward Daniel of Redman Lane, Mddx., cooper, who is to be my exec. Residue to my children John and Samuel when they are of age. Wits: Ann (x) Way, James Burn and John Perry. Pr. 1 Jun 1743 by named exec. (PROB 11/727/208).

Edward Tomlinson of Rotherhithe, Surrey, mariner [of the merchant ship *Rappahannock Merchant*, who died in Va., widower], dated 28 Oct 1740. To my eldest son Henry Tomlinson one shilling and no more. All my clothes to my youngest son John. Residue to my daughter Ann Tomlinson who is to be my exex. Wits: Elizabeth Standford, Marmaduke Humphreys and Ralph Kent, scrivener near Rotherhithe church. Pr. Jly 1743 by named exex. (PROB 11/728/246).

William Gill of London, gent., son and heir of Capt. John Gill, mariner, of Bridgetown, Barbados, deceased, dated 12 February 1740. To my sister and sole exex. Frances Gill, now of London, all the lands up the river near Charles Town, S.C., which my father bought of Nathaniel Snow, doctor, and all the estate to which I am entitled by the will of my said father. Wits: John Eaglesfield, Ann Eaglesfield his wife, and Catherine Payne. Pr. 10 Aug 1743 by named exex. (PROB 11/728/262).

Edmond Bennett [of Boston, N.E.], cook of H.M. ship *Squirrel* and pensioner of the Chatham Chest, dated 2 Jan 1736. My whole estate to Edward Westall of St. George's, Mddx., who is to be my exec. Wits: Henry Sheppard, Three Tuns, Crutched Friars, London, and Benjamin Bechinoe. Pr. 5 Oct 1743 by named exec. (PROB 11/729/302).

Thomas Southwick of London, mariner, now bound overseas, [of Va.], dated 4 Feb 1742. My whole estate to Mary, wife of Roger Hare of Clerkenwell, Mddx., silversmith, and she to be my exex. Wits: Thomas Brown and Abraham Ogier in Pope's Head Alley. Pr. 1 Dec 1743 by named exex. (PROB 11/730/369).

Catherine Snell of St. James, Goose Creek, S.C., spinster, dated 19 Sep 1741. (Copy from S.C. records). £1,000 current to my cousin Joshua Sanders. £500 current each to my cousins Catherine Sullivant and Anne Grange. £200 for the relief of the poor of this parish. £100 current each to my cousins Elizabeth Clarke Sanders (wife of my cousin Joshua Sanders), Joshua Sullivant, husband of Catherine

Sullivant, and Hugh Grange, husband of Anne Grange. The residue of my estate between the children of my cousins Joshua Sanders, Catherine Sullivant, Anne Grange and the late Wilson Sanders, i.e. John, Elizabeth and Joshua Sanders, Jane and Joseph Mackey, Hugh, Anne, Hannah, Thomas and Sarah Grange. My friends Rev. Mr. Timothy Millechamp and Mr. Hugh Grange to be execs. Wits: Bn. Smith, George Waring and Francis Holmes. AWW 5 Dec 1743 to James Crokatt, attorney for execs. (PROB 11/730/370).

Henry Cope Esq. [of N.Y.], Lieut-Col. of the American Regiment of Foot, dated Jamaica 5 Mar 1742. My whole estate to my wife Jane Cope and my daughter by my said wife, Jane Cope. My friends Murray Crymble Esq., Receiver-General of Jamaica, and Mr. Stephen Bayard, merchant in N.Y., to be execs. Wits: Thomas Clarke, Conyers Dobby and Charles Cross. Deposition at Trenton, New Jersey, 7 May 1742 by Capt. Thomas Clarke that he and others witnessed the above will. AWW 29 Feb 1743 to Richard Jeneway, attorney for Stephen Bayard in N.Y. (PROB 11/731/34).

1744

William Donning of Nurshill, Lidney, Glos., gent., dated 27 May 1743. To my wife Joanna Donning my tenement in Lidney called Purlier's Farm and all my other lands and tenements, and she to be my exex. Wits: Robert Porry and Edward Trye, clerk to Mr. Morgan Richard. Pr. 9 Feb 1744 by the relict. (PROB 11/731/35).

N.B. The testator's heir at law was his cousin once removed, William Donning of S.C. See NGSQ 65/136-141.

Roger Newberry Esq. of Windsor, [N.E., Captain in the American Regiment], now entered in H.M. service against the Spanish West Indies, [who died in the West Indies], dated 5 Sep 1740. £150 and one-third of my personal estate to my wife Elizabeth Newberry. £150 each to my sons Benjamin and Thomas Newberry. £100 each to my daughters Elizabeth, Hannah, Abigail and Sarah Newberry when they are 21 or married. My mulatto servant Tony *alias* Benony is to be released on reaching the age of 25. Execs: my wife and my brother Mr. Roger Wolcott Jr. Wits: Matthew Allyn, Henry Allyn and Esther Filley Jr. AWW 27 Aug 1744 to Christopher Kilby Esq., attorney for the execs. (PROB 11/734/198).

George Stewart Esq. of Boston, N.E., Captain of a Company in an expedition against the Spanish West Indies [who died there], dated 20 Sep 1740. One third of my estate to my wife Ruth Stewart.

Five shillings to my son Stewart and £50 to his son John Viscount Stewart. The residue to my daughter Mary with remainder to my next-of-kin or, if none, to the church of King's Chapel, Boston. Exec. to be Benjamin Faneuil. Wits: Mary Faneuil, Addington Davenport and John Read. AWW 27 Aug 1744 to Christopher Kilby Esq., attorney for exec. (PROB 11/735/202).

Thomas Freame Esq., at present in Philadelphia, Captain of a Company in Col. William Gooch's Regiment of Foot, ready to embark on a ship against the enemies of the King, dated 22 Sep 1740. One-fifth of my estate to the child my wife Margaretta now bears. The residue to my said wife and my son Thomas Freame. Execs: my said wife and her brother Hon. Thomas Penn Esq., one of the Proprietors of Penna., and Richard Hockley of Philadelphia, merchant. Wits: William Shaw, William Harper and Stephen Stapler. Codicil dated Newcastle 23 Sep 1740. Deposition in Philadelphia 10 Jly 1741 by William Harper that he and others witnessed the above will. Pr. 4 Sep 1744 by affirmation of Thomas Penn Esq. (PROB 11/735/214).

Moses Wright of H.M. ship *Victory* [of Boston, N.E.], dated 20 Mar 1744. My whole estate to my sister Ann Duglass of St. James, Mddx., and she to be my exex. Wits: Thomas Pain and Samuel Yeomans. Pr. 15 Nov 1744 by Ann, wife of (blank) Douglass. (PROB 11/736/271).

1745

William Aglionby of Savannah, Ga., dated 8 Aug 1738. My friend Mr. William Bradley of Savannah to be my sole legatee and exec. Wits: William Kellaway, James Habersham and Samuel Manet. Pr. 30 May 1745 by named exec. (PROB 11/739/130).

John Steel of St. Philip's Parish, Charles Town, S.C., vintner, [who died in Plymouth, Devon], dated 3 December 1742. Bequests to: my brother-in-law John Fitchett and my father Gilbert Steel in Britain. Residue of estate to my wife and sole exex. Mary Steel. Wits: John Martini, Rice Price and John Rattray. Pr. 5 June 1745 by the relict. (PROB 11/740/180).

John Dolphin [of Frederica, Ga.], gent., [bachelor], dated 1 Aug 1741 at the camp of St. Simon's, Ga. Since I arrived in this country I have received civility from my niece Mrs. Martha Heron, wife of Maj. (Alexander) Heron of Capt. Oglethorpe's Regiment of Foot, and I leave my entire estate to her. Since I left England, I may have become entitled to estates unknown to me and these to I leave to my said niece with remainder to her daughter Sarah Maidman, spinster. My said niece to be exex. Wits: George Cadogan, William Lyford and White Outerbridge. Pr. 20 Aug 1745 by Martha, wife of Alexander Heron. (PROB 11/741/220).

1746

Tobias Peirce, late of N.E. but now of London, mariner, dated 9 Dec 1745. My whole estate to my friends and execs. John Burrows of St. Ann's Parish, Middlesex, waterman, and Sarah his wife. Wits: Joseph Hester, notary, and William Woolgar his servant. Pr. 2 Jan 1746 by Sarah Burrows. (PROB 11/744/9).

Charles Dyson, mariner of H.M. ship *Hastings*, but now in hospital in Rochester, Kent, dated 8 Jan 1746. My entire estate to my brother Philip Dyson of the Court House, Princess Anne Co., Va., or, if he is dead, to my brother Francis Dyson of Va. My cousin John Dyson of Limehouse, Middx., gent., to be my exec. Wits: Edward Reed and William Stubbs. Proved 8 Jan 1746 by affirmation of named exec. (PROB 11/744/11).

James Pope of Madeira, merchant, dated 1743. My estate to my nephew John Barrett of Broseley (Salop.), who is to pay an annuity to my wife Margaret Pope. If my said nephew should die without heirs, my estate is to go to my relations of the Pope family. My estate in Manachty (*sic*), Wales, to my cousin Francis Pope of R.I. The rents of my two houses in Bristol to the use of the poor of the church of St. Thomas there. Execs: my nephew John Barrett, now resident in Madeira, and Mr. Thomas Beckford of London, merchant. Witnessed by many persons with Spanish names. Pr. 6 Feb 1746 after testimony as to the testator's writing. (PROB 11/745/59).

John Lloyd of Sarphley, St. James, Goose Creek, S.C., dated 27 Jly 1733. My 640 acres on Waccamaw River and slaves or £200 sterling, my land to the north-west of the Broad Path which goes past Thorowgood's plantation to Mr. Hume's plantation, where Mr. Richard Walker now lives, an annuity of £40 sterling, and a negro girl named Maria, one of the four I lately bought of Jenys and Baker, to my wife Sarah. To my brother Thomas Lloyd half of my 2,000 acres on Four Hole Swamp, reserving the other half to my half-brothers David, Richard, Edward and Hugh Lloyd. If my brothers Thomas or Richard Lloyd come to Carolina, they are to have £20 to pay their passage. The residue of my estate to my eldest son including the reversion of £162 per annum payable by the Exchequer upon the demise of my cousin Jane Griffith. Whoever marries my eldest daughter should take the surname of Lloyd to perpetuate the name. If I have no issue, my estate should descend to my brother Thomas Lloyd. The six family pictures hanging in the front parlour in my house at Sarphley to my wife and friends Ralph Izard and Benjamin Wareing, and they are to be execs. Wits: Samuel Prioleau, John Moultrie, John Ballyntine and John Lewis. Codicil of 28 Sep 1733. My house in Childsbury is to be sold. Wits: Elizabeth Atkin Jr., Joseph Russell and Thomas Steers. AWW 7 Jun 1746 to John Nickelson, adr. of the infant son John Lloyd deceased, and attorney for the daughter and only next-of-kin Sarah Lloyd, infant; the relict and other named execs. having died. (PROB 11/747/184).

John Watson of London, master mariner, [of Md., bachelor], dated 10 May 1743. £200 to my brother William Watson. £10 to my sister Jane Watson. A guinea for a mourning ring each to: Walter Cockram and his sister Mary; William Ferdyce and his spouse Margett; William Smith and his spouse Mary; and Robert Ragg, shipmaster of Abingdon. £20 to my friend Christopher Marshall of London, merchant, who is to be exec. The residue to my father Alexander Watson. Wits: John Stewart, James Stewart and George Steel. Pr. 23 Jun 1746 by named exec. (PROB 11/748/196).

Joseph Avery, late of Connecticut but now of the City of Bristol, mariner, dated 13 Mar 1745. A suit of mourning to my friend James Vincent of Bristol, clerk, and Betty Stone of Bristol, spinster. The residue of my estate to my friend Jane Day of Bristol, spinster, who is to be my exex. Wits: John Churchman, Ambrose Bartlett and James Murray. Pr. 7 Jly 1746 by exex. (PROB 11/748/197).

William Claiborne of Va., at present in London, merchant, [who died in Hackney, Middlesex], codicil dated 16 May 1746. I have made a will in Va. appointing execs. there. My exec. in London is to be Mr. John Hanbury of London, merchant. Wits: Edward Randolph Jr. and Benjamin Keene. Pr. 17 July 1746 by affirmation of named exec. (PROB 11/748/202).

John Prentis of New London, Connecticut, mariner, [late commander of H.M. ship *Defence*], at present of St. Martin in the Fields, Middlesex, sick of smallpox, dated 24 July 1746. I have made a will in N.E. and have goods in England and the United Provinces which are to go to my wife and children. Exec: Mr. William Bowdoin of Boston, N.E., merchant, now in the parish of St. Martin in the Fields. Wits: Margaret Ryan, William Hopkins and W. Bolleme. Pr. 5 Aug 1746 by named exec. (PROB 11/749/244).

Thomas Haynes of Warwick Co., Va., dated 1 Sep 1742. To my son Anthony Haynes my lands on Stony Creek where he now lives which I bought of Stephen Evans and lands between Wills Run and Rockey Run, except for 400 acres which I give to my son Thomas Haynes. In accordance with a bond of 11 Jan 1740 made on the marriage of my said son Thomas, he is to have the land on which I now live after my wife's decease and the plantation called Myers's and Prices'. In default of heirs to him, these lands are to descend to my son William Haynes or to my grandson Herbert Haynes, son of my said son Anthony. My 400 acres between Wills Run, Hickman's Line and Rockey Run in Prince George Co., mentioned in the marriage agreement, to my said son Thomas. To my son Richard Haynes lands in White Oak Swamp in Prince George Co., partly bought from Robert Moody, and in default of heirs to him, to my son Andrew Haynes. To the said Andrew Haynes my lands on the south side of Stony Creek from Mr. Keith's line on the east across Notway road to Wills Run on the west, part bought of Stephen Evans and part of Theophilus Field. To my said son William a lot in York Town bought of William Cary Jr. To my daughter Martha Haynes £20. To my granddaughter Martha Haynes, daughter of my son Herbert Haynes deceased, £20. My wife Martha is to have my plantation and the one on which my mother lives during her lifetime, and she is to provide my son William with a good education. Execs: my said wife and sons Anthony, Thomas and Andrew. Wits: Ann Haynes, Elizabeth Haynes and Lawrence Haynes. AWW 27 Sep 1746 to James Wilkes, attorney for Andrew Haynes in Va. (PROB 11/749/267).

Nathan Walker, Ensign of Maj. John Caulfield's detachment in the Isle of Ratan, late of Col. Gooch's American Regiment, dated Augusta 25 Nov 1744. The arrears of pay due to me to be remitted to my cousin John Gardner of R.I., merchant. Execs: Lieut. Jenkins of Caulfield's detachment and Lieut. Carre of Brig. Wolf's Regiment of Marines. Wits: Francis Hopkins, Alexander Cosby and John Lenn Barnett. Pr. 15 Oct 1746 by the surviving executor Andrew Carre. (PROB 11/750/314).

Edward Bradley of Philadelphia, glazier, dated 22 Mar 1743. To Ebenezer Kinnersley the £30 he owes me. £150 sterling each to my brothers Thomas and Joseph Bradley and my sister Ann Shepherd. £30 each to my nephews Edward Shepherd, son of the said Ann, and William Bradley, son of my said brother Joseph. To my wife Esther the residue of my estate including the revenue from the sale of land to William Houk, the right to a stable I took of Thomas Howard, my messuage on Front Street between the lots of Robert Strettle and George Shed, the rents of a tenement in Elbow Lane I bought of Joshua Carpenter, and my slaves named York and Daphne with their children. My said wife, Ebenezer Kinnersley of

Philadelphia, shopkeeper, and Thomas Leach of Philadelphia, shop-keeper, to be execs. in Penna.; my said two nephews to be execs. in Britain. Wits: Peter Turner, C. Brocden and Robert Strettle. Pr. 8 Nov 1746 by Edward Shepherd. (PROB 11/750/318).

William Warden, late of Charles Town, S.C., but now of Whitechapel, Middlesex, mariner, dated 15 Apr 1746. My tenement and ground in Charles Town to my wife Margaret Warden and my daughters Elizabeth and Catherine. Execs: my friend Mr. William Legoe of Whitechapel, weaver, and Mr. Stephen Coleman of Wapping Wall, Mddx., ship chandler. Wits: Thomas Smith, James Fraser and John Marmaduke Bagline, all of Goodmans Fields, London. Pr. 18 Nov 1746 by William Legoe. (PROB 11/751/341).

Nathaniel Higgins of Cape Cod, N.E., now a mariner of H.M. ship *Torbay* [but late of H.M. ship *Hornet*, bachelor], dated 23 November 1743. My estate to my shipmate and executor Thomas Brown of Hackney, Mddx. Wits: Abraham Scares and Henry Crick. AWW Nov 1746 to Sarah Browne, wife and attorney of Thomas Brown, now on H.M. ship *Nottingham*. (PROB 11/751/354).

Thomas Matthews [of Boston, N.E.], mariner of H.M. ship *Eltham*, dated 26 Nov 1746. My whole estate to my wife Hannah Matthews of Boston. Mr. Richard Crafts of Deptford, Kent, to be my exec. Wits: Peter Pride, John Nowell and Thomas Crafts. Pr. 3 Dec 1746 by named exec. (PROB 11/751/359).

1747

Ashby Utting Esq. [of S.C.], Captain of H.M. ship *Aldborough*, dated Charles Town, S.C., 27 Sep 1745. I confirm the settlement made on my wife Amy Utting. Mourning rings to: my mother-in-law Mrs. Amy Mighells; my brother-in-law Mr. Thomas Mighells; Mr. James Reeve of Lowestoft and his family; Mr. Caleb Aldred of Yarmouth; Mr. Gabriel Maningault and Jacob Motte of Charles Town, mer-chants. The residue of my estate to my said wife with remainder of half to the said Thomas Mighells and half to Elizabeth Neeve. Wits: Robert Whitchell, Christopher Gadsden and Thomas Easton. Pr. 13 Jan 1747 by the relict. (PROB 11/752/26).

William Brewer, late of Boston, N.E., now residing in Titchfield, Hampshire, mariner. To Clement Walcot of Titchfield my whole estate including my pay for service on the ships of war *Rose*, *Norwich*, *Royal Sovereign* and *Nottingham*, and he to be my exec.

Wits: William Murrant and Nicholas Meritt. Pr. 23 Mar 1747 by named exec. (PROB 11/753/63).

Alexander Dalrumble [of Salem, N.E., bachelor], of H.M. ship *Woolwich*, Capt. Joseph Lingen, dated 10 Mar 1747. My whole estate to my friends Paul Moor and Mary Moor of Ratcliffe, victualler, and they to be execs. Wits: John Buchanan and R. Pidgeon, attorney at law near the Three Cups, Lower Shadwell. Pr. 12 Mar 1747 by Paul Moor. (PROB 11/753/68).

Limpany White, Lieut. in Col. William Gooch's Regiment of Foot, [bachelor], dated Cartagena, West Indies, 3 April 1741. My estate to be divided between my sisters Katherine and Martha White and my brother Maurice White. My arrears of pay to be remitted to Katherine Duron, widow (of Charles Duron, physician,) of Second River, East New Jersey. AWW 5 Mar 1747 to the sister Martha White after testimony by Rev. Edmond White of Tooting, Surrey, and David Long of St. Andrew, Holborn, London, as to the testator's handwriting. (PROB 11/753/85).

Isaac Berthon, born at Chattellerault on 6 Aug 1663 and now in London, dated 12 May 1746. (Translated from French). £10,000 to Mr. Stephen Galhie, surgeon and apothecary of Stewart Street, Spitalfields, Mddx., and his wife Mary Galhie Berthon, daughter of my cousin german Michael Berthon now in N.Y. £2,000 to Elias Le Clerc, watchcase maker in Compton Street, Leicester Fields, Mddx., son of my cousin Jane Berthon, widow of Alexander Le Clerc, living at Amsterdam. £1,000 to Francis Ribot, mercer at the sign of the Peach, New Round Court, Strand, Mddx., and his wife Letysa Ribot Berthon, (my relation in the same degree as her sister Mary Galhie). £1,000 to Stephen Ledet, bookseller at Amsterdam, son of my cousin John Ledet and his wife Mary Berthon. £100 each to: Mr. Arne Berthon, merchant in Amsterdam, son of my cousin Francis Berthon, and Ledet his wife; John Berthon, jeweller, his brother Michael Berthon, engraver, and their mother-in-law Ann Berthon, widow of Paul Berthon, all living in the Greek Quarter. £1,000 to the French church in Threadneedle Street, London, for the poor. Execs: Mr. Claude Aubert, merchant of Austin Friars, London, Mr. Elias Le Clerc, Mr. Stephen Galhie and Mr. Francis Ribot. Wits: James Teissier and Alexander Eynard. Pr. 2 May 1747 by named execs. (PROB 11/754/116).

Edmund Cook of the Island (*sic*) of Md., [of Norwich, Norfolk, who died in St. John's, St. Mary Co., Md., bachelor], dated 29 Mar 1744. One shilling each to my sisters Abigail and Elizabeth. My estate in Lessingham near Hempstead, Norfolk, to James Brown of Md. in trust for my cousins and execs. Charles and Susanna Martin

of the City of Norwich. Wits: Thomas Smart and T. Snoud. Pr. 19
May 1747 by Charles Martin. (PROB 11/754/121).

Samuel Allen [of Boston, N.E., mariner], late of H.M. ship *Kent* but
now of H.M. ship *Maidstone*, Capt. Frederick Rogers, dated 23 Feb
1745. My whole estate to my wife Mary Allen in Boston. My friend
Daniel Gunn of Wapping, cordwainer, to be my exec. Wits:
Frederick Rogers and J. Chalkhill, clerk. Pr. 1 Jun 1747 by named
exec. (PROB 11/754/141).

John Fenwick Esq., late of S.C. but now of St. George, Hanover
Square, Middx., dated 22 Jly 1747. £50 to my son-in-law Isaac
Whittington Esq. A mourning ring to my kinsman Robert Fenwick
Esq. of Lincolns Inn. My estate in S.C. is much reduced in value
because of the failure of trade due to the war with France and
Spain, and I leave it with the residue of my estate to my son
Edward Fenwick who now resides there. To my daughter
(Elizabeth, Countess of) Deloraine £1,000 in addition to what I
have given her and her late husband, my coach and horses,
furniture, etc. £2,000 to my daughter Sarah. £100 current each to
my brother-in-law Col. John Gibbes, Andrew Rutledge Esq., and
my nephew Culcheth Golightly, all of S.C. £200 current to my
nephew John Gibbes, son of my late brother-in-law Mr. William
Gibbes, when he is 18. £500 in trust for my grandson John Scott
until he is 21. Execs: my daughter Deloraine and my said son
Edward. Wits: Thomas Compton, Thomas Adams and Elizabeth
Compton. Depositions 22 Jly 1747 by George Morley Esq. of St.
Clement Danes, Mddx., Silvia Brathwaite of St. George, Hanover
Square, widow, and Andrew Pringle of St. Margaret Pattens,
London, merchant, that they found the above will in the testator's
bureau and that its seal was broken by the execs. Pr. 23 Jly 1747
by Elizabeth, Countess of Deloraine, and 2 Nov 1747 by Edward
Fenwick Esq. (PROB 11/755/176).

Addington Davenport of Boston, N.E., clerk, dated 1 Feb 1745. £200
to Benjamin Faneuil Esq. £2,500 sterling each to my daughters Jane
and Elizabeth Davenport, when they are 24, and my friends Mr.
William Price of Boston, cabinet maker, and Mr. Powers Marriott
of Boston, shopkeeper, are to be their guardians. My daughters shall
not marry without their approval until they reach the age of 24 and
are to have all that belonged to my late wife. The residue, including
half of my father's estate which will come to me on the demise
of my mother Elizabeth Davenport, to my only son Addington. My
friend Mr. Joseph Dowse to be my executor with William Price
and guardian of my said son. Wits: Timothy Cutler, Thomas Gunter
and Benjamin Pollard. AWW 21 Aug 1747 to William Baker,
Alderman of London, attorney for Joseph Dowse and William Price

in Boston. Revoked Mar 1756 and granted to the son Addington Davenport on his coming of age. (PROB 11/756/203).

Thomas Bordley of Annapolis, Md., intending this day to depart for Great Britain, [who died in Greenwich, Kent], dated 4 Jun 1747. All my debts, and particularly that to Mr. Wakelin Welch, are to be paid. The residue of my estate in Great Britain to Mrs. Margaret Smith of Mark Lane, London, haberdasher. My half of our four lots in Annapolis to my brother John. My quarter part of Augustine Manor is to descend in due course to my brother Matthias Bordley in accordance with my father's indication. The residue in Md. to my sister Elizabeth Bordley and brother Beale Bordley. Martin Smith of Mark Lane, London, to be my exec. O'seers: Mr. Jenings and my brother Stephen Bordley. Wits: Mary Jenings, B. Young Jr., and Samuel Woods. Pr. 19 Sep 1747 by named exec. (PROB 11/756/222).

John Dyson of St. Ann, Middlesex, gent., dated 22 Sep 1747. Bequests to: Philip and Francis Dyson of Norfolk Town, Va., Peter and David Dyson, sons of my late uncle Francis Dyson; Sarah Bailey, daughter of my aunt Bailey, late of Little Moorfields, Middx., and her two sisters; the Quakers of Ratcliffe. Residue to my wife Priscilla, my brother-in-law Joseph Besse, and friend Silvanus Greville, shipwright, who are to be my execs. and pay an annuity to Sarah Bentley, daughter of Joseph Besse and wife of Thomas Bentley. Wits: Seymour Hocker and Thomas Hearle. Pr. Nov 1747 by the execs. named. (PROB 11/757/277).

Nathaniel King [of Boston, N.E.], mariner of H.M. ship *York*, dated Gibson Bay on board the said ship 31 Dec 1741. My whole estate to my wife Mary King of Boston who is to be my exex. Wits: Thomas Mandery, George Worden, Roger Coleman and O. Sutherland, clerk. AWW 27 Nov 1747 to Thomas Newman, attorney for the relict in Boston. (PROB 11/757/284).

John Burrington of St. George, Hanover Square, Mddx., dated 1 Apr 1747. To my friend and exec. Esquire Cary, gent., my whole estate including that on Cape Fear River, N.C. Wits: Anna de Beekers, Jane Maxwell and Jean Paguy. Pr. 14 Dec 1747 by named exec. (PROB 11/758/302).

Ebenezer Currie of Penna., at present in London, dated 28 Aug 1746. To John Groves who has served me with great fidelity 100 guineas. The residue to my father, Rev. John Currie of Kinglassie, (Fife, Scotland), wikth remainder to my mother Jean Currie. Mr. Samuel McAll Sr. of Philadelphia and Mr. John Seton of London, merchant, to be execs. Wits: Andrew Elliot and Andrew Seton. Pr. 2 Dec 1747 by John Seton. (PROB 11/758/304).

Mary Orpwood of St. Margaret, Westminster, Mddx, spinster, dated 4
Nov 1746. My house and lands to my exex. Mary Collins, daughter
of William and Elinor Collins of East Hanney, Bucks., (now Oxon.).
A legacy of £100 left to me by my grandfather Edmond Orpwood
of (Oxford Township), Philadelphia, and now in the hands of his
execs. Francis and John Knowles of Philadelphia, to Richard
Pomeroy of London, gent. Wits: Mary Rake, Mary Malbone and
Jonah Finlayson. AWW Dec 1747 to William Collins, father of the
named exex. until she is 17. (PROB 11/758/321).

1748

Paulin Brooke of [York River], Va., [bachelor], dated 4 Jly 1746. To
my friend Heneage Robinson £40 with which to redeem my negro
boy now in France and send him to Va. Five guineas to Mrs.
Catherine Giffard. A mourning ring to William and Sarah Watts,
Rebecca Stevens, Mr. John Maynard and his son. My friend William
Watts is to be exec. amd attend to my affairs in England. Wits:
William Richardson and John Atkinson. Pr. 15 Feb 1748 by named
exec. (PROB 11/759/38).

Charles Home of N.Y. City, gent., dated 15 Sep 1740. My whole estate
to my nephew Charles Home, son of Alexander Home of Leith,
Scotland, with remainder to his next eldest son who is to be
educated at the discretion of my exec. William Home Esq. of
Bastonrig (*sic*), Scotland. My execs. for America to be William
Jamison, James Headcorn and James Rochead, all of N.Y. City,
gents. Wits: Archibald Ramsay, John Innes and George Burnet. Pr.
12 Feb 1748 by William Home. (PROB 11/760/51).

William Lithgow of London, merchant, [of Wilmington, N.C.], dated
4 Jun 1740. All my household goods and furniture to my wife Mary
Lithgow. £20 to my mother Barbara Lithgow. £50 to my brother
David Lithgow. £10 each to my sisters Janet, Elizabeth and Anne
Lithgow, and my daughter-in-law Elizabeth Masters. One third of
my estate to my said wife and two thirds to Mary Lithgow, my
daughter by my former wife. My friends Mr. Nathaniel Fletcher of
London, merchant, Mr. Job Pearson of Clapham, Surrey, gent., and
Mr. Peter Thompson of London, merchant, to be execs. Wits: Mary
Brown, William Daman and George Augustus Prosser, attorney at
law, Portsmouth. Pr. 9 Mar 1748 by Nathaniel Fletcher. Further
grant in Jly 1754 to Sir Peter Thompson with similar powers
reserved to Job Pearson. (PROB 11/760/90).

Alexander Stewart of Maj.-Gen. James Oglethorpe's Regiment [who died in Frederica, Ga.], dated 7 Nov 1747. Half my personal estate to my eldest daughter Naney Stewart with an annuity of £12, and half to my sons Allan and Charles Stewart who may sell the same when they come of age. My house and half lot at Frederica to Hannah Mackay for the maintenance of Alexander Stewart, my natural son born of her. My execs. are to be Lt. Col. Alexander Heron, Capt. George Dunbar, Capt. Patrick Sutherland and Ensign White Outerbridge of the said regiment, Dougal Stewart Esq. of Appin, my brother James Stewart and Mr. Patrick Houston of Frederica. Wits: Samuel Mackay, Ronald Campbell and Roderick Haliburton. Pr. 5 May 1748 by James Stewart. (PROB 11/761/130).

Archibald Liddell of St. George, Mddx., commander of the *Elliott* galley, now bound on a voyage to S.C. [and who died in Charles Town], dated 4 May 1747. An annuity of £5 to my mother Lillie Band. The residue to my niece Anne Liddell, daughter of my brother Thomas Liddell, with remainder to my brother John Liddell. My execs. to be Archibald Elliott of London, merchant, and Abraham Creedlan of Wapping, Mdx., sailmaker. Wits: Nathaniel Edmonds, Charles Cozens and William Moon. Pr. 7 Jun 1748 by Archibald Elliott. (PROB 11/762/184).

Joseph Austell of Boston, N.E., mariner, now bound on a voyage overseas, dated 6 Nov 1743. I have determined the disposal of my estate in Boston by a will made there in Oct or Nov 1742 of which the execs. are my brother Isaac Austell of Wilmington near Philadelphia, farmer, Benjamin Bagnell Sr. and Benjamin Bagnell Jr. This will is to regulate my affairs in Europe which I entrust to my exec. there who is to be my cousin Moses Austell. Wits: Joseph Harrison, Ebenezer Tull and Gyles Lone, notary public in Exchange Alley. Pr. 7 Sep 1748 by named exec. (PROB 11/764/257).

William Grace of St. Katherine by the Tower, London, mariner, [master of the merchant ship *Owen*, who died in Boston, N.E.], dated 17 Apr 1744. My whole estate to Catherine Hunter of St. Katherine's, widow, who is to be my cxex. Wits: Thomas Galley and John Forber. Pr. 30 Sep 1748 by named exex. (PROB 11/764/267).

John Bayley [of Philadelphia], mariner of H.M. ship *Jersey*, commander Charles Hardy Esq., dated 18 Oct 1746. £20 to my friend Hugh Hagan, quartermaster of H.M. ship *Roebuck*, who is to be my exec. The residue to my wife Elizabeth Bayley of Philadelphia. Wits: William Stown and Thomas Johnston. Pr. 29 Oct 1748 by named exec. (PROB 11/765/290).

Lewis Jones, now living in St. Helena parish, Granville Co., [S.C.], clerk, dated 10 Feb 1744. My land on Port Royal Island and my

lot in Beaufort to be sold with slaves and stock. £400 sterling to
my brother John Jones. £150 sterling to my father's children by
his last wife. £150 sterling to my sister's children. £100 sterling
each to my nephews Lewis Jones and Hugh Jones. To my friend
John Jones, sister's son to the late Capt. Rowland Evans, 1,000
acres in the hands of Capt. Pooley. £50 sterling each to my friends
Gabriel Manigault and Charles Purry who are to be execs. with my
brother John Jones. A bible each to my godchildren: Margaret Ellis;
Allan McLean; John Scott, son of Capt. Edward Scott; Lucia
Palmer; John Palmer; Deveana Susannah Frankling; Lewis Reeve;
Catherine Barnwell; and Hugh Brian Jr. A bible each to the
godchildren of my late wife, Catherine Higg and Elizabeth Sysom.
£100 for the support of the school at Beaufort. £30 for the poor
of the parish of Llamoring (*sic*) where I was born. The residue to
my brother John Jones. Wits: William Harvey, Edward Wigg and
James Houston. Pr. in S.C. 13 Mar 1745. Pr. London 4 Oct 1748
by the brother John Jones. (PROB 11/765/300).

Mary Emerson [of Bristol, R.I.], widow, dated 24 Jly 1740. £50 to
my granddaughter Mary Bonsignor when she is 21 or married, and
the interest meanwhile to her mother, my daughter Sarah Bonsignor.
The residue of my estate to my daughter Mary Vonheinen who is
to be exec. with Mr. Richard Partridge of London, merchant. Wits:
Edward Webb, Abraham Wilson and Laurence Vale. Pr. 10 Nov
1748 by the affirmation of Richard Partridge. (PROB 11/765/324).

Edward Fottrell of Baltimore County, Md., [widower], dated 17 Feb
1741. To my son Edward Fottrell my mill, lands on Jones Falls
near Baltimore, 100 acres I purchased from William Peel, and a
negro boy called Tom. To my son Thomas Fottrell my three
contiguous lots in Baltimore and a negro boy called Paul. My
dwelling house is to be sold and the proceeds given to my daughter
Achsah Fottrell when she is 21 or married; she is also to have a
negro woman called Moriah. Basil Dorsey and Alexander Lawson
are to be execs. Wits: T. Sheredine, Frances North and Elenor
Linch. Codicil of 17 May 1741. William Payne, late of Cork,
Ireland, is to have the management of my mill house and lands
and to care for my children. Wits: Benedict Bourdillon, Janette
Janson Bourdillon and Lawrence Maynard. AWW 11 Nov 1748 to
William Black, attorney for the creditor William Chapman in Md.;
the named executors and the said children having been cited but
not having appeared. (PROB 11/765/325).

Abraham Huisman of N.Y. City, merchant, dated 4 May 1748. To
Hendrick Garret and Bonwina Helena, children born in wedlock to
Abraham Blancke and Maria Van Bulderen of Groningen in the
United Provinces, clothing, diamond rings, linen and plate, etc. £70

each to Joseph Murray Esq. and Richard Nicholls, gent., both of N.Y. City, who are to be execs. £300 current and one of my negroes to my servant Isaiah Crane. All my real estate is to be sold for the benefit of the children of Abraham Blancke. Joseph Mico of London, merchant, is to be exec. for England. Wits: George Harrison, John Burnet and Joseph Webb Jr. Codicil of 12 Jun 1748. £75 current to Mr. Simeon Soumaine. Pr. 29 Dec 1748 by Joseph Mico. (PROB 11/766/368).

1749

John Fernsley, mariner of the *Princess Louisa*, Capt. John Pinson, now bound to East India, [of H.M. ships *Lowestoft* and *Worcester*, who died in Boston Hospital, N.E., bachelor], dated 26 Mar 1741. My whole estate to my sisters Mary Crouchefer, [widow], and Sarah Fernsley and they are to be exexs. Wits: William Masterman and John Butler of Wapping. Pr. 4 Jan 1749 by exexs. (PROB 11/767/8).

Andrew Nicoll of N.Y. City, gent., Capt-Lieut. of Captain Hubert Marshall's Independent Company, [who died in N.Y. City], dated 28 Jun 1746. My 1,000 acres near the Highlands in Orange Co., N.Y., in the occupation of William Postles to be sold. £200 is to be put at interest for the maintenance and education of Susannah Nicoll, daughter of the late George Nicoll of N.Y. City, until she is 21, with remainder to her mother, Elizabeth Nicoll, widow. £30 current to Wellegonda Bayard of N.Y. City, widow. £20 current to George Burnet of N.Y. City, shopkeeper. £20 sterling to Helen Nicoll, relict of my late brother James of Aberdeen, Scotland, with remainder to Rev. James Orem, chaplain to the forces in this province. The residue of my estate to the said James Orem and Richard Nicolls who are to be execs. with George Burnet. Wits: John Burnet, James Emott and John McEvers Jr. Pr. 9 Feb 1749 by Rev. James Orem. (PROB 11/768/50).

Barnet Bond, formerly of Md. but now of Limehouse, Mddx., mariner, dated 25 Jan 1742. My freehold estates in Md. including one near Gunpowder River, one near the head of Bush River and one in Nodd Forest called the Land of Nod, to be divided: one third to go to my wife Alice Bond during her lifetime and two thirds to my daughter Mary Bond and such other child as my wife may now be pregnant with. My said wife to be exex. and trustee but, if she remarries, my cousin Mr. William Bond in Md. is to be trustee. Wits: Charles Barnard, John Lugg and Thomas Coulthred. Pr. 20 April 1749 by the relict, now wife of William Grimes, who made an affidavit that the testator had only one daughter, Mary, now living. (PROB 11/769/100).

N.B. The testator was for some years employed as the master of ships carrying transported felons to America and in 1743 was arraigned on a charge of murder on the high seas. He was acquitted after a lengthy trial.

Anthony Palmer, Lieut. in Lieut-Gen. Dalzel's Regiment in the Leeward Islands, being about to depart thither, [who died in Philadelphia], dated 24 Apr 1746. My whole estate to my wife Elizabeth Palmer and she and my friend Lieut. Robert Lowe are to be execs. Wits: Daniel Flexney and James Killpatrick. Pr. 8 May 1749 by Robert Lowe. Revoked and granted to the relict in Jly 1750. (PROB 11/770/156).

Eliakim Palmer of [St. Peter le Poor], London, merchant, dated 14 May 1749. On my marriage to my now wife Elizabeth, I agreed to distribute my estate in accordance with the custom of the City of London; accordingly I leave her £15,000. By his will my late father Thomas Palmer Esq. of Boston, N.E., devised to me and my brother Thomas a mansion house which he built at the foot of Fort Hill in Boston, and my part, now in the occupation of Charles Paxton Esq., I leave to my said brother. To Nathaniel Balston Esq. of Boston and my said brother all my houses, wharves and lands in Boston for the benefit of my sister Sarah, wife of Job Lewis Esq. of Boston, with remainder to my nieces Abigail and Hannah Lewis. £10 to Mrs. Mary Baker, relict of the late Dr. John Baker. £100 to John Faris, son of my cousin Mary Faris. £50 each to George Walker Esq. and Hon. John Lyte of Barbados. £100 each to my execs. Beeston Long Esq., Mr. Henry Norris Jr. of London, merchant, and my cousin William Palmer of London, attorney at law. £100 to my book-keeper Abraham Shand. A bond of 24 Jun 1730 whereby Archdale Palmer and his son Thomas Palmer became bound to my uncle Henry Palmer I leave to Anne Palmer, relict of my said late uncle Archdale Palmer. £10 to the congregation of Protestant Dissenters in Old Jewry, London. The residue of my estate to my son William Finch Palmer and to any child being carried by my wife. Wits: Eliza Norris, James Theobald and Judith Grover. Pr. 24 May 1749 by named execs. (PROB 11/770/157).

Anthony Moreton, [Lieut. in General Oglethorpe's Regiment of Foot, who died in Frederica, Ga., bachelor], dated Frederica 7 Sep 1747. My whole estate to my youngest brother Stephen Moreton, surgeon in the Navy, or my youngest sister Sarah Moreton. My execs. to be Rev. Thomas Bosomworth, Robert Paterson and Niel Holland, all in Frederica and landholders in Ga. Wits: James Simms and John Stronach. Pr. 11 Jly 1749 by Niel Holland. (PROB 11/771/223).

James Browne of Philadelphia, mariner, dated 8 Mar 1710. To my wife Sarah Browne my house and ground on the west side of Front Street, Philadelphia, where I now dwell, bounded on the north by Edward Church and on the west by John Smart. She is also to have the residue of my estate and be my exex. Wits: Richard Heath, Richard Walker and John Baily. Deposition in Philadelphia on 8 Jly 1710 by Richard Heath and Richard Walker that they were witnesses. AWW to William Lea, adr. of the relict, Sarah Lea alias Browne, late the wife of William Lea deceased. (PROB 11/773/303).

Nicholas Salisbury of Boston, Mass., shopkeeper, dated 4 Apr 1748. The late John Elbridge Esq. of Bristol devised £8,000 by his will (*pr. 27 Mar 1739, q.v.*) to his sister Sanders, her daughters and their children in N.E., by virtue of which my son Josiah Salisbury and my daughters Martha and Rebecca (my only children then living) had a share of £800 sterling, but my daughter Martha died on 7 Feb 1748. My wife Martha shall enjoy the said legacies until my children Josiah and Rebecca reach the age of 21. £300 sterling to my son Samuel. £150 sterling to my daughters Elizabeth and Sarah. £300 sterling to my son Stephen because he took nothing under the will of his grandmother Rebecca Sanders. £100 in bills to my brother Benjamin Salisbury. An annuity of £24 to my wife who is to have my dwelling house and land in Marlborough Street, Boston, with remainder to my son Samuel. My said wife to be exec. with my friends John Fairweather Esq. and John Salter the brazier. Wits: Robert Auchmuty, Robert Auchmuty Jr. and Josiah Torrey. AWW 7 Nov 1749 to Thomas Lane, attorney for the relict in Boston. (PROB 11/775/356).

David Thomson late of Carolina, merchant, at present in London and now bound for Va. [who died in York Town, Va.], dated 26 Jun 1746. Bequests to: my brother William Thomson of Jedburgh, Scotland, surgeon; my sister Margaret Thomson; my cousin Margaret Hardie of London, spinster; my cousin Joseph Davidson of London, bookseller, and his wife. Execs: Joseph Anderson of Edenton, N.C., gent., and the said Joseph Davidson. Wits: Thomas Browne of Pope's Head Alley, and Hugh Price. Pr. 29 Dec 1749 by Joseph Davidson. (PROB 11/775/389).

1750

Thomas Dickson [of Boston, N.E., surgeon of H.M. ship *Worcester* [*Gibraltar* and *Hawk*], dated 22 Jly 1748. Five guineas for a ring to my aunt Elizabeth Dickson, wife of William Mitchell of Forfar,

Scotland. One guinea each for a ring to my friends Mr. George
Patterson of Orange Street, St. Martin in the Fields, peruke maker,
and his wife. The residue to my sister Jane Dickson in Montrose,
Scotland. My friends Capt. James Ogilvy in King Street, St. James
Square, gent., and John Ouchterlony, merchant in Angel Court,
Throgmorton Street, London, to be my execs. Wits: Silvester
Gardner, William Complin and William Winter. Codicil of 14 Aug
1748. My gold watch to my friend Silvester Gardner of Boston,
N.E., physician, and he is to be my exec. for N.E., to dispose of
my black boy and send my seal ring to my first cousin Patrick
Dickson of Doe, Angus. To my cousin Mr. James Dickson of
Montrose my sword, etc. Wits: Nathaniel Thwing, John Whitney
and Jean Sinclair. Pr. 12 Jan 1750 by John Ouchterlony. Further
grant 2 Jun 1762 to the sister Jane Dickson. (PROB 11/776/8).

Russell Tompkins, late H.M. Storekeeper of Jamaica but now on the
Ruby of Philadelphia, Mr. William Edwards, bound to Philadelphia
[and who died in Penna.], dated at sea 17 Jly 1749. To my nephew
Jonathan Tompkins, orphan son of Jonathan Tompkins of Deptford,
Kent, £800 when he comes of age or as my brother John Tompkins
sees fit, and the interest thereon to be used for his maintenance.
£100 sterling to my nephew Nicholas Carr, son of Nicholas Carr
of Greenwich, Kent, bricklayer, and Mary his wife, when he comes
of age. £100 to my sister Sarah Tompkins of Deptford, Kent,
spinster. To my brother John Tompkins of Mitchell Grove near
Arundel, Sussex, the moiety of 18 negroes I left in Jamaica in the
care of Mr. William Willy, master shipwright. I give to the mulatto
woman named Jenny in Kingston, Jamaica, a negro wench named
Molley, a negro man named Handy and a horse called Diamond,
with remainder to the children of my brother and sister, John and
Elizabeth Tompkins. Execs. to be my brother John Tompkins and
George Hind, late of Jamaica but now residing in London, who is
to gather in my effects in the hands of Mr. John Myers of
Limehouse. Wits: Cony Edwards, William Flanagan and William
Imlay. Pr. 12 Jan 1750 by the brother John Tompkins. (PROB
11/776/30).

Elizabeth Hammerton of Charles Town, S.C., widow, [who died at
sea], dated 27 Oct 1738. My whole estate to my son Hollier
Hammerton when he is 21, with remainder to my brother Nathaniel
Hollier of Lynn, Norfolk, schoolmaster. My friends Ann de la
Brasseur, Joseph Barry, Adam Beauchamp and Thomas Bolton to
be execs. Wits: Maurice Lewis, John Rattray and James Varnor.
Codicil of 13 Jan 1739. If I die in the summer time when the
weather is hot, my corpse is to lie three days before interment; but,
if it is cold, it is to lie for four days. Wits: Clement Sackville and

John Rattray. Codicil of 6 Oct 1748. My clothes and furniture to Mary Roberts, widow. Wits: William Bee and John Rattray. AWW to Nathaniel Hollier, the son Hollier Hammerton having died and the other execs. having been cited but not having appeared. (PROB 11/776/16).

Charles Mackintosh of N.Y.C. [but late of St. Martin in the Fields, Middx., who died at sea], dated (blank) Feb 1747. My whole estate to my wife Susanna Mackintosh during her lifetime and she is to use the profits thereof for the maintenance of my children Phineas and Susanna until they come of age or are married. Execs: my said wife and my friends Stephen Bayard of N.Y.C. and Richard Alsop of New Town, Long Island. Wits: Elisha Parker, Par Parmiter and (---?---) Crofts. AWW 3 Feb 1750 to John Fell, husband and attorney of the relict, now Susanna Fell, in N.Y. Admon. of Jun 1749 to the principal creditor Alexander Mackintosh now made void. (PROB 11/777/51).

Andrew Mills [of N.Y.], purser of H.M. ship *Greyhound*, dated 12 Dec 1743. My whole estate to my wife Eleanor Mills of Hope, Hants., who is to be exex. Wits: J. Boy, John Bladen and Michael Grew. Pr. 5 Feb 1750 by the relict. (PROB 11/777/51).

Ruth Woodbridge of Barbados, now residing in Boston, Mass., [and who died there], widow, dated 23 Dec 1748. My whole estate to my mother Susannah Haggett during her life on condition that she pays £10 sterling to my sister-in-law Mary Alleyne, widow, and £300 sterling to my friend Col. Richard Wiltshire, with remainder to my sister Jane, wife of Nathaniel Haggett Esq., then to my nephew William Haggett. My said mother and brother-in-law to be execs. Col. Wiltshire is to manage my affairs in Boston. Wits: William Bowdoin, Thomas Willshire and Joseph Mannon. AWW 14 Feb 1750 to Edward Clark Parish, attorney for Nathaniel Haggett Esq. in Barbados, exec. to the relict Ruth Woodbridge. (PROB 11/777/65).

Dudley Woodbridge, Rector of St. Philip's, Barbados, shortly intending for North America, [late chaplain of H.M. ship *Sunderland*, who died in Barbados], dated 15 Mar 1748. Bequests to: my sister Mary Alleyne of Boston, N.E., relict of Maj. Abel Alleyne, formerly of Barbados but late of Boston; Andrew, son of Thomas Wade of St. Peter's, Barbados; John, son of Thomas Abel Payne of St. Lucy's, Barbados, planter. My wife Ruth Woodbridge to be exex. Wits: Thomas Abel Payne, Robert Wadeson and Samuel Armstrong. AWW 14 Feb 1750 to Edward Clark Parish, attorney for Nathaniel Haggett Esq. in Barbados. (PROB 11/777/65).

John Hambelton, seaman of H.M. ship *Canterbury*, [bachelor], dated 10 Sep 1748. My whole estate to my friends Thomas Mackenly and David Chanceler, mariners of H.M. ship *Cornwall*, and the said Mackenly to be exec. Wits: Moses Jevens and Joseph Drinkeld. AWW to Owen Gray, adr. of the named exec. Thomas McKenly deceased, and attorney for his principal creditor William Gale in N.Y., the legatee David Chancelor having died. (PROB 11/777/78).

William Lambert Esq. of Boston, Mass., dated 15 Apr 1748. (Copy from Mass. records). To my nephew William Lambert of Boston, sugar refiner, my house and land at the south end of Frog Lane, Boston, which I bought of Mr. Samuel Holyoke and an adjoining tract which I bought of James Bowdoin Esq. I have already given to Thomas Lambert half of the land in Frog Lane which I bought from John Bulston and the other half I now give to my niece Mary Pattin. I give to my said nephews Thomas and William Lambert and my niece Mary Pattin a house and land in Sherborne, Dorset, unless they have already been sold in accordance with my instructions to Messrs. Lane and Caswall of London, merchants. To my nephew William Lambert a picture of myself and one of my wife drawn by Mr. Smibert. A mourning ring to Thomas Lambert and his wife, William Lambert and his wife, William Pattin and his wife, and my nephew John Lambert, brother of Thomas and William Lambert. My negroes Cato and Phillis are to be sold. Exec. to be my nephew William Lambert. Wits: William Sheafe, Stephen Deblois and James Hill. AWW to Thomas Lane, attorney for the named exec. in Boston. (PROB 11/777/84).

John Parker of Morton, Thornbury, Glos., yeoman, [who died in Penna., bachelor], dated 25 Mar 1726. To my cousin Edward Gregory, son of William Gregory of Almondsbury, Glos., yeoman, by his late wife Mary, my messuages and lands in Thornbury, and he is to pay an annuity of £20 to my brother William Parker. £20 to John Gregory, another son of the said William and Mary Gregory, and £50 to his sister Martha Gregory. £5 each to my cousins Daniel and William Weare, and William and Israel Roach, sons of my cousin William Roach of Bristol, tiler. Half of my lands and tenements in Penna. to John Brenton, son of William and Jane Brenton of Birmingham, Penna., who is to pay £10 current each to his brothers and sisters. To Mary Wyeth, daughter of John Wyeth of Birmingham, Penna., 100 acres of my said lands. My lands and tenements in Kennett Township, Penna., to the said William Brenton on trust to apply the rents thereof for the benefit of the poor Quakers of Concord Monthly Meeting. £5 to the poor Quakers of Thornbury Meeting. Thomas Allway of Thornbury, mercer, to be guardian of the said Edward Gregory while he is a minor, and to be exec. with William Gregory. The residue of my estate to my brother William Parker. Wits: Bowy Clarke, William Burton and Mary Edwards.

AWW 5 Apr 1750 to the cousin german and next-of-kin Isaac Roach, the named exes. and the brother William Parker having died. (PROB 11/778/124).

James Wood, mariner [of Woolwich, Kent, who died in Md., bachelor], dated 26 Apr 1750. My clothing to my father-in-law Thomas Harrell. The residue of my estate to my mother Mary Harrell who is to be exex. but, if she dies, I appoint my friend Thomas Callies of Woolwich, butcher. Wits: Elizabeth Blakelock, John Blakelock and Thomas Reed. Pr. 26 Apr 1750 by the mother. (PROB 11/778/133).

John Fananbrouse, mariner of H.M. ship *Pembroke*, [bachelor], dated 25 Sep 1747. My whole estate to my friend Elizabeth Partridge living in Plymouth Dock, Devon, who is to be my exex. Wits: Thomas Fincher, John Ball and Francis Smith. AWW 7 May 1750 to Joseph Argent, attorney for the named exex. in Boston, N.E. (PROB 11/779/149).

John Law, mariner of H.M. ship *Pembroke*, [bachelor], dated 31 Oct 1747. My whole estate to my friend Elizabeth Partridge living in Plymouth Dock, Devon, who is to be my exex. Wits: Thomas Fincher, John Green and Francis Smith. AWW 7 May 1750 to Joseph Argent, attorney for the named exex. in Boston, N.E. (PROB 11/779/149).

Laughlin McGuiry [of N.Y.], mariner, now in the Bay of Honduras, [who died on the ship *Monmouth*, bachelor], dated 21 Dec 1749. My whole estate to my friend and shipmate Thomas Packer who is to be my exec. Wits: John Edwards, Captain, and John Palmer. Pr. 28 Jun 1750 by exec. named. (PROB 11/780/208).

William Gough of Bristol, woollen draper, dated 1 May 1748. Bequests to: my nephews Isaac and Ebenezer Burges; my nephew Thomas Gough, son of my late brother John Gough; my kinsman Nathaniel Merriman of Marlborough, (Wilts.), grocer; my late kinsman Nicholas Gough. Wits: Edward Webb, William Temple and Samuel King. Pr. 4 Jly 1750 by the nephew Isaac Burges. Revoked on his death and admon. granted to Henry Dorsey Gough in May 1767. Revoked on his death and granted to William Hoffman, attorney for James Carroll in North America, in Dec 1822. (PROB 11/781/230).

John Payne, late Lieut. of H.M. ship *Chichester* but now resident in Winterbourne, Glos., gent., dated 13 May 1750. Bequests to: my sisters Alice and Isabella Payne; my aunt Ann Chambers, her son William Chambers and his son Charles Chambers; my brothers William Laurence and Richard Payne; my brother-in-law Walter Rainstorp; my sisters-in-law Ann Heylyn, Sarah Rainstorp, Mary Rainstorp and Elizabeth Rainstorp; my wife Martha. My lands and tenements in Carolina, England and Ireland to be sold by my execs. for the benefit of my wife and her heirs. Execs: my said wife, John

Heylyn of Bristol, merchant, John Deverell the elder of Bristol, surgeon, and William Payne King, late of Coney Hatch, Mddx., gent. Wits: John Rainstorp, Jane Rourk and Caleb Esse. Pr. 4 Jly 1750 by the relict. (PROB 11/781/240).

William Sherley, citizen and apothecary of London, [of Va., bachelor], dated 16 Jun 1746. My whole estate to my friend Edward Bathurst Esq. of Goudhurst, Kent. Wits: Thomas Paris and Edward Lewis. Pr. 16 Jly 1750 by named exec. (PROB 11/781/244).

Richard Bennett of Queen Anne Co., Md., dated 25 Sep 1749. Very long will in which the following are principal beneficiaries: my cousin George Parker of Accomack Co., Va.; Lloyd Dulany, son of Daniel Dulany Esq. by my cousin Henrietta Maria; my cousin Mary McCubbins, daughter of Dr. Charles Carroll of Annapolis; my cousin Edward Neale of Queen Anne Co. and his daughter Eleanor by his late wife, my cousin Mary; my cousin Bennet Chew, son of my cousin Henrietta Maria Dulany, his brother Philemon Chew, and their sisters Margaret and Mary Chew; my cousin Priscilla Browne, wife of Mr. Charles Browne; Charles Blake, second son of my cousin John Blake, and his sister Mary Blake; my cousin John Blake, son of my late cousin John Sayer Blake, his brother Charles Blake, and their sister Henrietta Maria Blake; my cousin Philemon Blake; my cousin Ann Brookes and her sister Priscilla Browne; my cousin Margaret Smith, daughter of Capt. Richard Smith; my cousin Edward Lloyd, son of my cousin Edward Lloyd; my cousin Edward Tilghman, son of my sister Ann Tilghman; my cousin William Tilghman; my cousin James Chamberlaine and his sister Henrietta Maria Chamberlaine; my godson Thomas Wilson lately returned from Europe. Wits: Richard Archbold, James Tuite, James Walters, John Knock, John Tayler, James (x) Fetters and John Coursey. Appended to the will is a list of the testator's debtors showing their counties of residence. Codicils of 26 and 29 Sep 1749. AWW 22 Aug 1750 to John Hanbury and William Anderson, attorneys for Edward Lloyd in Md. (PROB 11/781/253).

Featherston Bayliff of Frederica, Ga., [surgeon's mate in Gen. Oglethorpe's Regt. in Ga., bachelor], dated Charles Town 14 Jun 1748. £50 sterling to my friend Mrs. Anne Bellinghurst of Frederica, widow. The residue of my estate to my mother Elizabeth Baylie (*sic*) with remainder to Featherston Molloy, eldest son of Francis Molloy of Piccadilly, (Mddx.), grocer, and Elizabeth Dawson, daughter of Matthew Dawson, attorney at law of Newcastle upon Tyne. Maj. William Horton, Capt. James McKoy and Lieut. Thomas Goldsmith to be execs. Wits: David Godin, Andrew Sputledge and James Campbell. Pr. 5 Sep 1750 by James McKay *alias* McKoy. (PROB 11/782/285).

Richard Annely [of N.Y., merchant], dated 25 Mar 1737. If I die before my arrival in N.Y. or thereafter, my brother Thomas Annely is to be my exec. and sell the goods received in partnership before 26 Dec 1735 and left on my departure from N.Y. with Mrs. Judith Bourdett, wife of Mr. Samuel Bourdett Jr. Deposition of 17 Oct 1750 by Walter Jenkins of St. Michael's, Bristol, gent., and Susannah Annely of St. Nicholas, Bristol, that in Sep 1743 they saw the testator sign his name many times and the writing on the will is his. Pr. 24 Oct 1750 by the named exec. (PROB 11/782/313).

Thomas Jenys of Charles Town, S.C., merchant, dated 19 Oct 1745. My whole estate, slaves and stock at Good Hope which I bought of Mr. Hugh Brian to my nephew Paul Jenys, with remainder to my nephew George Jenys or my right heirs in England. To the said Paul Jenys £3,000 sterling and all my estate in England of which my father was possessed, subject to the legacies chargeable. To my niece Mary Esler £1,000 sterling. To my friends Charles Pinckney Esq. and Andrew Rutledge Esq. £1,000 current each. To John Basnett £150 current. My sister-in-law Mrs. Elizabeth Gibbes, my friends Mr. Branfill Evance and Stephen Bedon, son of Stephen Bedon of Charles Town, and my nephew Paul Jenys to be execs. Wits: John Basnett, Edward Edgar and Thomas Dale. Pr. 26 Oct 1750 by Stephen Bedon Jr. (PROB 11/783/330).

William Knipe of Portsmouth, N.H., sailor of H.M. ship [*Centurion* and] *America*, commander Henry Barnsley, dated 5 Oct 1749. My wages and prize money for sea service to Dr. Robert Ratsey of the *America*, who is to be my exec. The residue of my estate to my friend Robert Glaster living at Whitehaven, Cumb., blacksmith. and he is to be exec. Wits: John Watson, Mary Dinello and John Maurice. Pr. 27 Nov 1750 to named exec. (PROB 11/783/360).

Christopher Blacklock [of Boston, Mass.], mariner of the *Mermaid* man of war now lying at Nantucket bound to sea, dated 23 Feb 1747. My whole estate to my wife Ruth Blacklock of Boston and she is to be my exex. Wits: Thomas Hammond, William Hassall and William Martin. AWW 1 Dec 1750 to John Coles, attorney for the relict in Boston. (PROB 11/784/376).

1751

Ann Gates of St. Botolph Bishopsgate, London. £100 to my son Thomas Gates now of Va. £40 to Ann Andrews who is to be my exex. Wits: John Archer and Samuel Fild. Pr. 9 Jan 1751 by Ann Andrews, spinster. (PROB 11/785/10).

John Linn of Md. but now of Bristol, mariner, dated 17 Nov 1750. My whole estate to my friend and sole exex. Sarah, wife of John Humphreys of Bristol, ship carpenter. Wits: Joshua Pope, Thomas Gore and Richard Tucker. Pr. 1 Jan 1751 by named exex. (PROB 11/785/15).

Samuel Wragg of London, merchant, [formerly of Holborn, Mddx., but late of Charles Town, S.C.], dated 14 Jun 1749. To be buried with my late wife in the vault I built in Beckenham, (Kent), churchyard. I have already conveyed to my son William Wragg all my lands on Ashley River, S.C., known as St. Gyles with 4,000 acres, 100 negroes and stock, and now leave him Dockon Plantation on Cooper River. To him and Robert Henshaw of Cook's Hall, London, gent., who are to be my execs., I leave 3,000 acres, part of my St. Gyles Barony, adjoining the lands I sold to Alexander Skene Esq. and 100 negroes, subject to the payment of the rents to my daughters Mary and Judith Wragg. £100 sterling towards the erection of a free school in the parish of St. George's on Ashley River. The residue of my estate to my said execs. Wits: David Barclay Jr. and Thomas Bromley. Codicil of 12 Sep 1750, now residing in Charles Town. If I die here my corpse is to be conveyed in my large canoe to my Barony where it is to be received by Rev. Mr. Guy and borne by four negro men: Joe, a wheelwright, Walbee, the carpenter, Newcastle, a cooper, and Stephen, the tradesman and husbandman. I am to be buried between two large cedar trees that I have already indicated. Andrew Rutledge Esq. and Mr. William Cattle Jr. are to be trustees of my estate in S.C. My negro woman Janey is to be freed. Wits: John Remington, notary, Joseph Shute and Benjamin Axford. Pr. 6 Jan 1751 by the son William Wragg Esq. Revoked Jly 1754 and granted to the daughters. (PROB 11/785/33).

George Forrester of N.Y.C., mariner. My whole estate, including what is due to me from my service in the *Sunderland* man of war and the privateer *Antelope* of N.Y., to my friend William Holt of N.Y.C., vintner, who is to be my exec. Wits: Charles Gilmore, Peter Van Vechter and John Bryant. Pr. 14 Feb 1751 by named exec. (PROB 11/785/45).

Edward Holding, mariner of the *Sandwich*, Capt. John Petre, [master of the *Friends Goodwill* who died in Boston, N.E., bachelor], dated 6 Mar 1746. My whole estate to my friend Mary Pomfrett of St. George's, Mddx., widow, who is to be my exex. Wits: John Holding, John Holland and Mary Johnson. Pr. 27 Feb 1751 by named exex. (PROB 11/785/49).

Jermyn Davers Esq., formerly of Rushbrooke, Suffolk, then of Va., who died at sea, bachelor] son of the late Sir Jermyn Davers of Rushbrooke, dated (blank) Jly 1744. My whole estate to my mother (Lady) Margaret Davers who is to be my exex. Deposition 22 Mar 1750 by Thomas Corbett and Paul Corbett of St. Martin Vintry,

London, sugar refiners, that the above will is in the testator's hand. Pr. 22 Mar 1751 by the named exex. (PROB 11/786/78).

John Nicholls [of Philadelphia who died at sea on the *Dorothy*], dated 8 Mar 1745. My whole estate to my sisters Ann Gregory and Mary Gould of Bristol. Charles Willing of Philadelphia, merchant, to be my exec. Wits: Christopher Marshall, Thomas Gilbert and Gr. Brigdall. Pr. 1 Mar 1751 by named exec. (PROB 11/786/87).

John Colleton of Fairlawns, St. John's parish, Berkeley Co., S.C. An annuity of £100 to my wife Susannah Colleton during her lifetime and she is to live at my Fairlawns or Exmouth Plantation until my eldest son comes of age when she is to have a house of her own. To my son John Colleton my Exeter Plantation of 1,500 acres in St. John's parish bounded on the east by Cooper River, on the south by the land of Thomas Broughton Esq., and on the west and north by Fairlawns Plantation, with remainder to my son Peter Colleton. £600 sterling to my daughter Hannah Colleton when she is 21 or married. An annuity of £60 to my father Sir John Colleton, Baron of Exmouth, Devon. £10 each for mourning to my aunt Kendall and my brother Robert Colleton. I give her freedom and £2 sterling to Jane Morris for her care of my son in his passage to England. The residue of my estate to my son Peter Colleton. Execs: my said wife, father, and son Peter Colleton. Wits: Mary Rowe, Henry Braddon and Mary Grill. Codicil of 15 Jun 1748 revising bequests to the children on the death of his daughter Hannah Colleton. Third codicil of 26 Sep 1749. Pr. 3 Apr 1751 by the only surviving exec. Sir John Colleton. Further grants Nov 1754 & Mar 1756. (PROB 11/787/107).

John Houghton of Charles Town, S.C., merchant, dated (blank) 1743. £100 sterling each to my mother and father, Edmund and Mary Houghton of Ashton, Northants. The residue of my estate to my wife Mary Houghton with the exception of my slaves whom I free. My friends John Owen of London, merchant, and Charles Shepherd of Charles Town to be execs. Wits: William G. Freeman and John Witherston. Pr. 27 Apr 1751 by surviving exec. John Owen. (PROB 11/787/113).

Thomas Brocas of Westminster, surgeon, [of Littleton, N.E., bachelor], dated 2 Apr 1748. One third of my estate to my friend Christopher Kilby Esq. of Spring Gardens, Mddx., who is to be my exec. The residue to be divided between: the children of my eldest brother Richard Brocas of Broad Street, London, tobacconist; my sister Sarah Brocas, now of London, spinster; my nephew William Brocas, son of my brother John Brocas of Boston, N.E., cabinet maker; my brother John Brocas and his younger son John Brocas Jr. Wits: Otis Little, Peter Annet and James Beckingham. Pr. 26 Jly 1751 by named exec. (PROB 11/788/200).

Stephen Nichols [of Newport, R.I.], mariner of H.M. ship *Vigilant*, Capt.
James Douglas, [who died in Louisburgh, bachelor], dated Louis-
burgh Harbour 25 Mar 1746. My whole estate to my friend Samuel
Pool. Wits: Seth Harvey, David Hawkins and Jonathan Hiddeon.
AWW 31 Jly 1751 to Benjamin Wickham, attorney for the named
exec. in Newport, no executor having been named. (PROB 11/789/216).

Elizabeth Colson [of Bethnal Green, Mddx.], now residing in Charles
Town, S.C.], widow, dated London 1 Jun 1744. £300 in stock, silver
plate, etc. to my son William Roper who is to be my exec. A ring
for mourning to my nephew Brewer and his wife and my nephew
George Colson, smith. Clothing etc. to my niece Elizabeth Brewer.
Wits: Laurence Marcroft and James Crockatt. AWW 17 Aug 1751
to James Crockatt, attorney for the named exec. in Charles Town.
(PROB 11/789/231).

John Ashley, late of Barbados but now of Blackheath, Lewisham, Kent,
dated 9 Oct 1750. My plantations etc. in Barbados and lands in
Penna. to my son John Ashley who is to fulfil the following bequests:
my negroes on Hatton Plantation named Toney and Nancy and the
latter's children Betty, Mulatto and Frances, and the revenues of my
Palley Plantation to my wife; £2,000 Barbados money to my daughter
Elizabeth Aynesworth Ashley when she marries or is 21. Execs:
James Theobald Esq. of Waltham Place, Berks., Solomon Ashley
Esq. of Westminster, Mr. William Whitaker of Dolphin Court, Lon-
don, merchant, my wife during her widowhood only, Mr. Christopher
Moe of Barbados, planter, and my said son. Wits: John Vaughan,
Samuel Jones and Thomas Collett. Codicil of 12 Oct 1750 makes
bequest to Mrs. Johanna Smith, daughter of Joseph and Sarah Cooper,
formerly of St. Martin's in the Fields. Wits: Richard Hotchkiss,
Francis McMahon and N. Maxwell. AWW Oct 1751 to creditor
George Prescott, the named execs. renouncing or not appearing.
(PROB 11/790/273).

Patrick Fitch [of N.Y. Province], mariner of H.M. ship *Launceston*,
Capt. Peter Warren, dated 25 Oct 1743. My whole estate to my wife
Abigail Fitch who is to be my exex. Wits: Peter Warren and W.
Tattam. AWW 10 Dec 1751 to John Dupre, attorney for the relict
in N.Y. (PROB 11/791/333).

1752

William Antram, mariner of H.M. ship *Boyne* [of H.M. ship *Mermaid*
who died in S.C., bachelor], dated 31 Oct 1743. My whole estate
to my mother Mary, wife of Jacob Minor of Gosport, Hants., mariner,

and she is to be my exex. Wits: George Huish, notary public, and George Huish Jr. Pr. 26 Feb 1752 by named exex. (PROB 11/792/27).

Stephen Bedon of Charles Town, S.C., but now of St. Clement Danes and Chelsea, Mddx., [who died in the City of Bristol], dated 20 May 1750. Half my estate in trust to my brother-in-law Isaac Nichols to pay the rents during her lifetime to my wife Ruth and, after her death, to my brothers Benjamin and George Bedon and my sisters Sarah and Rebecca Bedon. The other half of my estate to my said sisters. My cousin George Bedon to manage my business affairs in England. Execs: my said wife, my uncle Henry Bedon, my brother-in-law (Isaac) Nichols and my cousin George Bedon. Pr. 10 February 1752 by the cousin german George Bedon. (PROB 11/792/29).

Joseph Blake Esq. of Berkeley Co., S.C., [who died on the *Wilmington*, widower], dated 18 Dec 1750. £2,000 sterling and £1,000 current for the maintenance of my children Daniel, William and Ann Blake. To my son Daniel Blake the plantation where I live called Newington, a tract of Cypress Swamp between the lands of Mr. James Postell and Barnaby Brandford which I bought of James Postell deceased, land on Charles Town Neck between the High Road and Cooper River, 1,500 acres on Cumbee River between Mr. Hudson's line and the land I bought of Col. William Bull, and 597 acres in two tracts. To my son William Blake my plantation on Wadmelaw River and the new cut called Plainsfield between the lands of Mr. John Atkinson and Mr. Fuller, two tracts of 230 and 76 acres, and two tracts of 440 acres I purchased from Stephen Dowse. To my daughter Rebecca Izard 1,873 acres in Granville Co. on the head of Coosaw, Hatcher's and Chiliphinas Swamp, an island in Port Royal River called Catt Island, and another 286 acres in Granville Co. The residue of my real estate to my said two sons and my daughter Ann Blake. My daughter Rebeccah Izard and my sons Daniel and Ralph Blake to be execs. Wits: Jacob Molte, William Roper and Alexander Rigg. Deposition by John Ouldfield and William George, gents., both of S.C. but at present in London, that the above will has been copied from S.C. records. Pr. 20 Feb 1752 by Daniel Blake Esq.; admon. of Sep 1751 revoked. (PROB 11/792/30).

George Jones of Philadelphia, yeoman, designing to pass over the seas, [who died in Worcester], dated 22 Sep 1743. £20 current to Sarah Toms, daughter of Robert Toms, when she is 18. My seat in Christ Church, Philadelphia, to Thomas Howard of Philadelphia, joiner. £100 to Mary Howard, daughter of Thomas Howard, when she is 18. My horse and saddle etc. to Andrew Robertson, miller at Wesschicken (*sic*). £10 to Katherine Hinton provided she does not

marry until after my death. £20 current to Abraham Pratt of
Philadelphia, joiner. Residue of my estate to the children of my
late brother James Jones of Brogmore Green, Worcs., and my sister
Elizabeth Clay of Worcester and her children. Jonathan Robeson
Esq., Lawrence Anderson, merchant, and Jacob Duchee of Market
Street, shopkeeper, all of Philadelphia, to be execs. Wits: William
Cunningham, Warwick Coats and John Chapman. AWW 14 Feb
1752 to the sister Elizabeth Clay, widow. (PROB 11/792/39).

Walter Scott of Md., merchant, at present residing in [St. Benet
Gracechurch], London, dated 6 Feb 1752. To Walter Scott & Co.
of Glasgow, Scotland, my two lots at Portobacco, Md. To my friends
and execs. James Armour and John Stewart of London, merchants,
all my lands in Md. including those granted to me by Henry and
Sarah Wyne as follows: A tract of 300 acres known as Simpson's
Delight at Portobacco in Charles Co.; three parcels of lands known
as Wassall at Portobacco, London and Blocksith; 200 acres of land
at Nanjemy in Charles Co. known as Glovers' Point; 200 acres at
Pirealaway in Charles Co. known as Pithly; and three parcels of
land at the head of Wicomico River in Charles Co. known as
Burton's, Sudmore's Adventure and Susquetoanna. Wits: William
Maghie, John George and Richard Chare. Pr. 14 Mar 1752 by
named execs. (PROB 11/793/78).

Ruth Stuart of Boston, Mass., widow, dated 5 Mar 1752. All the real
estate that came to me by my late father Dr. John Cuffee to my
daughter Mary Johnson for the benefit of her children and grandchildren. Other bequests to my grandchildren Henry, Mary and
Hannah Johnson when they come of age and my son Sir John
Stuart, now in England, with remainder to his children by his second
wife. Execs: my friend Mr. Rufus Greene and my said son and
daughter. Wits: Francis Johonnot, Sanderson West and William
Skinner. Pr. 14 Jly 1752 by the son. (PROB 11/796/199).

Thomas Venables of the Northern Liberties of Philadelphia, dated 21
May 1750. To my wife and exex. Rebecca Venables my plantations
in the Northern Liberties, my houses in Philadelphia and my estate
in Barbados and England. Wits: Edward Jones and Lethea Howell.
AWW 20 Aug 1752 to Daniel Moore Esq., attorney for the relict
in Philadelphia. (PROB 11/796/224).

John Mallory, citizen and leatherseller of London, dated 23 May 1747.
To my wife (Mary) Mallory my estate at Stratford Langthorn, Essex,
and the lease of a house in the Strand, London. £100 each to St.
George's Hospital and the New Foundling Hospital in London. To
Mr. Galfridus Mann and Mr. Richard Cooke 20 guineas each for
mourning. My said wife to be exex. on condition that she pays
£4,000 to the said Mann and Cooke who are to undertake the

following trusts. £400 to the children of my brother William (Mallory) near James Town, King William Co., Va.; £300 to the children of my sister Elizabeth Palmer; £1,200 to the children of my brother Roger (Mallory); £300 to the children of my sister Quarles; £400 to the children of my brother Charles (Mallory); and £20 to the childrfen of my cousin Francis Mallory of James River, Va. Wits: Charles Waring, John Vickery and John Locher. Pr. 16 Dec 1752 by the relict. (PROB 11/798/303). See wills of Elizabeth Ross, pr. 1768, and William and Florisabella Mallory, pr. 1769.

1753

Mary Helden of Egham, Surrey, widow of John Helden, dated 23 Sep 1752. Bequests to: my sister Mrs. Deborah Batt; my kinsman Rev. William Netcutt and his wife; my brother Mr. Cornelius Helden; my nephew John Helden and his son Cornelius Helden; my nieces Sarah Bendal and Mary McConnel; my kinswoman Mrs. Deborah Hurt; my kinswoman Mrs. Mary Chadwell and her daughter Mrs. Mary Walker. My mortgage on Staines Bridge to my daughter (Mary) Foster and her children after the decease of my sister Deborah Batt. To my kinswoman Mrs. Elizabeth Brice in Carolina £10 a year during her life. One-sixth part of a plantation in Nevis which may come to me on the death of Mrs. Sophia Snow I leave in trust to the use of John Helden Hurt. The said Mary Foster to be sole exex. Wits: Sarah Marriott, Mary Ward and John Ward. Pr. 16 Jan 1753 by the named exex. Further grant 23 May 1780 to George Netcutt, son of William Netcutt. (PROB 11/799/15).

John Lewis of Charles Town, S.C., cordwainer, [who died in St. Thomas's Hospital, Southwark, Surrey], dated 25 Jun 1753. To my wife Sarah Lewis all my estate in Carolina during her lifetime and then to my brother Thomas Lewis of Leominster, Heref., miller, and his children Thomas, William and Elizabeth Lewis. £10 sterling out of the money owed to me in London to my mother Mary Lewis of Ludlow, Salop., widow. £5 each to John Taylor at the Globe and Runner in St. Saviour, Southwark, victualler, and Thomas Hardwick of Dowgate Hill, London, Customs Messenger, who are to be execs. with my said wife. Wits: Christiana (x) Wicks, Thomas Morgan and Sarah Eastman. Pr. 6 Jly 1753 by John Taylor and Thomas Hardwick. (PROB 11/803/210).

John Price, mariner of H.M. ship *Mermaid*, [who died in S.C., bachelor], dated 29 Mar 1751. My whole estate to my friend Mary Rea of Greenwich, Kent, widow, who is to be my exex. Wits:

Thomas Nottingham and P. Herringham. Pr. 18 Jly 1753 by exex.
named. (PROB 11/803/215).

John Russell Esq., Captain of H.M. sloop *Scorpion*, now at Brunswick,
Cape Fear, N.C., dated 13 Dec 1752. My whole estate to my wife
Alice Russell who is to be my exex. and to be assisted by Mr.
Robert Napper and Mr. Richard Quince, merchant in Brunswick.
Wits: Robert Napper, Thomas Buckle and Archibald Bruce. Pr. 6
Jly 1753 by the relict. (PROB 11/803/216).

Frances L'Escott of Charles Town, S.C., widow of advanced age, dated
24 Aug 1752. £100 current to Mrs. Mary Mazyck, wife of Isaac
Mazyck of Charles Town, merchant. £200 current to Ann, wife of
Mr. Henry Gray. £100 current to my grandson Benjamin Villepon-
toux. My negro boy Antony to my grandson Francis Villepontoux.
My negro woman Molly and her children to my granddaughter
Frances Villepontoux. £5 curent to Susanna Fountaine. One shilling
sterling to my grandson Paul Villepontoux. The residue of my estate
to my said grandchildren except Paul Villepontoux. Mr. Isaac Mazyck
and Mr. Zachariah Villepontoux to be my execs. Wits: Thomas
Corker, John Lewis and John Remington. AWW 26 Sep 1753 to
George Chardin Esq., attorney for execs. in S.C. (PROB 11/804/255).

Elias Dupee, late carpenter of H.M. ship *Bedford*, [of Boston, N.E.,
shipwright of the *Adventure*], dated 25 Sep 1749. My whole estate
to my friends John Thomas of Whitechapel, Mddx., victualler, and
Mary his wife who are to be my execs. Wits: Joseph Harris and
John Sharpe. Pr. 15 Oct 1753 by Mary Thomas. (PROB 11/804/267).

N.B. Copy of will of 30 Aug 1752 appointing his father Daniel Dupee
and brother Benjamin Dupee as execs. appears in PROB 20/816.

John Custis Esq. of Williamsburg, Va., dated 14 Nov 1749. A
handsome white marble tombstone mounted on pillars is to be
erected over my grave inscribed with my coat of arms of three
parrots and carrying the following words: "Under this marble stone
lies the body of the honourable John Custis Esq. of the City of
Williamsburg and parish of Bruton, formerly of Hungars parish on
the Eastern Shoar of Va. and County of Northampton, the place of
his nativity, aged (blank) years and yet lived but seven years (*sic*)
which was the space of time he kept a bachelor's house at Arlington
on the Eastern Shoar of Va. This inscription put on this stone by
his own positive orders." My body is to be carried to my plantation
called Arlington to be buried with my grandfather Hon. John Custis
Esq. where a large walnut tree formerly grew and is now enclosed
with a brick wall. My whole estate is to descend to my next male
heirs who carry the name of Custis. £200 to my friend Thomas
Lee Esq. £100 sterling to my friend John Blair Esq. and a mourning

ring to his wife. My plantation at Arlington which descended to me from my said late grandfather and my late father Hon. John Custis Esq. is to descend in the same manner as Smith's Island and Motton Island. By deed lodged in York Co. Court I have set free my negro boy christened John and called Jack, who was born of my slave Alice; a house is to be built for him on land I bought of James Morris near the head of Queen's Creek in York Co., a plan for which has been drawn by my friend John Blair Esq., and it is to be well furnished. When he is aged 20 the said Jack is to have a riding horse, two working horses and farming equipment, and meanwhile is to live with my son Daniel Park Custis and to be handsomely maintained. To Mrs. Ann Moody, wife of Matthew Moody, an annuity of £20 sterling during her lifetime. The residue of my estate to my said son who is to be my exec. Wits: Thomas Dawson, George Gilmer and John Blair Jr. Pr. 19 Nov 1753 by the named exec. Further grant 23 Sep 1784 to Wakelin Welch, attorney for Martha, wife of Hon. George Washington, the relict of Daniel Parke Custis. (PROB 11/804/287).

Enoch Stephenson of N.Y.C., dated 3 Feb 1736. To my wife Catherine Stephenson all my estate and my slaves Maria with her children Quaco and Sarah, a negro boy Qua and a negro girl Cato (*sic*). The house I bought of John Price in Port Royal, Jamaica, and two lots in King Street, N.Y., which I purchased of David Jennison, are to be sold and the proceeds invested for the maintenance of my said wife who is to be exec. with my brother Pennington Stephenson, at present residing in England, and my friends Peter Valert and Joseph Robinson, both of N.Y.C. My friend Col. Edwin Sandys is to be guardian to any children I may have by my wife and to provide for any who may travel to Jamaica. Wits: Gulm. Verplanck, Abraham Van Horne Jr. and William Heurtin. AWW 21 Dec 1753 to Robert Lindsay, attorney for the named execs. (PROB 11/805/325).

1754

William Scott of Cannon Street, St. Mary Abchurch, London, [of Charles Town, N.E.], surgeon, dated 18 Aug 1752. To be buried at St. Mary Abchurch. My freehold in Everton, Notts., known as the Pasture Grounds is to be divided between Rev. John Foss of Everton and my friend Philip Hall of Bread Street, London, grocer. The said Philip Hall is to be my exec. and to have the residue of my estate including my watch and sword. Wits: Elizabeth Willey, John Pinkard and Henry Shier of Cliffords Inn. Pr. 30 May 1754 by named exec. (PROB 11/808/150).

Henry Cosby Esq., commander of H.M. ship *Centaur* stationed in N.Y.C., dated 6 Oct 1753. My whole estate to my mother Hon. Grace Cosby, widow, who is to be my exex. My brother-in-law Joseph Murray Esq. of N.Y.C. to be o'seer. Wits: Peter Renaudet, Sidney Breese and Francis Cosigin. Codicil of same date. My gold watch to my sister Grace Murray. My clothes to my cousin Philip Cosby. Pr. 16 Aug 1754 by the mother. (PROB 11/810/222).

Peter Colleton Esq. of [Fairlawns, St. John's, Berkeley County], S.C., [who died at sea], dated 30 Nov 1740. Bequests to my brother Robert Colleton, my brother John Colleton, and my sister Susanna Colleton. Execs. to be my said brothers. Wits: Elianor Sandwell, Nathaniel Lade and William Hopton. Pr. 11 Nov 1754 by the surviving exec. Robert Colleton. (PROB 11/811/295).

Sir John Colleton of Withycombe Raleigh, Devon, dated 22 Apr 1751. To be buried at Withycombe in a coffin the same as my grandson Peter's. To my son Robert Colleton my lease at Exmouth, Devon, and my interest in an estate at Whetstone, Finchley, Mddx. To my grandson John Colleton, son of the late John Colleton of Carolina and Susannah his wife, all my other estate in Britain and America. Before the marriage of my said late son John Colleton to Susannah Snell, I settled on her my Barony of Fairlawns in S.C. which my son disposed of in his will. Other bequests to my unhappy daughter Elizabeth, late wife of Edward Hawley Esq., and Anne Collins, daughter of the late Rev. John Collins of Stoke, Devon. Execs: the said Anne Collins and Robert Colleton in trust for my grandson John Colleton. Wits: Finney Belfield, Allan Belfield and Endymion Walker. Pr. 13 Nov 1754 by Robert Colleton, 7 Mar 1755 by Anne Collins, and 2 Aug 1759 by the grandson Sir John Colleton. (PROB 11/811/295).

Allen Steel of Boston, Mass., mariner [of H.M. ship *Comet Bomb*, dated 7 May 1747. My whole estate to my wife Deborah Steel who is to be exex. Wits: John Hughes, Stephen Greenleaf and William Warden. AWW 7 Dec 1754 to Henry Sanders, attorney for the relict in Boston. (PROB 11/812/341).

1755

Richard Pike of Stoke Newington, (Mddx.), dated London 2 Sep 1752. All my lands in Penna. to my kinsman Samuel Hoare and Nathaniel Newberry of London, merchants, who are to be my execs. £2,000 to my niece Rachel Strangman. £500 each to: my nephews Joshua and Samuel Strangman; my nephews Joshua and Joseph Beale, and my niece Sarah Beale, children of Joshua Beale of Cork, (Ireland); my nephew Samuel Beale, son of my sister Rachel Beale. £100 to Sarah Foster. £50 to Mary Edes. Wits: Justus Denis Beck, William Braund and William Russell. Pr. 5 Apr 1755 by affirmation of execs. (PROB 11/815/111). See NGSQ 61/34.

John Graham of Wapping, Mddx., mariner, [of Charles Town, S.C., bachelor], dated 9 Jly 1753. My whole estate to my friend William Littleton of Wapping, victualler, who is to be exec. Wits: Josa. Cotton and Thomas Cotton, attorney in Red Lyon Street, Wapping. Pr. 28 May 1755 by named exec. (PROB 11/815/131).

John Cooke of St. James Santee, Craven Co., S.C., dated 4 Nov 1744. To my son George Cooke all my land called Varambeau after all the wood thereon has been sold, and my said son is to pay what is due to Varambeau. £20 current to my son-in-law John Ward for mourning. The residue of my estate to my children George Cooke, William Beresford Cooke, and Elizabeth, Sarah and Rebecca Cooke. My friend James Maxwell and my said son George Cooke to be execs. Wits: Thomas Akin, John Harleston and James Jennens. AWW 12 Jun 1755 to Elizabeth Cooke, spinster, attorney for the daughter Rebecca Cooke in S.C., James Maxwell having been cited but not having appeared, and the son George Cooke having died. (PROB 11/816/156).

Henry Perroneau of Charles Town, S.C., gent, dated 27 Jan 1753. £1,575 to be disposed of by my execs. as I have directed. £10,000 current to my wife Elizabeth Perroneau and the use of my house and land. £1,000 current to my son Henry Perroneau. To my son Arthur Perroneau, when he comes of age, £7,000 current and the residue of my real estate with the buildings in Broad Street, Charles Town, formerly belonging to the late Marmaduke Aish. To my son Robert Perroneau, when he comes of age, £7,000 current and the reversion of a lot on Queen Street. To my son James Perroneau, when he comes of age, £7,000 current, land on Broad Street I bought of Andrew Deveaux, a house and land on Bay Front between my brother Alexander Perroneau and Edward Croft, and lots on Old Church Street. £8,000 current to my daughter Elizabeth Perroneau when she is 21 or married. The residue of my personal estate to my six children Henry, Arthur, Robert, James, Elizabeth and Ann Perroneau. My brother Alexander Perroneau, my friend Mr. Benjamin Harriette and my son Henry Perroneau to be execs. Wits: John Moultrie, S. Perroneau and Isaac Holmes. AWW and two codicils 9 Aug 1755 to James Crokatt of London, merchant, attorney for execs. in S.C. (PROB 11/817/223).

Edward Braddock Esq., Maj-Gen. of H.M. Forces and commander-in-chief of an expedition now fitting out for America, dated 25 Nov

1754. All my real and personal estate to my friend Mary, wife of John Yorke, Lieut. in the Royal Regt. of Artillery, now on duty in Gibraltar, and John Calcraft Esq. of Brewer Street, Westminster, and they are to be my execs. Wits: Thomas Morgan, Joseph Oddy and James Rubins. Pr. 3 Sep 1755 by John Calcraft. (PROB 11/817/233).

Samuel Ogle Esq., Lieut-Gov. of Md., dated 11 Feb 1752. An annuity of £250, the contents of my house in Annapolis, my coach and horses, etc., to my wife Ann Ogle during her lifetime. To my son Benjamin Ogle my house and land in Prince George Co. with slaves and horses. £1,200 each to my daughters Mary and Meliora. The residue to my son Benjamin Ogle who is to be educated in England by his guardians and my execs., Benjamin Tasker Esq. and Col. Benjamin Tasker. Wits: George Steuart, Alexander Hamilton and Edmund Jenings. Codicil of 15 Apr 1752 with additional witness Ann Street. Pr. 1 Sep 1755 by named execs. (PROB 11/818/244).

James Steuart of Woolwich, Kent, shipwright, [who died in Charles Town, S.C.], dated 6 Jly 1749. My whole estate to my brother John Steuart Jr. of Dalguire, writer in Edinburgh. Mungo Murray of Deptford, Kent, shipwright, and Mungo Murray of Limehouse, Mddx., gent., to be execs. Wits: John Purse and John Rose. Pr. 17 Oct 1755 by Mungo Murray Jr. (PROB 11/818/270).

Simeon Soumaien [of Philadelphia], Lieut. in [Capt. Horatio Gates'] Independent Company of Foot from N.Y., dated at Wills Creek Camp 28 May 1753. My whole estate to my wife Aleathea Soumaien who is to be my exex. Wits: Thomas Bachea, Thomas Cresap Jr. and Nathaniel Gest. Pr. 22 Dec 1755 by relict. (PROB 11/819/328).

1756

Daniel Huger [of Berkeley Co., S.C.], dated 16 Nov 1754. £50 sterling to the church of Shoreditch parish in Oxon. (*sic*) near London, to be added to the annuity funded by Mr. Thomas Fairchild for a yearly sermon on the works of God in the vegetable creation. To my wife Ann Huger a tenement in Colleton Square which I bought of John Cordes, £1,000 sterling and £3,000 current. £200 current to Benjamin, Elizabeth and Lydia Perdrian, children of my cousin Benjamin Perdrian. My plantations called Limrick and Rice Hope, including lands I bought of Messrs. Gough and Horne, to my son Daniel Huger. Three tracts of 1,384 acres in Berkeley Co. at the head of Wando River which I bought of Mr. Thomas Lynch to my son Isaac Huger. My Cyprus Plantation with 500 acres I bought of Mr. James Boisseau, 3,425 acres near Savannah Bridge in Craven Co., the plantation of 1,070 acres called the Hagan on the eastern branch of Cooper River, which I bought of Mr. William Moore, and two tracts adjoining, to my son John Huger. To my son Benjamin Huger 1,500 acres adjoining my Cyprus tract and Mr. Esias Ball's land, which I bought of Mr. James Nicholas Mayraut, and 500 acres adjoining the lands of Mr. John Nicholson which I purchased from the Lords Proprietors. £2,000 sterling each to my sons Francis and Paul Huger. To my daughter Margaret Huger £1,000 and another £1,000 which is the hands of Col. Francis Lejan when she is 21 or married. The said Francis Lejan and his son Francis Lejan to be my execs. in S.C. My friends Gabriel Manigault, Elias Horry, Daniel Lescene and Thomas Cordes are to act as execs. in trust until my son Daniel Huger comes of age. Limited AWW 7 Jan 1756 to Thomas Corbett, attorney for Francis Lejan Sr. and Jr. in S.C. (PROB 11/820/11).

Charles Willing of Philadelphia, merchant, bound on a voyage to England, dated 28 Jly 1750. An annuity of £50 sterling to my father Thomas Willing of Bristol, merchant. To my eldest son Thomas Willing my house on Third Street where I now live and 30 acres on the west side of Schuykill I lately bought of James Humphrie. To my son Charles Willing the house on Front Street which I bought from the estate of Joshua Cart. To my son Richard Willing my house on Second Street where Capt. Charles Stedman lives, and my right to a grant of 500 acres in Penna. which I lately bought of the heirs of Christopher Forward. To my son Richard and my daughters Mary, Elizabeth and Abigall lots on Third Street and Fourth Street, late the estate of Thomas Story deceased. To my wife (Ann) the interest on £2,600 during her lifetime, my negro wench and my black horse and furniture. To my daughter Dolly (Dorothy) my negro girl Venus. Three guineas each to my brother Thomas Willing of London, merchant, and my sisters Dorothy Hand and Ann Willing. My said wife and son Thomas to be execs. Wits: D. Martin, Thomas Hopkinson and John Price. Pr. 15 Jan 1756 by the named execs. (PROB 11/820/23).

Culchett Golightly of St. Andrew's, Berkeley Co., S.C., planter, dated 14 Dec 1749. To my wife Mary Golightly £1,000 when my daughters come of age or are married and a yearly allowance at the discretion of my execs. To Rebecca Pinckney, youngest daughter of my friend Maj. William Pinckney, £1,000 current which is to be paid into the hands of her uncle Charles Pinckney Esq. The residue to my daughters Dorothy and Mary when they are 21 or

married with remainder to the children of my brother Fenwick
Golightly in the East Indies. My friend Mr. Thomas Everson is to
have the management of my Horse Shoe estate. My friends Hon.
Edward Fenwick and Charles Pinckney Esq. to be my execs. Wits:
Lionel Chalmers, John Gibbes and Lucy Ann Edwards. Pr. 18 Mar
1756 by Charles Pinckney Esq. (PROB 11/821/69).

Edmund Jennings Esq. of Yorkshire, dated 10 Mar 1756. To be buried
in the parish where I die. £1,300 to Mr. James Buchanan, merchant
in London, who is to pay £1,200 to Mrs. Sibilla Cowcher, widow,
and the remaining £100 to Mrs. Anna White, spinster. £1,700 to
Hon. Col. Richard Corbin of Va. to be placed at interest for the
benefit of my daughter Ariana Randolph, free of the control of her
husband, and after her death the principal sum to my grandson
Edmund Randolph. A year's wages and clothing to my servant
William Russell. To my nephew Edmund Jennings of Md. four
negroes from my plantation on the forks of Patuxent River, cattle
and horses. A mourning ring each to: Hon. Cecilius Calvert Esq.;
William Sharpe Esq.; Mrs. Chester of Bristol, widow; Mrs. Russell,
wife of James Russell of London, merchant; Hon. Philip Ludwell
of Va.; Mrs. Corbin, wife of Col. Corbin; Col. John Taylor of Va.;
Mrs. Brice, wife of John Brice Esq. of Annapolis; Stephen Bordely
Esq.; Elizabeth Bordely, spinster; Mrs. Harris of Kent Co., Md.,
widow, daughter of my late wife Ariana Jennings; Mrs. Harris,
widow of the late James Harris Esq.; Mrs. Shipping, widow, sister
of my said late wife; William, John, Matthias and Beale Bordely,
all of Md.; Margaret and Elizabeth Beckwith; Robert Porteus and
his daughter Nanney Porteus; Edward Thompson Esq. of Helperby,
Yorks., and his wife. The residue to my son Edmund Jennings who
is to be exec. with the said James Buchanan. Col. Richard Corbin
and John Brice are to be trustees for my estate in Va. and Md.
Wits: Alexander Sutherland, Jonathan Fleming and Lewis Clutterbuck. Pr. 24 Mar 1756 by Edmund Jennings. (PROB 11/821/72).

Robert Ellison Esq. of the City of Westminster, [Lieut-Col. of a Regt.
of Foot, who died in Albany, N.Y.], dated 2 Nov 1754. My whole
estate to my brothers and sisters Cuthbert and Henry Ellison Esqs.,
Catherine, wife of John Airey Esq., and Jane and Elizabeth Ellison.
My said brothers to be execs. Wits: John Calcraft, John Massey
and James Rubins. Pr. 28 Jun 1756 by Hon. Maj-Gen. Cuthbert
Ellison. (PROB 11/823/164).

Hubbard Brewen of Md., merchant, at present in London bound on a
voyage to Md., dated 31 May 1755. My whole estate to my mother
Ann Brewen of Brentingby (?Bruntingthorpe), Leics., with
remainder to my sisters Sarah Brewen of Brentingby and Ann, wife
of Henry Beestland of Market Overton, Rutland. Mr. John Philpot

of London, merchant, to be my exec. Pr. 31 Jly 1756 by named exec. (PROB 11/823/187).

Richard Morrey of Philadelphia, gent., dated 30 Aug 1753. To my wife Sarah all my lands in Penna. and leaseholds in the City of London. My said wife and my brother-in-law John Beazly are to be execs. and Mr. Jenkin Jones and Dr. William Chandler, both of Philadelphia, o'seers. Wits: James Graisbury, Paul Isaac Voto, Abraham Gardiner and Stephen Holwell. AWW 12 Nov 1756 to John Strettell, attorney for the surviving exec. John Beazly in Philadelphia, the relict having died. (PROB 11/826/303),

Thomas Wyatt of Boreham, Essex, yeoman, [who died in Md.], dated 14 Apr 1750. £10 to my niece Frances Jay. The residue to my brother Samuel Wyatt of Boreham who is to be my exec. Wits: E. Pryor and Samuel Rogers. Pr. 26 Nov 1756 by affirmation of named exec. (PROB 11/826/315).

Martha Lane of Blandford, Dorset, spinster, [who died in N.C.], dated 19 Dec 1754. To my nephew Thomas Fitzherbert, son of my sister Judith Fitzherbert, my one-fifth part of houses in London and my houses in Haselbury Bryan, Dorset, and Holwell, Somerset. To my nephew Richard Fitzherbert my quarter part of a house in Blandford, (Dorset), and my one-third part of a leasehold house in Bryans Piddle, Dorset, during the lives of my two sisters and Susannah Hill. £10 each to my nephew John Fitzherbert and my niece Susannah Hill. £20 to Henrietta Mary McCulloch, daughter of Henry McCulloch Esq., with whom I now live. A mourning ring to Rev. Mr. Gilbert Bushery of Swaffham, Norfolk, and his wife. All my clothing and linen to my sisters Christian and Mary Lane. Residue to my said nephew Thomas Fitzherbert who is to be exec. Wits: Daniel Turner of New Inn, attorney at law, Peter Sandiford, clerk to Mr. Combe, and Edmund Combe of New Inn, attorney at law. Pr. 15 Dec 1756 by named exec. (PROB 11/826/342).

1757

John Couzens [of Oswego, N.Y.], Ensign in Sir William Pepperell's Regt. of Foot, [bachelor], dated 4 Aug 1755. To my parents Samuel and Isabella Couzens residing in Dublin, Ireland, a Bill of Exchange for £100 drawn by Lieut. John Mitchell, paymaster to Col. Hugh Warburton's Regt., on Thomas Lovill Esq. in Warwick Street, (London), and sent by me on 6 May 1755 to John Calcraft Esq. in Brewer Street near Golden Square, (London). Remainder to my friend and exex. Mrs. Ann Hopper of South Shields, (Durham), who is to have my lots in the south suburbs of Halifax, Nova Scotia, and my houses and rents which are in the hands of Lieut. John Mitchell. Wits: James Campbell of Sir William Pepperell's Regt. and John Mills, Lieut. in Capt. Hubert Marshall's Independent Company. AWW 1 Feb 1757 to Henry Kidgell, attorney for the father in Dublin, the named exex. Anne Hopper, now wife of Edward Barron, renouncing. (PROB 11/827/42).

John Grave of Dublin, Ireland, but at present in Annapolis, Md., merchant, dated 3 Jan 1743. My whole estate to my brother and sisters Thomas, Elizabeth, Alice and Mary Grave. My said brother to be exec. Wits: Joseph Jening, rector of All Saints, Md., Joshua Hopkinson, clerk of Anne Arundel Co., and William Bermingham. Pr. 18 Jly 1757 by named exec. (PROB 11/831/221).

John Tilson of Boston, N.E., chief mate of the *Blackey*, commander John Osborne, bound from St. Kitts to London, dated 28 Jly 1757. My whole estate to my mother Rebecca Tilson of Boston, widow. Richard Comport of Milton Next Gravesend, Kent, innholder, to be my exec. Wits: Josa. Bramble, Robert Bramble and G. Parker. Pr. 2 Aug 1757 by named exec. (PROB 11/832/260).

John Clarke the younger of London, merchant, about to take a voyage to Va., [and late of Gloucester Co., Va., bachelor], dated 31 Jan 1749. My whole estate to my father and exec. John Clarke of Bugbrooke, Northants., merchant, with remainder to my mother Catherine Clarke or my sister Catherine Clarke. Wits: Richard Bennett, Edward Benton Jr. and James Bennett of Love Lane, Wood Street, London. Pr. 23 Nov 1757 by the father. (PROB 11/833/324).

John Lomas, late of Annapolis, Md., and now of Glasgow, Scotland, gent., dated 22 Oct 1754. To Walter Johnson, John Mill and George Spence of London, merchants, my whole estate, including my interest in the estate willed to me by my late brother Henry Lomas, in trust for the following uses. To my sister Mary Roson and annuity of £30 and to her husband John Roson £50. The interest on any residue to my friend James Johnson of Glasgow, merchant, during his lifetime, with remainder to his wife Margaret and her children. The said James Johnson to be exec. Wits: John Somervale, Robert Colquhoun and William McKenzie. AWW 22 Nov 1757 to John Mill, attorney for James Johnson in Va. (PROB 11/834/331).

Daniel Charlton of H.M. ship *Garland*, commander William Saltern Willet, [who died in Md.], dated 5 Jly 1753. My whole estate to Elizabeth Libbard of Portsmouth Common, Hants., widow, and she is to be my exex. Wits: John Birdsey and Thomas Burgen. Pr. 22

Dec 1757 by the named exec., now wife of Richard Dawley. (PROB 11/834/352).

Richard Edwards of Bradforton, Worcs., gent., [late of Eaton Town (?Edenton), N.C.], dated 30 Dec 1755. £200 to my cousin Ann Ashwin, daughter of the late John Ashwin of Bradforton, gent. My clothing to my nephew William Middleton. The residue to my execs. in trust William Daniel and Henry Murcott, both of Southam, Warw., who are to pay the interest thereon to my sister Rebecca, wife of Henry Middleton of Southam, mercer, with remainder to his children William and Rebecca Middleton. Wits: Richard Lyndon, Richard Roberts and J. Spicer. Pr. 8 Dec 1757 by Henry Murcott. (PROB 11/834/354).

Peter Smyth of Brentford Butts, (Mddx.), clerk, [chaplain of H.M. ship *Tilbury*, who died in America, widower], dated 19 May 1749. To Mary Chilcott, daughter of Rev. William Chilcott, minister of New Brentford, £200 when she is 21 or married, with remainder to her younger sister Charlotte Chilcott. £50 to their brother William Chilcott. The residue to the said Rev. William Chilcott who is to be exec. Wits: John Gunter and Ann (x) Clements. Pr. 8 Dec 1757 by named exec. (PROB 11/834/371).

George Towle, now of Bethnal Green, Mddx., [of the ship *Mary* who died in N.Y., bachelor], dated 3 May 1756. All my real estate is to be sold for the benefit of my brother-in-law William Coulson and his sister. My friend Matthew Stamford of Bethnal Green, dealer in coals, to be my exec. Wits: William Brown, William Ought and Francis Galloway. Pr. 1 Dec 1757 by named exec. (PROB 11/834/374).

1758

George Radford [of Dartmouth and Lympston, Devon, who died in N.Y., mariner], dated Dartmouth 18 Apr 1754. To my wife Dorothea Radford my whole estate and she is to be my exex. Wits: Ann Gely and Fishlake Chubb. Pr. 14 Mar 1758 by the relict. Sentence for validity of will 18 Feb 1761. (PROB 11/836/89).

Joseph Adams [of York Town, Va.], of H.M. ship *Wolf*, [but late purser of H.M. ship *Fox*], dated 1 Oct 1740. My whole estate to my wife Ann Adams who is to be exex. Wits: W. Dandrige and Charles Turner. AWW 19 Jun 1758 to Daniel Walton, attorney for the relict in York Town. (PROB 11/838/175).

Edward Smith of St. John the Baptist, London, [of H.M. Artillery in N.Y., bachelor], dated 22 Oct 1754. My whole estate to my uncle James Hannam of St. John the Baptist, smith, and he is to be my exec. Wits: Arthur Hannam and Mary Wintle. Pr. 17 Jly 1758 by named exec. (PROB 11/839/230).

Richard Larner [of St. Martin in the Fields, Mddx.], Lieut. in Maj-Gen. Richard O'Farrell's 22nd Regt. of Foot, [who died in Albany, North America], dated Halifax, Nova Scotia, 1 Aug 1757. My whole estate, including £100 in 3% Bank stock of 1726, to Ann Ashburn, daughter of William and Mary Ashburn of Keresley near Coventry, Warw., and she is to be my exec. Wits: Thomas Spencer and Paul Mangin, Lieuts. of 46th Regt. Deposition at Albany 16 Aug 1758 by Dirk Vanderheyden of London, merchant, resident in Albany, that the above will has been copied from N.Y. records. Pr. 25 Aug 1758 by exec., now wife of Thomas Lynes. (PROB 11/840/246).

Samuel Brookes of Dorchester, Mass., gent., dated 20 Aug 1757. £50 sterling to my brother Nehemiah Brookes. £310.10s. sterling to my uncle Thomas Brookes. Ten guineas to my cousin Henry Norris. £10 sterling each to my cousins Nehemiah and Samuel Nesbit. £20 sterling to the heirs of Rev. John Rastrick of Kings Lynn, Norfolk, who was living in Feb 1728(/9) when I was there. £200 sterling to Mrs. Eleanor Shippey and £50 more for the maintenance and education of her granddaughter Eleanor Spur. £150 sterling to Ann Shippey. £5 sterling to Abraham Shippey. £10 sterling to Jane Spur. £10 to Philip Shippey. £20 sterling to Isabella Shippey. £5 sterling to Abraham Spur. The residue, including my house and land in Dorchester where I live and three acres adjoining to the said Eleanor Shippey and her daughter Ann. A funeral ring to my friends Collis Oliver, Dr. Duglass, Rev. Thomas Prince, William Welsteed, Samuel Dunbar, Rev. Mr. Bowman, Capt. John Steel, Capt. John Smith, Mr. Jonathan Durand, Mr. Thomas Bromfield and Dr. Nathaniel Ames. Exec. for N.E. to be my friend Capt. John Homans of Dorchester; exec. for England to be Henry Norris of London. Wits: John Jeffries, Ebenezer Wiswall and Jeremiah Gridley. Pr. 25 Oct 1758 by Henry Norris. (PROB 11/840/287).

Henry Nicholson, Lieut. in Col. Amherst's Regt. of Foot, [who died in Louisburgh, bachelor], dated 18 Jan 1758. £50 to Capt. Sampson Barber of the Royal Dragoons. The residue to Capt. Richard Burton of the Royal Dragoons who is to be my exec. Wits: Henry De Vie, H. De Vie Jr., and John Freemantel. AWW 3 Oct 1758 to Sampson Barber Esq., attorney for Richard Burton Esq. in Germany. (PROB 11/841/303).

John Williams, mariner, now of H.M. ship *Nightingale* [but late of the privateer *Hornet* of N.Y., who died in hospital in France, bachelor], dated 15 Nov 1754. My whole estate to my mother Ann Williams of Deptford, Kent, widow, who is to be my exex. Wits: Dudley Digges, commander, and Charles Frankland, clerk. Pr. 27 Oct 1758 by the mother. (PROB 11/841/317).

Theophilus Young Lieut. in the 45th Regt. of Foot, [who died in Louisburgh], dated at Lunenburg, Nova Scotia, 15 May 1758. £400 to my brother John Young. £50 to my sister, wife of (blank) Cowper Esq. £300 to Mrs. Jane Anderson, housekeeper to my father Thomas Young Esq. of Hare Hatch, Berks. To my said father the residue of my fortune which came to me by my late mother Arabella, daughter of Sir Michael Biddulph. My said father to be exec. Wits: Patrick Sutherland, T. Gildart and Mary Gildart. Pr. 1 Dec 1758 by the father. (PROB 11/842/388).

1759

Augustine Frost, now at York Fort, North America. To the children of Margaret Stansly £100. To George Richardson, John Plumb, Humphrey Marton, Christopher Atkinson, James Davidson and Andrew Graham a half-guinea each. To my daughters Martha and Anna Maria Frost £10 each. Two guineas each to John Stevenson who belongs to the Post Office in England, and Thomas Hopkins, surgeon. Ten guineas to Anna, daughter of James Isham. The said James Isham is to be my exec. Wits: Thomas Hopkins, Christopher Atkinson and Andrew Graham. Pr. 10 Jan 1759 by named exec. (PROB 11/843/16).

James Mercer, Capt. in Col. Henry Conway's Regt. of Foot, [late of Gen. Webb's Regt. of Foot, who died in Albany, North America, bachelor], dated 6 Apr 1748. My whole estate to my sisters Mary, Jemima and Elizabeth Mercer. My uncle Mr. Richard Fenton, merchant in London, to be exec. Wits: John Pickford, Catherine Todo and Mary Pickford. Pr. Feb 1759 by the named exec. (PROB 11/844/65).

William Shrubsole of St. George, Hanover Square, Mddx., gent., [of S.C.], dated 19 Jly 1748. My whole estate to my wife and exex. Elizabeth Shrubsole who is now abroad with me but, if she dies before I return, to my brothers and sisters-in-law John Jamison, Martha Jamison, Josiah Woodward and Anne Joynson, all in Chester Co. Wits: John Jenkinson and Abram Loxley. Pr. 16 Mar 1759 by the relict. (PROB 11/845/109).

Sholto Douglas of London, mariner [of the *St. George* who died in North America], dated 28 Dec 1757. My whole estate to my friend John Dalglish of N.Y., merchant, who is to be my exec. Wits: Alexander Stewart, Peter Ewetse(?) and John Coo. AWW 4 Apr 1759 to Robert Mackoun, attorney for named exec. in N.Y. (PROB 11/845/125).

William Haslewood Lieut. [in the Royal American Regt., who died in North America, bachelor], dated 5 Apr 1756. To my father Edward Haslewood, mercer in Bridgnorth, (Salop.), all my money in the hands of John Winter Esq. and my clothing. My gold watch to my sister Catharine Haslewood and my gold sleeve buttons and shirt buckle to my brother Roger Haslewood. My silver shoe and knee buckles to my brother Edward Haslewood. Wits: George Haslewood and Thomas Arnold. AWW 4 May 1759 to the father, no exec. having been named. (PROB 11/846/169).

Robert Murdoch of Trenton, North America, dated 29 Mar 1758. All my estate in America and Ireland to be disposed of for the benefit of the children of Rev. Hugh Dixon at Gray Abbey near Belfast by my sister Isabel, and of James Riddle, merchant in Cumber near Belfast, by my sister Eleanor. The child commonly said to be mine by Rachel Stuart is to be treated kindly by my friends. The said Dixon and Riddle to be my execs. Wits: Robert Sterling and John Lees. Pr. 24 Jly 1759 by named execs. (PROB 11/848/242).

Henry Davers, [Lieut. of H.M. ship *Neptune*, who died in America, bachelor], son of Sir Jermyn Davers and Dame Margaretta of Rushbrook, Suffolk], dated 13 January 1759. My whole estate to my brother Sir Robert Davers and my sister Elizabeth Hervey with remainder to my brother Charles Davers, my sister Mary Davers and my brother Thomas Davers. Mr. Thomas Bilcliffe of King Street, Golden Square, to be my exec. Wits: Thomas Bilcliffe and Elizabeth his daughter, and Matthew Thornton. Pr. 11 Sep 1759 by named execs. (PROB 11/849/294).

Stephen Lavington Esq. of Antigua, being suddenly to depart for North America, [formerly of Arundell Street, St. Clement Danes, Mddx., but late of S.C.]. My freeholds in Antigua were conveyed by me on 3 Oct 1755 to the use of James Brebner Esq. and my sister Ann, his wife, and their issue. Parties to the deed were myself (Stephen Lavington Esq. of Argyle Street) and Jane my wife; the said James and Ann Brebner then of Argyle Street; James Gordon Esq. of Argyle Street; and Nathaniel Gilbert Sr. and Patrick Grant Esq., both of Antigua. Other bequests to my brother Samuel Lavington and my sister Elizabeth Gilbert. John Lightfoot Esq., Samuel Redhead Esq. and Dr. James Athill to be execs. Wits:

George Barret Collins, Richard Chapman and Edward Horne. AWW 8 Dec 1759 to Edward Codrington, attorney for execs. in Antigua. (PROB 11/851/405).

1760

Susanna Thurman, relict of Francis Thurman of N.Y.C., merchant, dated 23 Aug 1758. All my clothes to my daughter Elizabeth Thurman with remainder to my sisters-in-law Elizabeth, wife of Nicholas Roosevelt, and Gertruy Thurman. Rolls of cloth to my aunts Agnes, wife of Joseph Lockwood, Grace, wife of William Williams, and Sarah, wife of Isaac Brown. The residue of my estate in England and America to my son Richardson Thurman and my said daughter Elizabeth with remainder to my brothers-in-law Ralph Thurman and John Thurman and my said sisters-in-law. The said John Thurman, merchant, Nicholas Roosevelt, goldsmith, and Dirck Schuyler, merchant, all of N.Y.C., to be execs. Wits: Thomas Pettit, Abraham Bussing and John McKesson. Pr. 26 Jan 1760 by John Thurman. (PROB 11/852/40).

James Henderson of N.Y.C., dated 7 Oct 1743. To my wife Tessia Henderson the storehouse where I live and one in Prince Street adjoining the dwelling of Anthony Duane, and the use of my house during her lifetime. My farm at Greenwich and my land in Albany, Ulster Co. are to be sold with negroes and stock and the proceeds used for the benefit of my said wife and my daughters Margaret, Tessia, wife of Alexander Moore, Elizabeth, Catherine and Eve and Mary Henderson. My said wife and my daughter Margaret are to be exexs. Wits: Peter Renaudet, William Bascomb and John Kelly. Pr. 28 Feb 1760 by Tessia Henderson and the daughter Margaret, now wife of Joseph Haviland. (PROB 11/853/63).

Phineas Evans of South Weald, Essex, dated 7 September 1759, whose cousin, Edward Collins, was in Virginia. Will is listed as proved in Mar 1760 by Daniel Fox with powers reserved to Anna Taylor, spinster, under reference PROB 11/854/106 but there is no trace of it in the Register. See NGSQ 64/213 for a summary of the Chancery suit of 1761 in which Daniel Fox and Anna Taylor sued Sidney Collins, widow, Ann Collins of St Ives, Hunts., Ann Collins of Bromyard, Heref., etc. The testator's cousin, Edward Collins, went to Virginia in about 1756.

Benjamin Lay of Colchester, Essex, glover, [of Abington, Penna.], dated in the ninth month called March 1732. My wife Sarah is to be provided for according to her needs. A guinea each to the six children of my late brother William Lay of Fordham, Essex. £10 each to: Elizabeth Dennis of Layer Breton, Essex, singlewoman; Peter Flood of Layer Marney, Essex; and my nephew Philip Lay of London. £5 each to: my sister Sarah, relict of my said late brother William; John Bandock of Layer Breton, husbandman; Martha Potter Jr. of Copford, Essex; Mary, wife of Joseph Potter of Hatfield, Essex. £20 to Elizabeth and Mary Mash, daughters of John Mash of London, weaver. Small bequests of money to the following (Quakers), all of Essex: Christopher Choat of Easthorpe, gardener; Sarah, wife of William Reyner of Marks Tey, husbandman; Samuel South of Tendring, husbandman; John Sewell of Broomby (?Broomfield), husbandman; Elizabeth Bell of Feering, widow; Susan Bunns of Feering, widow; Widow Pettit of Gore Pitt near Feering; William Candler of Feering, miller; Susan Quarry of Colchester; Susan Spinks Sr. of Colchester; John Jeofferys of Colchester, sawyer; Syrus Scott of Colchester, weaver; Mary, wife of John Swinburn of Colchester, weaver; Mary, daughter of Michael Perry of Colchester; Ann, relict of John Hails of Colchester; Samuel Cook of South Halstead, weaver; Francis Harrison of Stebbing, thatcher; John Havens, woolcomber; Grizzle Babbs; Jane Hall. £100 to the Quarterly Meeting at Coggeshall or Colchester to be placed at interest for the transport of poor Friends to America. Philip Havens of Colchester, baymaker, Benjamin Bone of London, glover, John Mash of London, weaver, Emmanuel Liversedge of Dedham, dyer, Jonathan Furley of Colchester, linen draper, Ralph Thresher of Kelvedon, baymaker, and Elizabeth Kendall Jr. of Bradfield, Essex, are to be trustees. My said wife to be exex. Wits: Philip Goldsbury, John Raven and John Kendall. AWW 2 Jly 1760 by affirmation of Samuel Cook, the wife having died in the testator's lifetime. (PROB 11/857/290).

Sarah Waring (late Sarah Lloyd), of St. James, Goose Creek, S.C., widow, dated 24 Jan 1755. My personal estate to my sons John Lloyd Waring and George Waring. My plantation, 908 acres on Combahie River, and 2,000 acres on Four Hole Swamp, are to be divided between my said sons with remainder to my cousins James and Thomas Akin, sons of my uncle James Akin Esq. £100 current to my cousin Sarah Collins when she is 18 or married. My aunt Mrs. Elizabeth Akin and my friends Peter Taylor, George Austin, Benjamin Waring and Robert Hume are to be execs. Wits: Elizabeth Barnes, Mary Kirk and Edmund Barnes. AWW 4 Jly 1760 to Sarah Nickelson, widow, attorney for execs. in S.C. (PROB 11/857/292).

John Whitborn, [formerly of West Teignmouth, Devon, afterwards mate of the *Brislington*, but late of S.C., bachelor]. Will in the form of a letter dated Bristol 1 Sep 1756 to his sister. My accounts with Mr. Gomond, Mr. Meyler and Messrs. Devonshear, Reeve and Lloyd are to be settled. The account with Mr. Gomond in Bristol is for goods sent to Mr. Samuel Carne of Carolina. When I went from Carolina, I left money with Messrs. Austen and Lawrence. Mr. Henry West of Antigua owes me money. I left £400 in Oporto to be remitted to my father. My effects are to be shared between you and my brother, and my mother may keep what part she wants. On 1 Apr 1760 James Cornish, gent., and John Robins, mariner, both of West Teignmouth, depose that they knew the testator and that the letter is in his writing. AWW on same date to the brother Peter Whitborn. (PROB 11/855/178).

Carls Julin of Wapping, Mddx., mariner [of the *Charles Town Packet*, bachelor], dated 17 Mar 1759. My whole estate to my friends Johannes Scheelhase of Wapping, victualler, and Sarah his wife. Wits: Mary Kingston and Richard Rooke. Pr. 12 Aug 1760 by Johannes Scheelhase. (PROB 11/858/329).

Paschall Nelson Esq., late of Boston, N.E., but now residing in St. Margaret, Westminster, Mddx., dated 19 Jly 1759. To my nephew John Nelson of Portsmouth, N.H., merchant, all my lands on River Kenebee, Mass. He is to convey one-seventh of my lands in Mohawk Co., N.Y., to the children of my sister Lloyd and two-sevenths to the children of my sister Hubbard, 1,000 acres to John Temple Esq., late of Boston but now residing in London, 500 acres to John Lloyd of Stamford, Ct., merchant, 500 acres to Nathaniel Hubbard Esq. of Stamford, and 500 acres to Paschall Smith of Stamford, son of the late William Smith. The residue of my estate to my nephews John Temple and John Nelson and they are to be my execs. Wits: John Dagge of Ricmond Buildings, Soho, John Hudson of Charles Street, Westminster, peruke maker, and Jane Smith. Pr. 19 Sep 1760 by John Temple Esq. (PROB 11/859//366).

Richard Ayscough of N.Y.C., practitioner in physick and surgery, dated 22 May 1760. To my daughter Sarah Ayscough £500 sterling. To my brother John Ayscough Jr. £100 sterling. To my brother Thomas Ayscough £50 sterling. To my wife Anne Ayscough my house in Hanover Square, N.Y.C., during her lifetime, and afterwards it is to be sold. To my mother-in-law Anne Langdon, widow of Richard Langdon, £500 current. The residue of my estate to my wife and son Richard Ayscough. My said wife, my uncle Rev. Dr. Francis Ayscough and my friend Charles Williams of N.Y.C. to be execs. Wits: John Burnet, Cornelius C. Van Horne and Isaac Goelet. Pr. 22 Nov 1760 by Rev. Francis Ayscough. (PROB 11/860/412). Further grant in Jan 1768 to William Moore, husband of the relict Anne.

1761

Alexander Cairnes of London, lately residing in Leadenhall Street but now of Islington, Mddx., [who died in Va., widower], dated 1 Aug 1760. To my mother an annuity of £10 during her lifetime. To my brother David £200. To my sister Helen, who has a large family, £500 free of her husband's control. To my sister Margaret £200. To Martha Sayer *alias* Smith, lately in my service, £100 to pay her passage from Va., and £400 to her son James when he is 21. The residue to my friend and partner John Lidderdale of Throgmorton Steet, London, who is to be my exec. Wits: Ann Lowe and Cornelius Lowe. Pr. 10 Feb 1761 by named exec. (PROB 11/862/49).

Charles Ramsay, mariner of H.M. ship *Harwich*, Capt. William Marsh, [who died in America, bachelor], dated 3 Nov 1757. My brother John Ramsay of St. Martin in the Fields, Mddx., merchant, to be my sole legatee and exec. Wits: W. Marsh and John Hill. AWW 5 Feb 1761 to Henry Mills, attorney for named exec. in N.Y. (PROB 11/863/72).

James Bennet, now of the *James* in the transportation service, Capt. William Cooper, [who died in N.Y. Hospital, bachelor], dated 7 Mar 1760. My whole estate to my friend John Oswald of Shadwell, Mddx., rigger, who is to be my exec. Wits: James Cooper, Mark Webb and Edward B. Cooke. Pr. 3 Apr 1761 by named exec. (PROB 11/864/117).

James Abercrombie of Philadelphia, mariner, dated 11 Dec 1758 (copy from Penna. records). To my wife Margaret Abercrombie £1,000. The residue to my son James with remainder to my brother David Abercrombie, my sister Jannet Abercrombie, and John Stedman, son of my friend Alexander Stedman. My friends Charles Stedman, Alexander Stedman and Samuel McCall, all of Philadelphia, to be my execs. Wits: Robert Harper and Johannes George Waine. AWW 23 Jly 1761 to William Neate, attorney for execs. in Philadelphia. (PROB 11/867/239).

Nathaniel Shower, late of Boston, N.E., [widower], now purser of H.M. ship *Blandford*, dated London, 26 Jly 1755. One shilling to my daughter Susanna, wife of Capt. William Masswey. The residue to Nathaniel, Samuel, How (*sic*) and William Shower, my children by my first wife Alicia Shower, and my daughters Elizabeth and Ann Shower. My friend Sir Joseph Hankey of London to be exec. Wits: William Tudman of Birchin Lane, W. Eccleston, his clerk, and Benjamin Lloyd. AWW 13 Nov 1761 to the daughter Elizabeth Shower, the named exec. renouncing. (PROB 11/870/409).

1762

Joseph Temple of King William Co., Va., dated 20 Dec 1744. A mourning ring to my brother William Temple of Bristol. To my wife Ann Temple half of the plantation where I now live and my negroes Jenny, Alice, Angela, Rachel, Bew, Bristol, Peter and Phillis his wife, my four-wheel chaise and horses, with remainder to my son William. To my said son William the remaining half. To my son Joseph my 400 acres in King and Queen Co. and 1,250 acres in Spotsylvania Co. To my son Listum my 2,000 acres on Dushing Hole Swamp in Louisa Co. To my son Benjamin the 800 acres I bought of James Taylor and 180 acres of Frank Arnold's tract in Spotsylvania Co. which I bought of George Woodroff. To my son Samuel my 250 acres in Caroline Co. and the remaining part of my 1,390 acres in Louisa Co. with the land I bought of Samuel Maghee. To my daughter Hannah the mulatto girl named Doll. To my daughter Ann my negro girl Sarah. To my daughter Sarah my negro girl Polly. To my daughter Mary my negro girl Pheby. To my daughter Patte my negro girl Violet. The residue to my said sons and daughters. My wife and my son William to be execs. Wits: Edward (x) Watkins, Mary (x) Watkins, Phebe Pendleton and Elizabeth Roberts. Deposition 24 Oct 1760 by Hon. Philip Ludwell Esq., now of Cecil Street, Strand, Mddx., that the above will is a true copy from Va. records. Deposition 19 Jan 1762 by William Temple of St. Clement Danes, Mddx., gent., (son of the testator), to similar effect. Pr. 28 Jan 1762 by the son William Temple. (PROB 11/872/32).

Frederick Porter Esq., now resident in Roxbury, N.E., [of Boston, N.E., Capt. of the Third Batallion of the Royal American Regt.], dated 27 Dec 1760. My whole estate to my wife Mehettable during her lifetime and then to my daughter Mary. My gold watch and pistols to Matatiah Bourn Esq. John Bowdoin Esq., the said Matatiah Bourn and my wife to be execs. AWW 19 Feb 1762 to William Hodshon, attorney for exccs. in Boston. (PROB 11/873/72).

Peter Wraxall Esq. of N.Y.C., [Captain of an Independent Company of N.Y.]. £20 sterling to my father John Wraxall of Bristol. £400 sterling to Mrs. Ann Wraxall, my sister by my said father's first wife and my own mother, with remainder of £300 to my niece Elizabeth Wraxall, daughter of my brother Richard Wraxall, and £100 to my sister Mary Wraxall. £50 sterling to my said sister Mary Wraxall of Bristol. £20 current to my friend Sir William Johnson. All the residue to my wife Elizabeth Wraxall who is to be my exex. I am to be buried without any kind of expense which may border on ostentation. If my fortune would permit it, I should be equally an enemy to all the gloomy pomp. Deposition 10 Sep 1759 in N.Y.C. by Ann Devisme, wife of Philip Devisme of N.Y.C., merchant, and sister of Mrs. Elizabeth Wraxall, that she discovered the above will in a leather travelling case in the testator's study. Depositions on the same date by John Watts and Beverley Robinson Esqs. of N.Y.C. that the will is in the testator's hand. Pr. 13 Feb 1762 by the relict. (PROB 11/873/86).

John Metcalfe, now of King and Queen Co., Va., merchant, intending for Great Britain for the recovery of my health, [who died at sea, bachelor], dated 10 Jly 1760. An annuity of £20 sterling during her lifetime to my sister Mary Widders of Norwich (*sic* but ?Nantwich), Chesh. An annuity of £10 during her lifetime to Ann Metcalfe, widow of my late brother Samuel Metcalfe. To Ann, daughter of the said Samuel and Ann Metcalfe of Chesh., £200 sterling. To Samuel Metcalfe, son of the same, the ground rents of my tenements in Brook Street, Grosvenor Square, and of my houses in Bishop's Court, Clerkenwell Green. £50 sterling to my cousin Richard Widders, son of the said Mary Widders. Ten guineas to Mr. Heneage Robinson of London. Five guineas each for rings to my friends Mr. John Craven of London, Mr. David Ker of King and Queen Co., and Capt. John Foster of the same. £10 sterling each to my godchildren Elizabeth Foster, Peter Dudley, son of Capt. Robert Dudley, and John Didlake, son of James Didlake and Rhoda his wife. One guinea to my godson whose name I think is John, son of Joseph Rogers. £10 sterling to William Shackleford. To Thomas Metcalfe of Va. my negroes Sarah and Haney and the latter's child Marry. The remainder of my estate to my cousins Samuel and Thomas Metcalfe. My execs. to be Samuel Metcalfe and Mr. John Craven of London and Thomas Metcalfe and Mr. David Ker of Va. Wits: Nicholas Dillard, Richard Crittendon, Edward Price and James Price Jr. Pr. 11 Mar 1762 by Thomas Metcalfe. (PROB 11/874/118).

William Timbrill of St. Michael, Barbados, merchant, dated 25 Jly 1753. Bequests to: my son William Timbrill and my daughter Sarah Timbrill when they come of age; my mother Margaret Timbrill; my brother Thomas Timbrill; my uncle William Breedy; my uncle Lawrence Trent; my brother-in-law John Sober. My two lots of land and houses in Chester Town, Chester River, Md., now in the hands of John Bullen of Md., to be sold. Execs: Alexander Murray and Richard Milles. Wits: Thomas Morisone, Richard Carter and Edward Grove. Will entered at Barbados 25 Aug 1743. AWW 10 Dec 1762 to Joseph Price, husband of the daughter Sarah Timbrill, the named execs. having died. (PROB 11/882/530).

1763

George Haynes of St. George, Southwark, Sy., gent., dated 12 Jan 1763. To my wife Elizabeth Haynes all my personal estate, including what belonged to her former husband Thomas Adams (of N.E.) deceased, and 20 guineas for mourning. To my brother William Haynes 20 guineas for mourning. To my nephew William Haynes Jr. 10 guineas for mourning. To my friend Charles Ryder of Cheapside, London, mercer, 10 guineas. Other bequests to: Mrs. Elizabeth Jones, daughter of Benjamin Todd of Cowes, Isle of Wight, tallow chandler; my nieces Mary, wife of John Downing, Sarah Haynes, spinster, Ann Phillis Haynes, spinster, Elizabeth, wife of Abraham Selby, and Sarah Harris, spinster; Elizabeth and Mary Adams, spinsters, daughters of my said wife Elizabeth by her former husband. The residue to my said wife, my brother William Haynes, and Charles Ryder in trust to provide for the benefit of any children born of my said wife. Wits: Thomas Holt, Mary Cockram and Benjamin Hills, East Lane, Rotherhithe. Pr. 26 Jan 1763 by named execs. (PROB 11/883/20).

Frances Balgay, (formerly Wright), of St. Paul Covent Garden, Mddx., widow, dated 11 Jan 1763. £200 each to Col. William Miles, now in Germany and his wife, and Mrs. Ann Speed, wife of Mr. John Speed. £400 to Sarah Cooke and £50 to Ann Cooke, both of Maiden Lane, Covent Garden, spinster. £300 to Miss Quincey of Northants. £100 to Mrs. Seagrow. £250 to my niece Elizabeth Gordon. £150 to Mary Sawrey. To my execs. William Thomson of Throgmorton Street, London, merchant, William Frankcomb Esq. of Boswell Court, London, and John Gordon of Charles Town, S.C., £3,000 in trust to pay the interest on £1,000 to my sister-in-law Mrs. Ann Blenman, wife of Thomas Blenman, doctor in physick, during her lifetime; and the interest on the remaining £2,000 to provide an annuity of £60 to my son Richard Miles during his lifetime. The residue of my estate to my great nephews and great nieces. Wits: Ann Eccles and Joseph Hodges. Pr. 1 Mar 1763 by William Thompson and William Frankcombe. Double probate to John Gordon 3 Oct 1774. See NGSQ 65/142. (PROB 11/885/111).

Richard Mather Esq. [Capt. of the First Batallion of Royal Americans, who died in Pittsburg, America, bachelor], dated St. George Camp 28 Jun 1758. Will in the form of a letter to his brother Thomas Mather Esq. in Chester, Europe. We have a large army encamped here waiting to go from Ticonderoga, Crown Point, and are hourly expecting news from Louisburgh. As yet we have had no good news from that quarter. I wrote my last from N.Y. I have left £500

Penna. currency, which is near £300 sterling, in the hands of Mr. Stedman, merchant at Philadelphia, and whenever the Royal American accounts are settled here, there will be a considerable balance owing to me, all of which I leave to you. Depositions 18 Apr 1763 by the brothers Thomas Mather Esq. and Rev. Roger Mather, and Witter Cumming of Liverpool, Lancs., gent., that the above letter is in the testator's hand. AWW same date to the brother Thomas Mather. (PROB 11/886/190).

George Smith of Wapping, Mddx., [of the transport ship *Hercules*, who died in N.Y., bachelor], dated 26 Apr 1761. To my sister Barbara Gering £50 which is in the Bank of England. The residue of my estate to my friends and execs. Bearend Ehlers and George Fisher. Wits: David Palmer and Mary Lowe. Pr. 13 Apr 1763 by Bearend Ehlers. (PROB 11/887/210).

John Appy Esq., at present in the City of Albany, N.Y., [Secretary and Judge-Advocate of H.M. Forces in North America], dated 10 Jun 1758. Twenty guineas each to my execs. my father Peter Appy of London, merchant, and my friend Abraham Mortier Esq., Deputy Postmaster-General of the forces in North America. The residue to my wife Elizabeth Appy. Depositions on 27 Apr 1763 by the father Peter Appy of St. Stephen, Coleman Street, London, merchant, and Samuel Mestrezat of St. Dionis Backchurch, London, merchant, that the above will is in the testator's hand, and that, a few hours after his death, his relict Elizabeth was delivered of a daughter. The relict and child are both living in N.Y. Province. Pr. 10 May 1763 by the father. (PROB 11/887/210).

John Chichester [of Va.], dated 24 Sep 1753. To my wife Jeane Chichester the plantation where I live and my negroes and stock during her lifetime, with remainder to my daughter Mary Chichester and my brother Richard Chichester. £500 each out of my Va. estate to my said wife and to my daughter who is to be genteely maintained. £50 sterling each to my four sisters Elizabeth, Ellen, Mary and Hannah Chichester. £50 sterling to my brother Rawleigh Downman. A choice negro girl to Miss Elizabeth Griffin. My estate in England to my brother Richard Chichester. My friends James Ball Jr. and the said Richard Chichester to be execs. Pr. Lancaster Co., Va., 15 Mar 1754. Pr. London 28 May 1763 by Richard Chichester. (PROB 11/887/224). Further grant on 9 Jun 1803.

William Fenwick of London, merchant, now bound out on a voyage to sea, [of Boston, N.E.], dated 12 Mar 1738. Twenty guineas each for mourning to my father Mr. Edward Fenwick and my uncle Mr. Andrew Howard. One-fifth of my estate to my brother Henry Fenwick and the residue to my brothers and execs. Michael and

Samuel Fenwick. Wits: Robert Sedgwick, Jonathan Barnard and John Harrison. Pr. 13 May 1763 by the brother and surviving exec. Michael Fenwick. (PROB 11/887/228).

Ralph Izard of Berkeley Co., S.C., dated 13 Sep 1757. To my son Ralph Izard the plantation where I live called Burton, the land up Cypress Path left to me by my father, a tract called Mount Boone left to me by my brother Thomas Izard, a plantation in Cow Savannah, and a plantation on Combahie River given me by my said father and brother. To my son Walter Izard my plantation on Timothy Savannah which I bought from Mr. James Deveaux and land on Lady's Island left to me by my brother Thomas. To my daughters Sarah and Rebecca Izard the plantation left to me by my father-in-law Joseph Blake Esq. My execs. are to settle a plantation on my Combahie land given to my son Ralph. If Mrs. Galleghar is living in my family when I die, she is to have £30. My houses in Charles Town are to be repaired. My brother-in-law Daniel Blake and my friends Henry Middleton and Benjamin Smith Esqs. are to be execs. Wits: John Butler, Newman Swallow and Charles Atkins. AWW 18 May 1763 to Ralph Izard, attorney for the execs. in S.C. (PROB 11/887/236).

Edward Jackson of Boston, Mass., gent., dated 8 Jun 1757. To my wife Dorothy my negro Cato, my chaise and horse and household goods during her lifetime, except for a bed which I gave to my daughter Mary on her marriage. One-third of my goods, my desk and books, and a quarter of the ship *Bethel* to my son Jonathan. £14 each to my cousin Mrs. Elizabeth Elliott and my friend Mr. Dudson Hilcup. My real estate in Milton, including the slitting mill purchased of my father, and my other tenements in Boston are to be sold for the benefit of my children, and my farm at Braintree is to be disposed of at the discretion of my execs. My wife, Mr. Daniel Marsh, Mr. Samuel Sewall and Mr. Thomas Cushing are to be execs. Wits: John Williams, Benjamin May and Ebenezer Newell. Codicil of 11 Jun 1757 authorizing his execs. to settle any claims arising from his lawsuit with Charles Apthorp Esq. re property conveyed to him by Edmund Quincy Esq. and Charles Apthorp in the right of Samuel Turner of London, merchant. Wits: Joseph Pynchon, Thomas Hubbard and John Wendell. AWW 7 May 1763 to Nathaniel Paice, attorney for the surviving execs. Daniel Marsh, Samuel Sewall and Thomas Cushing in Boston, the relict having died. (PROB 11/887/236).

Daniel Collier, mariner, now of H.M. ship *Devonshire*, Capt. William Gordon Esq., [who died in N.Y., bachelor], dated 16 Nov 1757. My cousin Susannah Long of Greenwich, Kent, spinster, to be my legatee and exex. Wits: William Gordon, Captain, and Joseph Marriott, master. Pr. 14 Jun 1763 by named exex. (PROB 11/888/273).

James Rodgers of S.C., mariner, dated Charles Town, (blank) Jan 1762. £100 sterling each to Robert Raper, gent., and James and Sarah Lockhart of Wapping, Mddx. The residue is to be deposited in the Bank of England and the interest paid yearly to the said James and Sarah Lockhart for bringing up their children. Mr. John Beswicke of London and Mr. John Savage and Mr. Robert Raper of S.C. are to be execs. Depositions 22 Jan 1762 by William Ancrum of Charles Town, merchant, and Mr. Jackson Hale, clerk to Robert Raper Esq., that the above will is in the testator's hand. Pr. 9 Jun 1763 by John Beswicke. (PROB 11/889/303).

Thomas Smith of Penna., midshipman, now of H.M. ship *Cumberland*, Capt. William Brereton, dated 29 May 1757. All my wages etc. to my wife Mary Smith of Penna. My prize money, clothing, etc. to my friend and shipmate Samuel Cherry who is to be my exec. Wits: Edward Ashley, Nathaniel Chisholm and Benjamin Lyon. Pr. 6 Jun 1763 by named exec. (PROB 11/889/305).

Joanna Brooker of Boston, N.E., widow, dated 11 May 1759. To Charles and Thomas Wheeler of London £100 sterling. To my cousins Benjamin Alford of New London and Joanna Alford of Boston £10 sterling each. Other bequests to: my cousin Elizabeth Loring, her sister Sarah Vryland, and her son John Loring; Mrs. Margaret Stoddard, wife of Sampson Stoddard Esq. of Chelmsford, and their daughter Sarah Stoddard; Sarah Tyng, daughter of Col. Tyng of Dunstable; John Alford Tyng; Mrs. Elizabeth Waterhouse of Boston, widow; Johanna Davis, daughter of William Davis, merchant, when she is 21 or married; Mrs. Hannah Davis; Benjamin and Edward Davis, merchants; Sarah Wood, granddaughter of the late Rev. Mr. Harris of Boston, and Mary Juliana Pooring; Rev. Mr. Hugh Caner and Rev. Mr. Roger Price of Leigh, Essex, England; Mrs. Sarah Henshaw, daughter of Joshua Henshaw Esq.; Rev. Mr. Troutbeck; Mrs. Mary Juliana Auchmuty; Mrs. Christian Wainwright; William Walter of Roxbury; Henry Ewing Esq., late Naval Officer in Va., or his children. My real estate in Boston to King's College Chapel. My estate in Hartford and elsewhere in Ct. to the children of the late Edward Todd of Hartford, gent. Silvester Gardiner, Joshua Henshaw and John Winslow, shopkeeper, to be execs. Wits: Sarah Dupee, Elizabeth Allen and Benjamin Pratt. AWW 11 Aug 1763 to Edward Pearson, attorney for execs. in Boston. (PROB 11/890/370).

Ambrose Westley, [soldier of the 65th Regt. of Foot, who died in Charles Town, S.C., bachelor]. Will in the form of a letter dated St. Helier, Jersey, 19 Aug 1759, to his mother Mrs. Mary Westley at Aston Clinton, Bucks. I am much fatigued since I left you. We set out on our march through England three or four days after I got down to the Regiment. We took shipping at Southampton on 2 May and had a good voyage. We landed here on Sunday 20 May and were obliged to encamp for a month confined to a castle surrounded by the sea on all sides. I have been through several scenes of soldiership in a little time. Rum, brandy wine and cyder are cheap and plentiful but no beer is to be had. The inhabitants are mostly of French extraction so there is little English spoken but by our own Regiment. I believe it was the best day's work I have done these seven years when I enlisted. I have had a great deal of sickness which has taken off some very hearty young men and we have expected to have been attacked by the French. If I should not return, I desire you and my brother to be equal sharers of what I may be possessed of. Direct for me to Capt. Lloyd's Co. in Col. Hampton's Regiment in Jersey. Depositions 27 Oct 1763 by Mary Westley, widow, Elizabeth Westley of St. Clement Danes, Mddx., widow, and Joseph Smith of St. James, Westminster, Mddx., stationer, that the testator never returned to England after writing the above letter which is in his own hand. He died in S.C. in 1762. AWW granted same day to the mother. (PROB 11/893/492).

John Curle King of Hampton, Va., mariner, [formerly of H.M. ships *Port Royal* and *Orford*, who died in St. Martin in the Fields, Mddx., dated London 5 Nov 1763. To my mother Mary King of Hampton all my lands, houses and negroes, including my lands on Sawyer's Swamp and Blackbeard's Point in Hampton Co., with remainder to my sisters Mary and Rose King. One shilling to my brother William King. William Boyd and James Casey of Hampton, mariners, to be my execs. Wits: Robert Allen, Edward Mitchell and Thomas Douglass. Pr. 15 Nov 1763 by William Boyd. (PROB 11/893/515).

William Shearer of London, mariner, [master of the *Friendship*, who died in Boston, N.E.], dated 31 Mar 1762. My brother-in-law Mr. John Freeman of lower East Smithfield, St. Botolph, Aldgate, London, is to be my legatee and exec. Wits: Abraham Ogier, notary public, John Clement and William Comafleau. Pr. 2 Dec 1763 by named exec. (PROB 11/894/568).

1764

Thomas Robey the younger of Derby, gent., [who died in Philadelphia], dated Gravesend 7 Mar 1754. All my tenements and lands in Pinxton, Normanton and Heage, Derbys., and all my personal estate to my friend Francis Green of Clements Inn, London, gent., who is to be my executor. £500 each to my friends Francis Partridge, master of the Blue Boar Inn in Holborn, London, and William Hodgson, master of the Robin Hood Inn near Temple Bar, London. Wits: Thomas Hodgson, Robert Butler and John Dakeyne. Codicil of 29 Mar 1755 revoking the legacy to William Hodgson and bequeathing £100 to friend William Holland, coal merchant in Fetter Lane, London. Wits: Elias Pullen, David Amey and William Lance. Codicil dated Philadelphia, where I now reside, 8 Nov 1763, revoking bequest to Francis Partridge and making following additional bequests. To my friend William Whitebread Sr. of Philadelphia, innholder, 700 guineas. To my friend David McMurtrie of Philadelphia, merchant, 200 guineas. To John Reily of Philadelphia, conveyancer, 100 guineas. Wits: Thomas Paschall, John Head and Stephen Collins. Pr. 10 Apr 1764 by Francis Green. (PROB 11/898/153).

John Van Veghten of the City of Albany, now Major in the N.Y. forces, [who died in the Havannah], dated 19 May 1762. My whole estate to my wife Annatje Van Veghten who is to be my exex. Wits: Goose Van Shaick, Gerard De Peyster and John Vischer. AWW to Thomas Harris, attorney for the relict in N.Y. (PROB 11/898/158).

Robert Mackenzie, corporal of the 77th Regiment, [who died in Amboy], dated General Hospital in Amboy Barracks, 15 Sep 1762. My whole estate to Donald Mackenzie, sergeant in the said Regiment. Wits: Robert Stewart, Donald Gordon and Donald (x) McDonald. AWW 23 May 1764 to Donald Mackenzie, no exec. having been named. (PROB 11/898/189).

William Bicknell [of Annapolis, Md.], master sailmaker of H.M. ship *Richmond*, dated 19 Jan 1764. Two-thirds of my estate to my wife Ann Bicknell, inhabitant of Annapolis, and the residue to my brother Andrew Bicknell of Yeovil, Som., weaver. My effects on board this ship to my friend William Dicker. My said brother to be exec. Wits: Thomas Gibbs, purser, Stanley Douglas, Captain, and Thomas Fairbank, clerk. Pr. 22 Jun 1764 by the named exec. (PROB 11/899/212).

George Ingraham of N.E., seaman of H.M. ship *Grafton*, Capt. Hyde Parker, [but late of H.M. ship *Newcastle*], dated 9 Oct 1761. £4 sterling to Robert Curtain, seaman of H.M.S. *Grafton*. The residue to my wife Bethiah Ingraham of York, Mass., with remainder to my daughters Abigail and Mary Ingraham. Robert Smith of H.M.S. *Grafton* to be my exec. Wits: Richard Jasper and Thomas Stimpson. Pr. 28 Jun 1764 by the named exec. (PROB 11/899/229).

John Spooner of Boston, Mass., merchant, dated 11 Feb 1761. To my wife Sarah Spooner £400 current, an annuity of £120 while she nremains a widow, my chaise and horse, my negro man Prince and negro girl Venus, and household goods. My real estate to my son John Spooner who is to give security to my said wife, my friend Mr. Thomas Green and Mr. Daniel Waldo of Boston, brazier. £4,000 each to my sons William, Joshua, George and James Spooner, and £30 each to my grandsons John Jones Spooner and William Spooner. £6 each to Dr. Jonathan Mayhew and William Hooper Jr. £50 to my mother Sarah Wells. The residue to my son John. The said Thomas Green is to be guardian of my son Joshua, and he and my said wife guardians of my sons George and James. The said Thomas Green and my son John Spooner are to be execs. Wits: William Hall, Benjamin Clark and Robert Auchmuty. AWW 22 Jun 1764 to Sir William Baker, attorney for execs. in Boston. (PROB 11/899/243).

Philip Delegal, dwelling in the parish of St. Peter's Port, Guernsey, Capt. of a company in Lieut-Gen. Parsons' Regt. of Invalids now quartered in Guernsey, dated 22 Jan 1762. To my wife Eleanor Delegal living at Phillip's Bluff in S.C. my plantation there which I have already gifted to her, my son Edward and my youngest daughter Sophia. If my wife should not survive me, I bequeath £200 to my daughter Catherine, wife of Mr. Hugh Campbell of S.C., mariner. Other bequests to: my eldest son Philip Delegal of Little Ageehee, Ga., gent, and, if he be dead, to his children; my sons George and Edward Delegal of Ga., planters, to have 500 acres at Little Ageehee granted to me and my wife and now in the hands of my son Philip; my daughter Margaret, wife of (blank) of S.C., planter. My goods and effects to be sold and divided amongst my wife and my seven children. Execs: my said wife and son Philip. Wits: Andre Migault, George Hawley and Edward Knight. Pr. 14 Sep 1764 by Abraham Le Mesurier, attorney for Eleanor and Philip Delegal in Ga. (PROB 11/901/346).

1765

John Patterson Esq. of Farmington, Ct., [Capt. of the First Ct. Regt. of Foot], at present on an expedition against our northern enemies, the French, [who died in the Havannah], dated 11 May 1759. To my wife Ruth Patterson half the lot I bought of Serjeant Ebenezer Smith in the sixth division of land west of the reserved land in Farmington, my right to undivided land in Farmington, and all my personal estate, with remainder to my son John when he comes of age. To my daughter Mary, wife of John Peirce of Litchfield, half my tract in New Cambridge parish in Farmington which I bought of Aaron Aspenwell and a tract in the township of Harwington in Litchfield Co. which I bought of Joseph Curtiss. To my daughter Sarah, wife of James Lush of Farmington, the house where they now live, 5 acres of land I bought of Joseph Hart Jr., 7 acres I bought of Joseph Kellogg of New Hartford, and my right to 100 acres in the fourth allotment in the first division, west of the reserved land. To my daughter (blank), wife of Rev. Stephen Holmes of (blank) the other half of the tract I bought of Aaron Aspenwell and a negro girl Rose. To my daughter Ruth Patterson the land I now own which belonged to David Curtiss and lies west of Robert Woodruff's homelet, with the remaining part of my farm north and west. To my son John Patterson the remaining part of my farm and 5 acres in Weathersfield which I bought of Joseph Kellogg. My said wife and my son-in-law John Peirce of Litchfield to be my execs. Wits: Samuel Nevall, Timothy Pitkin and Ebenezer Smith. AWW 29 Jan 1765 to Phineas Lyman, attorney for the named execs. in Ct. (PROB 11/905/30).

James Pitkin of Hartford, Ct., [Lieut. of the First Ct. Regt. of Foot, who died in the Havannah, bachelor], dated 2 Jun 1761. To my mother Esther Pitkin my cow and the product of half my lands during her lifetime. All my lands, oxen and horse to my brother Daniel Pitkin who is to be my exec. Wits: Jonathan Stanley, James Bidwell and Elisha Pitkin. AWW 29 Jan 1765 to Phineas Lyman, attorney for the named exec. in Hartford, Ct. (PROB 11/905/30).

John Stanton Jr. of Groton, New London Co., Ct., [who died in the Havannah, dated 21 May 1762. To my wife Prudence Stanton all my personal estate until my sons come of age. To my son Samuel Stanton my homestead farm where I now dwell, bounded by the lands of William Morgan, William Williams Esq. and Jedadiah Leedes, and my silver hilted sword. My son Amos Stanton is to have a college education and £10 and a horse when he is 21. To my son Robert Stanton my 10 acres in Groton, bounded by the lands of Capt. Benjamin Adam, Joseph Colver and Jedediah Baly, and a negro boy Shoram. To my daughter Sarah Hamborough Billing my negro Tom and a mare. To mmy daughter Zerviat Fanning a negro boy called Jordan and my right of land in the New Town at Otter Creek as described in the deed executed to her by Col. John Henry Lydins of Albany. To my daughter Prudence Stanton £50 when she is 18 and my negro girl Lettice. Wits: William Williams, Joseph Williams and William Williams Jr. AWW 9 Jan 1765 to Phineas Lyman, attorney for the execs. in Ct. (PROB 11/905/34).

Isaac Thompson of New London, Ct., [Lieut. of the First Ct. Regt. of Foot, who died in the Havannah], dated 6 Jun 1761. To my brother and exec. Samuel Thompson all my lands in the township of New London (with the exception of one acre) and he is to take care of my father Mr. Isaac Thompson. To my brother Thomas Thompson one acre and part of the adjoining land belonging to the heirs of Rev. James Hillhouse which is to be laid out at my exec's. discretion. Wits: David Jewitt, Patience Jewitt and Sarah Jewitt. AWW 29 Jan 1765 to Phineas Lyman, attorney for the exec. in New London, Ct. (PROB 11/905/36).

Lachlan Shaw, [Lieut. of an Independent Company, who died in S.C.], dated Prince William parish, Indian land, S.C., 20 Feb 1761, now going on service against the Indians. All my estate in Europe to my son Lachlan and my daughter Bridget. Al my estate in America to my wife Mary and the child she carries. My said wife, James Parsons Esq. and Francis Kinloch Esq. to be my execs. Wits: James McPherson Jr. and Isaac McPherson. Deposition 6 Apr 1764 by Charles Ogilvie of Angel Court, Throgmorton Street, London, merchant, that he came to England in May 1761 after many years' residence in S.C. and knew the testator and his execs. well: the will is in the testator's hand. AWW 6 Feb 1765 to George Urquhart, attorney for the son Lachlan Shaw in Scotland, the other execs. having been cited but not appearing. (PROB 11/906/74).

Matthew Hatch of St. Leonard Eastcheap, London, [who died in Ga., bachelor], dated 26 Nov 176- (blank). To my friend Mr. Leonard Gorst my title and benefit of 50 guineas from the United Society of Blues held at the Ship tavern behind the Change, and being a free member thereof, all my estate. Wits: Henry Bell and William Dunkley Jr. AWW 12 Mar 1765 to Leonard Gorst, no executor having been named. PROB 11/907/101).

Charles Lake, Rector of St. James' parish, Ann Arundell Co., Md., dated 2 Nov 1763. My books and papers to Rev. Mr. Samuel Keene who is to be my exec. Wits: Thomas Deale, Hesther (x) Page and Samuel Sprawl. AWW 3 Apr 1765 to Messenger Monsey, doctor of physick, attorney for named exec. in Md. (PROB 11/908/148).

Thomas Saunders [of Newport, R.I.] of H.M. ship *Guernsey*, dated 7 Feb 1761. My whole estate to my friend Edward Wright, sergeant in H.M. Regt. of Foot in Gibraltar, who is to be my exec. Wits: Henry Jarmon and John Scott. AWW 6 Apr 1765 to Clark Gayton Esq., attorney for the exec. in Gibraltar. (PROB 11/908/158).

William Jones, now purser of H.M. ship *Coventry*, at present residing in N.Y.C., [and who died there], dated with codicil of same date N.Y.C. 6 Nov 1764. To my wife Rachel all monies in the hands of my agent Richard Kee of Tower Hill, London. To Dr. Peter Blair, surgeon of the said ship, £50. The residue of my estate to my brothers Adam, Theophilus and Deering Jones, my sisters Jane and Deborah, and my cousins John and William Wetherall and Mary and Eleanor Tyrell. My said wife to be exex. Wits: Peter Blair, James Smith, ----- Kempe and Thomas Bulbrook. Pr. 18 Jly 1765 by the relict. (PROB 11/910/261).

1766

Nicholas Baker of St. George's, Maryland, [widower], dated 28 Feb 1753. My whole estate consisting of 200 acres called Nicholas Baker's Choice in the Rich Bottom, now in the possession of John Taylor of St. George's, to my brother John Baker of Grays Inn Lane, St. Andrew, Holborn, London, gardener, with remainder to my sister Elizabeth Baker of the same. Wits: James Hugh, John Willson and Mary Willson. AWW 7 Jan 1766 to the sister Elizabeth, now wife of George Pell, no exec. having been named and the brother having died. (PROB 11/915/3).

William Goldsborough of Talbot County, Md., gent., dated 15 May 1750. My plantation in Island Creek, Talbot Co., to my wife Henrietta Maria Goldsborough during her lifetime with remainder to my nephew Greenbury Goldsborough, son of my brother John Goldsborough, and he is also to have my negro men Cato, Liverpool and Sparrow, my negro woman Sabina and her mulatto daughter Flora. To my nieces Mary and Ann Money, daughters of my late sister Mary Money, £20 sterling each. A mourning ring to my brothers Robert, Nicholas, Charles and John Goldsborough To my niece Caroline Goldsborough, daughter of my lately deceased brother Howes Goldsborough, £30 sterling when she is 16. To my son-in-law Thomas Robins a tract of 621 acres near Choptank Bridge in Dorchester Co. called Goldsborough lately surveyed to me. £100 sterling to my daughter-in-law Elizabeth Robins. £10 sterling each to my daughter-in-law Anna Maria Holliday and to Margaret, Henrietta Maria and Susanna Robins. The residue to my said wife who is to be my exex. Wits: William Thomas, Robert Harwood, Jacob Hindman, Tristram Thomas and Edward Knott. AWW 2 Jan 1766 to William Anderson, attorney for the relict in Md. (PROB 11/915/15).

Giles Phillipps Esq. of Ipswich, Suff., [but late of Pensacola, W. Fla.], dated 28 Sep 1764. My 10,000 acres in W. Fla. lately granted to me by the King to my wife Elizabeth Phillipps during her lifetime and then to my children, with remainder to my sister Joanna Preston, widow. My wife to be my exex. Wits: Thomas Crawley, John Page and John Brown. Pr. 24 Jan 1766 by the relict. (PROB 11/915/30).

Thomas Reade Rootes of Va., merchant, at present residing in [St. Faith's], London, dated 10 Feb 1766. All my estate in Va. to my wife Martha Reade during her lifetime and then to my son Thomas Reade Rootes to whom my said wife is to be guardian during his minority. I authorise John Hyndman of London, merchant, to settle my long and intricate account with Lyonel Lyde. The said Hyndman and John Smith of Mddx. Co., Va., are to be my execs. Wits: Lucy Paplay(?), John Collier and Charles Palmer. Pr. 21 Mar 1766 by John Hyndman. (PROB 11/917/116). Further grant in Mar 1767 to exec. John Smith.

Philip Brooks in Capt. Hellman's company of the 22nd Regt. of Foot, [who died in Mobile, W. Fla., bachelor], dated 15 Nov 1764. My whole estate to my friend and kinsman Robert Carson, corporal in the said Regt. Wits: Collin Robinson and William Starratt. AWW 30 Apr 1766 to Jane, wife of John Drummon, formerly Jane Irvine, adx. to the universal legatee Robert Carson deceased. (PROB 11/917/129).

Robert Carson, sergeant in Capt. John Campbell's company of the 22nd Regt. of Foot, [who died in Mobile, W. Fla., bachelor], dated 21 Feb 1765. My whole estate to my friend Jerret Irvine. Wits: Robert Taylor, William Jenkins and Samuel Jenner, Lieut. AWW 30 Apr 1766 to Jane Drummon, formerly Irvine, wife of John Drummon, and adx. of Jerrett Irvine deceased. (PROB 11/917/133).

Philemon Charles Blake of Queen Anne Co., Md., dated 13 Jan 1753. To my wife Sarah Blake the choice of any one of my tracts of land. To my son Philemon Charles Blake my plantation, originally consisting of several tracts, but lately resurveyed to my late father Mr. Charles Blake and called Blakeford, and two tracts called Lloyd's Meadows given to me by my aunt Alice Lloyd which lie near the head of Wye River. My said son is to convey to my son Charles Blake the land on Cosica Creek called Bennett's Regulation. A mourning suit and £10 current to Rev. Mr. James Bedwall. The residue to my four children Henrietta Maria, Philemon Charles, Elizabeth and Charles Blake. My wife is to be my exex. Wits: Susannah Tilghman, Juliana Carroll and Edward Neale. AWW 3 May 1766 to William Anderson, attorney for the relict in Queen Anne Co. (PROB 11/918/168).

Ambrose Bisaker, corporal in Capt. John Farmer's company of the 22nd Regiment of Foot, [who died in W. Fla., bachelor], dated 3 Feb 1765. My whole estate to my friend William Chipman who is to be my exec. Wits: Robert Tayler, William Collyar and Robert Lindsay, Lieut. Pr. 13 Jun 1766 by named exec. (PROB 11/919/212).

Arthur Dobbs Esq. of Brunswick, New Hanover Co., Governor of N.C., dated 31 Aug 1763. £100 to poor housekeepers of Ballymure and Kilroot, Co. Antrim, Ireland, and £100 to poor housekeepers of Carrickfergus, Ireland. I confirm the settlement I made on my son Conway Richard Dobbs on his marriage in Jly 1749 in which was included the several fortunes to my younger children. To my younger son Edward Brice Dobbs a sum of not more than £1,000 as indicated in my marriage settlement on my marriage to my first wife. To my wife Justina Dobbs all my slaves and moveables and the interest from my lands called Tower Hill in Johnston Co. £20 sterling to my brother Dr. Richard Dobbs. The residue to my son Conway Richard Dobbs. My said wife and two sons to be execs. Wits: John Hasell, Lewis De Rosset and John Sampson. Pr. 9 Jun 1766 by Conway Richard Dobbs. (PROB 11/919/220).

Samuel Eveleigh, formerly of Charles Town, S.C., merchant but now residing in Bristol, dated 20 Jun 1764. Bequests to: my brother-in-law George Eveleigh, his wife Elizabeth, and their children John, Elizabeth, Samuel, Thomas, Catherine and Ann Eveleigh; my son George Eveleigh, apprenticed to Mr. Thomas Pennington; Elizabeth, relict of Henry Newman of Arundel, Sussex; Mrs. Grace Foster, daughter of Mr. Farr, innkeeper of Arundel deceased; Mr. Hull of New Sarum, Wiltshire. Residue, including estate and slaves in Charles Town, 300 acres on Combaliel and 900 acres of marsh land adjoining, to my son Nicholas Eveleigh. Execs: Sir William Baker, merchant and alderman of London; George Austin Esq., merchant, late of Charles Town but now in England; Mr. Benjamin Stead, merchant, late of Charles Town but now in England; and my brother-in-law George Eveleigh. My said execs. are to be guardians of my children Nicholas and George Eveleigh. Wits: Thomas Pennington, Philip Harris and Abraham Biggs. AWW 30 Oct 1766 to the son Nicholas Eveleigh, the named execs. renouncing. PROB 11/922/369).

Thomas Whitehurst [of Brunswick, N.C., bachelor], Lieut. in the Royal Navy, dated 22 Mar 1765. To William Grinfill Lobb, youngest son of Jacob Lobb Esq., commander of H.M. sloop Viper, £50 which is in the hands of my agent Mr. George Marsh of Savage Gardens, Tower Hill, London. All my lands known as Styles Copp, six miles from Stafford in England, and subject to a lease to my uncle John Whitehurst, to my sister Ann Whitehurst who is to be exec. with the said Jacob Lobb. Wits: G. Eustace, Thomas Cobham and Thomas McGwire. Pr. 7 Oct 1766 by Ann Whitehurst. (PROB 11/923/391).

Simon Amory of Pensacola, W. Fla., gent., dated 28 Aug 1765. A guinea each to my brother Thomas Amory and Mary his wife, and my nephew John Amory and his wife. My niece Mary Paradise is to have two shillings a week to a total of £10. To Rev. Mr. Warner of

Taunton, Som., £10 for the good of the church. Five guineas each to Edmund Rush Wegg, H.M. Attorney-General, and Thomas Hardy, his clerk. The residue to my nephews and nieces Samuel, Mary, Ann, Henry and Thomas Amory. The said Edmund Rush Wegg and my brother Thomas Amory to be my execs. Wits: Patrick Reily, John Watts and David Ross. Letter dated Pensacola 4 Oct 1765 from Edmund Rush Wegg to Rev. Thomas Amory informing him of his brother's death there on 31 Aug 1765. Pensacola has been this summer fatal to many of its inhabitants. The gentleman who delivers this is William Amory, late of R.I, who came hither upon the invitation of your brother but, his expectations being frustrated, he is determined to visit you. Deposition 8 Nov 1766 by Rev. Thomas Amory of St. Michael Bassishaw, London, brother of the testator, that he received the above letter last July. Pr. 20 Nov 1766 by Rev. Thomas Amory. (PROB 11/923/395).

Henry Bouquet Esq., Brig-Gen. of H.M. Forces and Lieut-Col. of the Royal American Regiment, [who died in N.A.], dated Philadelphia 25 Jun 1765. £40 to the hospital in Philadelphia. To my friend Mr. Willing five tracts of 200 acres each in Trough Creek Valley, Md. To John Schneider, the boy who is bound to me, when he comes of age, £50 current to be paid by Col. Haldimand. All my estate in Europe to my father, if he be alive at my death; if not, to Col. Lewis Bouquet. My estate in America consisting of a farm in Frederick Co., Md., called the Long Meadow and the mill thereon, the deeds of which are in the possession of Hugh Roberts, is to be sold and the proceeds remitted to my friend and exec. Col. Frederick Haldimand. Wits: Benjamin Chew, John Turner and Thomas Turner. Pr. 13 Nov 1766 by the named exec. (PROB 11/923/398).

William Hewitt, surgeon and Ensign of the 28th Regt. of Foot, now residing in Charles Town, S.C., [and who died there, bachelor], dated 16 Feb 1763. Five guineas for a ring to Col. Welch and Capt. Arthur Price. Ten guineas to Dr. Lionel Chalmers. The residue to my brother Thomas Hewitt of Cork, Ireland, merchant, with remainder to his eldest son. The said Arthur Price and Lionel Chalmers to be execs. Wits: James Reid and John Remington. AWW 22 Dec 1766 to John Cole, attorney for the brother Thomas Hewitt in Cork, Ireland, the other execs. renouncing. (PROB 11/924/454).

1767

John Willett Esq., [formerly of St. Christopher's], of N.Y.C., merchant, [but late of St. Croix in W.I.], undated. My whole estate to my wife Frances Willett who is to be my exex. Wits: Charles Crooke, Andrew Barclay and Peter Hill. Pr. 9 Jan 1767 by the relict. (PROB 11/925/31).

Hector Beringer De Beaufain Esq. [of Charles Town, S.C.], dated 17 Oct 1766. £500 sterling each to my friends Col. John Schutz, Peter Simond of London, and George Schutz, son of Augustus Schutz. £500 current, my books and my share in the Charles Town Library Society to my friend David Rhind of Charles Town. £500 current and my house to the poor of both parishes of Charles Town. My pew in St. Michael's church to the poor of that parish. If William Dockwra is my clerk when I die he is to have £100 current. The residue of my estate to (blank) Beaufain, the only surviving son of my late brother, and he is to pay an annuity of £50 to my sister Cladie (*sic*) de Beaufain. George Schutz is to be my exec. for England and David Rhind for S.C. Pr. 10 Feb 1767 by George Schutz Esq. (PROB 11/925/36).

Francina Augustina Cheston of Kent Co., Md., widow, dated 3 Nov 1765. To my children James, Daniel and Fanny Cheston my silver plate, etc. My brother-in-law John Brice Esq. and my sister Brice are to be guardians of my said daughter, and my son William Stephenson guardian of my two sons. The residue to the said William Stephenson who is to be my exec. Wits: Thomas Ringold and Benjamin Binney. Pr. 10 Feb 1767 by the named exec. (PROB 11/925/39).

William Temple of King William Co., Va., but now resident in Bristol, dated 15 Mar 1763. Mr. John Snow of Bristol, merchant, and my brother Mr. Liston Temple of King William Co., Va., to be my execs. in trust. My estate in Great Britain to the said John Snow who is to remit the surplus to my said brother. Wits: Thomas Cocking, Young Green, William Spicer, John Scott and Ann Wall. Pr. 2 May 1767 by John Snow. (PROB 11/929/199).

William Billings, surgeon [of H.M. ship *Eolus* who died in Pensacola, W. Fla.], dated 28 Mar 1764. £300 in stocks and all other estate to John Billings, son of George Billings, upholder and broker in the Strand, London. The said George Billings to be my exec. Wits: James Caskie and James Turner. Pr. 2 June 1767 by George Billings, uncle of the testator. (PROB 11/929/206).

John Hawkins of St. Anne's, (Limehouse), Mddx., mariner [of H.M. ship *Essex* but late of H.M. ship *Juno*, who died in N.Y. Hospital], dated 13 Sep 1746. My whole estate to my wife Sarah Hawkins who is to be my exex. Wits: Joseph Hester, notary public, and William Woolgar, his servant. Pr. 30 Jun 1767 by the relict. (PROB 11/929/224).

Thomas Poizer, soldier in Capt. Campbell's company of the 22nd Regt. of Foot, [who died in in Mobile, W. Fla., bachelor], dated 24 May 1764. My whole estate to nurse Elizabeth Chipman of the said Regt. for the care and affection she has shown me, and she is to be my exex. Wits: Charles Parson, William Stairatt and John Vickers, Lieut. Pr. 13 Jun 1767 by Elizabeth, wife of William Chipman. (PROB 11/929/237).

Alexander Reade of Mddx. Co., Va., dated 11 Dec 1759. My houses and lots in Urbania which I bought of Samuel Price, the lots I bought of Mr. Ralph Wormeley, my books, medicines and utensils are to be sold and the proceeds used for the purchase of lands and negroes. To my mother Mrs. Elizabeth Foster an annuity of £10 sterling and £30. To my son John Reade my houses in Bedford, England. To my wife my negroes Lucy, Young George, Boy Peter and Sam. To my apprentice John Davise £10 for his faithful services. The lands I bought of John Davise and Col. Lewis Burwell are to be kept together. The residue of my estate is to be divided between my wife and my sons John and Charles who are to be sent to college. Ralph Wormeley Esq., Christopher Robinson Esq. and Maj. Francis Tompkies are to be execs. for Va. and Messrs. Freeston and Thornborough of London for Great Britain. Wits: John Gordon, William Moulson and Joseph Eagleston Jr. Pr. Va. 1 Jan 1760. Pr. London 15 Jly 1767 by the surviving exec. George Thornburgh, mistakenly wrought in the will as Thornborough. (PROB 11/930/281).

John Wardrop of Calvert Co., Md., merchant, [but late of All Hallows Staining, London], dated 22 Sep 1758. To my nephew Andrew Whyte my house in Lower Marlborough with stock, cattle, horses and negroes and £100 sterling. To my sister Jean Kelley an annuity of £20 sterling until her three youngest children come of age. To John and Jean Holden near Dundee, (Scotland), an annuity of £20 sterling. I give to my nephews and niece Alexander, Andrew and Jean Summers their bond to me of 10 Dec 1756. To Mrs. Ann Russell, wife of my friend James Russell, £100 sterling. To Mrs. Margaret Dedrusina £250 sterling. To Mrs. Sarah Clarke £250 sterling. To Miss Ann and Miss Helen Russell £250 sterling each when they come of age or are married. To Mr. Charles Grahame, my attorney in Md., my mulatto fellow William and half my sloop *Betsey* for him to buy a slave for his daughter Agenath Grahame. My friend Mr. James Russell of London to be exec. Wits: Hensey Johns, Samuel Galloway and Hancock Lee. Pr. 1 Jly 1767 by named exec. (PROB 11/931/288).

John Knolles of Bath, Som., apothecary, intending shortly to depart on a voyage to the island of Guadeloupe, W.I., as assistant apothecary at the public hospital there, [surgeon's mate of W. Fla. Hospital], dated 10 Dec 1761. My whole estate to William Street of Bath, apothecary, who is to be my exec. and trustee for my mother Elizabeth Knolles. Wits: John Chapman, Mayor of Bath, and John Burges, attorney at law in Bath. Pr. 2 Sep 1767 by the named exec. (PROB 11/932/344).

Raymond Calvert of Charles Town, S.C., dated 24 Oct 1766. My whole estate to my friend Emanuel Reller who is to be my exec. Wits: Lewis Plancke, Mathew Burnet and James Tranchpeire. Pr. 22 Aug 1767 by named exec. (PROB 11/931/302).

John Dalrymple Esq. [of Brunswick Co., N.C., reduced Capt. of Sir William Pepperell's Regt. of Foot], second lawful son of Sir John Dalrymple of Courland, Baronet of Scotland, dated 25 Feb 1743. My whole estate to my wife Martha Dalrymple with remainder to Hon. Roger Moore Esq. and my brothers and sisters William, Joseph, John and Samuel Watters, Sarah Lillington and Elizabeth Howes. My plantation of Spring Gardens is to be appraised and those of the name of Watters, beginning with the eldest, are to have the first offer of buying it. My said wife, Hon. Roger Moore, William and Joseph Watters are to be execs. AWW 8 Oct 1767, limited to the recovery of sums due from Richard Crosdill of Petty France, Westminster, to Alexander Duncan of Wilmington, N.C., attorney for the relict and only surviving exec. in Brunswick. (PROB 11/932/369).

Henry Watson of [St. George's, Prince George Co.], Md., gent, now residing in London, dated 17 Mar 1736. To my wife Lucy Watson during her lifetime all my personal estate, a dwelling house and lands in Md. called the Vineyard and Flint's Discovery of 200 acres which I bought of John Flint, and 367 acres in Prince William Co., Va., on the Woolshop Branch which I bought of William Scott, with remainder to my eldest son. £100 sterling to my sisters Anne, wife of John Tinney, and Henrietta Watson. £30 sterling to John Belt Sr. of Md. My execs. to be John Belt Jr. of Md., Peter Wright of London, sugar refiner, and Peter Oyles of Grays Inn, London, Cursitor in Chancery. Wits: Thomas Osborne Jr., James Jones and John Evans. AWW 7 Nov 1767 to the son John Watson, the relict and Peter Wright having died and John Belt not appearing. (PROB 11/934/433).

Francis Robins of Exeter, Devon, serge maker, dated 7 May 1764. Two guineas each to my brother John Robins of Kingston, (Devon), and my sister Elizabeth Frende. A silver cup to my niece Elizabeth Robins. One guinea to my niece Agnes Hurford. Five guineas to my cousin Francis Robins, son of my late brother Francis Robins of Boston, America, when he is 21. £10 to my sister Agnes, wife of Obidiah Creswell. I confirm the agreement whereby my sister

Meriam Robins is to receive £8 a year. To my daughter Rebecca Robins 600 guineas when she is ·21. My wife Rebecca is to have my house during her lifetime and £20, and she, Samuel Luscombe of Exeter, apothecary, Samuel Luscombe Jr. of the same, surgeon, and George Wrideat of the same, timber merchant, are to be my execs. Wits: Mary Kingdon, William Williams and James Bisgood. Pr. 7 Dec 1767. (PROB 11/934/460).

1768

William Grover Esq. of Reading, Berks., [late Chief Justice of E. Fla., who died at sea], dated 7 Jan 1766. My whole estate to my son John Grover of King's College, Cambridge, with remainder to my half-brother John Potenger. My said son to be exec. Wits: Ann Rafugeau, Sophia Stumbels and Bezaleel Stumbels. Pr. 23 Jan 1768 by the son. (PROB 11/935/15).

Adam Hill of Talbot Co., Md, mariner, dated 2 Mar 1767. To my mother Margaret Ramsay of Ayr, Scotland, the interest on £500 sterling in annual payments during her lifetime. To my natural son Adam Hill in London the annual interest on £200 sterling during his minority and £100 when he is 21 to put him into business. To my niece Eleanora Campbell of London silver plate etc. The residue to the children of my sister Elizabeth Donald of Ayr. My friends William Campbell of London and Ebenezer Mackie and Robert Campbell of Md. to be execs. Wits: John Crawford, Thomas Brereton and Patrick McCaull. Pr. 14 Mar 1768 by William Campbell. (PROB 11/937/111).

Thomas Nox, master of H.M. sloop *Hornet*, Capt. Jeremiah Morgan, [who died in Brunswick, N.C.], dated 28 Sep 1767. My whole estate to my cousins Michael Cashio Howard and Patrick Howard, both of Galloway, Scotland, but late living in Barge Yard, Bucklersbury, London, and they are to be my execs. Wits: John Randle, Thomas Smith and Jeremiah Cushing. Codicil of 28 Oct 1767 with further bequests to Mr. John Randle, Alexander Fraisure, John Randle Jr. and Mary Randle. Wits: Isaiah Pawisol, John Bacon and Hannah Pawisol. AWW 17 Mar 1768 to Thomas Howard, attorney for Michael Cashio Howard in Douai, Flanders, and Patrick Howard in Angiers, France. (PROB 11/937/120).

Eubule Ormsby, Ensign in Gen. Otway's Regt. of Foot, [Lieut. of the 35th Regt. who died in W. Fla.], dated 23 Feb 1756. To my three sisters Rebecca and Mary Ormsby and Catherine Stuart my interest in leasehold lands in Ballaghatrellick, Co. Sligo, (Ireland). My debts in Dublin are to be paid including six guineas to Robin Ormsby, four guineas to Gilbert Ormsby and two guineas to William Stennon. To my brothers George and John Ormsby five shillings each. My sister Mary Ormsby is to be my exex. Wits: George Robinson and James Lawler. Pr. 2 Jun 1768 by exex. (PROB 11/940/252).

Mary Dryden, widow of Adam Dryden of St. Martin in the Fields, Mddx., staymaker, dated 29 Apr 1760. Mr. John Greenough, whose father kept the Crown Inn in Wood Street, London, is to pay £100 to my son-in-law James Dryden of Charleston, S.C., and Eleanor his wife or, if they be dead, to their children. Other bequests to: Elizabeth Wills, sister of the said James Dryden, at boarding school in Salisbury, (Wilts.); my niece Mary Skilbeck to have the goods received by my brother John Skilbeck; Mordecai Reader of Hull, (Yorks.), plateworker; John West of St. Paul, Covent Garden, Mddx., peruke maker, and his sister Elizabeth; the household goods I left at Hull in the care of my sister Almand to her daughter Mary. The residue to my brother John Skilbeck of Hull who is to pay interest during her life to my sister Elizabeth Thompson. Execs. my said brother John Skilbeck and my goddaughter Mary Skilbeck. Wits: Mary Ealand and John Lane. Pr. 9 July 1768 by named execs. (PROB 11/940/275).

Henry Farrant, [formerly of Lanton, N'land], of Schenectady, Albany Co., N.Y., [Lieut. of a N.Y. Independent company under Capt. John Gordon], dated 22 Mar 1767. To my brother Godfrey Lee Farrant twenty shillings sterling. To my nephew Henry Jordice all my real estate on the east side of Hudson River and north side of Batton Kill, N.Y. My personal estate to Elizabeth Delemont of Schenectady. The residue to my wife Mary Farrant. Execs: John Sanders Esq. of Schenectady and John Steel Esq. of the Royal Exchange Assurance Office in London. Wits: Caleb Beck, Abraham Delemont and Nicholas Vedder. Pr. 12 Jly 1768 by John Steel. (PROB 11/940/277).

Edward Merrefield of Germantown, Philadelphia, innholder, dated 3 Nov 1766. To my sons Robert and John Merrefield one shilling each. The residue in this province to my wife Sarah. To my youngest son Vernon Merrefield, now residing in England, and to my said wife all my estate in England bequeathed to me by the will of my late brother Robert Merrefield. My friend Benjamin Goudy of Philadelphia and my said youngest son to be execs. Wits: James Dove, Edward Conner and Christian Lehman. Pr. 4 Jly 1768 by Vernon Merrefield. (PROB 11/941/289).

Francis Borland Esq. of Boston, Mass., dated 7 Mar 1763. To my wife Phebe Borland £1,000 sterling, my slaves, the household goods she brought to our marriage, and the use of my mansion house while she remains a widow. To my son Francis Lindall Borland, who has been long absent and I fear may be dead, all my lands in Billerica and Stourbridge, a messuage in Milk Street, Boston, where Joseph Calef now lives, and £1,000 current. £1,500 current to the children of my daughter Jane Winthrop. £7 each to Rev. Dr. Joseph Sewall and Rev. Mr. Alexander Cumming. The residue to my son John Borland who is to be exec. with my said wife. Wits: Joseph Russell, Lydia Russell and Oxenbridge Thatcher. AWW 20 Oct 1768 to William Mills, Edward Brice and Edward Wheeler, attorneys for the execs. in Boston. (PROB 11/942/370).

Peter Randolph Esq. of Chatsworth, Henrico Co., Va., [Surveyor-General of Customs for the Middle Western District of America], dated 4 May 1767. To my wife Lucy my plantation known as Chatsworth with slaves, horses and stock, my household goods and chariot during her lifetime and £50 sterling. To my son William my lands in Chesterfield Co. called Skin Quarter on Stanton River which I purchased of Robert Munford. To my son Beverley a tract in Cumberland Co. known as the Fork and two tracts of 1,300 acres on Roanoke River which I purchased of Thomas Nash. To my son Robert three tracts totalling 3,000 acres, i.e. lands on Bannister River purchased of Col. Bannister, lands on Dan River purchased of Thomas Douglas, and lands on Stanton River purchased of Hempton Wade. To my daughter Ann Fitzhugh £350 current. To my said three sons my two acres in Chesterfield opposite Chatsworth. The residue to my said son William. Col. Archibald Cary, Richard Randolph, John Wayles and Seth Ward Sr. to be execs. AWW 21 Oct 1768 to William Robertson Lidderdale, attorney for named execs. in Va. (PROB 11/943/393).

Thomas Willett of N.Y.C., merchant, being speedily to depart beyond sea, dated 26 Dec 1766. All my estate is to be sold and the proceeds divided between my wife Elizabeth and my son John and his sisters. My said wife and son, my sons-in-law Christopher Billop and Thomas Miller, and my friend Joseph Royal to be execs. Wits: George Ludlow, James A. Stewart and John Vanderbilk. Pr. 20 Oct 1768 by the son John Willett. (PROB 11/943/399).

Thomas Palmer of St. John's, King William Co., Va., dated 2 Sep 1752. To my son John Palmer 250 acres of land, part of a tract (described) where my mother-in-law Martha Whitworth now lives, my negro called Dick, a ewe and a lamb. To my son Thomas Palmer the plantation where he now lives with 120 acres (described) and my negro wench Judy. To my son Martin Palmer the plantation where he now lives with 100 acres (described). To my daughter Elizabeth Palmer three negro children January, Lot and Richard. To my son Daniel Palmer the residue of land adjoining my son John's. The residue of my estate to my wife Mary Palmer who is to be exec. with my son Nicholas Palmer. Wits: William Neale, Thomas Lipscomb and John Ellett. Pr. 3 Nov 1768 by Nicholas Palmer. (PROB 11/943/423).

Sir William Pepperell of Kittery, York Co., Mass., dated 1 Jan 1759. To my wife Mary the income from half my estate, and four of my negroes, my chariot and chaise and £1,000 sterling to be paid out of money in the hands of William Baker Esq. in London. I forgive my son-in-law Nathaniel Sparhawk Esq. the debt which he and his late partner Benjamin Colman owe me. My daughter Elizabeth Sparhawk and her children are to be supported as my execs. think fit, and she is empowered to dispose by her will of my farm in the upper parish of York called Scotland. To my grandson Nathaniel Sparhawk Jr. when he is 21 the lands in York Co. which I purchased of my son-in-law Nathaniel Sparhawk Sr., with remainder to the other children of my daughter Elizabeth Sparhawk. To my grandson Samuel Hirst Sparhawk, when he is 21, my house and land at Portsmouth and my farm at Newington, N.H., my farm at Lower Ferry in York where Daniel Crosby lives, and two acres at Kittery Point which I purchased of Thomas Allen and where he now lives. To my grandson Andrew Pepperell Sparhawk the new house I built for my deceased son Andrew Pepperell in Kittery and land at Sturgeon Creek in Kittery which I bought of Charles Frost, with remainder to my grandson William Pepperell Sparhawk. To my granddaughter whom I call Mary Pepperell Sparhawk, when she is 21, the house and land in Kittery I purchased of William and Henry Barter, and all my lands in Boston and Rutland in Worcester Co. To my sister Mary Prescot £30 sterling for mourning. I forgive my sister Margery Gunnison what she owes me and give her £20 sterling for mourning. To my sister Miriam Tyler my right to the house in Boston where she lives. To my sister Jane Tyler £20 sterling for mourning. I forgive my sister Dorothy Newmarch all that her husband Joseph Newmarch Esq. owes me. Other bequests to the following kinsfolk: John and Andrew Philips; Sarah Frost, my late brother's eldest daughter, and Joanna Frost, widow of Charles Frost Esq.; Capt. William Frost, his brother Andrew Pepperell Frost, and his sister Sarah Blunt; John Frost Esq.; the children of the late Margery Wentworth who was wife of Capt. William Wentworth; Jane Watkins, widow of Capt. Andrew Watkins; the children of the late Joel Whittemore; William Whittemore; the children of the late Margery Gerrish; the children of the late Elizabeth Hale; John Watkins; Mary, wife of Edmond Moody; and Dorothy, widow of Davy Pitman. The will makes provision for his Sparhawk heirs to change their name to Pepperell. My said wife and my friends Jeremiah Moulton Jr., Esq., Sheriff of York Co., and Mr. Benjamin Greenleaf of Kittery, merchant, to be execs. Wits: Joseph Decker, John Underwood, George Moody and Benjamin Parker Jr. Codicil of 4 Jly 1759 with additional witness Jeremiah Bragdon. Pr. 10 Nov 1768 by the grandson William Pepperell Esq., formerly William Pepperell Sparhawk. (PROB 11/943/424).

Elizabeth Ross of Elizabeth City Co., Va., (widow of Francis Ross), dated 20 Sep 1756. To my son-in-law Anthony Hawkins my right to a legacy left to me by the will of (my uncle) John Mallory in England. (See will proved in Dec 1752). The said Anthony Hawkins is to pay my daughter Ann Bean £40 current and my grandson Mallory Ross £30 current when he is 21. My negro woman Jean to the said Anthony Hawkins who is to be my exec. Wits: Curle Tucker, Thomas Dixon and Owen Dailey. Pr. 28 Nov 1768 by the named exec. (PROB 11/944/429).

Samuel Tarry of Rawleigh, Amelia Co., [of Mecklenburgh Co.], Va., dated 10 Jun 1757. To my daughters Frances, Mary and Rebecca Tarry £500 sterling each, when they are of age or married, from my lands in Cambs. and Hunts. in England which were devised to me by the will of my mother Mrs. Frances Tarry. I have ordered a conveyance of the said lands from Mr. Peter Sainthill, now of London, by power of attorney given to Mr. Christopher Smith, now in London, merchant. To my son George Tarry I give the land where I now live and half my lands in England when he comes of age. The other half of the said lands I give to my son Edward Tarry with my lands on the other side of Flat Creek. To my nephew John Pinnock £100 current when he is 21. If I should die before my son George comes of age, I ask that Mr. Thomas Yuille will take him and my son Edward to be maintained. My brother Edward Booker, Richard Booker Jr. and Edward Booker (sons of George Booker), and Abraham Green to be execs. Wits: Martha Bowker and Harman Thompson. AWW 22 Dec 1768 to John Tabby of Petersburgh, Va., attorney for the creditors Peter Johnston and Thomas Yuille in Va., the named execs. Edward, Richard and Edward Booker and the relict all having died. (PROB 11/944/469).

1769

Ezekiel David of London, merchant, about to proceed on a voyage to S.C. [of Charles Town, S.C.], dated 29 Mar 1766. My whole estate to Mr. Francis Magnus of London, merchant, who is to be exec. with Mr. Edward Brice of London, merchant. Wits: William Robe,

Thomas Read and James Withers. Pr. 16 Feb 1769 by Edward Brice. (PROB 11/945/41).

John McCrackan of Old Glenluce, Galloway, Scotland, [who died in New Haven, N.E.], dated 16 Jly 1763. My whole estate to my brothers Alexander, James and William and my sister Grisel Mc-Crackan. My father Andrew McCrackan in Barnsalie and my uncle James McDoul in the Strand, London, to be my execs. Wits: Samuel Bagnall and William Cockburn. Pr. 9 Feb 1769 by James McDouall. (PROB 11/946/56).

William Richardson Esq. of Kensington, Mddx., [but late of Cross Oak, Wilts., [who died in Pensacola, W. Fla.], dated 29 Aug 1760. £1,000 to my brother-in-law Rev. William Robinson. £100 each to Mr. John Gaspard Ringmacher of London, merchant, Mr. Samuel Commeline and Mr. Thomas Athawes of Cordwainers' Hall, London, gents. Twenty guineas each for mourning to Robert Jones Esq. of London, Philip de la Tour of London, doctor of physick, and Thomas Lloyd Esq. of James Street, Mddx. £30 to the Scotch Corporation in Blackfriars, London. My execs. in trust are to be the said Commeline and Athawes who are to invest the residue of my personal estate for the benefit of my wife, my sister Mary, and the said William Robinson. Wits: Edward Athawes Jr., Christopher Coleman, servant to Mr. Richardson, and Samuel Hains. AWW to the sister Mary, wife of Rev. William Robinson, the exec. Thomas Athawes having died, and the exec. Samuel Commeline renouncing. Further grants in 1794 & 1828. (PROB 11/946/62).

Charles Pinckney Esq. of Charles Town, S.C., dated 4 Jun 1751. To be buried in Charles Town near my mother and father and a gravestone to be inscribed. Principal bequests to: my brother Maj. William Pinckney, his wife and children; my friend William Bull; Mrs. Sarah Bartlet of London, widow, sister of my deceased wife, to be paid from my plantation Pinckneys Plains near Beech Hill; Mary Bartlet, my wife's niece; my nephew Charles Pinckney; my (now) wife Elizabeth, daughter of Hon. George Lucas, late Lieut-Gov. of Antigua; our daughter Harriet; our son Thomas; my plantation called Bellmount and house in Colleton Square to my wife during her lifetime; my son Charles Cotesworth Pinckney. My wife and William Bull Jr. to be guardians of my children. Wits: John Cleland, Alexander Vander Dusen and Alexander Gorden. Codicils of 12 Jly 1752 and 13 February 1756 (now resident in Ripley, Sy.). My uncle Richard Pinckney of Bishop Auckland, Durham, who died about 1726, was seized of estate there which descended to my eldest brother Thomas Pinckney who died in 1733 intestate and without issue; his estate descended to me but I did not return to England until 1 May 1753. Second codicil witnessed by George Morley, James Abercromby and Thomas Drayton. On 28 November 1758 George Morley of Somerset House, Strand, London, and John Chatfield of Cliffords Inn, gent., testified to the authenticity of the codicils. Proved 18 Mar 1769 by the son Charles Cotesworth Pinckney. (PROB 11/947/100).

William Russell Esq. of Savannah, Ga., now residing in Prescot Street, Goodmans Fields, [Whitechapel], Mddx., dated 21 Feb 1768. To my wife Jane Russell, now with me in England, my estate in Ga. including Lot. No. 6 in Jekyl Tything, Derby Ward, Savannah, a five acre lot in the same, and a tract of 700 acres in the south-east of the town, during her lifetime. Thereafter my said estate is to be sold by my execs. in trust Francis Harris, Henry Yonge, John Smith and Noble Wimberly Jones of Savannah, Esqs., and Mr. Joseph Clay of the same, merchant, for the benefit of the following: Joseph Clay, son of the said Joseph; Hannah Hunter, daughter of Dr. Joseph Hunter, formerly of Savannah; William Galache, son of the late James Galache of Savannah, gunsmith; and John Galache, son of John Galache, late of Savannah, carpenter. To the said Anna (*sic*) Hunter, now living with me, £300 sterling on her marriage. £100 sterling to the said James Galache, my wife's brother. My negro boy Charles and negro girls Molly and Charlotte to my said wife but the girls are to be freed when they are 25. The residue to my said wife who is also to act as exex. Wits: Thomas Laconena, Thomas Mason and John Talley. Pr. 6 Mar 1769 by the relict. (PROB 11/947/101).

James Stevens Esq. of Chippenham, (Wilts.), Second Lieut. [Capt.] in Royal Regt. of Artillery now in Minorca [but who died in N.Y., bachelor], dated 30 Oct 1767. The estate of my mother Ann Stevens, after her decease, I bequeath to my nephew Edward Stevens. Wits: Maj. Thomas James and Ann Stockton. AWW 3 May 1769 to the mother Ann Stevens, widow, no executor having been named. (PROB 11/948/183).

John Spooner of Boston, Mass., merchant, designing a voyage to Great Britain, dated 23 Jly 1768. The house and lands now in the possession of Christopher Clarke, which were demised by the will of my late father John Spooner of Boston to his heirs, are to descend to my son John Jones Spooner. One-third of the residue of my estate to my wife Margaret Spooner and two-thirds to my three children John Jones, William and Andrew Spooner. Andrew Oliver Esq. and Arnold Welles Esq, both of Boston, are to be execs. Wits: John Cutler, Josiah Tressenden and Joseph Carnes. AWW 19 May 1769 to Abraham Dupuis, attorney for the execs. in Boston. (PROB 11/948/186).

James Nevin Esq. of N.H., dated 31 May 1766. To my son George Nevin £5 and no more. To my daughter Margaret Nevin £5. The residue to my wife Isabella Nevin, my sons Andrew and James

Nevin, and my daughter Mary Nevin when they are 21. Thomas Lane of London, merchant captain, James Cummins of London, mariner, Theodore Atkinson Esq. of N.H., and my said wife to be my execs. Wits: Andrew Beckett, Richard Cock and John Evans. Pr. 1 Jun 1769 by Thomas Lane. (PROB 11/949/218).

John Worthington of Ann Arundell Co., Md., merchant, dated 22 Oct 1764. To my daughter Ann Dorsey my plantation of 160 acres called Wyatt's Harbour and Wyatt's Hills, which she and her husband Thomas Beal Dorsey occupy, with negroes and stock. To my son John Worthington my eleven tracts (named) totalling 2,600 acres in Ann Arundell Co., and 363 acres in Frederick Co., part of a tract called Whiskey Bridge. To my son Charles Worthington five tracts (named) in Ann Arundell Co. totalling 905 acres. To my son Samuel Worthington 1,000 acres in Baltimore Co. where he now lives. To my son Thomas Worthington three tracts totalling 1,620 acres on the north side of Patapsco River near Patapsco Falls in Baltimore Co. To my daughter Elizabeth, wife of Nicholas Dorsey, two tracts (named) totalling 109 acres near Patapsco River in Ann Arundell Co. Other bequests to: my granddaughter Helen Lynch; my grandsons John and William Worthington, sons of my late son William Worthington; my brother John Brice. My sons John and Charles Worthington to be my execs. Wits: Alexander Warfield, William Woodward and John McDonall. AWW 2 Jun 1769 to James Russell Esq., attorney for the execs. in Md. (PROB 11/949/228).

Thomas Brown of N.Y.C., merchant, intending soon to go to Europe, [and who died in St. Sepulchre, London], dated 19 Mar 1768. £500 current to poor inhabitants of N.Y.C. who are of the Church of England. £1,000 current to my daughter Ann, widow of John Smith of N.Y.C., leather dresser, and £1,000 current each to his sons Thomas and Richard Smith. £20 current to John Finglass, son of Capt. John Finglass of N.Y.C. £20 sterling to my cousin Ann Ghinn, widow of John Ghinn, £20 sterling to her youngest daughter, my goddaughter, and £10 sterling each to her two elder daughters. £100 sterling to Sarah Brown, widow of my late brother Richard Brown. £20 sterling for mourning to my cousin William Hardwick. The residue to my nephew and nieces Richard, Susanna and Sarah Brown, children of my said late brother Richard Brown. My friends Elias Desbrosses and Richard Light of N.Y.C., merchants, and William Hardwick of London, leather seller, to be my execs. Wits: James Dalzell, James Armstrong and James Emott. Pr. 18 Jly 1769 by William Hardwick. New grant made in Apr 1779. (PROB 11/949/235).

Robert Burridge, boatswain of H.M. ship *Launceston*, commander Edmund Affleck Esq., [who died in Va.], dated 13 Sep 1759. My whole estate to my wife Sarah Burridge of Charles parish, Plymouth,

Devon, and she is to be my exex. Wits: Edmund Affleck and John Johnston, clerk. Pr. 20 Jly 1769 by the relict. (PROB 11/949/235).

Isaac Mendes of Pensacola, W. Fla., dated 8 March in the year 5527 or 1767 according to Christian account, [and who died on 11 Apr 1767]. I am of the Jewish religion and desire my friend Alexander Solomons to perform my funeral according to the Jewish institutes. Many of my friends and creditors will suffer on account of the misfortunes I have met with and I recommend that the Bills of Exchange I had from Ensigns Briscoe and Powell be used towards the discharge of my debts. I entreat my relations Mr. Moses Da Costa, Abraham Levy and Lewis Mendes to consider the affluence with which God has blessed them and make up the deficiency of what I owe my creditors, and in particular to Mr. Conrad Van Bergen as he is a very poor man. Notwithstanding the many differences I have had with my mother, my brother Moses Mendes, and other relations, I forgive them. My friends Messrs. William Barrow, William Aird, Arthur Neil and Alexander Solomons to be my execs. Wits: Charles Blanchard, John Watkins and Jacob Allison. Pr. 21 Jly 1769 by William Barrow. (PROB 11/950/255).

George Seaman of Charles Town, S.C., gent., dated 14 Jan 1769. (An extremely long will). To my sister Elizabeth Seaman of Leith, Scotland, an annuity of £100 sterling during her lifetime and £200 sterling. To my cousin Naomi Ross, commonly called Lady Pitcane of Cromartie, £500 sterling and to her son Munro Ross of Pitcane £2,000 sterling when he is 21. To my cousins Catherine and Christian Brown of Leith £200 sterling each. To my cousin Helen Kendall of Leith £50 sterling. £2,000 sterling each to John Deas and William Lennox of Charles Town, merchants. £300 each to Mary, Catherine and Elizabeth Deas, daughters of David Deas of Charles Town, merchant, Catherine Lennox, daughter of the said James Lennox, and the South Carolina Society. £500 sterling to the Infirmary at Edinburgh or any other charitable institution there. £500 sterling to needy and honest housekeepers in Leith. To my daughter-in-law Elizabeth Deas, wife of the said John Deas, my negro woman Alice and the use of my other slaves, my pew in St. Philip's church and the use of my tenement on Charles Town Bay, now occupied by Newman Swallow, and of all my other tenements and plantations. Other principal bequests to: Seaman Deas, son of my daughter-in-law Elizabeth Deas; my sister-in-law Rachel Caw of Charles Town, widow; Emarintha, wife of John Richardson of E. Fla.; Archibald, son of the late Robert Brown of Goose Creek. My friends James Lennox, David Deas, John Deas and William Lennox to be my execs. Wits: Robert Williams Jr., Edward Pierce and Robert Dick. Pr. 24 Jly 1769 by John Deas. (PROB 11/950/264).

Joseph Shepherd deputy chaplain to the 21st Regt. of Foot, intending
to go to Mobile where the Regt. is stationed, [and who died in W.
Fla.], dated 12 Jun 1765. My personal estate is to be sold and the
interest on 2,000 marks paid to Miss Jeany Simpson, eldest daughter
of Rev. Alexander Simpson at Monymusk, (Scotland), with
remainder to my brother Rev. John Shepherd, missionary at Fair
Isle, and my nephews, the eldest sons of Mr. James Brown in the
Miln of Wester Goul(?), and Mr. Francis Smith Sclater in Aberdeen.
Capt. Archibald Grant Esq. is to be my exec. Depositions at
Aberdeen 24 Jun 1769 by Robert Young and Thomas Hutcheon,
factors to Sir Archibald Grant of Monymusk, that the testator died
in Florida in 1766 and that the above will is in his hand. Pr. 1
Aug 1769 by Archibald Grant Esq. (PROB 11/950/292).

William Mallory of Elizabeth City Co., Va., dated 26 Mar 1750. To
my son William Mallory all my lands in this Co., my plantation
in York Co., and my negroes Howell and Manuel. To my daughter
Fanny Mallory my negro girls Rose and Nell. To my daughter Mary
Mallory my negro girls Phillis and Judy. My wife (Mary) is to be
my exex. and to have the use of my estate until my said son is of
age. My friends John and William Allen are to be trustees. Wits:
William Armistead, Johnson Mallory and Edward (x) Wilson. Pr.
Va. 6 Nov 1750 by the relict. AWW London 11 Sep 1769 by the
son William Mallory, the relict having died. (PROB 11/951/316).
See NGSQ 61/125-131 for an account of the descent of this family
from Sir William Mallory of Yorks. who died in 1603.

Florasabella Mallory of St. John's parish, King William Co., Va.,
[spinster], dated 26 Nov 1758. My negro girl Sue to Mary Mallory,
daughter of my brother William Mallory. My negro woman Dinah
and her child Lucy to my nephew Thomas Avera. £50 to my said
brother William Mallory who is to be my exec. with my said
nephew. Wits: N----- Davis and George Hollings. Pr. King William
Co. 21 Dec 1758. Pr. London 11 Sep 1769 by the named execs.
(PROB 11/951/316).

Sir John St. Clair, Deputy Quartermaster-General of H.M. Forces in
America, now resident in Elizabeth Town, N.J., dated 26 Oct 1767.
To my wife Elizabeth, commonly called Lady St. Clair, enough
N.Y. money to make up a sum of £1,000 sterling on which she is
to receive interest annually during her life. All my real estate and
the residue of my personal estate to my son John St. Clair when
he is 21, with remainder to Maria Gage, daughter of Maj-Gen.
Thomas Gage, Elizabeth Elliott, daughter of Andrew Elliott Esq.,
Collector of Customs for N.Y., and Lauchland McClean Esq.,
Deputy Secretary of State. My said wife and Andrew Elliott Esq.
to be my execs. Wits: Daniel Coxe, John Crawford and Elias

Boudinot. AWW 15 Sep 1769 to Richard Mowland Esq., attorney for the relict, now wife of Dudley Templer Esq., and Andrew Elliott, both resident in America. (PROB 11/951/323).

Mary Inman, late of Chesterfield, Derbys., and now of Wapping, Mddx., spinster, [who died in S.C.], dated 16 Aug 1764. My quarter part of a water corn mill with 30 acres in Tapton near Chesterfield, now in the occupation of William Rickett and Thomas Handy, and all my other estate to my kinsman Thomas Pike of Wapping, timber measurer, who is to be my exec. Wits: Jo. Heaton, Valentine Flood and James Connor. Pr. 23 Nov 1769 by named exec. (PROB 11/952/384).

Mary Avory of Prince George Co., Va., [widow], dated 26 Oct 1766. All money due to me in England and all other estate to my children Charles and Molley Avory and they are to be my execs. Wits: Henry Batt Jr., William White and Clift Haselwood. Pr. 2 Dec 1769 by Charles Avera *alias* Avory and Molly Elliott, wife of Amos Elliott. (PROB 11/953/402).

1770

Cornelius Garret Van Horne of N.Y.C., merchant, dated 3 Sep 1747. To my wife Judith one-third of the rents of my houses and a sufficient allowance for her to maintain and educate my four sons Garrit, Augustus, Cornelius and David Van Horne. My two lots in N.Y.C. and one at Saratoga, Albany Co., N.Y., that came to me by my late wife Joanna, are to descend to my eldest son Garrit. All my other lands and tenements in N.Y.C. and the residue of my estate to my other sons. My said wife and sons and my brothers-in-law Simon Johnson and Peter Jay are to be my execs. Wits: Francis Johnson, Willem Hyer and Augustus Vallete. Pr. N.Y.C. 24 Oct 1769 by the surviving exec. Augustus Van Horne. AWW London 3 Mar 1700 by John Exley, attorney for the said Augustus Van Horne in N.Y.C., Simon Johnson and Peter Jay renouncing. (PROB 11/956/125).

Richard Dobbyn of Carrick, Tipperary Co., Ireland, but now of Savannah, Ga., dated 19 Sep 1759. To my wife Anastasia Dobbyn my two houses in Carrick and all my personal estate. My friend Capt. Edward Somerville is to be my exec. Wits: Adam Loyer, Thomas Smith and Elizabeth Baugh. Pr. Ga. 16 Dec 1759. AWW London 4 May 1770 to the relict, the named exec. having died. (PROB 11/957/183).

Pierre Barnier [of St. Ann, Westminster, Mddx., [who died in Philadelphia, bachelor]. £50 each to my mother and my brother John. £30 each to my sister Jean and my brother Jamy. £1 sterling each to the hospital of Geneva and the poor of the French church. My said mother to be my exex. Wits: Nicholas Bernard and Daniel McInnes. Pr. Philadelphia 7 Jun 1770. AWW London 7 Jun 1770 by the mother Ann Barnier. (PROB 11/958/220).

Alexander Stephens of Frederick Co., Va., [Lieut. of the Royal Americans under Sir Geoffrey Amherst], dated 12 Jan 1768. To my brother Adam my sword and sash. To my brother John all my lands, my negro Ambrose, all my servants for the time they have to serve, and my horse and saddle, and he is to settle my accounts with Mr. Hodge and Mr. Allison. To my brother Robert I give my brother Adam's bond to me for £60 sterling. To my two sisters I give the £40 which is in my agent's hands in London. Any residue and my gold buckles and buttons to Miss Pheby Seaman. My brother John is to be my exec. Wits: Jonathan Seaman, Robert Cunningham and Phebe Seaman. AWW 8 Jan 1770 to John Russell, attorney for the brother John Stephens in Va. (PROB 11/958/243).

Sir Henry Moore of Jamaica, Governor of N.Y., dated 11 Apr 1769. All my estate in Jamaica, Great Britain and elsewhere in trust to Henry Dawkins Esq. of Standlinch, Wilts., Edward Morant Esq. of Pilewell, Hants., Edward Long Esq. of Jamaica, Judge of the Vice-Admiralty Court, and John Gordon Sr. of St. Mary's, Jamaica, practitioner in physick. To my wife Catharina Maria Moore an annuity of £600 and she is to relinquish any claim to the jointure settled upon her by deed of 11 January 1750. To my daughter Susanna Jane, now wife of Capt. Alexander Dickson of the 16th Regt. of Foot, £3,000 sterling. The residue to my son John Henry Moore. My said wife is to be my exex. and guardian of my son. Wits: Francis Child, Robert Hull and Philip Livingston Jr. Pr. 7 Jun 1770 by the relict. (PROB 11/958/237).

Benjamin Heron Esq. of New Hanover Co., N.C., dated 4 Sep 1768. To my wife Alice my house in Wilmington with the negro slaves and furniture out of my Mulberry house. To my daughter Mary the tract called the Mulberry with a tract adjoining the river given to me by Job Howes, and a tract I bought of John Ashe Esq. To my daughter Elizabeth my plantation called Mount Blake which I bought of Mr. William Mount(?), the ferry house opposite and the eight acres adjoining. To my daughter Frances the house and land in the Sound which I bought of John Mott, the tract I bought of Mrs. Vail which is now occupied by Jenking Perry, a tract adjacent to Capt. Dubois' on Smith's Creek which I lately bought of Mrs. Bowen, and all my lots in Wilmington. I leave to my daughters

Mary and Elizabeth the families of negroes entailed to them by the will of their grandfather Job Howes. A diamond ring to my wife's sister Peggy (Marsden). To my nephew Charles Heron I give the £100 sterling owed me by Mark Robinson, commander of H.M. ship *Fowey*. The residue of my estate to my said three daughters. My said wife and my friends Lewis de Rosset, Frederick Jones of Swan Point and Samuel Swann Jr. to be my execs. Wits: Frederick Jones, Henry Burford and Charles Heron. Codicil of 12 Jly 1769. My wife and my daughters Mary and Elizabeth are near to embarking for England and, in the event of their demise, I leave my whole estate to my daughter Frances. To my sister-in-law Peggy Marsden £1,000. To my brother Charles Heron, apothecary and surgeon in Southampton, Hants., £500 sterling and to his son, my nephew Charles Heron, who lives with me, £500 sterling. Depositions 3 Jly 1770 by James Waller of Islington, Mddx., merchant, and Fountain Elwin of St. Andrew, Holborn, Mddx., that they have known the testator for several years and that the codicil is in his hand. Pr. 4 Jly 1770 by the relict. (PROB 11/959/266).

John Ross of Wapping, Mddx., mariner, [late of N.E.], dated 11 Apr 1766. My whole estate to my nephews and niece John, Isaac and Mary Garbutt of Harborough, Yorks., children of my late sister Elizabeth Garbutt. John Thompson of Shadwell, Mddx., ropemaker, is to be my exec. Wits: Jo. Heaton and Howell Parry. Pr. 27 Oct 1770 by the named exec. (PROB 11/961/376).

Samuel Cary Esq. of Charles Town [of Chelsea], Mass., dated 14 Nov 1763. My house and land in Boston now in the tenure of Widow Mary Minot to my son Samuel Cary. £10 sterling each to Rev. Mr. Hull Abbot and Rev. Mr. Thomas Prentice. The residue to my three sons Samuel, Thomas and Jonathan Cary. My brothers Richard and Nathaniel Cary are to be my execs. Wits: Edmund Trowbridge, John White and Isaac Foster Jr. AWW 8 Nov 1770 by his affirmation to Abraham Deterne, attorney for the execs. in Mass. (PROB 11/961/391).

Joseph Marsh of the sick Company of Marines of the Portsmouth Division [of H.M. ship *Romney*, who died in Boston, N.E.], dated 6 May 1767. My whole estate to my friend Thomas Marston of Portsmouth, (Hants.), and he is to be my exec. Wits: Charles Sempill and William Harwood. Pr. 7 Dec 1770 by the named exec. (PROB 11/962/442).

William Williamson, at present lodging with Mr. Tobias Johnson at the Four Lyons Inn, London, and intending to leave England, [of Charles Town, S.C.], dated 14 Apr 1766. £200 to Mrs. Susanna Widdows, now living with William Gordon Esq. of Rochester, Kent. £100 to Mrs. Margaret Padmore, wife of Mr. John Padmore, now

living at the Weavers' Arms in Middle Street, West Smithfield.
£100 to my friend Mr. Robert Halcrow, merchant in Mark Lane,
London. Wits: Isaac Friend and Edward Chidlow. Pr. 30 Dec 1770
by the named exec. (PROB 11/962/452).

1771

Lord Norborne Botetourt of Stoke, Glos., [of Va.], dated 26 Jly 1766
with codicil of 27 Aug 1766. All my manors and lands in trust to
Lord Viscount Barrington. My sister the Duchess Dowager of
Beaufort is to have the rents of my estates which, after her death,
are to be conveyed to the use of my nephew the Duke of Beaufort.
£5,000 each after the death of their mother the said Duchess of
Beaufort to my nieces Lady Henrietta Somerset and Lady Mary
Somerset. Annuities to: my cousin Maurice Berkeley, now living at
Hatfield School; Mrs. Jane Berkeley, now living at Mr. Akerman's
at Isleworth, Mddx.; George Norborne Vincent of Berkeley Square,
Mddx.; Lieut. Charles Thomson, now of the *Cygnet*, his mother
Margaret Thomson of Edinburgh, Scotland, and his sister Elizabeth
Thomson of Edinburgh; Mr. Thomas Wright of Byers Green, Dur-
ham; Mrs. Mary Hamilton of Petersham, Sy. £500 to the Gloucestershire Infirmary. I am to be buried in Stoke Church and carried to
my grave in the most private manner. My house in Grosvenor Square
and the residue of my estate to my nephew the Duke of Beaufort.
Wits: Charles Bragge, John Warner and John Taylor. Pr. 10 Jan 1771
by Henry, Duke of Beaufort. (PROB 11/963/4).

William Knight, at present at Roade, Northants., [of Williamsburg,
Va.], widower, dated 3 Jly 1768. To my brother and exec. Robert
Knight all my tenements at Roade in the occupation of John Hedge,
Margaret Linnell and Rebecca Knight, and my lands in Roade,
Ashton and Hartwell now rented by William Paine of Courteenhall.
Wits: William Steevens, Sarah Steevens and William Adkins. Pr. 2
Jan 1771 by the named exec. (PROB 11/963/22).

George Whitefield, at present residing at the Orphan House Academy
in Ga., [minister of the Gospel, of St. Luke, Mddx., who died in
Ga., widower], dated 22 Mar 1770. I leave the orphan house at
Bethesda, Ga., with the buildings lately erected and all else in Ga.
to "that elect Lady, that mother of Israel, that Mirror of true and
undefiled Religion, the Rt. Hon. Selina, Countess of Huntingdon . . ."
with remainder to my fellow traveller and friend Hon. James
Habersham Esq. to whom I leave my late wife's gold watch and

£10 for mourning. I leave the Tabernacle in London and the adjacent house, where I usually live when I am in London, the Tottenham Court Chapel and all other property in London to my friends Daniel West Esq. in Church Street, Spitalfields, and Mr. Robert Keen, woollen draper in the Minories. £50 to my friend Gabriel Harris Esq. of Gloucester who received me when I was helpless and destitute over 35 years ago. £500 to my servant and friend Mr. Ambrose Wright. £50 each to my brothers Mr. Richard Whitefield and Mr. Thomas Whitefield, my brother-in-law Mr. James Smith, hosier in Bristol, and Mrs. Frances Hartford of Bath. Bequests to the following at the Orphan House Academy in Bethesda: Mr. John Crane, now a faithful steward; Mr. Benjamin Stirk for his services at Bethesda; Peter Edwards; William Trigg; the three brothers of Mr. Ambrose Wright; and Mr. Richard Smith, attendant. £50 to Mr. Thomas Adams of Rodborough, Glos., my only surviving first fellow labourer. £10 each for mourning to: Rev. Mr. Howel Davis of Pembrokeshire; Mr. Toriah Joss; Mr. Cornelius Winter; and all my present assistant preachers. "I also leave a mourning ring to my hon. and dear friends and disinterested fellow travellers, Revd. John and Charles Wesl(e)y, in token of my indissoluble union with them in heart and Christian affection notwithstanding our difference in judgment about some particular points of doctrine. Grace be with all of them of whatever denomination that love our Lord Jesus, our common Lord, in sincerity." James Habersham Esq. to be my exec. (for Ga.). Wits: Robert Bolton, Thomas Dixon and Cornelius Winter. Limited AWW 5 Feb 1771 to Charles Hardy, Daniel West and Robert Keen. (PROB 11/964/88).

James Fry the younger of Southall, Mddx., tanner, [of Nottingham, Md.], dated 17 Apr 1770. £250 each to my son James Fry, my wife Rebecca Fry, my daughter Jane, wife of John Fyfield, and £250 for the maintenance of their daughter Jane. The residue to my said son. My execs. are to be William Molleson of Crutched Friars, London, merchant, and Ninian Pinckney of Stanhope Street, London, gent., who are also to be guardians to my granddaughter Jane Fyfield. Wits: R. Molleson, Robert Wrigglesworth and Richard Templer. Pr. 20 Mar 1771 by the named execs. (PROB 11/965/103).

Richard Penn Esq. of Stanwell, Mddx. [of St. Marylebone, Mddx.], dated 21 Mar 1750. An extremely lengthy will. My friends William Vigor Esq. of Taplow, Bucks., and Joseph Freame of London, banker, are to be execs. in trust for England; and my friends Lynford Lardner Esq. and Richard Peters Esq., both of Philadelphia, and Richard Hockley of Philadelphia, merchant, execs. in trust for America. My quarter part of the province of Pennsylvania has been regulated by articles of 1 May 1732 between myself and my brothers

John Penn Esq. now deceased and Thomas Penn Esq., and articles
of 31 January 1750 between my said brother Thomas and myself.
My family plate and picures are to go to my eldest son John Penn.
My rights and those of my late brother John Penn in N.J. are to
be sold and the proceeds remitted to my execs. in England. Principal
bequests to: my wife Hannah Penn; my son William Penn, born
since the decease of my brother John; my niece Philadelphia Hannah
Freame, only surviving child of my late sister Margaret Freame;
my great-nephews and nieces of half blood Springett Penn, Christiana Guilielma Penn, Robert Edward Fell (only son now living of
my late niece Guilielma Penn), Mary Margaretta Fell, and Guilielma
Maria Frances Fell. Wits: Ferdinand John Paris, Francis Eyre and
Robert Gwyn. Codicil of 15 Jan 1756. Codicil of 13 Mar 1760.
My younger son William Penn is lately dead. Codicil of 13 Jly
1768. A family vault is to be built in Stoke church, Bucks., and
the body of my son William, who died on 4 Feb 1760, is to be
taken from Penn church and buried at Stoke where I am also to
lie. Wits: John Lancaster, Val. Henry Allott and Henry Jodrell. Pr.
4 Mar 1771 by the relict. (PROB 11/965/119).

Alexander Simpson, master of H.M. ship *Swallow*, commander Philip
Carteret Esq., [of Norfolk, Va.], dated 14 Sep 1767. My whole
estate to my wife Ann Simpson of Norfolk, Va., and she is to be
my exex. Wits: Philip Carteret, E. Leigh and Thomas Watson. AWW
12 Jun 1771 to John Gathorne, attorney for the relict, now wife of
William George. (PROB 11/968/273).

William Worthington [of Ann Arundell Co., Md.], dated 25 Sep 1770.
To my daughter Ruth a tract of 200 acres called the Plains, part
of a tract called Pawson's Plains, with remainder to my granddaughter Ruth Davis. To my daughter Ruth Shaw £100 current and
a negro woman. To my grandson William Worthington Davis a
tract of 300 acres on the north of Magochy River called Homewards
Range, £100 current and two negro men when he is 21. To my
granddaughter Sarah Davis four tracts of 640 acres on the south
side of Magochy River and the negro woman that lives with her
father John Davis when she is 16. To my granddaughter Ruth Davis
a tract of 260 acres on the north side of Magochy River and three
negroes when she is 16. To my granddaughter Mary Ann Davis
three tracts of 250 acres on the south side of Magochy River when
she is 16. To my grandson William Worthington Shaw a negro boy
called James. The residue of my lands in Md. to my grandson
William Worthington. My son-in-law John Davis is to be my exec.
Wits: William Phillips, Samuel (x) Phillips and Samuel (x) Todd.
AWW 3 Sep 1771 to Silvanus Grove of London, merchant, attorney
for the named exec. in Md., limited to the recovery from William

and Mary Hunt, execs. of Capt. Thomas Hunt, who was sole exec. of William Hunt deceased, of debts due to tthe testator William Worthington. (PROB 11/971/393).

John Arey of the City of Oxford, carpenter, now bound to N.C. in the service of Anthony Bacon of London, merchant, [who died in N.C., bachelor], dated 15 Dec 1770. To my friend Henry Goodenough of the Prerogative Office, Doctors' Commons, London, all my personal estate, my house in St. Peter in the East, (Oxford), in the occupation of William Lyme, and my two houses in Holwell, (Oxon.), in the occupation of William Birkett and (blank) Piddington, milliners in Oxford. Wits: Gilbert Francklyn, Anthony Richardson and Bartholomew Ghetting. Pr. 4 Nov 1771 by Henry Trenchard Goodenough. (PROB 11/972/428).

John Suggitt of Newcastle-upon-Tyne, master and mariner, [late of Northampton Co., Va.], dated 16 Mar 1763. To my wife Jane Suggitt my tenement in Westoe, Durham, called Bentham Farm, in the occupation of Thomas Bruce, farmer, and my shares in the ships *Antelope* and *Blackett*, and she is to be my exex. Wits: Robert Wilson, Stephen Coulson and Robert Wilson Jr. AWW 9 Oct 1771 to Jane Selby, widow, mother and adx. of the named exex. (PROB 11/972/422).

Francis Fauquier Esq., Lieut-Gov. of Va., dated Williamsburg 26 Mar 1767. Principal bequests to: my wife and my two sons Francis and William; my brother-in-law Francis Woollaston. My lands in Va. are to be sold. Execs: William Nelson, Robert Carter, Hon. Peyton Randolph and George Wyllie. Wits: Thomas Everard, James Cocke and ---?--- Savage. Pr. 19 Dec 1771 by the son Francis Fauquier. (PROB 11/973/480).

James Gray surgeon [of Maj. Ogle's Battalion] of the 21st Regiment of Foot, [who died in Philadelphia], dated 13 Jun 1762. My whole estate to my father John Gray who is to be my exec. Wits: Mathew Smith, Josiah Marshall and William Collins. Pr. 18 Dec 1771 by the father. (PROB 11/973/482).

Aaron Quarles of St. John's, King William Co., Va., dated 19 Dec 1767. £50 to my son James Quarles. To my wife a feather bed, a mare, two cows and two negroes and the use of my land during her lifetime, after which it is to be sold. Negro servants to my children Tunstall and Catherine Quarles. A negro boy to my grandson Aaron Quarles Starke. The residue of my estate to my other children: Anne, Isbell, Aaron, John and Nathaniel Quarles, Jane Stanhope and Barbary Starke. My execs. to be Joseph Fox, Bartholomew Dandridge and John Quarles Jr. Wits: James Quarles, Solomon Quarles and Thomas Waller. Pr. Dec 1771 by John Quarles the younger. (PROB 11/973/496).

1772

Elizabeth Russell of Marblehead, Mass., widow, dated 15 Aug 1770. My farm at Wenham, Mass., purchased of Zacheus Goldsmith, Richard Goldsmith and Benjamin Rumball, my estate in the Great Swamp in Wenham and Plumb Island to my son Russell Trevet of Marblehead, merchant, during his lifetime with remainder to his son Samuel Russell Trevet. £100 to my granddaughter Elizabeth, wife of Thomas Wendall of Marblehead, merchant. South Sea stock to be shared between the said Samuel Russell Trevet and Elizabeth Wendall and my granddaughter Susannah, wife of Joshua Orme Jr. of Marblehead, gent. My uncle Elbridge's two pictures to my son James. Bequests to my great-granddaughters Elizabeth Russell Wendall and Elizabeth Russell Orme. My said son, Mr. Daniel Waldo of Boston, merchant, and Mr. William Gray of Boston, upholsterer, to be execs. Wits: Isaac Mansfield, Thomas Frothingham, Sarah Gerry and Willmut (x) Hubbard. Pr. 2 Jan 1772 by Russell Trevet. (PROB 11/974/22). Further grant in 1803.

Mary Goldhawk of Chertsey, Sy., widow, dated 22 Oct 1770. £100 to the Fishmongers' Company to discharge a bond for the support of Sarah Bury during the coverture of her worthless husband. £10 each to my cousin Martha Norman of Beccles, Suff., Martha Hayter of Haddon, Hunts., and my nieces Frances and Rebecca Lamm. A ring for mourning to my cousin Thomas Evance of S.C., Thomas Anguish Esq. and others (named). The residue of my estate to my nephew John Hayter who is to be my exec. Wits: John Stantial and Richard Smith. Pr. 25 Feb 1772 by the named exec. (PROB 11/975/51).

Abraham Taylor Esq. of Philadelphia but now of Bath, Som., dated 8 May 1764. An annuity of £200 and the use of my furniture, etc. to my wife Philadelphia Taylor during her lifetime. All my houses and lands in Penna., Md., N.J. or elsewhere in America, and all my personal estate to my son John Taylor who is to be my exec. Wits: Richard Brigden Fowell, attorney in Bath, John Brooke Brooke and William Hooper. Pr. with two codicils 10 Mar 1772 by the named exec. (PROB 11/976/113).

Nathaniel Walthoe Esq. of Williamsburg, Va., undated. My whole estate in England to my sister Mary Hart. £30 sterling each to my brothers and sisters. My estate in Virginia to my sister Henrietta and my nieces Mary and Martha Hart. £200 current to Mrs. Christiana Campbell, widow. My lost diamond ring to William Byrd Esq. and my watch to Crosley Thornton Esq. My execs. are to be Thomas Waller, stationer of London, Benjamin Waller and George

Davenport, both attorneys at law of Williamsburg. Depositions in
Va. 31 Oct 1770 by Robert Carter Nicholas Esq. and William
Pasteur, surgeon, that they well knew the testator and that his will
was found locked up with his other papers. Pr. 13 Jun 1772 by
Thomas Waller. (PROB 11/979/240).

Jeremiah Stanton of Richmond Co, [late of Staten Island], N.Y., dated
N.Y. 3 Oct 1767. One quarter of my estate in lieu of dower to my
wife Louisa Teresia Stanton and the rents and profits of the residue
during her life for the maintenance of herself and my children. The
remaining three-quarters to my son George Augustus Stanton and
my daughters Diana Maria and Louisa Stanton, when they come of
age or are married. My said wife, my brother John Stanton, Captain
in the Royal Navy, and my friend George Harrison of N.Y.C., gent.,
to be my execs. Wits: Peter Marquis de Conty, James Leadbetter
and Richard Harrison. Codicil of 19 Jun 1769. Since drawing up
my will, I have had another son William Edward Stanton and he
is to take his full share of my estate. Additional witness Morley
Harrison. Pr. N.Y.C. 14 Oct 1771. AWW London 3 Jly 1772 to
Isaac Lascelles Winn, attorney for the relict, to recover annuities
from the East India Co. (PROB 11/979/273).

Thomas Corker of Charles Town, S.C., merchant, dated 3 May 1768.
If I die married, £50 sterling is to go to my widow. To my brother
John Corker of Uttoxeter, Staffs., £50 sterling (*This entry crossed
out with a marginal note "erased because my brother has disobliged
me."*), and £20 sterling to each of his sons and daughters when
they are 21. To the two daughters of my late brother Daniel, now
in London, £250 sterling. (*This bequest also deleted*). To the
daughters of my late brother Nathaniel £250 each when they are
21. To Nathaniel Withers, son of Lawrence Withers, who was born
(in) this town and then went off and has not returned since, on
condition that he returns, I leave him my two tenements which
were conveyed to his mother Elizabeth Withers by Mr. John Breton
of Charles Town, merchant, (by mistake entered in the deed as
having been bought of Noah Boyer). If the said Nathaniel Withers
does not return, or any others claim to be "nearer in affinity than
I've done from records in England, which must be from the said
records and nearly to correspond to mine in most instances as the
marriage of our parents was in the same parish, then I think it best
to leave the affair to judicious arbitrators." The yearly income from
my estate is to be administered by the present minister of the
Congregational persuasion in Nantwich, Chesh., as a charity to
provide teachers for 20 boys and 10 girls so that they may read
and write English by the age of 12 or 14 and then put to a trade,
with preference being given to those of my name. My said brother

John Corker to be exec. (*this part erased*) with Mr. Josiah Smith Jr. of Charles Town, merchant. Wits: Daniel Frezvant, Thomas Horsey and Daniel Bell. AWW 4 Aug 1772 to James Poyas, attorney for the named exec. in Charles Town. (PROB 11/980/285).

John Taylor of Whitehaven, Cumberland, [of Savannah, Ga.], shipwright, dated 19 Feb 1765. I leave to my father John Taylor during his lifetime £110 which is in his hands: thereafter £40 is to go to my brother Walter Taylor, £40 to my sister Jane, and the residue of my estate with all my tenements to my brother William Taylor who is to be my exec. Wits: William Smith, Edward Comsteed and Margaret Smith. Pr. 2 Oct 1772 by the named exec. (PROB 11/982/386).

Henry Sampson of Bruton, Som., [Lieut.] in the 31st Regt. of Foot commanded by Gen. Henry Holmes, [who died in Florida], dated 14 Dec 1757. My whole estate to my brother Thomas Sampson of Bruton, surgeon and apothecary, who is to be my exec. Wits. Elizabeth Sampson and Thomas Sampson. Pr. 30 Dec 1772 by the named exec. (PROB 11/983/460).

1773

John Apthorp Esq. of Cambridge, Mass., dated 8 Oct 1771. My two daughters Grizzel and Catharine which I had by my first wife Sarah are provided for by my marriage settlement. £10,000 sterling to my wife (Hannah) to maintain herself and family until her children John Trecothick and Hannah and Frances Western are 21 or marry. My said wife is to have the use of my estate during her lifetime and thereafter it is to descend to my son John Trecothick. The residue to my said children John Trecothick, Frances Western and Hannah Western. Execs: my said wife, Barlow Trecothick Esq., George Apthorp Esq., my brother Thomas Apthorp and my brother-in-law Martin Howard Esq., Chief Justice of N.C. Wits: Stephen Greenleaf, Mary Greenleaf and Hannah Richards. Pr. 22 Feb 1773 by George Apthorp. (PROB 11/984/42).

Catesby Cocke Esq. of Prince William Co., Va., dated 13 Jun 1763. My estate to my executors in trust Richard Henry Lee Esq., Richard Lee Esq. of Westmoreland, Mr. Thomas Everard of Williamsburg and Mr. Thomas Jett, nephew of my late wife, for the following uses. One-third of my estate is to be used for the benefit of my son William Cocke, one-third for my son John Catesby Cocke and one-third for the maintenance of my daughter Elizabeth, wife of

Mr. John Graham. My son John Catesby Cocke is to have my negro Jack. I revoke a deed of trust I made to Rev. Charles Green and others as being contrary to the provisions of my will. Wits: R. Bernard, Katherine Vaulx, Younger Kelsick, Thomas Barnes, David London, Charles Mortimer, Andrew Bailie, Archibald Ritchie and James Mills. Pr. Va. 6 Nov 1772. AWW London 1 Mar 1773 to William Perkins and William Brown, attorneys for the sons William and John Catesby Cocke in Va., the named execs. renouncing. (PROB 11/985/97).

Hon. Richard Maitland [of N.Y.C.], Deputy Adjutant-General of H.M. Forces in N.A., dated 16 Feb 1771. My whole estate to my two natural sons Richard and Peter, children of Mary McAdam, and the child with which she is now pregnant. Execs: my brother Hon. Col. Alexander Maitland, Mr. William McAdam, merchant, and Rev. John Ogilvie, all of N.Y.C., Thomas Montcrieffe Esq, Major of Brigade, and Dr. William Bruce of the Royal Regt. of Artillery. Wits: John McDowall and Andrew Anderson. AWW 20 Jly 1773 to James Syme, attorney for execs. in N.Y.C., the brother Alexander Maitland renouncing. (PROB 11/990/303).

James Griffin of Oxford, Worcester Co., Mass., gent., [Lieut. in Gen. Shirley's Regt.], dated 2 Jly 1768. My estate to my wife Prudence provided she remains a widow; if not it should descend to the heirs of Mr. William Fairfield of Boston. £5 each to Joseph, son of Rev. Mr. Joseph Bowman of Oxford, Caleb, son of Rev. Mr. Caleb Curtis of Charlton, and Sarah, minor daughter of William Campbell of Oxford. My clothes to Dennis Haffron of Hockham. £6 to my nephew William Mackinstry of Taunton, physician. My largest Bible to Samuel Doghead, minor son of Capt. Samuel Doghead of Boston. Execs: Mr. William Watson of Oxford and my said wife. Wits: John Wilson, John Shamway and John Town Jr. AWW 24 Sep 1773 to Thomas Kast, attorney for the execs. in Mass. (PROB 11/991/360)

Joseph Potts of the Orphan House, Christ Church parish, Philadelphia, [Lieut. on half pay of the Royal Navy], dated 21 Oct 1768. £50 to my mother. £10 each to my sister and my wife's mother. The residue to my wife Meriam who is to be my exex. Wits: Richard Scow and Samuel Edwards. Pr. Penna. 24 Apr 1770. AWW London 3 Sep 1773 to Oliver Tomlin Esq., attorney for the relict in Penna. (PROB 11/991/368).

John Ripley [who died in Fort Augustus, E. Fla.]. dated Tower of London, 10 Nov 1769. My whole estate to my mother Mrs. Judith Ripley, if she survives me; if not to Elizabeth Ripley, daughter of Wessel Ripley. Wits: Samuel Sone, Thomas Powell and George Short. Pr. 7 Sep 1773 by the mother. (PROB 11/991/370).

Thomas Dixon of the Orphan House, Christ Church parish, Philadelphia, [but late of St. Botolph Aldgate, London, widower], dated 16 Mar 1764. My whole estate to my wife Mary Dixon who is to be my exex. Wits: Benjamin Stirk, Mary Stirk and Thomas Brownhill. AWW 22 Oct 1763 to the sister Ann Adams, widow, the relict having died in the testator's lifetime. (PROB 11/991/387).

1774

Thomas Hart of N.Y.C., mariner, dated 25 Aug 1761. My whole estate to my wife Ester Hart who is to be my exex. Wits: John Harrison, Simon Fleet and Hugh Gaine. Pr. 11 Jan 1774 by the relict. (PROB 11/994/16).

Elizabeth de Lancey of St. Mary le Bow, Mddx., widow, dated 4 Jan 1774. Bequests to: my mother Sarah Beresford, widow; Rev. Thomas Walker, late of Charles Town, S.C., but now in England; my friend Mrs. Izard, wife of Ralph Izard Esq. of Berners Street, London; my grandmother Mrs. Sarah Blakeway; my brothers Richard and James; my sisters (unnamed). Residue to my mother, my brother Richard Beresford Esq. and Rev. Robert Smith of Charles Town. By his will my late father provided for the division of his estate but this has not yet been done. A monument is to be placed in St. Philip's Church, Charles Town, to me and my deceased husband. Execs: Richard Beresford and Rev. Robert Smith. Wits: Elizabeth Hewett, Elizabeth Burnett and Angus Greenland. Pr. 1 Feb 1774 by Richard Beresford. (PROB 11/994/44).

James Short Esq. of Surrey Street, London, [of Va.], dated 10 Aug 1773. I cancel the bond for £411 owed me by my uncle Mr. Thomas Short. To Dr. Donald Monroe 10 guineas. £50 and the residue of my estate to my brother Mr. Thomas Short. Execs: Mr. Mungo Baikie of Orange Street, Leicester Fields, and Mr. Joseph Clarke of Tavistock Street. Wits: Matthew Duane and Peter Lyon. Codicil of 15 Jan 1774, of Va. but now of Lisbon. My clothing to my servant Peter Elliot. My body is to be conveyed to England to be buried near my uncle James Short at Southgate. Wits: Thomas Digges of Md. and John MacLean of Edinburgh, Scotland. Pr. 21 Feb 1774 by the named execs. (PROB 11/995/69).

Benjamin White of Princes Square, London, [of Boston, N.E., master in the Royal Navy on half pay], dated 3 Oct 1765. My whole estate to my wife Elizabeth White and my daughters Rebeccah and Elizabeth White. Henry Cort of Crutched Friars, London, gent., to be my exec. Wits: William Hoggart, Sarah Owen and J.S. Charouneau. Pr. 23 Mar 1774 by the named exec. (PROB 11/996/124).

John Wilmshurst [of Charles Town, S.C.], dated 9 Sep 1756. My whole estate to my daughter Elizabeth Wilsmhurst of Stepney, Mddx., who is to be my exex. Wits: William ---?--- and Edward Lever. Pr. 21 Jly 1774 by the named exex., now wife of John Dugleby. (PROB 11/1000/287).

Thomas Barnsley Esq., [of Bensalem, Bucks County, Penna., Capt. in the 60th Regt. of Foot], dated 10 Aug 1766. My whole estate, with the exception of a tract on Flagrum, to my wife Bersheba Barnsley provided she remains a widow; if not she is to have only one-third and the rest is to go to the children of my sisters in England. The names of my said sisters are: Mary, wife of Robert Shepherd, living in Sheffield; Sarah, a widow, living at Conisbrough; Anne, now deceased, whose children live in Sheffield; and Hannah, wife of Christopher Smith, living at Thorne, Yorks. To quartermaster John Clark a tract at Flagrum, Cumberland Co., Penna., the warrant for which is in the hands of Mr. Richard Tea. My wife and my friends William Redman and Gilbert Hicks are to be execs. Wits: John Clark and Gabriel Newman. Pr. 7 Sep 1774 by affirmation of the surviving execs., William Redman and Gilbert Hicks. (PROB 11/1001/328).

James Caldwell, now of H.M. ship *Royal Sovereign*, [seaman of H.M. ship *Captain*, who died in Boston Hospital, Mass.], dated 29 Apr 1757. My whole estate to my wife Agnes in Harhock(?) in the parish of St. Tringings (*sic*), Stirlingshire, Scotland, and she is to be my exex. Wits: P. Carteret, John Prosser and James Leitch. AWW 10 Sep 1774 to Andrew Rice, attorney for the relict in Falkirk, Scotland. (PROB 11/1001/330).

Robert White [of N.Y.], Commissary of Stores at Pensacola, W.Fla., bachelor], dated London, 30 Mar 1767. My whole estate to my brother Rev. Mr. Nathaniel White of Bow Churchyard who is to be my exec. Wits: James Hancox and Thomas Shipman. Pr. 8 Nov 1774 by the named exec. (PROB 11/1002/415).

1775

Andrew Elliott of Savannah, Ga., mariner, [formerly of Senegambia, Africa], dated 28 Sep 1771. £25 sterling each to my friends John Ross of London, merchant, and Thomas Davis of London, mariner, who are to be execs. The residue of my estate to my reputed daughter Isabella, daughter of Sylvia Elliott, who is also to have two free negro women living in Gambia reputed to be my daughters. Wits: John Holmes, Anthony Ellison and John Green. Pr. 5 Jan 1775 by the named execs. (PROB 11/1004/9).

John Mauroumet midshipman of the *Boyne* privateer of Dublin, [late Lieut. of the N.Y. Provincials who died in the Havannah], dated 15 Apr 1757. (Copy from S.C. records). My whole estate to my wife Anne Mauroumet *alias* Moraud, who is to be my exec. with Thomas Grollier and John Mairac, merchants. Wits: Robert Lestrange, John Dowling, Thomas Grollier Jr. and Samuel Hope. AWW 4 Jan 1775 to James McKenzie, now husband of the relict, Anne, in S.C., the other named execs., having died. (PROB 11/1004/20).

Job Blackburn of Cary Street, St. Clement Danes, Mddx., coal merchant, dated 24 Jan 1775. My estate to my execs. in trust William Harding of Teston, Kent, yeoman, and John Mead of Rupers Gardens, Sy., yeoman, to pay £20 and an annuity to my mother Esther Blackburn. Mourning rings for: Robert Green, steward to Lord Willoughby de Brooke; John Bowers of the Stamp Office; John Parish, servant to Hon. F. St. John; John Healde; Thomas Blackburn; Abraham Naylor of Dewsbury, (Yorks.); my nephew John Ward, gardener; Samuel Bewsel, gardener to Lord Willoughby de Brooke; Thomas Baker, servant to Mr. Mordaunt at Walton, Warw.; Hugh Hayes, gamekeeper to Lord Leigh; Mr. Parry of Tottenham Court, (Mddx). A silver cup to Joseph Tender, second son of Thomas Tender of Tottenham Court. Further bequests to: John, Job and Hannah Blackburn, children of my brother Joseph Blackburn; my sister Hannah Blackburn; my nephew John Richardson of Charles Town, S.C. Wits: John Fryer, Thomas Dearn and William Morris. Deposition 24 Apr 1775 by John Maides of Lambeth, Sy., that the testator died in the parish of St. Pancras, Mddx., and had intended him (named Mead in the will) to be exec. Pr. same day by named execs. (PROB 11/1006/31).

Francis Welch, late of N.Y.C. but at present of Knightsbridge in the parish of St. Margaret, Westminster, Mddx., merchant, dated 2 Jan 1775. One guinea to my wife Elizabeth Welch as a sufficient reward for her undutiful and merciless conduct towards me. £100 to my friend Mr. Robert Burdy. Ten guineas each to his brother Mr. Thomas Burdy and to Mr. George Surridge who are both clerks to my friend Richard Neave Esq. of Mark Lane, London, merchant. Ten guineas to Mr. Edward Thomas of Hoxton, Mddx., accountant. Five guineas to Mr. Thomas Farguson of Knightsbridge, victualler. The remainder to the said Richard Neave who is to be exec. Wits: James Dowdall, Robert Anderson and Susannah Moodie. Pr. 2 Mar 1775 by the named exec. (PROB 11/1006/121).

Henry Jerningham Esq. [of St. Mary's Co., Md.], dated 19 Nov 1772. (Copied from Md. records). I am in the faith and communion of that church in which my ancestors received the baptism in Britain 743 years ago. To Col. William Taylor of St. James Place, Westminster, aide-de-camp to His Majesty, my land called Cannon Hill in Sy. which I have leased with my uncle Sir George Jerningham. To my wife Catherine Jerningham the plantation where I reside and she is to keep my family. I have a survey being made for 8,000 acres beyond the Appalachian Mountains by contract with Capt. James Wood Esq. as it has always been my view to establish my family in the back country. If the survey is not completed when I die, my eldest son Charles shall be employed to take the 8,000 acres upon some of the waters beyond the Appalachians, of which he shall have 2,000 acres and my other children Frances Henrietta, Mary, Helloisa, Edwardina, Olivia, and my son Tobias the remaining 6,000 acres. If Mr. Athanasius Ford moves with his family to the western part of this continent, my family may choose to go with him. If any of my children marry so that they become inhabitants of St. Mary's or of Charles Co., they shall not be entitled to any legacy. My body is to be opened by Dr. Craig Medcalfe, my bowels put in a box with quicklime at my feet, the trunk of my body filled up with lime, and my coffin to be buried in the garden by my children. At the family's removal, my bones and those of my children are to be carried with them in a decent box painted black and are to be interred in the lands which my son Charles shall have by fee simple. If my family does not go beyond the mountains or with Mr. Ford, my son Tobias is to be bound to a merchant in Philadelphia or Penna. If any of my children contest moving out of Md., they are to be paid one shilling in lieu of their legacy. A mourning ring to my brother Nicholas Jerningham Esq. My said wife and daughter Frances Henrietta are to be exexs. for America and my brother Nicholas Jerningham for England. Wits: Eleanor Lancaster, George Slye and Ignatius Craycroft. Pr. 5 May 1775 by the daughter Frances Henrietta Jerningham. (PROB 11/1007/188).

William Forman Commissary and Paymaster of Artillery in N.A., now residing at the Tower of London, [and died in N.Y.], dated 3 Aug 1773. To my nephew John Morgan and my niece Jane Morgan, children of my brother and sister James and Sarah Morgan, 1,000 acres each in the township of Marlborough. To my nephew Edward William Forman, second son of my brother Richard Forman, all my lands known as the Artillery Patent. To Mrs. Ann Stockton of N.Y. my clothes except my two best suits which I give to my friends Samuel Tuder and John Antill of N.Y. Other bequests to the following, all of N.Y.: Margaret Antill, wife of the said John; Mr. Richard Nichols Colden, Miss Jane Colden, John Colden, Mr.

Alexander Colden and Mrs. Elizabeth Colden; Mrs. Mary Tuder; Mr. Thomas William Moore. Fifty guineas each to: my brothers Anthony, Henry, John, Greenfield and Sarah (*sic*) Forman; my mother Jane Forman; and my cousins William and Alice Forman now living at Waltham, (?Essex). The residue of my estate to my brother Richard Forman who is to be exec. with Mr. Alexander Colden. Wits: William Eaton, Mary Trested and Ann Wyatt. Pr. 13 Jun 1775 by the surviving exec. Richard Forman. (PROB 11/1008/230).

Robert Barrie, [assistant surgeon to H.M. Hospital in St. Augustine, E.Fla.], now residing in E.Fla. but shortly intending to depart for England, [who died at sea], dated 3 Apr 1775. My expenses, including the passage of myself and my family to England, are to be paid and the residue of my estate is to go to my execs. for the benefit of my wife Dorothy Barrie while she remains a widow; but, if she remarries, my son Robert Barrie is to inherit my estate when he is 24. If my said son dies without issue, my estate is to go to my mother and then to my two brothers. My said wife and my friend James Penman Esq. of St. Augustine's are to be execs. Wits: John Forbes, John Leadbetter and Thomas Hall. Depositions 24 Jly 1775 by Thomas Wooldridge of St. Botolph Aldgate, merchant, and Caleb John Garbrand of Pall Mall, St. James, Westminster, that they knew the testator and that the will is in his hand. Deposition 4 Aug 1775 by Dorothy or Dolly Barrie of Villars Street, St. Martin in the Fields, widow of the testator, that her husband died at sea in May 1775 while on passage to England. Pr. 12 Aug 1775 by the relict. (PROB 11/1010/300).

Richard Skinner, dated Charles Town, S.C., 22 April 1774, beginning tomorrow upon a voyage to the Mississippi in W.Fla. To my brother Robert Skinner of London my whole estate consisting chiefly of negroes shipped in the schooner *Rose*, Capt. Ogilvie, for the Mississippi River and other goods shipped with me in the King's packet, the *Comet*, from Charles Town to Pensacola. Depositions 29 Sep 1775 by William Lyon of the Stamp Office, of Drury Lane, St. Martin in the Fields, and Thomas Radley of South Audley Square, living with Hon. Augustus Keppel, Admiral of the Royal Navy, that the testator died in June 1775 near Mansack, W.Fla., and that the will is in his hand. AWW 30 Sep 1775 to Robert Skinner. (PROB 11/1011/360).

William Davies [of King George Co., Va.], now on the high seas and low in health, dated 8 Aug 1775. To my friend Rev. Llewellyn Llewellyn of Trecastle, Brecon, the value of a Bill of Exchange for £239 drawn on Messrs. Farrel and Jones, merchants of Bristol, and he is to pay 5 percent thereof during their lifetimes to my parents. The said Rev. Llewellyn is also to receive from the assignees of Perkins, Buchanan and Brown, late merchants of London, the proceeds from the sale of tobacco. John Hopkins, druggist in London, is to be my exec. Deposition 7 Sep 1775 by Charles Mortimer of Fredericksburgh, Va., doctor in physick, at present in St. Faith, London, that he well knew the testator who died in August 1775 on the ship *Jett* in the River Thames. The deponent came as a passenger in the same ship and saw the testator draw up his will. Deposition on same day by Howell Powell of Llywell, Brecon, to the same effect. Pr. 16 Oct 1775 by the named exec. (PROB 11/1011/370).

William Finnie [Lieut.] of the 61st Company of the Second Division of Marines, [who died in Boston, N.E.], dated Rubislaw, (Scotland), 25 Jly 1774. To my cousin-german and exec. George Skene Esq. of Rubislaw all the estate to which I may be entitled by contract of marriage with my wife Letitia Parker, and my right to 2,000 acres of servitude land in America which may be taken up on my behalf for my service in America during the last war. He is also to have my black slave Isham. The rents of my estate to my sister Katherine Finnie during her lifetime with remainder to the said George Skene. My gold watch to my agent Mr. John Ogilvie of Conduit Street, London. Wits: James Wallace and Al. Miln. AWW 21 Nov 1775 to named exec. (PROB 11/1012/416).

Elizabeth Hinton of Chelsea, Mddx., widow of Thomas Hinton, with no children now living, dated 29 May 1763. Family pictures and coat of arms to my niece Sarah, wife of John Moore of Horsley Down, (Southwark, Sy.), blacksmith. By the will of my mother Elizabeth Roulland, I am entitled to assign her estate. Bequests to: Mrs. Jane Raby, wife of Daniel Raby; Jane Raby, daughter of Daniel Raby Jr.; Mrs. Catharine Elizabeth Quanton; Daniel, son of Charles Cecil; my acquaintance Mrs. Mary Pesey of Kensington, widow. The residue of my estate and my mother's to go to the six children of my late half-brother Peter Francis de Prefontaine, i.e. the said Sarah Moore; Elizabeth, wife of Philip Trevis; and John, Mary, Peter Francis and Ann de Prefontaine of Philadelphia. My exec. is to be Mr. Francis Duroure of Throgmorton Street, London. Wits: Marianna Chauvin and Margaret Alderton. Pr. 14 Dec 1775 by the named exec. (PROB 11/1014/473).

Henry Morse of Williamsburg, Va., intending speedily on a voyage to Britain for the recovery of my health, dated 28 Aug 1775. £100 sterling to my mother Mary Morse of Westfield near Haverfordwest, South Wales. £100 sterling to the eldest child of Thomas Woodall Esq. of Hot Wells near Bristol. £100 sterling to John Morse, son of Thomas Morse of Saundersfoot near Tenby, Pembrokeshire. A

mourning ring to Mrs. Woodall, wife of the said Thomas, Anne
Bowen of Westfield, Martha Waller, wife of Benjamin Waller Esq.
of Williamsburg, and Mr. Robert Prentis of Williamsburg. The
residue of my estate to my brother Thomas Morse of Bristol.
Thomas Woodall, Benjamin Waller and Robert Prentis are to be
my execs. Depositions 23 Dec 1775 by Jacob Boak and Frederick
Jones, both of Leadenhall Street, London, linen drapers, that they
well knew the testator and that the will is in his hand. Pr. 29 Dec
1775 by Thomas Woodall. (PROB 11/1014/483).

Index of Persons

Names are arranged in accordance with original spellings. Testators are shown in bold type.

Abbitts, Francis 159
Abbott, Hull 249
  Richard 26
  William 130
Abell, George 171
  Thomas 171
  William 130
Abercrombie, David 218
  James 218,243
  Jannet 218
  Margaret 218
Abery, Harwood 105
  John 105
  Sarah 105
  Thomas 105
Achley, Anderson 20
  John 20
Acres, Samuel 87
Acrod, Benjamin 35
  John 35
  Lydia 35
  Phebe 35
  Priscilla 35
  Susanna 35
Adam, Benjamin 228
Adams, Capt. 114
  Abigail 96
  Abraham 96
  Ann 211,258
  Elizabeth 221
  James 158
  Joseph 211
  Mary 221
  Richard 41
  Robert 1
  Thomas 182,221,251
  William 158
Adamson, John 103
Addington, Isaac 39,44, 73
Addis, Millicent 9
  William 9
Aderne, Sir John 109
  John 109

Aderne, Margaret 109
  Mary 109
  Ralph 109
Adkins, William 250
Adley, Thomas 48
Adman, William 25
Adney, R. 65
Affleck, Edmund 244,245
Aglionby, William 176
Aird, William 245
Airey, Catherine 208
  John 208
Aish, Marmaduke 205
Akerman, Mr. 250
Akin, Elizabeth 216
  James 216
  Thomas 205,216
Akins, Thomas 128
Albertson, Albert 46
  Anne 47
Albin, James 78
Albyn, Benjamin 45
  Elizabeth 45
Alcock, William 140
Alderne, Charles 10
  Daniel 10
  Dorothy 10
  Edmond 11
  Edward 10
  Owen 10
  Thomas 10
Alderson, William 73
Alderton, Ann 105
  Margaret 263
Aldred, Caleb 180
  John 53,54
Aldworth, Charles 9
Alexander, Charles 73, 135
  James 146,147
  Jane 73
  John 73
  Joseph 124
  Mary 135

Alexander, Robert 73
  Sarah 114
  William 135
Alexon, Jasper 90
  Mary 90
Alford, Benjamin 224
  Joanna 224
  Samuel 9
Allcock, Anne 159
  Joan 159
  William 159
Allder, George 25
Allen, Andrew 167,172
  Anne 143
  Arthur 108
  Benjamin 118
  Catherine 108
  Edward 33
  Elizabeth 224
  James 158,173
  John 24,53,55,94,98, 108,148,172,246
  Margaret 172
  Martha 157
  Mary 182
  Nathan 157
  Robert 225
  Samuel 98,182
  Sarah 137
  Thomas 240
  William 72,172,246
Allerton, Isaac 71
Alleyne, Abel 191
  E. 155
  Mary 191
Allibon, Elizabeth 143
Allin, Ann 8
  Mary 8
  Thomas 151
Allip, William 134
Allison, Mr. 248
  Jacob 245
Allott, Val. Henry 252

Allright, Jone 19
  Margaret 19
  Thomas 19
  William 19
Allsell, Joseph 94
  Margaret 94
Allway, Thomas 192
Allyn, Henry 175
  Matthew 175
Almand, Mrs. 238
  Mary 238
Almy, Christopher 72
Alpen, John 29
  Robert 30
Alsop, John 38
  Stephen 191
Alstone, Clare 16
  Edward 16
  Isaac 16
  Joseph 16
  Mary 16
Alsup, George 105
Ambler, Elizabeth 168
  Richard 168
Ames, Nathaniel 212
  Richard 10
Amey, David 226
Amherst, Col. 212
  Geoffrey 248
Amory, Ann 233
  Henry 233
  John 232
  Mary 232
  Samuel 233
  Simon 232
  Thomas 232
  William 233
Amos, James 58
  Margery 58
  Solomon 58
Amyand, Claudius 164
  Isaac 164
  Justina 164
Ancrum, William 224
Anderson, Andrew 257
  Anne 36,52
  Henry 144
  Jane 213
  Joseph 189
  Lawrence 200

Anderson, Robert 114
  Robert 260
  Thomas 36,52,132
  William 194,230,231
Andrews, Ann 195
  Elizabeth 122
  John 122
  Rebecca 140
  Thomas 38
  William 122
Angell, Elizabeth 32
Anger, Elizabeth 46
  Thomas 45
Anguish, Thomas 254
Annaud, Alexander 169
Annely, Richard 195
  Susannah 195
  Thomas 195
Annesley, Anne 149
  Mary 149
Annet, Peter 197
Anson, G. 153
Ansted, John 42
Answorth, John 47
Anthony, David 28
  John 83
  Michael 45
Antill, John 261
  Margaret 261
Antram, Mary 198
  William 198
Antrim, John 103
Antrobus, Henry 104
Apletree, Nathaniel 51
Appy, Elizabeth 222
  John 222
  Peter 222
Apthorp, Catharine 256
  Charles 223
  George 256
  Grizzel 256
  Hannah 256
  John 256
  Sarah 256
  Thomas 256
Arbuckle, William 58
Arbuthnot, Robert 166
Archbell, John 48
Archbold, Richard 194
Archer, John 195

Arderne, John 119
  Ralph 119
Arey, John 253
Argent, Joseph 193
Arlington, Michael 116
Armiger, Anne 83
Armistead, William 246
Armour, James 200
Armstrong, George 153
  James 244
  Margaret 91
  Mary 91
  Matthew 91
  Samuel 191
Arnall, Goldsmith 52
  James 52
  Katherine 52
  Thomas 52
Arnett, Alexander 37
Arnold, Elizabeth 38
  Frank 219
  John 68,118
  Josiah 121
  Thomas 119,214
Arrowsmith, Hugh 45
  Obediah 157
Arslett, Thomas 144
Arthur, Anstace 128
  Bartholomew 128
  Christian 128
  Christopher 128
  Dominick 128
  Katherine 128
  Patrick 128
Arundell, Robert 128
Asby, John 128
Ash(e), Ann 122
  Benjamin 81
  Isabella 122
  John 32,87,122,248
  Mary 87
  William 87,122
Ashburn, Ann 212
  Mary 212
  William 212
Ashby, Isaac 146
Ashford, Jane 128
  John 128
Ashley, Edward 224
  Elizabeth 198

Ashley, John 198
Solomon 198
Ashwin, Ann 211
John 211
Askew, John 102
Aspely, Thomas 19
Aspenwell, Aaron 228
Assally, Susan 115
Atchison, David 136
George 136
Grizell 136
Jane 136
Jennett 136
John 136
Athawes, Edward 242
Thomas 242
Athill, James 214
Athy, William 37
Atkey, John 83
Atkin, Elizabeth 178
Atkins, Charles 223
James 46
Joseph 154
Robert 128
Thomas 9
Atkinson, Christopher 213
Francis 54
John 184,199
Nathaniel 31
Theodore 168,244
Thomas 141
Attes, Jane 89
John 89
Attwood, William 146
Aubert, Claude 181
Robert 136
Auchmuty, Mary Juliana
224
Robert 189,227
Audry, Capt. 13
Aunger, Sarah 110
Thomas 110
Austell, Isaac 185
Joseph 185
Moses 185
Austen, Mr. 217
Austin, Mr. 41
George 166,216,232
Joseph 32
Thomas 51

Austion, John 6
Richard 6
Avenill, Roger 14
Avera, Charles 247
Thomas 246
Avery, Anne 34
John 34
Joseph 178
Margaret 19
Aves, Samuel 91
Avis, Ar. 125
Samuel 91
Avory, Charles 247
Mary 247
Molly 247
Awburne, Richard 71
Axford, Benjamin 196
Axtell, Anne 40
Daniel 40
Elizabeth 40
Holland 40
Mary 40
Rebecca 40
Sibilla 40
Axton, Robert 69
Ayacat, Elyas 78
Aylward, William 91
Aynesworth, Elizabeth
198
Ayscough, Anne 217
Francis 217
John 217
Richard 217
Sarah 217
Thomas 217
Ayton, Thomas 29

Babbs, Grizzle 216
Bache, Elizabeth 27
Mary 27
Peter 27
Thomas 27
William 27
Bachea, Thomas 206
Bacon, Anthony 253
John 237
Mary 18
Richard 40
Samuel 18

Badcock, Joan 143
Baddy, Roger 66
Badham, William 49
Bagg, Roger 47
Bagline, John M. 180
Bagnall, Samuel 242
Bagnell, Benjamin 185
Baikie, Mungo 258
Bailey, Sarah 183
Bailie, Andrew 257
Baille, Mr. 111
Baily, John 189
Baker, Ann 61,64,154
Ebenezer 154
Edith 64
Elizabeth 61,230
Francis 154,157
George 116
Henry 154
Isabella 154
Joane 64
John 130,152,31,95,
154,157,188,230
Margaret 64
Mary 61,64,188
Nicholas 230
Richard 61
Samuel 165
Sarah 31
Stephen 154,157
Thomas 64,260
Sir William 227,232
William 182,240
Winifred 61
Baldin, Edward 38
Baldridge, Mr. 74
John 16
Balfoure, William 39
Balgay, Frances 221
Ball, Esias 207
John 193,222
Joseph 159
William 110
Ballard, Charles 123
Eleanor 123
Ballew, Abraham 93
Mary 93
Ballyntine, John 178
Balston, Nathaniel 188

Baltimore, Lord 36
  Lady 150
  Charles, Lord 150
Baly, Jedediah 228
Bamber, William 145
Band, Lillie 185
Bandock, John 216
Bankes, Richard 27
Bankston, Clement 83
Bannister, Col. 239
Bapty, Patrick 92
Barber, Charles 119
  Edward 13
  Elizabeth 155
  Mary 155
  Sampson 212
  William 155
Barbot, James 115
  John 115
  Mary 115
Barclay, Andrew 234
  David 196
  Margaret 70
Barker, Mary 154
  Robert 153
  William 2
Barkley, Robert 60
  William 128
Barlow, Elizabeth 111
  Samuel 111
Barnacot, Katherine 32
Barnard, Anna 169
  Charles 187
  Joel 9
  Jonathan 223
  Lettice 83
  Rachel 169
  Thomas 101
Barnardiston, Nathaniel
132,139
Barneby, John 15
Barnerd, Stephen 80
Barnes, Edmund 216
  Elizabeth 44,216
  James 17
  Jane 36
  John 167
  Merrick 44
  Sarah 81
  Thomas 44,257

Barnes, William 9
Barnett, John Lenn 179
Barnier, Ann 248
  Jamy 248
  Jean 248
  John 248
  Pierre 248
Barnsley, Anne 259
  Bersheba 259
  Hannah 259
  Henry 195
  Mary 259
  Sarah 259
  Thomas 259
Barnwell, Catherine 186
Barrett, John 177
  Patrick 17
  Sampson 114
Barrie, Dorothy 262
  Robert 262
Barrington, Viscount 250
Bar(r)on, Anne 210
  Edward 210
  James 110
Barrow, Ann 119
  Thomas 119
  William 245
Barry, Joseph 190
Barter, Henry 240
  William 240
Bartholomew, Isaac 93
Bartlet(t), Ambrose 178
  Anne 63
  Elizabeth 146
  George 82
  Mary 242
  Samuel 146
  Sarah 242
Barton, Ann 130,152
  John 152
  T. 101
  Thomas 130,146,152
  William 60,152
Bartram, Zachary 24
Barwick, John 145
Bascomb, William 215
Basnett, John 195
  Susanna 6
  William 6

Bass, Jeffery 88
  Sarah 121
Baston, Daniel 57
Bataille, John 75
Bate, William 21
Bates, Edward 55
  Mary 63
  William 63
Bath, Lawrence 112
Bathurst, Edward 194
Batt, Deborah 201
  Mary 87
  Samuel 87
  William 247
Baudouin, Claude 115
Baugh, Elizabeth 247
Baulke, William 6
Bayard, Stephen 175,191
  Wellegonda 187
Bayley, Elizabeth 18,185
  John 51,100,185
  Nathan 132
  Richard 10,13
  Robert 33
Bayliff, Elizabeth 194
  Featherston 194
Bayly, Armiger 65
  Arthur 104
  John 112,124
  Jonathan 102
Baynham, Robert 170
Baynton, Robert 124
Beadle, Robert 98
Beake, James 21
Beale, Col. 10
  John 118
  Joseph 204
  Joshua 204
  Rachel 205
  Sarah 205
  William 173
Beamore, Sarah 131
Bean, Ann 241
  Mary 134
Beard, Dionisia 9
  Richard 36
  Robert 9
Beardsly, Alexander 66
Beauchamp, Adam 190

Beaufort, Duchess 250
Henry, Duke 250
Beavans, Roger 104
Beazly, John 209
Bechinoe, Benjamin 174
Beck, Caleb 238
Justus Denis 205
Beckett, Andrew 244
Richard 86
Beckford, Thomas 177
Beckingham, James 197
Beckles, Maud 132
Thomas 132
Beckwith, Elizabeth 208
Margaret 208
Marmaduke 105
Bedford, John 135
Bedingfield, Ann 173
Thomas 173
Bedon, Benjamin 199
George 199
Henry 199
Rebecca 199
Ruth 199
Sarah 199
Stephen 195, 199
Bedson, William 120
Bedwall, James 231
Bee, John 172
Martha 172
William 191
Beeching, Margaret 167
Beesley, Martha 134
Samuel 134
William 134
Beestland, Ann 208
Henry 208
Belcher, Andrew 91
Belfield, Allan 204
Finney 204
Belin, P. 111
Bell, Daniel 256
David 104
Elizabeth 104, 216
Henry 229
Richard 47
Bellas, Edward 110
Stephen 116
Bellinger, Edmund 88
Bellingham, Richard 21

Bellinghurst, Anne 194
Belt, John 236
Bendal, Sarah 201
Beneat, Joseph 123
Benezet, Stephen 172
Benger, Dorothea 170
Elliott 170
Bennet(t), Mrs. 29
Dorothy 133
Edmond 174
Elisha 133
George 20, 27
James 29, 210, 218
John 63, 64, 112, 133
Jonathan 141
Mary 64
R. 151
Rebecca 91
Richard 117, 194, 210
Spencer 91
Benseks, Denis 52
Benskin, Edward 113
Frances 113
Benson, Earle 162
Thomas 111
Benston, William 162
Bentley, Sarah 183
Thomas 183
Benton, Edward 210
Beresford, Richard 258
Sarah 258
Berisford, Samuel 12
Berkeley, Jane 250
Maurice 250
Berkley, Edmond 114
Bermingham, William 210
Bernard, Nicholas 248
R. 257
Berrington, Elizabeth 14
John 14
Thomas 15
Berry, Elinor 90
James 23
Rebecca 23
William 23
Berthon, Ann 181
Francis 181
Isaac 181
Jane 181
John 181

Berthon, Ledet 181
Letysa Ribot 181
Mary 181
Mary Galhie 181
Michael 181
Paul 181
Besse, Joseph 183
Sarah 183
Bessill, Mary 107
William 107
Best, James 70
Beswicke, John 224
Betts, Thomas 92
Betty, Robert 95
Bevis, Benedict 112
Margaret 112
William 112
Bevor, William 141
Bew, Elizabeth 64
Mary 64
Rigault 64
Sarah 64
William 40
Bewes, Henry 121
Bewsel, Samuel 260
Bibb, Alexander 129
Bicknall, William 43
Bicknell, Andrew 226
Ann 226
Robert 42
William 226
Biddle, Daniel 70
William 19
Biddulph, Arabella 213
Sir Michael 213
Bidwell, James 228
Bigger, John 85
Biggs, Abraham 232
Bignall, Michael 35
Thomas 141
Bilcliffe, Elizabeth 214
Thomas 214
Billett, Joshua 133
Billing, Sarah H. 228
Billings, George 234
John 234
William 234
Billingsby, Benjamin 41
Billingsly, Hester 52
Richard 52

Billop, Anne 130
    Christopher 130,239
    Mary 130
    Thomas 130
Bilton, Edward 24
    Eli 110
Bincliffe, John 137
Binks, Samuel 154
    Thomas 154
Binney, Benjamin 234
Birch, Alice 75
    Elizabeth 75
    Ellinor 75
    Mathew 75
Birchall, Thomas 33
Birchfield, Francis 62
Bird, Adam 93
    Charles 19
    Robert 129
    Thomas 79,142
    William 145
Birdsey, John 210
Birkett, William 253
Birkley, Cuthbert 171
Bisaker, Ambrose 231
Bisgood, James 237
Bishop, Thomas 45
Bisill, William 81
Bissell, Mr. 123
    Margaret 123
Black, Ann 44
    William 171,186
Blackalar, Mary 94
    Philip 94
Blackburn, Esther 260
    Hannah 260
    Job 260
    John 260
    Joseph 260
    Thomas 260
Blackhurst, Roger 24
**Blacklock, Christopher
    195**
    Ruth 195
Blackman, Nicholas 27
Blackmore, Arthur 16
    Frances 16
    Humphrey 16
    Mary 16
    Rebecca 17

Blackmore, Sarah 16
    Susan 17
    William 165
Blacksley, John 115
Bladen, Catherine 84
    John 191
    Nathaniel 84
Blague, Margaret 26
Blair, Alexander 39
    John 203
    Peter 230
    William 47
Blake, Ann 199
    Charles 151,194,231
    Christopher 24
    Daniel 199,223
    Deborah 42,67
    Dorothy 151
    Lady Elizabeth 88
    Elizabeth 231
    George 44
    Henny 151
    Henrietta Maria 194,231
    Hester 24
    John 151,194
    John Sayer 194
    Joseph 199,223
    Mary 24,194
    Philemon 151,194
    Philemon Charles 231
    Ralph 199
    Rebecca 199
    Richard 80
    Ruth 24
    Sarah 231
    William 199
Blakelock, Elizabeth 193
    John 193
Blakeway, Sarah 258
    William 134
Blakey, Charles 93
Blanchard, Charles 245
    George 25
Blancke, Abraham 186
    Bonwina Helena 186
    Hendrick Garret 186
Bland, John 34
    Margaret 75
    Sarah 75
    Thomas 75

Blaney, George 119
Blare, Walter 81
Blatt, Elizabeth 61
    Rebecca 61
Blaunch, Frances 38
    Robert 38
Blenkern, John 82
Blenman, Ann 221
    Thomas 221
Blessingham, Thomas 64
Bletchley, John 42
Blissett, Hester 11
    Richard 41
Bloomfield, Frances 75
    Samuel 75
Bloxham, Nathaniel 76
Bluck, Amy 101
    John 101
Bludder, Emma 9
    Marmaduke 9
    Thomas 9
Blunt, Margaret 13
    Sarah 240
Blydenburg, Joseph 72
Boak, Jacob 264
Boardman, Charles 134
    Mary 134
Boddam, Charles 109
Boddell, Robert 110
Bodman, Henry 162
Bogan, Richard 24
Boisseau, James 207
Boldry, Philip 144
Bolleme, W. 178
Bolter, Mary 143
    Thomas 143
Bolton, Ann 122
    Richard 47
    Robert 251
    Roger 77
    Solomon 22
    Thomas 122,190
Bond, Alice 187
    Barnet 187
    James 130
    John 90
    Mary 187
    Susanna 130
    William 187
Bone, Benjamin 216

Bonham, Samuel 161
Bonifant, Francis 136
Bonner, Phebe 153
    Robert 59
Bonnet, Benjamin 156
    Francis 45
Bon(n)ifield, Abraham 79
    Lucy 79
    Mary 79
    Sarah 52,79
Bonsignor, Mary 186
    Sarah 186
Boodle, Robert 38
Booker, Edward 241
    George 241
    John 105
    Richard 241
Booth, Ann 10
    Hannah 130
    John 50
    Richard 30
    Sarah 50
    Thomas 10
Borch, John 78
Bord(e)ley, Beale 183
    Elizabeth 183,208
    John 183,208
    Matthias 208
    Stephen 183,208
    Thomas 183
    William 208
Bordon, Elizabeth 157
    John 168
Borland, Francis 238
    Francis Lindall 239
    Jane 239
    John 118,239
    Phebe 238
Bosomworth, Thomas 188
Bostick, Thomas 83
Botetourt, Lord
    Norborne 250
Botley, Elizabeth 141
    Thomas 141
Botting, John 53
Boudinot, Elias 247
Boughton, John 146,147
Boult, Benjamin 99
    Henry 116

Bound, Anne 154,157
    Isabella 154
    James 154,157
    John 154
    Sarah 154,157
Bouquet, Henry 233
    Lewis 233
Bourdett, Judith 195
    Samuel 195
Bourdillon, Benedict 186
    Janette Janson 186
Bourne, Abigail 72
    Benjamin 100
    Elizabeth 72,100
    Jesse Jacob 100
    Mary 100
    Matatiah 219
    Nehemiah 25
    Richard 100
    Samuel 100
Bovin, Is. 140
Bowater, John 89
Bowdoin, James 121,192
    John 219
    William 178,191
Bowell, Edward 42
    Rebecca 67
Bowen, Mrs. 248
    Anne 264
    Peter 33
Bower, William 33,43,172
Bowerman, James 54
Bowers, James 83
    John 260
Bowker, Edward 85
    James 85
    Martha 241
    Ralph 86
    Samuel 20
Bowler, Henry 173
Bowles, Elenor 138
    George 138
    James 133,138
    Jane 138
    Mary 133,138
    Phineas 133
    Rebecca 138
    Richard 52
    Thomazine 133
    Tobias 133

Bowman, Rev. 212
    Arthur Lone 144,156,158
    Joseph 257
Bowry, Francis 164
Bowtell, William 57
Bowyer, William 91
Boy, J. 191
    Samuel 106
Boyce, Roger 156
Boyd, Mr. 45
    Sir Thomas 24
    William 225
Boyer, Noah 255
Boyle, John, Lord 145
Boyltins, Hendrine 161
Boys, Joan 10
    John 10
    Joseph 10
    Mary 10
    Sybilla 10
    Thomas 10
    William 10
Boz, Robert 135
Brace, John 139
Braddock, Edward 205
Braddon, Henry 197
Bradley, Ann 179
    Benjamin 105
    Edward 179
    Esther 179
    James 105
    Joseph 126,179
    Lewis 153
    Thomas 179
    William 176,179
Bradshaw, Henry 64
    Mary 15
    Rose 64
    Thomas 62
Bragdon, Jeremiah 241
Bragge, Charles 250
Brailsford, Edward 149
    Samuel 149
Braine, Benjamin 70
    James 70
    John 70
    Margaret 70
    Mary 70
    T. 96
    Thomas 70

Braines, Thomas 109
Bramble, John 74
　Josa. 210
　Robert 92,210
Brandford, Barnaby 199
Brandon, Charles 12
　Thomas 121
Brandreth, Cicely 38
　William 38
Brant, James 19
Brasbridge, Thomas 48
Brathwaite, John 166
　Silvester 166
　Silvia 166,182
　Thomas 166
Braund, William 205
Braxton, William 54
Bray, David 144
　Henry 36,37
Brayne, William 37
Bread, Thomas 43
Brebant, ----- 86
Brebner, Ann 214
　James 214
Breeden, Samuel 133
Breedon, Mary 77
　Robert 77
Breedy, William 220
Breese, Sidney 204
Breintall, Joseph 146
Bremer, Edward 138
Brent, Elizabeth 105
　Humphrey 111
Brenton, Jane 192
　John 192
　William 192
Brereton, Sarah 58
　Thomas 28,237
　William 224
Brerewood, Charlotte 150
Bressey, Charles 125
　John 125
Bretevil, ----- 111
Breton, John 255
Brett, Catharina 105
　Sir Edward 38
　George 11
Brewen, Ann 208
　Hubbard 208
　Richard 14

Brewen, Sarah 208
Brewer, ----- 198
　Elizabeth 198
　William 180
Brewerton, George 72
Brewster, George 96
　Richard 3
Brian, Hugh 186,195
Briant, Christian 32
　George 71
　Henry 122
　Joseph 122
Brice, Mrs. 208
　Edward 239,241
　Elizabeth 201
　John 208,234,244
Brick, Mrs. 149
Brickdell, Edward 129
Bricker, John 142
Bridge, Benjamin 138
Bridges, P. 54
Brierly, William 131
Brigdall, Gr. 197
Brigge, John 65
Briggins, Peter 69,115
Bright, John 113,122
　Mary 122
Bringhurst, Edward 23
Brinley, Deborah 121
　Francis 120,121
　Hannah 120
Briscoe, Ensign 245
Britcher, Margaret 140
Broadbent, Mrs. 106
Broadhurst, Ann 77
　Elizabeth 77
　John 77
　Thomas 77
Brocas, John 197
　Richard 197
　Sarah 197
　Thomas 197
　William 197
Brock, William 92
Brockden, C. 180
　Charles 146
Brockson, Thomas 23
Brogden, William 138
Brome, John 141,148
　Thomas 31

Bromell, Isaac 5
Bromfield, Thomas 212
Bromley, Thomas 196
Bromsall, Mary 68
　Thomas 68
Bromwich, Anthony 55
Bronaugh, William 117
Brooke, Eli 106
　Francis 132
　John Brooke 254
　Paulin 184
　Thomas 86
Brooker, Joanna 224
　John 76
Brook(e)s, Mrs. 58
　Anne 58,194
　Mary 58
　Nehemiah 212
　Philip 231
　Richard 145
　Samuel 212
　Thomas 212
Brookesbancke, Isaac 28
　Sarah 28
　William 28
Brookhouse, William 63,82
Broome, Thomas 53
Broughton, Andrew 153
　Nathaniel 153
　Richard 87
　Thomas 153,197
Brouncker, Richard 133
Brown(e), Abigail 131
　Andrew 159,160
　Ann 244
　Archibald 245
　Arthur 168
　Bartholomew 69
　Benjamin 100,101
　Catherine 245
　Charles 194
　Christian 245
　David 109
　Edward 122
　Elizabeth 109
　Francis 159
　Henton 169
　Hester 122
　Isaac 215
　James 131,181,189,246

Brown(e), Johan 4
John 18,73,101,125,231
Katherine 36
Mary 6,160,184
Nicholas 6
Peregrine 83
Priscilla 194
Rebecca 101
Richard 244
Robert 33,245
Samuel 101
Sarah 101,180,189,
215,244
Susanna 244
Thomas 174,180,189,
244
William 17,101,211,257
Brownhill, Thomas 258
Brownsmith, Ann 22
Bruan, Humphrey 4
Bruce, Archibald 202
Thomas 253
William 257
Brudenall, William 119
Brulon, Daniel 115
David 115
Isaac 115
Brumwich, John 103
Brunifield, John 169
Bryan, John 153
Jonathan 172
Joseph 3
Mary 172
Bryant, John 196
Buchanan, George 143
James 208
John 181
Margaret 143
Neil 155
Buckerfield, Elizabeth 55
Buckland, Robert 9
Buckle, Thomas 202
Buckley, Jonas 108
Buckmaster, Edward 72
Bucknell, Elizabeth 14
Buckston, Francis 21
Buckworth, John 25
Budd, John 13
Bulbrook, Thomas 230

Bulkley, Edward 119
Elizabeth 119
Gersham 119
Peter 119
Sarah 119
Thomas 119
Bull, Elizabeth 13,137
Job 135
John 133,137
Jonathan 137
Samuel 137
William 199,242
Bullen, John 220
Bullivant, Benjamin 46
Bullock, Jane 116
Thomas 116
Bulston, John 192
Bunce, John 60
Bund, Thomas 155
Bunns, Susan 216
Bunting, Daniel 8
Burbridge, Richard 133
Burbydge, Richard 126
Burch, Mary 113
Burcombe, Anne 135
Jane 135
Mary 135
Stephen 135
Burdett, Charles 48
Burdon, Robert 47
Burdy, Robert 260
Thomas 260
Burford, Abigall 35
Henry 249
Burge, John 31
Mary 66
William 66
Burgen, Margaret 3
Thomas 210
Thomas 3
Burges, Ebenezer 193
Isaac 193
John 236
Burgess, Edward 118
Burgis, William 77
Burkett, B. 75
Burkitt, Ann 156
Burley, Anne 105,140
Elizabeth 134
Margaret 140

Burley, Mary 105
Susanna 134
Thomas 105
William 134,140
Burn, Alexander 50
Edward 166
James 174
Burnell, Hester 7
Thomas 7
Burnet(t), Edward 110
Elizabeth 258
George 184,187
Gilbert 140
John 110,187,217
Mary 140
Mathew 236
Samuel 110
Susan 17
Thomas 140
William 140
Burnham, Thomas 100
Burr, Elizabeth 163
Samuel 163
Thomas 60
William 128
Burridge, Robert 244
Sarah 244
Burrington, John 183
Burroughs, Jeremiah 162
John 81
Burrows, John 159,177
Sarah 177
Burslem, James 163
Burt, Philip 155
Burton, Alwine 13
John 97
Richard 212
William 48,192
Burwell, Lewis 235
Nathaniel 86
Burwood, William 82
Bury, Margaret 104
Sarah 254
William 104
Busby, Richard 72
Busher, Abraham 4
Anne 4
Jane 4
Bushery, Gilbert 209
Bussing, Abraham 215

Butcher, Nicholas 4
Butler, Anne 29
   C. 55
   Daniel 152
   John 187,223
   Katherine 18
   Lawrence 74
   Robert 226
   Samuel 22
   Thomas 70
   William 108
Buttall, Benjamin 126,143
   Charles 126,143
   Elizabeth 126
   George 126
   Humphrey 126,143
   John 126
   Joshua 126
   Mary 126,143
   Samuel 126,143
   Sarah 126,143
Butts, Mathew 60
Buttwell, Cornelius 58
Buy, John 106,115
   Mary 106,115
   Robert 106
   William 106
Buyes, Anne 4
   Orvis 4
   Petternel 4
Byard, John 68
Byorr, John 19
Byrd, William 254
Byres, James 88
Byrne, Owen 108
Byrom, Ann 84
Byton, Mr. 164

Cable, John 137
Cadd, Elizabeth 19
Cadogan, George 177
Cadwallader, John 126
Cage, William 115
Cailleau, Anne 115
   John Jacob 115
Cairnes, Alexander 218
   David 218
   Helen 218
   Margaret 218

Calcraft, John 206,208,209
Calderwood, Thomas 109
Caldwell, Agnes 259
   James 259
Calef, Joseph 239
Call, Daniel 73
Callaham, Owen 79
Callendrine, Mr. 41
   Mary 41
Callies, Thomas 193
Calvert, Benedict
   Leonard 142,150
   Cecilius 150,208
   Charles 21,142,150
   Charlotte 150
   Edward Henry 142
   Elizabeth 150
   Jane 150
   Margaret 142
   Raymond 236
Calwell, James 146
Camfield, Frances 60
   Jacob 100
Campbell, Capt. 235
   Mrs. 163
   Catherine 227
   Christiana 254
   Eleanora 237
   Hugh 227
   J. 92
   James 194,210
   John 231
   Lord Niell 147
   N. 112
   Robert 237
   Ronald 185
   Sarah 257
   William 50,237,257
Campion, Thomas 54,123
Candler, Bartholomew 60
   William 216
Cane, Abigail 108
   Francis 108
   Margaret 115
Caner, Hugh 224
Capell, ----- 119
Carberley, Samuel 138
Cardel, Isa. 129
Carew, Johanna 64
Carlton, George 11

Carmichael, Walter 160
Carne, Samuel 217
Carnes, Joseph 243
   Robert 78
Carpender, Alice 14
   Francis 14
   Helen 14
   Martha 61
   Mary 14
   Phillip 14
   Richard 14
   Simon 14
   Thomas 14
   Walter 14
   William 14
Carpenter, Anthony 128
   Elizabeth 53
   George 59
   John 40,101,140
   Joshua 179
   Katherine 101
   Margery 94
   Mary 59,140
   Samuel 66,76,98
   Thomas 4
   William 53
Carr, Isabel 156
   John 156
   Mary 190
   Nicholas 190
   Thomas 71,80
Carrack, James 127
Carre, Andrew 179
Carroll, Charles 117,
   151,194
   Dorothy 151
   James 193
   Juliana 231
   Mary 194
   Patrick 44
Carson, Robert 231
Cart, Joshua 207
Carter, Deighton 171
   Dorothy 15
   Joane 15
   John 15
   Jonathan 9
   Richard 50,220
   Robert 135,253
   Thomas 151

Carter, William 147
Carteret, Philip 252,259
Cartwright, Elizabeth 111
John 111
Thomas 129
Carvel, Robert 78
Car(e)y, Archibald 239
Daniel 26
Esquire 183
Henry 167
Jane 142
John 142
Jonathan 249
Mary 26
Nathaniel 249
Peter 62
Richard 142,249
Robert 91,171
Samuel 249
Thomas 142,249
Warren 142
William 179
Casey, James 225
John 54
Caskie, James 234
Cason, John 24
Rachel 24
Castell, William 106
Castle, Edmond 90
Elizabeth 23
John 45
Mary 23
Caswall, John 167
Kezia 167
Lydia 167
Susannah 167
Catchpoule, Mary 40
Cater, Susanna 95
Cattle, William 196
Caulfield, John 179
Causton, Henry 56
Thomas 56
William 56
Cavalier, John 140
Cave, William 167
Caw, Rachel 245
Cawthorne, William 27
Cay, Dorothy 161
John 161
Jonathan 161

Caydle, Joseph 70
Cecil, Charles 263
Daniel 263
Walter 69
William 145
Chaband, James 59
James 74
Chadborne, John 53
Chadwell, Mary 201
Chalke, Wiliam 40
Chalkhill, J. 182
Chalkley, George 93
Thomas 125
Chalmers, Lionel 233
Chamberlaine, Henrietta
Maria 194
John 158
James 194
Chambers, Ann 193
Charles 193
Elizabeth 76
Mary 76
Nicholas 76
Richard 76
Thomas 76
William 193
Champlyn, John 57
Chanceler, David 192
Chancellor, William 173
Chandler, Daniel 39
Elizabeth 18
Jacob 18
Mary 102,122
Richard 108
William 108,122,209
Chapman, George 116
Hannah 116
John 72,200,236
Richard 215
Susannah 22
William 186
Chard, John 77
Chardin, George 202
Chardon, Isaac 136
Chare, Richard 200
Charles, Peter 77
Charleton, Michael 63
Charlton, Daniel 210
Charouneau, J.S. 259
Charriot, Katherine 112

Chatfield, John 243
Chaundler, Richard 10
Chauvin, Marianna 263
Checkley, John 20
Samuel 39
Cheny, Joane 34
Robert 34
Cherry, John 86
Robert 86
Samuel 224
Cheshire, Elizabeth 113
Richard 114
Chester, Mrs. 208
Ann 61,63
Gamaliel 63
John 61
Joseph 61
Cheston, Daniel 234
Fanny 234
Francina Augustina
234
James 234
Chew, Benjamin 233
Bennet 194
Henrietta Maria 194
Margaret 194
Mary 194
Philemon 194
Cheyney, Katherine 101
Chichester, Elizabeth 222
Ellen 222
Hannah 222
Jeane 222
John 222
Mary 222
Richard 222
Chidlow, Edward 250
Chilcott, Charlotte 211
Mary 211
William 211
Child, Francis 248
Chipman, Elizabeth 235
William 231,235
Chisholm, Nathaniel 224
Choat, Christopher 216
Chois, Mr. 111
Chonan, John 124
Christian, Mrs. 170
Ewan 37

Christmas, Edward 18
  Susanna 18
Chrystie, John 113
Chubb, Fishlake 211
Chubbard, Richard 118
Church, Edward 189
  Robert 15
Churchill, Charles 132
Churchman, John 37,178
Clagett, M. 151
  W. 151
Claiborne, William 178
Clancay, Mary 131
Clapcott, William 57
Clarendon, Earl of 52
Clark(e), Anne 99
  Benjamin 227
  Bowy 192
  Catherine 210
  Christopher 38,139,243
  Elizabeth 15,133,154
  Frederick 73
  George 105
  Henry 133
  Jane 43
  Joane 17
  John 3,15,17,19,43,
    128,210,259
  Jon. 87
  Joseph 258
  Margaret 143
  Mary 1,15,17,74,120
  Raynes 1
  Richard 43
  Robert 15,43
  Ruth 143
  Samuel 98,145
  Sarah 235
  Sterling 171
  Thomas 12,39,72,79,
    102,175
  Timothy 121
  Walter 72
  William 15,17,48,68,97
Clarkson, David 127
Claxton, Hannah 8
  Robert 8
Clay, Elizabeth 152,200
  Joseph 243
  Robert 151

Clay, Sarah 152
  Stephen 151
  William 152
Claypoole, James 75
Clayton, Christopher 56
  Elizabeth 22,84
  John 22,79
  William 84
Cleare, Ambrose 61
  Anne 61
  Mary 61
Cleaveland, William 97
Cleaver, Mary 73
  Thomas 73
Cleland, John 242
Clement, John 124,225
  William 2
Clements, Mr. 56
  Anne 211
Clench, Brune 38
Cliff, Michael 153
Clifford, Mary 110
  Peter 110
  Thomas 167
Clifton, George 75
Cload, William 72
Clodius, Frederick 161
  Phillis 161
Cloke, Hannah 139
  Richard 139
Clopton, William 147
Clothier, Jane 117
  Robert 117
Clough, George 86
Cloyson, Hendrick 77
Cluny, David 82
Clutterbuck, Joseph 50
  Lewis 208
Coad, Mary 107
Coats, George 128
  Thomas 62
  Warwick 200
Coatsworth, Caleb 86
  Susannah 86
Coattam, John 73
Cobb, Alice 19
  Arthur 19
  Francis 19
  James 19
  Margaret 19

Cobb, Susan 19
  Sir Thomas 19
  Winifred 19
Cobham, Thomas 232
Cobley, Jennit 160
  Mary 20
Cochet, Anna 12
  Anne 12
  Nathaniel 12
  Robert 12
  Sarah 12
  Thomas 12
Cockburn, John 129
  Martha 129
  Thomas 129
  William 242
Cock(e), Catesby 256
  Elizabeth 256
  James 253
  John Catesby 256,257
  Richard 244
  Robert 139
  Sarah 96
  Thomas 156
  William 256
Cocking, Thomas 234
Cockram, Mary 178,221
  Walter 178
Cockrell, Christopher 57
Cockshudd, Edmund 97
  Jeffery 97
  John 97
  Thomas 97
Cockshutt, Thomas 85
Cockwell, Hester 119
Cod(d)rington, Edward 215
  Margaret 34
  Thomas 34
Codenham, Jane 72
  Robert 72
  William 72
Coggin, Ann 119
  Edward 119
Colchester, Richard 16
Colcutt, William 13
Colden, Alexander 262
  Elizabeth 262
  Jane 261
  John 261
  Richard Nichols 261

Coldham, John 165
Cole, Edward 145
  Elizabeth 62,116
  John 14,121,233
  Josiah 147
  Mary 73,89,116,121
  Michael 116
  Philip 116
  Rachel 116
  Susannah 82
  Thomas 116
  William 89
Coleman, Abraham 70
  Christopher 242
  Daniel 126
  Margaret 70
  Philip 159
  Roger 183
  Stephen 180
  William 159
Coles, Elizabeth 50
  Joane 50
  John 50,195
  Ruth 50
Colles, Mary 91
  Thomas 91
Colleton, Anne 51
  Arabella 25
  Charles 51
  Elizabeth 204
  Hannah 197
  Henry 25
  J. 166
  James 50
  Sir John 197,204
  John 50,197,204
  Katherine 50
  Sir Peter 50
  Peter 166,197,204
  Robert 197,204
  Susannah 197,204
  Ursula 25
Collett, Thomas 198
Colley, Alice 63
  Elizabeth 63
  Hugh 63
  Jonathan 63
  Michael 63
  William 63

Collier, Alexander 164
  Daniel 223
  John 231
Collings, Elizabeth 148
Collingwood, Gerard 148
Collins, Mr. 7
  Ann 204,215
  Edward 215
  Elinor 184
  Elizabeth 25,104
  George Barret 215
  James 126
  Jerome 54,91,111
  John 204
  Marie 25
  Mary 99,184
  Phillip 76
  Richard 25
  Sarah 216
  Sidney 215
  Stephen 226
  Terence 132
  Thomas 25,173
  William 42,97,104,
    173,184,253
Collyar, William 231
Collyer, Jane 14
  John 104
  Thomas 14
Colman, Benjamin 161,240
  William 37
Colquhoun, Robert 210
Colson, Elizabeth 198
  George 198
  John 49
  Sarah 49
Colston, William 75
Coltby, Philip 19
Coltman, Alice 19
  William 19
Colver, Joseph 228
Colvert, William 59
Colvill, Edmund 10
  Edward 53
  Elizabeth 53
  Jane 53
  John 53
  Stephen 53
  Susanna 53
  Thomas 53

Comafleau, William 225
Combe, Edmund 209
Comby, Martha 127
Comean, Margaret 169
Comer, John 161
Commander, Hercules 16
Commeline, Samuel 242
Complin, William 190
Comport, Richard 210
Compton, Elizabeth 182
  Thomas 182
Comsteed, William 256
Conant, John 126
Coneway, James 23
Conn, Thomas 8
Connaway, Thomas 74
Conner, Edward 238
  Elizabeth 139
  Lewis 139
Connop, John 90
Connor, James 247
Conway, Henry 213
  Margaret 11
  Robert 11
Conyers, John 39
Coo, John 214
Cook(e), Abigail 181
  Andrew 101
  Ann 66,101,221
  Bentley 96
  Ebenezer 101
  Edmund 181
  Edward B. 218
  Elizabeth 181,205
  George 205
  John 45,66,205,153
  Joseph 30
  Judy 142
  Kenner 102
  Martha 102
  Mordecai 27
  Philip 128
  Rebecca 205
  Richard 80,200
  Samuel 216
  Sarah 205,221
  Thomas 27,82,135
  Walsingham 55
  William Beresford 205
Cooles, Ursula 73

Coombe, Henry 129
    William 153
Coombes, Enoch 23
Coomes, Joan 5
    Thomas 5
Cooper, Anne 40
    Bartholomew 128
    Benjamin 28
    Daniel 147
    James 218
    Johanna 198
    John 147
    Joseph 81,198
    Richard 102
    Samuel 20
    Sarah 198
    Thomas 49
    William 56,116,125,
        128,218
Coote, James 36
Cooter, Matthew 121
Cope, Henry 175
    Jane 175
Copping, George 39
Coppocke, Martha 40
Copson, John 147
Corbett, Paul 196
    Thomas 164,167,196,
        207
Corbin, Mrs. 208
    Elizabeth 18
    Gawin 103,104
    Jane 103
    John 18
    Richard 208
Corddaux, Richard 144
Corderoy, Anne 20
    Francis 20
    Jasper 20
    William 20
Cordes, John 206
    Thomas 207
Corker, Daniel 255
    John 255,256
    Nathaniel 255
    Susan 17
    Thomas 202,255
    William 17
Cornelius, Elizabeth 173
    Richard 88

Corney, Robert 12
Cornish, James 217
Cornock, Daniel 150
    Samuel 150
Cornwall, Alexander 85
    Walter 85
Cornwell, Anne 34
    Anthony 54
    Thomas 54
Cort, Henry 258
Cosby, Alexander 179
    Grace 204
    Henry 204
    Philip 204
Cosens, John 163
    Stephen 46
Cosigin, Francis 204
Cosin, Ellinor 113
    John 49,52,113
Cossart, Peter 161
    Susannah 161
Cosse, Mary 19
Coster, Dorothy 32
Cottle, Edmond 170
Cotton, Ann 66
    Edward 32
    John 4
    Josa. 205
    Thomas 205
    William 66
Couch, Elizabeth 137
    James 62
Coulborne, William 13
Coulson, Stephen 253
    William 211
Coulter, Michael 161
Coulthred, Thomas 187
Coursey, Elizabeth 117
    John 194
    Otho 151
    William 117
Coutts, Hercules 95
    James 96
    Thomas 71
Couzens, Isabella 209
    John 209
    Samuel 209
Coverly, John 143
Covinton, Sarah 117

Coward, Christian 46
    William 46
Cowcher, Sibilla 208
Cowper, ----- 213
    Christopher 65
    Sarah 24
    Sir William 41
Cox(e), Anne 102
    Christian 103
    Daniel 52,246
    Edmund 42
    Elizabeth 40,132
    Grace 102
    Henry 135
    John 102
    Joseph 134
    Mary 102
    Nehemiah 42
    Russell 102
    Samuel 132
    Sem 104
    Thomas 102
    Thomas 36,102
Coyle, John 43
Cozens, Charles 185
Crabb, Samuel 53
Cradock, George 121
Crafts, Elizabeth 168
    John 168
    Richard 180
    Thomas 180
Cragg, Robert 162
Craig, John 103
Craige, George 169
Crampton, Richard 53
Crane, Griffin 89
    Isaiah 187
    John 251
    Thomas 31
Cranston, Anne Mary 157
Cranstone, Robert 58
Cranwell, Jonathan 110
Crashawe, Mr. 1
Craske, Sell. 36
Craven, Charles 110
    John 220
    Thomas 37
Crawford, Mr. 95
    John 237,246

Crawley, John 112
Thomas 231
Cray, John 137
Craycroft, Ignatius 261
Creake, Mary 111
Samuel 111
Creamer, John 117
Creedlan, Abraham 185
Cresap, Thomas 206
Creswell, Agnes 236
Obidiah 236
Creswick, Samuel 162,163
Crevatt, Capt. 37
Crew, Sir John 119
Crews, Emme 56
Richard 56
Crick, Henry 180
Crips, Thomas 155
Crispe, Edmond 11
Elias 11
Rowland 11
Samuel 11
Tobias 11
Crittendon, Richard 220
Cro(c)katt, Charles 166
James 166,175,198,205
John 166
Crockett, William 140
Croft, Childermas 164
Edward 205
Crofts, ----- 191
Croker, Alice 19
Cromartie, Adam 168
Marjery 168
Crome, Val. 6
Crommelin, Charles 165
Daniel 165
Crook, Watt 169
Crooke, Charles 234
Crosby, Daniel 240
Robert 136,155
Crosdill, Richard 236
Croskeys, Joseph 129
Cross(s)e, Anne 19
Charles 175
George 80
John 44
Richard 19
Samuel 19,74
Sarah 80

Crossmith, Mr. 173
Crouch, George 2
John 69
William 42,69
Crouchefer, Mary 187
Croucher, ----- 106
Crow, John 96
Crowley, Charles 56
Crowther, John 69
Cruger, Jacob Myna 81
Valentine 81
Cruickshank, Mary 93
Cruley, James 109
Crump, Isaac 114
John 121,127
Sarah 114
Crymble, Murray 175
Cudlipp, John 84,126
Margaret 126
Mary 70
Cuffee, John 200
Ruth 200
Culforth, J. 140
Culling, William 164
Cully, Abraham 51
John 51
Culpepper, Lady
Margaret 115
Culverwell, Anthony 1
Richard 1
Cumming, Alexander 239
Witter 222
**Cummings, Archibald
169**
George 169
Jane Elizabeth 169
Cummins, James 244
Cunningham, Archibald 92
David 24
Robert 248
William 200
Curling, Anthony 142
Curr, Daniel 138
Currie, Ebenezer 183
Jean 183
John 183
Curry, Ester 156
Samuel 156
Curson, W. 40
Curtain, Robert 226

Curtis, Caleb 257
Daniel 119
George 32
William 128
Curtiss, David 228
Joseph 228
Curtyce, Elizabeth 14
John 14
Mary 14
Richard 14
Cushing, Jeremiah 237
Thomas 223
Cussens, Richard 37
Custis, Daniel Park 203
John 202
Martha 203
Cuthbert, Eleanor 68
Robert 67,68
Cutler, John 243
Timothy 182

Dabdin, Henry 111
Da Costa, Moses 245
Dafforne, Ann 28
Benjamin 28
John 28
Dagge, John 217
Dagget, Martha 57
Dagnall, Ralph 57
Dailey, Owen 241
Daintrey, William 44
Dakeyne, John 226
Daking, Ann 63
Elizabeth 63
Samuel 63
Dalany, Daniel 160
Dale, Joan 3
Richard 3
Thomas 195
Dalglish, John 214
Dalley, Robert 81
Dalrumble, Alexander 181
Dalrymple, Sir John 236
John 236
Martha 236
Dalzell, James 244
Lieut.-Gen. 188
Daman, William 184
Danby, Earl of 65

Dance, Jeremy 15
Dandridge,
   Bartholomew 253
  W. 211
Dandy, Patience 13
Daness, Ebenezer 56
Dangerfield, Stephen 49
Daniel(l), Edward 60,174
  J. 140
  Richard 152
  William 211
Dansey, Thomas 122
Danson, Barbara 131
Danvers, Henry 40
Darby, John 127
  Martha 127
  Mary 165
Darnall, Mr. 144
  Elizabeth 145
Darvall, Frances 34
  William 34
Dassay, James 23
  John 23
  Raphe 23
Daston, John 67
Daulton, John 27
Davenport, Addington
  176,182
  Alice 111
  Annis 111
  Elizabeth 111,182
  George 255
  Jane 182
  Richard 111
  Thomas 111
  William 111
Davers, Charles 214
  Elizabeth 214
  Henry 214
  Sir Jermyn 196,214
  Jermyn 196
  Lady Margaret 196
  Dame Margaretta 214
  Mary 214
  Thomas 214
David, Ezekiel 241
  John 47
Davidson, James 213
  Joseph 189
Davie, William 46

Davi(e)s, Benjamin 224
  Edward 224
  Elizabeth 32,129
  Ellen 52
  Hannah 80,224
  Hester 52
  Howel 251
  Isaac 52
  Jane 131
  Johanna 224
  John 2,47,113,117,
    129, 252
  Lewis 80
  Mary 58
  Mary Ann 252
  Mathew 32
  N. 246
  Peter 162
  Philip 118
  Ruth 252
  Sarah 252
  Thomas 138,259
  William 11,**52**,224,**262**
  William Worthington
    252
Davise, John 235
Davison, Timothy 104
Davister, Mary 116
  Richard 116
Davoll, Ann 130
Davy, Mary 56
  William 56
Dawes, Nicholas 25
Dawkings, William 135
Dawkins, Henry 248
  James 54
  William 54
Dawley, Elizabeth 210
  Richard 210
Dawson, Elizabeth 194
  John 74
  Joseph 50
  Matthew 194
  Rigault 64
  Samuel 64
  Sarah 64
  Thomas 203
Day, Edward 79
  James 120
  Jane 178

Day, Jone 79
  Margaret 67
  Mary 120
  Richard 52
  Robert 27
  Sarah 75
Deakin, Peter 7
Deale, Thomas 229
Dean, William 80
Deane, Thomas 4
Dearing, Joseph 89,108
  Mary 89,108
Dearn, Thomas 260
Deas, Catherine 245
  David 245
  Elizabeth 245
  John 245
  Mary 245
  Seaman 245
Death, Anthony 92
Deaveaux, James 205
de Bary, Mrs. 94
De Beaufain, Cladie 234
  Hector Beringer 234
de Beekers, Anna 183
Debell, Paul 153
Deblois, Stephen 140,192
De Brissac, James 111
de Brooke, Lord Wil-
  loughby 260
Decker, Joseph 241
de Conty, Peter Marquis
  255
Dedrusina, Margaret 235
De Frene, Peter 128
De Giguillat, ----- 45
de la Brasseur, Ann 190
de la Croix, Abraham 161
  Susannah 161
Deladicq, Lawrence 46
de la Tour, Philip 242
De Lafontaine, Ch. 170
de Lancey, Elizabeth 258
  James 258
  Richard 258
De Lannay, Anne 136
De Lanne, John 136
  Mary 136
  Peter 136
  Susanna 136

De Lavall, Hannah 66
John 34,66
Margaret 34
Thomas 34
Delegal, Catherine 227
Edward 227
Eleanor 227
George 227
Margaret 227
Philip 227
Sophia 227
Delegat, Philip 139
Delemont, Abraham 238
Elizabeth 238
Dell, Mary 115
Thomas 115
Delony, Ann 173
James Matthew 173
Deloraine, Elizabeth,
Countess 182
Delpech, Isaac 136
Isaac 115,163
Delval, J. 145
Demayne, Francis 112
Denline, George 23
Dennes, Robert 3
Dennis, Mrs. 88
David 63
Elizabeth 216
John 46,79,83,98,99,
107
Denniston, Roger 43
Denny, Alexander 141
James 141
Lucy 141
Dent, Digby 169
Elizabeth 58
William 86
Denton, Frances 171
Luke 148
Matthew 171
Denwood, Living 13
De Peyster, Gerard 226
de Prefontaine, Anne 263
Elizabeth 263
John 263
Mary 263
Peter Francis 263
Sarah 263
Derickson, George 36

Derne, Christopher 20
de Rosset, Lewis 232,249
Desbrosses, Elias 244
Deterne, Abraham 249
Deveaux, James 223
Deverall, Benjamin 117
Jeremiah 117
John 117
Rachel 117
Susannah 117
Deverell, John 194
Deverill, Benjamin 105
De Vie, Henry 212
Devisme, Ann 220
Philip 220
Devonshear, Mr. 217
Dewbery, Thomas 81
Dewell, Richard 32
Dewxell, Margaret 9
Richard 9
Diamond, Richard 49
Dick, Margaret 143
Robert 245
Dickenson, Michael 63
Dicker, William 226
Dickinson, Francis 4
Lawrence 4
Philip 4
Dicks, James 28
Margaret 28
Dickson, Alexander 248
Elizabeth 189
James 190
Jane 190
Patrick 190
Susanna Jane 248
Thomas 189
Dicus, Charles 53
Didlake, James 220
John 220
Rhoda 220
Digges, Charles 145
Dudley 213
John 145
Susanna Maria 145
Thomas 258
Dillard, Nicholas 220
Dinello, Mary 195
Dinglass, James 104
Dismarett, Lydia 35

Ditcher, John 150
Dix, Jane 166
Dixon, Ann 258
Hugh 214
John 13
Josiah 67
Mary 258
Thomas 241,251,258
Dobbs, Arthur 232
Conway Richard 232
Edward Brice 232
Justina 232
Richard 232
Dobby, Conyers 175
Dobbyn, Anastasia 247
Richard 247
Dockwra, William 95,234
Doctour, Mr. 11
Dod, John 24,138
Mary 24
Dogett, Benjamin 92
Benjamin 94
John 94
Otgher 94
Doghead, Samuel 257
Dolley, William 169
Dolly, Daniel 131
Dolman, John 20
Dolphin, John 176
Donald, Elizabeth 237
James 168
Donalson, Andrew 146
Daniel 147
Mary 146
Doncastle, Mrs. 63
Doncell, John 127
Donevan, Daniel 73
Donkester, William 142
Donne, Anthony 170
John 170
Mary 170
Robert 170
Donning, Joanna 175
William 175
Donogan, Hugh 132
Doody, Samuel 62
Dorsey, Ann 244
Basil 186
E. 171
Elizabeth 244

Dorsey, Nicholas 244
  Thomas Beal 244
Dottin, Elizabeth 155
Doughty, Thomas 150
Douglas(s), Capt. 155
  James 118,198
  Sholto 214
  Stanley 226
  Thomas 225,239
  William 107,115
Douxsaint, James 111
Dove, James 238
  Thomas 134,135
Dover, Anne 90
  Edward 48
  Thomas 90
  William 90
Dovey, Elizabeth 27
Dowdall, James 260
Dowling, John 260
Downe, Abraham 151
  Elizabeth 151
  Joseph 151
Downer, William 88
Downes, Anne 167
  Christopher 135
  Samuel 167
Downing, Anne 104
  George 104
  John 221
  Joseph 104
  Mary 221
Downman, Rawleigh 222
Dowse, Joseph 182
  Stephen 199
Draper, Anne 5
  Jasper 5
  Lawrence 4
  Richard 4
  Thomas 4
Dray, William 29
Drayton, Thomas 243
Dreury, Eliza 136
Drew, Richard 67
Drinkeld, Joseph 192
Drinkwater, John 78
Droure, Francis 263
Drummon, Jane 231
  John 231
Drummond, John 61

Drumont, James 19
Dry, Jenny 98
  Mary 98
  Thomas 98
Dryden, Adam 238
  Constance 11
  Eleanor 238
  Elizabeth 238
  Francis 11
  Henry 11
  James 238
  Jonathan 11
  Martha 11
  Mary 11,238
  Robert 11
Drysdale, Hester 132
  Hugh 132
Duane, Anthony 215
  Matthew 258
Dubois, Capt. 248
Ducasse, Isaac 110
Duchee, Andrew 147
  Jacob 200
  Mary 147
Duckenfield, William 57
Duckinfield, William 119
Dudgeon, Patrick 79
Dudley, Peter 220
  Robert 220
Duglass, Dr. 212
  Ann 176
Dugleby, Elizabeth 259
  John 259
Duhigg, Walter 171
Duke, Ann 113
  Richard 113
Dulany, Daniel 194
  Henrietta Maria 194
  Lloyd 194
Dummer, Jeremy 163
Dumotier, James 111
  John 111
  Judith 111
  Peter 111
Dunbar, George 185
  Samuel 212
Duncan, Alexander 236
Dungey, Elizabeth 87
Dunkan, John 108

Dunkin, John 128
Dunkley, William 229
Dunn, Mrs. 22
  Adrianna 172
  Elizabeth 113
  George 94
  Joseph 113
  Samuel 172
  Thomas 12
Dunnidge, James 125
Dunsford, Martin 36
Dunster, Charles 146
  Margaret 146
Dunton, Elizabeth 149
  John 148
  Sarah 149
Dupee, Benjamin 202
  Daniel 202
  Elias 202
  Sarah 224
Duport, Simon 59
Dupre, John 198
Dupuis, Abraham 243
Durand, Jonathan 212
Durant, Elizabeth 89
Duron, Charles 181
  Katherine 181
Durousseau, Samuel 59
Durratt, John 103
Durzy, Benjamin 51
Duskin, Elizabeth 142
Dutton, Henry 135
  Peter 26
Dycke, Thomas 149
Dyer, Edward 34
  Hugh 106
Dyke, Daniel 29
Dymmock, William 43
Dyson, Charles 177
  David 183
  Francis 183
  Gravenor 27
  John 177,183
  Mary 27
  Peter 183
  Philip 177,183
  Priscilla 183

Eades, John **65**
  Mary 65
  Winifred 65
Eaglesfield, Ann 174
  John 174
Eagleston, Joseph 235
Ealand, Mary 238
Eales, Catherine 134
Earle, Robert 91
East, Benjamin 68
  Hannah 68
  John 68
  Mary 68
  Thomas 52
Eastlake, Samuel 64
Eastman, Sarah 201
Easton, John 72
  Thomas 180
Eaton, Edward 74
  William 262
Ebbitt, Edward 101
Eccles, Ann 221
Eccleston, Theodore 52,76
  W. 218
Echballs, Harman 17
Eckley, John **66,67**
  Sarah **66,**67
Edes, Mary 205
Edgar, Edward 195
  John 58
Edgcomb, Judith 35
Edge, Johanna 127
  John 69,**127**
  Martha 127
Edgington, Jeremy 21
Edmonds, Benjamin
  54,105,**168**
  Eddey 25
  Elizabeth 25
  Joane 25
  John 25
  Nathaniel 185
  Rebecca 168
Edmondson, Sarah 26
Edwards, Cony 190
  David 64
  Hugh 56
  Isabel 56
  Isabella 148
  John 56,193

Edwards, Mary 51,64,82,
  102,192
  Meridah 74
  Morris 102
  Peter 251
  Rebecca 211
  Richard 211
  Samuel 257
  Susanna 64
  Sweet 64
  William 190
Efford, Jane 67
  Richard 67
Egelsham, John 120
Ehlers, Bearend 222
Eirde, James 15
Elbridge, Mr. 254
  Aldworth 162
  John 154
  John 162,189
  Rebecca 162
  Thomas 162
Elford, John 154
Elkington, Anne 159
  George 159
  Richard 159
Ellery, Thomas 123
Ellett, John 240
Elliot(t), Amos 247
  Andrew 183,246,**259**
  Archibald 185
  Benjamin 138
  Elizabeth 103,223,246
  George 18
  Gilbert 146
  Isabella 260
  Katherine 18
  Margaret 18
  Molly 247
  Peter 258
  Robert 145
  Sylvia 260
  William 18
Ellis, Charles 29
  Edward 19
  Henry 13
  John 12,29,76
  Margaret 19,186
  Mary 19
  Owen 161

Ellis, Richard 22
  Thomas 93
Ellison, Anthony 260
  Catherine 208
  Cuthbert 208
  Elizabeth 208
  Henry 208
  Jane 208
  Robert 208
Elliston, Elizabeth 76
  John 76
  Mary 76
  Peter 76
Ellixon, Jasper 90
  Margery 90
  Mary 90
Ellwood, Thomas 61
Elly, George 138
Else, Thomas 82
Elsey, Hannah 101
Elson, Samuel 92
Elton, Mr. 107
  Andrew 40
Elwes, Anne 21
  Thomas 21
Elwin, Fountain 249
Ely, Thomas 59
Emerson, Grace 99
  James 97
  Mary 186
  Sarah 186
Emerton, Francis 77
Emory, Ann 117
  Arthur 117
Emott, James 187
  James 244
End, Joseph 107
  Rachel 107
England, Allen 163
  Betty 153
  John 163
  Joseph 163
  Mary 86
  Samuel 86
English, Garrett 52
Enosin, Mary 52
Enton, John 45
Epes, John 100
Erby, Elizabeth 47
  William 47

Ernall, Elizabeth 22
 Thomas 22
Erp, John 66
 Mary 66
Errington, Anthony 18
Erswell, Henry 156
Eskridge, George 97
Esler, Mary 195
Esse, Caleb 194
Eustace, Anne 135
 G. 232
 John 101
 Mary 101
Evance, Branfill 195
 Thomas 254
Evans, Alice 138
 Ann 137
 Barbara 137
 Edward 82
 Elizabeth 33
 Evan 138
 Hugh 6
 John 62,236,244
 Peter 126,169
 Phineas 215
 Richard 33
 Rowland 186
 Stephen 179
 Thomas 67,105
 William 37
Eveleigh, Ann 232
 Catherine 232
 Elizabeth 232
 George 232
 John 232
 Nicholas 232
 Samuel 232
 Thomas 232
Evens, Thomas 57
Everard, Thomas 253,256
Evered, Ralph 69
Everson, Thomas 208
Ewens, John 55
Ewer, John 70
Ewetse, Peter 214
Ewing, Henry 224
Exley, John 247
Eycott, Rachel 128
 Thomas 128
Eynard, Alexander 181

Eyre, Francis 252
 Kingsmill 136,139
Eyres, John 44

Facer, Henry 164
 James 164
 Martha 164
 Thomas 164
Fagan, Marcela 147
Fairbank, Thomas 226
Fairchild, Thomas 130,206
Fairclo, Thomas 125
Fairfax, Lady
        Catherine 115
 Catherine 116
 Frances 116
 Henry Culpepper 115
 Margaret 116
 Robert 115
 Thomas, Lord 115
Fairfield, William 257
Fairweather, John 189
Faldo, Charles 138
 Mary 138
 Thomas 77
Fallows, John 151
Fananbrouse, John 193
Fane, Charles 96
 George 96
 Henry 162
Faneuil, Andrew 161
 Anne 161
 Benjamin 161, 176
 John 161
 Judith 59
 Marian 161
 Mary 176
 Paul 59
 Peter 161
 Susannah 161
Fanning, Zerviat 228
Fanster, Elizabeth 73
Farbour, Katherine 41
Farewell, George 66
Fargusion, Robert 62
 Thomas 62
Farguson, Thomas 260
Faris, John 188
 Mary 188

Farley, Thomas 70
Farmar, Anne 130
 Brook 130
 Christopher 130
 Jasper 130
 Robert 130
 Samuel 130
 Thomas 130
 William 130
Farmer, Hannah 135
 Joan 159
 John 159, 231
 Mary 159
 Oliver 153
Farr, Mr. 232
 Grace 232
Farrant, Godfrey Lee 238
 Henry 238
 Mary 238
Farrel & Jones 262
Farrell, Agnes 134
 Daniel 134
 Edith 64
 James 160
Farthing, James 20
 Maria 145
Fary, Charles 54
 Francis 54
 Joseph 54
 Mary 54
 Robert 54
Fashion, William 68
Fast, Mary 161
Faulcon, Henry 71
Fauquier, Francis 253
 William 253
Fawkner, Elizabeth 119
 Everard 119
 Jane 119
 Sarah 119
 Susanna 119
Fazakerly, E. 127
Feddeman, Richard 128
Fegon, Ann 5
Felgate, Tobias 2, 3
Fell, Guilielma M.F. 252
 John 191
 Mary Margaretta 252
 Robert Edward 252
 Susanna 191

Fenning, Hannah 16
Fenton, Richard 213
Fenwick, Edward 182, 222
  Elizabeth 182
  Henry 222
  John 153, **182**
  Michael 222
  Robert 182
  Samuel 223
  Sarah 182
  William 222
Feram, John 41
Ferdyce, Margett 178
  William 178
Ferguson, Archibald 160
Fernald, John 77
Fernsley, John 187
  Mary 187
  Sarah 187
Fervis, William 106
Fetters, James 194
Fidler, Deborah 71
  James 71
Field, Abraham 80
  John 103
  Theophilus 179
Fielding, Ambrose 28
  Ann 28
  Edward 28
  Frances 103
  Henry 103
  Richard 28
Filby, Bridget 13
Fild, Samuel 195
Filley, Esther 175
Filmer, Lady Anne 21
  Sir Edward 21
  Edward 115
  Mary 22
  Samuel 21
Finch, E. 116
  Francis 5
  Grace 5
  Hannah 61
  John 5
  Mary 5
  Robert 60
Fincher, Thomas 193
Findlason, Wiliam 85

Findley, James 109
  Margaret 109
Finglass, John 244
Finlason, William 92
Finlayson, Jonah 184
Finnie, Katherine 263
  Letitia 263
  William 263
Firebrace, Henry 5
Fish, Joseph 171
Fisher, George 112, 222
  John 22, 57, 85
  Paul 157
  William 57
Fitch, Abiel 158
  Abigail 198
  Martha 158
  Patrick 198
  Sarah 158
  Thomas 158
Fitchett, John 176
Fithes, Anne 24
Fittar, James 130
Fitzharry, A. 53
Fitzherbert, John 209
  Judith 209
  Richard 209
  Thomas 209
Fitzhugh, Ann 239
  Henry 57
  Robert 57
  William 46
Flanagan, William 190
Fleet, Elizabeth 149
  Giles 149
  Henry 149
  John 149
  Mary 149
  Mathew 149
  Richard 149
  Simon 258
  William 149
Fleetwood, Anne 45
  Sir Gerald 41
  John 41
  Mary 41
  Richard 45
  Samuel 45
Fleming, Jonathan 208
  Marmaduke 19

Fletcher, Joseph 85
  Nathaniel 184
Fleurian, Peter 59
Flexney, Daniel 188
Flinge, Andrew 140
  Mary 140
Flint, John 236
  Thomas 88
Flood, Peter 216
  Valentine 247
Flower, Daniel 22
  Joseph Edward 160
Fluellin, William 19
Fly, John 62
Fog, Mary 84
  Robert 105
Fogwell, John 13
Follett, John 46
Foote, Elizabeth 58
  Francis 58
  George 58
  Henry 58
  Hester 58
  Richard 58
  Samuel 58
  Topham 58
Forber, John 185
Forbes, Anne 171
  Dryden 171
  George 171
  James 171
  John 171, 262
  Margaret 171
  Margery 171
  Robert 171
  Thomas 171
Ford, Athanasius 261
  George 87
  Jane 165
  Mary 90
  Philip 103
  Stephen 122
  Thomas 90, 166
  W. 88
Foresight, Arthur 77
Forman, Alice 262
  Anthony 262
  Edward Wiliam 261
  Greenfield 262
  Henry 262

Forman, Jane 262
  John 262
  Richard 261
  Sarah 262
  William 261, 262
For(r)est, Edmund 88
  John 96
Forrester, George 196
Forster, Edward 57
  Miles 60
  Robert 14
Fortune, Elias 78
Forward, Christopher 207
  Jonathan 109
Foss(e), Elizabeth 16
  John 203
Foster, Mr. 71
  Edmond 35
  Elinor 118
  Elizabeth 220, 235
  Grace 232
  Isaac 249
  John 56, 91, 220
  Joseph 86
  Mary 115, 201
  Rebecca 60
  Sarah 205
  Thomas 109
Fottrell, Achsah 186
  Edward 160, 186
  Thomas 186
Fountain, John 101
  Margaret 101
  Martha 101
  Robert 102
  Roger 102
  Susanna 202
Fowell, Richard B. 254
Fowler, Daniel 95
  Elizabeth 95
  James 95
  Roarry 95
Fowlis, Thomas 74
Fowlkes, Bridget 29
  John 29
  Mary 29
Fox, Charles 42
  Daniel 215
  Freeman 1
  George 159

Fox, James 66
  John 104
  Joseph 253
  Stephen 62
Foxcroft, Francis 63
Foye, Edward 69
Fraisure, Alexander 237
Frampton, Thomas 51
Frances, Thomas 113
Franceys, James 173
Francis, R. 171
  Tench 172
Francklen, Capt. 81
Francklyn, Gilbert 253
Frank, Thomas 130
Frankcomb, William 221
Frankland, Charles 213
  Frederick 136
  Sir Thomas 136
Frankling, Anne 102
  Deveana Susannah 186
  Elizabeth 102
  Jacob 102, 103
  James 44
  Mary 102
  Thomas 102
Fraser, James 180
  John 147, 171
Fraunces, Edward 168
  James 168
Fread, John 127
Freame, Joseph 251
  Margaret 252
  Margaretta 176
  Philadelphia Hannah 252
  Thomas 176
Fred, John 127
Freeke, Philip 154
Freeman, Charles 164
  Henry 79
  John 225
  Robert 5
  William G. 197
Freemantel, John 212
Freere, Elizabeth 25
  Toby 25
Freestan, Thomas 135
Freeston, Mr. 235
French, Robert 159
Frende, Elizabeth 236

Freshwater, Elizabeth 89
  Richard 89
  William 89
Frezvant, Daniel 256
Friend, Isaac 250
  Robert 145
Frigatt, Mrs. 103
Frinck, Sarah 69
  Thomas 69
Frisby, James 83, 84
  Peregrine 83
  Sarah 83
  Thomas 83, 84
  William 83
Froadsham, John 71
Fromantle, Sarah 149
Frost, Andrew P. 240
  Anna Maria 213
  Augustine 213
  Charles 240
  Joanna 240
  John 13, 240
  Martha 213
  Sarah 240
  William 240
Frothingham, Thomas 254
Fry, James 251
  Jane 251
  Rebecca 251
Fryer, John 260
Fukes, William 93
Fulham, John 110
  Ursula 110
Fuller, Mr. 199
  D. 116
  John 95
  Mudd 137, 147
Fullerton, George 96
  William 96
Furley, Jonathan 216
Furness, Elizabeth 129
  Jacob 129
  John 129
Furnivall, Thomas 109
Furse, Elizabeth 112
Furton, Henry 2
Furzland, Andrew 29
Fyfield, Jane 251
  John 251

Gabourel, Amos 158
  Jane 158
  Joshua 158
  Rachel 158
  Thomas 158
Gadsden, Christopher 180
Gage, Maria 246
  Thomas 246
Gaine, Hugh 258
Gainsborough, Thomas
  159
Galache, James 243
  John 243
  William 243
Galbraith, William 80
Gale, Christopher 152
  Edmund 152
  George 172
  John 75
  Mildred 75
  William 192
Galhie, Stephen 181
Galleghar, Mrs. 223
Galley, John 174
  Thomas 185
Galloway, Francis 211
  Samuel 235
Gamble, Henry 129
Gambling, Joseph 126
Games, Edward 130
Garbrand, Caleb John 262
Garbutt, Elizabeth 249
  Isaac 249
  John 249
  Mary 249
Gardiner, Abraham 209
  Christopher 94
  Silvester 224
Gardner, John 179
  Richard 99
  Silvester 190
  Timothy 22
Gardon, ----- 111
Garnett, Hannah 35
Garrard, Anne 4
Garrett, Amos 164
  Edward 91
  Elizabeth 164
  James 164
  Mary 164

Garrett, Sarah 164
  Seth 164
Garth, Catherine 166
Gate, Ann 7
  Judith 7
  Katherine 7
  Thomas 7
Gates, Ann 195
  Horatio 206
  Thomas 195
Gathorne, Thomas 252
Gault, Alice 60
  James 60
Gayton, Clark 229
Geary, Henry 56, 57
  John 56
  Joseph 56
Geast, Daniel 92
  John 92
Gee, Thomas 2
Geist, Christian 145
Gell, Robert 14
Gely, Ann 211
Geneves, Peter 115
Geneway, John 23
George, Ann 252
  John 200
  Thomas 96
  William 199, 252
Gerarde, Agnes 1
  John 1
Gering, Barbara 222
Gerrish, Margery 240
Gerry, Sarah 254
Gest, Nathaniel 206
Gester, Anthony 29
Ghetting, Bartholomew 253
Ghinn, Ann 244
  John 244
Gibb, James 71
Gibbon, Samuel 27
  Thomas 90
Gibbons, John 138
Gibb(e)s, Benjamin 167
  Elizabeth 195
  John 182
  Richard 21, 52
  Thomas 226
  William 182

Gibson, Ann 36, 154
  Daniel 134, 154
  Elizabeth 36
  John 36, 47
  Patience 36
  Thomas 13
  William 36
Giffard, Catherine 184
Gilbert, Abraham 38
  Elizabeth 214
  Francis 122
  John 27
  Moody 136
  Nathaniel 214
  Thomas 27, 38, 197
Gilchrist, Thomas 81
Gildart, Mary 213
  T. 213
Gildemaster,
  Christopher 156
  Daniel 156
  John Frederick 156
Giles, Anne 81
  George 81
  John 81
  Joseph 81
  Thomas 81
  William 81
Gill, Frances 174
  John 56, 174
  William 128
  William 174
Gilmer, George 203
Gilmore, Charles 196
Gilpin, Robert 38
Ginn, Elizabeth 164
Ginnott, Hester 63
Gipson, Martha 157
Girard, Peter 93
Gladman, Benjamin 44
Glaster, Robert 195
Gledhill, Mary 120
Glencross, Cane 136
  William 107, 136
Glissel, John 82
Glossopp, Anne 19
Glover, Nathaniel 131
Goade, Rebecca 166
  Solomon 166
Gobble, John 21

Gobell, Hannah 167
  John 167
Godard, George 112
Godber, Robert 97
Goddard, Edmund 33
  Hannah 33
  Mary 33
  William 165
Godin, Benjamin 134
  David 194
Godscall, Lady Anne
  21, 22
Godson, Agnes 80
  Richard 80
  Sarah 58
Godwin, Alexander 169
  Joseph 28
Goelet, Isaac 217
Goff, Peter 53
  Roger 153
Gold, Ursula 25
  William 25
Goldhawk, Mary 254
Goldney, Henry 42
Goldsborough, Caroline
  230
  Charles 230
  Greenbury 230
  Henrietta Maria 230
  Howes 230
  John 230
  Mary 230
  Nicholas 230
  Robert 230
  William 230
Goldsbury, Philip 216
Goldsmith, Richard 254
  Thomas 194
  Zaccheus 254
Goldthwait, Ezekiel 168
**Golightly, Culchett
  182, 207**
  Dorothy 207
  Fenwick 207
  Mary 207
Gomm, Joyce 47
Gomond, Mr. 217
Gooch, Col. 179
  William 176, 181

Goodenough, Henry 253
  Henry Trenchard 253
Goodfellow, Elizabeth 141
  Theophilus 141
  Timothy 141
Gooding, John 107
Goodman, Thomas 113
Goodson, Job 169
  William 42
Goodsonne, John 66
Goodwin, Anthony 39
  John 95
  Mary 135
  Nathaniel 111
  Thomas 16
Goodyear, Stephen 8
Gorden, Alexander 242
Gordon, Capt. 96
  Donald 226
  Elizabeth 221
  George 171
  James 214
  John 221, 235, 238, 248
  Mary 171
  William 65, 223, 224,
    249
Gore, Thomas 196
Goring, Henry 61
  John 61
  Lovet 61
Gorst, Leonard 229
Gorstelowe, John 159
Gossedy, Robert 30
Gotes, Elbathes 113
Gotley, Richard 37
Gouche, William 1
Goudy, Benjamin 238
Gouge, Caleb 1
  Thomas 90
  William 1
Gough & Horne 206
Gough, Henry Dorsey 193
  John 61, 193
  Nicholas 193
  Thomas 193
  William 193
Gould, Mr. 80
  Mary 197
Gouldney, Henry 52, 89
Gourdon, Francis 165

Gower, Elizabeth 42
Grace, John 78
  William 185
Gradwell, Jacob 69
  Thomas 69
Graeme, Elizabeth 132
  George 132
Graham(e), Agenath 235
  Andrew 213
  Charles 235
  Elizabeth 256
  James 152
  John 205, 257
  Thomas 109
  William 80
Graisbury, James 209
Grange, Anne 175
  Hannah 175
  Hugh 175
  Sarah 175
  Thomas 175
Granger, John 34
  William 15
Grant, Sir Archibald 246
  Archibald 246
  John 143
  Patrick 214
Grape, Arabella 150
  Esther 150
  James 150
  Mary 150
  Richard 150
  Samuel 150
Grascombe, Thomas 51
Grastis, Samuel 145
Grave, Alice 210
  Anne 29
  Elizabeth 210
  George 29
  John 210
  Mary 210
  Thomas 210
Graves, Richard 69
  William 167
Gray, Ann 202
  Edward 43
  Henry 202
  James 253
  John 253
  Owen 192

Gray, Robert 19
  William 254
Green(e), Abraham 241
  Barbara 17
  Charles 257
  Eleanor 11
  Frances 11
  Francis 226
  Hannah 79
  James 79
  John 5, 11, 38, 72,
    124, 193, 260
  Joseph 76
  Nicholas 4
  Robert 260
  Rufus 200
  Thomas 4, 126, 144, 227
  William 3, 144
  Winifred 5
  Young 234
Greenbury, Charles 86
  Rachel 86
  Tobias 4
Greenfield, Thomas 61
  Thomas Truman 171
Greenland, Angus 258
Greenleaf, Benjamin 241
  Mary 256
  Samuel 137
  Stephen 204, 256
Greenough, John 238
Greenshaw, Elizabeth 171
Greenwood, John 78
  Jonathan 162
Gregory, Ann 197
  Edward 192
  John 192
  Martha 192
  Mary 192
  Richard 21
  William 192
Greive, James 148
Greme, Alexander 170
  John 170
Grendon, Thomas 31
Greves, Adam 160
Greville, Silvanus 183
Grew, Michael 191
Grey, Elizabeth 27
  Henry 27

Grey, Thomas 131
Gridley, Jeremiah 212
Griel, David 79
Griffin, Elizabeth 222
  James 257
  Mary 52
  Prudence 257
  Thomas 58
Griffith, Andrew 4
  Francis 11
  Sir Henry 1
  Jane 178
  Pearce 162
  Thomas 17
Griffiths, James 94
  John 94
Grill, Mary 197
Grimes, Alice 187
  Elizabeth 114
  Joseph 49
  Thomas 148
  William 41, 114, 187
Grimsdalle, John 69
  Thomas 69
Grindall, Anthony 95
Grinsted, John 53
Grollier, Thomas 260
Grove, Edward 75, 220
  Joseph 93
  Silvanus 93, 252
Grover, John 237
  Joseph 97
  Jotham 97
  Judith 188
  William 237
Groves, Elizabeth 120
  John 76, 135, 183
  Samuel 120
  Sarah 120
  Thomas 39
Grymes, William 64
Gudridge, Ruth 50
Guest, John 92
  Thomas 92
Guilliames, George 73
Guillum, John 78
  Mary 78
  Peter 78
  Thomas 78

Guise, Brig. 173
  Elizabeth 148
Gully, William 98
Gundry, Daniel 97
  Deborah 97
Gunn, Daniel 182
Gunnison, Margery 240
Gunter, John 211
  Thomas 182
Guy, Rev. 196
Gwynn, David 32
  Robert 252
Gyles, John 92

Habersham, James 176, 250
Hackett, J. 137
  John 143
  Mary 143
  Thomas 143
Haddock, James 118, 142
Hadley, Dionysia 106
Haffron, Dennis 257
Hagan, Hugh 185
Haggett, Jane 191
  Nathaniel 191
  Susanna 191
Haig, Mary 60
  Obediah 60
  William 60
Haile, Elizabeth 37
Hails, Ann 216
  John 216
Haines, John 69
  Peter 69
  Samuel 242
Hake, Nathaniel 99
Halcrow, Robert 250
Haldimand, Frederick 233
Hale, Elizabeth 240
  Jackson 224
Halford, Mary 110
Haliburton, Roderick 185
Hall, Andrew 79
  Charles 68, 124
  Dorothy 145
  Elizabeth 118
  Francis 145
  George 134
  James 109

Hall, Jane 216
  Joan 17
  John 52, 138, 142
  Joseph 29
  Margaret 109, 142
  Philip 203
  Robert 118
  Thomas 262
  William 227
Hallam, George 65
  Winifred 65
Halleday, Elizabeth 50
Halley, Edmond 79
  Eleanor 79
  Francis 79
  Katherine 79
  Margaret 79
  Mary 79
Halliman, Josiah John 108
Halse, William 14
Halsey, Henry 173
Ham, Matthew 84
Haman, Anne 112
  Richard 112
Hambelton, John 191
Hamblin, John 28
Hamilton, Alexander 206
  Andrew 154, 172
  James 172
  John 97
  Margaret 172
  Mary 250
  Thomas 139
Hamlin, Elizabeth 81
Ham(m)erton, Edmond 139
  Elizabeth 190
  Hannah 139
  Hollier 190
  Pinchback 139
Ham(m)ond, George 63
  Thomas 48, 195
  William 147
Hampton, Col. 225
  Frances 123
  John 123
  Margery 123
  Mary 123
  Robert 123
Hamson, Daniel 109

Hanbury, John 172, 178, 194
Hance, Peter 93
  Sarah 93
Hancox, Edward 86
  James 259
Hand, Dorothy 207
Hands, Thomas B. 173
Handy, Thomas 247
Hankey, Sir Joseph 218
Hannam, Arthur 212
  James 212
Hanslapp, Elizabeth 70
  Henry 70
Hanson, Christian 89
  Robert 5
Harbin, Robert 62
Hardie, Margaret 189
Hardige, James 71
  Mary 75
Hardiman, Abraham 66
Harding, Edward 27
  Margaret 27
  Philip 172
  Robert 92
  William 172, 260
Hardridge, William 37
Hardwick, George 137
  Thomas 201
  William 244
Hard(e)y, Charles 185, 251
  Jonathan 29
  Joseph 29
  Thomas 233
Hardyman, John 67
Hare, Mary 174
  Roger 174
  Thomas 128
Hargrave, Henry 134
Harl(e)ston, Ann 128
  John 128, 205
Harman, Abraham 152, 166
  John 137
  Mary 137
Harper, Edward 125
  John 141
  Robert 218
  William 23, 176
Harradin, Edward 125
  Henrietta 125

Harrell, Mary 193
  Thomas 193
Harries, Joseph 165
Harriette, Benjamin 205
Harriman, Jane 94
Harrington, John 66
Harris, Capt. 165
  Mrs. 208
  Rev. 224
  Amos 119
  Anthony 159
  Francis 243
  Gabriel 251
  George 23
  Hanbury 25
  Hannah 49
  James 48, 154, 208
  Jane 26, 49
  John 4, 49, 68, 112, 149
  Joseph 202
  Mary 49, 68, 87, 108
  Philip 232
  Richard 25, 81, 87
  Robert 25
  Roger 92
  Samuel 49, 119
  Sarah 49, 221, 224
  Simon 68
  Thomas 68, 127, 226
  William 119
Harrison, Cuthbert 48
  Francis 216
  George 187, 255
  Hendrick 50
  John 2, 105, 132, 223, 258
  Joseph 185
  Margaret 58
  Morley 255
  Nathaniel 108
  Richard 65, 255
  Sarah 105
Hart, Andrew 126
  Ester 258
  Joseph 228
  Martha 254
  Mary 254
  Thomas 258
Hartford, Frances 251
Hartnell, Samuel 28

Hartry, John 17
Harveild, Isabella 120
  Luke 120
Harvey, Seth 198
  William 186
Harvison, Elizabeth 44
  Susan 44
Harwood, Joel 59
  John 105, 168
  Peter 151
  Richard 105
  Robert 230
  Swanley 105
  Thomas 105
  William 249
Hasell, John 232
Haselwood, Clift 247
  John 82
Haskett, John 140
Haslewood, Anne 35
  Catherine 214
  Cuthbert 35
  Edward 214
  George 214
  Roger 214
  William 214
Haslipp, Thomas 27
Hassall, William 195
Hassert, Arent 153
Hastings, Jeanet 92
  John 92
Hatch, Matthew 229
Hatt, Charles 165
Hatten, Martha 86
Hatton, Francis 164
  Henry 16
  John 16
  Samuel 16
  Susan 16
  Thomas 16
Haveningham, Maria 128
Havens, John 216
  Philip 216
Haviland, Joseph 215
  Margaret 215
Hawker, Gilbert 127
Hawkesworth, John 168
Hawkins, Mr. 71
  Anthony 241
  Arnaut 128

Hawkins, David 198
  Dorothy 39, 79
  Elizabeth 117
  Ernault 117
  Frances 38
  John 37, 38, 47, 117,
    120, 234
  Joseph 99
  Mary 120
  Rachel 38
  Sarah 234
  Susanna 99
  William 36, 38, 79, 86
Hawles, Sir John 65
Hawley, Edward 204
  Elizabeth 204
  George 227
  Henry 21
Hayes, Hugh 260
  John 61, 122, 158
  Mary 122
  Patrick 55
Hayles, John 7
  Ladd. 52
Hayman, Joseph 47
Haynes, Andrew 47, 179
  Ann 179
  Ann Phillis 221
  Anthony 178
  Elizabeth 179, 221
  George 221
  Herbert 159, 179
  Lawrence 179
  Martha 179
  Richard 179
  Sarah 159, 221
  Thomas 159, 178, 179
  William 179, 221
Hayter, John 254
  Martha 254
Hayward, Nicholas 51
  Samuel 51
Head, Ann 118
  Bigger 118
  John 226
  Mary 118
Headcorn, James 184
Heading, Margaret 76
  Richard 76
Healde, John 260

Heard, David 161
  Elizabeth 161
Hearle, Thomas 183
Hearse, James 51
Heartley, Francis 57
Heath, Benjamin 132
  Gilbert 108
  Henry 77
  James 100
  Richard 189
  Thomas 82
Heathcott, George 72
Heathfield, Richard 129
Heaton, Jo. 247, 249
  John 132
Heddell, Thomas 152
Hedge, John 250
Helden, Cornelius 201
  John 201
  ₒMary 201
Hellasar, Thomas 51
Hellman, Capt. 231
Hellyer, John 32
Helme, Arthur 74
  Jane 74
Helsing, John 122
Hemard, Anne 115
  Elizabeth 115
  Peter 115
Hemingway, Abraham 48
Henchman, Abigail 96
Henderson, Catherine 215
  Elizabeth 99, 215
  Eve 215
  James 215
  Margaret 215
  Mary 215
  Tessia 215
  William 99
Henly, Capt. 110
Henry, John 123
  Robert Jenkins 123
Henshaw, Joshua 224
  Robert 196
  Sarah 224
Herbert, Ester 156
  Henry 156
  Mary 32, 63
  Thomas 130
Herd, David 77

Heron, Alexander 176, 185
  Alice 248
  Benjamin 248
  Charles 249
  Elizabeth 248, 249
  Frances 248
  Martha 176
  Mary 249
  Sarah 176
Herringham, P. 202
Herriott, William 92
Hervey, Elizabeth 214
Hesselberg, Christen 137
  Inger 137
Hester, John 63
  Joseph 177, 234
  Mary 63
  William 63
Heurtin, William 203
Hewet(t), Ann 83
  Elizabeth 258
  Robert 164
Hewis, Henry 96
Hewitt, Thomas 233
  William 18, **233**
Hewson, William 5
Hext, Alexander 172
  Amias 172
  David 172
  Edward 172
  Francis 172
  Hugh 172
  John 172
  Martha 172
  Philip 172
  Thomas 172
Heylyn, Ann 193
  John 193, 194
Heyward, Mary 28
  Richard 28
Hiccocks, William 47
Hicks, Alice 125
  Gilbert 259
  Thomas 29
Hiddeon, Jonathan 198
Hide, John 139
Higg, Catherine 186
Higgins, Nathaniel 180
Higginson, ----- 43
  John 44

Higginson, Stephen 158
Higgs, Thomas 33
Hilcup, Dudson 223
Hill, Adam 237
  Alice 4
  Anne 59
  Bartholomew 5
  Charles 56
  Edward 53
  Elizabeth 4, 237
  George 4
  Isaac 104
  James 192
  Joan 82
  John 147, 218
  Mary 4, 113
  Naomi 131
  Peter 234
  Richard 4, 74, 78,
    125, 157
  Ruth 131
  Samuel 53
  Sarah 40
  Susannah 209
  Thomas 58, 59
  William 4
  Willoughby 82
Hiller, John 18
Hillhouse, James 229
Hilliard, Samuel 67
Hillington, Emanuel 104
Hills, Benjamin 221
  William 24
Hilton, Richard 4
  Robert 112
Hind(e), Anne 102
  George 190
  Joseph 152
Hindman, Jacob 230
Hinton, Anne 4
  Elizabeth 263
  Katherine 199
  Thomas 4, 263
Hippertree, William 73
Hissey, Sarah 46
Hitchcock, Ann 169
  Elianor 20
  Henry 169
Hitchinson, Nathaniel 20
Ho, George 139

Hoare, John 80
  Samuel 204
Hobbs, Catherina 65
  Thomas 65, 150
Hobson, Thomas 28, 71
Hocker, Joseph 19
  Rachel 19
  Seymour 183
Hockley, Richard 176, 251
Hodge, Mr. 248
Hodges, Anne 100
  Frances 143
  John 100
  Jory 143
  Joseph 143, 221
  Dame Mary 143
  Mary 126, 143
  Nathaniel 126, 143
  Valentine 143
Hodgkin, John 88
Hodgson, Francis 12
  Marina 108
  Thomas 103, 226
Hodshon, William 82, 219
Hoffman, William 193
Hogg, William 129
Hoggart, William 259
Hoggon, Alexander 105
Holdcroft, Henry 106
  Mary 106
Holden, Jean 235
  John 144, 235
Holding, Edward 196
  John 196
Holdsworth, John 85
Holland, Mr. 22
  David 80
  Elizabeth 44
  Francis 100
  Groningen 186
  Henry 56
  John 44, 196
  Joshua 44
  Martha 22
  Niel 188
  Thanks 44
  Thomas 118
  William 226
Holliday, Anna Maria 230

Hollier, Elizabeth 190
Nathaniel 190
Hollings, George 246
Zachary 94
Hollingsworth, William 94
Hollis, Thomas 139
Holloway, George 17
John 144
W. 112, 119
William 48, 124, 152
Hollyday, Ann 50
William 27
Holmes, Alexander 112
Edward 81
Elizabeth 58
Francis 66, 175
Gideon 145
Henry 256
Isaac 205
Jane 99
John 99, 260
Stephen 228
Thomas 33
William 102
Holt, Col. 110
Samuel 169
Thomas 221
William 196
Holwell, Mary 28
Stephen 209
Holyoke, Samuel 192
Homans, John 212
Home, Alexander 184
Charles 184
William 184
Homes, Richard 54
Homewood, Thomas 63
Hoo, Richard 124
Hoole, Edward 69
Hooper, Margaret 169
William 227, 254
Hope, Samuel 260
Hopkins, Charles 132
Francis 179
Jane 132
John 263
Thomas 213
William 178
Hopkinson, Joshua 210

Hopkinson, Matthew 103
Thomas 166, 207
Hopley, Mrs. 120
Randolph 120
Hopper, Ann 210
Hopton, William 204
Hornbe, Elizabeth 85
Robert 85
Horne, Edward 215
John 6
Horrall, John 22
Horrocks, Mary 16
Horry, Elias 207
Horsepool, William 111
Horsey, Stephen 13
Thomas 256
Horsmonden, Anthony 21, 30
Mary 21
Susan 21
Ursula 22
Warham 21
Horton, William 71, 194
Horwood, Henry 59
Joel 59
Hosea, John 105
Hoskins, Anne 76
Aurelius 76
Benjamin 73
Martha 76
Mary 76
Mercy 76
Millicent 46
Philip 87
Richard 76
Hospitt, Edward 36
Hotchkiss, Richard 198
Hothersall, John 51
Houchin, Mr. 15
Houghton, Edmund 197
John 197
Mary 197
Houk, William 179
Houlden, Agnes 1
Elizabeth 1
Katherine 1
Margaret 1
Richard 1
Houlton, John 167
Lydia 167

Housden, John 59
House, John 169
Houston, James 186
Patrick 185
How, John 40
Howard, Adam 160
Andrew 222
Christopher 46
Elizabeth 160
Francis 160
John 84, 108
Martin 256
Mary 91, 199
Matthew 160
Michael 160
Michael Cashio 237
Michael William 160
Patrick 237
Rebecca 8
Rochfort 160
Rose 160
Sarah 84, 160
Thomas 91, 179, 199
Howell, John 103
Lethea 200
Mary 103
Thomas 139
Howes, Elizabeth 236
Job 248
Thomas 75
Howford, Timothy 16
Howgill, James 164
Howkins, Thomas 42
Howlett, Rachel 36
Howse, John 103
Howson, Mary 113
Thomas 113
Hoyden, William 109
Hubbard, Mrs. 217
Nathaniel 217
Thomas 223
Willmut 254
Huckebutt, Joseph 37
Huckstep, Jane 55
Samuel 55
Hudley, Mathew 8
Hudson, Mr. 199
John 79, 217
Mary 13
Matthew 140

Hudson, Thomas 20
Huett, Mr. 116
Huger, Ann 206
 Daniel 206
 Francis 207
 Isaac 207
 John 207
 Margaret 207
 Paul 207
Huggins, Robert 29
Hugh, James 230
Hughes, Catherine 84
 Edward 84
 Hugh 114
 John 90, 204
 Mary 55, 133
 Robert 133
Huish, George 199
Huisman, Abraham 186
Huling, Walton 102
Hull, Mr. 232
 Edward 64
 Robert 248
Hume, Alexander 113
 Robert 113, 125, 216
 Sophia 125
 William 160
Humfrey, Nicholas 86
Humphreys, Charles 98
 John 196
 Marmaduke 174
 Sarah 196
Humphrie, James 207
Hunt, Andrew 69
 Annis 111
 Bernard 60
 Edward 86
 Hannah 16
 Isaac 23
 Jabez 158
 John 22, 28, 91, 99
 Joseph 113
 Mary 69, 158, 253
 Priscilla 158
 Ruth 69
 Susannah 149
 Thomas 16, 22, 69,
  111, 253
 William 118, 143,
  159, 171, 253

Hunter, Anna 243
 Catherine 185
 Hannah 243
 Joseph 243
Huntingdon, Countess
  Selina 250
Hunton, Elizabeth 90
 Mary 90
 Nathaniel 90
 Samuel 90
Hurd, Francis 154
 John 135
 Mary 154
 Nathaniel 153
Hurford, Agnes 236
Hurley, Vincent 98
Hurlock, Thomas 34
Hurt, Deborah 201
 John Helden 201
Huson, Elizabeth 142
Huss, Mary 121
Hutchenson, Mrs. 22
Hutcheon, Thomas 246
Hutcheson, Archibald 153
Hutchinson, Eliakim 121
 Elizabeth 120, 121
 John 130
 Joseph 88
 William 121
Hyam, Anne 157
Hyatt, Mary 137
Hyde, Mr. 129
 Ann 105
 Elizabeth 129
 Elizabeth Wigfall 130
 Herbert 160
 Jane 150
 John 57, 85, 125, 150,
  168
 Samuel 160
Hyer, Willem 247
Hyndman, John 231
Hyrne, Burrl. M. 149
 Henry 149

Ilmore, Henry 89
Imlay, William 190
Ince, Thomas 127
Ing, Thomas 128

Ingham, John 106
Ingleby, Sir Charles 112
Ingoldsby, Capt. 39
 Mary 39
Ingraham, Abigail 226
 Bethiah 226
 George 226
 Mary 226
Ingram, William 42
Inman, Mary 247
Innes, John 184
Innys, Paul 157
Iredell, Rebecca 162
Ireland, Anne 101
 Hannah 101
 Henry 101
 John 101
 Susannah 101
Iremonger, Anna 20
Ireson, Elizabeth 132
Irish, George 27
Ironmonger, Elizabeth
  27, 64
 Francis 64
 Samuel 64
 Sarah 64
Irons, Richard 41
Irvine, Jane 231
 Jerret 231
Isham, Anna 213
 James 213
Ive, John 101
Ives, Hannah 166
Ivory, Edward 96
Izard, Mary 73
 Ralph 73, 122, 167,
  178, **223**, 258
 Rebecca 199, 223
 Sarah 223
 Thomas 223
 Walter 223

Jackman, Catherine 108
 Joseph John 108
 Mary 108
 William 108
Jackson, Abraham 126
 Arthur 107
 Bartholomew 118

Jackson, Dorcas 126
  Dorothy 223
  Edward 223
  Elizabeth 107
  Francis 44
  John 129, 140
  Jonathan 223
  Mary 96, 223
  Mathew 153
  Rachel 107
  Thomas **96, 107, 112**
Jacob, **Henry 2**
  I. 28
  Joseph 157
  Salina F.A. 24
  Sarah 2
Jacobs, Thomas 89
Jacquelin, Elizabeth 168
  Mary 168
Jago, John 165
James, Edward 140
  Elisha 87
  Elizabeth 7, 137
  Frances 137
  Hannah 137
  Henry 136
  John 136
  Joseph 136, 137
  Katherine 39
  Mary 8
  Tablay 140
  William 12
Jamison, David 91, 92
  John 213
  Martha 213
  William 184
Janson, Anne 51
  Barbara 51
  Bryan 51
  George 51
  John 51
  Mary 51
  William 51
Jarmon, Henry 229
Jarrett, Johanna 81
Jarvis, Christopher 35
  Elizabeth 35
  Thomas 35
Jasper, Edward 160, 166
  Richard 226

Jauncey, John 173
  Mary 173
Jay, Frances 209
  Peter 247
Jeakins, Christopher 40
Jeay, William 22
Jefferie, Stephen 4
Jefferson, Welden 118
Jeffery, Josias 138
  Richard 169
Jeffrey, James 168
Jeffreys, Jeffrey 75
  John 32, 109, 212
  Peter 148
  Robert 148
  William 109
Jeneway, Richard 175
Jening, Joseph 210
Jenkin, John 29
Jenkins, Lieut. 179
  James 20
  John 37, 170
  Robert 60
  Walter 195
  William 231
Jenkinson, Abraham 170
  Jane 79
  John 112, 213
  William 79
Jennens, James 205
Jenner, Samuel 231
Jennifer, Michael 145
Jen(n)ings, Mr. 183
  Anne 7
  Ariana 208
  Edmund 150
  Edmund 206, 208
  Mary 183
  Thomas 9
Jennison, David 203
Jenvrem, Mr. 165
Jenys & Baker 177
Jenys, George 195
  Paul 195
  Thomas 157, 195
Jeoffreys, John 216
Jerningham, Catherine 261
  Charles 261
  Edwardina 261
  Frances Henrietta 261

Jerningham, Sir George 261
  Helloisa 261
  Henry 261
  Mary 261
  Nicholas 261
  Olivia 261
  Tobias 261
Jervis, Abigail 121
Jess, Martha 87
Jesses, Peter 46
Jesson, Ann 166
  Robert 166
Jett, Thomas 256
Jetter, Elizabeth 18
Jevens, Moses 192
Jewell, George 36
Jewitt, David 229
  Patience 229
  Sarah 229
Joanas, Mr. 78
Joans, Thomas 171
Jobson, Hannah 93
  John 93
  Katherine 93
  Mary 93
  Michael 93
  Samuel 93
  Sarah 93
Jocham, John 162
Jodrell, Henry 252
Johanna, F. 28
Johnes, William 1
Johns, Frances 71
  Hensey 235
  John 71
  Mary 71
  Richard 100
Johnson, Mr. 30
  Andrew 92
  Ann 173
  Bedingfield 173
  Daniel 55
  Elizabeth 51
  Ezekiel 173
  Francis 247
  George 99
  Hannah 18, 200
  Henry 161, 200
  James 210

Johnson, Jane 99
  John 34, 65, 90, 120
  Joseph 161
  Margaret 153, 210
  Mary 91, 99, 120,
    153, 196, 200
  Nathaniel 153
  Peter 49, 170
  Robert 104, **153**
  Simon 247
  Thomas 1, 33, 153
  Tobias 249
  Walter 210
  Sir William 219
  William 99
Johnston, Gideon 110
  John 245
  Peter 241
  Thomas 185
Johonnot, Francis 200
Jolly, John 166
Jones, Adam 230
  Barbara 85
  Charles 37, 162
  Deborah 230
  Deering 230
  Edward 84, 200
  Elizabeth 66, 221
  Evan 129
  Frances 155
  Frederick 249, 264
  George 199
  Henry 88
  Hugh 85, 186
  James 11, 200, 236
  Jane 230
  Jean 126
  Jenkin 209
  John 48, 85, **126**,
    147, 186
  Judith 35
  Kenelm 171
  Lain 155
  Lewis 185
  Livellet 97
  Margery 63
  Marie 25
  Mary 68, 129
  Noble Wimberly 243
  Owen 66

Jones, Phillip 84
  Rachel 229
  Richard 66, 72, 85,
    97, 118, 147
  Robert 59, 242, 91, 137
  Samuel 26, 48
  Susanna 26
  Theophilus 230
  Thomas 25, 38, **66**,
    83, 122
  William 23, **114**, 229
Jordan, Abraham 173
  Elizabeth 13
  Mary 126
  Robert 108
  William 13, 97
Jordice, Henry 238
Joseph, Benjamin 103
Joss, Toriah 251
Joursey, John 63
Joyce, Dorothy 12
  Henry 170
  John 12
Joyner, Theophilus 132
Joynson, Anne 213
Jukes, Dorothy 110
  Edward 110
Julin, Carls 217
Juxon, Sarah 38

Kast, John 97
  Thomas 257
Kay, Richard 63
Kea, Robert 108
Kearney, Michael 147
Kearsley, John 169
Keast, Joan 97
Keate, John 36
  Katherine 36
Keating, Martha 125
Keck, John 120
Kee, Richard 230
Keech, Elizabeth 41, 112
  Joanna 41
  Mary 41
  Sarah 41
  Simon 41
  Thomas 112
Keeling, Mary 66

Keen(e), Anne 82
  Benjamin 178
  Mary 68
  Robert 251
  Samuel 229
  Sarah 82
Keer, Anne 40
Kellaway, William 176
Kellogg, Joseph 228
Kell(e)y, Ellis 41
  Jean 235
  John 215
  Samuel 49
Kelsall, Richard 99
Kelsick, Younger 257
Kelsing, John 123
Kelson, Elizabeth 107
  James 107
Kemble, Thomas 37
Kemp(e), Mr. 230
  Cicely 99
  James 99
Kendall, Mrs. 197
  Elizabeth 216
  Helen 245
  John 216
Kennedy, Adam 65
  Anne 65
  Jane 65
  Margaret 65
  Mary 65
  Robert 65
Kenner, Benjamin 102
  Mary 102
Kenrick, Lettice 99
Kent, Mrs. 163
  Ralph 174
  Sarah 135
  Thomasine 26
Kenyan, Abraham 84
  Jabez 84
  Jacinta 84
  John 84
  Joseph 84
Kenyon, Eliz 96
  Samuel 96
Keppell, Augustus 262
Kerby, Edward 47
  Elizabeth 27, 134
  Lancelot 71, 80

Kerle, James 50
Kermish, Mary 75
Kerr, David 220
  Jane 140
  Thomas 140
Kerrett, Moses 168
Ketelby, Mrs. 136
  Abel 98, 136
  Robert 136
Key(e), Elizabeth 83
  John 83
  Leonard 79
  Philip 145
Keynell, Frances 2
  George 2
Kidder, John 131, 137
Kidgell, Henry 210
  Nicholas 134
  Sarah 134
Kiffin, William 29
Kiggell, Kentish 158
KIlburne, Charles 59
Kilby, Christopher 175,
  176, 197
Killpatrick, James 188
Kilner, Frances 98
King, Mrs. 23
  Amy 147
  Christopher 60
  Edward 81
  Elias 49
  Eusebius 99
  James Curle 225
  John 133
  Mary 59, 183, 225
  Nathaniel 183
  Obadiah 113
  Robert 123, 147
  Rose 225
  Samuel 193
  Thomas 79, 149
  William 34, 88, 100, 225
  William Payne 194
Kingdon, Mary 237
Kingked, John 55
Kingland, John 140
Kingston, Mary 217
  William 7
Kinloch, Francis 229
  James 88

Kinnersley, Ebenezer 179
Kinnorston, Margaret 118
Kinsey, Anne 33
  John 33
  Mary 33
  Ralph 33
  William 33
Kipping, Walter 137
Kirk, Mary 216
Kirke, Susanna 35
Kirkdell, John 104
Kirwan, Robert 159
Kistell, Charles 4
  Edward 4
  John 4
  Philip 4
Kitchin, Samuel 3
Kitchiner, Richard 83
Knapp, Thomas 102
Knewstubb, Richard 21
Knight, Mrs. 41
  Edward 227
  Gabriel 88
  Hannah 11
  Henry 27
  John 16, 133
  Plasance 89
  Rebecca 250
  Robert 250
  William 89, 250
Knipe, Anne 58
  William 195
Knock, John 194
Knolles, Elizabeth 236
  John 235
Knott, Edward 230
Knowles, Edward 87
  Francis 184
  John 49, 124, 184
  Mary 124
  Peter 24
  Samuel 70

Laconena, Thomas 243
Lacy, John 46
  Margaret 85
  Moses 73
  Patrick 74
Ladd, Richard 85

Lade, Nathaniel 204
Laindon, Mr. 155
Laithwait, Hannah 99
  James 99
Lake, Charles 229
  Martha 101
  Robert 101
  Susannah 101
  Thomas 55
  William 57
Lakin, James 32
Lamb(e), Joshua 62
  Susan 62
  Thomas 24
Lambert, Anne 82
  Edward 34, 82
  John 192
  Margaret 82
  Thomas 192
  Vincent 82
  William 90,192
Lambkin, Thomas 45
Lambly, William 17,18
Lamboll, Thomas 157
  William 106,115
Lamm, Frances 254
  Rebecca 254
Lamport, Daniel 133
Lancaster, Eleanor 261
  John 252
  Samuel 53
Lance, William 226
Lanchester, William 97
Landon, Thomas 34
Lane & Caswall 192
Lane, Christian 209
  Elizabeth 91
  John 43,66,238
  Judith 209
  Margaret 79
  Martha 209
  Mary 34,43,103,104,209
  Thomas 48,88,167,
    189,192,244
  Timothy 29
  William 90
Lang, George 2
  James 135
Langdon, Mr. 166
  Anne 217

Langdon, Richard 217
Langhorne, Mary 39
Sir William 39
Thomas 39
Langley, Elizabeth 67
John 67
Margaret 67
Richard 67
Thomazine 67
William 67
Lanman, Chrisogon 132
Johan 132
John 132
Samuel 132
William 108,132
Lanterow, Ethelred 31
William 31
Lardner, Lynford 251
Larner, Richard 212
Larwens, Mary 59
Laskam, Mr. 4
Lason, ----- 125
Laud, Francis 139
Laundis, Thomas 17
Laurence, William 193
Lavington, Ann 214
Jane 214
Samuel 214
Stephen 214
Law, David 92
John 193
Lawes, Thomas 8
Lawler, James 238
Lawrence, Mr. 217
Dorothy 156
John 156
Mary 170
Richard 170
Robert 44
Theodosia 150
Thomas 74,76
Lawry, Agnes 60
Arthur 60
Christian 60
Gawen 60
James 60
Mary 60
Rebecca 60
Lawson, Alexander 156,186
John 132

Lay, Benjamin 215
Philip 216
Sarah 215
William 216
Lea, Sarah 189
William 189
Leach, Thomas 180
Leadbetter, James 255
Leader, William 132
Lear, Elizabeth 120
John 120
Leath, Robert 101
Leather, Richard 10
Leaver, Mary 87
Thomas 90
Le Bessin, Mr. 111
Le Clerc, Alexander 181
Elias 181
Jane 181
Le Counte, Ann 173
James 173
Ledbetter, John 262
Ledet, John 181
Mary 181
Stephen 181
Lee, Anne 135
Elizabeth 135
Francis 88
George 130
Hancock 135,235
Isaac 135
John 17,135
Lettice 130
Martha 130
Richard 17,68,135,256
Richard Henry 256
Samuel 132
Sarah 135
Thomas 134,202
Leedes, Jedadiah 228
Lees, John 214
Leeth, Jane 99
Thomas 99
Legg, T. 46
Thomas 67
Legoe, William 180
Lehman, Christian 238
Leigh, E. 252
Lord 260
William 61

Leitch, James 259
Lejan, Francis 207
Le Jeune, Jerome J. 165
Leman, Hickford 147
Leman, William 100
Le Mesurier, Abraham 227
Lennox, Catherine 245
James 245
William 245
Le Noble, Henry 59
Lenthall, Frances 127
John 126
Philip 126
Le Palle, Jean 73
Le Sage, John 157
Lescene, Daniel 207
L'Escott, Frances 202
Le Serurier, Mr. 59
Leslie, Andrew 149
John 50
Lessons, David 74
Robert 74
Lester, Joseph 162
Lestrange, Robert 260
Letchworth, Thomas 10
Lever, Edward 259
Ezekias 157
Levett, Elizabeth 142
John 142
Margaret 142
Robert 142
Levitt, Christopher 1
John 13
Richard 13
Sybilla 13
Levy, Abraham 245
Lewis, Mrs. 74
Abigail 188
Edward 104,194
Elizabeth 201
George 62
Hannah 188
James 66,67
Job 188
John 57,178,201,202
Joseph 157
Mary 201
Maurice 190
Sarah 26,188,201
Stephen 26

Lewis, Thomas 26,201
William 201
Ley, Humphrey 15
Judith 15
Mary 15
Libbard, Elizabeth 210
Liddell, Anne 185
Archibald 185
John 185
Lillie 185
Thomas 185
Lidderdale, John 218
William Robertson 239
Lidgett, Ann 63
Charles 63
Mary 63
Peter 63
Light, Richard 244
Lightfoot, John 214
Ligon, Thomas 24
Lillington, Sarah 236
Lilly, John 65
Samuel 112
Lillywhite, Elizabeth 116
Paul 116
Limbre, William 4
Linch, Elenor 186
Lindsay, David 82
Robert 203,231
Lindsey, ----- 170
Ling, John 11
Joseph 24
Samuel 73
Lingen, Joseph 181
Lingom, Margaret 21
Lining, John 150
Linn, John 196
Linnell, Margaret 250
Linsey, Alice 12
Lipscomb, Thomas 240
Lirland, Jeremiah 108
Lithered, Thomas 154
Lithgow, Anne 184
Barbara 184
David 184
Elizabeth 184
Janet 184
Mary 184
William 184
Little, Otis 197

Littlepage, Edmund 103
Joseph 103
Richard 103
Littleton, William 205
Liversedge, Emmanuel 216
Livingston, Ann 122
Elizabeth 118
John 118
Margaret 118
Philip 248
William 122,139,162
Llewellyn, Llewellyn
262,263
Robert 16
Lloyd, Capt. 225
Mr. 217
Mrs. 163,217
Alice 231
Alles 53
Benjamin 218
David 66,76,177
Edward 11,26,55,66,
177,194
Elinor 125
Evan 11
Grace 55
Henrietta Maria 55
Hugh 177
James 55,153,160
John 8,75,121,126,
177,217
Mary 55,138
Philemon 55,151
Richard 177
Robert 62
Sampson 67
Sarah 177,216
Simon 11
Thomas 11,66,138,
177,178,242
William 11
Lobb, Jacob 232
William Grinfill 232
Lober, Garttree 72
Margaret 72
Loch, William 100
Locher, John 201
Lock, Mrs. 153
William 87
Locker, James 124

Lockey, John 17
Lockhart, James 224
Sarah 224
Lockwood, Agnes 215
Joseph 215
Loddington, Thomas 11
Lodovick, Charles 87
Lofthouse, John 163
Logan, George 130
Loggin, John 168
Lomas, Henry 210
John 210
Mary 210
London, David 257
Lone, Gyles 185
Jacobus 144,156,158
Long, Alice 132
Augustine 132
Beeston 188
David 181
Edward 248
Elizabeth 132
Richard 3
Susannah 223
William 89
Longman, Richard 20
Lonsdale, John 44
Susanna 44
Lord, John 71
Lordor, John 144
Loring, Elizabeth 224
John 224
Jonathan 158
Lotherbury, Bridget 172
Lothrop, Susanna 1
Lott, Charles 88
Lougher, Walter 137
Loughman, Daniel 18
James 18
Jane 18
John 18
William 18
Loure, Thomas 76
Loutitt, Ichabod 127
Love, Joseph 46
Loveday, Samuel 17
Lovell, Sarah 41
Lovelock, John 135
Jone 135
William 135

Lovemore, Richard 149
Lovett, Richard 95
Lovill, Thomas 209
Loving, Thomas 54
Lowd, Deborah 110
Lowdham, Hannah 16
Lowe, Ann 144,218
  Bennet 144
  Cornelius 218
  Dorothy 145
  Elizabeth 144,145
  Henrietta Maria 144
  Henry 144
  Johanna 81
  John 93
  Joseph 43
  Mary 145
  Micajah 81
  Nicholas 144
  Robert 188
  Sarah 81
  Susanna 81
  Susanna Maria 145
  Thomas 144
Lowfield, ----- 125
Lowther, ----- 106
Loxley, Abram 213
Loyer, Adam 247
Lucas, Anne 36
  Charles 123
  Elizabeth 123,242
  George 242
  John 126
  Robert 123
  Thomas 19,138
  William 123
Lucy, Ann 54
Ludlow, George 239
Ludwell, Philip 208,219
Luffingham, Ann 148
Lugg, John 187
Luke, George 71
Lunn, Thomas 55
Luscombe, Samuel 237
Lush, James 228
  Sarah 228
Lutwich, Susannah 148
  William 148
Lyddall, Barbara 86
  James 34

Lyddall, John 85
Lyde, Edward 121
  Katherine 120
  Lionel 120,231
Lyden, Joan 111
Lydins, John Henry 228
Lyford, William 177
Lyman, Phineas 228*,229
Lyme, William 253
Lynch, Francis 108
  Helen 244
  Thomas 207
Lynd, Benjamin 101
  Mary 101
  Samuel 121
Lyndon, Richard 211
Lynes, Ann 212
  Thomas 212
Lyon, Benjamin 224
  John 12
  Peter 258
  William 262
Lyte, John 188
Lythall, Samuel 163

Macaire, **Francis 45**
MacCallow, John 146
MacConell, Alexander 65
MacCulloch, John 147
MacDowall, Alexander 147
Macham, Joseph 140
Mackay, Hannah 185
  Samuel 185
Mackclannan, James 74
Mackenly, Thomas 191
Mackenzie, Alexander 155
  Anne 155
  Donald 226
  Duncan 155
  Elizabeth 155
  Glenn 155
  Robert 226
Mackey, Hester 95
  Jane 175
  John 173
  Joseph 175
Mackie, Ebenezer 237
Mackinstry, William 257

Mackintosh, Alexander 191
  Charles 191
  Phineas 191
  Susanna 191
Mackoll, John 85
Mackoun, Robert 214
Mackworth, Sir Thomas
  148
Maclaning, Jane 74
MacLean, John 258
MacMillan, James 83
Macphederis, Mary 168
Maghee, Samuel 219
Magill, Dr. 138
Magnus, Francis 241
Magregory, Margaret 87
Mahier, John 121
  Katherine 121
  Mary 121
  Richard 121
  Richard 121
Mahos, Mr. 121
Maides, John 260
Maidman, Sarah 177
Mainstone, John 46
Mairac, John 260
Maiston, Nathaniel 92
Maitland, Alexander 257
  Peter 257
  Richard 257
Makill, D. 138
Malbone, Mary 184
Males, Daniel 131
Maling, Abigail 93
  Elizabeth 93
  Hannah 93
  Samuel 93
  Thomas 93
Mallard, William 153
Mallett, Winifred 58
Mallortie, David 156
  James 156
Mallory, Charles 201
  Elizabeth 201
  Fanny 246
  Florasabella 246
  Francis 201
  John 200,241
  Johnson 246
  Mary 200,246

Mallory, Roger 201
    Sir William 246
    William 200,201,**246**
Manchester, Abigail 112
Mandell, Col. 163
    Nicholas 146
Mandery, Thomas 183
Manet, Samuel 176
Mangin, Paul 212
Manigault, Gabriel 153,
    164,180,186,207
Manley, Mr. 71
Man(n), David 13
    Galfridus 200
    Jane 13
    Joanna 98
    John 26,27
    Manley 29
    Nicholas 32
    Richard 34
    Thomas 73
Manning, Jacob 94
    John 71
    Joseph 73
    Thomas 73
Mannon, Joseph 191
Mansfell, Nicholas 44
Mansfield, Isaac 254
Manstidge, Emanuel 3
    Isaac 3
    Joan 3
    Robert 3
    Thomas 3
    William 3
Manton, Edward 49
Manwaring, George 116
    Martha 58
    Mary 57
    Thomas 57
Mappell, Katherine 93
    Payne 93
Mapson, Elizabeth 14
    George 14
    James 14
    Joan 14
    Susanna 13
    Thomas 13
March, Elizabeth 90
    Hunton 90
    John 90

March, William 53
Marcroft, Laurence 198
Marden, William 90
Mariartee, Daniel 142
Marion, Joseph 168,170
Markey, Thomas 105
Markham, Lewis 74
Markin, Nicholas 105
    Sarah 105
    Thomas 105
Marlar, John 34,44
Marler, Jacob 120
Marlow, Thomas 116
Marnasse, Theodore 111
Marriner, William 133
Marriott, Mrs. 52
    Benjamin 160
    George 116
    John 54
    Joseph 224
    Powers 182
    Rachel 169
    Sarah 201
    William 116,125
    Zechariah 148
Marrow, William 145
Marsden, Peggy 249
Marsh, Anne 51,69
    Daniel 223
    Elizabeth 117
    George 232
    Joseph 249
    Mary 68
    Peter 55
    Sarah 117
    Thomas 117
    William 51,**54**,218
Marshall, Christopher
    178,197
    George 119
    Hubert 187,210
    John 106,**113**,121
    Josiah 253
    Martha 106
    Sarah 113
Marsham, Robert 61
Marston, Thomas 249
Martell, Peter 68
Marten, John 28

Martin, Ann 120
    Charles 181
    D. 207
    Elizabeth 120
    George 120
    John 67,120
    Mary 120
    Richard 52,**120**
    Ruth 162
    Susanna 181
    Thomas 111
    William 20,195
Martine, Andrew 65
    George 65
Martini, John 176
Marton, Edward 131
    Humphrey 213
    Oliver 89,131
Martyn, Alexander 22
    Jane 76
    Michael 76
    Richard 76
    S. 150
    Sarah 76
Marwood, Isaac 50
Mash, Elizabeth 216
    John 216
    Mary 216
Maslyne, John 4
Mason, Edward 68
    Elizabeth 97
    James 80
    John 116,147,157
    Mary 68,147
    Robert 97
    Thomas 147,**243**
    William 93,130
Massey, John 208
Masswey, Susanna 218
    William 218
Masterman, William 187
Masters, Elizabeth 184
    Peter 2
Mather, Increase 91
    Martha 40
    Richard 221
    Roger 222
    Thomas 40,221
Mathew, John 131
Mathewes, Robert 20

Mathews, Edward 170
    Franklyn 170
Matthew, Thomas 132
Matthews, Elizabeth 44
    Hannah 180
    Samuel 117
    Susanna 44
    Thomas 180
Maude, David 146
Maurice, John 195
Mauroumet, Anne 260
    John 260
Maxwell, James 205
    Jane 183
    John 127
    N. 198
    Robert 58
May, Benjamin 223
    George 9
    John 123
    Mary 123
    Susan 9
    Thomas 114
    William 123
Maybank, Ann 129,130
    David 129
    Elizabeth 129
    Joseph 129,130
    Susanna 129,130
Mayhew, Jonathan 227
Mayleigh, Thomas 93
Mayling, Thomas 93
Maynard, Benjamin 155
    Henrietta 135
    Henry 135
    James 14
    John 184
    Lawrence 186
Mayne, Mr. 88
    Jo. 11
Maynwaring, Ruth 56
Mayo, Alice, 45
    Anne 45
    Elizabeth 45
    George 45
    Israel 45
    John 45, 87
    Margaret 45
    Mary 87
    Phebe 45

Mayo, Rebecca 45
    Sarah 45
Mayraut, James N. 207
Mayvill, George 11
Mazyck, Isaac 202
    Mary 202
McAdam, Mary 257
    Peter 257
    Richard 257
    William 257
McAll, Samuel 183
McCall, John 172
    Samuel 218
McCartey, Florence 53
McCaull, Patrick 237
McClean, Lauchland 246
McConnel, Mary 201
McCrackan, Alexander 242
    Andrew 242
    Grisel 242
    James 242
    John 242
    William 242
McCubbins, Mary 194
McCulloch, Henrietta
        Maria 209
    Henry 209
McDonald, Donald 226
McDonall, John 244
McDoul, James 242
McDowall, John 257
McEvers, John 187
McGuiry, Laughlin 193
McGwire, Thomas 232
McInnes, Daniel 248
McIntosh, Thomas 147
McKay, James 194
McKenzie, Anne 260
    James 260
    William 210
McKesson, John 215
McKoy, James 194
McLain, Hector 138
McLean, Allan 186
McMahon, Francis 198
McMurtrie, David 226
McPherson, Isaac 229
    James 229
McWilliams, Mary 171
    William 171

Mead(e), Frances 41
    Francis 41
    John 112,260
    Mary 48
    Robert 61
Meads, T. 54
Meakin, Ann 27
Meanes, Thomas 89
Measures, Alice 111
    Matthew 111
Medcalfe, Craig 261
Medgate, Charles 43
Medley, William 18
Medlicott, Henry 70
Meeke, Robert 109
Meeres, John 23
Meers, James 39
Meese, Anne 33
    Frances 33
    Henry 33
    John 33
Melham, William 48
Mendes, Isaac 245
    Lewis 245
    Moses 245
Mercer, Elizabeth 213
    James 213
    Jemima 213
    Mary 213
    Thomas 103
Meredith, Joseph 95
    Mary 34
    Susanna 15
    William 37
Meritt, Nicholas 181
    W. 41
Merrefield, Edward 238
    John 238
    Robert 238
    Sarah 238
    Vernon 238
Merricke, Giles 37
    Susannah 92
Merriman, Nathaniel 193
Merriott, George 141
    Penelope 141
Merrydale, Richard 3
Merzeau, John 120
Messell, Gerrardus 49
Mestrezat, Samuel 222

Metcalfe, Ann 220
Charles 62
Christian 103
John 91,**220**
Lassells 103
Mary 220
Samuel 220
Thomas 220
Methuen, William 88
Mew, Elizabeth 24
Ellis 24
Hester 24
James 24
Jane 24
Mary 24,30,72
Noel 72
Patience 72
Peter 24
Richard 72
Samuel 24
Sarah 24
Meyer, Henry 93
Meyler, Mr. 217
Mickilman, John 29
Micklethweight, Mr. 11
Mico, Joseph 187
Middleton, Arthur 149, **166**
Benjamin 25
Christopher 142
Elizabeth 25
Henry 167,211,223
Rebecca 25,211
Richard 158
Sarah 149,166
Thomas 25,167
William 167,211
Miers, Walter 93
Miffant, James 136
Migault, Andre 227
Mighells, Amy 180
Thomas 180
Milam, Ebenezer 30
Mildred, Thomas 157
Mileham, John 19
Mathew 19
Miles, Richard 221
William 221
Mill, George 25
John 210

Mill, Richard 92
Millechamp, Jane 167
Timothy 167,175
Millener, Mrs. 155
Miller, Alice 9
Anne 36
Emma 9
Isaac 58
John 169
Richard 44,147
Thomas 239
Milles, Richard 220
Millew, David 110
Mills, Andrew 191
Ann 28
Edward 50
Eleanor 191
Elizabeth 89
Hannah 89
Henry 218
Honor 9
James 257
John 89,210
Mary 89
Richard 46
Stephen 132
Thomas 9
William 9,239
Millus, George 61
Miln, Al. 263
Milner, Jeremiah 134
Joseph 156
Milners, Per 39
Milton, Anne 13
Mary 79
Nathaniel 50
William 79
Milward, Robert 105
William 1
Minor, Jacob 198
Mary 198
Minot, Mary 249
Minskipp, John 148
Minton, Elizabeth 75
Misher, George 54
Mitcheler, Alexander 13
Mitchell, Capt. 52
David 140
Edward 225
Elizabeth 189

Mitchell, John 138,209
Mary 140
Thomas 92
William 123,189
Mitton, Edward 48
Moe, Christopher 198
Mohan, Dinah 72
Molins, George 46
Moll, John 27
Molleson, R. 251
William 251
Mollison, Margaret 131
Molloy, Featherston 194
Francis 194
Molte, Jacob 199
Molyneux, Thomas 70
Money, Ann 230
Mary 230
Monroe, Donald 258
Monsey, Mesenger 229
Montcrieffe, Thomas 257
Montgomerie, Robert 50
Moodie, Susannah 260
Moody, Ann 203
Edmond 240
Eliezer 39,73,79
George 241
James 82
Mary 240
Matthew 203
Robert 179
Moone, Alice 32
Christian 32
Dorothy 32
George 32
Hugh 32
Katherine 32
William 185
Moor(e), Alexander 215
Anne 128,217
Catharina Maria 248
Daniel 200
Edward 46
Elizabeth 4,15
Sir Henry 248
James 67
John 41,124,263
John Henry 248
Martha 131
Mary 41,181

Moor(e), Paul 181
  Richard 49
  Roger 236
  Sarah 263
  Susanna Jane 248
  Tessia 215
  Thomas 19,131,169
  Thomas William 262
  William 168,207,217
Morant, Edward 248
Moraud, Anne 260
Mordaunt, Mr. 260
Mordit, Mrs. 152
More, George 135
  Samuel 122
Morgan, Bridget 21
  Christopher 81
  Christopher 88
  Gabriel 88
  George 21
  James 81,88,261
  Jane 261
  Jeremiah 237
  John 88,261
  Jone 88
  Lydia 88
  Robert 88
  Samuel 85
  Sarah 88,261
  Susanna 26
  Thomas 201,206
  William 98,117,118,228
Morisone, Thomas 220
Morley, George 182,242
  James 7
  John 7
  Katherine 7
  Thomas 7
Morrey, Richard 209
  Sarah 209
Morrice, Jane 135
  Mary 135
Morris, Charles 161
  James 203
  Jane 197
  William 260
Morrison, Thomas 132
Morse, Henry 263
  John 263
  Mary 263

Morse, Thomas 263
Mortier, Abraham 222
Mortimer, Charles 257,263
Mor(e)ton, Ann 67
  Anthony 188
  Deborah 42,67
  Elinor 42
  John 42,67
  John Joseph 149
  Joseph 41,67,88
  Rebecca 42
  Sarah 188
  Stephen 188
Moseley, Anne 63
  Sir Edward 63
Mosley, Sir Anthony 3
Mosse, Benjamin 33
  Mary 63
Motte, Jacob 180
  John 248
Motteux, Benjamin 131
  John Anthony 131
  Moses 131
Moulson, Foulke 26
  Gaines 27
  Peter 26
  William 235
Moult, Dorothy 11
  Francis 11
  Lucy 11
  William 11
Moulton, Jeremiah 241
Moultrie, John 178,205
Mounsell, Henry 54
Mount, William 248
Mountford, John 48
Mountjoy, Mary 69
  Thomas 80
Mousat, James 118
Moutravers, Johanna 134
Movelty, Nathan 116
  Sarah 116
Mowland, Richard 247
Moyle, John 132
Muchalt, Ann 27
Mudge, Frances 162
Mugleworth, Peter 120
Muller, Albert 137
  Jochim 137
  Lyder 137

Mulligan, John 58
Muncreef, Elizabeth 151
  John 151
  Mary 151
  Richard 151
Munday, Elizabeth 161
  Richard 161
Mundell, John 58
  William 58
Munford, Robert 239
Murcott, Henry 211
Murdoch, Eleanor 214
  Isabel 214
  Robert 214
Murrant, William 181
Murray, Alexander 220
  Grace 204
  James 178
  Joseph 187,204
  Mungo 206
Musgrave, Peregrine 66,67
Mustard, Christian 19
Myatt, Jonathan 142
  Joseph 142
  Philip 142
  William 142
Myers, John 190
Myles, Walter 22
Mynterne, Alice 2
  Byngey 2
  John 2
  Nathaniel 2
  Samuel 2
  William 2

Naish, William 135
Nall, John 56
  Mathew 56
  William 56
Napier, Bouth 114
  George 170
  Patrick 20
  Robert 114
Napper, Ann 12
  Richard 12
  Robert 202
Nash, Elizabeth 122
  Frances 47
  George 10

Nash, Hester 122
  Joseph 47
  Mary 122
  Nicholas 122
  Thomas 239
  William 122
Nayler, John 99
Naylor, Abraham 260
Neale, Edward 194,231
  John 41
  Mary 145,194
  Sarah 41
  William 240
Nean, Henry 153
Neate, William 218
Neave, Richard 260
Nedham, Cor. 77
Needham, Walter 40
Neele, Dorcas 97
  Rose 97
Neeres, Robert 109
Neeve, Elizabeth 180
  Hannah 26
  John 26
  Mary 26
  Sarah 26
Negus, John 22
Neil, Arthur 245
  Lawrence 154
Neilson, John 173
  Mary 173
  Richard 173
  Samuel 173
  William 173
Nelmes, Francis 6
Nelson, Gilbert 84
  John 150,217
  Mathew 150
  Paschall 217
  Robert 34
  Thomas 18,61
  William 253
Nepton, William 12
Nesbett, Alexander 106
Nesbit, Nehemiah 212
  Samuel 212
Netcutt, George 201
  William 201
Netter, Richard 41

Nevall, Samuel 228
Neve, Gabriel 133
Nevett, Arthur 32
  Hugh 32
  John 32
  Richard 32
  William 32
Nevill, Elizabeth 61
  George 45
  John 61
  Martha 61
  Mary 61
  William 155
Nevin, Andrew 244
  George 243
  Isabella 243
  James 243
  Margaret 243
  Mary 244
New, Elizabeth 146
  Thomas 146
Newall, John 84
  Martha 84
Newberry, Abigail 175
  Anne 157
  Anne Mary 157
  Benjamin 72,175
  Elizabeth 157,175
  Hannah 175
  Margaret 157
  Martha 157
  Mary 157
  Nathaniel 204
  Patience 157
  Roger 175
  Sarah 157,175
  Thomas 175
  Walter 157
Newby, John 109,110,
    135,148
  Thomas 110
Newcombe, Crispin 99
Newell, Andrew 169
  Ebenezer 223
  Eunice 169
  Joseph 169
  Mary 169
Newham, Roger 70
Newland, George 69
  John 13

Newman, Barbary 20
  Elizabeth 232
  Gabriel 259
  Henry 232
  Roger 86
  Susannah 86
  Thomas 183
Newmarch, Dorothy 240
  Joseph 240
Newton, James 79
  John 55
  Jonathan 6
  Joseph 52
  Samuel 65
  Sarah 6
  Thomas 6,121
Nicholas, Robert C. 255
  Thomas 146
  William 152
Nicholls, Ann 73,197
  John 25,197
  Lewis 74
  Mary 197
  Richard 187
  Simon 25
Nichols, Isaac 199
  Stephen 198
Nicholson, Anne 118
  Benjamin 118
  Catherine 49
  Edward 118
  Elizabeth 118
  Francis 136,139
  Henry 212
  James 118
  John 49,207
  Joseph 118
  William 118
Nickelson, John 178
  Sarah 216
Nickolls, Jeremiah 72
  Mary 72
  Robert 72
  William 72
Nickols, Randolph 92
  Sarah 92
Nicoll, Andrew 187
  Elizabeth 187
  George 187
  Helen 187

Nicoll, James 187
  Susannah 187
Nicolls, Richard 187
  Stephen 167
  William 159
Nightingirl, John 154
Nisbett, Alexander 139
Noble, Robert 66
Noore, Anne 49
  John 49
  Naomi 49
  Rachel 49
  Sarah 49
Norman, Edward 23
  Hannah 147
  Martha 254
Norris, Eliza 188
  Elizabeth 110
  Francis 119
  Henry 188,212
  Samuel 19
North, Frances 186
  Francis 125
  Stephen 125
Northen, Bryan 106
Northey, Mr. 149
  William 70
Norton, Edward 65
Norwood, Richard 17
  William 151
Nossiter, John 13
Nottingham, Richard 1
  Thomas 202
Nowell, John 180
  Martha 106
  Thomas 106
Nowland, Richard 149
Nox, Thomas 237
Noyes, Dorothy 69
  Esther 69
  Joseph 69
  Mary 69
  Nicholas 100
  Peter 69
  Sarah 69
Nunn, John 85
Nurden, John 119
Nurse, Joseph 139
Nuttmaker, James 20
Nye, John 48

Oakings, Hester 17
  Joseph 17
Oakley, Adrianna 172
  Richard 100
Oare, Jane 53
  John 53
Oddy, Joseph 206
O'Farrell, Richard 212
Ogburne, John 120
Ogden, Alice 85
  Thomas 85
Ogier, Abraham 174,225
Ogilvie, Capt. 262
  Charles 229
  John 257,263
Ogilvy, James 190
Ogle, Maj. 253
  Ann 206
  Benjamin 206
  Mary 206
  Meliora 206
  Samuel 206
Oglethorpe, Gen. 176,
  188,194
  James 185
Oker, Abraham 20
Olbie, William 162
Oldfield, John 144
Oldis, Elizabeth 6
  Nathaniel 6
  Thomas 6
Oldner, Alice 138
  George 138
Oliver, Andrew 158,243
  Collis 212
  Daniel 131
  Samuel 82
  Thomas Fitch 158
Olivier, Daniel 115
Olliffe, Thomas 61
Opie, Edward 82
  Helen 82
  John 82
  Lindsay 82
  Sarah 82
  Susannah 82
  Thomas 82
Oram, Roger 122
Ordway, Richard 33
Ore, John 60

Orem, James 187
Ormandey, John 74
Orme, Elizabeth R. 254
  Joshua 254
  Susannah 254
  William 141
Ormsby, Catherine 237
  Eubule 237
  George 238
  Gilbert 238
  John 238
  Mary 237
  Rebecca 237
  Robin 238
Ormston, Joseph 146
Orpwood, Edmond 184
  Mary 184
Orr, Thomas 109
**Orrery, Charles Earl
  of 145**
Orton, John 123
Osborne, Edward 6
  John 210
  Thomas 50,236
  William 159
Osgood, Anna 88
  Anne 89
  Hester 52
  John 51,89
  Mary 52
  Obadiah 52,88
  Rebecca 52,89
  Salem 51,88
  Sarah 52
O'Sheal, David 153
Oswald, John 218
Oswin, Christopher 122
  Thomas 122
Ottway, Gen. 237
  Gresham 113
  John 22
  Thomas 22
  William 22
Ouchterlony, John 190
Ought, William 211
Ouldfield, John 199
Outerbridge, White 177,
  185
Outridge, Daniel 55
  John 55

Ouzeel, Beatrice 81
Ovens, Thomas 157
Overman, John 147
Owen, Mr. 103
  Charles 76
  Elizabeth 8,160
  Frances 160
  Humphrey 171
  Jeremiah 160
  John 24,153,169,197
  Joseph 11
  Owen 147
  Robert 149
  Sarah 259
  Thomas 160
Owens, Anne 21
Owles, William 84
Owsebie, John 4
Oxenbridge, Clement 39
  John 39
  Katherine 39
Oxenden, George 140
  Sarah 140
Oxley, Walter 6
Oyles, Mary 98
  Peter 236
  Philip 98
  Sarah 98
  Thomas 98

Pack(e), Elizabeth 144
  Francis 24
  Graves 144
  James 77
  Richard 144
Packer, Thomas 193
Packwood, John 17
Padmore, John 249
  Margaret 249
Page, Alice 114
  Anne 103
  Edmund 103
  Elinor 125
  Elizabeth 103,114
  Francis 114
  Hannah 103,123
  Hesther 229
  James 2
  John 65,114,231

Page, Mann 114
  Martha 114
  Mary 114
  Matthew 114
  Nathaniel 2
  Nicholas 15
  Richard 103
  Robert 103
  Thomas 152
  William 123
Pagett, Joakim 41
  Rebecca 106
Paguy, Jean 183
Paice, Nathaniel 223
Pain(e), Andrew 7
  James 136
  John 60
  Susanna 98
  Thomas 176
  William 98,250
Painter, Katherine 36
  Nicholas 36
  Roger 36
Paley, T. 85
Palfray, Warwick 94
Palmer, Anne 188
  Anthony 188
  Archdale 188
  Charles 231
  Daniel 240
  Eliakim 188
  Elizabeth 188,201,239
  Henry 132,133,188
  John 158,186,193,
    239,240
  Lucia 186
  Martin 239
  Mary 240
  Nicholas 240
  Sarah 188
  Thomas 188,239
  William 138,188
  William Finch 188
Paplay, Lucy 231
Paradise, Mary 232
Parepoint, Mehittable 118
Pargiter, Edward 41
  Elizabeth 41
  George 41
  John 41

Pargiter, Robert 41
  Samuel 41
  Thomas 41
  William 41
Paris, Ferdinando John
  172,252
  Thomas 194
Parish, Edward Clark 191
  John 260
Parke, Graves 108
  Richard 61
Parker, Alexander 42
  Anne 42
  Arthur 158
  Benjamin 241
  Dorothy 26
  Elisha 191
  Elizabeth 26,42
  Ellen 42
  G. 210
  George 194
  Grace 26
  Hyde 226
  John 15,42,192
  Letitia 263
  Mary 42
  Richard 95
  Robert 163
  Sarah 26
  Thomasine 26
  William 25,171,192,193
Parkes, Andrew 3
  John 3
  Susan 3
Parkhurst, George 4
Parkman, John 120
Parmeter, John 69
Parmiter, Par 191
Parmoore, John 13
Parnell, Bridget 131
  Elizabeth 131
  James 131
Parr, Arthur 99
  Thomas 161
Parris, Dorothy 69
  John 115
  Samuel 69
Parrott, William 140
Parr(e)y, Mr. 260
  Henry 107

Parr(e)y, Howell 249
John 11,84
Mary 84
Parson, Charles 235
Sarah 157
Parsons, Gen. 227
Humphrey 39
James 229
John 50,148
Thomas 79
William 47
Partridge, Elizabeth 101, 193
Francis 226
Katherine 101
Martha 101
Mary 101
Richard 186
Robert 101
Thomas 101
Paschall, Thomas 226
Passmore, William 115
Pasteur, William 255
Paston, Elizabeth 99
John 99
Mary 99
Robert 105
Samuel 99
Paterson, Jane 136
Robert 188
Patten, Nathaniel 156
Patterson, George 190
John 227,228
Mary 227
Ruth 227,228
Sarah 228
Pattin, Mary 192
William 192
Pattison, George 122
Isabella 170
Jane 122
John 170
Thomas 34
Paul, Richard 123
Paulding, William 172
Pawisol, Hannah 237
Isaiah 237
Pawlett, John 118
Martha 53
William 53

Paxton, Alexander 166
Charles 188
Payne, Alice 193
Catherine 174
Edmund 92
George 142
Isabella 193
John 191,193
Katherine 92
Martha 193
Richard 193
Thomas Abel 191
William 186
Peacock, John 154
Peale, Thomas 23
Pearce, Ann 54,142,154
Henrietta 157
James 154,157
Mary 96
Thomas 154
Pearse, William 15
Pearson, Edward 224
Job 184
William 125
Peasley, William 29
Peck, Dorothy 70
Jane 70
Robert 104
Thomas 70
Peele, Lodowick 14
William 186
Peere, Dorothy 15
Elizabeth 15
Joane 15
Robert 15
Thomas 15
Peers, Henry 132
Sarah 132
Peirce, John 228
Joshua 168
Mary 228
Tobias 177
William 71
Peirson, John 46
Pell, Elizabeth 230
George 230
Pemberton, Mrs. 163
John 66
Margaret 66
Pemmell, Margaret 26

Pendleton, Phebe 219
Pendrill, Lawrence 75
Sarah 75
Penman, James 262
Penn, Christiana G. 252
Elizabeth 61
Guilielma 252
Hannah 252
John 60,131,252
Richard 251
Springett 252
Thomas 176,252
William 33,61,103,252
Pennant, Thomas 4
Penniman, Moses 168
Rebecca 168
Pennington, Thomas 232
William 40
Penny, Alan 9
John 12,125
Pennyston, Prescott 122
Pepin, Alexander 45
Pepper, Edward 3
Pepperell, Andrew 240
Elizabeth 240
Margery 240
Mary 240
Sir **William** 209,240,236
William 241
Percivall, Andrew 55
Essex 55
James 55
Mary 55
Samuel 55
Perdrian, Benjamin 206
Elizabeth 206
Judith 59
Lewis 59
Lydia 206
Perkins Buchanan & Brown 263
Perkins, William 257
Perroneau, Alexander 205
Ann 205
Arthur 205
Elizabeth 205
Henry 205
James 205
Robert 205
S. 205

Perry, Mrs. 136
  Anne 104
  Elizabeth 172
  Jenking 248
  John 149,174
  Mary 216
  Micajah 48,64,81,86,88,
    108,114,120,136
  Michael 216
  Philip 143
  Richard 88,108,114,136
Persehouse, P. 65
Pert, Edward 22
  Frances 33
  Francis 33
Pesey, Mary 263
Peter, Tabitha 172
Peters, Edward 152
  Elizabeth 152
  James 152
  John 152
  Richard 251
  Sarah 152
  Warren 152
Peterson, Gilbert 127
  Peter 36
Petre, John 196
Pett, Arabella 25
  Arthur 1
  Elizabeth 1
  Florence 1
  Samuel 25
  William 1
Petter, Thomas 14
Petteres, Henry 4
  Rebecca 4
Pettit, John 63
  Thomas 215
  Widow 216
Pett(e)y, Francis 49
  Richard 146
  Sarah 49
  William 10
Pewsey, George 5
  Rebecca 5
Phelp, Barney 168
Philips, Andrew 240
  George 43
  Neel 162
Philipson, Christopher 106

Philiptes, Adr. 96
Phillimore, Robert 133
Phillip, Robert 138
Phillipps, Elizabeth 230
  Giles 230
  Joanna 230
  Adolph 105
  Alice 22
  Andrew 161
  Anne 43
  Caleb 48
  Charles 22
  Elizabeth 48
  George 67
  Gillam 161
  Henry 22
  Hester 22
  Joan 5
  John 10,22,49,64,
    135,240
  Judith 22
  Lewis 22
  Margaret 22
  Mary 101,135,161
  Paul 80
  Samuel 252
  Sarah 135
  Thomas 22
  William 33,135,252
Philpot, John 208
Philpotts, John 15
Phipherd, Caleb 59
Phipps, Mrs. 136
  Dame Mary 91
  Neel 162
  Spencer 91
  Sir William 91
Pick, John 151
Pickering, Robert 113
Pickford, John 213
  Mary 213
Piddington, ----- 253
Pidgeon, R. 181
Pierce, Edward 245
Piggot, Jone 25
  Nathaniel 108
  Ralph 108
Pike, Joseph 20
  Richard 204
  Sarah 148

Pike, Thomas 83,247
Pilkington, Edward 10
  Ellen 10
Pilsworth, John 87
Pim, Charles 84
  Elizabeth 84
Pimms, John 44
Pinckney, Charles 195,
  207,242
  Charles C. 242
  Harriet 242
  Ninian 251
  Rebecca 207
  Richard 242
  Thomas 242
  William 207,242
Pine, Arthur 18
  John 62
Piner, Thomas 134
Pinkard, Archibald 21
  John 203
Pinkny, Mary 83
Pinnard, Richard 51
Pinnock, John 241
Pinson, John 187
Pitcane, Lady Naomi 245
Pitchford, William 7
Pitkin, Daniel 228
  Elisha 228
  Esther 228
  James 228
  Timothy 228
Pitman, Davy 240
  Dorothy 240
Pitt, Robert 153
Pitts, Bartholomew 154
  Francis 163
Plancke, Lewis 236
Plater, George 84,150
Platt, Francis 52,89
  John 154
  Rebecca 52,89
Pleadwell, Edward 159
  John 18
Plesto, Catherine 134
  Dorothy 134
  Edward 134
  John 134
Plowden, Edmund 138
  Sir Edward 65

Plowden, Francis 65
  Thomas 65
  Thomazine 65
Plumb, John 213
Plummer, Benjamin 168
  Thomas 168
Plumpton, Dorothy 116
  Elizabeth 38
Plumstead, Clement 102,
  153
  Mary 102
  Sarah 102
  Thomas 146,150,157
Plunkett, Ann 160
  Christopher 160
Pocock, Lydia 143
Pointer, John 90
  Mary 90
Poizer, Thomas 235
Pole, Godfrey 108
Pollard, Benjamin 182
  William 100
Pollett, Samuel 40
Polly, Mary 131
Poly, L. 145
Pomeroy, Mr. 108
  Richard 184
  Theo. 77
  Thomas 60,89
Pomery, Alice 84
  Owen 2
Pomfrett, Mary 196
Pool(e), John 35
  Joseph 37
  Samuel 198
Pooley, Capt. 186
Pooring, Mary Juliana 224
Pooyd, Mark 54
Pope, Andrew 120
  Charles 37
  Elizabeth 37
  Francis 177
  James 177
  Joanna 37
  John 37
  Joshua 196
  Margaret 37,177
  Mary 37
  Nathaniel 37,80
  Richard 37

Pope, **Thomas 37**
Pordage, Dorcas 39
Poreton, Dorothea 141
  Penelope 141
  Sarah 141
Porry, Robert 175
Porter, Frederick 219
  Mary 219
  Mehettable 219
  Thomas 93,127
Porteus, Nanney 208
  Robert 208
Portlock, Elizabeth 86
Postell, James 199
Postles, William 187
Potenger, John 237
Potter, Joseph 216
  Martha 216
  Mary 216
  William 50
Potts, Elinor 83
  Joseph 257
  Meriam 257
  Richard 83
Poulson, Edward 60
  Prudence 60
Poulter, Edward 123
  Elizabeth 123
  Hannah 16
  John 16,123
  Mary 16
  Thomas 16
Poultney, John 48
Powell, Ensign 245
  Howell 263
  James 132,149
  John 93
  Rebecca 119
  Thomas 257
Power, Charles 94
  Elizabeth 133
Powers, George 169
  Mary 169
Powles, John 67
Powry, George 34
Poyas, James 256
Poynter, John 18
Poythres, Francis 31
Pratt, Abraham 200
  Benjamin 224

Pratt, Cresswell 144
  Elizabeth 144
  James 144
  John 114,143
  Keith William 144
  Mary 137
  William 144,161
Predix, Gabriel 59
  Susanna 59
Preeson, Isabel 124
  Margaret 124
  Thomas 124
  Zerubabel 124
Prenderges, Thomas 13
Prentice, Thomas 249
Prentis, John 178
  Robert 264
Prescott, George 198
Preston, Hannah 102
  James 23
  Joanna 230
  Margaret 23,102
  Rebecca 23
  Richard 23
  Samuel 23,102
  Sarah 23
  Thomas 23
Price, Ann 3
  Arthur 233
  Edward 220
  Elizabeth 13,24
  Hugh 189
  James 220
  Jane 24
  John 3,17,201,203,207
  Joseph 220
  Margaret 3
  Martha 3
  Morris 5
  Olive 3
  Rice 176
  Richard 3,24,135
  Robert 126
  Roger 24,224
  Samuel 235
  Sarah 220
  Walter 101
  William 24,182
Prichard, John 170
  Katherine 170

Prichard, Luce 170
  Luke 55
  Ruth 170
Pride, Peter 180
Priest, Francis 138
Prigg, Samuel 105
Primrose, Alexander 133
  Henry Alexander 133
  Margaret 133
Primus, John 60
Prince, Thomas 158,212
  William 103
Pringle, Andrew 182
Print, Hannah 102
Prioleau, Philip 172
  Samuel 178
Prise, Joanna 29
  John 29
Pritchard, Ann 44
  Mary 67
  Roger 67
Procter, Edward 64
Prosser, George A. 184
  John 259
Prout, Joseph 64
Provoast, Elias 45
  Johannes 45
Pruning, Thomas 133
Prusen, John 53
Prynn, Abigall 35
  Dorothy 35
  Judith 35
  Nicholas 35
Pryor, E. 209
  Thomas 51
  William 65
Pugh, Ruth 170
Pullen, Elias 226
Pultney, Daniel 166
  Margaret 166
Punchard, Francis 21
Purnell, William 23
Purry, Charles 186
Purse, John 206
Pye, Anne 58
  Edward 21,58
Pyke, Benjamin 76
  Eleanor 79
  Mary 76,121
  Richard 79

Pyke, Susan 79
  Thomas 79
  William 79
Pynchon, Joseph 223
Pyne, Elizabeth 18
  Hannah 18

Quanton, Catherine E. 263
Quarles, Mrs. 201
  Aaron 253
  Anne 253
  Barbary 253
  Catherine 253
  Isbell 253
  James 253
  Jane 253
  John 253
  Nathaniel 253
  Solomon 253
  Tunstall 253
Quarrington, James 107
Quarry, Susan 216
Quelch, Benjamin 129
Quick, John 94
Quiller, Thomas 39
Quilter, Joseph 147
  Thomas 44
  Thomas 80,90
Quince, Richard 202
Quincey, Miss 221
  Edmund 223
Quiney, Adrian 10
  Richard 10
  Thomas 10
  William 10
Quinton, Walter 66

Raby, Daniel 263
  Jane 263
Rackstraw, Grace 41
  William 41
Radford, Dorothea 211
  George 211
Radley, Thomas 262
Rae, James 81
Rafugeau, Ann 237
Ragg, Mary 111
  Robert 178

Rainstorp, Elizabeth 193
  John 194
  Mary 193
  Sarah 193
  Walter 193
Rake, Mary 184
Ralstone, Thomas 12
Ramsay, Archibald 184
  Charles 218
  John 218
  Margaret 237
Randal, William 151
Randall, Henry 6
Randle, John 237
  Mary 237
Randolph, Ann 239
  Ariana 208
  Beverley 144,239
  Deborah 84
  Edmund 208
  Edward 84,144,178
  Elizabeth 84
  Isham 100
  John 144
  Lucy 239
  Peter 239
  Peyton 253
  Richard 239
  Robert 239
  Sarah 84
  William 100,239
Ranger, John 49
Ranolds, Samuel 147
Rant, Edward 134
Raper, Robert 224
Rastrick, John 212
Ratford, Sarah 74
Ratsey, Robert 195
Rattray, John 176,190,191
Ravaud, Mark Anthony 134
Raven, John 216
Rawlins, Jane 99
  John 10,15
  William 99
Rawson, Edward 15,21
Ray, Paul 46
Raye, Mr. 113
Rayment, Elizabeth 15
  Robert 15
Raymond, Abel 167

Rayner, Jane 116
Raynold, John 111
Rea, Mary 201
Read(e), Alexander 235
  Charles 235
  Elizabeth 87
  George 19,37
  Henry 59
  Isaac 18
  James 86
  John 138,161,165,
    176,235
  Joseph 165
  Margaret 37
  Mary 18,44
  Owen 138
  Rachel 19
  Richard 20
  Robert 87
  Samuel 44
  Thomas 18,242
Reader, Mordecai 238
Reading, Nathaniel 148
  William 148
Readman, Robert 75
Reasley, William 59
Reddall, James 148
Redding, Henry 69
Reddish, Nicholas 166
  Ward 13
Reddock, Mary 9
Redhead, Samuel 214
Redman, William 259
Reed, Anthony 17
  Charles 60
  Edward 177
  Henry 100
  Isaac 54
  Nathaniel 154
  Patience 157
  Thomas 193
  William 82
Reef, John 149
Reeks, Nicholas 152
Reeve, Mr. 217
  Ambrose 160
  James 180
  Lewis 186
Reid, James 233
Reif, Jonas 82

Reily, John 226
  Patrick 233
Reller, Emanuel 236
Remington, John 196,
    202,233
Remnant, John 173
Renaudet, Peter 204,215
Renells, John 98
Renoff, Katherine 121
Renton, Joseph 171
Reny, Jacob 71
Revell, Thomas 166
Reyner, Sarah 216
  William 216
Reynolds, Elizabeth 146
  Francis 31
  Joseph 146
Rhett, Catherine 96
  Sarah 96
  William 96,116
Rhind, David 234
Rhodes, Charles 81
Ribot, Francis 181
Rice, Andrew 259
  Anne 128
  David 127
  Jane 127
  Katherine 127
Rich, Thomas 167
Richard, Morgan 175
  Nicholas 59
Richards, Elizabeth 123
  George 35,40,43
  Hannah 256
  John 14
  Robert 51
  Sarah 43
  Thomas 63
  William 123
Richardson, Anna 77
  Anthony 253
  Benjamin 162
  Elizabeth 77,94
  Emarintha 245
  George 94,213
  James 104
  Jim 104
  John 77,245,260
  Joseph 146
  Katherine 101

Richardson, Mary 77,
    149,242
  Nathaniel 150
  Peter 94
  Rebecca 154
  Richard 36,106,146
  Samuel 77
  Sarah 77
  Stephen 77
  Thomas 157
  William 146,184,**242**
  Zachariah 154
Richason, John 159
Richmond, John 121
Ricken, John 8
Rickett, William 247
Ricketts, William 116
Rickman, James 148
Riddle, James 214
Rider, Henry 91
Ridgen, John 167
Ridley, Mary 120
  Nathaniel 108,120
Rigby, Sir Alexander 130
Rigg, Alexander 199
Rimes, Elizabeth 164
Ringmacher, John G. 242
Ringold, Thomas 234
Ripley, Elizabeth 257
  John 257
  Judith 257
  Wessel 257
Rise, Elizabeth 132
  John 22
Ritchie, Archibald 257
Rives, Alexander 89
Rivet, Barbe 163
  Daniel 163
  Enoch 163
  Lewis 163
  Rose Elizabeth 163
  Susanna Louisa 163
Roach, Henry 28
  Isaac 193
  Israel 192
  William 192
Roades, Ann 26
Robbonce, Henry 122
  William 122
Robe, William 241

Robert, Col. 75
Roberts, Edward 126
  Elizabeth 73,77,219
  Hugh 233
  John 9
  Mary 43,191
  Nicholas 77
  Richard 211
  Thomas 72
Robertson, Alexander 166
  Andrew 199
  Isham 108
  William 108
Robeson, Joseph 200
  William 82
Robey, Thomas 225
Robins, Agnes 236
  Elizabeth 230,236
  Francis 236
  Henrietta Maria 230
  John 109,124,217,236
  Margaret 230
  Meriam 237
  Rebecca 237
  Susanna 230
  Thomas 230
Robinson, Andrew 56
  Anne 82
  Beverley 220
  Catherine 168
  Christopher 235
  Collin 231
  Frances 75
  Francis 48
  George 238
  Heneage 184,220
  Humphrey 17
  Isabel 168
  John 155
  Joseph 203
  M. 168
  Mark 249
  Robert 35,109
  Samuel 69
  Sarah 83
  Septimus 172
  Susan 17
  Thomas 83,163
  William 59,138,242
Robison, Henage 86

Robison, John 146
  Richard 54
Robotham, Ann 66
  George 66
  Mary 66
Robson, Isaac 98
  Mary 98
Rochdale, Richard 5
Roche, Anstace 128
  Francis 128
  Patrick 128
Rochead, James 184
Rock, Mary 62
Rodgers, James 224
Rodman, Henry 162
  Thomas 157
Rodway, John 128
Rogers, Abraham 5
  Anne 141
  Bridget 141
  Christian 141
  Edward 5
  Elizabeth 141
  Frederick 182
  Joan 5
  John 5,139,141,220
  Joseph 220
  Lidia 5
  Peter 81
  Richard 141
  Richard 5
  Robert 141
  Samuel 209
  Theophilus 141
  Walter 15
  William Christopher 141
Rokeby, Elizabeth 141
  Rebecca 141
Rolfc, William 127
Rolle, Dorothy 128
  Feddeman 128
  Francis 128
  Henry 128
  Redmond 12
  Robert 128
Rolt, Edward 40
Romein, Mary 169
Romman, Richard 123
  William 122
Rooff, Jon. 152

Rooke, Richard 217
  Whittington 162
Rooles, Richard 59
Roosevelt, Elizabeth 215
  Nicholas 215
Roost, Elizabeth 79
  William 79
Rootes, Martha Reade 231
  Thomas Reade 231
Roper, Randall 17
  William 198,199
Rose, John 206
  Robert 19,171
Rosier, John 75
Roson, Mary 210
Ross, ----- 150
  Ann 241
  David 233
  Elizabeth 110
  Elizabeth 241
  Francis 241
  John 249,259
  Mallory 241
  Munro 245
  Naomi 245
Rossor, Adam 149
Rotheram, Mary 119
Roulland, Elizabeth 263
Round, Samuel 86
Rourk, Jane 194
Routh, Zaccheus 138
Rowe, George 77
  Hannah 11
  Mary 197
  Owen 10
  Phebe 77
  Samuel 11
Rowland, John 26,108,120
Rownd, Edward 123
  James 123
  William 123
Rownson, Jane 73
Rowse, ----- 18
Roy, Daniel 146
  Margaret 146
Royal, Joseph 239
Roydon, Elizabeth 56
  Robert 56
  William 56

Royse, Daniel 39
  John 39
Rubins, James 206,208
Ruby, Christopher 141
Ruck, John 63,82
Ruddle, William 160
Ruddock, William 70
Rudkin, Jane 76
Rudle, Samuel 122
Ruggles, George 2
Rumball, Benjamin 254
Rush, John 174
  Samuel 153,174
  William 74
Rushworth, Jane 141
Russell, Alice 202
  Ann 235
  Daniel 166
  Elizabeth 163,**254**
  Helen 235
  Henry 94,**151**
  James 208,235,244,254
  Jane 243
  John 118,**202**,248
  Joseph 178,239
  Lydia 239
  Mary 8
  Philip 102
  Rachel 118
  Thomas 8
  William 151,205,208,**243**
Rust, John 71
Rutland, Benjamin 164
Rutlidge, Andrew 153,
  182,195,196
  Sarah 172
Rutton, John 85
  Thomas 92
Ryan, Margaret 178
Ryder, Anthony 17
  Charles 221
  Elenor 106
Ryley, John 106
  Nathaniel 106
  William 106
Rymer, Elizabeth 159
  Hugh 159
  Mary 159
Rymes, Edward 85
  Elizabeth 85

Sabbartony, John 61
Sackville, Clement 190
Sadler, Elizabeth 112
  John 7,10,**112**
  Mary 7
Safford, John 120
St. Andre, Nathaniel 140
St. Clair, Lady Elizabeth
  246
  Sir John 246
  John 246
Sainthill, Peter 241
St. John, Hon. F. 260
Sale, Anne 99
  Henry 99
  John 99,150
  Mary 99
  Nathaniel 99
Salisbury, Benjamin 189
  Elizabeth 189
  Josiah 189
  Martha 189
  Nicholas 189
  Rebecca 189
  Samuel 189
  Sarah 189
  Stephen 189
  William 5
Sally, Mary 108
Salter, Dorcas 91
  Elliot 150
  John 189
  Thomas 91
Salwey, Anthony 25
  Dorothy 25
  Helen 25
  Joane 25
  Richard 25
Sam(p)son, Elizabeth 86,
  256
  Henry 256
  John 232
  Samuel 111
  Thomas 126,256
Sander, Jane 8
Sanders, Elizabeth 175
  Elizabeth Clarke 175
  Henry 204
  Humphrey 85
  John 175,238

Sanders, Joshua 174,175
  Michael 57
  Rebecca 163,189
  Wilson 175
Sandford, Peter 72
  Robert 163
  Thomas 105,139
Sandiford, Peter 209
Sandwell, Elianor 204
Sandys, Edwin 203
Sargeant, Peter 91
Sargent, Stephen 47
Sarjanton, John 106
Sarsafitt, Edward 66
Saunders, Elizabeth 62
  John 103
  Lovet 62
  Thomas 229
  William 70,83
Savage, ----- 253
  Elizabeth 99
  Henry 99
  John 224
  Mary 121
  Perez 78
  Thomas 15,121
Saveige, William 83
Sawarey, Nathaniel 77
Sawrey, Mary 221
Sayer, Charles 139
  George 116
  James 218
  Martha 26,218
Sayers, Mr. 151
Scammell, William 165
Scandrith, Capt. 107
Scarlett, Nathaniel 45
Scarth, Jonathan 125
Scheelhase, Johannes 217
  Sarah 217
Schencking, Benjamin 167
Schneider, John 233
Schutz, Augustus 234
  George 136,234
  John 153,234
Schuyler, Dirck 215
Sclater, Francis Smith 246
  Mary 45
Scordy, William 63
Scorey, William 56,91

Scorry, William 82
Scott, Anne 145
　Bridget 110
　Catherine 148
　Edward 110,134,186
　Elizabeth 81
　Gustavos 80
　James 80,110
　Jane 80
　John 80,153,182,186,
　　229,234
　Jonathan 49
　Mary 126
　Rebecca 80
　Sarah 80
　Syrus 216
　Thomas 145
　Walter 200
　William 110,164,**203**,
　　236
Scow, Richard 257
Scrimshire, John 109
Scrivener, John 106
Scrope, John 162
Seager, Anthony 110
Seagrow, Mrs. 221
Seale, Richard 85
Seaman, Elizabeth 47,245
　George 245
　John 47
　Jonathan 248
　Pheby 248
Seares, Abraham 180
Seaton, George 32
Seddon, Charles 60
Sedgwick, Robert 223
Sedwall, Stephen 101
Sedwell, Amelia 155
Scignoret, Peter 134
Selby, Abraham 221
　Elizabeth 221
　Jane 253
Selwood, John 37
　Mary 69
Sempill, Charles 249
Senth, Peter 59
Sergeant, Mary 91
Sergent, Henry 25
Seton, Andrew 62,183
　John 183

Sevencraft, Sarah 105
Sewall, Rev. 158
　Joseph 239
　Samuel 223
Seward, Abraham 15
Sewell, Adam 169
　John 216
Seymour, Arthur 169
　Edward 149
　Francis 149
　John 95
　John Webb 149
　William 149
Shackleford, William 220
Shakespeare, Jonathan 116
Shallder, John 131
Shamway, John 257
Shand, Abraham 188
Sharman, Samuel 126
Sharp(e), Abraham 94
　Benjamin 116
　John 202
　Lionel 86
　Mary 132
　Peter 23
　Simon 12
　Thomas 165
　William 208
Sharpey, Richard 46
Shaw, Bridget 229
　Eliz 97
　John 106
　Lachlan 229
　Mary 229
　Richard 73,110
　Ruth 252
　William 176
　William Worthington 252
Shawser, Samuel 28
Shea, Patrick 166
Sheare, William 12,192
Shearer, William 225
Shed, George 179
Sheen, John 113
Sheers, John 69
Sheffield, Hannah 33
Shelley, Gyles 96
Shemans, Benjamin 126
Shephard, William 157

Shepherd, Ann 179
　Charles 197
　Edward 179
　John 246
　Joseph 246
　Mary 259
　Robert 259
Sheppard, Benjamin 22
　Daniel 7
　David 97
　Frances 7
　Henry 174
　John 7
　Samuel 7
　Thomas 47
　William 7,47
Sheredine, T. 186
Sherge & Forte 170
Sherley, William 10,**194**
Sherman, James 69
Sherrard, Francis 147
Sherwin, Samuel 91
Shickles, Thomas 159
Shier, Henry 203
Shiller, Roger 25
Shilling, Daniel 30
Shipard, Peter 150
Shipman, Thomas 259
Shipp, Thomas 122
Shippen, Edward 76,102
　Elizabeth 102
Shippey, Ann 212
　Eleanor 212
　Isabella 212
　Philip 212
Shipping, Mrs. 208
Shipton, Cornelius 91
Shirley, Gen. 257
Short, George 257
　James 258
　Thomas 29,258
Shower, Alicia 218
　Ann 218
　Elizabeth 218
　How 218
　Nathaniel 218
　Samuel 218
　William 218
Shrimpton, Elizabeth 73,77
　Samuel 72,77

Shrubsole, Elizabeth 213
  William 213
Shute, Anne 38
  Benjamin 38
  Elizabeth 38
  Joseph 38, 196
  Samuel 38
Shyling, Daniel 33
Sibbet, Robert 157
Sibley, Stephen 107
Silater, Thomas 98
Silk, John 131
  Martha 131
  Tobias 131
Silver, Ann 164
  Margaret 77
Sim, William 118
Simcock, Samuel 34
Simkins, Francis 101
  J. 26
  Thomas 49
Simms, Anthony 171
  James 188
Simond, Peter 234
Simonds, Ann 14
Sim(p)son, Alexander
  246, **252**
  Ann 252
  James 139
  Jeany 246
  John 139
  Love 139
  Mary 139
  Nathan 109
  Thomas 139
  Sir William 87
  William 48, 139
Sinckler, John 59
Sinclair, Jean 190
  Robert 81
  William 146
Sisle, Henry 119
Skamadine, William 73
Skelton, Mrs. 106
Skene, Alexander 196
  George 263
Skilbeck, John 238
  Mary 238
Skilton, Elizabeth 52
Skinn, Judith 16

Skinner, Elizabeth 90
  John 90, 156
  Mary 90, 130
  Richard 262
  Robert 50, 85, 262
  Samuel 147
  Thomas 90
  William 130, 200
Slack, Elizabeth 89
Slade, Catherine 108
  Mary 108
  Richard 108
  Thomas 108
Slany, Mary 44
Slater, Elianor 107, 148
  Henry 45, 86
  John 107, 148
  Mary 45
  Mary 86
Slone, James 158
Slye, George 261
Smallwood, Henry 168
  John 99
  Thomas 99
Smalman, Elizabeth 98
  Richard 99
  Samuel 99
Smart, Ann 119
  John 119, 189
  Thomas 182
Smibert, Mr. 192
Smile, James 129
  Janet 129
  John 129
  Mary 129
Smith, Capt. 18, 20
  Alice 159
  Ann 146, 244
  Barbara 222
  Benjamin 96, 223
  Bn. 175
  Christopher 137
  Christopher 241, 259
  Daniel 87
  Dorothy 87
  Ebenezer 227, 228
  Edmund 122
  Edward 85, 212
  Francis 29, 193
  George 137, 146, 222

Smith, Guy 114
  Hannah 259
  Jacob 30
  James 32, 61, 127, 148,
    154, 165, 230, 251
  Jane 217
  Jehosaphat 30
  Johanna 198
  John 5, 10, 20, 30, 45,
    127, 146, 168,
    212, 231, 243, 244
  Joseph 225
  Josiah 256
  Katherine 131
  Margaret 30, 183, 194,
    256
  Marie 13
  Martha 134, 218
  Martin 183
  Mary 30, 39, 146, 168,
    178, 224
  Mathew 253
  Mebello 77
  Oliver 39
  Paschall 217
  Philip 158
  Richard 26, 54, 32, 85,
    87, 122, 194, 244,
    251, 254
  Robert 10, 162, 171,
    226, 258
  Samuel 87, 131
  Sarah 6
  Simon 38
  Susanna 26
  Thomas 14, 30, 41, 43,
    87, 127, 134, 180,
    224, 237, 244, 247
  Walter 23
  William 10, 15, 56, 106,
    141, 146, 151, 178,
    217, 256
Smithett, Proteza 54
  Robert 54
Smithson, Thomas 66
Smyth, Peter 211
Snead, Mary 102
Snell, Catherine 174
  Susanna 204
Snelling, Samuel 47

Snoud, T. 182
Snow, John 234
    Nathaniel 174
    Sophia 201
Soames, John 96
Sober, John 220
Soffrith, George 76
Soley, Robert 18
Solguard, Capt. 129
Sollers, John 25
Solley, Thomas 132
Soloman, Anna 35
    Elias 148
Solomons, Alexander 245
Somerset, Lady Henrietta
    250
    Lady Mary 250
Somervale, John 210
Somerville, Edward 247
Sommers, Sir John 65
Sondel, Thomas 29
Sone, Samuel 257
Sonman, Peter 156
Soso, Thomas 86
Souldsby, Margaret 44
Soumaien, Aleathea 206
    Simeon 206
    Simeon 187
South, Robert 96
    Samuel 216
Southake, Cyprian 40
Southcot, Leonard 29
Southell, Anna 57
    Seth 57
Southwick, Thomas 174
Spaine, John 99
Sparhawk, Andrew P. 240
    Elizabeth 240
    Mary Pepperell 240
    Nathaniel 240
    Samuel Hirst 240
    William Pepperell 240
Sparke, John 50
    Robert 72
Sparkes, John 3
Sparrow, Benjamin 167
    Robert 159
Speed, Ann 221
    Elizabeth 6
    John 221

Speed, Robert 6
    Sarah 6
    William 6
Speermaine, David 73
    Elizabeth 73
    Launce 73
Spence, George 210
    Jonathan 66
    Mary 97
    Patrick 97
    Thomas 97
Spencer, Charles 112
    Frances 71,83
    Francis 71
    John 71
    Lettice 83
    Mottrom 71,82
    Nicholas 71
    Thomas 212
    William 71,83
Spenston, Agnes 162
    James 162
Speven, Lydia 151
    William 151
Spicer, Alice 75
    Arthur 75
    Elizabeth 75
    J. 211
    John 75,104
    Lydia 75
    William 234
Spinage, Joseph 102
Spinks, Susan 216
Splitt, Martha 92
Spooner, Andrew 243
    George 227
    James 227
    John 227,243
    John Jones 227,243
    Joshua 227
    Margaret 243
    Sarah 227
    William 227,243
Sporle, Peter 154
Spotswood, Alexander 170
    Anna Catharine 170
    Butler 171
    Dorothea 170
    John 170
    Robert 170

Spratt, Helen 58
Sprawl, Samuel 229
Sprigg, Margaret 142
    Thomas 118
Springett, Harbert 36
    Margaret 62
Spur, Abraham 212
    Eleanor 212
Spurrell, George 142
Spurrier, Samuel 152
Sputledge, Andrew 194
Stac(e)y, Benjamin 110
    Hannah 110
    Jeremiah 110
    John 110
    Katherine 110
    Mary 110
    Randolph 58
    Richard 58
    Samuel 110
Stafford, Charles 112
Stafford, Richard 66,67
Stagg, John 123
Staining, John 2
Stairatt, William 235
Stamford, Matthew 211
Standbridge, John 34
Standford, Elizabeth 174
Stanhope, Jane 253
Stanley, Dorothy 24
    Edward 24
    Elizabeth 24
    Hugh 24
    John 24
    Jonathan 228
    Mary 26
    Michael 26
    Samuel 26
Stansly, Margaret 213
Stantial, John 254
Stanton, Amos 228
    Diana Maria 255
    George Augustus 255
    Jeremiah 255
    John 228,255
    Louisa 255
    Louisa Teresia 255
    Prudence 228
    Robert 228
    Samuel 228

Stanton, Sarah Ham-
borough 228
  William 152
  William Edward 255
Stanyan, Elizabeth 65
  Susanna 65
Stapler, Stephen 176
Staples, Sarah 161
Stapleton, Darby 127
  Hester 89
  Peter 156
Stargicall, John 116
Starke, Aaron Quarles 253
  Barbary 253
  Elizabeth 88
  Frances 88
  John 88
  Martha 88
  Sarah 88
  Thomas 88
Starratt, William 231
Statch, John 170
Staunton, Richard 142
Stead, Benjamin 232
Stedman, Mr. 222
  Alexander 218
  Charles 207,218
  John 218
Steel(e), Allen 204
  Deborah 204
  George 178
  Gilbert 176
  John 176,212,238
  Mary 176
  Thomas 137,140
Steere, Ralph 49
Steers, Elizabeth 36
  Thomas 178
Steevens, Sarah 250
  William 250
Stelfax, John 111
Stennon, William 238
Stephen, Mary 74
  Robert 74
Stephens, Adam 248
  Alexander 248
  Anne 88
  Christopher 79
  Dorothy 25
  Edward 160

Stephens, Frances 21
  John 248
  Joseph 161
  Richard 25
  Robert 248
  Samuel 21
Stephenson, Catherine
  203
  Enoch 203
  Mary 163
  Pennington 203
  William 234
Stepkin, Charles 43
  Elizabeth 43
  Theodosia 43
Sterling, Robert 214
Sterry, Charity 37
  William 37
Steuart, George 206
  James 206
  John 206
Steuert, Andrew 59
Stevens, Alexander 61
  Ann 243
  Edward 243
  James 146,243
  John 151
  Joseph 56
  Mariane 124
  Mary 124
  Nathaniel 162
  Philip 85
  Rebecca 184
  Robert 124
  William 5,167
Stevenson, Alexander 71
  Allen 71
  Ambrose 131
  Bridget 131
  James 71
  John 71,213
  Thomas 131
**Stewart, Alexander
  185,**214
  Allan 185
  Charles 185
  Dougal 185
  George 175
  James 178,185
  James A. 239

Stewart, John, Viscount
  176
  John 178,200
  Mary 176
  Naney 185
  Robert 226
  Ruth 175
Stichfield, John 73
Stimpson, Thomas 226
Stinte, Thomas 66
Stirk, Benjamin 251,258
  Mary 258
Stock, Jonathan 152
Stocker, Amos 31
  Anthony 31
  Ephraim 31
  Joan 31
  Joseph 31
  Mary 31
  Obadiah 31
  William 31
Stocking, Francis 140
  Thomas 140
Stockton, Ann 261
Stoddard, Mr. 15
  Margaret 224
  Sampson 224
  Sarah 224
Stolpys, John 46
Stone, Betty 178
  James 58
  Margaret 28
  Sarah 28
  William 28
Stoninge, Paul 16
Stoodly, John 143
Storke, Samuel 137,163
Storrs, Othniel 163
Story, Avis 17
  John 103
  Katherine 17
  Ralph 17
  Robert 17
  Rowland 17
  Thomas 207
  William 168
Stout, Henry 60
Stow, John 10
  Thomas 10
Stower, Philip 61

Stown, William 185
Stowy, Daniel 166
Strachan, Margaret 166
Strachey, Arabella 40
  Martha 40
  William 40
Straing, Hannah 16
Strangman, Joshua 204
  Rachel 204
  Samuel 204
Stratfold, Thomas 89
Stratford, Francis 163
Stratton, Alexander 96
  Anthony 55,66
Strayne, John 90
Streatfield, John 127
Street(e), Mr. 113
  Ann 206
  Benjamin 68
  Daniel 68
  Hannah 68
  Mary 113
  William 236
Stretch, Hannah 174
Strettell, John 209
Strettle, Robert 179
Strickson, John 38
Stringer, Joseph 62
  Louisa 160
  Samuel 142,160
  Stephen 152
  William 11
Stringfellow, Catherine 157
Stronach, John 188
Strong, John 47
Strother, Benjamin 117
Strotton, Elizabeth 122
Stuart, Catherine 237
  Deborah 138
  Isabella 62
  Sir John 200
  Joseph 138
  Rachel 214
  Ruth 200
  William 137
Stubbs, William 177
Stuckey, John 68
Studd, Ralph 113
Stumbels, Bezaleel 237
  Sophia 237

Sturdivant, Chichester 100
  Daniel 99
Sturgis, John 123
Sturt, William 84
Suckle, T. 57
Sudbury, Hesther 148
  John 148
Sudell, Rachel 38
Suffield, John 110
Sugden, Isaac 137
Suggitt, Jane 253
  John 253
Sullivan, Daniel 95
  Margaret 95
Sullivant, Catherine 175
  Joshua 175
  Robert 47
Summers, Alexander 235
  Andrew 235
  Elizabeth 37
  Hannah 37
  Jane 37
  Jean 235
  John 37,43
  Mary 37
  Peter 37
  Sarah 37
Sumner, W. 150
Surridge, George 260
Sutherland, Alexander 208
  O. 183
  Patrick 185,213
Sutton, Janet 146
  Thomas 146
Swaine, Elizabeth 95
  William 100
Swallow, Lucretia 90
  Newman 223,245
  Sarah 90
Swan, John 54,76
  Thomas 145
Sway, Henry 104
Sweetland, George 91
Swetnam, Joseph 12
Swett, Joseph 56
Swift, Elizabeth 35
  James 35
  Judith 35
  Sarah 35

Swinburn, John 216
  Mary 216
Swinton, John 60
Swordfeger, Mrs. 145
Sybada, Kempo 12
  Mary 12
Syme, James 257
Symes, John 97
Symme, Andrew 71
Symmonds, Joseph 157
Symonds, Richard 111,116
  Sarah 111
Symons, John 9
Symson, Paul 71
Sysom, Elizabeth 186

Tabby, John 241
Talbot, John 149
Taliaferro, Margaret 105
  Robert 105
Talier, James 63
Talley, John 243
Tankersly, Charles 80
Tanner, Mary 149
  Robert 149
Tapley, Martha 169
Tarry, Edward 241
  Frances 241
  George 241
  Mary 241
  Rebecca 241
  Samuel 241
Tasker, Benjamin 206
Tate, Mary 158
Tattam, W. 198
Taverner, William 62
Tavernor, Jeremy 29
  Robert 29
Tavor, John 95
Tayer, John 169
Tayler, Etheldred 108
  John 82,194
  Richard 137
  Robert 231
  Sarah 137
Taylor, Abraham 172,
  254
  Anna 215
  Bryan 158

Taylor, Daniel 8
    Edmond 8
    Elizabeth 111
    Esther 153
    Everard 158
    Francis 158
    Freeman 158
    Humphrey 111, 117
    James 219
    Jane 256
    John 23, 119, 201, 208,
        230, 250, 254, **256**
    Margaret 8
    Mary 111, 117, 158
    Peter 216
    Philadelphia 254
    Rebecca 8
    Richard 9
    Robert 8, 231
    Samuel 8
    Thomas 46, 76, 147
    Walter 256
    William 8, 256, 261
Tea, Anne 61
    Richard 259
    Thomas 61
Teale, John 148
Teate, Matthew 73
Teere, Elizabeth 33
    Thomas 33
Teissier, James 181
Temple, Ann 219
    Benjamin 219
    Hannah 219
    John 217
    Joseph 219
    Liston 219, 234
    Mary 219
    Patte 219
    Samuel 219
    Sarah 219
    William 193, 219, **234**
Templer, Dudley 247
    Elizabeth 247
    Richard 251
Tenant, Elizabeth 139
    James 139
    Samuel 139
Tench, Frederick 150

Tender, Joseph 260
    Thomas 260
Tendring, Robert 27
    Sarah 27
Teppets, Robert 155
Terrell, Charles 30
    Mary 30
    Richmond 30
    Robert 29
    William 29, 30
Test, Daniel 102
    Mary 102
Tew, Elizabeth 11
    Nicholas 11
Thacker, Barbara 51
Thatcher, George 6
    Oxenbridge 239
    Thomas 78
Theed, John 86
Theobald, James 188, 198
Thexer, Stephen 61
Thistleweat, Catherine 125
Thomas, Capt. 113
    Alexander 8
    Anthony 94
    Benoni 107
    Edmond 35
    Edward 260
    Gabriel 102
    Henrietta 125
    James 102
    John 6, 78, 98, 165, 202
    Jon. 114
    Mary 7, 66, 202
    Micah 102
    Richard 46, 60
    Samuel 8
    Tristram 230
    William 8, 100, 134, 230
Thom(p)son, Agnes 162
    Alexander 48, 166
    Ann 50
    Benjamin 162
    Charles 250
    Clare 6
    David 189
    Edward 29, 208
    Elizabeth 238, 250
    Francis 103
    George 6

Thom(p)son, Hannah 48
    Harman 241
    Isaac 229
    Jacob 69
    James 89, 113, 155, **162**
    Jane 165
    Johanna 162
    John 90, **165**, 249
    Margaret 189, 250
    Peter 184
    Robert 165, 166
    Roger 135
    Samuel 52, 75
    Susanna 69
    Thomas 155, 159, 229
    Timothy 119, 147
    William 74, 162, 189, 221
Thornburgh, George 235
    William 50
Thornbury, Samuel 76
Thornton, Crosley 254
    Henry 89
    Matthew 214
    Nicholas 40
    Posthumus 156
Thorold, George 92
Thoroton, Richard 4
Thorowgood, Thomas 139
Thorp(e), Benjamin 124
    Elizabeth 98
    Henry 98
    Jane 127
    John 127
    Mary 127
    Thomas 98, **127**
    William 99
Thresher, Ralph 216
Throckmorton, Albion
    22, 68
    Alice 22, 68
    Bromsall 68
    Edward 22
    Frances 22
    Gabriel 22, 68
    John 22, 32
    Mary 22, 68
    Raphael 22
    Robert 68
    Sarah 22
    Susanna 68

Thrupp, Francis 82
Thurman, Elizabeth 215
 Francis 215
 Gertruy 215
 John 215
 Ralph 215
 Richardson 215
 Susanna 215
Thurmur, Anne 21
 John 21
Thurston, Elizabeth 64
 John 64
 Mary 64
 Robert 64
Thweats, James 100
Thwing, Nathaniel 190
Tice, George 47
Tichburn, Elizabeth 166
Tick, William 23
Tilbury, Martha 92
 Thomas 92
Tilden, Freegift 6
 Hopestill 6
 John 134
 Joseph 6
 Lidia 6
 Nathaniel 6
Tilghman, Ann 194
 Edward 194
 Richard 134,151
 Susannah 231
 William 194
Till, William 172
Tiller, Moses 56
Tilly, Sarah 41
 Susan 152
Tilson, John 210
 Rebecca 210
Tilsted, Thomas 23
Timbrell, Henry 128
Timbrill, Margaret 220
 Sarah 220
 Thomas 220
 William 220
Timson, Anna Maria 155
 Elizabeth 155
 John 155
 Juxon 155
 Mary 155

Timson, Samuel 155
 William 155
Tinney, Anne 236
 John 236
Tinsley, Mary 169
Tippett, Richard 92
Tisley, Samuel 158
Titcom, Thomas 123
Tithick, Mrs. 48
Titt, Richard 140
Tittery, Joshua 172
Tizack, Elizabeth 49
 John 56
Tobee, William 8
Todd, Ann 30
 Avarilla 30
 Benjamin 221
 Christopher 30
 Edward 224
 Elizabeth 221
 Frances 30
 Humphrey 107
 Johanna 30
 Samuel 252
 Thomas 30
 William 55
Todder, Anthony 121
Todo, Catherine 213
Tomlin, Oliver 257
 William 160
T(h)omlinson, Ann 174
 Edward 174
 Henry 40,174
 John 174
 Richard 168
 Robert 168
Tompkies, Francis 235
Tom(p)kins, Elizabeth 190
 John 190
 Jonathan 190
 Russell 190
 Sarah 190
Toms, Lettice 13
 Robert 199
 Sarah 199
 William 33
Tongue, John 45
Tookerman, Katherine 132
 Richard 132
Tookey, Job 57

Topping, Anne 49,113
 Elizabeth 49
 Hannah 47,49
 Joseph 47
 Samuel 47,49
 William 113
Torkinge, John 169
Torrey, Josiah 189
Torver, William 156
Tovey, Anne 27
 Nicholas 27
Towers, Henry 3
 Margaret 3
Towle, George 211
Town, John 257
Townrow, George 24
Townsend, Ann 148
 Hannah 79
 James 148
 Mary 148
 Patrick 79
 Philip 109
 Robert 93
 Solomon 121
 William 79
Towsey, John 96
 Thomas 96
Traheron, Philip 95
Traiell, James 113
 Margery 113
Tranchpeire, James 236
Traverse, Henry 13
Traweek, George 141
 Robert 141
Trecothick, Barlow 256
 John 256
Tregonow, Valentin 43
Trench, Alexander 150
 Hester 150
Trent, James 62
 Lawrence 220
 William 63
Tressenden, Josiah 243
Trested, Mary 262
Trevet, Russell 254
 Samuel Russell 254
Trevis, Elizabeth 263
 Philip 263
Trewbody, Charles 104
Trigg, William 251

Trinder, Barbara 36
Trobell, John 112
Trott, John 74
  Nicholas 110
Trotter, Jonathan 97
Troutbeck, Rev. 224
Trowbridge, Edmund 249
Trull, Mary 103
Truman, Robert 124
Trumper, Honor 171
Try(e), Edward 175
  Frances 76
  Ralph 76
Tubb, James 29
Tuberville, Edward 105
Tublay, Roger 143
Tucker, Curle 241
  Henry 138
  Nathaniel 117
  Richard 196
Tuckey, John 117
Tuckwell, William 61
Tuder, John 34
  Mary 262
  Samuel 261
Tudman, William 218
Tuite, James 194
Tull, Dorothy 70
  Ebenezer 185
  Nathaniel 51
  Richard 70
Turbut, Foster 117
  Maryann 117
  Michael 117
  Samuel 117
  William 117
Turfrey, Edward 92
Turner, Charles 211
  Daniel 209
  Elizabeth 53
  Henry 49,128
  Ignatius 55
  Jacob 127
  James 234
  John 54,128,135,233
  Margaret 54
  Peter 180
  Samuel 128,223
  Thomas 53,233
  William 92

Turpin, James 30
Tustian, Ralph 13
Tute, Elizabeth 161
  John 161
Tutet, Cephas 45
Tuttie, John 11
  Rachel 11
  Samuel 11
  William 11
Tyler, J. 141
  Jane 240
  Miriam 240
  Samuel 165
  William 50
Tyley, Samuel 138
Tyllott, Bathiah 135
  Philip 135
Tym, John 33
Tyms, Richard 35
Tyndale, G. 157
Tyndall, G. 135
  One. 163
Tyng, Col. 224
  John Alford 224
  Sarah 224
Tynte, Edward 98
Tyrell, Eleanor 230
Tysoe, John 33

Undee, Ann 120
Underdowne, John 133
  Mary 133
Underhill, Anne 81
  Mary 45
Underwood, John 241
Ungle, Mary 67
Upington, John 47
  Robert 47
  Sarah 47
  Walter 47
Uriell, George 162
  Rebeccah 162
  Ruth 162
Urquhart, George 229
  John 171
Usher, Jane 99
  John 99
Utting, Amy 180
  Ashby 180

Uxbridge, Henry Earl of
  145

Vail, Mrs. 248
Vale, Lawrence 186
Valert, Peter 203
Valette, Ann 140
  Peter 140
Vallete, Augustus 247
Valner, Margaret 169
Van Bergen, Conrad 245
Van Bulderen, Maria 186
Vander Dusen,
  Alexander 242
Vanderbilk, John 239
Vanderford, Charles 117
Vanderheyden, Dirk 212
Vanderneden, Gerard 116
Vandrose, John 152
Van Horne, Abraham
  140,203
  Augustus 247
  Cornelius 247
  Cornelius C. 217
  Cornelius G. 247
  David 247
  Garrit 247
  Judith 247
  Mary 140
Van Shaick, Goose 226
Van Swieten, Ouzeel 81
Van Vechter, Peter 196
Van Veghten, Annatje 226
  John 226
Varambeau, ----- 205
Varnor, James 190
Vass, Ezekiah 48
Vaudry, Samuel 64
Vaughan, Arthur 170
  John 158
Vaulx, Katherine 257
  Robert 29
Vaus, Samuel 116
Vaux, Richard 43
Vedder, Nicholas 238
Venables, Rebecca 200
  Thomas 200
Vernon, Anne 128
  Christopher 128

Vernon, Jane 128
  John 128
  William 128
Verplanck, Gulm. 203
Vetch, Margaret 118
  Samuel 118
Viall, Mary 121
  Samuel 133
  Sarah 133
Vicaridge, John 124
Vickers, John 235
Vickery, John 201
Vigor, William 251
Vikarage, Hester 74
Villepontoux, Benjamin
  202
  Frances 202
  Francis 202
  P. 156
  Paul 202
  Zachariah 202
Vincent, Capt. 52
  George Norborne 250
  James 178
Vinter, Thomas 140
Vischer, John 226
Vocher, Martha 8
Vonheinen, Mary 186
Voto, Paul Isaac 209
Vryland, Sarah 224

Waad, Edward 57
Wade, Andrew 191
  Christopher 39
  Dyer 66
  Hempton 239
  Nathaniel 78
  Rachel 39
  Thomas 191
Waden, George 75
Wadeson, Robert 191
Wadham, John 111
Wager, Prudence 42
Wagstaffe, James 54
  Mary 54
Waine, Johannes George
  218
Wainwright, Christian 224

Wait, Alice 121
  Robert 133
  Samuel 121
Wakeham, Joseph 95
Walbank, Agnes 153
  Edward 153
Walcot, Clement 180
  Humphrey 84
Waldenfield, Samuel 103
Waldo, Daniel 227, 254
Walke, Anthony 139
Walker, Ann 94
  Christopher 94
  Cornelius 28
  Dorothy 115
  Elizabeth 94, 103
  Endymion 204
  Flower 94
  Frances 28
  George 116, 188
  Hannah 16
  Henderson 57
  Isabell 94
  John 164
  Joseph 114, 132
  Margaret 116
  Mary 28, 201
  Matthew 114
  Nathan 179
  Richard 94, 177, 189
  Robert 60
  Steward 19
  Thomas 16, 28, 32, 94,
    258
  William 16, 43, 65, 94
  Winifred 19
Walklyn, Joshua 63
Wall, Andrew 65
  Ann 234
  Stephen 12
Wallace, James 19, 263
Waller, Benjamin 171,
    254, 264
  Henry 18
  James 249
  Martha 264
  Thomas 79, 253, 254
Walley, Mary 173
Wallice, Margaret 146

Wallin, Hannah 16
  John 16
Wallis, George 62, 170
  John 150
  Robert 146
  Thomas 38, 39
  William 82
Walsh, Thomas 32
Walter, Abel 155
  Alleyne 155
  Elizabeth 155
  Henry 155
  James 155
  John 155
  Lucy 155
  Mary 155
  Meynell 155
  Richard 155
  William 155, 224
Walters, David 83
  James 194
Walthall, William 22
Walthoe, Henrietta 254
  Mary 254
  Nathaniel 254
Walton, Charles 93
  Daniel 211
Walworth, Sir William 5
Wancklen, James 39
Waple, Henry 109
  Osmund 109
  Thomas 109
Waples, George 7
Waplington, Richard 95
Warburton, Hugh 209
Ward, Francis 53
  Henry 27, 53
  J. 60
  James 53
  John 38, 45, 79, 201,
    205, 260
  Joseph 107
  Margaret 84
  Mary 19, 79, 201
  Seth 239
  Thomas 3, 97
Warden, Catherine 180
  Elizabeth 3, 180
  Margaret 180
  William 180, 204

Wardrop, John 235
Wareham, William 131
Warfield, Alexander 244
Waring, Basil 21
  Benjamin 178,216
  Charles 201
  George 175,216
  John Lloyd 216
  Sampson 21
  Sarah 216
  Thomas 122
Warkeman, Samuel 121
Warman, Stephen 118
Warmingham, Charles 155
Warner, Rev. 232
  Edward 127
  Elizabeth 90
  Francis 140
  John 18,154,167,250
  Jonathan 141
  Mary 127
  Richard 127
  Samuel 127
  Susannah 167
Warr, Hannah 90
  John 90
Warren, Edward 109
  James 124
  Peter 170,198
  Sarah 158
Warriner, John 154
Warwell, John 46
Warwick, Ann 92
Washington, Anne 74
  Augustin 74
  George 203
Washington, John 37,74
Washington, Lawrence
  37,71,**74**
  Martha 203
  Mildred 74
Waterhouse, Elizabeth 224
  John 19
Waterman, Temperance 6
Waters, Arabella 40
  Christian 147
  Dorothy 116
  Elizabeth 40,124
  Ester 125
  John 40,124

Waters, Littleton 124,125
  Mary Hammond 147
  Richard 124,125
  Sarah 125
  William 124
Waterson, William 150
Wathan, Mary 58
Wathen, James 47
Watkin, Thomas 39
Watkins, Andrew 240
  Charles 171
  Edward 44,219
  Jane 6,240
  John 171,240,245
  Mary 171,219
  Philip 154
  Richard 6
  William 29,171
Watkinson, Godfrey 29
Watley, John 17
Watson, Adam 95
  Alexander 178
  Anne 236
  David 50
  Henrietta 236
  Henry 236
  Jane 178
  John 147,178,195
  Lucy 236
  Richard 38
  Thomas 252
  William 178,257
Watt, George 60
  James 139
  John 60
Watters, John 236
  Joseph 236
  Samuel 236
  William 236
Watts, Ann 156
  Daniel 131
  Dorothy 156
  George 162
  Isabel 156
  John 156,220,233
  Richard 156
  Sarah 158,184
  Thomas 129
  William 10,184
Waugh, John 107

Way, Ann 174
  Hannah 154
  Richard 154
Wayles, John 239
Wayne, John 154
  Sarah 154
Wayte, Benjamin 46
  Elizabeth 46
  John 46
Weale, Benjamin 157
Weardale, William 14
Weare, Daniel 37,192
  Hannah 37
  Mary 37
  Peter 37
  Thomas 37
  William 192
Weaver, John 87
  Mary 87
  Thomas 11
Webb, Gen. 213
  Anne 100
  Daniel 149
  Edward 186,193
  Elizabeth 100
  Hannah 52
  Isaac 149
  James 153
  Joseph 187
  Margaret 8
  Mark 218
  Michael Smith 149
  Rebecca 61
  Sarah 100
  Thomas 76,97
  William 8,74,100
Webber, Daniel 143
  Susanna 143
Webster, John 29
  Nathaniel 71
Weedon, Ann 48
  James 48
  Mary 48
  Thomas 48
  William 48
Weekes, Abraham 65
  Anne 102
  Francis 65
  Hobbs 65
  Margaret 24

Weekes, Thomas 54,65
Wegg, Edmund Rush 233
Welborn, Elizabeth 99
Welce, Mary 52
   William 52
Welch, Col. 233
   Elizabeth 260
   Francis 260
   Mary 13
   Wakelin 183,203
   William 1
Welden, Anthony 150
Weldon, Anthony 51
Wellin, Dorcas 34
   Thomas 34
Wellings, Thomas 129
Well(e)s, Abraham 126,143
   Anthony 75
   Arnold 243
   Elizabeth 126
   Jane 123
   John 77,143
   Jonathan 165
   Mary 143,167
   Sarah 77,227
   Toby 36
Welstead, William 132
Welsteed, William 212
Wemm, Capt. 85
Wendall, Elizabeth 254
   Elizabeth Russell 254
   Thomas 254
Wendell, John 223
Wentworth, Ebenezer 121
   John 12
   Margery 240
   William 240
Wesley, Charles 251
   John 251
   Timothy 115
West, Anne 13,68
   Anthony 6
   Benjamin 68
   Daniel 251
   Elizabeth 238
   George 170
   Hannah 68
   Henry 217
   Isabella 170
   John 25,68,238

West, Mary 68
   Michael 7
   Richard 68,69
   Sanderson 200
   Sarah 68
   Stanley 119
   Thomas 69
Westall, Edward 174
Western, Frances 256
   Hannah 256
Westley, Ambrose 224
   Elizabeth 225
   Mary 224
Westoll, Parnall 31
Weston, John 112
Wetherall, John 230
   Mary 230
Weymss, John 146
Whaley, James 153
Wharley, Daniel 42
Wharton, Ann 44
   Bethia 43
   Dorothy 44
   G. 76
   John 106
   Martha 44
   Rachel 102
   Richard 43,106
   Ruth 106
   Sarah 43
   Thomas 54,57,102,106
   William 43,59,63,106
Whatley, Stephen 163
Whearley, Abraham 42
   Anne 43
   Daniel 43
   Henry 42
   Sarah 43
Wheatcraft, John 51
Wheate, William 10
Wheatley, Jeremiah 165
   John 48
Wheeler, Charles 224
   Edward 239
   Francis 13
   Sarah 127
   Thomas 224
Wheelwright, John 157
Wheller, Samuel 83
Whetcombe, Simon 3

Whincopp, Thomas 54
Whistler, Mary 64
Whitacre, Benjamin 150
Whitaker, Alexander 1
   Benjamin 150,166
   Frances 1
   Jabez 1
   Samuel 1
   William 1,198
Whitborn, John 216
   Peter 217
Whitbourne, Elizabeth 47
Whitchell, Robert 180
White, Anna 208
   Anne 20
   Benjamin 258
   Daniel 74
   Dorothy 20
   Edmond 181
   Elizabeth 258
   Frances 91
   James 20
   John 13,20,91,146,249
   Josiah 20
   Katherine 20,181
   Limpany 181
   Martha 181
   Maurice 181
   Nathaniel 259
   Philip 91
   Priscilla 35
   Rebecca 258
   Richard 35,142
   Robert 259
   Sampson 24
   Thomas 35,105
   William 20,21,60,247
Whitebread, William 226
Whitefield, George 250
   Richard 251
   Thomas 251
Whitehart, Henry 12
Whitehead, Mary 31
   Philadelphia 32
   Richard 31
Whitehorne, George 124
   Katherine 124
Whitehurst, Ann 232
   John 232
   Thomas 232

Whitemill, John 88
Whitfield, Nathaniel 44
Whithall, Simon 30
Whithorne, Gabriel 49
Whiting, Robert 27
Whitley, Roger 139
Whitmore, Benjamin 56
Whitney, John 190
Whittemore, Joel 240
    William 240
Whittingham, John 83
Whittington, Isaac 182
Whittle, Dorothy 26
Whitworth, Martha 239
Whorlton, John 167
Whyte, Andrew 235
Wiche, Mrs. 39
Wickeat, Jacob 169
Wickens, Thomas 80
Wickham, Benjamin 198
    Eleanor 109
    John 29
    Moses 109
    Nathaniel 46
Wickhams, John 44
Wicking, Elizabeth 30
    John 30
    Richard 30
Wickins, Elizabeth 30
Wick(e)s, Christian 201
    Prudence 29
Widders, Mary 220
    Richard 220
Widdows, Susanna 249
Widmore, Elizabeth 149
    Richard 149
Wigfall, Joseph 129
Wigg, Edward 186
Wiggett, Margaret 18
    Susannah 18
    Thomas 18
Wig(g)ington, Ann 125
    Benjamin 143
    Elizabeth 143
    George 50,143
    Henry 125
    Humphrey 143
    Mary 143
    Samuel 143
    Sarah 126,143

Wig(g)ington, Thomas
    126,143
Wight, John 61
Wilby, John 10
Wilcocke, Samuel 112,
    151,162
Wildman, John 119
    John 77,78,86
Wilford, Roger 6
Wilk(e)s, Elizabeth 135
    James 179
    Job 159
Wilkins, Comford 148
    Elizabeth 38
    Katherine 38
    Michael 38
    Nicholas 30
    Rebecca 25
    Richard 148
    Theodore 38
Wilkinson, Ann 6
    Christopher 117
    Elizabeth 156
    Hannah 6
    John 122
    Joseph 156
    Mary 6
    Sarah 44
    Thomas 6
    William 6,57,138
Willdy, Benjamin 57
    Elizabeth 58
    Joseph 58
    Martha 57
    Mary 57
Willett, Elizabeth 239
    Frances 234
    John 233,239
    Richard 92
    Thomas 239
    William Saltern 210
Willey, Alice 38
    Elizabeth 203
Williams, Mrs. 84
    Ann 213
    Ayliffe 152
    Charles 217
    Daniel 153
    David 146
    Elizabeth 102

Williams, Esther 153
    George 43
    Grace 215
    Hester 24
    Jeremiah 157
    John 153,171,**212**,223
    Joseph 228
    Mary 102,157
    Morgan 104
    Rachel 102
    Robert 245
    Thomas 29
    William 215,228,237
Williamson, William
    82,249
Willing, Mr. 233
    Abigall 207
    Ann 207
    Charles 197,207
    Dorothy 207
    Elizabeth 207
    George 135
    James 135
    Mary 207
    Richard 135,207
    Thomas 105,135,207
Willis, Mr. 133
    Edward 125
    Francis 46
    Samuel 49,52
    Susanna 65
Willison, Elizabeth 138
    Robert 138
Willmutt, Richard 41
Willoughby, Henry 80
    James 54
Willox, George 172
Wills, Mr. 141
    Ann 42,68
    Elizabeth 2,238
    Francis 163
    Henry 70,111
    Joan 51
    John 2
    Samuel 35,51,52,56,92
    Thomas 42,68
Willshire, Thomas 191
Willy, William 190
Wilmer, Mrs. 141
    Benet 141

Wilmer, William 141
Wilmshurst, Elizabeth 259
John 259
Wilsheir, Richard 114
Wil(l)son, Abraham 186
Ann 66
David 80
Edward 246
George 161
John 126,134,230,257
Jonathan 15
Josiah 118,143
Lingan 143
Mary 230
Robert 62,126,253
Rose 160
Samuel 84
Thomas 194
William 50
Wiltshire, Richard 191
Windham, Joseph 143
Windsor, Viscount 145
Winfield, Edward 123
John 7
Thomas 7,123
Winn(e), Mrs. 39
Alexander 76
Isaac Lascelles 255
Thomas 40
Tobiah 39
Winslow, John 224
Winter, Cornelius 251
John 2,214
Mary 107
William 107,190
Winthrop, Adam 37
Ann 101
Jane 239
John 101
Waite 44
Wintle, Mary 212
Wise, John 36
Lawrence 29
William 36
Wiseman, Philip 92
Wiswall, Ebenezer 212
Wither, Mary 40
Withers, Elizabeth 24,255
Godfrey 110
Henry 24

Withers, Hester 24
James 242
Lawrence 255
Nathaniel 255
Samuel 24
Thomas 24
Witherston, John 197
Withinson, Thomas 133
Witter, James 12
Wolcott, Benjamin 101
Roger 175
Wolf, Brig. 179
Wolley, William 62
Wolseley, Winifred 58
Wonham, Anne 4
Wood, Edith 9
Edward 57
James 193,261
Jo. 83
Julian 9
Martha 57
Mary 9,193
Richard 9
Robert 4,9
Sarah 224
Thomas 48
William 9,52,60
Woodall, Thomas 263,264
Woodard, Elizabeth 164
Henry 164
Mary 164
William 164
Woodbridge, Dudley 191
Ruth 191
Woodburn, Mrs. 141
Woodel, John 134
Martha 134
Woodland, Elizabeth 50
Woodleif, Mrs. 31
George 31
Woodnett, Elizabeth 41
Woodroffe, George 219
John 17
Woodrop, William 166
Woodruff, Robert 228
Woods, Mrs. 126
Samuel 183
Woodward, Josiah 213
Richard 159,160
Sarah 101

Woodward, Thomas 33
William 244
Wooldridge, Thomas 262
Woolgar, William 177,234
Woolhead, Alice 101
Martha 101
Woolhouse, Richard 149
Woollaston, Francis 253
Woolmer, John 99
Thomas 99
Woolnough, Henry 152,162
Rebecca 162
Woolward, Sarah 57
William 57
Wooten, Turner 118
Worden, George 183
Worgan, William 21
Worley, Sir John 58
Worlick, Mary 35
Wormeley, Ralph 235
Wornel, Edward 134
Sarah 134
Worrall, Roger 38
Worth, John 24
Wortham, Mr. 64
Worthington, Ann 244
Charles 244
Elizabeth 244
James 153
John 244
Ruth 252
Samuel 244
Thomas 244
William 244,252
Worthy, John 148
Wortley, Sarah 90
Wotton, Anne 57
Simon 57
Susanna 57
Wragg, Joseph 160
Judith 196
Mary 196
Samuel 128,130,136,
136,149,152,196
William 196
Wraxall, Ann 219
Elizabeth 219
John 219
Mary 219
Nathaniel 120

Wraxall, Peter 219
  Richard 219
Wrench, William 66
Wrenn, Francis 120
  Thomas 120
Wrideat, George 237
Wrigglesworth, Robert
  251
Wright, Alice 19
  Ambrose 251
  Ann 56,176
  Bazell 123
  Benjamin 91
  Broughton 107
  Duncan 146
  Edward 229
  Elizabeth 56
  Frances 221
  Francis 74
  James 12
  Jane 59
  John 136,150
  Margaret 56
  Mary 127
  Moses 176
  Nicholas 79
  Peter 236
  Richard 71,127
  Sarah 115
  Thomas 250
  William 115,172
Writt, Anne 74
Wyatt, Ann 262
  George 12

Wyatt, Samuel 209
  Thomas 209
Wyborne, Thomas 46
Wych, Benjamin 156
Wyeth, John 192
  Margaret 157
  Mary 192
Wyett, Davey 36
  John 36
Wyld, Anne 105
  Elizabeth 105
  Martha 105
  Mary 105
Wyllie, George 253
Wyne, Henry 200
  Sarah 200
Wynne, Joshua 30
  Mary 31
  Robert 30
  Thomas 30
Wyron, Elizabeth 41
  Grace 41
  John 41
  Mary 41
  Sarah 41

Yale, Elihu 62
  Thomas 62
  Ursula 62
Yardley, John 51
Yates, Catherine 134
  Richard 67
  Sarah 67

Yeascombe, Robert 134
Yems, Mary 32
  Nathaniel 32
Yeo, Leonard 7
Yeomans, John 48
  Samuel 176
  William 160
Yerbury, Richard 109
Yesline, Jonas 126
Yonge, Edward 115
  Henry 243
  Robert 112
York(e), John 73,206
  Mary 206
  Robert 168
Young, Arabella 213
  Arthur 100
  B. 183
  Edward 151
  John 152,213
  Mary 128,145,151
  Nathaniel 89
  Robert 150,246
  Samuel 86
  Theophilus 213
  Thomas 213
  William 105
Yuille, Thomas 241

Zachary, Thomas 72
Zankey, William 89
Zouch, Francis 75

Index of Ships

Accamacke 18
Adventure 82,107,202
Advice 55,80*
Alborough 52,140,151,180
America 12,195
Amity 78,126
Anne 28,49,50,151
Anne & Mary 74,99
Antelope 196,253
Assurance 5,47
Augustine 30

Baltimore 52,87
Barnardiston 50
Bayly 119
Bedford 202
Bendish 20
Benjamin 85
Bethel 223
Betsey 235
Betty 122
Bever 46
Blackett 253
Blackey 210
Blandford 126,218
Blessing 1
Boughton 113
Boyne 198,260
Brislington 216
Britannia 83,98,111
Brunswick 162
Bugill 145

Canterbury 191
Captain 259
Carolina Merchant 109
Catherine 62
Centaur 204
Centurion 195
Champion 131
Charles 20,62,98
Charles Town Packet 217
Charming Peggy 135
Chatham 140
Chester 62,106
Chichester 193
Colchester 168
Comet 262

Comet Bomb 204
Concord 7,34,153
Consent 2
Cornwall 192
Coventry 229
Culpepper 37
Cumberland 224
Cygnet 250

Daniel & Anna 151
Defence 178
Defiant 56
Deptford 45,46,54
Devonshire 223
Dispatch 71
Dolphin 74,109,124,171
Dorothy 197
Dove 60
Dreadnaught 52
Due Return 2
Duke of York 32
Dunkirk 53,172

Eagle 89
Easter 123
Edgar 45
Edward Francis 73
Eliott 185
Elizabeth 12,64,116,124
Elizabeth & Martha 97
Eltham 180
Eolus 234
Ephraim 48
Essex 53,74,122,234
Europa 161
Exeter Merchant 43
Expedition 48,50

Fairfax 76
Feversham 105
Five Sisters 145
Forward 137
Fowey 249
Fox 147,211
Friends Goodwill 196
Friendship 121,225

Garland 210
George 123

Gibraltar 189
Gloucester 88
Golden Fleece 36
Gooch 144
Goodwill 112
Goodwin 166
Grafton 226
Grantham 12
Greenwich 56
Greyhound 92,129,191
Guernsey 229

Hamilton 109
Hampton Court 169
Happy 153
Hartford 107
Hartwell 88
Harwich 218
Hastings 177
Hawk 189
Henrietta 142
Hercules 222
Hope 20,49,58,112,161
Hopewell 3,123
Hornet 180,212,237
Humphrey 165

India King 82
Industry 50,97
Isabel 124

Jacob 48
James 2,3,54,92,218
Jane & Margaret 78
Jersey 185
Jett 263
John 39,107
Juno 234

Kent 134,182
Kinsale 148

Lancaster 97
Launceston 198,244
Levite 91
Lichfield 167
Little John 80
Lowestaff 96
Lowestoft 187

Loyal Rebecca 29
Lumley Castle 54
Lyme 116
Lyon 1,167

Maidstone 96,182
Marmaduke 5
Martha & Hannah 119
Mary 54,146
Mary & Francis 109
Maryland Factor 85
Maxwell 158
Mediterranean 165
Mermaid 109,195,198,
    201
Molly 150
Monmouth 193
Montague 111

Namur 154
Nassau 135
Neptune 46,214
New England Chacer 135
New York 112
New York Postilion 113
Newberry 129
Newcastle 226
Newport 57
Nicholson 91
Nightingale 110*,212
Norwich 180
Nottingham 180*

Old Neptune 90
Olive Tree 90
Orford 225
Owen 185
Owners Adventure 59

Paget 79
Patsey 144
Peach Blossom 149
Pearl 116,173
Pembroke 66,116,193*
Phoenix 15,169
Planter 13
Play 60
Plymouth 141
Port Royal 225
Portsmouth 77
Potomack Galley 80

Preservation 67,90
Preston 69
Primrose 4
Prince Royal 127
Princess Louisa 187
Prosperous Ann 148
Providence 93,96,97

Rappahannock
    Merchant 174
Recovery 29
Relief 15
Resolution 113
Restoration 74
Richard & Martha 26
Richard & Sarah 88
Richmond 51,53,66,226
Robert 93,135
Rochester 104
Roebuck 185
Romney 249
Rose 44,160,162,171,
    180,262
Royal Katherine 56
Royal Oak 110
Royal Sovereign 85,180,
    259
Royal William 73
Ruby 94,190
Rumney 94
Rumsey 113
Ruth 54

St. Albans 60
St. George 214
St. Thomas 44
Salisbury 20,24
Samuel 101
Samuel & Henry 45
Sandwich 196
Sarah 69,148
Sarah & Hannah 105
Scarborough 141
Scorpion 202
Sea Horse 129
Seaford 126
Severn 88
Sheerness 59
Shoreham 77,111,113
Smyrna Factor 83

Society 38,59,78,108
Sorlings 109
Southampton 82
Squirrel 170,174
Star Bomb 104
Success 135
Suffolk 97
Sunderland 191,196
Susan 70
Susanna 39,156
Sussex 92
Swallow 37,252
Swan 47

Tartar 133,134
Thomas & Anne 40
Thomas & Elizabeth 85
Thomas & Richard 40,53
Three Brothers 148
Tilbury 211
Torbay 134,180
Triton 93
Truelove 41
Tunstone 114
Tyger 54,80

Unicorn 36
Unity 1,17

Victory 176
Vigilant 198
Viper 232

Warspight 26
William 146,162
William & Sarah 152
Wilmington 199
Winchelsea 106,152
Windsor 170
Wolf 164,211
Woolwich 181
Worcester 187,189

York 48,183

Index of Places

This index includes place names and locations as described in the original documents but excludes the metropolitan city of London and American colonies unless particular parishes or localities are shown. The inclusion of an asterisk indicates that the name occurs more than once on that page.

Canada

Louisburgh 198,213,221
Newfoundland 64,78
Nova Scotia,
   Halifax 210,212
   Lunenburg 213

Carolina North

Brunswick 202,232*,237
Brunswick Co. 236
Cape Fear 158,202
Cape Fear River 183
Edenton 189,211
Johnston Co. 232
New Hanover Co. 232,248
New River 153
Pascotank River 131
Salmon Creek 119
Smith's Creek 248
Spring Gardens 236
Swan Point 249
Tower Hill 232
Wilmington 184,185,
   236,248

Carolina South

Albemarle Co. 57
Ashley River 73
   St. George's 196
   St. Gyles 196
Beaufort 186
Beech Hill 242
Bellmount 242
Berkeley Co. 73,152,
   166,199,206,223
   Christ Church 129,130
   St. Andrew's 207
   St. John's 197,204
Boshee Plantation 73
Cassahatchey Creek 160

Catt Island 199
Charles Town 45,69,99,
   110,129,134,136*,
   139,141,150,151,
   153,154,157*,160*,
   164,166,167,171,
   174,180*,185,190,
   194,195,196,197,
   198,199,201,202,
   205,206,221,223,
   224*,232,233,234,
   236,238,241,242,
   249,255,259,260,262
Bay 172
Bay Front 205
Broad Street 130,205
Colleton Square 206,
   242
Neck 199
Old Church Street 205
Queen Street 205
St. Michael's 234
St. Philip's 96,172,
   176,245,258
Childsbury 178
Chiliphinas Swamp 199
Coeshah Island 149
Colleton Co. 87,122
Combahie River 216,223
Combaliel 232
Cooper River 69,167,
   196,197,199,207
Coosaw Swamp 199
Craven Co. 205,207
Cumbee River 199
Custopinum 57
Cypress Barony 128
Cypress Swamp 199
Cyprus Plantation 207
Danho 87
Day's Creek 155
Dockon Plantation 196

Dorchester 167
Edistow River 126,143
Exeter Plantation 197
Exmouth Plantation 197
Fairlawns 197,204
Flatly Creek 57
Fort King George 139
Four Hole Swamp 177,216
Good Hope 195
Granville Co. 150,155,
   160,185,199
Hagan Plantation 207
Hatcher's Swamp 199
Horse Shoe Plantation 208
Lady's Island 223
Limrick Plantation 206
Little River 57
Mount Boone 223
New London 126,143
Newington Plantation 199
Owen's Lodge 160
Owendan 129
Pascobank River 57
Phillip's Bluff 227
Plainsfield 199
Port Royal 94,150,156
Port Royal Island 185
Port Royal River 199
Prince William 229
Providence Island 140
Raplioe 150
Red Bank 155
Rice Hope Plantation 206
St. Helena 185
St. James, Goose
   Creek124,155,166,
   174,177,216,245
St. James Santee 205
Sarphley 177
Savannah Bridge 207
Timothy Savannah 223
Trench Island 150

Carolina South *(cont'd.)*
Varambeau 205
Waccamaw River 177
Wadmelaw River 199
Wando River 207
Wassamscue Swamp 167
Westfield 122

Connecticut

Black Point 92
Farmington 227
Groton 228
Guildford 29
Hartford 146,224,228
Harwington 228
Litchfield 228
Middletown 56
New Cambridge 228
New Hartford 228
New Haven 242
New London 56,118,
    178,224,229
New London Co. 228
Newhaven 29
Stamford 217

Florida East   237

Fort Augustus 257
St. Augustine 262

Florida West   256

Mansack 262
Mississippi River 262
Mobile 231*,235,246
Pensacola 230,232,234,
    242,245,259,262

Georgia

Augusta 179
Bethesda 250
Frederica 176,185,188,194
Little Ageehee 227
Orphan House Academy
    250
Savannah 176,243,247,
    256,259
St. Simon's 176

Maine   43

Piscataqua 46,62
Recompense Island 43

Maryland

Ann Arundell Co. 25,36,
    75,118,210,229,
    244,252
Annapolis 110*,115,127,
    142,145,151,160,
    164,170,183,194,
    206,208,210,226
All Saints 210
Annapolis, King Wil-
    liam School 150
Augustine Manor 183
Baltimore 86
  Baltimore Field 83
Baltimore Co. 30,118,
    144,186,244
Barbados 145
Barren Island 23
Barrons Neck 117
Batchelor's Delight 118
Beaver Marsh 117
Bell Town 170
Bennett's Lowe 145
Blocksith 200
Broadneck 171
Break Neck Hill 138
Broad Oak 83
Burtie's Journey 83
Bush River 187
Calvert Co. 21,24,57,
    100,156,161,235
  Christ Church 85,161
Cecil Co. 27,36,49,145,
    147,171
Charles Co. 58,87,108,
    145,261
Cherry Tree plantation 101
Chester River 30,36,55,220
Chester Town 220
Choptank 23,149
Choptank Bridge 230
Choptank River 23,55,101
Clark's Directions 118
Cocks 83
Cooke Point 101

Cosica Creek 30,231
Coursey Creek 117
Coursey Neck 151
Courseys 151
Covell's Cove 118
Covell's Troubles 118
Delabrook Manor 145
Dorchester Co. 34,36,
    101,145,230
Dorset Co. 66
Double Creek 117
Eastern Shore 24
Elk River 171
Elk Thicket 118
Elsie River 27
Eltonhead Manor 100
Essex Co. 171
Frederick Co. 233,244
Frisby's Addition 83
Frisby's Farm 83
Frisby's Forest 83
Frisby's Meadows 83
Frisby's Points 83
Frisby's Prime Choice 83
Frisby's Wild Chase 83
Glovers' Point 200
Golden Grove 145
Green Oak 144
Gunpowder River 187
Hardgrove's Choice 83
Hog Neck 138
Island Creek 230
Jaspers 117
Jones Falls 186
Kent Co. 134,208,234
King's Creek 66
Land of Nod 187
Langfords Bay 55
Little Choptank 23
Lockwood's Adventure 118
London Town 118,200
Long Neglect 151
Lower Marlborough 235
Manokin 124
Marlborough 118
Masson's 138
Mattaponney Creek 170
Mine Tract 170
Mitchell's Chance 118
Nanjemy 200

Maryland *(cont'd.)*
Nicholson's Manor 118
Nodd Forest 187
North East 163
Nottingham 251
Patapsco Falls 244
Patapsco River 244
Patuxent 23,84
Patuxent Iron Works 170
Patuxent River 61,208
Pawson's Plains 252
Petaphs River 86
Pirealaway 200
Piscatua 147
Pithly 200
Pocomoke River 48
Poplar Neck 118
Portobacco 200
   Creek 108
   Wassall 200
Prince Co. 145
Prince George Co. 118,
   142,206
   St. George's 236
Principio 163
Puddington's Harbour 118
Queen Anne Co. 117,
   160,194,231
Rappahannock 24
Red Lion Branch 117
Rich Bottom 230
Rissendale 151
Rockey Point 118
St. George's 230
St. James 229
St. John's 181
St. Mary's Co. 138,144,
   171,181,261
St. Mary's Court House 145
St. Thomas's Creek 138
Scotch Creek 138
Simms' Forest 171
Somerset Co. 123,124,172
Spotsylania Co. 170
Sprie's Hill 145
Susquetoanna 200
Talbot Co. 36,66,128,
   149,160,230,237
   Epsom 66
   The Freshes 144

Trough Creek Valley 233
Tuckahoe 36,66
Tukahoe Branch 117
Tuckahoe Creek 55
Tully's Delight 117
Turkey Island 118
Waters' River 124
Whiskey Bridge 244
White Banks 151
White Marsh 83
White River 151
Wicomico River 200
William & Mary
   College 170
Williams' Addition 118
Wye River 36,55,151,231

Massachusetts

Barrington 121
Billerica 239
Boston 15,16,20,30,37,
   39,43,46,53*,54*,
   56*,57,58,59,63,64,
   76,78,79*,83,91,96,
   97,101,104,106,
   107,113,120*,121,
   124,125,127,129,
   132*,133,135,137*,
   142,148,156,157,
   158*,161,162,167,
   168*,170,174,176,
   178,180*,182*,183,
   185*, 189*,191*,
   193,195,196,197,
   200,202,204,210,
   217,218,219,222,
   223,224,225,227,
   236,240,243,249*,
   254,257,258,263
Exchange Tavern 72
Fort Hill 188
Frog Lane 192
Hospital 187,259
King's Chapel 175,224
Marlborough Street 189
Milk Street 238
The Salutation 121
Town Dock 72
Braintree 168,223

Cambridge 100,256
   College 158
Cape Cod 180
Charlestown 54,83,87,
   92,119,163,169,
   203,249
Charlton 257
Chelmsford 224
Chelsea 249
Dorchester 131,212
Dunstable 43,224
Elizabeth Island 62
Fairfield 97
Gloucester 26
Harvard College 100
Haverell Line? 43
Hingham 93
Hockham 257
James Town 121
Kenebee River 217
King's Province 120
Kingston 120
Kittery 240
Kittery Point 240
Littleton 197
Lower Ferry 240
Lynn 55
Marblehead 254
Milton 223
Nantucket 169,195
Narragansett Co. 120
   Stoke Hall Farm 44
Newport 121
Norton 121
Oxford 257
Pemaquid 163
Plumb Island 254
Quonouaquatt Island 121
Roxbury 62,121,219,224
Rumney Marsh 133
Rutland 240
Salem 78,94,98,100,
   167,181
   North Field 101
Scotland 240
Stourbridge 239
Sturgeon Creek 240
Sudbury 69
Tarpaulin Creek 62
Taunton 121,257

Massachusetts *(cont'd.)*
Wenham 254
Windsor 175
Worcester Co. 240,257
York 37,226
York Co. 240

New Hampshire

Newington 240
Portsmouth 168,195,
    217,240

New Jersey

Allen Town 157
Amboy 226
Burlington 148,153
Cooper's Creek 102
Elizabeth Town 60,246
Gloucester Co. 102
Middlesex Co. 146
Perth Amboy 146
St. Lawrence's Brook 156
Second River 181
Trenton 175,214

New York

Albany 208,212,213,
    215,222,226
Albany Co. 238,247
Albany Fort 104,142
Artillery Patent 261
Batton Kill 238
Bentley 130
Crown Point 221,247
Ecopus 34
Flushing 157
Great Barnes Island 34
Greenwich 215
Harlem 34
Hempstead 157
Highlands 187
Hudson River 34,238
Innion's Land 130
Long Island 157
    Gravesend 34
    New Town 191
Marlborough 261
Mohawk Co. 217

New York City 34,81,
    87,91,184,186,187,
    191,196,204,215,
    217,219,229,233,
    239,244,247,255,
    257,258,260
    Fort 140
    Hanover Square 217
    Hospital 218,234
    King Street 203
    Prince Street 215
Orange Co. 187
Oswego 209
Otter Creek 228
Rareton River 130,147
Reed's Island 147
Richmond Co. 255
Saratoga 247
Schenectady 238
Smith's Fly 34
Staten Island 130,255
Ticonderoga 221
Ulster Co. 215
Yonkers Mill 34

Pennsylvania

Abington 215
Bensalem 259
Birmingham 192
Bucks Co. 172,259
Chester Co. 115
Concord 192
Cumberland Co. 259
Delaware Bay 102
Delaware River 172
Flagrum 259
Germantown 238
Kennett Township 192
Kent Co. 72
Newcastle 95,176
Newcastle Co. 58
Oxford Township 184
Philadelphia Co. 102
Philadelphia 56,66,67,
    92,93,98,102,115,
    122,125,126*,
    135*,139,140,146,
    150,153,154,159,
    165, 166, 169,172,

    176,183,185*,188,
    190,197,206,209,
    218,222,225,233,
    238,248,251,253,
    254,261,263
Arch Street 169
Christ Church 169,
    199,258
Elbow Lane 179
Fourth Street 207
Front Street 179,189,207
Market Street 200
Northern Liberties 200
Orphan House 257,258
Second Street 207
Third Street 207
Pittsburg 221
Radnor T'ship 67
Ridley 115
Schuykill 207
Sussex Co. 102
Wicocoa 172

Rhode Island

Bristol 186
James Town 121
Newport 157,198,229
    Rocke Farm 72
Providence Plantation 72

Virginia

Abingdon 159
Accawacke 11
Accomack 11,18
Accomack Co. 41,121,194
Acquamat 84
Amelia Co. 241
Arlington 202,203
Bannister River 239
Bellfound? 173
Blackbeard's Point 225
Bristol 99
Bruton 155,173,202
Butumocke 141
Cape Henry 46
Caroline Co. 219
Charles City 30
Charles City Co. 81
Chatsworth 239

Virginia *(cont'd.)*
Cherry Point 82
Cherrystone 121
Chesterfield Co. 239
Clifts 37
Cople 130
Copley 97
Cumberland Co. 239
Dan River 239
Dushing Hole Swamp 219
Elizabeth City Co. 241,246
Elizabeth Co. 7
Flat Creek 241
Frederick Co. 248
Fredericksburgh 263
Gloucester Co. 43,64,68,
    114,144,159,210
Hampton 225
Hanover Co. 144
Henrico Co. 100,239
Hickman's Line 179
Hog Island 66
Hungers parish 202
Hunger's Creek 124
Hunting Creek 74
Isle of Wight 120
Isle of Wight Co. 108
James City Co. 144
James River 15,47,82,
    95,112,161,201
James Town 1,32,201
Jordans parish 30
Joseph's Mount 108
King & Queen Co. 55,
    103,219,220
King George Co. 262
King William Co. 219,234
    St. John's 239,246,253
Kingcopsco 71
Kynothan 6
Lancaster Co. 75,222
Lawnes Creek 108
Louisa Co. 219*
Lynn Haven 102
Madade Creek 144
Magochy River 252
Manigo 2
Mannikin Town 155
Martin's Hundred 6,13
Martins Brandon 112

Martins Hope 112
Mathodack River 74
Mattox 80
Mecklenburgh Co. 241
Middlesex Co. 173,231,
    235
Motton Island 203
Myers' Plantation 179
Nansemond 95,153
Nansemond Co. 120
Nasswadax Creek 11
New Kent Co. 30,61,68,
    114,144
    St. Peter's 85
Nomini 71,82
Norfolk 252
Norfolk Co. 95,139
Norfolk Town 183
North River 32
Northampton Co. 11,
    124,202,253
Notoway River 108
Orange Co. 170
Petersburgh 241
Point Comfort 66
Pope's Creek 37,71,80
Potomack 82
Potomack River 37,46,
    80,107
Price's Plantation 179
Prince George Co. 99,
    100,179,247
Prince William Co. 236,
    256
Princess Ann Co. 139
    Court House 177
Quarry Creek 107
Queen Mary's Port 144
Queen's Creek 155,203
Rappahannock River 38,
    68,135
Rawleigh 241
Richmond, Head's Mill 104
    St. Mary's 104
Richmond Co. 75
Roanoke River 239
Rocky Run 179
Round Hills 74
St. Martin's Hundred 3
Sassafras River 83

Sawyer's Swamp 225
Sittenburne 75
Skin Quarter 239
Skitles Creek 144
Smith's Island 203
Spotsylvania Co. 219
Stafford Co. 51,74,107
Stanton River 239
Stocks Quarter 74
Stony Creek 178
Strabane 80
Stratton 55,61
Summerton 95
Surry Co. 108
Urbania 235
Ware 43,64
Warwick Co. 178
Washington 74
Westmoreland 256
Westmoreland Co. 37,
    71,74,80,82,97,130
White Oak Swamp 179
Williamsburg 106,107,
    108,144,173,202,
    250,253,254,256,263
Wills Run 179
Woolshop Branch 236
York Co. 108,155,173,
    203,246
York River 29,41,68,
    103,113,122,133,
    155,184
York Town 76,168,179,
    189,211

West Indies 132

Antigua 25,65,145,214,
    217,242
Barbados 20,25,29,38,
    42,50,59,69,70,73,
    76,100,101,132,
    155,158,167,170,
    188,191,198,200
Bridgetown 174
St. Lucy's 191
St. Michael 220
St. Peter's 191
St. Philip's 191

West Indies *(cont'd.)*
Bermuda (Somers Is.)8,
    12,84
Cartagena 169,181
Curacao 127
Guadeloupe 235
Havannah 226,227,228,
    229,260
Jamaica 12,39,47,57,82,
    91,115,175,190
    Bere 168
    Kingston 94,140,190
    Port Royal 104,139,203
    St. Mary's 248
Leeward Islands 53,188

ENGLAND

Bedfordshire

Bedford 235
Cople 71,83
Potsgrove 101
Woburn 101

Berkshire

Abingdon 101
Arborfield 19
Barcledon 96
Berkcome 124
Binfield 31
Bollington 84
Burghfield 14
Clewer 9
Cookham 4
Eton 147
Hare Hatch 213
Kingston Lisle 150
Longworth 41
Millington 84
New Windsor 150
New Windsor 41
Radley 14
Reading 14,78,79,89,
    96,106,115,237
    Bread Street 41
    London Street 106
    St. Lawrence 52
Streatley 105
Thatcham, Coldash 123

Tilehurst 14
Up Lambourne 4
Waltham Place 198
Warfield 84
Whitley 19
Windsor 147
Wokingham 150

Buckinghamshire

Aston Clinton 225
Aylesbury 61
Bierton 89
Buckingham 8
Burnham 145
Chalfont St. Giles 61,69
Chesham 56
Denham 3
East Hanney 184
Hedgerley Green 69
High Wycombe 115
Langley 52
Langley Green 89
Leighton Buzzard 101
Olney 23
Penn 252
Princes Risborough 69
Stonedeane 61
Taplow 251
Walton Fields 61
Warrington 22
Whelpley Hill 56

Cambridgeshire

Cambridge, King's
    College 160,237
    Trinity College 116
Ellington 6
Wisbech 100

Channel Islands

Guernsey, St. Peter's
    Port 227
Jersey 121,158
    St. Helier 224

Cheshire

Allostock 33
Altrincham 63

Arderne 109
Bickton 109
Chester 71,221
Congleton 142
Great Budworth 33
Hudsfield 77
Macclesfield 77
Middlewich 73
Moss Side 63
Nantwich 220,255
Sale 63
Uskinton 119
Waverton 26

Cumberland

Cockermouth 162
Whitehaven 162,195,256
Workington 156

Derbyshire

Chesterfield 29,247
Derby 12,225
Findern 66
Hartshay 98
Heage 225
Mickleover 12
Normanton 225
Pinxton 225
Stidd 153
Tapton 247

Devonshire

Barnstaple 4
Cotleigh 87
Dartmouth 211
Exeter 9,50,51,99,143,236
Exmouth 204
Fremington 32
Kingston 236
Lundy Island 107
Lympston 211
Moreton 126
Northam 4
Pilton 132
Plymouth 1,17,64,176,193*
    Charles 244
Stoke 204
Topsham 33,112,126

Devonshire *(cont'd.)*
Torbay 62
Uplyme 36
West Teignmouth 216
Withycombe Raleigh 204

Dorset

Allington 97
Blandford 209
Bryans Piddle 209
Haselbury Bryan 209
Portland 18
Purbeck 64
Sherborne 192

Durham

Bishop Auckland 242
Byers Green 250
Houghton 93
South Shields 210
Westoe 253

Essex

Boreham 209
Bradfield 216
Braintree 148
Broomfield 216
Codham Hall 71
Coggeshall 216
Colchester 215, 216
   All Saints 18
Copford 216
Dedham 216
East Ham 90
Easthorpe 216
Feering 216
Fethes 21
Fordham 216
Great Maplestead 29
Great Totham 56
Gueddy Hall 51
Hatfield 216
Hornchurch 20, 126
Kelvedon 216
Langham 18
Layer Breton 216
Layer Marney 216
Leigh 224

Leytonstone 51
Marks Tey 216
Mountnessing 33, 90
Much Farindon 135
Nasing 135
Plaistow 163
Romford 51
Roydon 135
Ruddock's Manor 135
Shenfield 90
Sible Hedingham 29
South Halstead 216
South Weald 215
Stebbing 216
Stratford 141
Stratford Langthorn 200
Stratford Langton 17
Temple Mills 70
Tendring 216
Thundersley 147
Waltham 262
West Ham 70, 88
Wimbish 151
Witham 56
Woodford 92

Gloucestershire

Almondsbury 192
Bagendon 128
Barton Regis 37
Bragington 99
Bristol 29, 37*, 47, 69, 77,
   80, 82, 87, 100, 105,
   107, 117, 120, 134,
   135, 136, 137, 146*,
   154, 157, 162, 165,
   178, 189, 192, 193,
   196, 197, 199, 207,
   208, 217, 219*, 232,
   234, 251, 262
Castle Green 52
Hot Wells 263
King Street 162
Leonards Lane 152
The Marsh 27
Old Market Street 152
Royal Fort 162
St. James 162
St. Michael's 195

St. Michael's Hill 162
St. Nicholas 195
St. Philip & Jacob 37
St. Thomas's 177
   Temple 157
Brookthorpe 9
Charfield 37
Cheltenham 102
Dorsington 99
Gloucester 9, 14, 251
Harescombe 9
Lidney, Nurshill 175
Redland 163
Rodborough 251
Stinchcombe 135
Stoke 250
Tewkesbury 102
Thornbury 192
Tiddington 102
Upton 102
Westbury on Trym 162
Whaddon 9
Winterbourne 193

Hampshire

Andover 36
Bicton 53
Boldre 88
Bramley 41
Gosport 198
Hope 191
Lasham 65
Longparish 149
Lower Wallop 108
Ludshott 65
Martin Worthy 149
Pamber 41
Pilewell 248
Plymouth 11
Portsmouth 140, 173,
   184, 249
Portsmouth Common 210
Rookley 65
Southampton 78, 107,
   109, 225, 249
Titchfield 180
Wansted 65
Winchester 149
Yateley 138

Herefordshire

Almeley 67
Bodenham 67
Bromyard 215
Clehonger 10
Docklow 67
Foy 2
Hereford 10,14
Hope under Dinmore 15
Kimbolton 67
Kings Pyon 14
Kingsland 67
Kingston 14
Lawton 67
Ledbury 157
Leominster 201
Madley 10
Vowchurch 10

Hertfordshire

Bayford 45
Cheshunt 7
Dunsley 56
Flaunden 98
Gosmore 171
Hatfield School 250
Hertford 48,60,148
Hitchin 16
Hunsdon 43,112
Rickmansworth 48
Stanstead Abbots 110
Totteridge 11
Tring 56
Ware 110
Wiggington 56

Huntingdonshire

Barford 71
Blunham 71
Brampton 22
Ellington 68
Haddon 254
Huntingdon 22
Little Paxton 68
St. Ives 215
St. Neots 71
Straughton 39

Isle of Wight

Cowes 78,221

Kent

Ashton 75
Beckenham 196
Benenden 53
Bersted, Milgate 115
Bethersden 53
Bexley 38
Blackheath 198
Blendon Hall 38
Broadstairs 142
Broomfield 115
Canterbury, St. George 31
    St. Mildred 31
Charlton 39
Chatham 15
Coptree 75
Cranbrook 10,53
Deal 36,108,133
    Royal Exchange 133
    Royal Oak 133
Deptford 45,54,76,91,
    111,129,130,180,
    190,206,213
    King Street 129
    Queen's Gate Yard 91
Dover 166
East Sutton 21,115
Goudhurst 194
Gravesend 39,85,92,225
Greenwich 76,106,134,
    183,190,201,223
    Crane Street 106
Ham 21
Hernehill 31
High Halden 53
Lenham 21
Lewisham 198
Lynton 21
Maidstone 10,75
Margate 142,151
Milton next Gravesend
    92,210
Orlestone 127
Rochester 170,177,249
Ruckinge 127
St. Peter in Thanet 142

Staplehurst 53
Teston 260
Upton 142
West Malling 76
Whitstable 30
Woolwich 193,206

Lancashire

Great Harwood 97
Knowsley 98
Liverpool 98,99,159,222
Manchester 63,73,96
    Clayton Bridge 109,119
Preston 69

Leicestershire

Ashby Folvill 11
Bruntingthorpe 208
Leicester 87
Packington 163

Lincolnshire

Gedney Manor 111
Laworth 99
Lincoln Close 99
Manby 94
Scothorne 12
Sutterton 138
Welby Manor 111
Whaplode 111

London & Middlesex

Abchurch Lane 36
Aldermanbury 23,88
    Love Lane 153
Aldersgate 169
Aldgate 44,67,80,97,147
All Hallows, Barking 170
All Hallows Staining
    79,235
All Saints, Lombard
    Street 71
Argyle Streetr 214
Arundell Street 214
Austin Friars 181
Barbican 29
Bartholomew Close 69,115
Berkeley Square 250

London & Middlesex
(cont'd.)
Berners Street 258
Bethnal Green 13,114,
153,198,211
Birchin Lane 125,150,218
Bishopsgate 103
Bishopsgate Street 158
Blackfriars 1,242
Boswell Court 221
Bow Churchyard 259
Bread Street 203
Brentford Butts 211
Brewer Street 209
Bridewell Hospital 52
Broad Street 153,197
Bromley by Bow 88
Brook Street 220
Brownlow St. 98
Bucklersbury 237
Budge Row 139
Bunhill Fields 68
Cannon St. 4,203
Cary Street 260
Cecil Street 219
Chancery Lane 132
Charing Cross 8
Cheapside 14,26,168,211
Chelsea 199,263
  Manor Street 143
Chiswick 146
Clements Inn 125,167,226
Clerkenwell 15,174
  St. John Street 69,89
  St. John's Lane 169
Clerkenwell Green 220
Cliffords Inn 203,243
Conduit Street 263
Coney Hatch 194
Cooks' Hall 196
Cordwainers' Hall 242
Coverlid Fields 102
Creechurch 17
Crutched Friars 161,251,
  258
Danish Lutheran Church
  137
Doctors' Commons 127,253
Dolphin Court 198
Dowgate Hill 201

Drury Lane 262
Duke's Place 112
Ealing 124
Edmonton 24
Enfield 103
Fenchurch Street 38,79
Fetter Lane 152,226
Finchley 204
Fleet Prison 95,130
Fleet Street 41
Fore Street 103
Friday Street 20
Golden Square 209,214
Goswell Street 101
Gracechurch Street 52,
  89,130,150,157
Grays Inn 116,163,230,236
Great Minories Street 29
Great Stanmore 7
Greek Street 103
Grosvenor Square 220
Gutter Lane 6
Hackney 8,10,35*,70,
  178,180
Hammersmith 134
Hatton Garden 69
Hayes 3,48
Hendon 169
Highgate 126
Holborn 19,39,131,196
  Dean Street 148
  Red Lion Street 170
Hornsey 70
Horseshoe Alley 103
Hoxton 121,260
Inner Temple 7,61,92,121
Isleworth 250
Islington 22,47,136,218,
  249
Kensington 242,263
King Street 190,214
Kingsbury 5
Knightsbridge 260
Leadenhall Street 218,264
Lee River 70
Leicester Fields 258
  Compton Street 181
Liberty of the Tower 30
Lime Street 61,103

Limehouse 5,20,98,111,
  162,177,187,190,
  206,234
Nightingale Lane 134
Lincolns Inn 84,131,182
Lincolns Inn Fields 65
Little Moorfields 86,183
Little St. Helen's 95
Lombard Street 52,88,146
London Bridge 48
Long Acre 52,89
Love Lane 210
Maiden Lane 221
Mark Lane 40,183,250,260
Middle Temple 39,51,
  89,108,164
Mincing Lane 79,133
Minories 47,139,251
Mint 5
Moorfields 6,103
Navy Office 94,116
New Brentford 211
New Foundling Hospital
  200
New Inn 146,209
New Street 148
Nonsuch 48
Norton Folgate 28
Old Artillery Ground 89,136
Old Jewry 188
Orange Street 190
Pall Mall 262
Paternoster Row 8
Paul's Chain 8
Pescod Street 102
Pewterers' Hall 103
Piccadilly 194
Plow Court 52
Plumtree Street 101
Pope's Head Alley 174,189
Poplar 31,62,116,127
Prescot Steet 243
Princes Square 258
Queen Street 167
Ratcliffe 1,20,70,88,98,
  133,137,147,181,183
  Broad Street 137
  Brooke Street 116
  Highway 90
  Marine Square 112

London & Middlesex
(cont'd.)
Ratcliffe Cross 158
Redman Lane 174
Ruislip 3
St. Andrew Holborn 38,
40,82,127,134,169,
181,230,249
St. Andrew Hubbard 2
St. Andrew Undershaft 16
St. Ann's 177,183
St. Augustine 40
St. Bartholomew by
Exchange 11,51
St. Bartholomew the
Less 26
St. Bartholomew's
Hospital 8,26
St. Benet Gracechurch 200
St. Botolph Aldgate 17,
18,27,29,30,33,47,
85,95,125,127,151,
162,225,248,262
St. Botolph Bishopsgate
48,71,85,87,195
St. Bride's 63,68,95,138
St. Catherine Creechurch
33,83,88,114
St. Clement Danes 3,65,
110,125,182,199,
214,219,225,260
St. Dionis Backchurch 222
St. Dunstan in East 47,
58,88
St. Dunstan in West 106,
126,128
St. Edmund Lombard St. 42
St. Edmund the King 36,127
St. Faith 231,263
St. Gabriel Fenchurch
Street 63,127
St. George, Hanover
Square 136,182,
183,213
St. George the Martyr 137
St. George's 133,174,
185,196
St. George's Hospital 200
St. Giles Cripplegate 43,
64,79,116,148,167

St. Giles in Fields 81,82,
98,101,104
St. Gregory 16,22
St. Gregory by St.
Paul's 135
St. James 176
St. James' Square 190
St. James' Street 242
St. John Baptist 6,212
St. John Walbrook 6
St. Katherine by Tower
2,161,185
St. Katherine's Precinct
85,164
St. Leonard Eastcheap 229
St. Luke 157,250
St. Margaret Lothbury 102
St. Margaret Moses 165
St. Margaret Pattens 182
St. Martin in Fields 23,27,
38,41,113,123,129,
139,146,155,156,164,
178,190,191,198,212,
218,225,238,262*
Hungerford Market 140
Spur Alley 140
Villiers Street 125
St. Martin le Grand 103
St. Martin Outwich 70
St. Martin Vintry 196
St. Mary Abchurch 18,
35,103,203
St. Mary at Hill 16
St. Mary le Bow 258
St. Mary Wolnoth 44
St. Marylebone 251
St. Michael Bassishaw 5,
16,233
St. Michael Cornhill 41,44
St. Michael Crooked
Lane 5,65
St. Mildred Poultry 24
St. Olave, Hart Street 40
St. Olave, Old
Jewry 35
St. Pancras 260
St. Paul, Covent Garden
45,111,221,238
St. Paul's Churchyard 171
St. Peter Cornhill 38,159

St. Peter le Poor 28,188
St. Sepulchre 68,244
St. Stephen, Coleman
Street 76,158,222
St. Stephen Walbrook
10,112
St. Thomas Apostle 86
Savoy 84
Shad Thames 119,152
Shadwell 29,32,34,36,48,
49,52,54,58,59,60*,
65, 72,77,89,96,101,
108,113*,119,122,
123,133,161,162,
169,171,218,249
Blewgate Fields 90
Cock Hill 119,147
King David Fort 44
Lower Shadwell 181
Upper Shadwell 77,
90,93
Shoreditch 28,109,124,
158,206
Smithfield 132
East 76,151,162,225
West 250
Snow Hill 68
Soho 217
Somerset House 243
South Audley Square 262
Southall 251
Southgate 258
Spitalfields 52,115
Brick Lane 167
Church Street 251
Stewart Street 181
Spring Gardens 197
Staines Bridge 201
Stanhope Street 251
Stanwell 121,251
Stepney 1,12,19,25,28,29,
32,35,39,40,41,43,
46,49,50,53,54,59*,
60*,65,71,73*,74,80,
84,88,90,92,93,98*,
99,105,108,109,111,
116,126,127,128,
135,136,140,141,
142*,143,147,148*,
161,163,259

London & Middlesex
(cont'd.)
Cock Hill 167
Garland Court 134
Greenbank 19
Love Lane 167
Manor 90
Mile End 86,95
Stoke Newington 40,204
Strand 173,200,219,234,
242,243
Bear Tavern 173
Beaufort Street 155
Essex Street 167
New Round Court 181
Stratford by Bow 70
Surrey Street 258
Tabernacle 251
Tavistock Street 258
Temple 131,158
Temple Bar 226
Thavies Inn 42
Theobalds 38
Threadneedle Street 48,
111,115,136,181
Throgmorton Street 190,
218,221,229,263
Tottenham Court 260
Tottenham Court Chapel
251
Tower Hill 166,230,232
Tower of London 257,261
Trinity Lane 102
Twickenham 63
Wapping 17,28,34,46,
49,50,51,52,70,73,
76,92,98,107,113,
126,131,133,144,
148,162,168,182,
185,187,217,222,
224,247,249
Hermitage 18,168
Hermitage Bridge 67,94
New Crane 34
New Stairs 56
Old Gravel Lane 153
Red Lyon Street 205
Union Stairs 126
Wall 73,122,123,180
Warwick Street 209

Watling Street 91
Well Close Square 137
Westminster 21,33,55,152,
197,198,208
Brewer Street 206
Charles Street 217
Clarges Street 171
Compton Street 153
King Street 120
Petty France 236
St. Ann 115,248
St. James 50,94,109,
113,118,225,262
St. James Place 261
St. James's House 113
St. Margaret 3,38,61,
107,115,116,173,
184,217,260
Westminster School 160
Tothill Fields 120
Whetstone 204
White Bear Court 100
White Hart Court 52
Whitechapel 37,46,55,
69,79,83,90,102,
110,124,128,143,
180,202
Dockhead 18
Goodmans Fields 52,
130,180,243
Rosemary Lane 149
Whitehall 150
Wood Street 210,238

Norfolk

Blofield 90
Hempstead 181
Hilborough 140
Kings Lynn 212
Lessingham 181
Lynn 190
Norwich 181
Swaffham 209
Yarmouth 17,180

Northamptonshire

Ashby St. Leger 51
Ashton 197,250
Ashwell 53

Bugbrooke 210
Courteenhall 250
Daventry 51
Hartwell 250
Heathencote Fields 116
Moreton Pinkney 141
Northampton 141
Roade 250
Scaldwell 89
Sywell 141
Towcester 7,116,125
Weldon 73

Northumberland

Benwell 62
Kenton 62
Lanton 238
Newcastle upon Tyne
194,253

Nottinghamshire

Everton 203

Oxfordshire

Abingdon 178
Banbury 69,159
Burford 101
Cropredy 159
East Hanney 184
Holwell 253
Mollington 159
Oxford 102,253
St. Peter in the East 253
Thame 103
Wardington 159

Rutland

Market Overton 208
Normanton 148

Scilly Isles 78

Shropshire

Astley 41
Aston Botterell 65
Bridgnorth 214
Broseley 177

Shropshire *(cont'd.)*
Little Ness 5
Ludlow 201
Nordley Wood 41
Shrewsbury 21

Somerset

Bath 42,99,235,251,254
Bathford 149
Berrow 42
Bridgwater 72
Bruton 256
Catcott 50
Frome 88,172
Holwell 209
Raddington 31
St. Gregory Stoke 36
Taunton 3,233
Weston 42
Wiveliscombe 31
Yeovil 226

Staffordshire

Callowhill 62
Kingstone 62
Lichfield 61
Over Penn 27
Stafford 232
Styles Copp 232
Tamworth, Alder Mill 163
Uttoxeter 61,255

Suffolk

Beccles 254
Bury St. Edmunds 124
Chelmondiston 90
Chevington 80
Holton 35
Ipswich 4,90,230
Lowestoft 180
Newmarket, Cornhill 173
Rushbrooke 196,214
Thorndon 33

Surrey

Battersea 41
Bermondsey 48,54,55,
    93,98,129,131,137,
    145,154,165

Camberwell 40,104,167
Cannon Hill 261
Carshalton 81
Chertsey 254
Christ Church 167
Clapham 167,184
Cobham 22
Dorking 173
Egham 201
Epsom 119,150,160
Kingston on Thames 38,
    125,173
Lambeth 67,103,151,260
Petersham 250
Redriffe Wall 98
Ripley 242
Rotherhithe 15,20,33,114,
    119,121*,127,131,146,
    161,166,169,172,174
East Lane 221
Jacob Street 145
Rotherhithe Wall 145,148
Rupers Gardens 260
Southwark 63
Bermondsey Street 87
Dockhead 84
Horsleydown 93,263
Long Lane 129
Red Lion Street 122
St. George 53,56,221
St. George Martyr 104
St. John 152
St. Margaret's Hill 104
St. Olave 73,84,87,
    90,112,113,127
St. Olave Street 164
St. Saviour 19,67,78,
    122,138
Globe & Runner 201
St. Thomas 13,26,73
St. Thomas' Hospital
    55,201
Tooley Street 125
Tooting 155,181
Wandsworth 69

Sussex

Arundel 190,232
Ewhurst 55

Fairlight 95
Horsham 22
Mayfield 7

Warwickshire

Bishopston 99
Coleshill 171
Coventry 51,212
Exhall 51
Farnborough 159
Fillongley 131
Keresley 212
Merevale 163
Newland 51
Polesworth 163
Rugby 164
Southam 211
Stratford on Avon 10,99
Walton 260
Welcombe 99

Westmorland

Waitby 106
Wharton 106

Wiltshire

Alderbury 149
Bishops Canning, Cote 122
Bradford 149
Bremhill 49
Calne 49
Charlcutt 49
Chippenham 135,243
Collingbourne Abbots 25
Compton 149
Cross Oak 242
East Coulston 87
Hillmarton 49
Hurst 115
Kingswood 45
Lacock 149
Limpley Stoke 149
Marlborough 193
Monkton Farley 149
New Sarum 232
Rodbourne 149
Salisbury 238
Sarum 141

Wiltshire *(cont'd.)*
Soluth Wraxall 149
Standlinch 248
Winsley 14
Woodborough 122

Worcestershire

Areley 89
Bradforton 211
Brogmore Green 200
Bushley 13
Severn Stoke 25
Worcester 25,46,134,
    143,199

Yorkshire

Aike 158
Beverley 142
Burton Agnes 1
Conisbrough 259
Dewsbury 260
Downham Park 136
Harborough 249
Helperby 208
Hull 238
Langtoft 158
Lockington 158
Northallerton 94
Richmond 136
Scarborough 158
Sheffield 259
Slaithwaite 109
Thorne 259
Whitby 156
York 1

WALES

Aberystwyth 164
Anglesey 85
Carmarthenshire 94
Grone 62
Haverfordwest 263
Haverfordwest 67
Llamoring 186
Llantwit Major 8
Llywell 263
Manachty 177
Raglan 126

Rudbaxton 67
Saundersfoot 263
Swansea 129
Tenby 263
Trecastle 262
Westfield 263
Wrexham 62,126

SCOTLAND

Aberdeen 187,246
Appin 185
Ayr 237
Ayrshire 96
Barnsalie 242
Bastonrig 184
Cameron 115
Courland 236
Cromartie 245
Dalguire 206
Doe 190
Dundee 58,235
Edinburgh 129,139,146,
    166,173,206,250,258
    Infirmary 245
Fair Isle 246
Falkirk 259
Forfar 189
Galloway 65,237,242
Glasgow 81,200,210
    Crawford's Dock 141
Inverness 62
Jedburgh 189
Kinglassie 183
Leith 184,241
Melrose 129
Montrose 166,190
Monymusk 246
Nelson 71
Old Glenluce 242
Paisley 71
Perthshire 147,155
Poterhead 92,144
Prestonpans 92
Rubislaw 263
Scotland 155
Stirling 81
Timvale 58

IRELAND 22,24,36,
    80,148

Ballaghatrellick 238
Ballymure 232
Belfast, Cumber 214
    Gray Abbey 214
Carrick 247
Carrickfergus 232
Cork 80,146,161,186,
    205,233
Dublin 135,150,160,
    209,210,238,260
Kilroot 232
Limerick 128
Londonderry 123
New Ross 38
Sligo Co. 238
Tipperary Co. 247
Westmeath 160

EUROPE

Denmark 165
Flanders, Douai 237
France 82,91,146,165,213
    Angiers 237
    Chattellerault 181
    Lyons 45
    Pont en Royan 45
    Rochell 161
Germany, Bremen 156
    Lubeck 34
    Nuremberg 7
Gibraltar 206,229
Holland 12,178
    Amsterdam 17,137,
        161,181
    Rotterdam 156,165
Minorca 243
Norway 137
Portugal, Bilbao 78
    Lisbon 78,97,135,166
    Oporto 217
Spain, Cadiz 78
Sweden 62
Switzerland, Geneva 248

OTHER AREAS

Africa

Barbary, Mackeness 78
Guinea 73, 76
Madeira 158, 159, 177
Senegambia 259
Tangier 20

East Indies 208

India, Fort George 62
    Bombay 88
    Fort St. George 119